# KAUA'I

Making the Most of Your Family Vacation

6th Edition

Dona Early & Christie Stilson

PRIMA PUBLISHING

In affiliation with
PARADISE PUBLICATIONS

**KAUA'I, A Paradise Family Guide**



| | | | |
|---|---|---|---|
| First Edition: | May 1988 | Second Edition: | May 1989 |
| Third Edition: | January 1991 | Fourth Edition: | October 1995 |
| Fifth Edition: | September 1997 | Sixth Edition: | March 2000 |



Illustrations: Janora Bayot
Maps: John Stenersen
Layout & Typesetting: Paradise Publications
Published By Prima Publishing, Roseville, California

PRIMA PUBLISHING and colophon are registered trademarks of Prima Communications, Inc.

Library of Congress ISSN data on file
ISBN 0-7615-2423-1

00 01 02 HH 10 9 8 7 6 5 4 3 2 1

Printed in the United States of America

HOW TO ORDER:

Quantity discounts are available from Prima Publishing, 3000 Lava Ridge Court, Roseville, CA 95661; (800) 632-8676. On your letterhead include information concerning the intended use of the books and the number you wish to purchase. Single copies are available from Prima Publishing or Paradise Publications.

**Visit us online at www.primalifestyles.com**

# *CONTENTS*

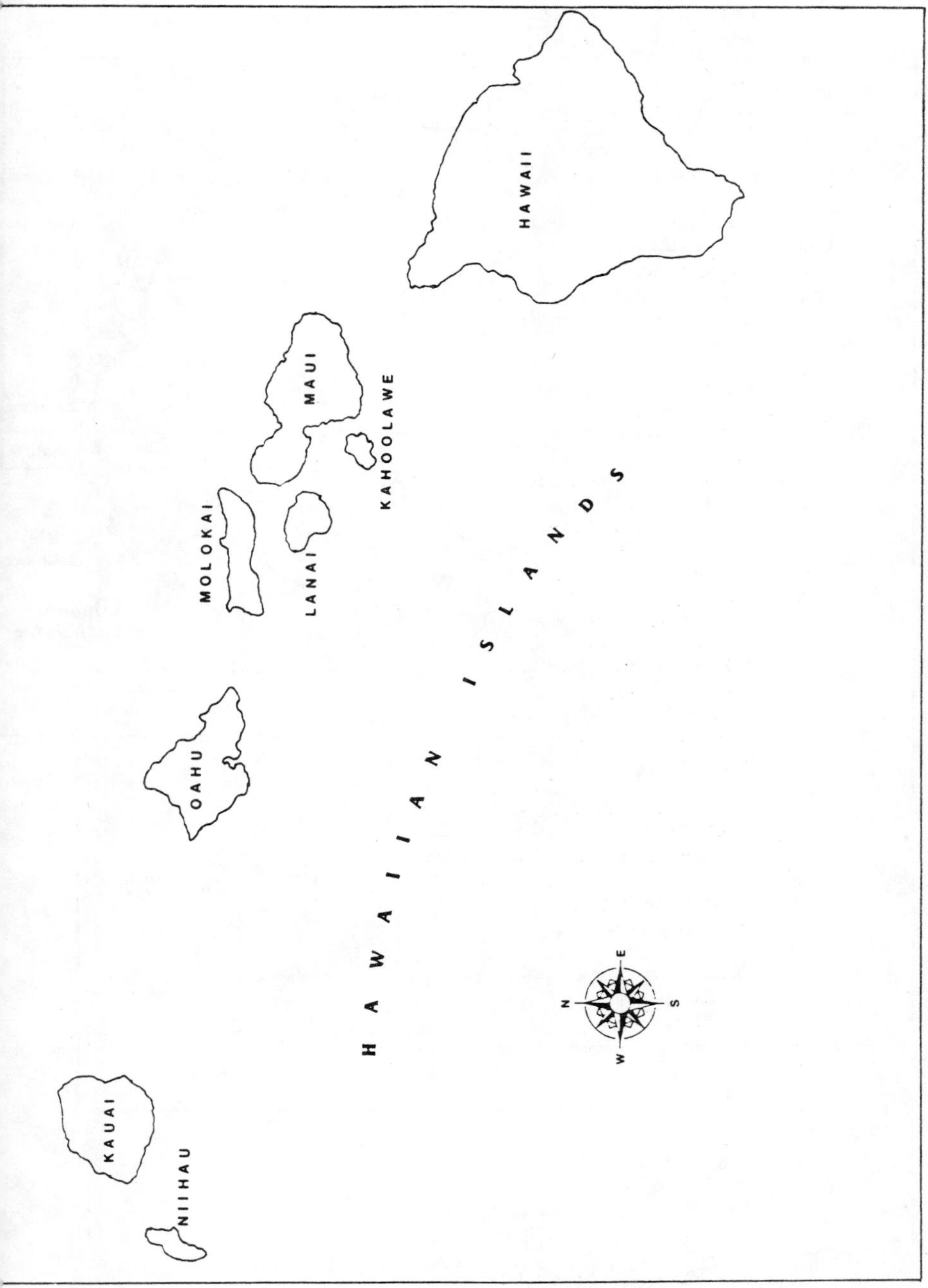
HAWAII
MAUI
KAHOOLAWE
MOLOKAI
LANAI
OAHU
KAUAI
NIIHAU
HAWAIIAN ISLANDS
N
E
S
W

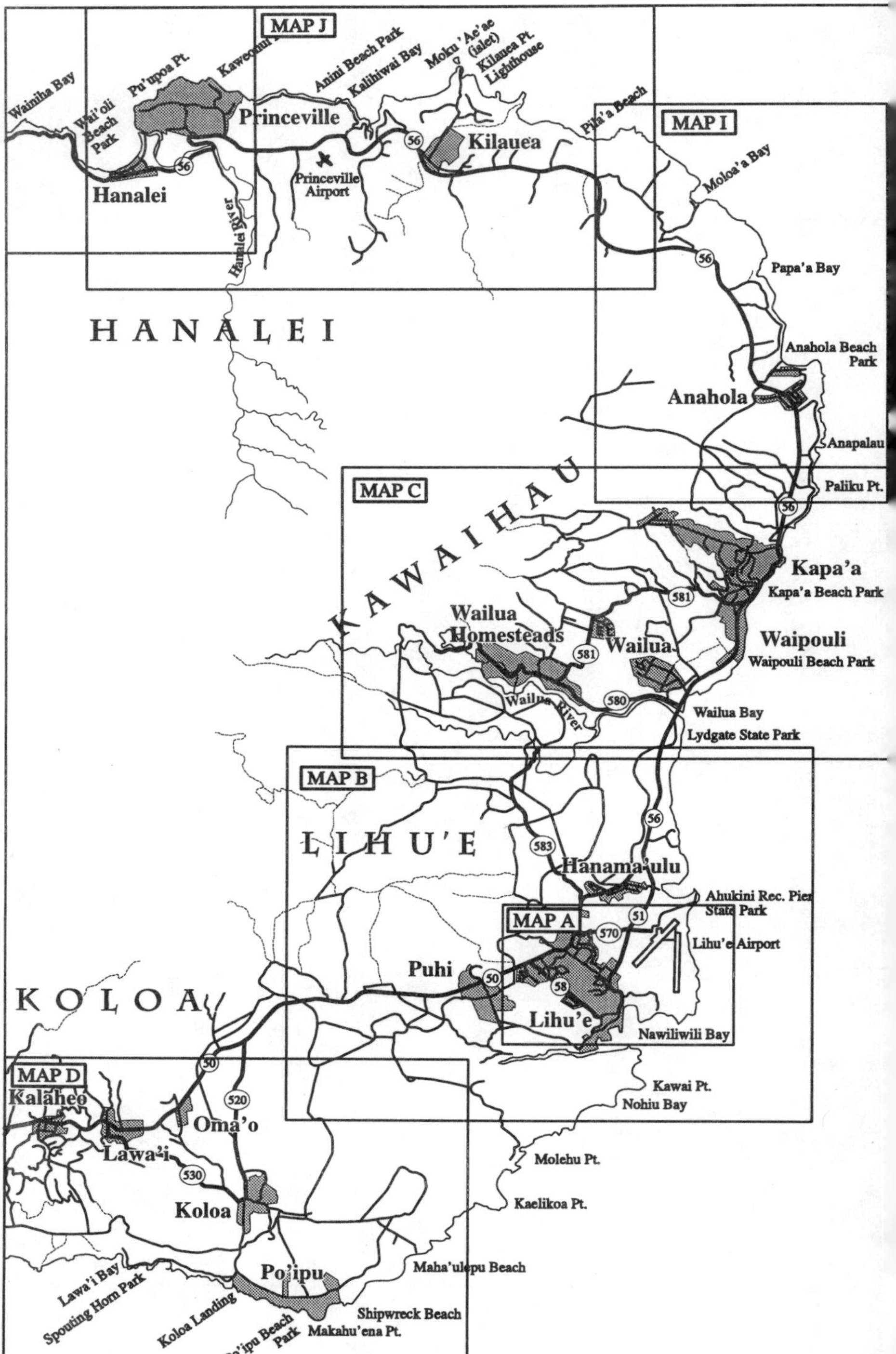

MAP J
MAP I
MAP C
MAP B
MAP A
MAP D
Wainiha Bay
Wai'oli Beach Park
Pu'upoa Pt.
Princeville
Anini Beach Park
Kalihiwai Bay
Moku 'Ae'ae (islet)
Kilauea Pt. Lighthouse
Kilauea
Pila'a Beach
Hanalei
Hanalei River
Princeville Airport
Moloa'a Bay
Papa'a Bay
HANALEI
Anahola Beach Park
Anahola
Anapalau
Paliku Pt.
KAWAIHAU
Kapa'a
Kapa'a Beach Park
Wailua Homesteads
Wailua
Waipouli
Waipouli Beach Park
Wailua River
Wailua Bay
Lydgate State Park
LIHU'E
Hanama'ulu
Ahukini Rec. Pier State Park
Lihu'e Airport
Puhi
Lihu'e
Nawiliwili Bay
KOLOA
Kawai Pt.
Nohiu Bay
Kalaheo
Oma'o
Lawa'i
Koloa
Molehu Pt.
Kaelikoa Pt.
Po'ipu
Maha'ulepu Beach
Lawa'i Bay
Spouting Horn Park
Koloa Landing
Po'ipu Beach Park
Shipwreck Beach
Makahu'ena Pt.
56
581
580
583
51
570
50
58
520
530

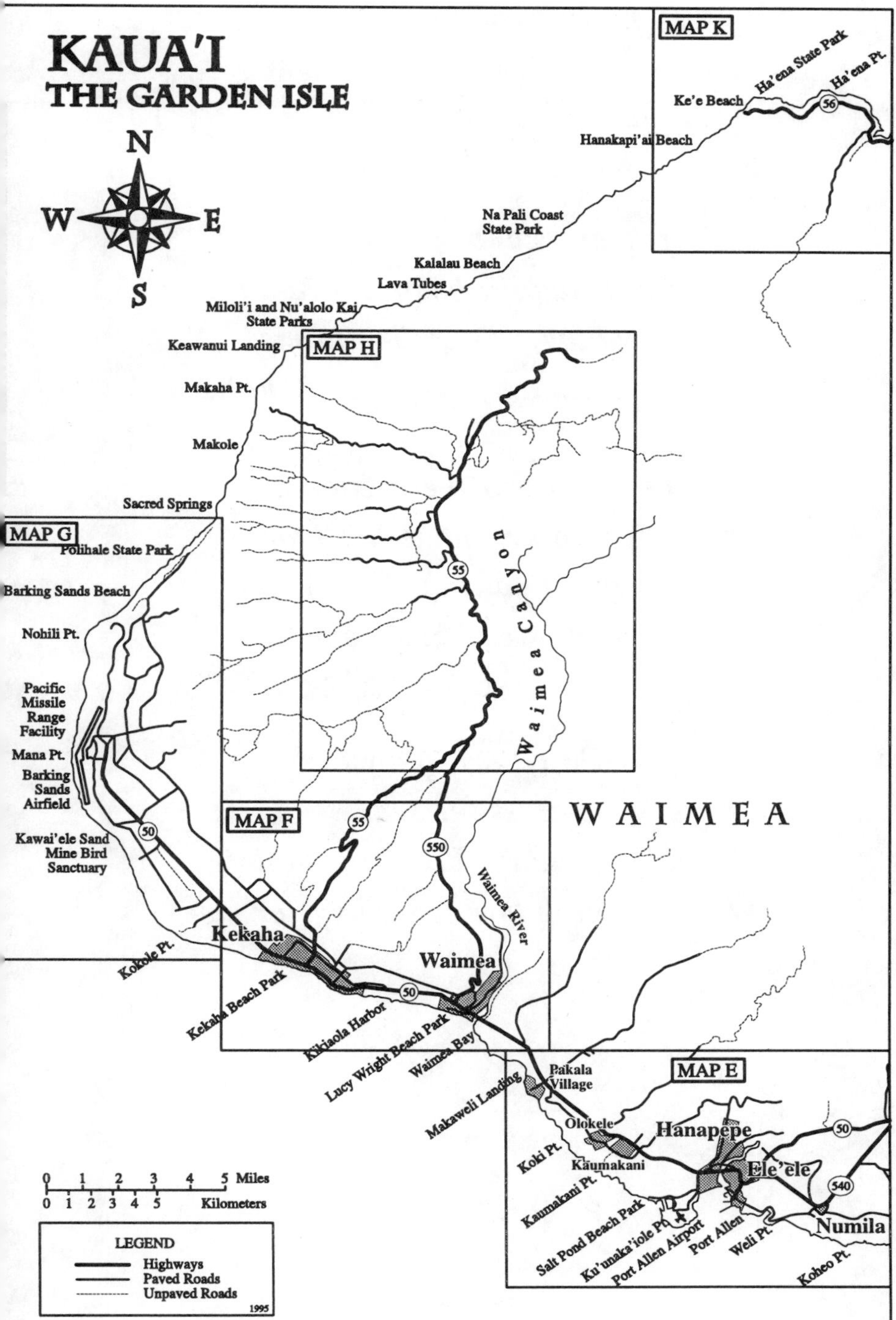

KAUA'I
THE GARDEN ISLE
N
W
E
S
MAP K
Ha'ena State Park
Ha'ena Pt.
Ke'e Beach
56
Hanakapi'ai Beach
Na Pali Coast
State Park
Kalalau Beach
Lava Tubes
Miloli'i and Nu'alolo Kai
State Parks
Keawanui Landing
MAP H
Makaha Pt.
Makole
Sacred Springs
MAP G
Polihale State Park
Barking Sands Beach
Nohili Pt.
Pacific
Missile
Range
Facility
Mana Pt.
Barking
Sands
Airfield
Kawai'ele Sand
Mine Bird
Sanctuary
55
Waimea Canyon
WAIMEA
MAP F
55
550
50
Waimea River
Kekaha
Kokole Pt.
Waimea
Kekaha Beach Park
Kikiaola Harbor
Lucy Wright Beach Park
Waimea Bay
Makaweli Landing
Pakala
Village
MAP E
Olokele
Hanapepe
Ele'ele
50
540
Koki Pt.
Kaumakani
Kaumakani Pt.
Salt Pond Beach Park
Ku'unaka'iole Pt.
Port Allen Airport
Port Allen
Weli Pt.
Numila
Koheo Pt.
0 1 2 3 4 5 Miles
0 1 2 3 4 5 Kilometers
LEGEND
Highways
Paved Roads
Unpaved Roads
1995

*There's an island, across the sea,*
*Beautiful Kaua'i, beautiful Kaua'i.*
*It's calling, It's calling to me,*
*Beautiful Kaua'i, beautiful Kaua'i.*

*In the mist of Fern Grotto,*
*Mother Nature made her home,*
*And the falls of Wailua,*
*Where lovers often roam.*

*So I'll return to my isle,*
*Across the sea,*
*Beautiful Kaua'i, beautiful Kaua'i,*
*Where my true love is waiting for me.*

By Randy Farden

# INTRODUCTION

Kaua'i is called "The Garden Island," and even to those unfamiliar and unacquainted with this serene and special place, the reasons are obvious and well deserved. It is lush and green, the most verdant of all the Hawaiian Islands. Rich in flora and fauna, it is an "Eden" within a paradise of unsurpassed natural beauty. There are more waterfalls, more rivers and more birds than on any of the other islands. It is abundant with wild fruit and flowers and provides a loving shelter to many endangered species. Yet it is only within the past decade that the full impact of this nickname has been realized, that Kaua'i has truly become "The Garden Island."

After two major hurricanes, the island has literally gone back to its roots. It has been replanted, grown back from new seeds and blossomed as much as any living garden. With each devastating hurricane, Kaua'i has grown and grown back - and grown back again. Like a plant or tree that needs to be pruned so that it will grow and blossom, Kaua'i has emerged from each disaster stronger and more beautiful than before. With each rebuilding and new restoration, its people have come closer together and are more appreciative of what they have. Their island has become precious. It is impossible to take nature for granted, whether in its destruction or in its simple beauty.

While it has been eight years since Hurricane Iniki, Kaua'i is still feeling a few lingering effects. Kaua'i has been much longer in its recovery from Iniki than Hurricane Iwa a decade prior. Tourism, once tolerated and grudgingly acknowledged, was sorely missed and is now seen as a remarkable gift. Because the people of Kaua'i worked hard to rebuild their island and give it new life, they take particular delight in the opportunity to share, not only with each other, but with those lucky enough to visit their special island. "The Garden Island" has also become "The Welcoming Island" as visitors are embraced with more love, enthusiasm, and *aloha spirit* than ever before.

So now that you know you have made the right decision in choosing Kaua'i for your vacation, you should also know that you have made the right decision in choosing KAUA'I, A PARADISE FAMILY GUIDE for your companion. From the family values "buzz words" of the 90's we know that "family" can mean anything. *Ohana*, the Hawaiian word for relative or family, is also used for an extended family of friends, neighbors or co-workers. Even visitors who share a common love and respect for the islands are often described as "part of the *ohana*." Your co-authors of this book have felt this "*ohana*" ever since they first visited the islands. In 1983, Dona moved to Maui to live permanently. Christie first visited the islands in 1978, and became so infatuated that she kept returning year after year.

Both your authors are visitors to Kaua'i and look at Kaua'i from a visitor's perspective. As authors who travel in very different modes (Christie, who travels as a family with two children, and Dona as a single adult), we can share our island experiences from different "family" viewpoints. Kaua'i offers the perfect location for a romantic interlude, a vacation with family or a wonderful destination to spend time relaxing with friends. There is plenty of information on traveling with children, as well as older adults who might be a part of your family. (By the way, if you don't have children or seniors to travel with, you might want to consider renting one or two after you read up on some of the freebies and discounts they get!)

You will notice that Kaua'i is divided into three distinct visitor destination areas along the North, South and East coasts of the island. Each area has characteristics uniquely their own, so reading up on them will help you decide just which part of Kaua'i you would like to make your temporary home. The Paradise Guidebooks are all formatted to help you do just that by listing all the accommodations and restaurants by area - section by section - along with sights and attractions particular to that neighborhood. Recreational activities are listed by category - after all, you choose activities by what interests you, not where they are located. General Information is in the front of the book. Overall facts and advice to help you with your vacation plans (as well as your general knowledge) are all in this section, but specific areas of information are emphasized for easy reference. Maps are located throughout the book - see the index for map pages to correspond with the areas you are most interested in.

Because the Hawaiian islands - and especially Kaua'i - are growing and changing almost daily, it can be difficult to keep up, especially given the particulars of printing and publishing a guide book. Anything can happen in a few weeks or months with the ongoing changes and continuing growth of Kaua'i, and it probably has! Unfortunately, that means that any guidebook is out of date before it is ever in print. However, as a small press, Paradise Publications is able to work up to within weeks of the date this book goes to print. That said, this is one of the most up-to-date and accurate guidebooks on the market. The previous edition of this guidebook had to be rewritten from scratch after Hurricane Iniki. Nothing could be left to assumption, so everything was carefully and thoughtfully updated. To further ensure that our guidebook is as up-to-date as possible, Paradise Publications also produces *The Kaua'i Update*, a quarterly newsletter to augment the information in this book. Paradise Publications is the only publisher to do so, so as facts in the book change, you'll be able to get the latest updates within months.

If your vacation plans include stopovers to one or more of the other islands, Paradise Publications also publishes *Maui, A Paradise Family Guide* by Dona Early and Christie Stilson and *Hawaii: The Big Island, A Paradise Family Guide* by John Penisten. (See ORDERING INFORMATION at the back of this volume.) If you would like a complimentary copy of our *Kaua'i Update* newsletter, send a self addressed stamped envelope along with your request and we will be happy to provide you with a sample of the most recent issue. We also publish the *Maui Update* and you are welcome to request a sample copy of this publication as well.

Of course there are other Kaua'i guidebooks and it doesn't hurt to get a second opinion. Most of the reviews in this book are based on our personal preferences, so you might wish to read others for different points of view or emphasis on other aspects of Kaua'i. We're so confident you'll find this Kaua'i Guide invaluable that we don't mind recommending the competition as well! There is the relative newcomer to the guidebook field, *The Ultimate Kaua'i Book* by Andrew Doughty. Jocelyn K. Fujii has a section on Kaua'i in *The Best of Hawai'i* as does Sean Pager in *Hawai'i: Off the Beaten Path*. Ray Reigert in his *Hidden Hawai'i* and Moon Publication's *Kaua'i Handbook* also have varied information with different emphasis.

The primary difference between guidebooks (ours from theirs) seems to be in choosing the information to use. We have tried to list ALL the accommodations, restaurants, and activities, not just our favorites or a select few. Of course, with a limited amount of time and resources, we have not been able to review each and every hotel, recreational activity or restaurant. Those which we have not been able to personally review have plenty of basic facts to assist you in making your decision. To further assist you in the selection of your accommodations, restaurant, activity or beach locations, we have added our personal recommendations or "Best Bets" to each chapter of this guide.

We also invite you to please write us with your viewpoints and experiences (they are what make the Paradise Guidebooks and Updates special and uniquely personal) and we will share them with our readers. Send directly to the authors by writing: Paradise Publications, 8110 SW Wareham, Portland, OR 97223 or E-mail us at: <Paradyse@worldnet.att.net>.

We have a few people to thank. Our gratitude to Kawaikapouokalani Hewett for permission to use words to his song "Hanalei in the Moonlight." To Chucky Boy Chock for permission to use "Ta Pua Elama" and "Na Nai'a Hulahula" and to Randy Farden for permission in using his song lyrics. To Kim Morris, because Kaua'i is his favorite island. A big hug and special thanks to Maren and Jeff Stilson for their patience while mom spent hours at the computer. An extra, and very notable thanks to Maren who is blooming as a budding editor.

*Aloha!*

*Dona and Christie*

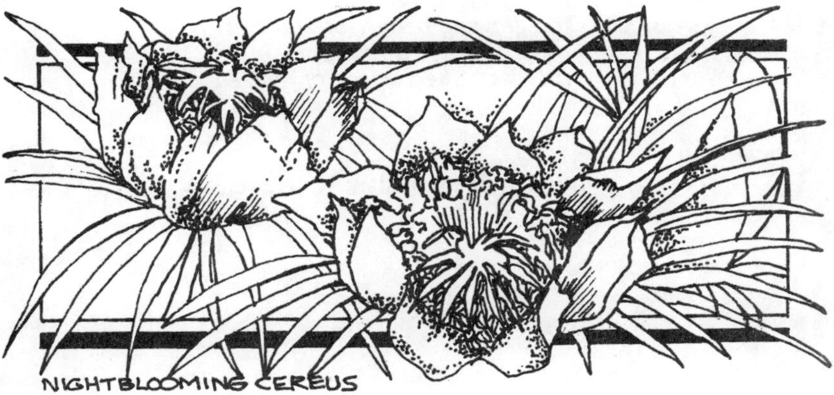

# *HANALEI IN THE MOONLIGHT*

*Hanalei in the moonlight*
*Silver shadows on the sea*
*Hanalei in the moonlight*
*A kiss, sweet memories*

*Hanalei in the moonlight*
*Lovers hand in hand*
*Hanalei in the moonlight*
*Strolling barefoot in the sand*

*Chorus:*
*E ho'i mai 'oe, e ku'u ipo*
*E ho'i mai 'oe, e ku'u ipo*
*I ka nani o Hanalei*

*Return to me my love*
*Return to me my love*
*To the beauty of Hanalei*

*E ku'u ipo, eia ho'i au*
*Ka u'i mālama a o Hanalei*
*'O ka pā kōnane a ka mahina*
*'Ōlinolino mai i ka 'ili o ke kai*

*Here I am my love*
*The glowing beauty of Hanalei*
*The brilliance of the moon*
*Glitters on the surface of the sea*

By Kawaikapuokalani K. Hewett

# GENERAL INFORMATION

## *OUR PERSONAL BEST BETS*

BEST FOOD SPLURGE: Sunday Brunch at the Kaua'i Marriott (with or without champagne) and the champagne Sunday Brunch or Friday evening seafood buffet at the Princeville Hotel.

BEST SUNSET AND COCKTAILS: South Shore: The Beach House, Brennecke's, or The Point at Sheraton Kaua'i in Po'ipu. North Shore: the lounge off the lobby at the Princeville Hotel with the sunset over Bali Hai. In Lihu'e, Whalers Brewpub at the Kaua'i Lagoons offers microbrewed beers with a spectacular view of the ocean and lighthouse as a backdrop.

BEST SUNSET DINING VIEW: North Shore: The Bali Hai Restaurant with views of Hanalei Bay and the Hamolokama mountains and waterfalls. The Hanalei Cafe at the Princeville Resort. South Shore: The Beach House restaurant in Po'ipu.

BEST BEACH SUNSET: From Ke'e Beach with the Napali for a backdrop or at the other end of the Napali coast at Polihale Beach.

BEST DAILY BREAKFAST BUFFET: Hyatt Regency Kaua'i.

BEST DINNERS IN PARADISE: Gaylord's, A Pacific Cafe, and Roy's.

BEST LUAU VALUE: Check the local Kaua'i newspapers for advertisements listing local luaus that might be held by churches or other organizations as fund raisers-a great value and you're sure to enjoy some great food!

BEST ROMANTIC DINING: Tidepools at the Hyatt. The Hanalei Cafe at the Princeville Hotel. Gaylord's at Kilohana

BEST FAMILY DINING: Barbecue Inn, Eggbert's

BEST FAMILY DINING ATMOSPHERE: Keoki's Paradise for the great tropical atmosphere, the homey feel of Auntie Ono's and the fun of an old-fashioned ice cream parlor at Beezers.

BEST PIZZA: Brick Oven Pizza in Kalaheo. Pau Hana wins for unusual toppings and best pizza on the North Shore. Kaua'i Aloha Pizza at the Coconut MarketPlace is great for to-go pizza. We've heard good things about Pizzetta in Koloa.

BEST COOL TREATS: Lappert's Ice Cream at one of their many locations. A shave ice at Halo Halo Shave Ice in Lihu'e or anything from Beezers.

BEST SALAD BAR: Duke's Canoe Club

BEST TAKE-HOME FOOD PRODUCTS: Fresh papaya salsa or Hanapepe-made taro chips from People's Market in Puhi. "Nuts-o-wot" roasted peanuts from Waimea. Flavored breadsticks (garlic nuts, chile or red salt) from Kilauea Bakery. Fresh produce from People's Market in Puhi and Made in Kaua'i products located roadside in Hanalei. (Note: some produce must be pre-inspected to go through airport agricultural checks, including pineapple and papaya!) After a "jittery" start we are now hearing good things about Kaua'i Coffee! (Available at retail stores or you can buy direct from Kaua'i Coffee Company at their visitor center in Kalaheo or by calling 1-800-545-8605.)

BEST (AND MOST AFFORDABLE) SEAFOOD RESTAURANT: Keoki's Paradise.

MOST CONVENIENT SHOPPING HOURS: Walmart in Lihu'e which opens at 6 am (Sundays at 8 am) and stays open nightly until 10 pm!

BEST ALOHA WEAR: Liberty House and Hilo Hattie. The "aloha wear" at Aloha Wear also comes highly recommended (as shown by the van of seniors we saw shopping for their Lei Day muumuus!)

BEST CHEAP ALOHA WEAR: While not for every traveler, the Salvation Army can be a great place to pick up some Hawaiian clothes to wear on your vacation. A muu muu for less than $5 is great for a beach cover-up or for wearing to a luau. There are two Salvation Army thrift store outlets. Hanapepe (4465 Puolo) is open Tuesday-Friday 9 am-noon and Saturday 9 am-3 pm. Hours for the Lihu'e location (4028 Rice St. by Mid-Pac Auto) are Tuesday-Saturday 10 am-4 pm. The Kaua'i Humane Society Thrift Shop (3100 Kuhio Hwy.) is open Tuesday-Friday 9:30-5:30; from 10 am-2 pm on Saturday.

BEST LEIS: People's Market in Puhi or the Blue Orchid in Koloa. Also, inexpensive leis can be found inside the Honolulu airport or at the lei stands outside.

MOST SPECTACULAR RESORT GROUNDS: Hyatt Regency Kaua'i.

BEST ROMANTIC ADVENTURE: A trip up the Wailua River to Fern Grotto in a kayak for two. A horse and carriage ride at Kilohana Plantation.

BEST EXCURSIONS:

| | |
|---|---|
| *Most spectacular*: | a helicopter tour. |
| *Most unusual*: | a kayaking trip around the Napali coast. |
| *Best adventure on foot*: | the first two miles of the Kalalau trail on the Napali coast. |
| *A world away*: | a helicopter tour of the isolated island of Ni'ihau. |
| *Unusual land tour*: | Hawai'i Movie Tour: the island and some special island sights! |

BEST CHANCE OF GETTING RAINED ON: The Wai'ale'ale Crater, the wettest spot on earth!

BEST BEACHES:

*Most scenic* -- Lumaha'i Beach or Ke'e on Kaua'i's North Shore.
*Unspoiled* -- Maha'ulepu, Honopu and Lawa'i Kai.
*Best for kids* -- Salt Ponds, Lydgate Beach Park, or Po'ipu Beach for protected kiddie wading area.
*Best dolphin spotting* -- Kauapea (Secret) Beach has fresh springs and dolphins can sometimes be spotted!

BEST RECREATION AND TOURS: See the beginning of the RECREATION & TOURS chapter for ideas!

BEST KAUA'I GET-AWAY-FROM-IT-ALL RESORT: Princeville Resort or The Kilauea Lakeside Estate (a private lakefront home).

MOST AFFORDABLE GET-AWAY-FROM-IT-ALL-ON-THE-NORTH-SHORE CONDO: Sealodge.

BEST HOTEL VALUE: Kaua'i Coconut Beach

BEST CONDO VALUE: Banyan Harbor

BEST BOOKING AGENT: We were impressed with Suite Paradise, they offer particularly good rates for week long stays if you are looking for a Po'ipu destination. And they are open Saturday and Sunday for taking your reservations!

BEST DISCOUNTS: We are disappointed to report that there really are not any great island discounts or coupon books. Many of the visitor magazines offer coupons. The rental car drive guides have coupon pages, Avis has an insert in their's with additional discounts. Aston properties gives guests a complimentary coupon book. We'll keep on the lookout for new, improved and better discounts and coupon books!!

*Entertainment Book* coupon discounts continue to offer discounts at several Kaua'i hotels and condominiums. *Entertainment Book* is printed in most major cities around the country and contains coupons for dining and activities in that area. In addition, they carry discounts for accommodations in other regions of the U.S., including Hawai'i. These may be useful in planning where you stay. However while we have recommended it previously, the HAWAI'I volume has very little to offer the visitor to Kaua'i for the $40 price tag. The outstanding restaurants that previously made this a must-purchase are no longer included.

The 1999 edition for Hawai'i lists the following properties on Kaua'i: Aston at Po'ipu Kai, Aston Kaua'i Beach Villas, Kaua'i Coast Resort at the Beachboy, Banyan Harbor, Best Western Plantation Hale, Embassy Vacation Resort, Kaua'i Coconut Beach Hotel, Kaua'i Sands Hotel, Kiahuna Plantation, Makahuena at Po'ipu, Marc Hale Moi Cottages, Marc Pali Ke Kua at Princeville, Marc Pono Kai Resort, Marc Princeville Pu'u Po'a, Outrigger Kaua'i Beach.

Many restrictions apply with limits on availability and categories of rooms. For example, they may require a five night maximum stay, exclude Christmas holidays or require that you make reservations more than 90 days prior to arrival. They only offer a few rooms at these discounts, so make your travel plans well in advance if you want to take advantage of any vacation bargains!

Check your local area Entertainment Book for possible discounts on Hawai'i accommodations. If you are still interested in the activity and restaurant coupons in the Hawai'i edition (which also has accommodation discounts) -- be an informed shopper and ask which Kaua'i merchants, hotels, and condos are included before you buy it. They change dramatically from year to year. When you go to book a property with either your local or the Hawai'i book be sure you know the current prices of the property. Some of the discounts are as much as 50%, others are much less because the rack prices they base the discounts on can be much steeper than if you book your accommodation through a different rental agent. We found that the Kaua'i Coconut Beach Hotel currently had the best discounts (check their "specials" even without an Entertainment Book!) For information contact Entertainment Publications at their Honolulu office at (808) 737-3252 or write them at 4211 Waialae Ave., Honolulu, HI 96816. You can also check your phone book under Entertainment, Inc.

***The beach activities are subject to weather and ocean conditions!***

BEST SNORKELING: Beginners -- Po'ipu Beach and Lydgate. Intermediate -- Tunnels (only for strong swimmers).

BEST BODY SURFING: Shipwreck Beach.

BEST SURFING: In front of the old Waiohai called "Acid Drop," Beach House, or Hanalei Bay.

BEST WINDSURFING: Beginners -- 'Anini.
Intermediate -- Tunnels or Mahaulapu.

BEST SWIMMING: Po'ipu Beach, Hanalei Bay, Salt Ponds.

BEST FLOWERS: Sunshine Markets around the islands;
People's Market in Puhi.

BEST NIGHT SPOTS: Gilligan's is now the only real nightclub on the island, but many restaurants and lounges offer live music and entertainment.

UNUSUAL GIFT IDEAS: Hawaiian motif needlepoint canvases and fabrics or an original Oriental doll quilt from Kapai'a Stitchery in Lihu'e. Mouse pads with Hawaiian designs may be the perfect gift for all your internet friends (available at Big Kmart and probably elsewhere) or be an angel and bring home one of Uncle Eddie's Aloha Angels dressed in a variety of muu muus, hula skirts, sea shells, or tapa cloth. These collectible ornaments have their own shop at the Hanapepe Cafe and are also sold at the Sheraton, Marriott, and Princeville hotels or by catalog. Movie buffs will enjoy The *Kaua'i Movie Book*, a full-color account of films,

TV shows and documentaries all shot on Kaua'i. Available at bookstores or support the non-profit Wilcox Foundation at (808) 245-1198. The Kaua'i Products Store at Kukui Grove not only has a nice selection of locally-made products, they also have homemade fudge! Made fresh daily on the premises, it comes in tropical flavors like chocolate or vanilla macadamia, Kona coffee, and pina colada. Roy's has a do-it-yourself chocolate souffle kit for making his signature dessert at home. Or purchase some tropical scented lotions, soaps, or candles from Island Soap & Candle Works. Scented with island fragrances like plumeria, torch ginger, or pikake, they are all hand-made using natural ingredients and even more fun -- you can watch them being made at their factory and gift shop in the Kong Lung Center in Kilauea or Koloa Town!

REALLY UNUSUAL GIFT IDEAS: "Uncle" Bill Ford makes custom Hawaiian coconut golf clubs -- a souvenir novelty gift that actually works! Contact him at PO Box 1403 Koloa, Kaua'i, HI 96756, call (808) 742-9250 or Email: unclebillford@webtv.net. And here's a really "novel" idea: Po'ipu-based Paradise Works will create a custom, personalized romantic adventure novel as a remembrance of your visit to Kaua'i. You just need to fill out a questionnaire with information about your trip to Kaua'i. Cost is $29.95. They are located at Accents at the Hyatt Regency Kaua'i. Call (808) 742-2457, FAX 742-9146 or visit their website <www.ParadiseWorks-Inc.com>.

BEST T-SHIRTS: The Red Dirt shirts are a way to take a little bit of Kaua'i home with you, but our favorites are Crazy Shirts: more expensive than the run-of-the-mill variety, but better quality. And now they come in flavors! Coffee, chocolate, beer, *Li Hing Mui* (local Chinese plum), and chile pepper colored tee's look - and smell - yummy! (Well, maybe not the beer. . .) They come in clever packages (the coffee shirt comes in a coffee bag); they're preshrunk - and colorfast!

## *BEST FREE STUFF:*

Kaua'i maps from The Hawai'i Visitors Bureau or the Chamber of Commerce.

A tour of the Guava Kai Plantation in Kilauea.

The Kamalani playground for the kids at Lydgate Park.

Free bi-monthly lectures and field tips on a variety of Kaua'i history topics through the Kaua'i Historical Society. (808) 245-3373

Free movies at the Princeville Hotel for resort guests and dining guests.

Free camping permits at state parks on Kaua'i.

Na Pali Eco Adventures sponsors whale slide shows during the winter season. This presentation is complimentary at various locations around the island. Check with (808) 826-6804 for days, times, and location.

Every Friday, the local galleries in Hanapepe host "Art Night" with at least one of them providing refreshments and an art demonstration. Decorative lighting adds to the mood for visitors to enjoy a festive stroll, watch artists doing portraits, and enjoy the hula show and local Hawaiian music.

A scenic drive along Kaua'i's North Shore.

Free admission to the Fayé Museum -- exhibits and photos of a pioneer sugar family at Waimea Plantation Cottages. Open 9-9 daily.

The Royal Coconut Grove Lounge (at the Kaua'i Coconut Beach Resort) has free pupus every afternoon from 4:30-5:30 pm.

Outrigger Kaua'i Beach Hotel offers daily arts & crafts demonstrations (quilting, seed leis, nut ornaments) in their lobby.

Sunset torchlighting ceremony at the Hyatt Regency.

Free coffee tasting at the Kaua'i Coffee Company Visitor Center & Museum

A free Dune Walk Tour guided by the Kaua'i Historical Society is offered every other Monday 9-10 am at the Hyatt Regency. The tour's focus is on prehistoric native Hawaiian sites and sand dunes of Makawehi.

Many free produce swap meets pop up around the island on various days.

Free introductory scuba lessons at resort pools.

Waimea Town Celebration in February; Koloa Plantation Days in July.

Free Yoga class offered 10 am-noon on the second Saturday of each month at the Institute for Yoga Science at Kaua'i Village in Kapa'a. Call (808) 828-0999.

The public is invited to Special Hawaiian Exhibits offered each morning in the Aupaaka Terrace at the Kaua'i Marriott. The exhibits and times vary daily but include Coconut Frond Weaving, Hula Dance Class, Hawaiian crafts, and displays of Hawaiian quilts, featherwork, and Ni'ihau leis.

Free self-guided tour of Moir Cactus Gardens and Hawaiian Gardens at the Kiahuna Plantation in Po'ipu. (Plants are marked.) Call (808) 742-6411.

Not quite free, but for a small donation, we think this counts: Enjoy a hike with an interpretive guide along the many trails of the Koke'e area. Offered during summer months only by the Koke'e Natural History Museum.

The Koke'e Natural History Museum also offers free guided and trail clearing hikes (through the Research Conservation Program) from June through mid-September. The museum sponsors a number of environmental and cultural festivals throughout the year. For further information contact them at PO Box 100, Kekaha, HI 96752 or call (808) 335-9975.

The Exhibition Hall at Kukui Grove Shopping Center is a cooperative effort between the Garden Islands Arts Council, Kaua'i Society of Artists. The Exhibition Hall regularly features the most creative and energetic efforts of the art community. In 2000, for example, the Exhibition Hall will welcome "Chalk Talks" where artists will be challenged to create temporary works of art on the sidewalk using colored chalk. An example of previous activities included an autumn "Lights, Lanterns and Luminaries" and an event called "Hello, Mr. Postman" where artists will design unique and innovative mail receptacles. Sounds fun!

Watch jewelry being designed and created at The Goldsmith's Gallery in the Kinipopo Shopping Village in Wailua.

Free daily hula and Polynesian shows (5 pm) at the Coconut MarketPlace. The center is located 15 minutes north of Lihu'e between the Wailua River and Kapa'a. To check their current schedule call (808) 822-3641.

Free hula and Tahitian Dance at Po'ipu Shopping Village, 5 pm Mon & Thurs.

Free shuttle between Kukui Grove Shopping Center and Po'ipu Resort area. Call the shopping center office at (808) 245-7784 for pick-up points and time schedule. (Some pickup points as far as Wailua.)

A two-hour guided Crater Hill hike is offered daily at the Kilauea Point National Wildlife Refuge. It'll cost you $2 admission to the Refuge, but the guided hikes are free. Early reservations are recommended. Call (808) 828-0168 or sign up at the visitor center.

Special events and children's activities at Borders Books at the Kukui Grove Shopping Center.

Take a self-guided tour of the Hawaiian artifacts, museum-quality art and handcrafted items at the Kaua'i Heritage Center of Hawaiian Culture & the Arts at Kaua'i Village in Waipouli (Kapa'a). They also offer a varied number of video presentations, lectures and workshops. Many of them are free.

Ma's in Lihu'e gives you a free cup of coffee when you order a meal!

Free hula show Friday at 6pm at Kukui Grove Center

A Sunday service in Hawaiian at the Waioli Hui Church in Hanalei or the Waimea Foreign (Foreign, in this case, means English speaking!) Hawaiian Church to enjoy the exceptional choir and appreciate the great acoustics! Lihu'e Lutheran is a quaint 150-year-old church that also features Hawaiian music. 6 pm at the Kukui Grove Center.

On the first Saturday of the month, admission is free at the Kaua'i Museum. This monthly event features special family activities. You can obtain a calendar of events by writing 4428 Rice St., Lihu'e, HI 96766 (808) 245-6931.

Lae nani condominiums in Kapa'a offers a cultural tour of the *heiau* located makua of the property.

Kaua'i's wilderness areas: Waimea Canyon; Koke'e State Park; Alakai Wilderness Preserve; Napali Coast State Park.

The public is invited to *E Kanikapila Kakou*, a free, 12-week Hawaiian music program that features local composers each week. Held every Monday (Feb-May) at 7pm at St. Michael's and All Angels Parish Hall. Call 246-3994 for schedule and more information.

Watching the sunset from Ke'e Beach on the North Shore or from Polihale Beach on the western coastline.

The many and varied annual events that are offered at no charge. (See monthly calendar listing).

Free copy of *Kaua'i Update* newsletter! Send a self-addressed stamped envelope to us at Paradise Publications and indicate you'd like the latest copy of our Kaua'i newsletter.

BEST GIFT FOR FRIENDS TRAVELING TO KAUA'I: Send a self-addressed, stamped envelope for a complimentary copy of the *Kaua'i Update* newsletter. (Subscriptions also available.) Or purchase them a copy of their own *Kaua'i, A Paradise Family Guide*.

# *HISTORY OF KAUA'I*

Our brief history will focus on just the island of Kaua'i. Please refer to our recommended reading section for information which will augment the history of the Hawaiian islands in general.

Although it is not the usual way to begin an historic narrative, this history of Kaua'i will begin in September 1992. The aftermath, now more than seven years, continues to leave a few lingering effects. On September 11th, life was forever altered on Kaua'i when hurricane force winds swept across the island. Few structures were left undamaged and although some hotels, condominiums and other island businesses were able to quickly rebuild, others have taken years to recover. Still other business closed their doors forever. But from the destruction sprang new growth and rebirth. In spite of insurance nightmares, hotels were renovated and remodeled, new restaurants opened and old ones were refurbished and improved. As we go to press there are but three hotels that are yet to reopen.

Hurricane Iniki left a heavy footprint throughout the island in the way it altered physical attributes and geography; the way it impacted important commercial industries like tourism, fishing, and agriculture; and the way it affected the attitudes, philosophies, lifestyles and even lives of its people. Many residents left after the second hurricane to hit the island within only ten years. Many others felt that with two hurricanes behind them they could probably face anything and be stronger for it. The facts about Hurricane Iniki were sent out to millions on the international news. Every devastating detail was reported, and we eagerly watched the good and bad news as it unfolded. But now that the day-to-day effects have diminished and the facts have become historical statistics, they can be neatly and benignly tucked into the section on Weather and its sub-category: Hurricanes. That done, let's go back seven years plus a few million to the creation of Kaua'i, The Garden Island.

Far beneath the warm waters of the Pacific Ocean is the Pacific Plate, which moves constantly in a northwest direction. Each Hawaiian island was formed as it passed over a hot vent in this plate. Kaua'i, the oldest of the major islands in the Hawai'i chain, was formed first and has since moved away from the plume, (the source of the lava) so it is no longer growing. But the ocean that created these islands millions of years ago has all but swallowed them back, leaving only atolls of coral reef. The archipelago known as Hawai'i spans 1,523 miles with 132 islands, shoals and reefs that reach as far west as the Aleutian Islands of Alaska. The Big Island is now the youngest in the chain and is continuing to grow. A new island called Lo'ihi (which means "prolonged in time"), southeast of the Big Island, is growing beneath the surface of the Pacific and is expected to emerge from the oceanic depths in about a million years. All islands other than the major eight come under the jurisdiction of the City and County of Honolulu. Midway Island, previously under the control of the U.S. Navy, is now a part of the National Wildlife Refuge and tours are now available there, departing from Honolulu! But, the islands we tend to think of as comprising the State of Hawai'i are the eight islands within the 400 southernmost of the island chain: Hawai'i, Maui, Kaho'olawe, Lana'i, Moloka'i, O'ahu, Ni'ihau and Kaua'i.

## *History*

The northernmost islands of the "eight" major islands, Kaua'i and Ni'ihau, were created together, emerging from the surface of the sea at the same time. They are actually dissected domes separated by the shallow 17-mile wide Kau'lakahi Channel. Lehua to the north and Ka'ula to the south are two tiny uninhabited islets that are part of Ni'ihau and Kaua'i County.

The interpretations of the name Kaua'i prove to be varied. Harry Franck, in his 1937 publication entitled *Roaming in Hawai'i,* noted that the translation was "to light upon" or "to dry in the sun." The reason might possibly be because driftwood landed on the shores of Kaua'i more often than on other islands. It lies very much in the path of the trade winds and of ocean currents. He continues: "The more commonly accepted meaning of the name is 'fruitful season or time of plenty,' because in olden times Kaua'i was the only island of the group which never suffered from famine on account of drought. In very ancient times, it was known as Kaua'i-a-mano-ka-lani-po, which freely translated means 'The fountain-head of many waters from on high and bubbling from below.'"

Kaua'i is young in geological terms, but its birth probably began about 6 million years ago and continued for about 3 million years. It lay dormant for another 1.5 million years before having a resurgence of volcanic activity which created the eastern portions of Kaua'i over the course of more than 1.5 million years. The most recent volcanic activity occurred on the southern shore more than 40,000 years ago. Compared with Maui's most recent volcanic activity which occurred only 200 years ago, Kaua'i is the grandfather in the chain of major Hawaiian islands. Kaua'i is much smaller today than when it was first formed. Over eons of time the crashing waves and storms eroded the North Shore, reducing the island's diameter from over 30 miles to 25, a small price to pay in return for the dramatic result of the erosion: the splendor and majesty of the incomparable Napali Coast.

Kaua'i's other phenomenon of nature, Waimea Canyon, was formed when a huge fault broke open and was further eroded by the Waimea River. Kawakini and Wai'ale'ale are the twin peaks of the single shield volcano that formed the island. Mt. Wai'ale'ale is considered the wettest place on earth. Harry Franck's book, *Roaming in Hawai'i,* tells that "in very ancient days the topmost peak was called Ka-wai-kini, 'waters in multitudes' and survey maps still record that appropriate old name. But today it is more familiarly known as Wai'ale'ale (which means 'rippling waters' or 'sparkling waters'), for the surface of the little lake at the summit is never still."

Due to the years of erosion, Kaua'i has many land characteristics unique in the Hawaiian islands. With a total of 136 miles of coastline, Kaua'i has more sandy beaches per square mile than any other of the major islands. The Napali coast on the North Shore is another of mother nature's wondrous creations, rising as much as 3,000 feet from the sea.

Kaua'i is also home to Hawai'i's only navigable rivers, seven of them, in our opinion! (Official reports vary, citing as few as five and as many as nine!) Kaua'i today is a blend of 555 square miles of desert, mountains, beaches and rain forests, making it Hawai'i's fourth largest island.

Life began in the waters surrounding the island in the form of marine creatures. Fish, mammals and microscopic animals found homes under the sea while generations of coral polyps attached themselves to the barren volcanic rock and ultimately created a coral reef. Kaua'i remains on the fringe of the coral reef system. Thus, many of its beaches lack a protective reef and require more caution.

On land, life began slowly, sporadically and quite by accident. Spores of ferns and moss, as well as tiny seeds, were carried by the winds. The few that survived altered the composition of the barren rock by breaking it down into bits of debris and fertile soil. Insects were tossed about by storms and washed ashore on floating debris. Birds blown off course began to colonize, not only populating the island with their own species, but with larger seeds and grasses that they inadvertently carried on their feet, feathers, or in their intestinal tracts. The introduction of each species of flora or fauna was a rare event, taking thousands of years. With no predators, birds flourished. The only mammals to arrive without the help of man were the seal and the bat, and neither provided any threat to the birdlife of the islands. Since the mongoose was never introduced to Kaua'i, the birds continue to flourish here.

Just as the creation of life is explained in two equally valid interpretations -- the scientific and biblical -- the population of the Hawaiian Islands must be explained both by legend and science in equal measures of credibility. Kaua'i was the first home of the Hawaiian volcano goddess, Madame Pele (until her sister drove her out) as well as being the first Hawaiian island populated by the Polynesians.

Although the dates vary greatly, sometime between 200 A.D. to 700 A.D., the first Polynesian explorers came to Kaua'i from the Marquesa Islands. Findings suggest that their ancestors came from the western Pacific, perhaps as far as Madagascar. Centuries later, they were followed by the Tahitians, who came via The Big Island, and from their word manahune (or outcast) came the reality-based legend of the menehune, the Hawaiian leprechaun. Driven out by her sister, Madame Pele moved to the Big Island taking her fire with her. She now makes her home in the volcanoes of Manua Kea and Mauna Loa and is no longer associated with Kaua'i.

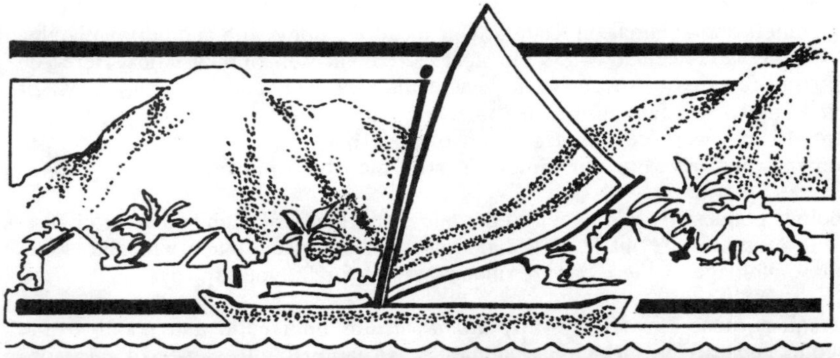

The Polynesians and Tahitians, however, settled on the island between the 11th and 14th centuries and began much of what we know as Hawaiian culture on the island of Kaua'i. The Polynesians brought their double-hulled canoes, laden with the food staples of taro and breadfruit as well as pigs, chickens and dogs (presumably the required quarantine time was more lenient back then), which supplemented their diet of fish. They also introduced a number of plants, including ginger and sugar cane (to name just a few). It was fortunate they arrived so well prepared, as Kaua'i offered them little in the way of edible plants. It is estimated that by the 1700's, the Hawaiian population may have risen as high as 300,000 persons, spread throughout the main eight-island chain.

Taro is the root from which poi is made, and it was used not only as a food by early Hawaiians, but as a dye for their tapa cloth and also to seal the lengths of the cloth together. It was used medicinally: rubbing a raw root stock on a wound was said to stop bleeding; the raw leaf stem rubbed on an insect bite was reported to reduce swelling and alleviate pain, and undiluted poi was used as a poultice for skin infections. The root would last for months without spoiling and, at one time, more than 300 varieties of taro were found in the islands. Today, fewer than 90 varieties are cultivated.

The Tahitians initiated a class system and the concept of *kapu* or *taboo*, which was composed of rigid sanctions and religious laws. However, they also introduced the pleasures of surfing, kite flying, the beauty of leis and the idea and spirit of *aloha*.

Four principal gods, Kanaloa (the god of the land of departed spirits), Kane (the god of war), Ku (the god who oversaw sacrifices) and Lono (the god of harvest and peace), formed the basis of the Hawaiian religion until the missionaries arrived. The stone foundations of *heiau*, the ancient religious temples, can still be found throughout the islands. The governing chief was called the *Ali'i*, and it was he who kept order by establishing various *"kapus."* It was *kapu*, for example, for men and women to dine together. It was not until the death of King Kamehameha that the appointed regent of Hawai'i, Ka'ahumanu, broke the kapu system when she persuaded Liholiho, heir of Kamehameha, to eat with her and his mother, Keopulani, in public.

The lower portion of the Wailua River was the sight selected as sacred by the high chiefs and kahunas on Kaua'i. This location, along with another at Waialua on O'ahu, were deemed two of the most sacred places in all the islands. Here you will find remains of seven *heiaus* where the early Hawaiians worshipped their gods. Future members of the *ali'i* were born at the sacred birthing stone located here. Rituals were an important part of their life, both in birth and in death. Human sacrifices were sometimes a part of the rituals performed.

Another goddess, Kapo, queen of the lei, is still honored each year on Lei Day. While most leis are made of island flowers, feather leis made with the exotic yellow plumage of the *o'o* were once reserved for Polynesian royalty.

The all-purpose Hawaiian word "*aloha*" means both hello and goodbye and encompasses all the principles, subtleties, variations and essence of the word "love."

Where science and legend exist side by side, you will discover some distinct differences about the islands. A business would not consider construction without first receiving a blessing of the land and often several more blessings during the construction. When a business prepares for a grand opening, *ti* leaves stretched across the threshold are gently untied (never cut), and the *kapuna* (minister/priest) will enter the building with holy water, words of reverence and gratitude to the creator. This is followed by a welcome to the family and friends. Perhaps this explains the power and strength of the people to rebuild and why these islanders have such hospitable and nurturing spirits. It has a base in reality in the *aina* -- the land -- and comes out as the spirit of *aloha*.

The islands were left undisturbed by western influence until the 1778 arrival of Captain James Cook. In search of the Northwest Passage, he first spotted and visited Kaua'i on January 19, 1778. His arrival was heralded by the local people, as his ship was believed to be a *heiau* for the god Lono. Cook stopped briefly at Ni'ihau and continued on to O'ahu and Maui. He brought with him to the island of Ni'ihau, melon, pumpkin, and onion seeds. On a later voyage, Cook was killed in a brawl on the Big Island of Hawai'i.

The arrival of Europeans brought not only tremendous changes for the Hawaiian culture, but also the introduction of diseases which killed the Hawaiian people in huge numbers.

One scholarly speculation is rarely spoken of in the history of the Hawaiian islands, but we feel it is at least interesting enough to bear mentioning. The sketches of early Hawaiians show them adorned with their ceremonial cloaks and unusual helmet-shaped headgear. It has been theorized (although rejected by historians) that perhaps Gaetan, a Spanish explorer enroute from the Philippines to Mexico in 1542, may have accidently stumbled across the Hawaiian islands. The headdress of the royal regalia does bear a striking resemblance to helmets worn by the early Spanish conquistadors, and the colors chosen by the Hawaiians for this garb are the royal Spanish colors. Another question these authors would like to address is the apparent knowledge of metal by the early Hawaiians. There are no ore deposits in the Hawaiian islands, yet when Cook arrived on Kaua'i and natives came aboard, they began clamoring for and seizing metal items. In *Kaua'i The Separate Kingdom*, Edward Joesting writes, "The Hawaiians had a knowledge of the importance of metal and eagerly sought these objects (from Cook) in trade for provisions." How did these 18th century Hawaiians know the importance of metal? How had they become introduced to the usefulness of it? Could there be some truth to this theory? Then again, it is perhaps merely coincidence.

Kamehameha the First was born on the Big Island of Hawai'i about 1758. He was the nephew of Kalaiopi, who ruled the Big Island. When Kalaiopi died, his son came to power, only to be subsequently defeated by Kamehameha in 1794. The great chieftain, Kahekili, was Kamehameha's greatest rival. He ruled not only Maui, but Lana'i and Moloka'i, and also had kinship with the governing royalty of O'ahu and Kaua'i. King Kahekili died in 1794, leaving control of the island to his sons, Kalanikupule. A bloody battle (more like a massacre since Kamehameha used western technology, strategy, and two English advisors) in the Iao Valley resulted in the defeat of Kalanikupule in 1795.

In the early 1790s, when Kamehameha was attempting to gain control of all the islands, The King of Kaua'i, Kaumuali'i, realized he had the advantage of having an island more removed from the rest of the Hawaiian chain. He had no interest in relinquishing his power to Kamehameha. The first attempt to overtake Kaua'i was made by Kamehameha in the spring of 1796. Encountering a storm, many of his soldiers never reached the island, being forced to turn back. Others who reached the island were killed at Maha'ulepu Beach. A later attempt by Kamehameha was thwarted when typhoid struck his soldiers. Without a fight, Kaumuali'i agreed to turn over his island to Kamehameha. Kaahumanu, the widow of Kamehameha I, wishing to further establish the loyalty of Kaumuali'i, forced the last King of Kaua'i into marrying her. Still doubtful of his allegiance, Kaahumanu went a step further. Kealiiahonui, the son of Kaumuali'i, still lived on Kaua'i and his potential power as an opposing force prompted her to take him as her second husband. When the missionaries arrived and found this polygamous practice abhorrent, Kaahumanu released Kealiiahonui from his marriage vows.

The last King of Kaua'i, Kaumuali'i, died on May 28, 1824, on the island of O'ahu, never returning to his home island of Kaua'i. Some histories report that he died on Maui. This information, however, is incorrect. He fell ill, quickly worsened, and died on O'ahu. Following the funeral services, his body was taken to Maui for burial. Kapiolani, royal wife of Kamehameha I, had become close friends with Kaumuali'i. Prior to the death of Kapiolani, an arrangement had been reached that at his death Kaumuali'i would be laid to rest next to her. Thus his burial is in Lahaina on the island of Maui.

Kaua'i was briefly inhabited by the Russians during the reign of Kaumuali'i. The Russian traders erected several forts. The remains of one, Fort Elizabeth, can still be found at the mouth of the Waimea River. Little remains but a few mounds of dirt at Fort Alexander, located on the bluff at Princeville. Another earthen fort in the Hanalei area called Fort Barclay, after a Russian general, has eroded completely away. Georg (with no "e") Scheffer was a German who worked for the Russian American Company. This trading company sent Scheffer to recover goods from one of their vessels that had gone aground off the coast of Kaua'i. When the ship was beached, King Kaumuali'i had seized the shipload of pelts, as well as everything else on board, stating that it now belonged to him.

Georg, a botanist and a physician, arrived first on O'ahu. After aiding the royal family when they were ill, he soon had endeared himself to the King. Scheffer reached Kaua'i in the spring of 1816 and expected that he might need force to regain the merchandise held by Kaua'i's King. He was surprised when Kaumuali'i warmly offered to return it. For a number of reasons, Kaumuali'i was eager to be on good terms with the Russians. Gifts were exchanged and Scheffer was later given the entire valley of Hanalei and subsequently bestowed Russian names on the Hanalei Valley, calling it Schefferthal and renaming the Hanapepe River the Don. King Kaumuali'i figured he could better protect his island from Kamehameha with the Russians as allies. Scheffer promised the King Russian protection. In *Kaua'i: A Separate Kingdom*, Edward Joesting writes, "The co-monarchs of Kaua'i (Kaumuali'i and Scheffer) now plotted the conquering of these islands. On July 1, 1816, they entered into a secret agreement.

When Kamehameha learned of this plan in 1817, Scheffer was ordered out of the islands. Interestingly, Georg Scheffer spent his last years in Brazil, having purchased a title for himself. He died Count von Frankenthal in 1836.

Kamehameha united all the islands and made Lahaina (on Maui) the capital of Hawai'i. It remained the capital until the 1840's when Honolulu (on O'ahu) became the center for government affairs.

Liholiho, the heir to Kamehameha I (also known as Kamehameha The Great), ruled as Kamehameha II from 1819 to 1824. Liholiho was not a strong ruler so Kaahumanu, the widow of Kamehameha I, proclaimed herself prime minister during his reign. (While Kaahumanu is said to have been the most favored wife of Kamehameha I, she did not have the bloodline of the *ali'i* royalty and therefore could not be his royal wife.) Kaahumanu ended many of the *kapus* of the old religion, thus creating a fortuitous vacuum which the soon to arrive missionaries would fill. The first missionaries arrived with their families from New England. On Kaua'i they were welcomed in 1821 and established mission houses around the island.

The missionaries caused drastic changes to the island with the education of the natives both spiritually and scholastically. It was the missionaries who set up guidelines that forbade the native women to visit the ships in the harbor. Also, horrified by the bare-breasted Hawaiian women, the missionary women quickly set about to more thoroughly clothe the native ladies. The missionary women realized that their dresses would not be appropriate for these more robust women and, using their nightwear as a guideline, fashioned garments from these by cutting the sleeves off and enlarging the armholes. The muumuu was the result, and translated means "to amputate or to cut short."

Many of the missionary descendants became successful planters and the island was blanketed with fields of green sugar cane. Sugar was to prove vital to the economic future of Kaua'i. The Polynesians who migrated from the Central Pacific brought with them the first varieties of *Ko*, or sugar cane. The early Hawaiians had many varieties of this grass which was used as a sweetener, as medicine for childbirth, and reportedly, as an aphrodisiac. The first successful sugar plantation in Hawai'i was established in Koloa (which means the place of long cane) in 1835 by Ladd & Company. William Hooper, a junior partner in Ladd & Company, established the plantation for that company by leasing 980 acres for $300 a year from King Kamehameha III. During the Civil War, Louisiana's shipping of sugar had been cut off which created a void that Hawai'i would step into. This was also the first sugar to be exported from the islands.

While the first workers in the sugar cane industry were Hawaiians, the increasing development brought workers from the four corners of the globe, which has helped shape much of Kaua'i's history and cultural diversity. During the next few decades, immigrants began arriving from both Asia and Europe to work in the fields and mills. In 1838, a few Chinese laborers were working for Hooper, but it was not until 1852 that the first contract laborers from China arrived in Hawaii. In 1868, more than 150 Japanese laborers left their homeland to work in the islands.

The first Portuguese contract laborers were recruited in the Azores and arrived in 1877. By that year, in the height of the sugar industry on Kaua'i, eight plantations had been established. They included Ele'ele, Grove Farm, Hanalei, Kapa'a, Kawaihau, Kilauea, Koloa, and Lihu'e. Castle and Cooke recruited a group of 629 Norwegian men, women and children who arrived in 1880. Larger groups of Chinese and Japanese immigrants continued to arrive in the 1880's. In 1902, the first Korean laborers arrived and they were followed by laborers from the Philippines in 1906.

A number of various crops have been attempted in Kaua'i, but for a variety of reasons, some of them proved successful, others failed:

The financial adviser to King Kamehameha I, a Spaniard named Don Francisco De Paula Marin, introduced to the islands produce which would soon thrive in the warm tropical climate: limes, guavas, pineapples, and mango. Guava quickly flourished in the islands and today it grows wild around Kaua'i in addition to being commercially grown. The Guava Kai Plantation operates 480 acres of orchards in Kilauea and offers a free self-guided tour.

In the 1860's, rice cultivation was attempted in Hanalei, Wailua, and Kapa'a. Labor proved too expensive and production ceased after only a few years.

Silk production was tried experimentally in Koloa and Hanalei between 1836 and 1845. Exports of raw silk by 1844 were small and the problems of droughts and insect pests caused heavy losses. Another factor was the difficulty in finding skilled labor -- "but G.W. Bates blamed the destruction of the industry, upon the religious zeal of the natives, who refused to feed the silkworms on Sunday." (Source: *Hawai'i and Its People* by A. Grove Day.)

A try at tobacco in Hanalei was a failure due to heavy rains. While it proved more successful on the south shore, it was never harvested commercially. One of the other more unusual crops was tapioca, which was attempted in Koloa.

Today, tourism is Kaua'i's major industry, while sugar continues to be the island's largest agricultural crop. Papaya, guava and coffee are also becoming increasingly important as the island diversifies its agricultural economy. In fact, Kaua'i now has the largest producing coffee plantations in the state. White shrimp, raised in state-of-the-art aquaculture ponds in Kekaha, has recently become a successful export.

Kaua'i has also become well-known on the big screen. The beauty of the island with its spectacular scenery has allowed Kaua'i to play a role in more than 50 movies and full-length television features. *Jurassic Park, Uncommon Valor, Flight of the Intruder, Raiders of the Lost Ark, Blue Hawaii, Outbreak, King Kong* and *South Pacific* are only a few. More recently, Disney's *George of The Jungle* and the sequel to *Jurassic Park, The Lost World,* were partially filmed on Kaua'i. You may have noticed in the original *Jurassic Park* that when they showed an island map it was even shaped like the island.

The selection of Kaua'i for the location may be more than coincidence as the author of *Jurassic Park*, Michael Crichton, resides at least part of the year on the North Shore of the island! For more information on Kaua'i in the movies check the RECREATION & TOURS section. We have a complete list of films shot on the island and information on a Movie Tour.

While visiting the Hawaiian islands, you may never see some of the native species of birds and plant life. Most of the remaining endangered native species can now only be found in protected areas. The more aggressive species that have been introduced over the past centuries have encroached on these fragile native ones and many endemic varieties have become extinct. Several refuges and botanical gardens on Kaua'i offer the visitor the rare opportunity to see these species at close proximity. See *Garden Tours* in the Recreation Chapter.

The Hawaiian State Flag was designed for King Kamehameha I in the first part of the nineteenth century. The British Union Jack in the corner acknowledges the early ties the islands had with England. The eight horizontal stripes of red, white and blue signify the eight major islands in the Hawaiian chain. King Kalakaua composed the state's national anthem, "Hawai'i Pono i".

A history of Kaua'i cannot be complete without a discussion of the *Menehune*, which were alluded to previously. An early account in the logs of Captain Cook tells of a people he found in Hawai'i that were smaller in stature and lighter skin-toned than most other Hawaiians. He described them as being a servant class. But are the menehune the stuff of myth or fact? The folklore says that the Menehune would work at night, creating vast projects such as the Menehune (or Alekoko) Fishpond, (still seen today, located off Nawiliwili Road) and the Menehune Ditches. Among the speculated theories, perhaps the most probable is that the Menehune were people from Tahiti who called themselves Manahune. In earlier times, while still in Tahiti, they had been conquered by warriors from the nearby island of Raiatea. It was theorized that the term Manahune might mean "conquered people" and thus could be construed to mean that they were lower in the social order rather than smaller in size. A census conducted in the early part of the nineteenth century showed that there were 65 Menehune living in the Wainiha Valley. Archaeologically, there have never been any bones that indicate a dwarf population was ever present on Kaua'i. While the Menehune are a part of island storytelling throughout the Hawaiian chain, they seem to have their roots on Kaua'i. If something goes wrong, you can blame it on the Menehune! So, if you lay down your sunglasses for just a minute, and discover them in the next room a little later, you can figure that the *Menehune* must have been up to their mischief. If something is unexplainable, then it probably was the Menehune. Whatever the facts, the legends of the Menehune are colorful and adds to the richness of the island's folklore.

There are a number of good books that will cover the history of the island and its people. The bibliography lists a number of resources. The most in-depth is *Kaua'i: The Separate Kingdom* by Edward Joesting, which is well-researched and recommended for those looking for a complete island history. *The Kaua'i Papers*, published by the Kaua'i Historical Society, is a collection of historical accounts told by some of Kaua'i's most prominent persons. Between 1914 and 1957 members and invited guests presented 115 papers to the Historical Society.

This is the published collection of just some of these papers. The authors were primarily island born and raised. While some are short stories, others offer more in-depth coverage of island events. The account of Queen Emma's visit to the Alaka'i Swamp is told by Eric A. Knudsen, and John M. Lydgate recalls the early days of Waimea. *The Kaua'i Papers* is a wonderful book that brings the early history of the plantation days on Kaua'i to life. Other books with good general historical background on all the islands is *Hawaii, an Informal History* by Gerrit Judd and *Shoal of Time* by Gavan Dawes.

## HISTORY OF NI'IHAU

Ni'ihau, located 17 miles west of Kaua'i, continues to be Hawai'i's only privately owned island and visitation is allowed only by special request. The island of Ni'ihau is slightly more than 47,000 acres with dimensions of 18 miles by 6 miles. The highest elevation is 1,281 feet at Paniau. Lake Halali'i is 841 acres and although the largest inland lake in Hawai'i, it is more a salt flat that only becomes a lake (with a depth of five or six feet) during heavy rains. Mullet are raised in the lake until the waters recede, then they are caught and sent to market.

The contemporary human history of the island of Ni'ihau began when Mrs. Eliza McHutchenson Sinclair, a widow, relocated from New Zealand. Although she considered the purchase of a piece of beachfront property on O'ahu (which we now know as Waikiki,) in 1863, she visited the island of Ni'ihau following a brief rainy spell and found it quite to her liking. She purchased the 46,000 acre parcel from King Kamehameha IV for the price of $10,000 on January 20, 1864. It was not until later that she discovered Ni'ihau suffers from a serious shortage of water, which continues to this day. Eliza Sinclair enjoyed only three long and hot summers on her new island before purchasing land on the western side of Kaua'i in Makaweli. Additional acreage was purchased in Hanapepe and this formed the bulk of the land used by the Gay & Robinson sugar plantation. Abrey Robinson inherited control of the family estate when Eliza died in 1893 at the age of 92. Abrey, born in 1853 in New Zealand, studied law at Boston University

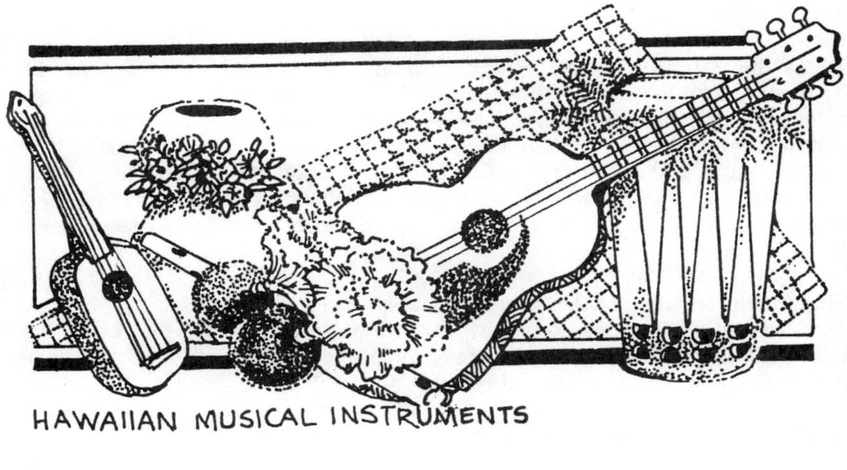

HAWAIIAN MUSICAL INSTRUMENTS

before returning to Kaua'i. He implemented some plans to improve the island by undertaking reforestation, initiating irrigation systems, and introduced to the island Arabian horses, cotton and honey.

In 1898 Hawai'i became a territory of the United States and Abrey began limiting outside influences and also began raising cattle and sheep. While crops proved difficult due to the arid climate, they have found that kiawe charcoal is a product they can produce.

It was not only O'ahu that became involved in World War II. Following the attack on Pearl Harbor, a lone Japanese pilot encountering engine failure was forced to ditch at Ni'ihau (nearly landing on an outhouse). The pilot was captured by the Ni'ihauans and resident Howard Hawila Kaleohano seized the documents he was carrying. Later these papers would assist in the breaking of the Japanese communication code. While five men made the trip across the channel to Kaua'i for help, the prisoner apparently managed an escape, taking his machine guns with him. The spunky Ni'ihau residents, however, had become fed up with this intruder's poor manners and overpowered him. One island resident, Benjamin Kanahele was shot three as times as he tried to convince the pilot to act more civilized. Following the hit by a third bullet, Benjamin became so angry that he promptly grabbed the pilot and threw him against the wall with such force that the pilot was killed.

At the time of Cook's visit, the population may have numbered as many as 10,000 individuals. By the time of the Sinclair purchase, the island had a population of 1,008. Dogs were raised by the Ni'ihauans for food and the Sinclairs ordered the destruction of all the canines to safeguard the new herds of sheep and cattle. More than 700 *kanakas* (people) left the island rather than destroy their dogs. The island population currently numbers in the neighborhood of 230 persons, 95% of whom are descendants of the Robinson Family (whose matriarch was Eliza Sinclair), speaking Hawaiian and maintaining the customs of old Hawaii. The island offers one paved road, no telephones and power is limited to that supplied by a generator. There are a few cars and transportation is mostly provided by donkeys and horses. The town of Pu'uwai is where the local residents live.

Today the island continues to be a working cattle and sheep ranch and has become famous for its beautiful shell necklaces. Made from very small shells collected on the island's beaches, the colored strands range in speckled hues from yellow to blue or white. The necklaces are very intricate and it may take hundreds of shells to find one or two that are in perfect condition. The price of these necklaces range from hundreds to thousands of dollars. Look for them on display at gift and jewelry stores and appreciate the craftsmanship of these fine pieces of Hawaiian art.

For more information on this remote island, an excellent resource is *Ni'ihau: The Traditions of an Hawaiian Island* by Reriorterai Tava and Moses K. Keale, Sr. Published in 1989, it is an outstanding account of the history of the island and its people from ancient to modern times.

# *KAUA'I NAMES AND PLACES*

AHUKINI - altar (for) many (blessings)

ALAKA'I - to lead

'ELE'ELE - black

HA'ENA - red hot

HANAKAPI'AI - bay sprinkling food

HANALEI - crescent bay

HANAPEPE - crushed bay (due to landslides)

HA'UPU - recollection

KAHANA - cutting

KA-HOLUA MANU - the sled course (of) Manu

KA-LA-HEO - the proud day

KA-LALAU - the straying

KA-LAMA - the torch

KA-LIHI KAI - seaward Kalihi (the edge)

KA'LIHI WAI - water Kalihi

KANAKA-NUNUI-MOE - sleeping giant

KA-ULA-KAHI - the single flame (streak of color)

KA-UMU-ALI'I - the royal oven

KA-WAI-KINI - multitudinous water

KA-WAI-HAU - literally this translates to ice water. (Apparently the name denotes a reference to an American missionary lady who drank only ice water.)

KE-KAHA - the place

KIKI A OLA - container (acquired) by Ola

KI-LAU-EA - spewing, much spreading (referring to volcanic eruptions)

KILOHANA - lookout point or best, superior

KOKE'E - to bend or to wind

KOLOA - place of long cane, the word "ko" means sweet sugar cane grass. Another source says it was named for the steep rock formation called "Pali-o-koloa."

KO'OLAU - windward

LIHU'E - cold child

MANA - arid

MILO-LI'I - fine twist (as sennit cord)

NA-MOLO-KAMA - the interweaving bound fast

NA'PALI - the cliffs (This is one word, not two!)

NA-WILIWILI - the wiliwili trees

NIU-MALU - shade (of) coconut trees

NOUNOU - throwing

PO'IPU - completely overcast or crashing (as waves)

POLI-'AHU - garment (for the) bosom (referring to snow)

POLI-HALE - house bosom

PRINCEVILLE - no Hawaiian translation, this area was named for the young Prince of King Kamehameha IV and his wife, Queen Emma. They visit the North Shore of Kaua1i in 1860 with their son Prince Ka Haku o Hawai'i. Plantation owner Robert Wyllie selected this name in honor of the young prince.

PUHI - blow

PU'U KA PELE - the volcano hill

WAI'ALE'ALE - rippling water or overflowing water

WAI-LUA - two waters

WAI-PAHE'E - slippery water

For more information on Hawaiian place names consult *Place Names of Hawai'i* by Mary Kawena Pukui, Samuel H. Elbert and Esther T. Mookini.

# *ISLAND FACTS AND FIGURES*

While the islands are known as Hawaii, the largest single island in the chain is also dubbed Hawaii. Confusing to say the least! The islands as a total unit have their own nickname, state flower, bird, tree, and fish. However, each individual island also has its own unique identity. Here is a little background on each.

**THE HAWAIIAN ISLANDS**

Nickname: The Aloha State
State Flower: Hibiscus
State Tree: Kukui
State Bird: Nene Goose
State Fish: Humuhumunukunukuapuaa
State Mammal: The Humpback Whale
State Capitol: Honolulu

**KAUA'I**

Nickname: The Garden Island
Island color: Purple
Flower: Mokihana (fragrant berry)
County Seat: Lihu'e
Area: 550 sq. miles
Length: 33 miles
Width: 25 miles
Coastline: 90 miles
Highest point: 5,243 ft. Kawaikiki

**O'AHU**

Nickname: The Gathering Place
Island color: yellow/gold
Flower: Ilima
County Seat: Honolulu
Area: 595 sq. miles
Length: 44 miles
Width: 30 miles
Coastline: 112 miles
Highest point: 4,003 feet at the top of Ka'ala Peak

*Island Facts and Figures*

**MAUI**
Nickname: The Valley Isle
Island Color: Pink
Flower: Lokelani (cottage rose)
County Seat: Wailuku
Area: 729 sq. miles
Length: 48 miles
Width: 26 miles
Coastline: 40 miles
Highest point: 10,023 ft. Haleakala

**KAHO'OLAWE**
Nickname: Lonely Island
Island Color: Gray
Flower: Hinahina
Area: 45 sq. miles
Length: 6 miles
Width: 10 miles
Coastline: 20 miles
Population: currently only goats
Highest point: 1,477 ft. Moa'ulanui

**MOLOKA'I**
Nickname: Friendly Island
Island Color: Green
Flower: White Kukui Blossom
Main Town: Kaunakakai
Area: 260 sq. miles
Length: 38 miles
Width: 10 miles
Coastline: 88 miles
Highest point: 4,961 ft. Kamakou

**LANA'I**
Nickname: The Private Island
Island Color: Orange/gold
Flower: Kaunaoa
Main Town: Lana'i City
Area: 140 sq. miles
Length: 18 miles
Width: 13 miles
Coastline: 47 miles
Highest point: 3,366 ft. Lana'ihale

**HAWAI'I**
Nickname: The Big Island
Island color: Red
Flower: Red Lehua
(flower of the Goddess Pele)
County Seat: Hilo
Area: 4,038 sq. miles
Length: 93 miles
Width: 76 miles
Coastline: 266 miles
Highest point: 13,796 ft. at the peak of Mauna Kea

**LOHI**
Still under water off the coast of the Big Island of Hawai'i, but continuing to grow due to volcanic activity.

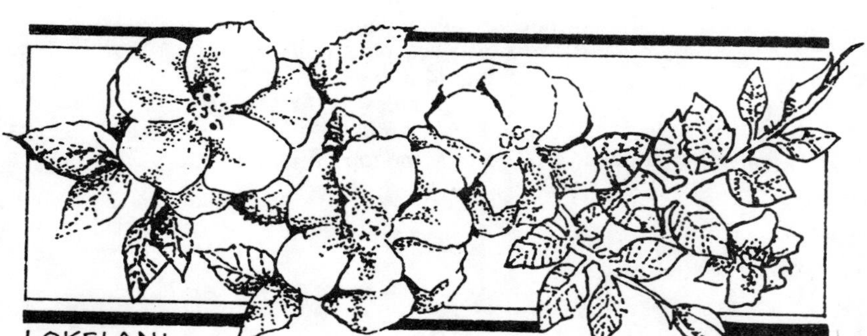

LOKELANI

The Hawaiian language was first written down by American missionaries. Using the written language they created an alphabet with only twelve letters, five of which are vowels. The key to the language is to remember to pronounce each letter, except for some vowels which run together as one. In some cases, substitute the "v" sound when "w" appears. The - ‘ - symbol you see is a glottal stop and instructs you to say each letter separately (such as *ali‘i*). Also, pick up a copy of *Instant Hawaiian*, this small handy guide will have you speaking like a *kama‘aina* in no time!

Following are some of the more commonly used Hawaiian words that you may hear:

## *HAWAIIAN WORDS AND THEIR MEANINGS*

ali‘i (ah-lee-ee) chief
aloha (ah-loh-hah) greetings
hale (Hah-lay) house
hana (HA-nah) work
hana hou (ha-nah HO) to do it again
Heiau (heh-ee-ah-oo) temple
haole (how-lee) a caucasian
kai (kye) ocean
kahuna (kah-HOO-nah) teacher, priest
Kama‘lanaina (Kah-mah-ai-nuh) native born
kane (kah-nay) man
kapu (kah-poo) keep out
keiki (kayee-kee) child
lana‘i (lah-nah-ee) porch or patio
lomi lomi (loh-mee-LOH-mee) to rub or massage
luau (loo-ah-oo) feast
makai (mah-kah-ee) toward the ocean
malihini (mah-lee-hee-nee) a newcomer or visitor
mauka (mah-oo-kah) toward the mountain
mauna (MAU-nah) mountain
mele (MAY-leh) Hawaiian song or chant
menehune (may-nay-hoo-nee) Hawaiian dwarf or elf
moana (moh-ah-nah) ocean
nani (NAH-nee) beautiful
ono (oh-no) delicious
pali (PAH-lee) cliff, precipice
paniolo (pah-nee-ou-loh) Hawaiian cowboy
pau (pow) finished
poi (poy) a paste made from the taro root
pua (POO-ah) flower
puka (POO-ka) a hole
pupus (poo-poos) appetizers
wahine (wah-hee-nay) woman
wiki wiki (wee-kee wee-kee) hurry

## *WHAT TO PACK*

When traveling to paradise, you won't need too much. Comfortable shoes are important for all the sightseeing. Sandals are the norm for footwear, although with periods of heavy rains, some close toed shoes might be recommended. Dress is casual for dining, although a few restaurants require men to wear sport shirts with collars. Clothes should be lightweight and easy care. Cotton and cotton blends are more comfortable for the tropical climate than polyesters. Shorts and bathing suits are the dress code here! A lightweight jacket with a hood or sweater is advisable for evenings and the occasional rain showers, especially on the North Shore! If you are headed for a stay on the North Shore (particularly in the winter months) we've found it advantageous to throw in a pair of slacks and a sweater or sweatshirt. The only need for warmer clothes is if your plans should include hiking at higher elevations or visiting the Koke'e area. Tennis shoes or hiking shoes are a good idea for longer hikes.

Sunscreens are a must and we recommend you toss in a bottle of insect repellent. A camera, of course, needs to be tucked in and perhaps your video camera. A hat with a brim is a good idea for protecting the head and neck from the sun while touring or just sitting on a beach. Binoculars are an option and may be well used if you are traveling between December and April when the whales arrive for their winter vacation, or used to enjoy the incredible sea and land birds found on the Garden Isle. Special needs for traveling with children are discussed in the next section. Anything that you need can probably be purchased once you arrive. Don't forget to leave room in those suitcases for goodies that you will want to take home!

## *TRAVELING WITH CHILDREN*

Traveling with children can be an exhausting experience for parents and children alike, especially when the trip is as long as the one to Kaua'i. Unfortunately, there are currently no direct flights from the mainland to Kaua'i. Your trip to the island includes a stop on O'ahu and a transfer to one of the outer island airlines.

Packing a child's goody bag for the long flight is a must. A few new activity books or toys that can be pulled out enroute can be sanity-saving. Snacks (boxes of juice are a favorite with younger children) can tide over the little ones at the airport or on the plane while awaiting your food/drink service. The new squeeze-it juice drinks are also very portable and can be frozen in their plastic bottle, providing a cool drink when the need arises. A thermos with a drinking spout works well and is handy for use during vacations. A change of clothes and a swim suit for the little ones can be tucked into your carry-on bag. (Suitcases have been known to be lost or delayed.) Another handy addition is a small night light, as unfamiliar accommodations can be somewhat confusing for little ones during the bedtime hours. Disposable diapers are a real travel convenience, but are very expensive in the islands. You might wish to fill up any extra space in that suit-case with these! And don't forget a strong sunscreen!

Children may have difficulty clearing their ears when landing. Many don't realize that cabins are pressurized to approximately the 6,000 foot level during flight. To help relieve the pressure of descent, have infants nurse or drink from a bottle, and older children may benefit from chewing gum. If this is a concern of yours, consult with your pediatrician about the use of a decongestant prior to descent.

***CAR SEATS:*** By law, children 3-4 years of age must have seat belts unless they are in a federally approved car seat. Federally approved car seats are required for all children from birth up to three years.

While some rental agencies do have car seats for rent, you need to request them well in advance as they have a limited number. The one -- and only -- car seat we have rented had seen better days, and its design was only marginal for child safety. Prices run about $5-15 per day. After that single experience, we always brought our own car seats with us. Several styles are permitted by the airlines for use in flight, or it may be checked as a piece of baggage.

***BABYSITTING:*** There are no full-time childcare services on Kaua'i. Arrangements for childcare can be made through your hotel concierge and the front desk at most condominiums will be able to assist you. Service is expensive and will run you about $10 per hour. As you can easily figure from the rates, spending much time away from your children can be costly. Consider the feasibility of bringing your own sitter, it may actually be less expensive, and certainly much more convenient. This has worked well for us on numerous occasions. Grandmothers work well too!

***CRIBS:*** Many condominiums and most hotels will be able to provide you with a rental crib. Prices run about $5 per day, $30 per week. There are many portable, cribs that can be packed into a large duffle bag. They weigh under 20 pounds and can be purchased for about the same price as a 10-day rental.

Ready Rentals (808) 823-8008 or 1-800-599-8008 has cribs, car seats, high chairs, strollers and more for rent on a daily or weekly basis. They offer Jerri Zoomer strollers and even twin baby strollers.

***FOR EMERGENCIES***: See listing under HELPFUL INFORMATION in this chapter.

***DINING:*** You'll soon discover, if you have not already, that a children's menu is often referred to as a "Keiki Menu." A few restaurants that offer menus (or child-size portions) for the young traveler include: Barbecue Inn, Whalers Brewpub, Buzz's Steak & Lobster, Duke's Canoe Club, Gaylord's, Bali Hai, JR's Plantation, Oki Diner, Kountry Kitchen, Chuck's Steak House, Keoki's Paradise, Wailua Family Restaurant, Waipouli Deli, and The Bull Shed. You can get a "Kitten's Menu" at TomKat's; feed the "Little Cowboys" at JR's Plantation; or ask for the "Menehune Menu" at any of the three Camp House Grill locations. A Pacific Cafe and The Beach House will serve any item on their menu at half size for half price. And kids (under 12) eat free at the Kuhio Dining Court at the Holiday Inn SunSpree Resort! Be sure to ask for children's menus or prices wherever you dine.

***BEACHES - POOLS:*** A precaution on the beach that is often neglected is the application of a good sunscreen -- always reapply after swimming! It is easy to forget that in the cool pool or ocean, you are still getting those strong rays of sun.

There is a natural kiddie wading pool at Po'ipu Beach Park that is ideal for toddlers and very young swimmers. The handy nearby access to bathrooms can be a plus for the traveling family, too! To the west of Po'ipu Beach is a small protected cove known as Baby Beach. This can be accessed from Spouting Horn Road to Ho'ome Road. Good swimming locations for the younger set might also be found at Lydgate Beach Park and at Salt Pond Beach Park. At both locations you'll find an ocean pool made from boulders. Kids will love exploring a variety of sea creatures found in the tidepools here and at 'Anini Beach. Several beaches do have lifeguards on duty. Unfortunately, many people underestimate the power of the ocean and drownings occur far too often on Kaua'i. Beaches are generally not posted with flags (as on some other islands) if the surf is creating conditions which are unsafe. Most beaches only have a generic warning sign posted. If the surf is up, choose a different activity that day, or just enjoy a picnic on the beach. Some beaches are fine for children in the summer, but are definitely NOT an option during the higher surf of winter.

The Kamalani playground at Lydgate Beach Park will give your lively young ones a chance to expend some of their energy. The park's volcano slide, tree-house, spider web rope ladder, tire swings, and caves were designed especially with active 6-10 year olds in mind! Another wonderful new playground is the park at the entrance to the Princeville Resort on the North Shore.

Few resorts have pools with the very young traveler in mind. The Point, a south shore condominium, has a toddler pool. The Outrigger Kaua'i Beach also has a keiki pool as does Kaua'i Coast Resort at the Beachboy (formerly known as the Kaua'i Beachboy Hotel). We recommend taking a life jacket or water wings (floaties). Packing a small inflatable pool for use on your lanai or courtyard may provide a cool and safe retreat for your little one. Typically resorts and hotels DO NOT offer lifeguard services.

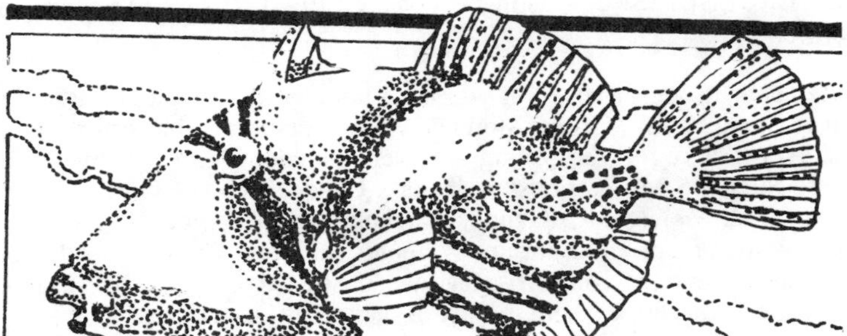

HUMUHUMUNUKUNUKUAPUAA

***CHILDCARE PROGRAMS***: Some of these youth programs are seasonal, offered just summer, spring and Christmas holidays. A few are available year round. Generally, only resort guests can partake of these childcare programs, however, sometimes they are open to non-hotel guests.

**Holiday Inn Sunspree Resort Kaua'i** has various activities offered in their Children's Activity Center when the hotel is full. Free to hotel guests. (808) 823-6000.

**The Hyatt Regency Kaua'i Resort & Spa's** daily Camp Hyatt program offers children 3 through 12 the opportunity to have fun while learning about island life. The Camp's learning adventures -- covering such topics as archaeology, Hawaiian crafts, local history and ecological preservation -- are part of the resort's overall commitment to responsible tourism development for Kaua'i. In addition to its learning adventure program, the regular Camp Hyatt schedule includes a variety of activities including cruising down the 150-foot waterslide, face painting, tennis and Hawaiian arts and crafts like seashell sculpture, sand crafts, shell bracelets, Hawaiian leaf stencil painting, and more. Camp Hyatt is available seven days a week to resort guests ages 3-12. Children under three may attend when accompanied by a babysitter. Camp hours are from 9am to 4pm. The cost of $45 per child includes lunch and a Camp Hyatt t-shirt, in addition to all the supervised activities. (Half day sessions are also available.) There is a ratio of one counselor for every four children, or one for every two children between the ages of 3 and 5. Exclusive Camp Hyatt programs can be arranged for groups staying at the resort. (Kinda makes you want to be a kid again, huh?)

Night Camp is available from 4-10pm daily, providing children 3-12 years with a variety of supervised activities including games, Hawaiian crafts and computer and video games. The cost for Night Camp is $10 per child.

There are also special Holiday Activities for children during the Christmas season, Easter and Halloween. Easter Sunday is the only day of the year that Camp Hyatt is closed. Instead, children are invited to take part in the annual Easter Egg Parade which winds its way through the resort groups and ends with an Easter Egg Hunt and Festival. For Halloween, Camp Hyatt kids are assisted in making their own special costumes then taken on a trick-or-treat excursion through the various hotel departments.

During the summer season, the resort hosts complimentary Family Fun Theater Nights on Wednesdays in the Alii Gardens. The event offers popular movies that were filmed on Kaua'i along with popcorn and soft drinks.

Rock Club Just for Teens is held during the summer season. It offers a "cool" activity room where teens can gather to socialize. Offered daily from 11:30am until 7 pm, Rock Club offers a variety of unsupervised teen-oriented activities such as music videos, ping-pong, darts, as well as popcorn and other munchies. The Rock Club is complimentary to teens 13 to 17 years. (808) 742-1234.

The Kiahuna Keiki Klub at the **Kiahuna Plantation** is for registered resort guests and is offered Monday through Friday 9 am until 3 pm. It is offered during the summer as well as during spring and winter breaks. Kids are exposed to the Hawaiian culture through activities like lei making, 'ukulele lessons, hula dancing, and story telling. Other activities include beach walks, lagoon fishing and arts & crafts. Activities are based on the age level of the children participating. Cost is $15 per child for half day session, $30 for full day. (808) 742-5411.

**Kaua'i Marriott Resort and Beach Club** features a program for 5-12 year olds called Kalapaki Kids. Provided for hotel guests only, activities include boogie boarding, hula, traditional Hawaiian games, crafts or making ice cream sundaes! The program is available year round. Rates run $25 (9-11:30am) $30 (11:30am-3pm) or $45 for the full day. Pass per child runs: Three day $120, five day $190, seven day $252. (808) 245-5050.

**Outrigger Kaua'i Beach Resort's** Keiki Klub is summer fun for children 5-12 years of age. Activities include beach combing, ukulele lessons, movie, pool play, Hawaiian face painting, swan/duck feeding, fishing derbies. Also included are excursions to Smith's Tropical Paradise and Fern Grotto! Full day program 8:30am-3:30pm is $30. Also available are 8:30am-11:30am (without lunch) $15, 8:30am-12:30pm with lunch $20.00, 12:30pm-3:30pm without lunch $15, 12:30pm-3:30pm with lunch $20. (808) 245-1955.

The **Princeville Hotel's** Keiki Aloha program is available for children ages 5-12 years of age and is designed with play in mind. Qualified youth counselors plan a full schedule of activities including snorkeling/beach play, sandcastle creations, Hawaiian arts & crafs, shell collecting and more. The program runs year round, but is closed Sundays. The program was complimentary during summer 1999, but check to see if there is a charge in the future! Charges other than summer are $50 for full day for the first child, $40 each additional child. Does not include lunch. $10 per hour for one child and $1 for each additional child from the same family for childcare. (808) 826-9644.

**Sheraton Kaua'i Resort** entertains young guests with their Keiki Aloha Children's Program. Activities range from lei making and other Hawaiian arts & crafts to kite flying and ukulele lessons. The program is available year round. Price is $45 for a full day of play, $25 for half day. (808) 742-4016.

***SHOPPING:*** The Coconut MarketPlace is one of the best all around family malls on Kaua'i. Lots of small shops ensure that there will be something for every member of the family. While mom visits the art galleries, fashion and jewelry stores, the younger members will enjoy the Gecko Store or the Islander Trading Co. to see the parrots. You'll find mother-daughter outfits at Made for Mom & Me -- or match with your pets at Sweet Blossoms & Gypsy's Pet Corner! If everyone wants something different for lunch, it shouldn't be a problem. There's Kaua'i Aloha Pizza, Taco Dude, the Fish Hut, or Eggbert's, just to name a few. MarketPlace phone (808) 822-3641. On the North Shore, pull off the road at Kilauea and stop in at the Little Grass Hut next to Mango Mama's. Unique gifts and whimsical toys along with "Baskets of Aloha" are sold to benefit the Na Kamalei School. At Princeville Center, there's the Kaua'i Kite and Hobby Company, and in Hanalei visit Rainbow Ducks, Toys, and Clothing.

***MOVIE THEATERS:*** The twin Coconut MarketPlace Cinemas adjoin the shopping center and offer bargain matinees before 6 pm. Recording (808) 822-2324. For information (808) 821-2402.

Kukui Grove Cinemas has four screens in their theater which is across the street from the Kukui Grove Shopping Center. Phone (808) 245-5055 to hear a recording.

***OTHER ACTIVITIES WITH KIDS:*** The Kaua'i Children's Discovery Museum offers island-wide exhibitions, events, and programs in science, culture, arts, and nature. Science on the Move (November-February); StarNight Planetarium (June-August); Coral Reef Kids Camp (July-August) For more information on what and where call them at (808) 823-8222.

Storybook Theatre of Hawai'i involves children in good storytelling activities and invites them to watch the filming of Cablevision's *Russell the Rooster Show*, weekdays at 6 am and 3 pm, weekends at 8am. Call or FAX (808) 335-0712. A multi-media center is being developed in Hanalei. A long way from being finished, they are the producers of this cablevision kids show. Their long-term goal is to have a center where youth will do all aspects of the television production, from script writing to behind the camera stuff. Awesome goals!

Older children will enjoy a luau. The Kaua'i Coconut Beach has a program which offers a free luau for each child with a full-paying accompanying adult on several evenings each week. Call (808) 822-3455 for current schedule.

The free hula show at the Coconut MarketPlace (currently Mon, Thurs & Sat at 5 pm) often features child performers. The younger children in your traveling family might enjoy this casual, outdoor performance.

You'll find a Fun Factory game arcade at the Waipouli Town Center next to Foodland. They are open Monday-Thursday, 10 am-10 pm, Friday & Saturday till midnight.

Visiting Waimea? Take time to stop at Darri's Delites for shave ice, pastries, popcorn, and even better is their full service crackseed. (This Asian treat is actually a form of flavored and dried fruit with the pit still in it.) Located at 4492 Moana Rd. along Kaumuali'i Highway. (808) 338-0113.

Paradise Fun is an air-conditioned, indoor play facility for children ages 6 months and up. Now located in their new larger facilities at the Kukui Grove Shopping Center, they offer a snack bar, video arcade, big screen tv, and soft playground. All children must be accompanied by an adult 18 or older unless you take advantage of their drop-off while you shop childcare! Hours of operation: 9:30am-6 pm, till 9 on weekends. Admission from $2.50-6.95 depending on age. A great place to go on a rainy day! Phone (808) 241-7050.

Joe-Jo's Clubhouse at 9734 Kaumaulii Hwy. in Waimea is a small store, but fun and festive. A good place to take the kids after the scenic wonders of Waimea Canyon. Joe-Jo's has balloons plus nachos, hot dogs, pizza pockets, saimin, cookies, and shaved ice with over 60 flavors. Open 10 am-6 pm daily. (808) 338-0056.

Borders Bookstore in the Kukui Grove Shopping Center has thoughtfully created a play corner. They also have a children's book section and a large Hawaiian book section. They schedule events, from storytelling to clown visits. And it's all free!

Keiki Adventures Kaua'i specializes in guided Eco Tours for kids! Hiking, swimming, snorkel tours, exploring dry caves and ancient Hawaiian ruins are just a few of the activities that include healthy lunch and snacks, footwear, rain gear, day packs and hiking sticks. 1191 Kuhio Hwy., Kapa'a, HI 96746. Phone or FAX them at (808) 822-7823, or call toll-free 1-800-232-6699.

Lihu'e Lanes is now a completely smoke-free bowling alley. They currently offer daytime specials: $6 Mon-Fri, between noon and 2:30 pm; $10 on Saturdays 3-5 pm. A great idea on a rainy afternoon. They also have a snack bar with a kid friendly menu which includes pizza, burgers and even cinnamon toast! Located in Lihu'e at the Rice Shopping Center. (808) 245-5263.

***EXCURSIONS:*** Hiking, mountain biking, bass fishing at one of the reservoirs, or a horseback tour of the beach and sand dunes, a trip to the Kilauea Lighthouse, a visit to Spouting Horn or the North Shore's unusual wet and dry caves! Kaua'i abounds with natural beauty that will be enjoyed by the traveler of any age.

Waipo'o Falls is a good and fairly easy hike for families. Kayaks are available for two, so pair up with one of the kids and enjoy the scenic wonders on one of Kaua'i's navigable rivers. The Wailua River trip is picturesque and affords a chance to hear the "Hawaiian Wedding Song" performed when the tour boats arrive at Fern Grotto. Stay around after the tour boat leaves and enjoy the silent beauty of this unique location. Check *KAYAKING* in the RECREATION & TOURS section of this guide. Older children will also enjoy horseback riding, or trying their skills at boogie boarding at Po'ipu Beach Park next to the kiddie pool.

## *ESPECIALLY FOR SENIORS*

More and more businesses are beginning to offer special savings to seniors. RSVP booking agency offers special rates for seniors who book their accommodations through them. They are listed in the Rental Agents section of our accommodations chapter. Remember that AARP members get many travel discounts for rooms, cars and tours. Whether it is a boating activity, an airline ticket or a condominium, be sure to ask about special senior rates. And be sure to travel with identification showing your birthdate. Check the yellow pages when you arrive on Kaua'i for the senior discount program logo. Look for a black circle with white star in the ads.

The County of Kaua'i, Office of Elderly Affairs at 4444 Rice St. #105, Lihu'e, HI 96766 (808) 241-6400 provides advocacy to elderly persons and their families.

The Lihu'e Chapter of AARP has monthly membership meetings at 1 pm on the second Monday of each month at Lihu'e Neighborhod Center. Call the AARP office at (808) 246-4500 or stop by 4212A Rice St. (look for the sign in back) to pick up brochure information or just to visit and "talk story."

Kaua'i Senior Centers, 4491 Kou Street, Kapa'a, HI 96746. (808) 822-9675. They sponsor centers in Kilauea, Kapa'a (main office), Lihu'e, Koloa, Kalaheo, Kaumakani, Kekaha, Hanapepe, and Waimea. They provide programs including dancing lessons, quilt making and health classes, 8 am-noon.

Kukui's at the Kaua'i Marriott and the Outrigger's Hale Kipa Terrace have AARP discounts and Chuck's Steak House offers a senior dinner menu. Jolly Roger has a great $7.95 lunch and dinner menu for seniors while Wailua Family Restaurant offers almost a dozen all-day $9.99 senior dinners (including salad bar!) from 10 am. Kaua'i Coconut Beach has early bird dinner specials in their Flying Lobster restaurant; Holiday Inn SunSpree Resort offers them at the Kuhio Dining Court. Buzz's Steak & Lobster has a nightly early bird for $8.95 with salad bar and Al & Don's (at the Kaua'i Sands Hotel) offers senior dinners from $5.95. At Local Boy's Drive Inn in Lihu'e, seniors can enjoy a cup of coffee or cold drink for a quarter and free refills! Seniors and others will find inexpensive hot lunches (average price $3.10) at the Wilcox Hospital in Lihu'e. Love's Bakery at 4100 Rice St. offers senior specials Tuesdays and Fridays. Gaylord's, Kaua'i Coconut Beach, and Princeville all offer senior discounts on their luaus.

Kukui Grove Shopping Center has a gathering place for seniors to enjoy coffee and refreshments, exercise, talk story, do crafts -- they are even putting in computers so you can email the grandkids back home! Call (808) 245-7784 for hours and more information.

The Salvation Army can be a real treasure trove for the adventurous shopper. A muumuu for a couple of dollars is perfect for that luau. Locations in Lihu'e and Hanapepe.

Kaua'i has some interesting annual events for seniors: The Annual Seniors Extravaganza showcases talented seniors (January/Kaua'i War Memorial Convention Hall); rubber ducks race down the Waimea River at the Kaua'i Senior Center's Quacker Race (September/Lucy Wright Park); and First Hawaiian Bank's "Prime Time Health Fair" offers displays, information, and exhibits along with entertainment and bingo (October/Kukui Grove Shopping Center.)

A number of airlines have special discounts for seniors. Some also have a wonderful feature which provides a discount for the traveling companion that is accompanying the senior. Coupon books for senior discounts are also available from a number of airline carriers.

The local Kaua'i Bus offers discounts for senior citizens.

## *TRAVEL TIPS FOR THE PHYSICALLY IMPAIRED*

Make your travel plans well in advance and inform hotels and airlines when making your reservations that you are a person with a disability. Most facilities will be happy to accommodate. Bring along your medical records in the event of an emergency. It is recommended that you bring your own wheelchair and notify the airlines in advance that you will be transporting it. Other medical equipment rental information is listed below.

Additional information can be obtained from the State Commission on Persons with Disabilities on Kaua'i at 3060 Eiwa St. Room 207, Lihu'e, HI 96766 (808) 274-3308 which can provide general information on accessibility for private and public facilities on Kaua'i. For information on accessibility features and technical assistance regarding access standards contact the Commission on Persons with Disabilities, 919 Ala Moana Blvd. #101, Honolulu, HI 96814. (808) 586-8121 or inter-island toll free 1-800-468-4644. On Kaua'i call the toll free local number, 1-800-274-3141 for a directory of individual extensions.

Contact Parents with Special Keikis c/o Easter Seal Society of Hawaii, Kaua'i Service Center 3115 Akahi, Lihu'e, HI 96766. (808)245-7141. They provide support and education for parents of children with disabilities.

Although primarily for community services for residents, another good resource is the Kaua'i Center for Independent Living. Contact them at 4340 Nawiliwili Road, Lihu'e at (808) 245-4034.

***ARRIVAL AND DEPARTURE:*** On arrival at the Lihu'e airport you will find the building easily accessible for mobility impaired persons. Parking areas are located in front of the main terminal for disabled persons. Restrooms with handicapped stalls (male and female) are also found in the main terminal.

***TRANSPORTATION:*** The only public transportation is The Kaua'i Bus which charges riders $1 per ride. Seniors, students, or disabled with ID are 50¢. A monthly pass for persons with disabilities runs $12.50. Caregivers traveling with eligible individuals will not be charged a fee. All buses are lift equipped. Carry-on baggage is limited to 9" x 14" x 22". Food and drinks are prohibited. As part of their ADA paratransit service, door to door pickups are available for qualified individuals. Reservations must be made 24 hours in advance; ID may be required. Each bus has a destination sign on the front and curb-side of each bus which displays a route number. Schedules are available which show the route the bus travels and the times along that route. Route 100: Kekaha-Koloa-Lihu'e. Route 200: Lihu'e-Koloa-Kekaha. (Both have limited service to Koloa; only one stop pre day.) Route 300: Discontinued. Route 400: Hanalei to Lihu'e. Route 500: Lihu'e to Hanalei. Route 600: Lihu'e-Kapahi-Lih'ue. Route 700 circles the Lihu'e area.

For additional information phone the County Transportation Office at (808) 241-6410 between the hours of 7 am and 5 pm on Monday-Saturday.

***ACCOMMODATIONS:*** Each of the major island hotels offer one or more handicapped rooms including bathroom entries of at least 29" to allow for wheelchairs. Due to the limited number of rooms, reservations should be made well in advance. Information on condominium accessibility is available by calling State Commission on Persons with Disability on Kaua'i at (808) 274-3308. They publish the "Aloha Guide to Accessibility" available for $3-5 per category section. Gaylord's restaurant at Kilohana has handicapped access and Victoria Place B&B and Po'ipu B&B Inn are a few of the Bed and Breakfasts that have a handicapped accessible room.

***ACTIVITIES:*** Espirit de Corp Riding Academy has horses trained to handle physically-challenged riders. (808) 822-4688. Ocean Quest Watersports Co. offers diving tours and classes for the "Differently Abled." They advise you to call before you arrive as some paperwork is required for this program. Toll free: 888-401-3483. County of Kaua'i Parks & Recreation sponsors integrated programs for youngsters with developmental disabilities. (808) 241-6668. ARC of Kaua'i provides recreational programs for persons with disabilities, transportation provided. (808) 245-4132. Call Easter Seals of Hawai'i on Kaua'i regarding other activities (808) 245-7141.

***BEACHES:*** Lydgate State Park, Hanalei Pavilion Beach Park and Salt Pond Beach Park are the only beach parks which currently are considered to have disabled access, but their facilities may not meet the ADA guidelines for disabled access.

***MEDICAL SERVICES AND EQUIPMENT:*** *A.B. Medical Inc.* (808) 245-4995. They rent and sell medical equipment and supplies, including appliances and access devices. 24-hour emergency service is available. *American Cancer Society* (808) 245-2942. They provide equipment including walkers, wheelchairs, etc. on loan without charge for home use, with priority to persons with cancer. *Garden Island Oxygen Supplies* (808) 245-1931. They rent, sell and service oxygen tanks and ancillary equipment. *Home Infusion Associates* (808) 245-3787. Rents and sells medical equipment including wheelchairs. *Ready Rentals* (808) 823-8008 or 1-800-599-8008 also offers wheelchair rentals. *Kaua'i Hospice* (808) 245-7277 has hospital beds. In addition to their Maui outlet, *Gammie Home Care* recently opened in Lihu'e at 3215 Kuhio Hwy. (808) 632-2333. <www.gammie.com> They can provide medical equipment rentals, from walking aides to bathroom accessories or wheelchairs as well as oxygen services. It is again recommended that you contact any of these services well in advance of your arrival.

***Accessible Vans of Hawai'i*** has been renting vans to travelers with disabilities visiting Hawai'i since 1979 and has now expanded their service to Kaua'i. These special vans feature lower floors, electric sliding ramps for wheelchair users plus a 4-point safety securement wheelchair tie-down system. The front passenger seat is removable to allow for excellent sightseeing and viewing from the van. Accessible Vans rent by the day, week, month or long term. Deliveries and pickups may be arranged for the Lihu'e Airport or Nawiliwili Harbor as well as hotels, island tours, or even private homes. Accessible Vans of Hawai'i works with the Kaua'i Center for Independent Living to have a local contact and delivery person for their special-needs clients. Rentals of one or two days are $109 per day, 3-4 days is $99 and it drops for longer rentals. Collision damage insurance waiver is $12 daily. Email: avavans@maui.net or their website at <www.accessiblevans.com>. Reservations 1-800-303-3750 or FAX (808) 879-0649.

KAMEHAMEHA BUTTERFLY

# *WEDDINGS & HONEYMOONS*

With tropical waterfalls, lush gardens and idyllic beachfront settings, a wedding ceremony on Kaua'i can fulfill all your dreams.

While the requirements are simple, here are a few tips (based on current requirements at time of publication) for making your wedding plans run more smoothly. We advise you to double check the requirements as things change!

Both bride and groom must be over 18 years of age. (16 years old with written consent from parents or legal guardians.) Blood tests and birth certificates are not required, but you do need a proof of age such as a driver's license or passport. You do not need proof of citizenship or residence. If either partner has been divorced, the date, county and state of finalization for each divorce must be verbally provided to the licensing agent. If a divorce was finalized within the last three months, then a decree must be provided to the licensing agent.

A license must be purchased in person in the state of Hawai'i. The Department of Health can give you names of the licensing agents on the island. You need to make appointments with these licensing agents. Both bride and groom must appear in person before the agent.

If you have questions, the local registrar on Kaua'i can be contacted at (808) 241-3495. Recording with information (808) 241-3498. The fee is currently $50 cash, no checks. There is no waiting period once you have the license, but the license is valid for only 30 days.

One wedding agency informed us that your personal vows for a Catholic wedding require special arrangements between your home priest and the Kaua'i priest. If both bride and groom are practicing Catholics, the Church requires that you marry within the church building, unless you are granted special permission from the Bishop in Honolulu.

Check with the Chamber of Commerce on Kaua'i for information regarding a pastor. Many island pastors are very flexible in meeting your needs, such as an outdoor location, etc. For $7 ($8 on a credit card charge) they will mail you a wedding packet the includes a Kaua'i Vacation Planner, list of wedding coordinators, photographers, florists, churches, and a marriage license application. Kaua'i Chamber of Commerce, 4272-B Rice St. or PO Box 1969, Lihu'e, HI 96766. Phone (808) 245-7363, Website: <www.kauaichamber.org>

Appointments must be made with the marriage license agents on Kaua'i. The current list (subject to change):

*Kawaihau District:* Lynn Kubota (808) 822-5122; Grace Apana or Walter Smith, Jr. (808) 821-6887.

*Lihu'e District:* Theresa Koki or Annabelle Pacleb (808) 274-3100.

*Hanalei District:* Dayna Santos (808) 826-7742.

*Koloa District:* Val Coyaso (808) 332-7076.
For copies of current requirements and to receive necessary forms, write in advance to the State of Hawaii, Department of Health, Marriage License Section, PO Box 3378, Honolulu, HI 96801. (808) 586-4544.

*"A Wedding in Paradise"* can be found at <www.aweddinginparadise.com> The site offers information on wedding related services and information on unusual and adventurous options. They also have an "estimator" which allows the viewer to calculate expenses.

The Kaua'i Wedding Professionals Association Directory & Bridal Guide is a great source of information. In addition to comprehensive listings and information on all their members, they offer helpful tips on wedding requirements, planning, and photography. For a copy of the booklet, send $3 to KWPA, PO Box 761, Kapa'a, HI 96746. Website: <www.kauaiwedpro.com>

## *WEDDING BASICS:*

The Hyatt Regency Kaua'i and other island hotel resorts frequently offer "honeymoon" or "romance" packages. Since these vary seasonally, inquire with the property when making your reservations.

*Wedding Chapels:*
Aloha Church, Assembly of God, (808) 241-7717

Chapel By the Sea at Kaua'i Lagoons, Lihu'e. Extraordinarily beautiful site, albeit very expensive!! Call (808) 241-6021 or see listing under Wedding Companies.

Koloa Church, founded in 1835, is located at 3269 Po'ipu Rd. Outdoor weddings also available. Write them at PO Box 668, Koloa, HI 96756. (808) 742-9956

*Butterflies!!*
Butterflies Over Hawaii, 644 Kamalu Rd., Kapa'a, HI 96746. This Kaua'i-based company does the helicopter flower drop one better by releasing from 10 to 100 Hawaiian Monarch butterflies at your wedding or special event. (Released at the moment of pronouncement at your wedding, it symbolizes both your - and their - transformation and new beginnings!) The butterflies are raised in greenhouses with protective care and their graceful release is a humane and environmental alternative to throwing rice or releasing balloons. The butterflies' survival rate upon release is close to 100%. Prices range from $74.95 to $499.99 for release of 100 butterflies. (808) 245-8838, FAX (808) 245-8846 or call 1-888-BUTRFLI toll free. Email: butrfly@aloha.net Website: <www.butterfly-hawaii.com>

*Formal wear rentals:*
Leonor's Formal Wear offers tuxedo rentals and also sells wedding and bridesmaids dresses. (808) 245-2292

*Limousines:* Kaua'i Limousine (808) 245-4855, 1-800-764-7213.

*Catering:*
Heavenly Creations, custom catering and a personal chef. Special wedding and honeymoon services include a romantic dinner on the beach or a personalized treasure hunt leading to a secluded beach and a champagne picnic or buried treasure of goodies. Phone or FAX (808) 828-1700 or call toll-free 1-877-828-1700. <www.aubergines.com/heaven/>

*Video tape services:*

| | |
|---|---|
| Hawaiian Creative Video | (808) 822-5784 |
| I DO Video Productions | (808) 823-6130 |
| Video Lynx | (808) 821-1379 or toll free 1-888-310-3038. |

*Photographers:*

| | |
|---|---|
| Islandwide Photography | (808) 823-0200 |
| Linc Rydell Photography | (808) 822-2520 |
| Rainbow Photography | (808) 828-0555 or toll free 1-888-828-0555. |
| The Wedding Photographer | (808) 245-2866 |

***WEDDING COMPANIES:***

A basic wedding package costs anywhere from $250-750. Add a few extras and the price will boost to $500-1,800. Although each company varies the package slightly, a basic package will probably include assistance in choosing a location (public or private), getting your marriage license, selecting a minister and a varying assortment of amenities such as champagne, a small cake, or leis. Video taping, witnesses, or music are available for an extra charge. There are a variety of beautiful public facilities at which you may be married. However, wedding companies do have a variety of private locations which may be rented for an additional fee ($50-$250). Smith's Tropical Paradise has one of the most affordable. Many resorts offer assistance with wedding planning.

"Beautiful Seas" wedding packages are available for couples who choose marriage aboard ship in Hawai'i on ***American Hawai'i Cruises***. It includes the services of an official to perform the ceremony, a small wedding cake, live Hawaiian music, a flower lei and floral headpiece for the bride and a lei or boutonniere for the groom, champagne and keepsake flutes, photography service and a 24 5X7 photos in a souvenir album. The wedding package price is $695 plus cruise fares. See Weddings & Honeymoons in this chapter for information on tests and licenses. For honeymooners that marry on the Mainland on a Saturday, they don't have to "miss the boat" to enjoy a Hawaiian Islands honeymoon cruise. While the normal departures are on Saturday from Honolulu, the "Sea and Shore" honeymoon enables couples to board the ship in Nawiliwili, Kaua'i. After six days on board ship, the honeymooners will enjoy a seventh night at a Waikiki Hotel. Call 1-800-765-7000.

Bali Hai Weddings, PO Box 1723, Kapa'a, HI 96746. (808) 821-2269. Toll free 1-800-776-4813. Contact Marcia Kay Sacco. Add to the Essentials Package ($350) a variety of options including a sunset cruise, photographer, flower arch way, horse and carriage, conch shell ceremony, or limousine from $35-250. Assistance with travel and honeymoon accommodations.

Chapel by the Sea at Kaua'i Lagoons, 3351-A Hoolaulea Way, Lihu'e, HI 96766. (808) 241-6021. FAX (808) 241-6008. Toll free 1-800-724-1686. Weddings are scheduled 5 times daily. The use of the chapel, floral arrangements, lei or bouquet, minister and solo musician runs $1,200. Photography packages start at $300, edited video $425. Add a ride in a private white wedding carriage $400 or white limousine $250. Cake and champagne options $2-300. <www.chapel@hawaiian.net>

Coconut Coast Weddings and Photography, PO Box 385, Hanalei, HI 96714. (808) 826-5557. Toll Free 1-800-585-5595. FAX (808) 826-7177. Complete packages with special emphasis on scenic North Shore locations and photography. Packages from "Barefoot & Basic" ($250) to an "Orchid Wedding" that includes video, butterfly release, and limousine ($1,550). Specialty locations ($895-1,725) They also offer travel services for wedding & honeymoon packages $1,800-$5,095) E-mail: <cocowed@aloha.net> Website: <www.kauaiwedding.com>

Gaylord's at Kilohana, 3-2087 Kaumuali'i Hwy (mailing address: PO Box 1725, Lihu'e, HI 96766.) (808) 245-1087, FAX (808) 245-7818. A basic wedding package begins at $550 and includes your choice of setting, a non-denominational minister and a one hour use of a wedding carriage. They can arrange for intimate or large receptions. You can also arrange to hold your wedding at their luau, the food and entertainment are already there and so are the "instant" family and friends! Email: gylords@aloha.net or Website: <www.gaylordskauai.com>

Hyatt Regency Kaua'i, (808) 742-1234. The Hyatt's wedding department offers extensive wedding services. The wedding coordinator can provide you with a list of "10 Helpful Tips for Getting Married on Kaua'i" to help you plan your wedding before you leave home. Unusual and romantic, the resort will even arrange to order a replica of an award-winning Hawaiian bridal gown (*holoku*) for the bride-to-be. The Victorian-styled Hawaiian holoku wedding dress was designed by Maile Jean Amorin, and is a replica of her grandmother's wedding gown. Wedding packages $1,200 - $1,750. Vow renewal packages start at $730.

Island Weddings & Blessings, PO Box 603, Kilauea, HI (808) 828-1548, FAX (808) 828-1569. Toll free 1-800-998-1548. A "Simple and Special" wedding begins at $295. Their "Island Romance Package" includes a wedding ceremony, officiant, witness, tropical outdoor location, two leis, and 24 photos or a video for $625. The "Island Memories Package" adds a bouquet, boutonniere, and champagne toast for $735. They offer non-denominational as well as religious ceremonies. Videos and other options available. E-mail: <wedding@aloha.net>

Kaua'i Aloha Weddings, 356 Likeke Place, Kapa'a, HI 96746. (808) 822-1477, FAX (808) 822-7067. This Hawaiian owned and operated company offers couples the opportunity of having their marriage performed by ordained ministers in the Hawaiian language. Each ceremony begins with the blowing of the conch shell followed by a special Hawaiian language blessing and lei exchange for the couple. Packages range from $295 to $1,095 for ceremonies which include Hawaiian songs sung to the accompaniment of a slack key guitar and hula dancer. E-mail: haunani@aloha.net or Website: <www.hshawaii.com/kvp/kauaialoha/>

Kaua'i Coconut Beach Resort has a full time on-property wedding coordinator. They offer a variety of wedding packages. 1-800-760-8555.

Kaua'i Fantasy Weddings, PO Box 3671, Lihu'e, HI 96766. (808) 245-6500. Photo packages or wedding packages available from $375-1,600. Hans Hellriegel has been a photographer for thirty years. He says each wedding is unique and he always falls a little in love with each bride. He has taken wedding couples to the beach, up into the mountains, to a church, with ceremonies held at sunrise, at sunset or during the day.

David Kelly is a "Ceremonial Wedding Guide." Licensed by the state to perform marriages, he also provides island nature hikes and tours. (808) 822-3052.

Mohala Wedding Services, PO Box 1737, Koloa, HI 96756. (808) 742-8777, 1-800-800-8489, FAX (808) 742-8777. Jona and Jim Clark work as a team to put together your wedding package. Jim is an ordained minister who performs the ceremonies, Jona and her musical partner sing the "Hawaiian Wedding Song." A Japanese garden setting, a beachside wedding, a sunset ceremony on a Kilauea estate on the North Shore with Bali Hai as a back drop or choose a garden *heiau* or gazebo with a waterfall. Packages run $300-1,450. Private locations run slightly more. Other options include cake, flowers, limo or carriage, musicians, tuxedo rental and video as well as a Hawaiian dove-releasing ceremony from $50-365. E-mail: mohala@hawaiian.net or Website: <www.mohala.com>

Smith's Motor Boat Service, Inc. offers wedding packages in the Fern Grotto and in the Smith's own gardens. Wedding times for the Grotto are currently only 8:30 am, 11:30 am, 4 pm and 5 or 6 pm. As for ceremonies in their gardens, the hours are more flexible. They do not do ceremonies on major holidays. Fern Grotto packages run $575-$925 (with optional video $235-295). They include your own private boat with entertainers, minister, photography, leis, and assorted extras. Wedding packages in the Smith's Tropical Paradise Gardens run $185-$465. They also offer a special candle and torchlight wedding ceremony at 6 pm for $1,075. 174 Wailua Rd., Kapa'a, HI 96746. (808) 821-6888 or FAX (808) 821-6887. Email: smithswedding@hawaiibc.net

Tropical Dream Wedding, PO Box 422, Lawa'i, HI 96765. (808) 322-5664, 1-888-615-5655. FAX (808) 332-0811. They specialize in custom wedding planning and also offer island concierge services, vacation activity planning, and travel arrangements. Wedding packages from $399 -- but their aloha spirit is free! Email: kkkauai@aloha.net or Website: <www.hi50.com/tdw>

Wedding in Paradise, PO Box 1728, Lihu'e, HI 96766. (808) 246-2779, 1-800-733-7431. A basic package with a non-denominational minister and a choice of locations begins at $295. Their average packages run about $680 and include photography, leis, musician, and bouquet. They provide a set of photographs with their brochure which gives a good feeling for their location selections. Wedding sites include Terrace Garden in the Limahuli Valley, Fern Grotto Wedding (basic package $900), Japanese Garden in Kukuiolono or a private white sand beach estate on Pakala Beach. Hosted weddings are $880 and include a wedding coordinator, table with linens, chairs, champagne, beverage and cake. Other options include photography, leis, videography, music and flowers dropped from a helicopter. Website: <www.paradiseservices.com>

Weddings on the Beach, PO Box 1377, Koloa HI 96756. (808) 742-7099, 1-800-625-2824. Fern Grotto wedding packages start at $575 or get married at an oceanfront estate for $435. Wedding coordinator Judy Neale offers ocean view or ocean front weddings from $285 and an "Everything" wedding package for $1,100. Or how about an ocean adventure where your wedding site is aboard a 56 ft. sailing trimaran? The two-hour sunset cruise wedding runs $1,400 with flowers, video, photos, toast, and buffet all included on board. Limousine service, video, food and beverages, musicians, flowers, and photography services are available as options. And if you'd like to receive a complimentary 8x10 color print or an extra copy of your original video, just mention this book! Email: judyn@hawaiian.net or Website: <www.weddingsonthebeach.com>

## *PARTIES & RECEPTIONS*

Kilohana offers an assortment of "theme parties" available for business or personal celebrations. A Paniolo Hoedown, a Garden Party, a Murder Mystery, a Kilohana Luau, South Pacific, Polo, Rock Around the Clock, Mad Maxx, or Casino Party are among the possibilities available. For information contact Kilohana, PO Box 3121, Lihu'e, HI 96766. Call (808) 245-5608.

# *HELPFUL INFORMATION*

***FREE INFORMATION:*** Racks located at the shopping areas can provide helpful information and lots of brochures! Some of them have coupons, which (if it was something you were planning on doing anyway) may save you a few dollars. The Kaua'i Visitors Bureau and the County of Kaua'i have compiled a free *Illustrated Pocket Map* which you can pick up at their Lihu'e office or order by calling their toll-free number (see below.) It is a nicely done island map that gives a lot of in-depth information. The Chamber of Commerce also has a helpful free map (with "real" streets!) which you can pick up at any Big Save or McDonald's. Or call the Chamber office at (808) 245-7363. The Kaua'i Visitor Information Hotline, begun after Hurricane Iniki to keep visitors apprised of the recovery process, continues its services. This hotline offers live tourism industry updates, directly from Kaua'i. The phones are staffed by local volunteers and the number is good for all the U.S. and in Canada. Phone 1-800-262-1400, 5 am-4 pm daily Hawaiian standard time. (A recording on the weekends.) Or send them your toll free FAX 1-800-637-5762.

***KAUA'I VISITORS BUREAU:*** 4334 Rice St., Room 101, Lihu'e, Kaua'i, HI 96766 (808) 245-3971, FAX (808) 246-9235.

***PO'IPU BEACH RESORT ASSOCIATION:*** PO Box 730, Koloa, HI 96756. (808) 742-7444. FAX (808) 742-7887. They also have a toll-free number 1-888-744-0888. E-mail: <info@poipu-beach.org> or look up their electronic brochure on the internet at <www://poipu-beach.org> The Po'ipu Beach Resort Association provides up to date information on accommodations, activities, dining, shopping, transportation and service in the Po'ipu, Koloa and Kalaheo areas of Kaua'i. Contact them to request a free 36-page guide.

***WEST KAUA'I VISITOR & TECHNOLOGY CENTER:*** 9565 Kaumualii Hwy., Waimea (808) 338-1332. HOURS: Open daily 9am-5pm. Pictorials, graphics, and displays with touch-sensitive screens provide information on all of Kaua'i's activities, not just Waimea.

ORCHIDS

***TELEVISION:*** We anticipate that you'll be much too busy enjoying the island to do much television viewing. The KVIC station on either channel 3 or channel 18 (depending on your area of the island) will have on-going programs aimed at you, the visitor. It's a guided tour from your room that might offer you a little more insight at something you might not have planned on doing! NOTE: the island's two cable services have combined and are in the process of merging all the stations so they be reached at the same channel throughout the island. In the meantime, the following are channels on basic cable service. (Numbers may vary according to area on the island.)

| | |
|---|---|
| 2 | KHON (FOX) |
| 3 | KFVE or KVIC (Visitor Information Channel) |
| 4 | KITV (ABC) |
| 5 | KFVE (or HBO) |
| 6 | Local programs |
| 7 | Local Origination (part-time) or QVC |
| 8 | KHNL (NBC) |
| 9 | KGMB (CBS) |
| 10 | PEG (Educational Access) |
| 11 | KHET (PBS) |
| 12 | PEG (Public Access) |
| 13 | Government Access |
| 14 | TBS (Turner Broadcasting Systems) or Headline News |
| 15 | L/O (Local Origin) or CNN |
| 18 | KVIC (Visitor Information Channel) or ESPN |
| 19 | Program Guide |
| 20 | QVC or The Learning Channel |
| 21 | PPV- L/O or The Discovery Channel |
| 22 | CSPN or TBS |
| 23 | ESPN or E! Entertainment Network |
| 24 | TDC (The Discovery Channel) |
| 25 | TLC (The Learning Channel) |
| 26 | USA |
| 27 | CNN |
| 28 | CNN-HN (Headline News) |
| 29 | AMC (American Movie Classics) |
| 30 | MTV (Music Television) |
| 31 | VH-1 (Video Hits One) |
| 32 | TNN (The Nashville Network) or Nickelodeon |
| 33 | COM (Comedy Central) or Lifetime |
| 34 | Lifetime or Nashvile Network |
| 35 | TNT or MTV |
| 36 | NICK (Nickelodeon) or VH-1 |
| 37 | America's Health or CNBC |
| 38 | CNBC or CSPAN |
| 39 | Weather Channel or A&E (Arts & Entertainment) |
| 41 | E! Entertainment Network or Home & Garden |
| 42 | ESPN 2 or AMC |

***RADIO:*** KONG at 57AM/93.5FM has the largest signal on the island. They play 80's and 90's adult contemporary as well as Hawaiian and offer local news, surf, weather, and what's happening on Kaua'i.. KFMN-97FM also has adult contemporary, but KUAI at 720AM is a bit more eclectic: they play mostly Hawaiian along with adult contemporary, hits from the past, young country and also offer news features, local news and sports. KKCR at 91.9FM is Kaua'i's non-profit community radio. Weekday mornings offer Hawaiian and Slack Key music. Other weekly programs include Vintage Hawaiian Music, Monday evening Sunset Jazz, Saturday "Rocks!" and Sunday morning classic music. Email: kkcr@Hawaiian.net or visit their website at <www.kkcr.org> A new FM station was expected to premiere in the fall of 1999 at 98.1FM.

***EMERGENCIES:*** The main hospital in Kaua'i is found in Lihu'e. G.N. Wilcox Memorial Hospital is located at 3420 Kuhio Hwy., Lihu'e. Phone (808) 245-1100.

The following provide general out-patient health services to persons requiring health care:

Kaua'i Medical Clinic (Main Clinic) 3420-B Kuhio Highway, Lihu'e (808) 245-1500

Kaua'i Medical Clinic (Koloa) 5371 Koloa Rd. (808) 742-1621

Kaua'i Medical Clinic (Kilauea) Kilauea & Ola Sts. (808) 828-1418

Kaua'i Medical Clinic (Kapa'a) 4-1105 Kuhio Hwy. (808) 822-3431

Kaua'i Medical Clinic (Ele'ele) 4392 Waialo Road (808) 335-0499

As of 1997, Wilcox Hospital and the above clinics are Kaiser Permanente affiliated providers and now serve Kaiser members. Call 1-800-966-5955 for benefit information.

See the section on Helpful Information for additional numbers. Calling 911 will put you in contact with local fire, police and ambulances.

***PERIODICALS:*** *The Garden Island* newspaper is published six days a week. They can be reached at 3137 Kuhio Hwy., PO Box 231, Lihu'e, HI 96766 (808) 245-3681. Subscriptions are available by mail. The other island newspaper, the *Kaua'i Times*, was purchased in 1995 by *The Garden Island* newspaper. The publication, sort of a two for one arrangement, now includes the *Kaua'i Times* which comes out on Saturday. Subscription runs $15 per month.

Call (808) 245-3681 for information. Both the *Honolulu Star Bulletin* and *The Honolulu Advertiser* can be contacted 605 Kapiolani Blvd., Honolulu, HI 96813.

If you are relocating to the islands, a copy of the Kaua'i *phone book* is a handy resource. Call GTE on Kaua'i at 1-800-888-8448 and they'll drop it in the mail free of charge. (If you have no plans to move, there is a $15 fee for the volume.)

The Chamber of Commerce offers an extensive Relocation Packet which includes the *Kaua'i Data Book* (demographics & statistics), detailed map, and information on businesses, schools, rental management companies, accommodations, auto shipping, and the local newspaper. Send $15 to Kaua'i Chamber of Commerce, Box 1969, Lihu'e, HI 96766 or call (808) 245-7363 to charge to your credit card ($16). Email: kcofc@aloha.net or Website: <www.kauaichamber.org>

*101 Things to Do On Kaua'i* is available free at stands around the island, or it can be ordered by sending $5 to 101 THINGS, PO Box 388, Lihu'e, HI 96766. Many of the ideas are suggestions for free activities, such as a walking tour of Koloa town or a visit to local *heiau* sites.

*Kaua'i Magazine* is available at bookstores or magazine stands for a cover price of $5 per copy. This quarterly full-color magazine contains a calendar of events, local columnists, and in-depth articles on Kaua'i's people and places. "Business, Community, and Lifestyle" is the focus of *Inside Kaua'i*, a bi-monthly magazine available for $4 an issue.

As mentioned previously, there are a number of free publications, small booklets that are available at racks around most visitor areas. Most of these free publications offer lots of advertising. However, they do have coupons which will give you discounts on everything from meals to sporting activities to clothing. It may save you a bit to search through these before making your purchases. We found the *Beach & Activity Guide Kaua'i* to be particularly helpful and informative with a lot of detail and cross referencing! *Menu* magazine is a great resource for restaurants that shows actual menus and appetizing color photos.

***WEBSITES:*** As cyberspace continues to boom, this is category continuing to develop for our guide! We have intermingled some websites throughout the text, but we have found it almost impossible to list the website for every business. Instead, we are using the code <WWW> to indicate that they do have a website. Either searching the net or calling the business for their website address are two options if you are interested in viewing it. E-mail addresses, however, are more difficult to find. So, we have included e-mail addresses throughout the text for some business as space allows. Following are some general websites that might be of interest to you! These will have links to assist you with other information. Please note that the "<" is not part of the URL address, it simply indicates where the address begins and ">" indicates where it ends.

*Po'ipu Beach Resort Association* has a website at <www.poipu-beach.org>

*Kaua'i Vacation Planner* <www.hshawaii.com/kvp/> is a good site with activities, feature stories, maps, calendar of events, weddings, shopping, dining and transportation information. The general information about what to see around the island is well laid out. You can also order a print copy. Put out by the Kaua'i Visitors Bureau, you should know that it is not a complete listing of dining, recreation, and other options. While there are a few exceptions, most of the listings are folks that are members of the Kaua'i Visitors Bureau. Via their website, you can also order a print copy of this 72 page guide and have it mailed to you. Current website price is $7.50, but you can get a free magazine copy by calling 1-800-262-1400.

Any individual or organization can add to the calendar website of the Hawai'i Visitor and Convention Bureau regardless of whether or not they are a Kaua'i Visitors Bureau or HVCB member. Check out: <www.gohawaii.com> Another visitor industry website can be found at <http://www.visit.hawaii> Also try <www.kauai-hawaii.com> These new websites also have Hawai'i information: <www.mele.com> is a site for Hawaiian music. The *Kaua'i Film Commmission* sponsors a site at <www.filmkauai.com> which includes Quicktime Virtual Reality 360 degree shots of some scenic spots on Kaua'i. Some of the listings for <www.sunjose.com> are a little awkward to use. For books, they just mention their generic categories and in searching it didn't seem that there was a complete listing of titles available. However, in the "fabric" section there are a number of Hawaiiana fabrics pictured with a section of Polynesian fabrics as well as an assortment of items from jewelry to hats, gift wrap to mouse pads, videos, clothing and other forms of art.

The *Garden Island* newspaper has a new website with abbreviated information of the daily paper. <www.kauaiworld.com> *101 Things to Do on Kaua'i* is a local free publication that can also be accessed at website <www.kauai101.com> The *Hawai'i State Vacation Planner* offers accommodation, restaurant, activity and other listings for the state with individual sections for Kaua'i and the other Hawaiian islands. <www.hshawaii.com> Discover current statistics for Kaua'i at the *Hawai'i State Data Book* at <www.state.hi.us> *Kaua'i Chamber of Commerce* is at <www.kauaichamber.org> Hawai'i State Government has comprehensive business listings within the state government <www.hawaii.gov? or download forms and other information from the Business Registration Divsion of the State Government at <www.businessregistrations.com>

*Haddon Holidays* is one of many companies that offer packages to Hawaii. You can visit their website at <http://www.haddon/com> *Pleasant Hawaiian Holidays* has a site at <http://www.2hawaii.com> or *Hawaiian Hotels & Resorts* at <http://www.HawaiiHotels.com> And you can reach *Marc Resorts* at <http://www.marcresorts.com>

*Even if you book through a travel agent, you might be interested in checking airline flight schedules and prices on the internet. With some, you can even book your reservation:*

| | |
|---|---|
| American Airlines: | <http://www.americanair.com> |
| Continental Airlines: | <http://www.flycontinental.com> |
| Delta Airlines: | <http://www.delta-air.com> |
| Northwest Airlines: | <http://www.nwa.com> |
| United Airlines: | <http://www.ual.com |
| Aloha Airlines: | <http://www.alohaair.com/aloha-air/> |
| Hawaiian Airlines: | <http://www.hawaiianair.com> |

*America On-Line* has an "Aloha Chat." It happens the second and fourth Wednesday of each month between 9-11pm EST at keyword: Travel Cafe. No commercialism, just people asking questions about and sharing their experiences in Hawaii. It has proven to be a very popular chat site and might be an interesting resource for people to "tap" in and find out answers to questions they have from real people (like the authors of this book!) and not companies trying to sell stuff. The catch is you have to be an AOL customer!

Kaua'i made products and crafts are available on the World Wide Web. *The Kaua'i Products Council* has its site at: <www.kauaiproducts.org> All items featured are from Kaua'i and are handcrafted and produced by local artisans and craftsmen. You can also check on the Calendar of Events page to see what local craft shows, expos, and festivals might be happening.

***SUN SAFETY:*** The sunshine is stronger in Hawai'i than on the mainland, so a few basic guidelines will ensure that you return home with a tan, not a burn. Use a good lotion with a sunscreen, reapply after swimming and don't forget the lips! Be sure to moisturize after a day in the sun and wear a hat to protect your face. Exercise self-control and stay out a limited time the first few days, remembering that a gradual tan will last longer. It is best to avoid being out between the hours of noon and three when it is the hottest. Be cautious of overcast days when it is very easy to become burned unknowingly. Don't forget that the ocean acts as a reflector and time spent in it equals time spent on the beach.

***FOR YOUR PROTECTION:*** Do not leave valuables in your car, even in your trunk. Many rental car companies urge you to not lock your car as vandals cause extensive and expensive damage breaking the locks.

***ISLAND FAUNA:*** There are few dangerous land and sea creatures in Hawai'i. And not to be alarmists, it makes common sense to use good judgment. Mosquitos were the gift of a ship called the *Wellington*, which arrived on Maui in 1826. They soon spread to the other islands and can be most irritating in the wetter, forested areas. It is worth packing a bottle of repellent. The only other insect that is to be avoided is the centipede. One guidebook we read said that you'll almost never encounter one. We have seen them on several occasions, right at a condominium. Generally they show up only when the landscape crews are trimming the palm trees and they are knocked to the ground. One groundskeeper told us that if you step on one end they can swing up the other end around your sandal and inflict a sting. If you see one; avoid it, the sting is extremely painful.

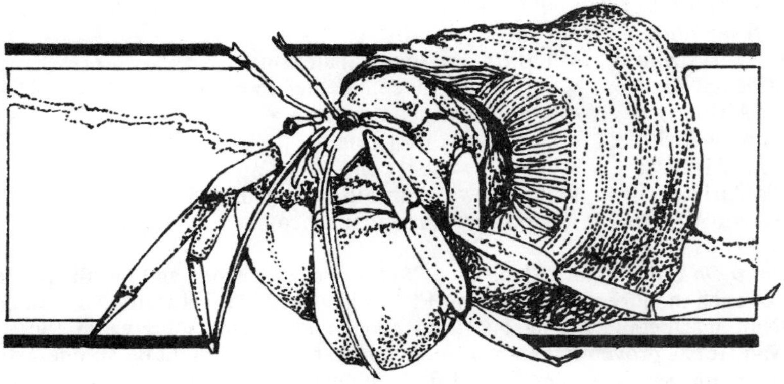

Hawai'i has no snakes and it is with very serious concern that a snake or two has been seen, caught and destroyed in the islands over the past decade. Great care is taken to ensure that none come to the islands unintentionally as part of cargo and dogs are even trained to sniff them out. The brown tree snake is among the most feared, for on Guam it has virtually destroyed their wild bird population.

The bufo toad is a very friendly fellow that can be found all around the islands, but generally is more noticed after a heavy rain, or unfortunately flattened on a road. In 1932 this frog was brought from Puerto Rico to assist with insect control. They don't mind being held, and can be turned over and seem to love having their stomachs rubbed. However, on the bufo toad you will notice a lump behind their head which carries a poison. The poison awaits a sharp blow or puncture to cause it to squirt out. A handy defense for this amphibian and dogs or cats quickly learn not to bother them. The poison can cause them to become seriously ill or can be fatal. We have also been told their body secretions can be irritating to the skin, especially eyes, and we suggest you just enjoy watching them instead.

On Kaua'i you'll see no mongoose, the only major Hawaiian island without these animals which prey on birds and their eggs. Consequently, Kaua'i is blessed with more birdlife than other islands.

The other Hawaiian creature that cannot go without mention is the gecko. They are finding their way into the suitcases of many an island visitor in the form of tee-shirts, sunvisors and jewelry. This small lizard is a relative of the chameleon and grows to a length of three or four inches. They dine on roaches, termites, mosquitos, ants, moths and other pesky insects. While there are nearly 800 species of geckos found in warm climates around the world, there are only five known varieties found in Hawaii. They are the only lizards which can vocalize, and different species make different sounds. The house gecko is the most commonly found, with tiny rows of spines that circle its tail, while the mourning gecko has a smooth, satiny skin and along the middle of its back it sports pale stripes and pairs of dark spots. The mourning gecko species is parthenogenic. That means that there are only females which produce fertile eggs -- no need for a mate! Smaller species have a life expectancy of five to seven years and larger geckos in captivity have reached 20 years of age.

The stump-toed variety is distinguished by its thick flattened tail. The tree gecko enjoys the solitude of the forests, and the fox gecko, with a long snout and spines along its tail, prefers to hide around rocks or tree trunks. Females make sure their eggs are well hidden before leaving them for ever more. The little ones will hatch in one to three months, breaking out of their eggshell with a specially designed "egg tooth" attached to their nose.

The first geckos may have reached Hawai'i with early voyagers from Polynesia, but the house gecko may have arrived as recently as the 1940s, along with military shipments to Hawaii. Geckos are most easily spotted at night when they seem to enjoy the warm lights outside your door. We have heard they each establish little territories where they live and breed so you will no doubt see them around the same area each night. They are very shy and will scurry off quickly.

Sometimes you may find one living in your hotel or condo. They're friendly and beneficial animals and are said to bring good luck, so make them welcome.

Birdlife abounds on Kaua'i, and no doubt the first you will note are the chickens!

Wild chickens? Yes! The wild chickens that you may see in the area of Koke'e and the lodge are descendants from the ones brought by the Polynesians, but you will find chickens just about everywhere you turn on Kaua'i these days. Hurricane Iwa, and to a greater extend Hurricane Iniki, caused a number of domesticated chickens to escape and they are obviously proliferating in paradise. Those descendants of the Polynesians have now inter-mixed with the domestic varieties that you will see many diverse colorations, particularly on the roosters. The roosters can be a bit of a nuisance in rural areas where their alarm wake-up calls are not always appreciated!

The songbirds of Hawai'i owe a great deal of credit to Mrs. Dora Isenberg. The *New York Herald Tribune* (September, 1938 edition) carried the following historical background: "Thanks to the efforts of one woman, the Hawaiian Islands are now the home of thousands of gaily colored songbirds from all parts of the world. Mrs. Dora Isenberg began her hobby of importing songsters forty years ago in celebration of Hawaii's joining the United States [as a territory]. After permitting them to get acclimated in her garden on Kaua'i Island, Mrs. Isenberg gave the birds their freedom. Her first attempts were unsuccessful when fourteen larks from the Orient were released and never heard of again. But, undismayed, Mrs. Isenberg continued her efforts, and many other people took up the hobby, with the result that today the islands boast thousands of such imported birds as the Peko thrush, African ringneck dove, Mongolian thrush, Chinese thrush, Bleeding Heart dove, meadow-lark, tomtit, and cardinal."

The goats found in the Koke'e area are descendants of those brought to the islands by Captain Cook. They have done significant damage to the vegetation and hunting for them is allowed. A pair of binoculars, or even a sharp lookout at one of the Waimea Canyon viewing areas and you might spot one or more. They blend in so well that we almost failed to spot one goat that was within a few hundred yards.

***AQUATIC SAFETY:*** Drinking of fresh water from streams, waterfalls and/or pools is not safe at any location. While there are many micro-organisms and parasites that can wreak havoc with your system, one of the most dangerous is Leptospirosis. This finds its way into rivers and streams in the urine of rodents and cattle and can be fatal. The symptoms are flu-like and because they do not result until 1 - 4 weeks after contamination, people who are infected may not connect their illness with a possible contamination weeks earlier. It can also be contracted through the skin if there are open sores or cuts. Be sure to pack your own drinking water should you do any hiking. As for cautions you should use in and around the ocean, please refer to our chapter on Beaches.

## *HELPFUL PHONE NUMBERS:*

| | |
|---|---|
| EMERGENCY: Police - Ambulance - Fire | 911 |
| NON-EMERGENCY POLICE: | |
| Non-emergency requests | 241-6711 |
| Crime Stoppers | 241-6787 |
| Weather | 245-6001 |
| Poison Control | 1-800-362-3585 |
| Sexual Assault Crisis (YWCA) | 245-4144 |
| YWCA Shelter | 245-6362 |
| Consumer Protection | 274-3200 |
| Kaua'i County Office of Elderly Affairs | 241-6400 |
| Transportation for Elderly or Handicapped | 241-6400 |
| Transportation: Airports Division | 246-1401 |
| Transportation: Highway Division | 274-3111 |
| Kaua'i Chamber of Commerce | 245-7363 |
| Po'ipu Beach Resort Association | 742-7444 |
| The Kaua'i Bus | 241-6410 |
| DIRECTORY ASSISTANCE: | |
| Local | 1+411 |
| Inter-island (charge) | 1-808-555-1212 |
| Long distance outside area code (charge) | 1+ area code+555-1212 |
| HOSPITALS: | |
| Wilcox Memorial in Lihu'e: | 245-1100 |
| West Kaua'i Medical Center-Waimea | 274-3901 |
| Kaua'i Visitors Bureau | 245-3971 |
| Time of Day | 245-0212 |
| LAND AND NATURAL RESOURCES: | |
| Division of State Parks | |
| State Parks Camping Permits | 274-3444 |
| Main Office | 274-3446 |
| Koke'e | 335-5871 |
| Wailua Marina | 822-5065 |
| Division of Aquatic Resources | 274-3344 |
| Forestry & Wildlife | 274-3434 |

The *Aloha Pages* in the front of the phone book has various hotline numbers to call for community events, entertainment, etc. on Kaua'i. While the call is free, the companies pay to be included, so information is biased. The front section of the telephone book also has some great street maps.

# *GETTING THERE*

# *-- AIRLINES AND MORE*

***CRUISING THE ISLANDS:*** One pleasant way to see the Hawaiian islands is aboard the ***American Hawai'i Cruises*** ship, the *S.S. Independence*. This 1,021 passenger, 682-foot ship provides comfortable accommodations and friendly service during its seven-day sail around the islands. In 1993, American Hawai'i Cruises was acquired by The Delta Queen Steamboat Co. public company, now American Classic Voyages, Co. In late 1999, American Hawai'i Cruises acquired the *Nieuw Amsterdam* from Holland America Line. This new U.S. flag ship will be renamed *ms Patriot* and join the *Independence* in service in December, 2000. The 704-foot *ms Patriot* will offer nine passenger decks, five lounges, two restaurants, a fully equipped spa and fitness center, two outdoor pools and a 230-seat theater. (Note: Two new U.S. flag 1,900 passenger, state-of-the-art cruise ships will enter service in Hawaiian waters in early 2003 and 2004.)

On board either *The Independence* or the *MS Patriot* you'll enjoy some outstanding Hawaiiana programs. Hawaiian costumes, hands-on Hawaiian museum exhibits, cabins with Hawaiian names, traditional Hawaiian church services, menus filled with Hawaiian specialties, and tropical flowers in every room are among the changes which bring the essence of Hawai'i on board. American Hawai'i Cruises has Kumu (Hawaiian teachers) on board to instruct passengers about the culture and history of Hawaii. Both ships offer fully handicap-accessible suites.

Currently the ***S.S. Independence*** departs Honolulu on Saturdays. It travels a seven day route from Honolulu to Nawiliwili, Kaua'i; Kahului, Maui; Hilo, Hawai'i and Kona, Hawai'i. Also available are a number of "Theme Cruises" which range from Big Band cruises to one which combines with Hawai'i's Aloha Festivals. The ship comes into port at each of the major islands for a day (or in some cases two) for touring.

"Beautiful Seas" wedding packages are available for couples who choose marriage aboard ship in Hawai'i on ***American Hawai'i Cruises***. It includes the services of an official to perform the ceremony, a small wedding cake, live Hawaiian music, a flower lei and floral headpiece for the bride and a lei or boutonniere for the groom, champagne and keepsake flutes, photography service and a 24 5X7 photos in a souvenir album. The wedding package price is $695 plus cruise fares. See Weddings & Honeymoons in this chapter for information on tests and licenses. For honeymooners that marry on the Mainland on a Saturday, they don't have to "miss the boat" to enjoy a Hawaiian Islands honeymoon cruise. While the normal departures are on Saturday from Honolulu, the "Sea and Shore" honeymoon enables couples to board the ship in Nawiliwili, Kaua'i. After six days on board ship, the honeymooners will enjoy a seventh night at a Waikiki Hotel. See Weddings & Honeymoons in this chapter for information on tests and licenses.

American Hawai'i Cruises offers shore excursions which include opportunities for passengers to discover the "hidden" Hawaii. Trips include the opportunity to hike through a rain forest to discover a hidden waterfall. The idea of a cruise is to give you a taste of each of the islands without the time and inconvenience of traveling by plane in-between islands. In fact, it would be impossible to see all the islands in a week in any other fashion. For additional information contact American Hawai'i Cruises 1-800-765-7000 or FAX (504) 585-0630.

***AIRLINE INFORMATION:*** The best prices on major air carriers can often be arranged through a reputable travel agent who can often secure air or air with car packages at good prices by volume purchasing. Prices can vary considerably so comparison shopping is a wise idea. Be sure to ask about senior citizen and companion fare discounts.

Another alternative is to book a package trip through one of several agencies which specializes in Hawai'i travel. While Creative Leisure uses major airlines (we were quoted on United), others use charter services.

"Airfare Only" is available through Sunquest on their Sun Country Charters and Pleasant Hawaiian Holidays who use commercial carriers including Delta Airlines, Hawaiian Airlines, United Airlines and American TransAir.

***Avalon Travel*** offers "theme" tours to Kaua'i that range from Culinary (with an emphasis on dining and exploring Hawaiian Regional and Pacific Rim cuisine) to Art & Garden (visit artists' homes and explore the "Garden Isle") to Wellness and Rejuvenation Retreats (created for those interested in personal growth, natural healing and spiritual enrichment). Their annual KauaiQuest 2000 is a "Festival of Spirit & Discovery" offered every October to coincide with Kaua'i's Aloha Festival Events. They promise their "insider" tours/retreats to be educational, cultural, and inspirational with "programs designed for those who wish to experience the local culture and environment on a deeper and more authentic level." These "land only" tours run seven days/six nights and are priced from $1,599. (Price includes lodging, meal plan, presentations, professional guide, and land excursions.) Call Karol Avalon at 1-888-552-7375; Email: karol@avalontravel.com or visit their website at <www.avalontravel.com>

***Classic Aloha Vacations*** PO Box 627, Hanalei, HI 96714. 1-800-200-3576 or toll free FAX 1-888-826-7155. Website: www.classic-aloha.com or Email: cav@aloha.net Classic Aloha offers a nice selection of properties on all the islands, with photos of each. Their staff of five agents on three islands are happy to answer any questions you may have! As a Hawai'i wholesaler who sells to agencies all over the mainland and Canada, the website allows them to offer excellent rates on hotels, condos, car and airfare.

***Creative Leisure*** 1-800-426-6367, (808) 778-1800. While you may not find the most inexpensive packages, Creative Leisure utilizes moderate to expensive, higher end condominiums and hotels (which include Whaler's Cove, Hyatt Regency, Po'ipu Kai, Embassy Vacation Resort, Princeville Hotel, Kaua'i Beach Villas, The Cliffs, Pali Ke Kua, Lae nani, Lanikai, Kiahuna Plantation, Waimea Plantation Cottages and Kaua'i Marriott). They offer the advantage of traveling any day you choose and the option of staying as long as you want. Rates are for the entire unit, not per person. Year-round discount airfares are available on United and you will receive full Mileage Plus credit for all United Airlines and Aloha Airlines travel booked through them. TravelGuard insurance is also available. You can combine and include other islands as a part of your package, or even a stopover in San Francisco. Customer service is a high priority with them, and it shows! PO Box 750189, Petaluma, CA 94975.

***Pleasant Hawaiian Holidays*** ★ 1-800-242-9244. Founded in 1959 as Pleasant Travel Service in Point Pleasant, New Jersey, Ed Hogan and his company have grown and expanded to provide a range of airfare, air only, and land only options. They work in conjunction with American Trans Air direct to Maui and Honolulu from L.A. and San Francisco. They also utilize Hawaiian Airlines, United, and Delta. Rental cars also available. <http://www.2hawaii.com>

Kaua'i properties include the Hyatt Regency Kaua'i, Princeville Hotel, Whaler's Cove, Aston Po'ipu Point, Kaua'i Marriott Resort, Hanalei Bay Resorts & Suites, Outrigger's Kiahuna Plantation, Aston Kaua'i Beach Villas, Outrigger Kaua'i Beach Hotel, Kaua'i Coconut Beach Resort, Islander on the Beach, and Plantation Hale. A $45 fee will waive any cancellation or penalties should you have to adjust your travel plans. Their "Last Minute Desk" is for those of you trying to find space on short notice -- right up to the day of departure!

***Suite Paradise*** ★ is a condominium rental agency which specializes in the "Best of Po'ipu." In addition to accommodations they offer very attractive rates on car/condo packages. They can arrange ticketing on regularly scheduled airlines (United, Delta, Northwest, TWA, Continental and Hawaiian) at discounts with their air ticketing affiliate. Call Suite Paradise at 1-800-367-8020 to request information on all their vacation options. They have a wonderful, helpful staff. Contact Suite Paradise to receive information on these airline contacts. See their URL at <http://suite-paradise.com> or e-mail: <mail@suite-paradise.com>

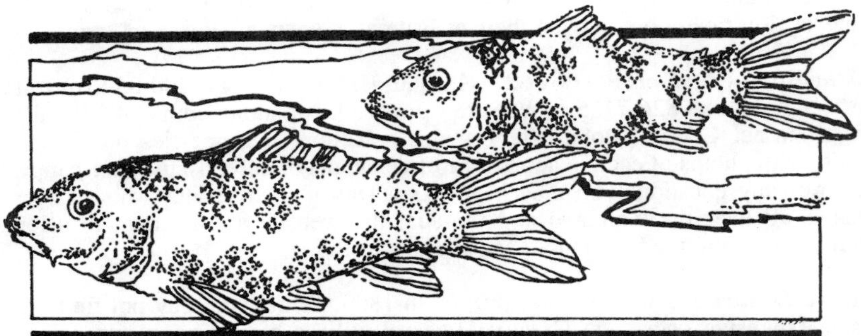

KOI

***Sunquest Holidays*** 1-800-357-2400 - isn't the new kid on the block, but they are new to serving Hawai'i bound vacationers. If you are from the midwest, you might be familiar with Sun Country which began in 1983 and has been flying to exotic Caribbean destinations. In the spring of 1997 they added Hawai'i, utilizing Los Angeles as their gateway to the Pacific. This means that if you live in the Southern California area you might get a great deal, but the rest of us have to make our own travel arrangements to the LAX airport. They do, however, fly (DC-10's) every day of the week which allows you to customize the length of your vacation stay. Land only, air only and combination packages including rental cars are available for O'ahu, Maui, Kaua'i and The Big Island. They offer some unique and intriguing incentives! By booking early you can take an extra $20 off the published airfares. Sunquest Holidays also offers FREE children's holidays for youngster up to 19 years of age. You get one free child per two full-paying passengers, when sharing a room and using existing bedding. A minimum seven night stay is required. Other children qualify for package discounts, which are still a good deal! Travel protection insurance, in the event you have to cancel at the last minute, is available as is travel insurance. Dollar Rent a Car handles the ground transportation (Hawai'i Rental Vehicle Surcharge of $2 per day not included in prices) and Aloha Airlines is the carrier used for inter-island flights. Single or multiple island packages are available. For airfare only, rates are staggered based on the day of the week you depart and the time of the year. Some very outstanding week long package rates. Worth calling to request a catalog.

***Remember!*** Be sure to check all the air carriers. Experience has taught us that a little leg work pays off! Sometimes the best deal may be through one of these agencies, but if you have the time, it may be worth a thorough investigation (and you may be pleasantly surprised). During one trip we discovered that United airlines had a promotional special that far and away beat these packages and even the charters!! Always make sure you let the airline know if you are flexible on your arrival and departure days. You may be able to squeeze into some price cut promotion that offers an even better value on your flight dollar.

The main airport in central Kaua'i, at Lihu'e. There has long been talk regarding a runway extension of the Lihu'e Airport. Extending the runway would allow for direct international flights and larger planes from the U.S. Mainland. The legislature has appropriated funds for review of this project.

In Princeville, on the North Shore, there is a small airstrip. It is used for small planes and helicopters and recently inter-island commercial service has resumed with Princeville Air, an affiliate of Hawai'i Helicopter, offering interisland (to O'ahu) service.

### *FLIGHTS TO THE ISLANDS*

Most of the airlines have their own websites. These are especially handy for getting an idea of flight schedules. See websites in preceding section for their world wide web addresses.

The major American carriers that fly from the mainland to the Honolulu International Airport on O'ahu, Hawai'i are:

ALOHA AIRLINES ★ - They recently (February,2000) initiated service to the US mainland using all new Boeing 737-700s. For the first time in the over 53-year history of the airline, they are offering two daily roundtrip flights to the West Coast: one between Oakland, California and Honolulu, and the other between Oakland and Maui. For reservations and information, call 1-800-367-5250 U.S. & Canada. Their Honolulu number is (808) 484-1111, on Kaua'i (808) 245-3691.

AMERICAN AIRLINES - Toll free from the mainland and all island 1-800-433-7300. Five flights per day to Honolulu with connections to inter-island carriers.

CANADIAN AIRLINES INTERNATIONAL - 1-800-426-7000. Over a dozen weekly flights from Vancouver to and from Honolulu. Then connecting inter island carriers to Kaua'i.

CONTINENTAL AIRLINES - 1-800-525-0280 toll free from mainland. Flights to Honolulu with connecting inter-island carriers to Kaua'i.

DELTA AIR LINES - 1-800-221-1212. They fly non-stop out of Atlanta, Dallas, Fort Worth, San Francisco and Los Angeles into Honolulu. Inter-island carriers will connect you to Kaua'i from there.

HAWAIIAN AIRLINES - Toll free from the mainland 1-800-367-5320; in Honolulu (808) 838-1555; on Kaua'i or from the neighbor islands, call 1-800-882-8811. Hawaiian offers both scheduled and charter flights from San Francisco, Los Angeles, Portland, Seattle, and Las Vegas direct to Honolulu with service connecting hourly to Kaua'i. They use DC 10's on the mainland and DC9's in Hawaii. Hawaiian is proud of their "*Mea Hookipa*" service which includes award-winning Hawaiian Regional Cuisine (in First Class), innovative in-flight audio selections which feature Hawaiian musicians and singers (also an award-winning service), and cultural narratives by flight attendants shared in "talk story" style.

Loosely translated, *Mea Hookipa* means to "act as a good host to guests." If you plan to do a lot of island hopping, Hawaiian's "Island Pass" offers unlimited travel on all islands for 5, 7, 10, or 14 days. (Approximately $229-409). Check with Hawaiian or your travel agent. for coupon books which can bring the cost down to about $55 for a one-way ticket.

NORTHWEST AIRLINES - 1-800-225-2525. They are partners with Hawaiian Air for flights from Honolulu to Kaua'i.

PLEASANT HAWAIIAN HOLIDAYS ★ - 1-800-242-9244. They use L-1011's on their American Trans Air flights from San Francisco and Los Angeles. (With a seat configuration of 3-4-3, we were told by a tall individual to stay away from the middle 4 seats, which seem to have less leg room.) They use Hawaiian, Delta, and United in their packages which offer different planes. Many of their United flights offer direct service from Los Angeles to Lihu'e. From Honolulu they work with Hawaiian Airlines connecting with their convenient hourly shuttle to Kaua'i.

TWA - 1-800-221-2000 toll free from the mainland and inter-island. One flight daily to and from Honolulu through their hub city, St. Louis.

UNITED AIRLINES ★ - United Reservations & Flight information: 1-800-241-6522. United has more flights to Hawai'i from more U.S. cities than any other airline. Currently they fly direct from Los Angeles to Lihu'e offering one flight daily that leaves around 5 in the evening and arrives at approximately 8 pm. (In 1999 they also initiated direct flights from San Francisco to Lihu'e during the summer. We were unable to find out how long they might continue this service, but if you plan to travel between June-September, you might inquire. And, of course, we'll let you know more in our KAUA'I UPDATE!) If you choose to go through Honolulu, you can book in conjunction with their Aloha Airlines partner to Kaua'i which will usually give you a better fare. However, we encountered one trip where we could get to Honolulu on United, but they had no convenient connections left to Kaua'i. Remember, you can still book that through one of the inter-island carriers yourself separately.

### *INTER-ISLAND FLIGHTS*

Hawai'i is unique in that its intrastate roads are actually water or sky. For your travel by sky, there are several inter-island carriers that operate between Honolulu and Kaua'i. If you plan on doing frequent inter-island excursions, some allow you to purchase a coupon book of six or so tickets that work out to being a small discount per ticket over a single ticket purchase.

Travel agents schedule at least an hour and a half between arrival on O'ahu and departure for Kaua'i to account for any delays, baggage transfers, and the time required to reach the inter-island terminal. The flight time from O'ahu to Lihu'e on Kaua'i is just 25 minutes. Currently there are no inter-island carriers using the Princeville airport. When returning from Kaua'i to Honolulu, make sure you have plenty of time before your connecting flight to the mainland. Otherwise you might make your flight, but your baggage won't!

Traveling from the main carrier to the inter-island terminal can be rather exhausting and confusing. You will probably need to take one Wiki Wiki bus to a drop-off point and then pick up another to take you to the inter-island terminal.

If you do arrive early, check with the inter-island carrier. Very often you can get an earlier flight which will arrive on Kaua'i in time to get your car before returning to pick up your luggage when it arrives on your scheduled flight.

If you are traveling "light" and have brought with you carry-on luggage only, be advised that what is carry-on for the major airlines may not be carry-on for the inter-island carriers. For example, those new small suitcases with wheels and long handles that extend out to pull along behind you MUST be checked by many of the inter-island carriers. Knowing this in advance, you may be able to pack those items that are more fragile in a smaller tote bag.

ALOHA AIRLINES ★ - For reservations and information, call 1-800-367-5250 U.S. & Canada. Their Honolulu number is (808) 484-1111, on Kaua'i (808) 245-3691. Aloha operates over 180 flights daily throughout the islands using an all-jet fleet of nineteen Boeing 737s. They offer e-ticketing, first class service, Drive-Thru Check-In at Honolulu and porter-assisted Curb-Side Check-in at both Honolulu and Lihu'e. They have two flights that offer non-stop service between Kaua'i and Maui. (Aloha also operates charter service to Midway, Johnson, and Christmas Islands plus long-range and inter-island charter flights upon request.)

This airline keeps on schedule and has always had one of the lowest passenger complaint records of all U.S. Airlines. In fact, Consumer Reports magazine (June, 1999) gave Aloha their highest rating for "Superior Value" in both customer satisfaction and low rates (the same reason they have always earned our "star") which the airline backs up with a service guarantee!

When making reservations, you might inquire about any special promotions, AAA membership discounts, passes, or coupon books that are currently available. For a flat rate (approximately $320 depending on the season) you can buy a 7-day pass which allows unlimited travel on Aloha Airlines to all islands. (Sort of Hawai'i's version of a Eurail Pass!) If you have a family or plan lots of inter-island excursions, you can purchase their "Lantern Ilima" coupon book of six tickets which can reduce the current standard one-way fare of $93 to as low as $53.) Be sure to check into their Fly/Drive packages for rental cars - they offer some really great deals, especially during slow season. For 5,000 United Mileage Plus miles, you can receive a free round trip ticket! Current flight schedule is available on the world wide web at <www.alohaair.com/aloha-air/>

ISLAND AIR - This sister airline to Aloha serves Hawai'i's smaller community and resort destinations, but no longer offers service to or from Kaua'i.

HAWAIIAN AIRLINES - They offer an hourly shuttle service to Kaua'i flying on their McDonnel Douglas DC9's. If you plan to do a lot of island hopping, Hawaiian's "Island Pass" offers unlimited travel on all islands for 5, 7, 10, or 14 days. (Approximately $299-409). Coupon books are available which can bring the cost down to about $55 for a one way ticket. Check with Hawaiian or your travel agent. Toll free from the mainland 1-800-367-5320; on Kaua'i or from the neighbor islands, call (800) 882-8811. Tickets for Hawaiian Airlines may also be purchased from ATM machines at selected Bank of Hawai'i outlets.

PRINCEVILLE AIR - In early 2000, Princeville Air (part of Hawai'i Helicopters) began offering nonstop service between the Princeville Airport and Honolulu International Airport. At press time we were advised that a nine passenger, twin-engine Navajo Chieftain would be used with service expected to be twice daily. Fares will be similar to those offered by Aloha and Hawaiian Airlines from Lihu'e to Honolulu. Flight time will be less than 60 minutes. Hawai'i Helicopters operates a commuter service between Kapalua and Moloka'i and Lana'i with a 24-passenger Sikorsky S-61. It is the largest passenger helicopter in the state. 1-800-994-9099. On Kaua'i 826-6591. Website: <www.hawaii-helicopter.com> If you arrive at the Princeville Airport from Honolulu, Avis is the only rental car company. Taxis are also available or check with your hotel or Princeville Air about shuttle service.

*LIHU'E AIRPORT:* Congratulations! It has been a long day of travel, but now you're here! Most visitors to Kaua'i will arrive at the island's major air terminal. The Lihu'e Airport covers 804 acres and is located on the southeast coast of the island of Kaua'i, about 1 1/2 miles from the town of Lihu'e. It is a blissfully simple airport with only a handful of gates and one baggage claim area. In addition to the chairs at the individual gates, there is a small centralized seating area surrounded by convenient pay phones and a gift shop. The airport operates two runways and offers passenger and cargo transportation. Currently the runway length does not allow direct international or overseas domestic air service by large aircraft, but there has long been talk regarding a runway extension of the Lihu'e Airport. Extending the runway would allow for direct international flights and larger plans from the U.S. Mainland. The legislature has appropriated funds for review of this project.

When you arrive (mid-day only), you'll find an unexpected greeting of Kaua'i aloha: live music at the Lihu'e airport every Monday, Wednesday and Friday from 9am until noon. And at baggage claim, there is a self-service counter with guava juice (from Guava Kai Plantation) plus flavored and regular coffee from Kaua'i Coffee - all complimentary! There is also a closed captioned video that is shown in the baggage claim area which provides safety information on roads, beach and ocean usage, and hiking trails as well as crime prevention. (And have your baggage claim check handy -- this airport actually checks!!)

***IMPORTANT!!! ARRIVAL AND DEPARTURE TIPS!*** During your flight to Honolulu, the airline staff will provide you with a visitor information sheet. This is used by the Hawai'i Visitors and Convention Bureau to track the number of visitors and their island destinations. This is also the opportunity to report any animals, fruits, vegetables or plants that will need to be inspected upon arrival in Honolulu.

***AGRICULTURAL INSPECTION:*** On your return, you will have to take your checked as well as carry-on baggage through agricultural inspection. Where your luggage will be inspected will depend upon your travel plans. If you are checking baggage at the Lihu'e airport which will be transferred directly to your connecting flight in Honolulu, then you will need to go through the agricultural inspection at the main entrance of the Lihu'e airport before proceeding to the airline ticketing counter to check in. Don't bother checking your carry-on baggage at this point, as you will just have to do it again in Honolulu. If you have a connection on O'ahu, you will arrive in Honolulu and begin trekking from your inter-island flight to your mainland carrier. Almost mystically an agricultural inspection center will appear. Don't bother looking, they seem to just find you! (In case this is your first trip, they look just like a "regular" airport baggage security center.) At this point you will need have your carry-on baggage inspected. You'll be amazed to see the apples, oranges and other fruits stacked up on the agricultural inspection centers, Even though they may have originally come from the mainland US, they will not pass inspection to get back there! Any fruits which you wish to take home, i.e. papaya and pineapple, can be specially boxed, inspected and sealed from reputable island retailers. Generally, you will not have trouble with flowers and/or leis. If you are unsure what is transportable, contact the U.S. Department of Agriculture at (808) 245-2831.

***DISTANCES FROM THE LIHU'E AIRPORT TO OTHER AREAS***
As mentioned previously, you'll have no trouble following signs to the baggage claim area. It is a simple matter of crossing the street to pick up a shuttle to take you to the nearby rental car agencies. From the Lihu'e airport it is a 20 minute drive to Kapa'a, 30 minutes to Po'ipu, 60 minutes to Hanalei, 75 minutes to Ha'ena, and 90 minutes to the Waimea Canyon, barring traffic tie ups.

# *GETTING AROUND*

An insider tidbit for you. The Kaua'i phone book has a couple of pages of very good color maps. Since every condo and hotel will have a copy, you might find this a handy and helpful reference!

We pause here with a brief aside. It seems most appropriate in the category of "getting around" the island, in general, to make note of this interesting fact. The street addresses may easily confuse you as you are trying to locate a particular establishment. You may see a number such as 3-5920 next to 5924, as an example. The number in front of the dash stands for the area of the island. 0-1 is Waimea, 2 is Koloa, 3 is Lihu'e, 4 is Kapa'a and 5 is Hanalei. That seems fairly clear, but it can get a little confusing as to where the cut off point is for each of those areas. Another problem is some people use the first number and the dash and some do not. So, all we can say is, good luck!

The only public transportation is The Kaua'i Bus which charges riders $1 per ride. Seniors, students, or disabled with ID are 50¢. Monthly bus passes are available for $25 which provide unlimited rides. A monthly pass for senior citizens, students, and persons with disabilities runs $12.50. Caregivers traveling with eligible individuals will not be charged a fee. Carry-on baggage is limited to 9" x 14" x 22". Food and drinks are prohibited. Each bus has a destination sign on the front and curb-side of each bus which displays a route number. Schedules are available which show the route the bus travels and the times along that route. Route 100: Kekaha-Koloa-Lihu'e. Route 200: Lihu'e-Koloa-Kekaha. (Both have limited service to Koloa; only one stop pre day.) Route 300: Discontinued. Route 400: Hanalei to Lihu'e. Route 500: Lihu'e to Hanalei. Route 600: Lihu'e-Kapahi-Lih'ue. Route 700 circles the Lihu'e area. For additional information phone the County Transportation Office at (808) 241-6410 between the hours of 7 am and 5 pm Monday-Saturday. Trans Hawaiian Kaua'i sponsors the Coconut Coast Trolley which operates between 10am and 10 pm daily. The Trolley runs north between the Kaua'i Marriott and the Coconut Marketplace; south between Kapa'a Town and the Wailua Marina. A feeder shuttle provides transfer (by reservation) from Po'ipu, Lihu'e, and Nawiliwili Harbor. One-way service is $2; a one-day pass is $5. Call (808) 245-5108 for schedules and more information. There is a free shuttle between Kukui Grove Shopping Center and the Po'ipu Resort area sponsored by Kukui Grove and Grove Farm Land Corporation. (Daily from 8:45-4:30 pm). Call the shopping center office at (808) 245-7784 for pick-up points and schedule. A free shopping shuttle, with two routes, is also sponsored by Hilo Hattie. One offers pick up four times daily at the Kaua'i Sands, Aston Kaua'i Beachboy, Kaua'i Coconut Beach Hotel, Holiday Inn Sunspree and Outrigger Kaua'i Hotel. The second route has pick ups and drop offs twice daily to and from the Hyatt Regency Kaua'i, Embassy Vacation

Resort Po'ipu Point, Kiahuna Plantation, Sheraton Kaua'i Hotel and Lawa'i Beach Resort. Other hotel or condominium pickups are available, but space is limited and reservations are required. The shuttle drops off at the Hilo Hattie store in Lihu'e. Call Hilo Hattie at 245-3404.

***FROM THE AIRPORT:*** After arriving, there are several options. Taxi cabs, because of the distances between areas, can be very costly, i.e., $32 from Lihu'e to Po'ipu ($65 Lihu'e to Princeville). That would pay for your economy rental car for the first day or two!

***LIMOUSINE SERVICE:*** Kaua'i Limousine (808) 245-4855 or 1-800-764-7213. E-mail: <klimo@hawaiian.net>

***LOCAL TRANSPORTATION:*** If you don't choose a rental car, you will find The Kaua'i Bus does service island-wide and taxi companies are available.

Akiko's Taxi (808) 822-7588
City Cab (808) 245-3227 (Cell phone 639-7932)
Kaua'i Cab Service(808) 246-9554
North Shore Cab & Tours (808) 826-6189
Scotty Taxi (808) 245-7888 (Cell phone 639-9807)
South Shore Cab (808) 742-1525 (24-hour and emergency service)

**RENTAL CARS AND TRUCKS:** Given the status of public transportation on Kaua'i, a rental car is still the best bet to get around the island and, for your dollar, a good buy. The rates vary, not only between high and low season, but from week to weekend and even day to day! (One rate we were quoted on a Wednesday had gone up $8 by Saturday!) The best values are during price wars, or super summer discount specials. Prices vary as much within the same company as they do between companies and are approximated as follows: Vans $60-117, small Jeep $47-98 (popular and in limited supply, so make reservations well in advance), Mid-size $32-55, Compacts $30-45. Add to the rental price a 4% sales tax, a $2 per day highway road tax, and at some companies, a new "vehicle license fee" that tags on another 15-36¢ per day. Some rental car agencies have also been discussing the reinstitution of mileage charges of 25¢ a mile or more. Be sure to inquire! Another aside here is to point out that probably the first person who will greet you on Kaua'i is the car rental company agent. It is unfortunate that "jolly" John at Alamo cannot be synthesized and reproduced *en masse* (or cloned like English sheep). He was funny, patient, helpful, and spent time explaining a few extra directions and giving advice on where to eat. He was not hurried and made sure we had all our questions answered. And, he was not aware that our business was travel writing! Alamo gets their star, not only for their low rates, but for having such a bonafide aloha-spirited employee!

A trend that poses good news for travelers is that the inter-island airlines, as well as many condos and hotels, are offering rental cars at discounts greater than if you were to book directly. Aloha Airlines offers some very competitive rates with your inter-island tickets. Some resort hotels and condominiums are offering a free rental car as a part of their package. Be sure to ask about these!

On Kaua'i there are currently no companies which rent camping equipment. Vans are available from a number of agencies, but camping in them is not encouraged.

The policies of all the rental car agencies are basically the same. Most require a minimum age of 21 to 25 and a maximum age of 70. A few require a deposit or major credit card to hold your reservation. All feature unlimited mileage with you buying the gas ($1.64-$1.87 per gallon). Shell's Island Service Station in Kalaheo takes 5¢ off a gallon every "Super Saturday" and several other stations in nearby areas have followed suit offering similar weekend discounts. As a rule, Hanamau'lu Shell still seems to have gas a few cents cheaper and the folks that work there are nice too! You might consider filling up before you return your car as the rental companies charge between $2.35 (Alamo) up to $3.20 (Hertz et.al) per gallon to do it for you. Please note that there are limited gas stations located on the North Shore!

Insurance is an option you may wish to purchase, which can run an additional $15-19 a day. A few agencies will require insurance for those under age 25. Most of the car rental agencies strongly encourage you to purchase the optional collision damage waiver (CDW) which provides coverage for most cars in case of loss or damage. We suggest you check with your own insurance company before you leave to verify exactly what your policy covers. Some credit cards now provide CDW (Collision Damage Waiver) for rental cars if you use that credit card to charge your rental fees (usually a practice with Gold Cards). This does not include liability insurance, so you need to check to see if your own policy will cover you for liability in a rental car. Rental companies prohibit cars on any unpaved roads, like Polihale. The rental agencies will provide you with a map showing restrictions. Should you travel on these roads they will hold you responsible for any damage.

Discounts are few and far between. You might be able to use some airline award coupons or entertainment book coupons, but they are often very restrictive. If you are a member of AAA you can receive a discount on rental cars. (Then there is buyer beware ... we sampled one on-line company "Hawaii on Sale." We encountered multiple problems and found them completely unorganized, irresponsible and unreliable. We had a similar report back from the person who originally recommended them!) In our research, we found that Alamo had the best rates of the car rental companies with a further 20% off those if you book through the internet at <www.goalamo.com> Check with Aloha Airlines for some great rates with their inter-island fly and drive packages. And remember that weekly rates are always a better value, even if you're only there for six days. The rental booths are at the Lihu'e airport and pick-up and return areas are conveniently located to the airline terminal and easy to find. Preferred customers get only a slight advantage by picking their cars up at the airport. The rest of the companies offer a convenient shuttle bus to travel the short distance to their rental office.

In Princeville there is only Avis.

## *RENTAL CAR LISTING:*

ALAMO RENT A CAR ★
1-800-327-9633
Lihu'e:
(808)246-0645

AVIS
1-800-331-1212
Hyatt Regency:
742-1627
Princeville:
(808) 826-9773

BUDGET
1-800-527-0700
Lihu'e:
(808) 245-1901

DOLLAR
1-800-800-4000
Inter-island:
1-800-342-7398
Lihu'e:
(808) 245-3651

HAWAIIAN RIDERS
(808) 822-5409
Kapa'a
Exotic Cars:
Hummer, Prowler
Miata, Porsche,
also Jeeps & Geo
Trackers

HERTZ
1-800-654-3131
Lihu'e:
(808) 245-3356

NATIONAL
1-800-227-7368
Lihu'e:
(808) 245-5636

SEARS RENT A CAR
contracts w/ Budget
1-800-451-3600

TOOLMASTER HAWAII
Pickup & Truck
rentals
(808) 246-1111

THRIFTY
1-800-367-5238
Lihu'e:
(808) 245-7741

WESTSIDE U-DRIVE
(808) 332-8644

# *GROCERY SHOPPING*

Grocery store prices may be one of the biggest surprises of your trip. While there are some locally grown foods and dairies, most of the products must be flown or shipped to the islands. The local folks can shop the advertisements and use the coupons, but it isn't so easy when traveling. To give you an idea of what to expect at the supermarket, here are some non-sale grocery store prices. Bread $2.39 and up, bananas $.99 /lb., strained baby food 55-69¢ per jar, chicken $1.79/lb., hamburger $1.99 /lb. and up, mayonnaise $2.59, Starkist Tuna $1.29, disposable diapers 12 count $6.79, 32 oz. ketchup $2.29 , skim milk $4.59 a gallon.

Look for the *Sunshine Market*, an outdoor farmer's market held at different locations around the island. We suggest a call to the Office of Economic Development (808) 241-6390 to check on their schedule, but currently they run: Monday-Koloa Ball Park at noon; Tuesday-Kalaheo Neighborhood Center at 3:30 pm; Wednesday-Kapa'a New Town Park in Kahau at 3 pm; Thursday-Hanapepe Park at 3:30 pm and Kilauea Neighborhood Center at 4:30 pm; Friday-Vidinha Stadium parking lot in Lihu'e at Hoolako Street 3 pm; Saturday-Kekaha Neighborhood Center on Elepaio Road at 9 am. Private Farmer's markets are also held Saturday AM/Kilauea Lighthouse Road; Tuesday AM/Hawaiian Farmers of Hanalei (Waipia); Monday 3 PM/Kukui Grove Shopping Center; West Kaua'i Agriculture Assoc. several times a day at Po'ipu Road at Cane Haul Road; and Haupu Growers, L.L.C. daily on Koloa Bypass Road.

Hanalei Town Farmers Market, a mobile market operated by Michael O'Reilly Rowan, specializes in farm fresh organic fruits and vegetables grown in the area. He's located across the street from Postcards Cafe and in front of Kayak Kaua'i in Hanalei.

If you are a devoted ad shopper (even on vacation), check the Wednesday paper for grocery specials. On the South Shore you can shop at Big Save in Koloa. On the East shore there is a Big Save in Kapa'a and a 24-hour Safeway at Kaua'i Village. In Lihu'e you'll find a Big Save and in the Kukui Grove Shopping Center, a Star Market. In Waipouli, the Foodland is open 24 hours a day and has a full service Bank of America in the store, not just an ATM! On the West Side there is a Big Save in Waimea and in Ele'ele. On the North Shore, choose between the Big Save in Hanalei or Foodland in Princeville. All major stores accept Visa or Mastercard. These larger stores offer the same variety as your hometown store and the prices are better than at the small grocery outlets. The best part of shopping for food in Hawai'i is discovering the interesting specialty markets. You'll find wonderful fresh fish, fruit, vegetable and pupu markets in all the towns. "Health" foods can be tracked down at Papaya's in Kapa'a or Vim 'N Vigor in Lihu'e.

# *ANNUAL KAUA'I EVENTS*

**JANUARY**
- New Year's Day Bowl Bash with big screen tv at Kukui Grove Shopping Center (808) 245-7784
- Christmas Bird Count. Koke'e Natural History Museum. (808) 335-9975.
- Annual Hula Ho'ike. Kaua'i War Memorial Convention Hall (808) 823-0501
- Rainbow Arts Festival. Family fair with visual and performing arts. Hanapepe Town Park. (808) 335-0712

**FEBRUARY**
- Chinese New Year. Celebrations around the island.
- Celebration in Waimea, usually the third weekend in February. "Sugar Mill Events" feature local food specialty booths, games, crafts, a fun run, canoe race, amusements, and entertainment. (808) 338-9957.

**MARCH**
- March 26 is Prince Kuhio Day, a State Holiday.
- Prince Kuhio Festival Celebration. Call (808) 822-5521 or 826-9272
- Prince Kuhio Outrigger Canoe Race, Hanamaulu to Wailua Beach, Garden Island Canoe Racing Association. (808) 822-1944

**APRIL**
- Annual Business Canoe Race, Hanamaulu Beach, Kaiola Canoe Club.
- April through August is Polo season at Anini Beach Polo Field (808) 822-3740
- Kaua'i Humane Society Fundraising Dinner, Hyatt Regency (808) 355-5255

**MAY**
- May 1st, Lei Day, is celebrated around the island with programs that include a contest and concert
- Annual Banana Poka Round Up and Forest Education Fair at Koke'e Natural History Museum. (808) 335-9975.
- Prince Albert Music Festival. Annual Princeville Hotel event dedicated to the only child of Queen Emma and King Kamehameha IV: Prince Albert Edward Kauikeaouli Lei O Papa A Kamehameha. (808) 826-6559.
- Annual Traditional Hawaiian Music Competition at War Memorial Convention Hall (808) 245-8508
- Hawai'i Hotel Association "Visitor Industry Charity Walk" with entertainment, food, and 2,000 walkers on a 5k route. Kukui Grove Pavilion.

**JUNE**

- Taste of Hawai'i at Smith's Tropical Paradise (808) 821-6895. The first of Hawaii's food festivals with over 50 of the state's top chefs participating in what has been called "The Ultimate Sunday Brunch!" Sponsored by Rotary.
- King Kamehameha Day celebrations around the state.
- King Kamehameha Ho'olaulea Festival. Parade, food booths, arts & crafts, entertainment (808) 337-1671
- Annual Ha'ena to Hanalei 8-mile run. Sponsored by Hanalei Civic Canoe Club
- O Bon Festival Season (June-August) Buddhist tradition in which spirits of ancestors are welcomed with prayers, offerings, and bon dances with food, game & crafts booths after. Fri. & Sat. nights at Buddhist temples around the island.
- "Made on Kaua'i Trade Show." Homemade & homegrown Kaua'i products exhibition at Kukui Grove Center.
- Kaua'i Ocean Festival. Swimming, surfing, canoe, and board races, volleyball, food booths, entertainment. The two-day festival benefits the Kaua'i Food Bank.

**JULY**

- 4th of July celebration at Vidinha Stadium: Concert in the Sky with fireworks, crafts, and food. Kaua'i Hospice fundraiser. (808) 245-7277
- Koloa Plantation Days. Week-long celebration of old Koloa Town's history & heritage (808) 332-9201.
- Annual Chili Cook-Off to benefit Kaua'i Humane Society, Kaua'i Village in Kapa'a (808) 822-4904.
- Kukui Grove Shopping Center Anniversary celebration with music, food, and prizes. (808) 245-7784.

**AUGUST**

- August 21 - Admission Day, a state holiday.
- Trout season opens in Koke'e State Park.
- Tahiti Fete, Kukui Grove Shopping Center Pavilion. Cultural exchange festival with Tahiti. Welcome luau at Lydgate Park. (808) 821-0098

**SEPTEMBER**

- Na Wahine Hula, Women's hula competition at Hyatt Regency (808) 742-1234
- Mokihana Festival, annual musical event featuring folk arts workshops, flowerless lei contests and ukulele jam. (808) 822-2166.
- Kaua'i Composers Contest & Concert, Outrigger Kaua'i Beach (808) 245-1955

**OCTOBER**

- Aloha Festivals, island-wide. Hawaiian ceremonies, parade, concerts, sports, hula, and other events that reflect the Aloha Spirit! (808) 821-2070
- Annual "*Eo e emalani i Alakai* Festival" commemorating Queen Emma's journey to Koke'e and the Alakai Swamp with hula and music outdoors at the Koke'e Lodge. (808) 335-9975.
- Kaua'i Community Oktoberfest, Kaua'i Veteran's Center (808) 332-7376
- Coconut Festival with food, crafts, games, & entertainment. Kapa'a Beach Park (808) 822-1141.
- Hanapepe Coffee Festival. Parade, music, art -- and coffee! (808) 335-0046.

**NOVEMBER**
- Hawai'i International Film Festival 1-800-752-8193 or (808) 528-FILM.
- PGA Grand Slam - Po'ipu Bay Resort Golf Course.
- Kapa'a Town Veteran's Day Parade
- Hawaiian Christmas Fair, Princeville Golf Club House
- Malama Pono Holiday Fundraiser, Kaua'i Marriott. Entertainment, pupus, silent auction (808) 822-0878.

**DECEMBER**
- Kilohana Craft Fair at Kilohana
- Kaua'i Museum Christmas Craft Fair.
- Kaua'i Chorale Christmas Concert at KCC Performing Arts Center 245-8270
- Christmas Fantasy Faire. Crafts, food, refreshments, entertainment 828-0014
- Parade of Lighted Floats and caroling in Waimea (808) 338-9957.
- Santa's Village, Christmas parade, craft fairs, and holiday entertainment at Kukui Grove Shopping Center. (808) 245-7784.

**THESE EVENTS ARE HELD EACH MONTH (DATES VARY)**

CJM Country Stables Rodeo (808) 742-6096

"Wonder Walk" Guided hike at Koke'e Natural History Museum (June-Sept) (808) 335-9975

Family Saturday at Kaua'i Museum with free admission for the whole family (808) 245-6931

Friday Art Nights in Hanapepe (808) 335-0046

Kaua'i History Program Series: lectures and field trips by Kaua'i Historical Society (808) 245-3373

*E Kanikapila Kakou*: 12-week (Feb-May) Hawaiian music program; held every Monday evening (808) 246-3994

Note: These annual events often change dates and have been known to switch months! We have included phone numbers wherever possible. For the exact dates of many of these events, write to the Hawai'i Visitors and Convention Bureau, 2270 Kalakaua Avenue #801, Honolulu, HI 96815, and request the Hawai'i Special Events Calendar. The calendar also gives non-annual information and the contact person for each event. A more complete listing for Kaua'i events can be obtained from the Kaua'i Visitors Bureau at 4334 Rice St., Room 101, Lihu'e, Kaua'i, HI 96766 (808) 245-3971, FAX (808) 246-9235. Check the local papers for dates of additional events. The *Kaua'i Update* newsletter will also advise you on current events!

# *WEATHER*

When thinking of Hawai'i, one visualizes bright sunny days cooled by refreshing trade winds, and this is the weather at least 300 days a year. What about the other 65 days? Most aren't really bad - just not perfect. Although there are only two seasons, summer and winter, temperatures remain quite constant. (The North Shore, however, tends to be slightly cooler and rainier.) Following are the average daily highs and lows for each month and the general weather conditions.

| | | | |
|---|---|---|---|
| January | 80/64 | July | 86/70 |
| Feb. | 79/64 | August | 87/71 |
| March | 80/64 | September | 87/70 |
| April | 82/66 | October | 86/69 |
| May | 84/67 | November | 83/68 |
| June | 86/69 | December | 80/66 |

*Winter:* Mid-October through April, 70 - 80 degree days, 60 - 70 degree nights. Tradewinds are more erratic, vigorous to none. Kona winds are more frequent causing wide-spread cloudiness, rain showers, mugginess and even an occasional thunderstorm. 11 hours of daylight.

*Summer:* May through mid-October, 80 degree days, 70 - 80 degree nights. Tradewinds are more consistent keeping the temperatures tolerable, however, when the trades stop, the weather becomes hot and sticky. Kona winds are less frequent. 13 hours of daylight. Summer type wear is suitable all year round. However, a warm sweater or light-weight jacket is a good idea for evenings and trips such as to Koke'e. If you are interested in the types of weather you may encounter, or are confused by some of the terms you hear, read on. For further reference consult *Weather in Hawaiian Waters*, by Paul Haraguchi, 99 pages, available at island bookstores.

Average water temperature ranges between 74 degrees in February to a warm 80 degrees by October. For additional information on surf conditions on Kaua'i call the Weather Information Recording at (808) 245-6001 or Marine Forecast / Hawaiian Waters for their recording at (808) 245-3564.

***TRADE WINDS:*** Trade winds are an almost constant wind that blows from the northeast through the east and are caused by the Pacific anti-cyclone, a high pressure area. This high pressure area is well developed and remains semi-stationary in the summer causing the trades to remain steady over 90% of the time. Interruptions are much more frequent in the winter when they blow only 40 to 60% of the time.

***KONA WINDS:*** The Kona Wind is a stormy, rain-bearing wind blowing from the southwest, or basically from the opposite direction of the trades. It brings high, rough surf to the resort side of the island - great for surfing and boogie-boarding, bad for snorkeling. These conditions are caused by low pressure areas northwest of the islands. Kona winds strong enough to cause property damage have occurred only twice since 1970. Lighter non-damaging Kona winds are much more common, occurring 2 - 5 times almost every winter (Nov-April).

***KONA WEATHER:*** Windless, hot and humid weather is referred to as Kona weather. The interruption of the normal trade wind pattern brings this on. The trades are replaced by light and variable winds and, although this may occur any time of the year, it is most noticeable during the summer when the weather is generally hotter and more humid, with fewer localized breezes.

***KONA LOW:*** A Kona low is a slow-moving, meandering, extensive low pressure area which forms near the islands. This causes continuous rain with thunderstorms over an extensive area and lasts for several days. November through May is the most usual time for these to occur.

***RAIN:*** Paradise would not be paradise without it and parts of Kaua'i do tend to receive more than the other islands. With the Northeast trade winds reaching the North Shore of Kaua'i first, they deposit a greater share on this coastline. The Hanalei/Princeville area receives up to 45 inches per year. The East side fares better, receiving only 30 inches per year. The south and western coastlines receive between 5 and 20 inches per year. And then there is Mt. Wai'ale'ale, officially the wettest place on earth with a record 665.5 inches of rain falling in 1982. More average years will result in 450-475 inches of rain fall on this, Kaua'i's second highest peak.

***HURRICANES:*** Hurricanes (called typhoons when they are west of the 180 degree longitude) have done damage to the Hawaiian islands on several occasions. The storms which affect Hawai'i usually originate off Central America or Mexico and most of the threatening tropical cyclones have weakened before reaching the islands, or have passed harmlessly to the west. Their effects are usually minimal, causing only high surf on the eastern and southern shores of some of the islands. At least 21 hurricanes or tropical storms have passed within 300 miles of the islands in the last 33 years, but most did little or no damage. Hurricane season is considered to be July-November. Hurricanes are given Hawaiian names when they pass within 1,000 miles of the Hawaiian islands.

In August of 1950, Hurricane Hiki went to the north of Kaua'i, but still brought 70 mile per hour winds to the island. In 1957, Kaua'i felt the force of two hurricanes which also passed nearby. Both Hurricane Della (in September of that year) and Hurricane Nina (which followed in early December) skirted a mere 100 miles from the southwestern shore of Kaua'i, bringing high winds and high surf. Hurricane Dot struck the island in August of 1959, with winds nearing 100 miles per hour. In this decade before much development, major damage was restricted to crops. Hurricane Iwa of November 1982 passed between Ni'ihau and Kaua'i with gusts up to 100 mph causing extensive damage to crops and property.

Hurricane Iniki (which means piercing wind) struck Kaua'i with incredible force in September 1992. Strangely it was within weeks of Hurricane Andrew's blow to Florida. As Iniki traveled across the Atlantic, crossing into the Pacific, it had time to develop winds that blew at 165 miles per hour with one gust at Napali on the Makaha Ridge which recorded a speed of 227 miles per hour. Iniki was considered a Category Four (Category Five is the highest) hurricane. Trees were uprooted, homes were destroyed, property damage was extensive and island wide. Power and phone lines were down for weeks. Due to the remoteness of the island, help was slower to arrive to Kaua'i than to Florida. While the news media continued to focus on Florida for weeks following Hurricane Andrew, after a few days of coverage, Kaua'i was almost forgotten. Residents refer to Iniki (and Iniki Day) as 911. A little pun since it occurred on September 11th, 9-11!

Kaua'i has been much slower to recover from this latest natural disaster. Only two major resorts, the Hyatt Regency and Princeville had reopened within two years following the hurricane. The Sheraton Kaua'i didn't open again until the end of 1997. The former Westin Kaua'i reopened in July of 1995 as the Kaua'i Marriott Resort and at press time, the Wai'ohai Resort is expected to reopen as a part of the Marriott Chain. Po'ipu Beach Hotel remains closed. The Coco Palms is being discussed as a possible timeshare.

Even good things can result from tragedies. Within hours of Hurricane Iniki, Kaua'i residents were pulling together to begin to normalize their lives. They began with neighbors helping neighbors. No one was untouched, but those with dwellings suffering only minor damage were welcoming neighbors into their homes. We were told that Stephen Spielberg, just finishing up his *Jurassic Park* filming, offered his private helicopter to bring in much needed medical personnel. Kaua'i continues to rebuild and grow stronger because of Iniki. Government agencies have begun to work in closer harmony, to make plans for the safety of the population of Kaua'i should any other disaster strike the island and its people.

***TSUNAMI:*** A tsunami is an ocean wave produced by an undersea earthquake, volcanic eruption, or landslide. Tsunamis are usually generated along the coasts of South America, the Aleutian Islands, the Kamchatka Peninsula, or Japan and travel through the ocean at 400 to 500 miles an hour. It takes at least 4 1/2 hours for a tsunami to reach the Hawaiian Islands. A 24-hour Tsunami Warning System has been established in Hawai'i since 1946. When the possibility exists of a tsunami reaching Hawaiian waters, the public will be informed by the sound of the attention alert signal sirens. This particular signal is a steady one minute siren, followed by one minute of silence, repeating as long as necessary.

Immediately turn on a TV or radio; all stations will carry CIV-Alert emergency information and instructions with the arrival time of the first waves. Do not take chances, false alarms are not issued!! Move quickly out of low lying coastal areas that are subject to possible inundation.

The warning sirens are tested throughout the state on the first working Monday of every month at 11 am, so don't be alarmed when you hear the siren blare! The test lasts only a few minutes and CIV-Alert announces on all stations that the test is underway. Since 1813, there have been 112 tsunamis observed in Hawai'i with only 16 causing significant damage.

Tsunamis may also be generated by local volcanic earthquakes. In the last 100 years there have been only six, with the last one November 29, 1975, affecting the southeast coast of the island of Hawaii. The Hawaiian Civil Defense has placed earthquake sensors on all the islands and, if a violent local earthquake occurs, an urgent tsunami warning will be broadcast and the tsunami sirens will sound. A locally generated tsunami will reach the other islands very quickly. Therefore, there may not be time for an attention alert signal to sound. Any violent earthquake that causes you to fall or hold onto something to prevent falling is an urgent warning, and you should immediately evacuate beaches and coastal low-lying areas.

There have been two tsunamis in recent history which struck Kaua'i doing serious damage to property and taking human life. In 1946 and in 1957 the tsunami did the most destruction to the North Shore of Kaua'i. A tsunami alert is always taken seriously, but fortunately the most recent (1995) tsunami generated a wave of only two inches.

For additional information on warnings and procedures in the event of a hurricane, tsunami, earthquake or flash flood, read the civil defense section located in the forward section of the Kaua'i phône book.

***TIDES:*** The average tidal range is about two feet.

***SUNRISE AND SUNSET:*** In Hawaii, day length and the altitude of the noon sun above the horizon do not vary as much throughout the year. This is because the temperate regions of the island's low latitude lie within the sub-tropics. The longest day is 13 hours 26 minutes (sunrise 5:53 am, sunset 7:18 pm) at the end of June, and the shortest day is 10 hours 50 minutes (sunrise 7:09 am and sunset 6:01 pm at the end of December). Daylight for outdoor activities without artificial lighting lasts about 45 minutes past sunset.

KAUAI NATURE PATROL
Janora Bayot

# *MAP INDEX*

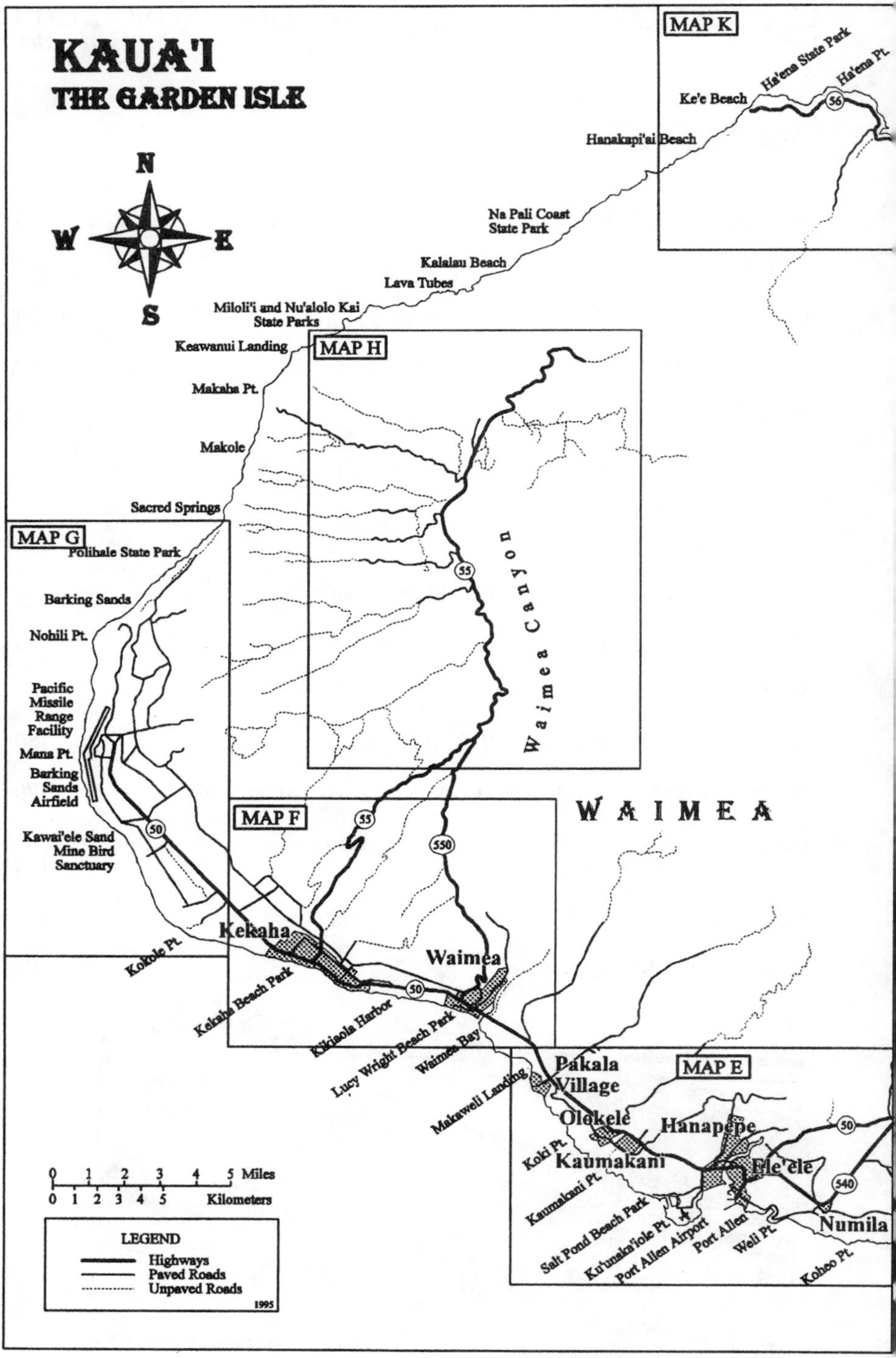

KAUA'I
THE GARDEN ISLE
N
S
W
E
MAP K
Ha'ena State Park
Ha'ena Pt.
Ke'e Beach
56
Hanakapi'ai Beach
Na Pali Coast State Park
Kalalau Beach
Lava Tubes
Miloli'i and Nu'alolo Kai State Parks
Keawanui Landing
MAP H
Makaha Pt.
Makole
Sacred Springs
MAP G
Polihale State Park
Barking Sands
Nohili Pt.
Pacific Missile Range Facility
Mana Pt.
Barking Sands Airfield
Kawai'ele Sand Mine Bird Sanctuary
55
Waimea Canyon
WAIMEA
MAP F
55
550
50
Kekaha
Kokole Pt.
Kekaha Beach Park
Kikiaola Harbor
50
Waimea
Lucy Wright Beach Park
Waimea Bay
Makaweli Landing
Pakala Village
MAP E
Olokele
Hanapepe
50
Koki Pt.
Kaumakani
Ele'ele
540
Kaumakani Pt.
Salt Pond Beach Park
Ku'unaka'iole Pt.
Port Allen Airport
Port Allen
Weli Pt.
Numila
Koheo Pt.
0 1 2 3 4 5 Miles
0 1 2 3 4 5 Kilometers
LEGEND
Highways
Paved Roads
Unpaved Roads
1995

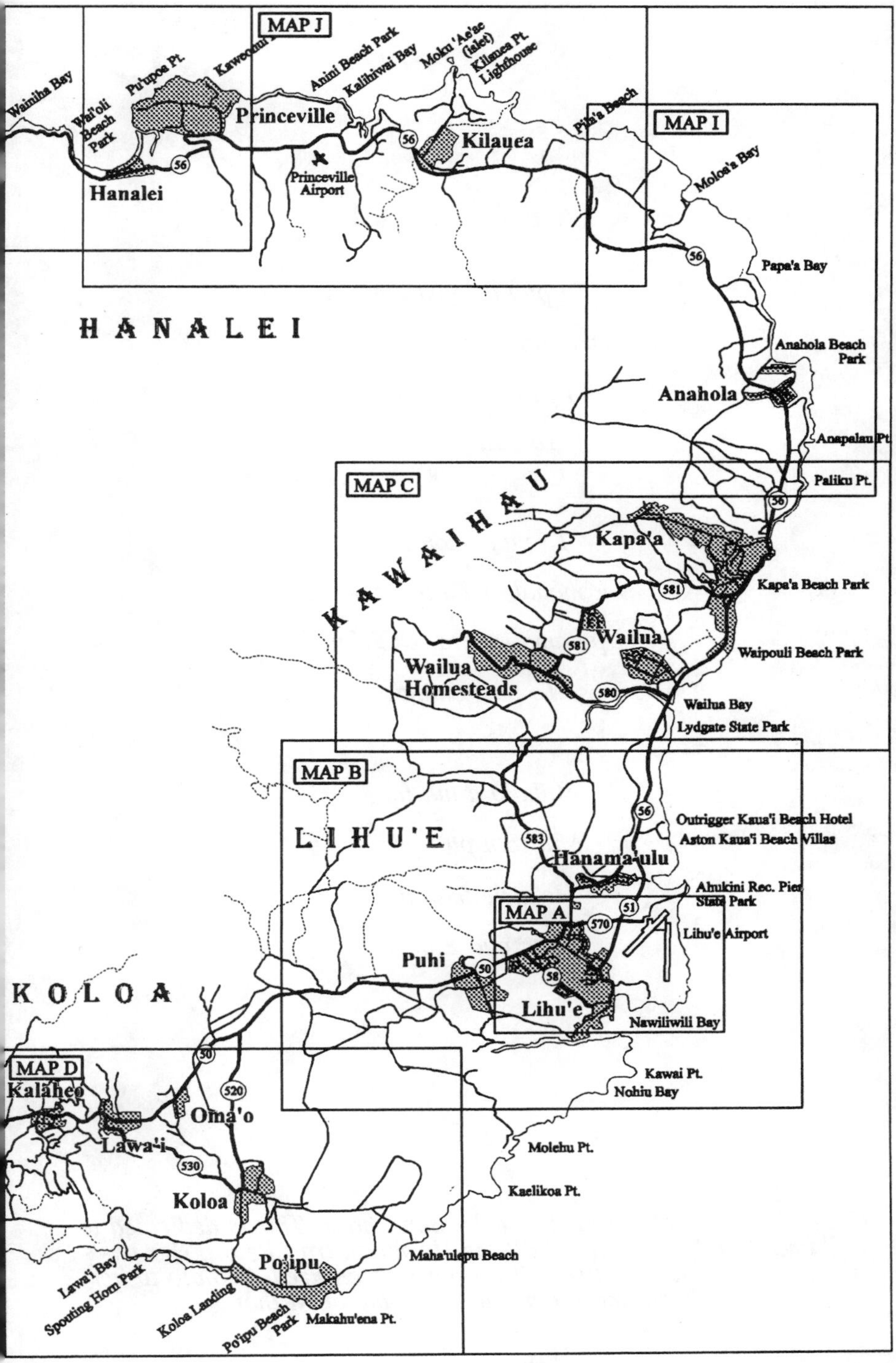
MAP J
Wainiha Bay
Wai'oli Beach Park
Pu'upoa Pt.
Princeville
Anini Beach Park
Kalihiwai Bay
Moku 'Ae'ae (islet)
Kilauea Pt. Lighthouse
Kilauea
Hanalei
Princeville Airport
Pila'a Beach
MAP I
Moloa'a Bay
Papa'a Bay
HANALEI
Anahola Beach Park
Anahola
Anapalau Pt.
Paliku Pt.
MAP C
KAWAIHAU
Kapa'a
Kapa'a Beach Park
Wailua
Waipouli Beach Park
Wailua Homesteads
Wailua Bay
Lydgate State Park
MAP B
LIHU'E
Outrigger Kaua'i Beach Hotel
Aston Kaua'i Beach Villas
Hanama'ulu
Ahukini Rec. Pier State Park
MAP A
Lihu'e Airport
Puhi
Lihu'e
Nawiliwili Bay
KOLOA
Kawai Pt.
Nohiu Bay
MAP D
Kalaheo
Oma'o
Lawa'i
Molehu Pt.
Koloa
Kaelikoa Pt.
Po'ipu
Maha'ulepu Beach
Lawa'i Bay
Spouting Horn Park
Koloa Landing
Po'ipu Beach Park
Makahu'ena Pt.

## *TA PUA ĒLAMA*

*Ta pua a ‘o Ni‘ihau*
*Onaona me ta ho‘ohihi,*
*I ta nui lehulehu,*
*Ta pua Ēlama.*

*Ta pua o tou lei,*
*E mohala mau loa ana,*
*I pulama ia e ta lehulehu,*
*Ta pua Ēlama.*

*Mahalo a nui loa,*
*Mai to‘u pu‘u wai,*
*He mele teia nou,*
*E ta pua Ēlama.*

*Used with the permission of Chucky Boy Chock. This is dedicated to Elama Kanahele, who did all the Hawaiian translation. Her patience, time and expertise will always be treasured. Mahalo to her ‘Ohana and the beautiful people of Ni‘ihau.*

# WHERE TO STAY WHAT TO SEE

## *INTRODUCTION*

In the fall of 1999, Kaua'i offered 3,486 hotel rooms, 3,139 condominium units, 24 cabins, 230 bed & breakfasts, 312 vacation rental homes and apartments, 24 lodges, 87 cottages, and 80 hostel units. This was prior to the opening of several major hotels (including the Waioha'i, Po'ipu Beach (to be demolished) and Coco Palms all scheduled to open in 2000), which will add a substantial number of rooms to the inventory.

The island can easily be divided into three main areas, with perhaps some sub-areas: Princeville and Hanalei -- North Shore; The East/Central region; and the third which we have grouped into one area that includes the South and West shores. This last area covers Po'ipu Beach and the Koloa areas, and continues to the west side to include the accommodations in the Waimea and Koke'e areas. This chapter contains a list of essentially all of the condominiums that are in rental programs as well as the island's hotels.

Bed & Breakfasts are a booming business and an alternative that has become increasingly popular over the years. Kaua'i, in particular, seems to have more prominently listed B & B units than the other islands. This again can probably be traced to Hurricane Iniki. When businesses were closed or destroyed, many whose homes needed to be rebuilt and renovated anyway looked into a B & B as a way to create their own jobs and/or additional income. Now that tourism is back in business, they are too, and there are dozens of B & B's that are ready, able, and happy to welcome guests.

Traditionally B & B means a room in a private home (usually with a shared entrance) and those range from $55 a night. Condos, cottages, and studios with private entrances and/or baths range from $60 to $200 a night. Bed & Breakfast homes are sprinkled around the island and we have listed them within the areas of the island where they are located.

Also included at the conclusion of this chapter are several of the Bed & Breakfast agencies which handle many more homes than we have been able to include in this volume. Many have websites and we'll list some of those for you to review! Refer to RENTAL AGENTS at the conclusion of this chapter. Note that very few Bed & Breakfast facilities accept any type of charge cards. Some do not allow children.

Remember when calling Hawai'i to adjust for the time difference. Most offices are open during business hours Hawai'i standard time and some only weekdays. Bed & Breakfast homes would no doubt really appreciate calls during the day or evening (Hawai'i time).

***HOW TO USE THIS CHAPTER:*** For ease in locating information, the properties are first indexed alphabetically following this introduction. In each of the three distinctly different geographical areas, we have divided the condominiums and listed them in order of price and then alphabetized them for quick reference.

Keep in mind that in providing directions, we may refer to the Hawaiian terms of *mauka*, which means towards the mountains and *makai*, which means towards the ocean. On these islands it is much less cumbersome to utilize this form of indicating direction than the standard north, east, south, and west!

Often the management at the property takes reservations, but some do not. In some cases there are several rental agents handling units in addition to the on-site management and we have listed an assortment of these. We suggest that when you determine which condo you are interested in that you call all of the agents. Be aware that while one agent may have no vacancy, another will have several. The prices we have listed are generally the lowest available (although some agents may offer lower rates with the reduction of certain services such as maid service on check in only - that means your room is clean when you arrive - rather than daily maid service). You may find that one of the package air/condo/car options will be an all-around better value than booking each of these separately.

Prices are listed to aid your selection and, while these were the most current available at press time, they are subject to change without notice. As island vacationers ourselves, we found it important to include this feature rather than just giving you broad categories such as budget or expensive. After all, one person's "expensive" may be "budget" to someone else!

For the sake of space, we have made use of several abbreviations. The size of the condominiums are identified as studio (S BR), one bedroom (1 BR), two bedroom (2 BR), and three bedroom (3 BR). The number in parentheses refers to the number of people that can occupy the unit for the price listed and that there are enough beds for a maximum number of people to occupy this unit, i.e. 2 BR (max 4). The description will tell you how much it will be for additional persons over two, i.e. $10/night. Some facilities consider an infant as an extra person, others will allow children free up to a specified age. The abbreviations o.f., g.v., and o.v. refer to oceanfront, gardenview, and oceanview units. Some of the prices may be listed with a slash dividing them. The first price listed is the high season rate, the second price is the low season rate. More and more properties are going to a flat all-season rate. A few include the summer months as high season, and a few others have complicated matters by having a three season fee schedule. The abbreviation <WWW> means that there is a website available. Due to space, we simply can't list all the URL addresses.

All listings are condominiums unless specified as a (Hotel). Condos are abundant, and the prices and facilities they offer can be quite varied. We have tried to indicate our own personal preferences by the use of a ★. We felt these were the best buys or special in some way. However, it is impossible for us to view all the units within a complex, and since condominiums are privately owned, each unit can vary in its furnishings and its condition.

***WHERE TO STAY:*** As for choosing the area of the island in which to stay, we offer these suggestions:

SOUTH SHORE: Along the south shore you'll find it generally sunnier in the Po'ipu area with generally the best beach conditions. During the winter months the south shore beaches are generally safer.

NORTH SHORE/HANALEI: If you want incredible scenery, lots of lush green vegetation and are eager to get just a little further away from civilization, then Princeville may be for you. With varied accommodations you can choose between luxury and moderate. During the winter months, high surf can make the North Shore ocean conditions very dangerous.

EASTERN SHORE: Affectionately known as the Coconut Coast, you'll find the best selection of affordable accommodations. Centrally located, you can easily drive to either the south or North Shore for the many varied activities they offer.

NEW DEVELOPMENTS: Reports indicate that the new Kukui'ula Resort project on Kaua'i's south shore is nearing final approval. The $125 million Alexander & Baldwin Inc. proposed development would include a 350-room resort and timeshare property overlooking Kukui'ula Bay.

***HOW TO SAVE MONEY:*** Kaua'i has two price seasons. High or "in" season and low or "off" season. Low season is generally considered to be April 15 to about December 15, and the rates are discounted at some places as much as 30%. Different resorts and condominiums may vary these dates by as much as two weeks and a few resorts are going to a flat, year-round rate. Ironically, some of the best weather is during the fall when temperatures are cooler than summer and there is less rain than the winter and spring months. (See GENERAL INFORMATION - *Weather* for year-round temperatures).

For longer than one week, a condo unit with a kitchen can result in significant savings on your food bill. While this will give you more space than a hotel room at a lower price, you may give up some resort amenities (shops, restaurants, maid service, etc.). There are several large grocery stores around the island with fairly competitive prices, although most things at the store will run about 30% higher than on the mainland. (See GENERAL INFORMATION - *Grocery Shopping*.)

Most condominiums offer maid service only on check-out. A few might offer it twice a week or weekly. Additional maid service may be available for an extra charge. A few condos still do not provide in-room phones and a few have no pool.

(A few words of caution: condominium units within one complex can differ greatly so, if a phone or other amenity is important to you, ask!) Some may offer free local calls while others will tack on an extra $1 per local call. Many have added microwaves to their kitchens. Some units have washers and dryers in the rooms, while others do not. If there are no in-room laundry facilities, you will generally find that most have coin-operated laundry facilities on the premises. Travel agents will be able to book your stay in the Kaua'i hotels and also in most condominiums.

If you prefer to make your own reservation, we have listed the various contacts for each condominium and endeavored to quote the best price generally available. A little phone work can be very cost effective! Rates vary between rental agents, so check all those listed for a particular condominium. We have indicated toll free 800 or 888 numbers for the U.S. when available. Some toll free numbers are not valid from Canada or inter-island. For additional Canadian toll free numbers, check the rental agent list at the end of this chapter. Look for an (808) area code preceding the non-toll free numbers. You might also check the classified ads in your local newspaper for owners offering their units for rent, which may be even a better bargain. Although prices can jump, most go up only 5-10% per year. To the prices listed, you will need to add sales tax of 4% plus a transient accommodations tax which is currently 7.25%

***GENERAL POLICIES:*** Condominium complexes require a deposit (usually equivalent to one or two nights stay) to secure your reservation and insure your room rate against price increases. Some charge higher deposits during winter or over Christmas holidays. Generally a 30 day notice of cancellation is needed to receive a full refund. Most require payment in full either 30 days prior to arrival or upon arrival, and some do not accept credit cards. Night owls beware! Many condos have initiated early check-out times of 11 am or even 10 am, although some are compensating by providing an earlier check-in of 2 pm (instead of 3 pm). The usual minimum condo stay is three nights with some requiring one week in winter.

Christmas holidays may have steeper restrictions with minimum stays as long as two weeks, payments 90 days in advance and heavy cancellation penalties. It is not uncommon to book as much as two years in advance for the Christmas season.

ALL CONDOMINIUMS HAVE KITCHENS, TV'S, AND POOLS UNLESS OTHERWISE SPECIFIED. Most condominiums have ceiling fans, but many have no air conditioning. After arriving from a long flight with a car full of luggage, one of the most unpleasant surprises may be to discover that you are on the third floor of a condominium complex that does NOT have an elevator. A surprising number of multi-level complexes are equipped only with stairs.

Monthly and oftentimes weekly discounts are available. Room rates quoted are generally for two. Additional persons run $10 and up per night per person with the exception of the high class resorts and hotels where it may run as much as $25 to $35 extra. Many complexes can arrange for crib rentals. (See GENERAL INFORMATION - *Traveling with Children.*) We have tried to give the lowest rates generally available, which might not be through the hotel or condo office, so check with the offices as well as the rental agents. Variations in prices may be due to the amenities of a particular unit or the general condition of the condo. When contacting condominium complexes by mail, be sure to address your correspondence to the attention of the manager. The managers of several complexes do not handle any reservations, however, so we have indicated to whom you should address reservation requests. If two addresses are given, use the P.O. Box rather than street address for your correspondence.

## *CONDOMINIUM AND HOTEL INDEX*

# *CENTRAL AND EASTSIDE*

### *Kapa'a - Lihu'e - Nawiliwili - Wailua - Waipouli*

In this section we will begin at Lihu'e and travel up the west coast in a northerly direction to Hanama'ulu, Wailua, Waipouli, and Kapa'a.

# *INTRODUCTION*

Kaua'i's main airport is located in Lihu'e, so this is probably the first place you'll see. It's not exactly the garden spot of the Garden Isle, but it is the least touristy and most "normal" area. This is the county seat where all the government and business offices are located and the place to find everyday necessities like the post office, discount shopping, banks, churches, and a library. It also offers the best selection of inexpensive local restaurants.

Hotels, motels, and condos in Lihu'e are inexpensive and convenient to the airport, but with the exception of only two resort areas, accommodations are very basic. Even if you stay at another property for the duration of your stay, they are worth considering for a night if you have a late evening arrival or an early morning departure. And don't worry about being too far away from the "good stuff." The Anchor Cove and Pacific Ocean Plaza shopping centers are very close, as is the Kaua'i Museum, and there are plenty of restaurants in the area - from funky local dining and ethnic places to fine dining selections. The Outrigger Kaua'i Beach Hotel & adjacent Aston Kaua'i Beach Villas along with the Kaua'i Marriott Resort & Beach Club are the only resorts with the Outrigger and Aston Villas slightly north of the general area.

Along the Central or Coconut Coast area are an abundance of affordably priced hotels and condominiums and there is plenty of wonderful natural beauty to be enjoyed as well.

# *WHAT TO SEE*

## *LIHU'E*

The word Lihu'e means "open to chill" and according to the *Kaua'i Talking Guidebook*, the town was named in 1837 by the Governor who relocated from the Big Island. His home town there (also called Lihu'e) had a cooler climate and was a more appropriate name than here on Kaua'i.

Because of our unusual island-state, mayors in Hawai'i govern counties which consist of one or more islands rather than areas of land. The island of Kaua'i (along with Ni'ihau) is a county of the state of Hawai'i and Lihu'e is the county seat. The historic county building was built in 1913 and, with its sprawling lawn and tall palm trees, it is a focal point of Lihu'e. Although government agencies are not usually high on one's list of visitor attractions, you may find the need to visit one or more while you're here on Kaua'i.

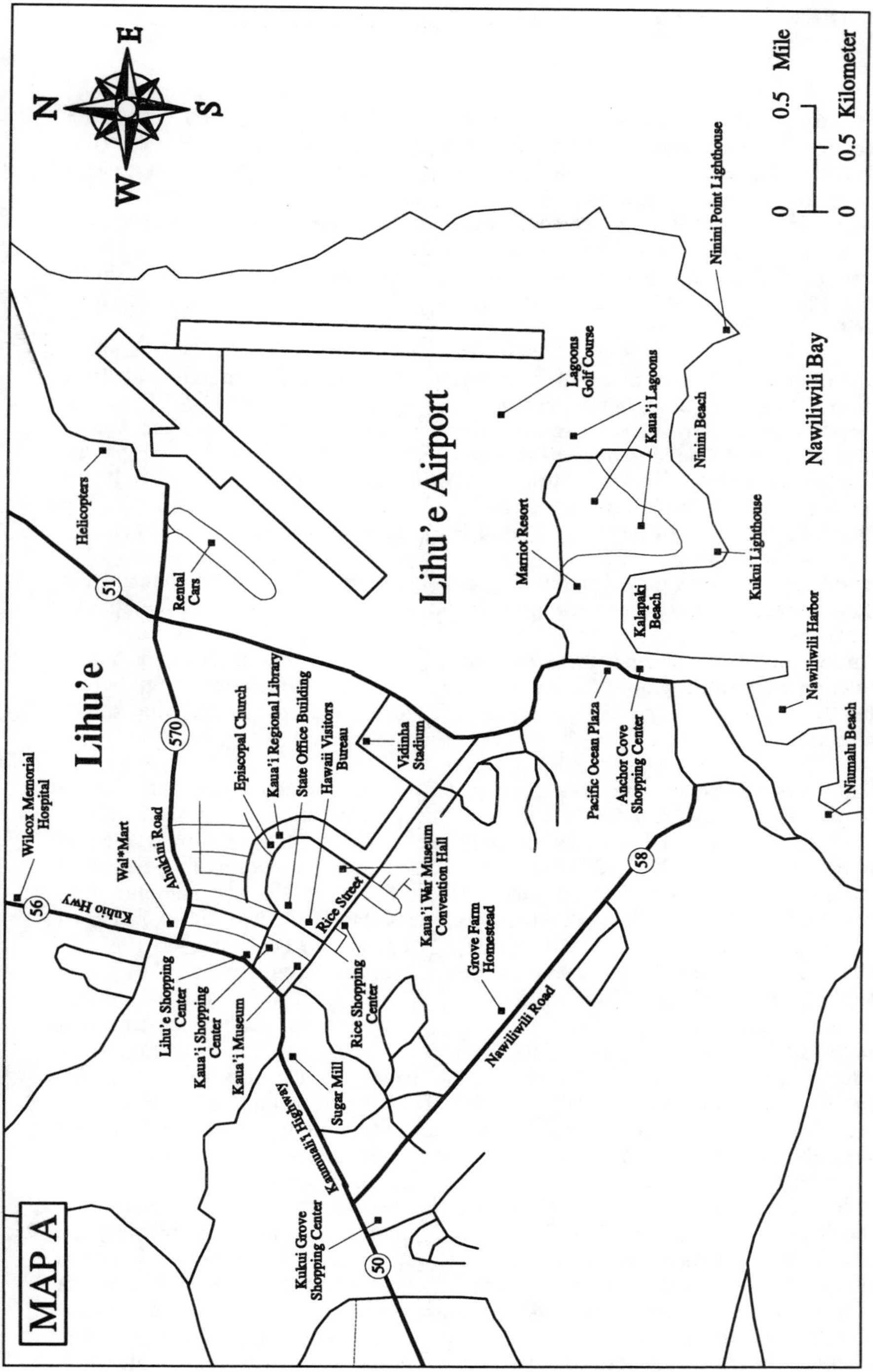
MAP A
N
E
S
W
0 0.5 Mile
0 0.5 Kilometer
Lihu'e
Lihu'e Airport
Wilcox Memorial Hospital
Wal*Mart
Ahukini Road
Kuhio Hwy
56
570
51
58
50
Helicopters
Rental Cars
Episcopal Church
Kaua'i Regional Library
State Office Building
Hawaii Visitors Bureau
Vidinha Stadium
Rice Street
Kaua'i War Museum Convention Hall
Lihu'e Shopping Center
Kaua'i Shopping Center
Kaua'i Museum
Rice Shopping Center
Grove Farm Homestead
Sugar Mill
Kaumuali'i Highway
Nawiliwili Road
Kukui Grove Shopping Center
Pacific Ocean Plaza
Anchor Cove Shopping Center
Marriot Resort
Lagoons Golf Course
Kaua'i Lagoons
Kalapaki Beach
Kukui Lighthouse
Ninini Beach
Ninini Point Lighthouse
Nawiliwili Harbor
Niumalu Beach
Nawiliwili Bay

The ***Kaua'i Visitors Bureau*** is always a good place to start to pick up some brochures and ask for information. It is located at 4334 Rice Street, Room #101. The ***State Parks and Recreation Department*** - a place you will need to go to if you plan on doing any camping, hiking, or generally any nature-oriented trips -is located in the State Building at 3060 Eiwa. This is where you will be able to pick up your permits. Phone (808) 274-3444 Division of State Parks - Camping permits. The ***County Parks and Recreation Department*** is at 4444 Rice, Suite 150. Phone (808) 241-6670 or for permits and reservations phone (808) 241-6660.

If you spend any time at all in Lihu'e you'll become quite familiar with Rice Street. It seems this single road can get you anywhere you want to go! From the Kaua'i Visitors Bureau, you can turn from Rice onto Hardy to reach the ***Kaua'i War Memorial Convention Hall*** and the Regional Library. The library has an excellent selection of Hawaiian titles, many of which are now out-of-print. If you are a Hawaiiana buff, you might like to include this on your itinerary! (The Kaua'i Community College has a good Hawaiiana section in their library).

If you are hot after a day of sightseeing and shopping, take a short detour to Halo Halo Shave Ice. It is part of ***Hamura Saimin*** and it, too, is just off Rice Street.

Further along Rice Street is the ***Rice Shopping Center***. It houses the island's only bowling alley, a Filipino bakery, and a couple of local style eateries. But before that, you'll find the main post office and, just across the street, the Kaua'i Museum.

The ***Kaua'i Museum*** ★ is a great place to get acquainted with the island's history. It is located at 4428 Rice Street in the Wilcox Building that was originally constructed in the 1920's as the first public library. Mrs. Emma Mahelona Wilcox offered $74,000 in February of 1922 for the construction of a permanent library in memory of her husband, Albert Spencer Wilcox. The building, designed by Hart Wood, was dedicated on May 24, 1924. In 1954 work began to create a Kaua'i Museum and it officially opened on December 3, 1960. In 1969 the adjacent Albert Spencer Wilcox Library building became the central building of the Kaua'i Museum Complex. The original museum building was named after William Hyde Rice. The museum offers a combination of permanent and changing exhibits. Some tell the story of the island's volcanic creation while other displays explain the role immigrants have played in creating the multi-cultural community that exists here today. The ancient people and their culture, the discovery by Captain Cook, missionary occupation, royal families, and agricultural history are all explored. Their 30 minute aerial film tour of Kaua'i provides a great base for planning your island excursions. Art, music, dance, religion, language, farming, surfing, healing, and the transition from royalty to statehood are all covered. The Kaua'i Museum gift store has quite possibly the best selection of Hawaiian titles as well as some wonderful handcrafted gift items. There is no admission charge if you wish to visit only the gift store, just advise them at the front counter. The museum is free to all on the first Saturday of each month. They have periodic special presentations and family activities. Open weekdays 9 am-4 pm, Sat. 10 am-4 pm, closed Sunday. (808) 245-6931.

The museum that housed the Hawaiiana collection of hotelier Grace Guslander (at the Coco Palms Hotel prior to Hurricane Iniki) has plans to reopen at another site in the near future. Currently, the ***Kaua'i Historical Society*** is involved in various historical and educational activities on the island, including an informative historical "dune walk" that is offered in conjunction with the Hyatt Regency. They also work in partnership with the Kaua'i Museum and Grove Farm Homestead and sponsor Elderhostel programs. They do maintain an office in Lihu'e, but they are not open to the general public. Their 3,000 volume collection, however, is available to the public for research and education, Monday through Friday, by appointment only. Donations and contributions are welcomed. Family membership is $25 per year. Contact them at (808) 245-3373.

Rice Street ends at the Lihu'e Shopping Center where it meets the Kuhio Highway. If you turn right and travel north for a few miles, you will find ***Hilo Hattie***, a mainstay for traditional aloha wear. They also sell an assortment of packaged Hawaiian food products and giftware items.

Just up the street is a branch of the national chain, ***Walmart***. This drug and sundry store has most things you might have forgotten to pack. Although we still like the comfortable feeling of a ***Longs Drug Store***, Walmart does have clothes and a larger selection of most items and you can't beat their long hours of operation! They open at 6 am (Sundays at 8) and stay open nightly until 10 pm!

If you choose to head south on the highway, it becomes the Kaumualii Highway (Route 50) and a short drive will take you to the ***Kukui Grove Shopping Center***. (The new 10-hole Grove Farm Golf Course at Puakea is nearby, so those golf lovers could partake of a short game while others in your group shop!) Kukui Grove is the island's largest shopping center and is the location for Liberty House, the major department store. The Kaua'i Products Store has a lovely selection of locally made quilts, muumuus, jewelry, lotions, keiki clothing -- even homemade fudge! Nature's of Hawai'i offers unusual Hawaiian curios and aloha wear. The Soul Garden Bath & Body Shop features organic soaps, lotions, bath & shower gels, oils, and blend-your-own Hawaiian fragrance products. And you don't want to miss a stop at Dollar Plus, where all items are priced at $1.25. There are several restaurants and eateries to be found in the mall, but better and more reasonable dining will be found back in the town of Lihu'e.

Turning left (south) onto the Kaumualii Highway from the Kukui Grove Shopping Center - on the same side of the road as Kaua'i Community College - you'll find a viewing area. This is a good location to pull alongside the road and glance at the Hoary Head Mountain Range which appears beyond and behind the Kukui Center. Look closely and you will see the ***profile of Queen Victoria***. Her head is slightly tipped back and she has a crown perched on the top of her head. A finger is pointing up as if she is reprimanding someone in the distance beyond. Just beyond is Puhi, once a plantation town. The old plantation store stood until it was destroyed in 1992 by the hurricane. A new post office was built at the end of 1999 along with new housing for the People's Market and several other new shops. But before you reach Puhi, there is the legendary plantation estate of Kilohana. ***Kilohana*** ★ is reminiscent of the grandeur and elegance of an earlier age. At the time when sugar was king on the island and prosperity reigned, plantation owners would build luxurious homes.

One of the grandest on Kaua'i was the home of Gaylord Parke Wilcox and is known as Kilohana. Built in 1935, this 16,000 square foot Tudor mansion was designed by a British architect named Mark Potter. The property was named for the large cinder cone which is located above and behind the property.

The grounds are carefully landscaped and inside furniture came from the exclusive and expensive Gump's in San Francisco. The Kilohana Shops and Galleries are well deserving of a bit of wandering, before or after you enjoy your meal at Gaylord's Courtyard Restaurant.

You'll find several tour options for exploring this 35-acre estate. The Canefield Tour is a step back into the history of sugar cane on Kaua'i. A wagon ride takes you back in time to 1835 with historical background on the property. Our guide was interesting and informative and nonplussed by the rain showers as our wagon, drawn by two Clydesdales, navigated through the fields.

In 1865 the second sugar plantation, the Lihu'e Plantation, was established along the Wailua River. It was the first to bring immigrant workers and to use stone grinders in the processing of the cane. George Norton Wilcox, the son of island missionaries returned to the island in 1864 following his studies at Scheffield (Yale) in engineering. He purchased 900 acres of wasteland for $10,000. When he broached the subject of irrigation, others thought he was crazy. He proceeded to dig a ditch 11.2 miles in length to bring water from Mt. Wai'ale'ale. The ditch, dug by hand, took two years to complete. His introduction of foreign immigrants from the Philippines, Germany, Australia, Japan, and elsewhere was the start of the cultural diversity that is evident in the islands today.

George was concerned that most of the workers would chose to return to their homelands following their contract. He approached them inquiring what would entice them to remain. Their answer resulted in Grove Farm providing single-family, 300 sq. ft. homes for the workers. These camp houses were designed after those used in logging camps in Oregon and Washington and were sent to Hawai'i in ready-to-assemble units. The only differences between these cabins and those in the Pacific Northwest logging camps were the lanais which were added to the front and the use of tin for the roofs. (Because of the cane burning and risk of flying cinders, a wooden roof would have been a fire hazard.) He also introduced chemical fertilization, developed hybrid strains of cane, and when the depression struck the country, George diversified. He died in 1933 at the age of 89 leaving everything to his nephew Gaylord. Gaylord built the 16,000 sq. ft. Kilohana home for his wife Ethel. Gaylord continued management of the company and ensured its continued success to this day. This sugar cane tour takes about an hour, but may not be a lively enough experience to keep the interest of youth. Those interested in a deeper background on the Wilcox family might enjoy the more lengthy tour at the Grove Farm Homestead.

The carriage ride is a shorter, more romantic excursion around the grounds. Carriage rides are available daily 11 am-6:30 pm. Horse dawn Sugar Cane Tours are set up by advance reservations, (808) 246-9529. Admission to Kilohana and its grounds is free, carriage rides are $8 adults/$4 children. Sugar Cane Tours are $21 adults/$10 children. Kilohana and the shops open daily at 9:30 am.

Gaylord's serves Sunday brunch 9:30 am-3 pm, lunch Monday to Saturday 11 am-3 pm, and dinner nightly from 5 pm. Located just outside Lihu'e, travel east along Kaumualii Highway, Route 50. Kilohana is on your left just before the town of Lihu'e. If you are arriving from the north or east, travel Kuhio Hwy., Route 56 south and west through Lihu'e. Bear right at the traffic light at the end of Kuhio Hwy. Kilohana will be 1.4 miles down Kaumualii Highway on your right. Kilohana (808) 245-5608.

Returning to the Kukui Grove Shopping Center, but at the opposite (Nawiliwili) end, is ***Big Kmart***. Adjacent is ***Borders Books and Music*** which is worth a stop. This is a bookstore chain, but in addition to books it there is also a terrific selection of music and videos as well as the drifting scent of espresso from their in-store cafe! They offer special events (free!) and their children's corner is a nice touch for the traveling family. 4303 Nawiliwili Rd., Lihu'e, HI 96766. (808) 246-0862. Also on Nawiliwili Rd. is the ***Grove Farm Homestead*** ★ which provides visitors with a fascinating look into the island's past. Kaua'i's history can be traced to the beginnings and growth of the sugar plantations. Grove Farm, one of the earliest sugar plantations, was founded in 1864 by George Wilcox, Gaylord's uncle. Today, this historic museum showcases the old sugar days and Hawai'i's politics from the monarchy to statehood. A two-and-one-half hour tour takes visitors through the original home, which was enlarged in later years to accommodate a growing family. The property, which includes the gracious old Wilcox home and the cottage of the plantation laundress, is situated amidst tropical gardens, orchards, and rolling lawns. The tours are small and intimate and the guides knowledgeable about the island's sugar industry and its history. Minted ice tea (with homegrown mint) and Grove Farm icebox cookies baked in an old wood stove in the farm house (Miss Mabel's favorite!) are served for refreshments. This living legacy was left by Miss Mabel Wilcox, the last surviving niece of George Wilcox, who wanted her family home to be preserved. She lived here until the time of her death in 1978. The property opened to the public in October of 1980. Most visitors miss touring the Grove Farm Homestead because reservations have to be booked weeks in advance. This is quite possibly Kaua'i's best cultural experience and is well worth a phone call ahead as you plan your island itinerary. Cost is $5 per person with tours available on Monday, Wednesday, and Thursdays. Reservations are required and can be made up to three months in advance. (808) 245-3202, PO Box 1631, Lihu'e, HI.

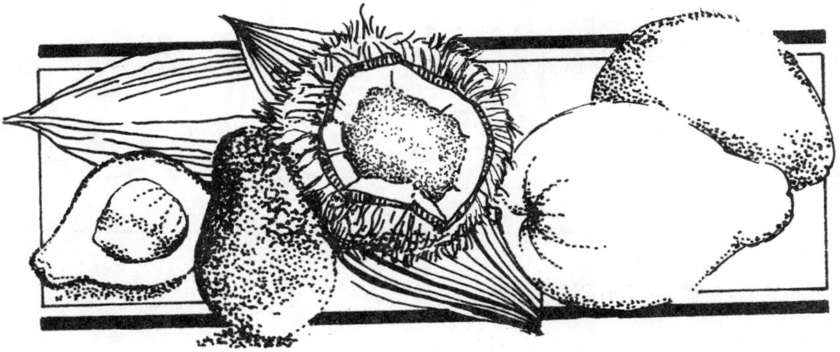

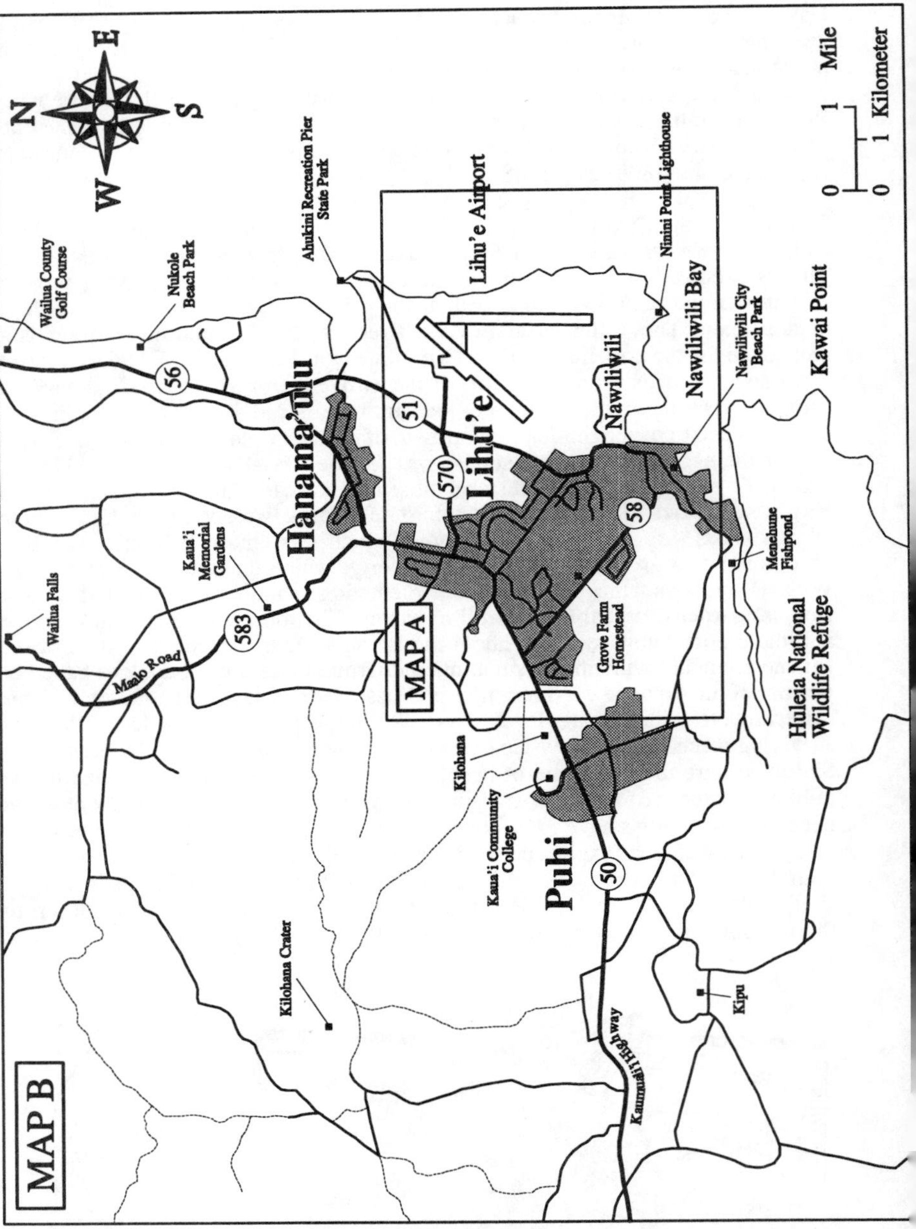

MAP B
MAP A
N
E
S
W
Mile
Kilometer
0
1
0
1
Wailua Falls
Wailua County Golf Course
Nukole Beach Park
Ahukini Recreation Pier State Park
Lihu'e Airport
Ninini Point Lighthouse
Nawiliwili Bay
Nawiliwili City Beach Park
Kawai Point
Nawiliwili
Hanama'ulu
Lihu'e
Kaua'i Memorial Gardens
Maalo Road
Grove Farm Homestead
Menehune Fishpond
Huleia National Wildlife Refuge
Kilohana
Kaua'i Community College
Puhi
Kilohana Crater
Kipu
Kaumuali'i Highway
56
51
570
583
58
50

## *NAWILIWILI*

Following Nawiliwili Road past Kukui Grove and the Grove Farm Homestead will take you toward the harbor. The route you travel is through scenic Lihu'e, again following Rice Street but in the opposite direction from before. Here, Rice Street becomes Hwy. 51 and will take you down past the Kaua'i Marriott Resort and on toward the harbor.

The ***Kaua'i Marriott Resort & Beach Club***, was formerly the Westin Maui and prior to that the Kaua'i Surf. It is located above the Nawiliwili Harbor at Kalapaki Bay. Following serious damage from Hurricane Iniki, the hotel sat vacant for several years before Marriott chose to take over the property and convert it into a combination timeshare and hotel. Major renovations converted the European style of this lavish resort to one with a Hawaiiana atmosphere. The much-improved property is now more fitting to the style of the islands. This hotel is the tallest building on Kaua'i: following the construction of the Kaua'i Surf, zoning laws changed building codes so that no building on Kaua'i could be taller than a palm tree. Next door at Kaua'i Lagoons is the Terrace Restaurant and further along, the Whalers Brewpub. Wedding services are available in the romantic gazebo.

Continuing on toward Nawiliwili Harbor, you will pass the ***Anchor Cove Shopping Center*** and the ***Pacific Ocean Plaza***, visitor-oriented shopping areas located across the street from each other on Rice Street. Nawiliwili was named for the abundant wiliwili trees that once thrived in this area. Nawiliwili Harbor became Kaua'i's main deep water harbor upon its completion in 1930. Following the completion of the harbor, Lihu'e became the island's major city. ***Nawiliwili Park*** was refurbished in 1995. A cement foundation destroyed by Hurricane Iniki was removed and play areas, barbecues, and picnic tables were added. Since then the park has also added professional volley ball courts. If you have some recreational time consider stopping by the kayak rental at Nawiliwili's small boat harbor which offers half day trips up the river past the Menehune Fish Pond. (Refer to RECREATION chapter for specifics.)

SPINNER DOLPHINS

The ***Menehune Fish Pond*** is a spot you may easily miss. Follow Hwy. 51 toward the Nawiliwili Harbor and look for the Wilcox Road sign. Follow it left onto Niumalu Road. Then turn right onto Hulemalu Road where a sign (the last time we checked) indicates the Menehune Fish Pond. From this turn-off it is another 6/10 of a mile to the lookout which will be on your left. The fish pond appears to be just a small pond adjacent to the Huleia River (or Huleia Stream, depending on the map you follow). Portions of *Raiders of the Lost Ark* were filmed along this waterway. Again, no historical background exists about the building of this pond, but legend tells that it was done by the menehune who were interrupted during their nighttime work and quit, leaving the pond unfinished with *pukas* (holes) in it! Some years ago a family tried to rebuild the gates to make the fish pond once again a working proposition, but plans or events changed and it was never made operational. The only way to see this up close is to do it by kayak along the Huleia River. Tours up the river - which begin near the Nawiliwili boat harbor - are available from a company called Kaua'i by Kayak.

The access road to the pond is posted as "No Trespassing" and while that doesn't stop some people from venturing beyond, we prefer to let the property owners maintain their legal rights.

Located along the Huleia River is the ***Huleia National Wildlife Refuge***, which is home to the endangered koloa duck. In 1973, 241 acres were purchased to provide a habitat for water birds. The lands, once taro and rice fields, are now breeding and feeding grounds for a variety of waterfowl. The refuge is located in a relatively flat valley along the Huleia River which is bordered by a steep wooded hillside. There are 31 species of migratory birds which inhabit the area, 18 of which were introduced. A special permit is issued annually to a commercial kayaking business for access through an upland portion of the refuge. The refuge, adjacent to the Menehune Fish Pond, is not open to the public. If you continue exploring the roads beyond the Menehune Pond you'll find some nice vistas of the Huleia Wildlife Refuge. We also found a little fruit stand that had piles of papaya. The papayas were each labeled with a black marker indicating the price. We picked out the one we liked, dropped the money in the can, and were on our way. Oh, wondrous Kaua'i!

## *WHERE TO SHOP*

Pacific Ocean Plaza and Anchor Cove are located across the street from each other on Rice Street as you head towards Nawiliwili. The ***Pacific Ocean Plaza*** has several boutiques along with Cafe Portofino, Kaua'i Chop Suey, and Tokyo Lobby restaurants. At ***Anchor Cove*** you will find a Crazy Shirts outlet, a Wyland Gallery, and J.J.'s Broiler.

If you plan to be on Kaua'i for a while, especially if you are staying in a condo and plan to make some of your own meals, check out the ***Holsum/Orowheat Thrift Store*** at 4252 Rice Street (at the corner of Rice and Hardy) for great bargains on bread and packaged baked goods. (Visitors always ask how people can afford to live in Hawai'i when groceries are so expensive. This is one of the ways!) They are open Mon-Fri from 8 am-4 pm, Sat. until 3. Sunday 9 am-2 pm.

Try to go on a Wednesday when their day-old products (or those nearing their expiration date) are further discounted for mo' bettah bread bargains. Call (808) 245-6113. There is also a ***Loves Bakery*** at 4100 Rice St. with discounted bread items and specials for seniors on Tuesday and Friday. Open 9 am-4:30 pm and

Just south on Hwy. 50 is the ***Kukui Grove Shopping Center***. Located at 3-2600 Kaumualii Highway, it is the largest shopping center on Kaua'i, but small by mainland standards. This mall has been impacted by the economic downturn around the islands and many shop fronts are empty. You will find Liberty House, Longs Drug Store, Big Kmart, convenient ATM's, a Star Market and a Borders Bookstore along with specialty shops and restaurants. For those movie devotees, there is a nearby four-screen cinema. Kukui Grove has a complimentary shuttle service to the shopping center with pick-up points from Po'ipu to Wailua. For shuttle service information call (808) 245-7784.

***Kaua'i Fruit and Flower Co.*** is on the *makai* side of the road as you leave Hwy. 50 and travel north on the Kuhio Highway toward Kapa'a. Stop by and visit Chucky Boy Chock (and Whitney, the dog) and sample the pineapple juice! This is the real stuff, straight from the pineapple. Or try the Dole Whip, a pineapple soft serve ice cream. In the 1960's the building was an old wood mill where Mrs. Chock's grandfather used to work and do wood carvings. They still sell wood carvings as well as other art work and gift items, plus there is a flower shop with protea and orchids. The main part of the operation is produce and you can purchase pre-packaged and pre-inspected pineapples, papayas, onions, and tropical flowers to take home. Mail orders, too! 1-800-943-3108 from the mainland. (808) 245-1814.

Following Hwy. 583 toward Kapa'a (just before it meets with Hwy. 56), you'll pass another longtime shopping landmark, the ***Kapai'a Stitchery.*** This shop will be of interest to anyone who enjoys sewing, especially quilters. They have a large selection of brightly colored fabrics, Hawaiian quilt squares, and supplies, plus a variety of craft items. Needlepoint fanciers will appreciate the beautiful hand-painted canvasses of local settings. The store is open 9 am to 5 pm Monday through Saturday.

Just beyond Kapai'a Stitchery there is a fork in the road where we will turn from shopping and return, once again, to sightseeing. A sign indicates the direction onto Ma'alo Road, also labeled Hwy. 583. This is a rather narrow, rutted road that winds through cane fields. At slightly more than three miles from the turn-off onto Ma'alo Road you will arrive at ***Wailua Falls***. (You'll recognize it from the opening of *Fantasy Island*!) There is parking where the road dead ends. A picturesque camera shot can be taken at this vista. There is a path which leads down to the base of the falls. The trail is dangerous, steep, and slippery. Many have been seriously or fatally injured and we suggest you enjoy the falls from the lookout above. Wailua, whose name means "two waters," was once actually two rivers which have merged into one. The river below is the largest navigable river on the island of Kaua'i and should definitely be explored during your Kaua'i stay.

Retrace your route back down to Hwy. 56 and continue northward. At mile marker #2 along Hwy. 56 you will be in ***Hanama'ulu*** where you'll find the Hanama'ulu Restaurant & Tea House, J.R.'s Plantation restaurant and a Shell Gas Station. Back in 1875, Hanama'ulu was a plantation camp. Cane was transported by oxen to Lihu'e until a mill was built in town. It continued to operate until 1918.

The ***Outrigger Kaua'i Beach Hotel***, a few miles beyond, has several popular evening activities including a disco and a comedy club. The ***Aston Kaua'i Beach Villas*** are located next door. Near mile marker #4 is the ***Wailua Golf Course***. Green fees on this municipal course are $20-25 weekdays and $30-35 weekends for eighteen holes of play. The golf course runs into the ***Lydgate Park*** area (where you will also find the ***Holiday Inn SunSpree Resort***). This is one of the island's safest beaches with two pools made of lava rock. One is very shallow, the other slightly deeper. There is also a lifeguard on duty. The fish are able to swim into the pools and are very tame. You might like to pick up a bag of fish food at one of the dive shops or check Safeway. This is a great place to give those wanna-be snorkelers a chance to try out this sport. The ***Kamalani Playground*** is a terrific spot to let the kids burn off all that extra energy!

## *WAILUA*

This area is a three-mile length along the Kuhio Highway. The region was of special religious importance to the *kahuna* and *ali'i* of ancient times. In fact, it is considered to be one of the two most sacred spots in all of the Hawaiian Islands. The ***Wailua River*** cuts back into a verdant valley with many splendors to be shared. The name Wailua means "two waters" as the Wailua River was originally two rivers.

A recent addition to transportation alternatives on Kaua'i is the Coconut Coast Trolley operated by Trans Hawaiian Kaua'i from 10am to 10pm daily. Their most recent (1999) posted fare structure is $2 for a one way ticket or $5 for an all-day pass. (Phone 245-5108.) Northbound stops include Maui Marriott, Hilo Hattie, Outrigger, Holiday Inn Sunspree, and the Coconut MarketPlace. Southbound stops include Kapa'a Town--ABC Store, Kaua'i Village, and Smith's/Waialealae Boats. A feeder shuttle provides transfer from Po'ipu, Lihu'e and Nawiliwili Harbor. This is a demand type of service and they reserve the right to not stop or pick up at locations based upon lack of demand. They suggest you call and make reservations 245-5108 to insure stops at Hyatt Regency, Embassy Vacation Resort, Kiahuna Plantation, or Sheraton Kaua'i.

A river cruise up to ***Fern Grotto*** is an excellent way to learn how Hawaiian royalty lived. The river and its surrounding land were once part of the royal grounds. Boat cruises run upriver daily to this natural rock cavern filled with maidenhair ferns. Boats depart every half hour from 9 am to 3:30 pm. (There is no departure at 12 noon.) Smith's boats have musical entertainment on board. With a $15 charge for adults, $7.50 for children, it is certainly a pleasant way to spend an hour and a half. The Fern Grotto gift shop was one of the few places we found that had authentic Hawaiian plant starts packaged to pass through customs. You may wish to rent a one or two person kayak at the mouth of the Wailua to enjoy this lovely river at your own pace.

The 30-acre ***Smith's Botanical Gardens*** is situated alongside the Wailua River and provides a wonderful opportunity to learn the names of the island's flowering trees and plants. Peacocks, ducks, colorful bantam roosters, and other birds inhabit the gardens, too. Bird food is available and carrying a sackful is almost certain to attract an entourage.

Smith's meandering pathways will take you onto a Japanese island, through a sweet-smelling hibiscus garden, into a bamboo forest, and past a variety of fruit and nut trees. Along the way you'll see a replica of an Easter Island statue and grass huts representing several island cultures. The gardens are fairly empty in the mornings; they open at 8:30 am and close at 4 pm. A luau is held here on Monday, Wednesday, and Friday evenings.

Turn *mauka* (toward the mountains) at the Coco Palms onto Kaumo'o Road for a short, but interesting, detour. Where the ***Wailua River*** meets the sea was, in ancient times, the place where Kings were born. Located along the Wailua River and winding upward toward Mount Wai'ale'ale are a series of seven *heiaus*.

Located on a part of Lydgate State Park is the ***Hauola O' Honaunau***, or ***Temple of Refuge***. The refuge and the *Hikina Heiau* are distinguished by a low wall which encircles them. It was at this site that *kapu* breakers were sent to atone for their deeds. Following this punishment, they could then return forgiven. Six of these religious sites are located within a mile of the mouth of the Wailua River. Some are easily spotted, while one is more difficult to view since it is located in an abandoned sugar cane field. The *Malae Heiau* is located in the corner of a canefield on the left side of the road just prior to the Wailua Bridge. It is somewhat hidden by a clump of trees and so overgrown that exploring it is nearly impossible. This is the largest *heiau* on the island, measuring 273 feet x 324 feet.

At 2/10 of a mile past the Coco Palms is a *heiau* that is actually mislabeled and information in publications has continued the erroneous details. Don and Bea Donohugh, authors of the first three editions of this Paradise Guide, enlisted an archeologist to visit the site to confirm their suspicions. The archeologist verified that the site marked as the *Holoholoku Heiau* was actually the location of an old pig pen. The *heiau* itself no longer exists, but its location would have been at the cemetery located on the top of the hill. Some books on Kaua'i say that the *heiau* was converted to a pig pen, but this would seem inaccurate given the archeological investigation. If a *kapu* (a rule or law) was broken, the penalties were stiff. Often death was the penalty for just having your shadow cast on an *ali'i*. However if you could reach a special *heiau*, like the Holoholoku, it would be a place of refuge and you could return forgiven. Behind the pig pen is the birthing stone, the spot where royalty were born. The early Hawaiians tried to "improve" their royal line and one way they felt this was possible was to inter-marry. It was not uncommon for a brother to marry a sister. As the years progressed, due to diseases and other causes, the numbers of *ali'i* diminished. A common woman could be chosen to give birth at this special and sacred site and her child would then become an *ali'i*. The ***Wailua River State Park*** is another 2.7 miles on the left and here you will also find the ***Poli'ahu Heiau***. This interpretive center along the scenic bluff explains the importance of the Wailua River Valley to the Hawaiians in earlier times. Wailua was a center for the Hawaiian *ali'i* (royalty) and *kahuna* (priests).

The fertile valley soil and plentiful supply of fresh water were ideal for supporting the large Hawaiian population which once inhabited this region. Adjoining the overlook is the *Poli'ahu Heiau*. The stones were brought from the bluffs to build this religious site which was used for ceremonies until the traditional ways were abolished in 1819. This is named after Poliahu, the goddess of snow and a sister to Pele. This is also believed to be a *luakini heiau*, which means a place of human sacrifice. An undesirable person was preferable: a prisoner of war, a person who had broken a *kapu* or sometimes a slave, but never a woman. They were generally killed in their sleep and then placed as an offering upon the altar. A large enclosure of black lava rock was once the personal temple of Kaua'i's last king, Kaumuali'i. This temple was reportedly built by the menehune.

You will see a dirt road just before the interpretive center. While very unimproved and rutted, the road is marked by a sign indicating the way to the ***Bell Stone.*** You will find two large rocks which appear to be a gateway. By following the path to the end you will be treated to another lovely view of the Wailua Valley. You will have to experiment to discover which of these stones made a resonant sound when struck. At the birth of a royal child, the stone was pounded to signal the arrival of a new member of the *ali'i*.

Just beyond, at 2.8 miles, is the ***Opaeka'a Falls*** lookout on the right side of the road and the Wailua River lookout on the left. Both are easily accessible and there is a paved parking lot with restrooms. The Opaeka'a Falls lookout affords a wonderful opportunity to see this 40 foot waterfall. This lovely waterfall has multiple cascades and flows year round. After walking the viewpoint trail, you can cross the highway for a view of the Wailua River and the Kamokila Hawaiian Village.

The family-owned and operated business, ***Kamokila Hawaiian Village***, is a re-creation of a Hawaiian village with huts, canoes, refurbished taro fields and demonstrations of lei making, poi making, and other native arts & crafts. Located opposite Opaeka'a Falls, the Kaumo'o Road entrance is just past the Wailua Bridge. Visitors can take a narrated cultural tour, a canoeing adventure on the nearby Wailua River, or kayak to Fern Grotto to discover a secret waterfall and pool. Village Tour $5, Village and Kayak Adventure $25. Open Monday-Saturday 8 am-5 pm. For kayak reservations or information on tour packages call 823-0559. Email: kamokila@hawaiian.net

Also along Kuamo'o Road, travel for 4 1/4 miles and turn left on Kaholalele Road (address is #107) to see where a $16 million ***Hindu Temple*** will be made from imported stone and materials. It is expected to take 5-20 years for construction to be completed. They offer weekly visitors' day tours. (808) 822-3012 or (808) 7032 for information.

## *WAIPOULI*

The Waipouli area of Kaua'i offers some excellent hiking opportunities. A section on hiking from Craig Chisholm's *Kaua'i Hiking Trails* is included under hiking in the RECREATION chapter of this guide.

The lush tropical region of this area is synonymous with Kaua'i. ***Sleeping Giant Mountain*** offers a majestic backdrop for this region. In her book, *Legends of Old Hawai'i*, Betty Allen retells the legend of the Sleeping Giant.

To summarize it, this tale began long ago in Kapa'a where a fisherman and his wife lived. This fisherman always caught the largest of fish and one day when he pulled in his net he found the biggest fish he had ever caught. When the fish began to cry he realized it was no ordinary fish, but an *akua* (good or evil spirit) and took it home to his wife. The only thing that kept the fish from crying was when they fed him poi. His appetite was enormous, so people from all around came to feed him. The fish then transformed into a young giant that grew larger and larger as they continued to feed him poi and sweet potatoes. He grew so large that he could no longer walk and he lay down. They sent for a *kahuna* who told them that they needed to sing to the giant, but he would not reveal which song should be sung. The villagers began to sing to the giant, but to no avail. A small girl named Pua-nai was nearby looking at the rocks on the ground. Suddenly she began to sing a song she had never heard before and the giant miraculously changed to stone. They say that the giant sleeps yet today. (As long as he still sleeps, hikers can walk on his "forehead" and stand on his "face.")

Continuing up Kamao'o Road 4.8 miles, you will pass an Agricultural Research Station. Continue on to the Wailua Reservoir which is one of several fresh water fishing areas on Kaua'i. Several hiking trails have their trail heads in this area.

At 5.45 miles, you will enter the Hawai'i State Forest Reserve. If you plan a day of hiking, the location of the ***Kuilau Ridge Trail*** head is at 5.5 miles and just beyond is the ***Keahua Arboretum***. The Arboretum has suffered from hurricanes and neglect, but still offers a quiet retreat for a picnic. Several streams cross the road from here on in and, depending on the waterflow and your rental car, you may choose not to proceed further. As you retrace your path down the road, look off to the left side just beyond the Agricultural Research Station, for a small pull out. A view of the reservoir with Sleeping Giant Mountain behind is a fine reward.

RED CRESTED CARDINAL

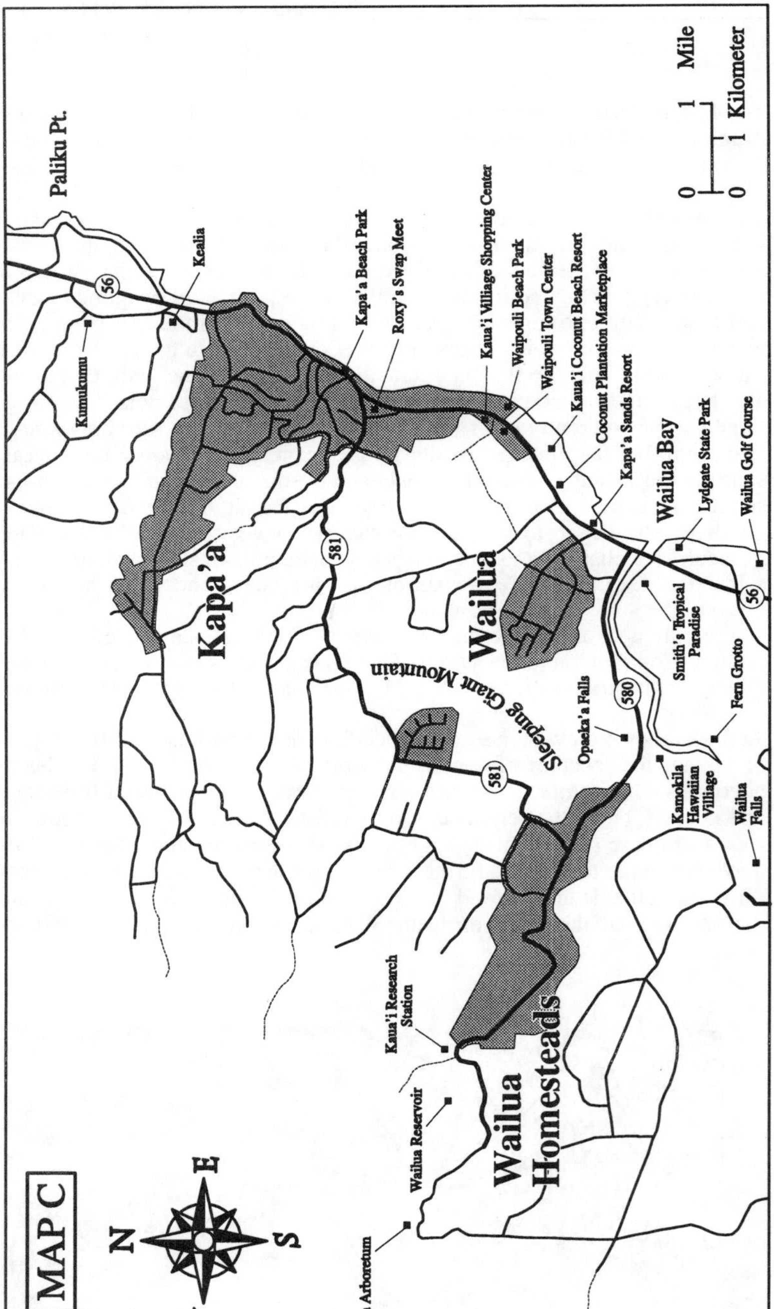

MAP C
N
E
S
W
Paliku Pt.
Kealia
56
Kumukumu
Kapa'a Beach Park
Roxy's Swap Meet
Kaua'i Villiage Shopping Center
Waipouli Beach Park
Waipouli Town Center
Kaua'i Coconut Beach Resort
Coconut Plantation Marketplace
Kapa'a Sands Resort
Wailua Bay
Lydgate State Park
Wailua Golf Course
0 1 Mile
0 1 Kilometer
Kapa'a
581
Wailua
Sleeping Giant Mountain
Smith's Tropical Paradise
Fern Grotto
580
Opaeka'a Falls
Kamokila Hawaiian Villiage
Wailua Falls
Kaua'i Research Station
Wailua Reservoir
Wailua Homesteads
Keahua Arboretum

Back down to the Highway and the Coco Palms Resort, reset your odometer at zero and turn northward and continue towards Kapa'a. On your left you'll see what is left of the ***Coco Palms Resort***. This area of palms was once the dream of a German plantation owner who, in the early 1800's, hoped to raise coconuts and sell copra, or dried coconut meat, to the mainland. From the copra, coconut oil can be made. His dreams were dashed, but the tall and elegant trees remain. There has been a some talk of settlement on the Coco Palms Resort, but the renovations have not yet even begun as we go to press. The status of this lovely old property is unquestionably the query we are asked most. We'll keep you abreast in our KAUA'I UPDATE newsletter.

*Miss Sadie Thompson* was filmed here and the scene where Tatoo on *Fantasy Island* goes flying by in the jeep was also filmed in this coconut grove. Should you see the ghost of Elvis around, it is because he was also here during a portion of his filming of the movie *Blue Hawai'i*. You, too, can have a Blue Hawai'i wedding. Entertainer Larry Riviera (who used to perform with Elvis) still serenades wedding parties and includes an Elvis-style barge ride as part of the ceremony. You won't have to wear hard-hats, but we understand weddings held on the grounds must include one security guard with each three guests as protection against those falling coconuts!

At a brief 6/10 of a mile past the intersection of Kaumo'o Road you will pass the largest shopping center on the east coast of Kaua'i. The ***Coconut MarketPlace*** has something for everyone. Located between the Wailua River and Kapa'a, it is open daily from 9 am-9 pm. Phone (808) 822-3641. This is one shopping center the kids may enjoy more than most with shops such as *The Gecko Store, Crazy Shirts,* and plenty of inexpensive eateries. A selection of jewelry and art galleries as well as a two-screen movie theater are also found here. Two of the more interesting shops are operated by Patrick and Mary Dunn. Their *Islander Trading Company* specializes in Hawaiian articles from decades ago. Old ukuleles, Aloha shirts, Hawaiian ceramics and prints make interesting perusing. New items include Hawaiian rubber stamps, seashells, and other gift items. It also has a bird store and you can pay for a handful of feed to share with some of the colorful parrots and macaws. *Island Accents* looks like an abundant flower shop, but everything is artificial! *Nutcracker Sweet* is an eclectic book and gift shop. Other unusual shops include *Bodacious* which features Petite thru Plus clothes, *Ye Olde Ship Store* (with scrimshaw ships in a bottle and ships' models), *Y Knot a Tie,* and *Russian Treasures*. You'll find Hawai'i keepsakes, quilts, handmade dolls, and other gift items at *Made for Mom & Me* or bring home a souvenir for your pets at *Sweet Blossoms & Gypsy's Pet Corner*! There is Polynesian and Hawaiian entertainment daily (at 5 pm) and it is free! The restaurants (Kaua'i Aloha Pizza, Taco Dude, the Fish Hut, Eggbert's, and Buzz's to name a few) remain open even after the shops close.

The relatively new Kapa'a bypass is an old cane road that was converted to a narrow two-lane alternate route to alleviate the traffic congestion through Kapa'a Town. The bypass road runs alongside the Kuhio Highway (56) and can be accessed from Wailua near the Coconut MarketPlace to the traffic light in Kapa'a Town. But unless you're in a hurry, we suggest continuing along Kuhio Hwy.

At 1.3 miles past the Coco Palms begins the row of strip malls that line the highway between Wailua and Kapa'a. The first is the ***Waipouli Town Center***, not to be confused with the other two "Waipouli" malls. A *Foodland* grocery store, *Fun Factory* (video arcade), *Blockbuster* (video rentals), *Lizard Lounge & Deli* and the popular *Waipouli Restaurant* are here. The neighboring McDonald's and a small stream divides this center from the next.

***Kaua'i Village*** in Kapa'a, is an eight-acre shopping center featuring over 30 stores and restaurants. Tenants include *Longs Drug Store, Waldenbooks, Crazy Shirts*, and a variety of gift shops. The restaurants at Kaua'i Village range from fine dining at *A Pacific Cafe*, to more casual eateries like *Papaya's* and *Pony Island Cantina* as well as the newest of the *Camp House Grills*. The new *Kaua'i International Theatre* is also here. The 62-seat playhouse offers six shows per season with guest performers and other entertainment in between productions.

The shopping village is distinguished by its turn-of-the century plantation architectural design, landmark three-story clock tower, garden courtyard, and two Whaling Wall murals by internationally-known environmental artist Wyland. There is plenty of room in the open air courtyard graced with a ten-foot waterfall and a series of landscaped ponds and streams to relax while other members of your group are off shopping. Or take a self-guided tour of the Hawaiian artifacts, art, and handcrafted items at the *Kaua'i Heritage Center of Hawaiian Culture & the Art*. The Village also has a Hawaiian Garden with indigenous (without human aid) and endemic (found only in Hawaii) plants growing with plaques which label them and provide some historical information.

Only 1/10 mile ahead is the next in a string of malls and mini-malls. ***Waipouli Plaza*** is the location of *King & I Thai Cuisine*. ***Waipouli Complex*** is another 2/10 of a mile and the last mall before Kapa'a. Here you'll find the *Aloha Diner* and the *K.C.L. Barbecue Drive Inn*. It is also the home of *Popo's Cookies*. The bakery makes coconut, chocolate chip, macadamia, and their new "granola great" cookies for all retail outlets. But you can buy them fresh and cheaper here! They also have "hard ice," thirst-quenching ice cakes in strawberry-cream, grape, orange, and lemon-lime. Open Monday-Friday, 8:30 am-3 pm, Saturday 9 am-2 pm, closed Sunday. (Hint: Grandma has a tendency to get cranky, so come back when Tennile is there - she is friendly and personable and as sweet as the cookies!)

## *KAPA'A*

Kapa'a was a center for rice cultivation until sugar cane replaced it as the major agricultural industry in the 1920's. Life went along peacefully for this quiet town on Kaua'i's western shore until tourism discovered Kapa'a in the 1970's.

The ***Hongwanji Temple*** is located across the street from the *Big Save Market*. A little further, turning onto Waikomo Road, is the ***Jodo Mission***.

There are several roads which travel into the island to follow and/or cross the Kapa'a Stream and lead to ***Ho'opi'i Falls***. Along Hwy. 56, Kawaihau Road is the first option. Follow this road which then intersects with Hauaala Rd. Just outside of Kapa'a, turn onto Mailihuna Road, which also connects with Hauaala Road. Hauaala Road meets Kealia Road, and if you follow it northeast, you will reach the Kaneha Reservoir.

## *WHERE TO SHOP*

At Wailua Village, in a historic sugarcane shack, you'll find *Bambulei*. They have collectibles, antique Hawaiian memorabilia, jewelry, silk and linen Aloha shirts, one-of-a-kind lamps, tacky treasures and things that are both funky and elegant. Caffe Coco is located next door.

Across the street at the ***Kinipopo Shopping Village*** (356 Kuhio Hwy.), *The Tin Can Mailman* specializes in used and rare books with an emphasis on Hawaiiana and South Pacific subjects. Owner Will Mauck also stocks art prints such as Matson menus and botanical prints. There are plenty of new books, too. Open Tuesday, Wednesday & Friday, 10:30 am-5:30 pm, Thursday from 2 pm, and Saturday 11 am-5 pm.

The town of Kapa'a is a small town gone tourist, but it is still a very pleasant place to dine or shop. The Sunnyside Market (open 8 am-7 pm) at ***Roxy Square*** still sells fresh produce and take home food products, but has expanded to include crafts, gifts, snacks, beverages, coffees, candy, and tee-shirts -- even shrunken heads! This new market has a more permanent appearance than the previous version and now houses Dori's Garden Cafe, a small outlet for sandwiches, salads, and smoothies. *William & Zimmer* specializes in gifts and furniture made from koa wood.

Across the street is a new store operated by the Kauai Historical Society. The *Kauai History Shop* (245-3373) is located in the historic Kawamura building. Staffed by volunteers from 10am-4pm weekdays, they offer local gifts, books and a map of the island *heiau* (temples). Also check out *Kia Gallery* for an eclectic assortment of crafts, jewelry, artwork, clothing, mats, vases, and household items. On the corner is Beezers, an old-fashioned ice cream parlor that offers some cool treats! And further down, is the Pono Market filled with lots of island favorites in their deli!

North of Kapa'a Town, you'll find the Kountry Kitchen family restaurant and next to that you'll see *Two Frogs Hugging*. This whimsical little shop offers hundreds of unique and unusual gift items from banana & coconut leaf baskets and notebooks to wooden flowers and candlesticks as well as pottery items, treasure boxes, teak and mahogany furniture -- and yes, carved statues of "Two Frogs Hugging!" The *Black Pearl Gallery* is a jewelry store located in the same building.

## *BEST BETS*

***Banyan Harbor*** or ***Garden Island Inn*** - convenient and inexpensive. ***Outrigger Kaua'i Beach Hotel*** and ***Aston Kaua'i Beach Villas*** - resort surroundings and amenities in a separate coastal area, yet close to the airport and downtown Lihu'e. ***Kaua'i Coconut Beach*** - this may be the best travel bargain with the use of an Entertainment discount card. ***Kaua'i Marriott Resort & Beach Club*** - a little more expensive, but a lovely and luxurious atmosphere. ***Bed & Breakfast*** - Try Rosewood B&B - it is simply wonderful!

## *PRIVATE HOMES*

### MAKANA CREST

Seattle (206) 242-4866 or Kauai (808) 245-6500. PO Box 3671, Lihue, HI 96766. Email: mokihana@hawaiian.net This cottage is 750 square feet with two furnished bedrooms and a bathroom with a shower. One bedroom has a queen bed, the other twins. A microwave, dishwasher, basic utensils included in the kitchen and cable TV provided. The guest cottage is on the acreage of the owners home. The property is landscaped with citrus and macadamia trees, and a 90 foot fish pond. The view features 5,000 foot Mt. Wai'ale'alae Crater. They also can arrange weddings! Your hosts are Hans & Karen Hellriegel.
*Rates are $100 per day (three day minimum) or $600 per week.*

### ROSEWOOD ★

Rosemary and Norbert Smith have expanded their vacation rental accommodation pool. In addition to their Rosewood Bed & Breakfast accommodations they also handle a number of homes, cottages and villas in the Coconut Coast area and southern Kaua'i coast. Contact (808) 822-5216, or FAX (808) 822-5478 or E-mail: <rosewd@aloha.net> NO CREDIT CARDS. Their home properties include Victorian Cottage (two bedroom/one bath) $115, Thatched Cottage (one bedroom one bath $85), Bunkhouse accommodations which are small rooms with shared baths $40-50, Traditional B&B in the main plantation home with king bed, private bath and breakfast included. Other properties include a one time cleaning fee $65-75 and the rates are: Hale Lani 2BR 2 BTH $125; Hale Pilialoha in Po'ipu with 2BR 2BTH near Baby Beach $150; Sleeping Giant Cottage 1BR $75; Plantation Hale Condo 1 BR $95; and others. Prices are double occupancy. Minimum stay three nights. All properties are non-smoking.

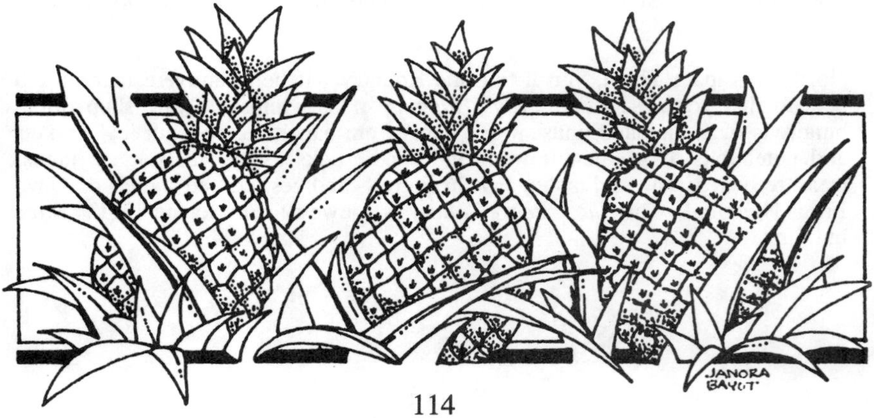

## *BED AND BREAKFASTS*

**ALOHA COUNTRY BED & BREAKFAST**
505 Kamalu Road, Kapa'a, HI 96746. (808) 822-0166, FAX (808) 822-2708. Email: wery@aloha.net Located on the east coast of Kaua'i behind Sleeping Giant Mountain. From the outside, the main house (5,000 sq. ft. on a 2-acre estate) looks like a Spanish villa. On the inside, there is a "choice" of lounge areas: a comfy, Victorian sitting room with plush flower-patterned cushions and plump pillows. Or the central living room remodeled with black and green marble, black leather couches, HIGH ceilings, and an enormous fireplace. Upstairs, the private luxury suites are decorated in beautiful woods, with antique furniture, canopy beds, and large walk-in closets. The primary residence suite offers a king-size bed, TV, refrigerator, microwave, sitting and dining area, and private bath with jacuzzi. *Rates including breakfast: Suite I, $65, Suite II with jacuzzi $75.* Detached units include a luxury apartment with queen bed, day bed, TV, full kitchen, sitting and dining area, and large open deck, *$80.* Studio apartment includes queen bed, sitting and dining area, kitchenette, a kind of mini-house with all rooms condensed into one, *$75;* Two bedroom cottage includes one room with full size bed another with queen bed, living room with kitchenette, one bath, TV *single/double $90 or 3-4 persons $150. Breakfast is not included with detached units.* Fresh flowers in all rooms and all have ceiling fans and separate bathrooms. Cottages and studios have kitchens or kitchenettes. Non-smokers only. The owner also operates the Manoa Valley Inn on Oahu.

**ALOHILANI BED & BREAKFAST INN**
1470 Wanaao Rd., Kapa'a, HI 96746 (808) 823-0128 or 1-800-533-9316. Hosts Sharon Mitchell and William Whitney offer their home which takes its name from the Hawaiian words meaning "Bright Sky." Located above Kapa'a town, their rates include breakfast of fresh squeezed juices, tropical fruits, and home baked breakfast breads and muffins. They offer the Malulani Guest Cottage at $99 per night, $650 weekly for two. The Kumulani guest cottage has a fully equipped kitchen and is set apart among the trees. It features ocean and mountain views, a king-size bed, and a living room area with sleeper sofa at $89 per night, $595 per week. Pa'ana a ka la "Sunshine" Atrium features wide French doors which open onto a lanai with a valley view. It has a queen size bed, sleeper sofa, and small refrigerator and microwave at $89 per night, $595 per week. In addition they have a two bedroom condominium across from Kalapaki Beach which rents for $650 per week or $1995 per month. <WWW>

**CANDY'S CABIN**
5940 Ohe St., Kapa'a, HI 96746. (808) 822-5451. Located in the Wailua Homesteads, your hostess is Candace Kepley. A studio apartment with a king-size bed, living area, private bath, lanai, and refrigerator. Very roomy and adequate for a family. If you choose breakfast, you'll find some home baked goodies. Stroll around the grounds and see the family of mallard ducks that visit from the nearby stream. Located 15 minutes from the Lihu'e airport. *Rates for two run $65 per night, No minimum stay.*

**HALE KAHAWAI BED & BREAKFAST**
185 Kahawai Place, Kapa'a, HI 96746. (808) 822-1031, FAX (808) 823-8220. Four rooms from which to select include a daily tropical breakfast. This B & B is located on Kuamo'o Ridge overlooking the Wailua River Gorge. A guest lounge is equipped with a 35" screen stereo cable TV. Your hosts Tom & Arthur want you to know that Hale Kahawai is "straight friendly." Three night minimum stay. Visa and Mastercard accepted. *Room rates for a private apartment run $90; room with shared bath $70, with private bath $80.*

**HOUSE OF ALEVA**
5509 Kuamo'o Rd., Kapa'a, HI 96746. (808) 822-4606. Hosts Ernest and Anita Perry offer two upstairs rooms with a bath to share. A single room downstairs has a private bath. *$55 per night per couple, $40 per night single. (Rates include all additional Hawaiian taxes.)*

**KAKALINA'S B & B**
6781 Kawaihau Rd., Kapa'a, HI 96746. Toll free 1-800-718-1018. E-mail: klinas@aloha.net <WWW> (808) 822-2328, FAX (808) 823-6833. Located on a three-acre working tropical flower farm in the foothills of Mt. Wai'ale'ale your hosts are Bob and Kathy Offley.

Their Hale 'Akahi unit is two rooms on the ground floor with a private entrance featuring king-size beds, shower, deep bath for soaking, and kitchenette. The Hale 'Elua unit is a ground floor studio with queen size bed, ceiling fan and private bathroom with shower and full-size kitchen. Each unit has color TV, microwave oven, refrigerator and laundry facilities. Hale Kolu is a 1-BR located above Hale Elua with an oceanview. A mile away is their other vacation rental, The Ginger Room. This one-bedroom home does not include the breakfast feature, but it offers a queen size bed, living room, dining room, full kitchen and private bath. *Rental rates run $75-85 with discounts for weekly stays.*

**KEAPANA CENTER**
5620 Keapana Rd., Kapa'a, HI 96746. (808) 822-7968, 1-800-822-7968. Email: keapana@aloha.net Website: <www.planet-hawaii.com/keapana/> Located on six acres. Rates include continental breakfast and use of jacuzzis.
*Room with shared bath $55 double, $45 single; room with private bath $75 double, $70 single.*

**LAMPY'S BED & BREAKFAST**
6078 Kolopua Street, Kapa'a, HI 96746. Phone or FAX (808) 822-0478. Located five minutes from Wailua Bay. Each of the three bedrooms is furnished with country decor and offers a private entrance and private bath. Tom and Lampy Lowy retired to Kaua'i in 1987 after 30 years as residents in Las Vegas, Nevada. After the decision was made to build a wing on their home for a B&B they opened in March of 1989. *Single rates are $50 nightly - double rates $55 nightly. Studio $65. Extra persons $10 additional. Weekly rates. No Credit Cards.*

**MOHALA KE OLA**
5663 Ohelo Rd., Kapa'a, HI 96746. Toll free 1-888-GO-KAUAI. Phone or FAX (808) 823-6398. <WWW> Host Ed Stumpf invites you to "Rejuvenate in Paradise" at Mohala Ke Ola, their Bed & Breakfast retreat. Located above the Wailua River Valley near Opaeka'a Falls on the eastern shore of Kaua'i, they have mountain and waterfall views. Breakfast of fresh island fruit on a private terrace, enjoy the pool, and relax in the jacuzzi. You can enjoy a Hawaiian Lomi Lomi massage or rejuvenate with other body treatments included shiatsu, acupuncture, and Reiki. Quiet and peaceful surroundings along with a congenial and friendly atmosphere. Ed will greet you at the airport or assist if you need some shopping help. He also speaks fluent Japanese and is very knowledgeable about sightseeing and activities. They offer four guest rooms, each with a private bath, and all non-smoking. The entire property was recently renovated with all new furniture. They have also added a new pond and more tropical landscaping. Three night minimum requested. *Rates are $65-105.*

**ROSEWOOD BED & BREAKFAST ★**
872 Kamalu Rd., Kapa'a, HI 96746. (808) 822-5216, FAX (808) 822-5478. E-mail: rosewd@aloha.net -- This home, located in Wailua Homesteads, was formerly an old Macadamia Nut Plantation Home. The area is rural with rolling pastures and grazing cattle framed by a wide mountain range with Mt. Wai'ale'ale in the center. After a nighttime shower, many waterfalls are visible with vivid rainbows. Since they moved to the islands 17 years ago, Rosemary and Norbert Smith have been restoring their home. A second cottage with two bedrooms, designed after the main house is called the "Victorian Cottage."

A smaller one designed with a Hawaiian look, is called the "Thatched" and a third option is their "Bunkhouse" which has proven popular with European visitors and hikers. The one-acre grounds include two ponds with small waterfalls plus lots of fruit and flowering trees and bushes. "Thatched" is a one bedroom cottage with a king-size bed, screened lanai, kitchenette with hot plate, microwave and small refrigerator. The toilet and sink are indoors, but the hot/cold shower sits outside enclosed in the garden surrounded by native plants.

The "Victorian Cottage" offers two bedrooms and one bath, also an outdoor hot/cold shower. The master bedroom is downstairs with a queen bed, upstairs is a loft bedroom with two twin beds. A sofa opens into a sleeper bed. The kitchen is full sized and includes a dishwasher, and a washer/dryer. The unit has a television and telephone with fax. The two "traditional" units in the main house each have a private bath. They have a king bed, which can be converted to two twins. Breakfast is left in the cottages, and, for main house guests, is served in the kitchen.

The bunkhouse has three separate rooms and a shared outside shower. Each room has its own sink, toaster, coffee maker, and small refrigerator. The larger room offers a microwave. Bunkhouse #1 has twin bunk beds, Bunkhouse #2 has a sofa bed that opens to a queen plus a queen bed in the loft. Bunkhouse #3 consists of a Queen bed in the loft. None of the bunkhouse units include breakfast or maid service. Breakfast may be provided for an additional $5 per day per person. All units are non-smoking. Conveniently located just four miles from beaches, shopping, and restaurants. Also available for rent is a one bedroom condo at Kapa'a Shores and several area homes and cottages. (See Private Homes for rental homes.) *Victorian $115; Thatched $85; Traditional $65; Bunkhouse #1 and #3 $40 per day; Bunkhouse #2 $50 per day.*

## *BUDGET*

**HALE LIHU'E MOTEL**
2931 Kalena St., Lihu'e, HI 96766. (808) 245-2751. Twenty two one-bedroom units, some with kitchenettes. No air conditioning, but rooms have table fans. Inexpensive and spartan two-story, frame building located near the main business area of downtown Lihu'e. Walking distance to local restaurants, government offices, churches, and banks. Rates including tax are the cheapest in an already inexpensive area. A little unkempt and rundown; not really what you'd envision paradise to be. *Single, double or triple occupancy $22/$25/$30; with kitchenette single $30, double $40, triple $50. Weekly discounts available.*

**KAUA'I INTERNATIONAL HOSTEL**
4532 Lehua St., Kapa'a, HI 96746. (808) 823-6142 <www>. The hostel has forty beds, full kitchen facilities, baths, and showers. One week maximum stay. Daily hikes and excursions explore waterfalls, beaches, and off-the-beaten-track places. Located in the heart of Kapa'a across the street from the beach and park. Airport pickup available for $10.
*With VIP hostel membership $15 per night plus tax. Private rooms available for $37 per night. Slightly higher for non-members.*

**MOTEL LANI**
4240 Rice St. (PO Box 1836) Lihu'e, HI 96766. (808) 245-2965. Email: tkn@hawaiian.net At the corner of Rice and Hardy, the center of the Lihu'e business district. They have ten units, each with shower and one double or two twin beds. Some rooms have air conditioning and no TV, others have a TV and a ceiling fan. There is also a tv in the lobby for guest use. Like Hale Lihu'e, inexpensive and very basic: "A place to sleep." *Rates are $32-50 per night two people, two night minimum. Rates for one night slightly higher.*

**TIP TOP MOTEL**
Located in downtown Lihu'e. PO Box 1231, Lihu'e, HI 96766. (808) 245-2333. These air conditioned rooms are spartan and basic. In operation since 1916, well not exactly: they actually moved to their present location in the early '60's. Maybe that is why they note on their brochure that they are "Kaua'i's Newest Motel." The restaurant and cocktail lounge are still here along with a new sushi restaurant and smaller version of their famous bakery. These no frills accommodations are stark, very basic and, of course, cheap! All units are air conditioned. *Single or double $45 (includes tax) plus $10 key deposit.*

## *INEXPENSIVE*

**BANYAN HARBOR CONDOMINIUM RESORT ★**
3411 Wilcox Road, Lihu'e, HI 96766. 1-800-4-BANYAN or (808) 245-7333, FAX (808) 246-3687. RESERVATIONS: The management company, Outrigger Lodging Services (OLS), also operates the front desk and runs the property's on-site rental program. 1-800-4BANYAN (422-6926) US & Canada. Email: banyan@aloha.net and Web: <www.vacation-kauai.com> RENTAL AGENTS: Maui & All 1-800-663-6962. Prosser Realty 1-800-767-4707.

There are 148 units on a hilltop near Kalapaki Bay, some have a view of the Nawiliwili Harbor. This property has been remodeling over the last several years and since OLS took over in 1997, the rates, always a VERY good value, have actually gone down! (Hence earning and keeping our prestigious star!) Tennis court, refurbished pool and decking area, plus a separate recreation area with wet bar, shuffle board, etc. Public volleyball courts across the street. The room renovations have created crisp, clean rooms with television, and air conditioning now in all units. Bathroom lighting is still a bit dim in some of the units, but additional renovation is planned to replace the older fixtures. Washer/dryers, full kitchens (with microwave, coffee maker & starter coffee packet, and dishwasher) and dining area. Townhouses have harbor views. Very convenient to the airport and an easy walk to shops and restaurants of Anchor Cove and Pacific Ocean Plaza or a short walk to the Marriott. The large front office is comfortable with an amiable, friendly staff and there is plenty of parking. Adjoining the property is a large tree orchard with the second largest banyan tree in Hawaii. Like many others, they have also gone to partial timeshare.

*OLS operates the management and front desk. Their rates: 1 BR $85-110; 2 BR $95-140; Room and car packages $99-119. (And be sure to take advantage of their latest offer: mention this book and they'll give you a free upgrade (from a one to a two-bedroom) with any room or package rate!)*

**GARDEN ISLAND INN ★**
Located in Nawiliwili. 3445 Wilcox Rd., Lihu'e, HI 96766. 1-800-648-0154, FAX (808) 245-7603, (808) 245-7227. Renovated 21-room hotel with tropical decor and a cheery cottage-feel to each of the rooms. Wilcox Road has been closed to through-traffic so the property is now on a quieter cul-de-sac (though there is still a lot of activity during the day). Owners Steve and Susan Layne will be happy to help you with sightseeing recommendations. They'll also provide golf

clubs, camping and beach equipment, and you can help yourself to bananas and tangelos from the trees on the property. A short walk to the Kaua'i Marriott, Kalapaki Beach and Anchor Cove Shopping Center (with J.J.'s Broiler) and just across the road from Nawiliwili Beach Park. All rooms have refrigerators, wet bars, TV, microwaves, and coffeemakers. Studios and one-bedroom suites on the third floor. All units are non-smoking and most now have A/C. Comfortable, friendly and cheap, too! They also have a unit at the Banyan Harbor which they rent. <www.gardenislandinn.com> *g.v. $65-75; o.v. $85; 1 BR suites $95-125.*

**HOTEL CORAL REEF**
1516 Kuhio Hwy., Kapa'a, HI 96746. 1-800-843-4659, (808) 822-4481. The main building opened early in 1995 following restoration as a result of Hurricane Iniki. Ground floor rooms are tiled, upstairs rooms are carpeted. Good, clean rooms with limited views. The oceanfront building offers beach views and is equipped with refrigerators and a choice of single or double beds. Beachfront is not suitable for swimming. Pay telephone and television in lobby. Daily maid service. Grocery store and restaurants nearby. Located within walking distance of a public swimming pool. Room and car packages available.
*O.f. and o.v. rooms range from $59-89; m.v. suites $79. Senior discounts.*

**KAUA'I INN**
2430 Hulemalu Road, Lihue, HI 96766, 1-800-245-9000. Email: kauaiinn.com With over 100 years of Aloha on Nawiliwili Bay, this place exudes old Hawaiian charm. Tucked below the Hapu Mountains and the Huleia River on three acres are 48 Plantation style units which were completely restored and opened in December 1999. Affordable and convenient, just 7 minutes to the airport, amenities include swimming pool, refrigerator and microwaves in each unit, complimentary breakfast bar, guest laundry, fax and email access. Handicapped units available. Innkeepers are Tom and Jami McKnight. Rates $79-145.

## *MODERATE*

**COCO PALMS (HOTEL)**
(808) 822-4921. The lastest word we have on the shuttered Coco Palms Resort centers on its purchase by Lincoln Consulting Group, a company out of Newport Beach, California. They plan on purchasing the property (which has sat decaying for seven years) and replacing the 396 room hotel with 232 timeshare units. The only Coco Palm structures that are expected to be spared are the Blue Hawai'i wedding chapel and one King cottage which will be convered into a an Elvis Presley museum. The project is expected to cost $60 million and include a four-story concrete building with 30-60 foot setabcks from the road. (The original buildings were set back 60-70 feet.) Each of the timeshare units is expected to be 2 BR 2 bath units. There will also be 20 resort hotel units in a 10 one-story bunaglows which will resemble Hawaiian huts. Some investigation is on-going regarding the ponds to see if they have historical value and what can be done to restore them. A spa and tennis facility and three bungalows will be constructed at the rear of the site where the existing tennis courts are located. It was reported that a combination hotel/timeshare arrangement would not be possible because funding is more difficult for hotels than timeshare properties. Across the street,

The Seashell Restaurant will also be restored. No estimate for time to complete this restoration was announced. Currently the permit process continues.

**HOLIDAY INN SUNSPREE RESORT**
3-5920 Kuhio Hwy., Wailua, HI 96746. 1-888-823-5111. (808) 245-3931, FAX (808) 822-7339. RENTAL AGENT: Management is Holiday Inn. OTHER RENTAL AGENTS: Hawaiian Pacific Resorts 1-800-367-5004. Maui & All Islands 1-800-663-6962.

This property has undergone a number of ownership changes in the last few years. The most recent was in mid 1997 when it was announced that Equinox, a California based company purchased the property for a reported $3.6 million, a fraction of the previous sales. (Editorial comment: At a half-million decrease per year, Dona and Christie figure they can buy this place out of their royalty payments in the year 2027!) Equinox Hotel Management is the fourth owner of the resort since 1986. The resort reopened as Holiday Inn Sun Spree Resort.

The 216-room resort has undergone a multi-million dollar renovation under the new owners. Sunspree Resorts, which operates under the Holiday Inn umbrella, aims at providing affordable, full-service, activity-oriented properties in prime leisure destinations. The line between condos and hotels seems to be blurring with hotels offering more condo-like conveniences and condos offering more hotel amenities. A junior suite, for example, has a wall-sized kitchen alcove with cabinets, mini-sink and refrigerator, microwave, toaster, coffee maker (and coffee supplies) plus a basic set of dishes and utensils. The property offers two swimming pools, a jacuzzi, fitness room, tennis, volleyball and shuffleboard.

The open lobby has a nice old Hawaiian feel to it. They put the accommodate in accommodations and have created a hotel value with condominium amenities. Even the basic rooms have a mini-fridge and coffee maker with starter fixings. Daily maid service, laundry facilities. Restaurants and lounges include the Kahanu Snack Bar and Kuhio Dining Court. There are meeting facilities available. They have a good location on Lydgate Park and the park offers a great playground for kids. Holiday Inn Sunspree Resort Kaua'i has various activities offered in their Children's Activity Center when the hotel is full and is free to hotel guests. The Coconut Coast Trolley stops here and goes to the local shopping centers. *Garden view $150, Ocean view $175, Junior Suite $195; 1 BR $250, Cottage $270.*

**ISLANDER ON THE BEACH ★**
484 Kuhio Hwy., Kapa'a, HI 96746. (808) 822-7417, 1-800-847-7417, FAX (808) 822-1947. RENTAL AGENTS: Managed by Aston Properties 1-800-922-7866. Pleasant Hawaiian Holidays 1-800-242-9244. Total of 196 units in three story buildings. A small understated lobby is tasteful and reminiscent of a simple, old fashioned Hawaiian plantation. Very pleasing grounds and rooms and an excellent value for your vacation dollar. The hotel features an outdoor pool and spa, restaurant and lounge on the property. All rooms offer king or two double beds, air conditioning, wet bar, refrigerator, microwaves in oceanfront units and suites, color TV and in-room coffee makers. Laundry facilities. Rooms are on the small side. Third and fourth persons are charged $20 per person per night.

No charge for children 17 and under when sharing parents room. Room and car packages available. Located on 6.5 oceanfront acres, next to the Jolly Roger Restaurant, and across from the Coconut MarketPlace. This is one of the best beaches on the eastern shore. Check with Aston regarding any seasonal specials that might include rental car, complimentary breakfast or the 5th night free. Complimentary crib on request at time of booking. In late 1999, Terry and Helene Kamsen and Steve and Gloria Cohen purchased the hotel for $5.2 million and plan on putting $1.5 milion worth of improvements into the property. Visit their website at: <http://www.islander-kauai.com>
*Garden view $120; partial o.v. $130; o.v. $150; o.f. $165; Junior Suite $250.*

**KAHA LANI**
4460 Nehe Rd & Leho., Lihu'e, HI 96766 (808) 822-9331. Managed by Aston Resorts 1-800-922-7866. Rental Agent: Maui & All 1-800-663-6962. Two and three story buildings with a total of 74 units. More an attractive, homey apt. building than a resort. Pool, BBQ area, laundry facilities, putting green, and tennis court. Full kitchens with complimentary coffee starter kit. High ceilings, private phones plus lanais, ceiling fans, and daily maid service. One bedroom units have two bathrooms. Located next door to the golf course on the beachfront at Lydgate Park, one of the islands better beaches.

Kaha Lani is difficult to find unless you know to turn on Leho from the highway, but when you do, you'll be glad for the quiet seclusion. You're surrounded by a "choice" of landscaping: the soothing ocean front with small stretches of sandy beach, tropical gardens, or the dramatic craggy rock and a red dirt road that borders the property and leads to other beach areas. The Kamalani playground at Lydgate Park will amuse the children in your party for hours! Ask Aston reservations about special package or promotional options such as Island Hopper Rates if you plan on visiting other islands.
*1 BR o.v. $190/175, o.f. $215/190; 2 BR o.v. $250/230, o.f. $265/245;*
*3 BR o.v. $370/335, o.f. $460/410*

**KAPA'A SANDS**
380 Papaloa Rd., Kapa'a, HI 96746. (808) 822-4901, 1-800-222-4901, FAX (808) 822-1556. The postal address is Kapa'a, but they are located in Wailua. Minimum maid service daily with full linen change for stays of 7 nights or longer. Twenty-four individually owned studio and two bedroom condominiums. Units all have telephone, color TV, microwaves, and ceiling fans. Conveniently located behind Kinipopo Shopping Village and a short walk from additional shops and restaurants at the Coconut Plantation MarketPlace. Swimming pool, laundry facilities, and attractive lana'is and grounds. Located on a pleasant beachfront. If you are up early in the morning (and sometimes in the afternoon) you can watch sea turtles feeding off the reef just in front of the property.
*Studio o.v. $85; studio o.f. $99 (max 2); 2 BR o.v. $114 (max 4); 2 BR o.f. $129 (max 4). Extra charge of $10 per night for the 5th person in 2 BR unit.*

**KAPA'A SHORE**
4-0900 Kuhio Hwy., Kapa'a, HI 96746. 1-800-827-3922, FAX (808) 822-1457. RENTAL AGENT: Kaua'i Vacation Rentals 1-800-367-5025. Eighty-one units, one and two bedroom condos in a three story buildings. Three night minimum stay, seven night minimum over Christmas holidays. Weekly and monthly discounts. Laundry facilities, some rooms have ceiling fans. Pool, tennis courts, and jacuzzi. *Kauai Vacation Rates: Only 1 BR available for rental $550 per week*

**(ASTON) KAUA'I BEACH VILLAS**
4330 Kaua'i Beach Drive, Lihu'e, HI 96766. (808) 245-7711. RENTAL AGENT: Managed by Aston Properties 1-800-922-7866. OTHER RENTAL AGENTS: Maui & All 1-800-663-6962. Pleasant Hawaiian Holidays 1-800-242-9244. Pahio Vacations offers 4 night 5 days packages 1-800-852-5317. Three floors (no elevator) 150 units located on 13 acres. As you approach the beach, you'll be greeted by an "Aloha" that is a little different here!

These condominiums, along with what is now the Outrigger Hotel, once comprised the Kaua'i Hilton. It is a short, pleasant walk along a pathway leading to the Outrigger pools, then on to restaurants shops, etc. They share the Outrigger resort amenities, but are managed and run separately. The Aston pool (and whirlpool) are centralized, on an attractive raised deck reminiscent of a ship's pool deck. There are plenty of lounge chairs with BBQ grills nearby and elsewhere around the property. Rooms have a safe, washer/dryer, TV/VCR, and pay movies. Clever room decorating matches the shower curtain with the bed quilt. The beds were particularly comfortable with velvety soft blankets and sheets. Lanais, maid service in all units. Air conditioning in bedroom suites only. Inquire about Aston's promotional rates, special packages or Island Hopper Discounts.
*Aston Rates:*
*1 BR $185-200/170-185 (max. 4); 2 BR g.v. $255/235; 2 BR o.v. $320/290*
*Pahio VIP Services (Selling timeshares) offers: 1 & 2 BR $145-190*

**(ASTON) KAUA'I COAST RESORT AT THE BEACHBOY**
484 Kuhio Hwy., Kapa'a, HI 96746. (808) 822-3441. Aston Hotels & Resorts 1-800-922-7866. Rental Agent: Maui & All 1-800-663-6962.

Currently 243 units in three stories, but soon to change! Pool, tennis courts. Rooms have air conditioning, television, and lanais. No kitchens, but they do have a bar size refrigerator. Daily maid service. Located next door to the Coconut Plantation MarketPlace.

In 1999 it was announced by Shell Management Hawai'i that the Kauai Beachboy Hotel would be renamed the Kauai Coast Resort at the Beachboy. The resort is expected to undergo a $10 million renovation and construction program into the year 2001. The 243 hotel units will be converted into 108 vacation ownership units with 69 one-bedroom, 33 two-bedroom and six hotel rooms. The parent company, Shell Vacations operates 12 other vacation ownership resorts in California, Arizona, Canada and Hawaii. On Kaua'i, their other proprties are Lawa'i Beach Resort and Pono Kai Resort. The renovation will be conducted in three successive six-month phases. Aston will continue management of the property and rentals during the renovation.

No restaurant on the property at this time, but we are told that Shell is seeking an operator for the 5,000 square foot oceanview restaurant. Currently guests receive a complimentary continental breakfast.

In late 1999, a number of renovations were underway! Guests will enjoy new improvements to the swimming pool which will feature waterscapes, a children's pool and a jacuzzi along with extensive new landscaping. Also in progress is a new building for their Activity and Fitness Center. Constuction is underway on the resort's entrance waterfall as well as one 81-unit wing of the hotel which will be transformed into 36 vacation ownership condominium suites. This is the first of three buildings to be transformed into new suites and it should be completed early in 2000.

*Std. hotel room g.v. $120 (1-2); o.v. $135 (1-2); o.f. $155 (1-2).*
*1 BR 1 BTH Suite with kitchen o.v. $185; o.f. $195. Additional persons $12 per night. (Aston offers special package rates, such as Island Hopper Plans... so be sure to inquire!)*

**KAUA'I COCONUT BEACH (HOTEL)** ★
PO Box 830, Kapa'a, HI 96746. (808) 822-3455, FAX (808) 822-1830, 1-800-22-ALOHA. This is a Hawaiian Hotels & Resorts Property, also known as Pleasant Hawaiian Holidays. Located on 10.5 acres at Waipouli Beach. The resort was built in 1978, Ed & Lynn Hogan purchased the property in 1985 and ITT Sheraton continued to manage it until January 1992. Renovated and rededicated in January 1995, the redecoration project included new hand-carved custom furniture for many of the resort's 311 rooms. The rooms are in pastels and reflect the plantation era. The resort features a swimming pool/jacuzzi, three tennis courts, coin laundry, and a restaurant on the property. Rooms provide lanai, refrigerator, coffeemakers with free coffee, air conditioning. A handicapped room is also available. Summer program available for children accompanied by a parent. Offered free to guests June 1-August 31, the activities include hula, lei making and other Hawaiian arts and crafts each morning. They also offer a "Kids Eat Free" policy for families dining on-property. Demonstrations of Hawaiian crafts are given daily year-round as is their traditional torch-lighting ceremony each evening. There is a complimentary summer children's program. Children under age 17 may stay free in rooms with their parents when using existing bedding. The proximity to nearby Kaua'i Shopping Village (with a Safeway) and just a few blocks to the Coconut MarketPlace make it ideally situated. On the down side, the parking area, while large, can be very crowded and finding a spot can be a little difficult at times. The hallways have poor lighting, making them very dark. All in all a fairly good value, especially if they continue to maintain the quality of their rooms and grounds. Be sure to check the Entertainment book for half price coupons on your stay. The discount makes this a recommended accommodation!

A buffet breakfast is served at their Voyage Room Restaurant and is included with some of their room packages. The restaurant also serves a la carte and buffet lunches. Dinner is served at the Flying Lobster Restaurant. Nightly entertainment is at Cook's Landing Lounge. Their luau and Hawaiian revue received the Hawai'i Visitors Bureau Kahili Award.

The resort offers wedding service, and their on-property coordinator can assist you with all your wedding arrangements, from a marriage license to flowers and musicians.
*Current promotions include "Ohana" $142-165 per night which allows family to reserve a second room free. "Kaua'i Comeback" includes standard room with economy rental car from $142-237 (depending on view); or the "Coconet" $91-121 which includes a buffet breakfast for two. Check for their internet specials from $75 per night.*

**KAUA'I SANDS**
420 Papaloa Rd., Kapa'a, HI 96746. (808) 822-4951. RENTAL AGENT: Sand & Seaside Hotels, 1-800-367-7000 U.S., 1-800-654-7020 Canada, Local (808) 922-5333. This Americanized Japanese complex has Hawaiian/Japanese decor. The black and white exterior could be painted more attractively. The rooms don't get much sun, but this keeps them cool and keeps the dark-colored spreads and carpets from fading - they look brand new. Self-service laundry. They are on a beachfront, but it is better for sitting and ocean watching than for swimming and sunbathing. Rooms are air conditioned. Al & Don's Restaurant overlooks the ocean. Located in Wailua, it is located between Papaloa Road and the Coconut Plantation MarketPlace. Discounts for AAA members and seniors. Free room upgrade for 50+ seniors, free welcome breakfast for two, daily free breakfast for AAA members.

*Standard $98, with car $127; Deluxe Poolview $125, with car $154; Kitchenette Pool $135, with car $164.*

**LAE NANI**
410 Papaloa Rd., Kapa'a, HI 96746. (808) 822-4938. Located adjacent to the Coconut MarketPlace in Kapa'a. RENTAL AGENT: Outrigger Resorts 1-800-OUTRIGGER. Kaua'i Vacation Rentals 1-800-367-5025. Maui & All 1-800-663-6962.

They offer 84 units in three story buildings. 1 BR units are 800 sq. ft., 2 BR 2 BTH units are 1,072 sq. ft. These apartments are spacious with nice island-style decor and furnishings; light colors with cane and bamboo accents. Amenities include oceanfront swimming pool, tennis courts, daily maid service if booked with Outrigger, barbecue, and picnic area. All units have ceiling fans, private lanais, and full kitchens with microwaves. Laundry facilities are available on the property, but not in most units.

The central office has a particularly friendly and helpful staff -- meet them when you check in, stop by for your complimentary newspaper, or to mail (postage-free) the set of complimentary postcards that Outrigger provides for you on your arrival! This property has some outstanding oceanfront vistas. While the units are a little older and perhaps not as contemporary in style, they are very roomy, and comfortable.

Lae nani is situated on seven acres of lovely grounds. A small man-made rock pool along the bay has been created. The rocky promontory along the beach is a remnant of an early *heiau*. A free historical brochure describes *A Self-Guided*

*Tour of Wailua* for you to explore this and other ancient Hawaiian sites in the area. Check with Outrigger for a variety of packages and programs including senior discounts, first night free, room & car, and family plans. Note that Outrigger price includes daily maid service.
*Kauai Vacation Rental Rates: 1 BR o.v. $800 week; 2 BR $950 week.*
*Outrigger Resorts:*
*1 BR g.v. $165; o.v. $195; o.f. $225; 2BR g.v. $220; o.v. $250; o.f. $295*

**OUTRIGGER KAUA'I BEACH (HOTEL)**
4331 Kaua'i Beach Drive, Lihu'e, HI 96766. (808) 245-1955. Outrigger Hotels Hawai'i 1-888-805-3843, US & Canada, 0014-800-125-642 Australia, FAX 1-800-456-4329. OTHER RENTAL AGENTS: Maui & All 1-800-663-6962. Pleasant Hawaiian Holidays 1-800-242-9244.

There are 341 units in a five-story building on 25 landscaped oceanfront acres. This property opened the day after Hurricane Iniki struck the island and has had continuous service ever since. The Outrigger is located three miles north of Lihu'e on Nukoli'i Beach (which means the beach of the kole fish). It provides a secluded setting for sunbathing, swimming, and snorkeling (with free scuba lessons available through the resort) but the beach can be unsafe for water activities at times. Three swimming pools (2 adult, 1 keiki) and a spa amid lush tropical gardens and rockscaped waterfalls. Four tennis courts (two lighted), lobby shops, activity desk, and fitness club. Wailua Golf Course nearby. Meeting and banquet space. No laundry facilities.The rooms have daily maid service, air conditioning, refrigerator, television, direct dial phones, and private lanais. Rooms tend to be a little damp during rainy season, but black-out curtains and particularly comfortable beds are conducive to a good night of sleep.

Voyagers Club is an exclusive concierge-level of rooms and suites. At check-in, Voyagers Club guests are presented with personal "membership" cards that provides exclusive access to the Voyagers Club Lounge and entitles guests to special privileges at restaurants and shops around the islands. Guests can also receive a customized vacation itinerary at the start of their trip. A survey form completed at check-in is fed into a computer which provides personalized information on dining, entertainment, and activities. Guest rooms, offer ocean views, coffee makers in rooms and local daily newspaper Monday through Saturday. The Voyager Lounge offers complimentary continental breakfast 6:30-10:20 am and cocktails and pupus in the evening from 6-8 pm.

Hale Kipa Restaurant is open for breakfast, lunch, and dinner and offers specialty buffets on selected nights. Snacks and light lunches are available poolside at Cascades or in the Mele Lounge which also offers nightly Hawaiian entertainment. Cocktail lounge. Gilligan's Disco is open Thursday, Friday and Saturday evenings. Enjoy dancing to the latest hits on Friday and Saturday evening from 9:30 with a $5 cover charge. Fee is waived for hotel guests. A variety of arts & crafts classes and twice weekly "coffee clatches" are some of the activities that were started to entertain guests in the aftermath of Hurricane Iniki when there was little to do off-property. They proved so popular that they've been kept on ever since. A new Outrigger amenity is an attractive set of complimentary Hawaiian postcards that the front desk will mail for you -- postage-free -- anywhere in the world!

A Keiki Klub Summer Program is available for children 5-12 who are guests at the resort. The program is available Thursday through Monday from 8:30 am-3:30 pm. Children are exposed to Hawaiian culture through activities such as lei-making, Hawaiian language games, Hawaiian legends and storytelling, hula lessons, and Hawaiian arts and crafts. Other activities include movies, fishing derbies, beach combing, and shell collecting as well as excursions to Smith's Tropical Paradise and Fern Grotto tours. Half day sessions are $15 per child. Full day program is $30 per child. Cost includes activities, excursions and refreshments. Lunch is provided only in the full-day program.

Additional persons $20 per night, children 17 and under free when sharing with parent in existing beds. Check with Outrigger for a variety of packages and programs including senior discounts, first night free, room & car, and family plans. Also discounts for seniors, AARP and travel club.
*1 BR mt.v. $180, pool view $200; ocean view $225; Voyager Club $290; and suites from $410-545.*

**PALI KAI COTTAGES**
Five units on a bluff at Kukui'i Point that overlooks Nawiliwili Harbor and Kalapaki Bay. RENTAL AGENT: Kaua'i Vacation Rentals 1-800-367-5025. Surrounded by the Marriott complex and lagoons and on a bluff overlooking Kalapaki Bay. 1 & 2 bedrooms, all have two baths and sleep four.
*Kauai Vacation Rentals has 1 BR $800 weekly, 2 BR $1,000 weekly.*

**PLANTATION HALE**
484 Kuhio Highway, Kapa'a, HI 96746 (808) 822-4941, 1-800-775-4253. Now a Best Western Franchise. RENTAL AGENT: Outrigger Lodging Services (OLS) which is a branch of, but different from Outrigger Resorts. Visit their website: <www.plantationhale.com> OTHER AGENTS: Maui & All 1-800-663-6962. Pleasant Hawaiian Holidays 1-800-242-9244.

A total of 151 rooms in ten two-story buildings, located in the Coconut Market-Place, across the street from the beach. A good spot to stay if you don't plan on getting a rental car. The convenience of the mall provides multiple choices for restaurants and shopping. All units are one bedroom with kitchenettes and refrigerators. No dishwashers. New spas and a pool deck were recently installed. Three pools, BBQ area, and laundry facilities. Air conditioning and daily maid service. Non-smoking rooms available. Second floor units have balconies, first floor have patios.

A one block walk to the beach. The location of this property is between the road leading to the Coconut Beach Hotel and the highway. The last time we stayed here, the street noise was a bit loud, but we understand they have made improvements which seem to have alleviated the problem. We'd recommend requesting one of the oceanview rooms. Rooms now have pay per view movies. There are televisions in both the living room and bedroom to help ease any program disputes! *1 BR $110-125*

**PONO KAI RESORT**
1250 Kuhio Hwy., Kapa'a, HI 96746. RENTAL AGENT: Marc Resorts Hawai'i 1-800-535-0085, toll free FAX 1-800-633-5085, local (808) 922-9700. Maui & All 1-800-663-6962. Kaua'i Vacation Rentals 1-800-367-5025. Amenities include pool, jacuzzi, sauna, BBQ's. Units have ceiling fans, telephones, lanais, full kitchens including microwaves. Lighted tennis courts, shuffleboard, covered recreation area with kitchen facilities, tables and chairs, concierge/activity desk, video rentals. There is an attractive lagoon and bridge leading into the property from the front office and further along, a small Hawaiian garden with pathways for a short, but pleasant stroll. The exterior has recently been repainted to lighter shades over the existing brown. Very central location on the edge of Kapa'a town. (An interesting aside is that this used to be a pineapple cannery!)
*Marc Resorts offers:*
*1 BR g.v. $179/169; 1 BR o.v. $199/189; 1 BR o.f. $229/209; (max 4);*
*2 BR g.v. $229/209; 2 BR o.v. $249/229; 2 BR o.f. $269/249; (max 6).*

**ROYAL DRIVE COTTAGES AND KEALOHA RISE**
147 Royal Dr., Kapa'a, HI 96746. (808) 822-2321. Email: sand@aloha.net <www.royaldrive.com> Sandy Meyers offers two guest cottages that can be arranged with two twin beds or made up as a single king-size. A kitchen offers the convenience of a refrigerator, microwave, and other serving and dining essentials. A private bath and ceiling fans. With plenty of fruit trees in the garden, there may be ripe papayas or bananas to sample. *They have a 1 BR Cottage ($80), 1 BR House ($120) or 2 BR home ($150) plus cleaning fees.*

**WAILUA BAY VIEW**
320 Papaloa Rd., Kapa'a, HI 96746. Located overlooking Wailua Bay. RENTAL AGENT: Linda Owen 1-800-882-9007 or Email: <lro@ix.netcom.com> Prosser Realty 1-800-767-4707, (808) 822-3651. Kaua'i Vacation Rentals 1-800-367-5025. Maui & All 1-800-663-6962.

The apartments are lengthwise, so the living room is at the end facing the ocean and as the name implies, provides a beautiful bay view. Full kitchens, microwaves (in some units), dishwasher, washer/dryers. All units are air conditioned. King or queen beds, sleeper sofa in living room. Swimming pool and BBQ's. Walking distance to shops and restaurants. Daily maid service. Located on the beachfront with tennis courts across the street.
*1 BR $85-140/$80-120 (1-4, max. 4)*

## *EXPENSIVE*

**HALE AWAPUHI**
RENTAL AGENT: Kaua'i Vacation Rentals 1-800-367-5025. Prosser 1-800-767-4707. Maui & All Islands 1-800-663-6962. Just nine units in this property with oceanfront pool. Convenient to shops, restaurants and The Coconut Marketplace. *Dlx groundfloor corner unit o.v. 2 BR 2 BTH (1-4) $250/210; 2 BR w/loft (1-4) $320/280; First floor 2 BR 2 BTH (1-4) non-smoking $190/170; 2 BR 2 BTH second floor non-smoking (1-4) $210/190.*

**KAUA'I MARRIOTT RESORT & BEACH CLUB** ★
3610 Rice Street., Lihu'e, HI 96766. (808) 245-5050. MARRIOTT RESERVATIONS: 1-800-228-9290. OTHER RENTAL AGENTS: Pleasant Hawaiian Holidays 1-800-242-9244.

Located on 51 acres overlooking Kalapaki Bay, the Kaua'i Marriott Resort & Beach Club consists of 356 hotel rooms (the Kaua'i Marriott) and a community of 232 one and two bedroom Vacation Ownership villas named Marriott's Kaua'i Beach Club. The villas overlook Kalapaki Beach and Nawiliwili Bay.

The Kaua'i Surf was the original property on this location which in the late 1980's was redesigned by Chris Hemmeter and reopened as the Westin Kaua'i. The Westin was designed with a heavy European influence and a style that many felt was out of place on Kaua'i. Hurricane Iniki's devastation on this property was massive and the hotel remained closed until Marriott stepped in to take over operation. They chose a new approach, combining time share with a hotel property. The $30 million renovation incorporated Hawaiian history and culture into the new interior design, while keeping within the existing architectural elements and scale of the buildings. The result, we are happy to say, was a much improved image for the Kaua'i Marriott - not nearly as ostentatious or garish, and more reflective of the tropical elegance of Kaua'i. The most significant change was the replacement of the Roman pool in front with a much more subtle lagoon and more natural landscaping. This single element has made a big difference. The pink and beige color scheme is warmer and less showy, but the property is still luxurious just in a more appropriate way. Of course much of the Westin structures remain, the marble columns and such, but they have made an effort to make them less focal. (But they still have the fat marble rabbit that "spits up" into the pool. One of those headshaking things that the resort was stuck with....)

The elevator down to the lobby is still attractive and fun, kind of like Pirates of the Caribbean at Disneyland. The rooms are attractively furnished and spacious -- not too much excess furniture. Convenient in-room amenities include a mini-fridge, free HBO, and hair dryers.

Our night-owl Dona also appreciates their (relatively) late check-out of noon! They still offer their complimentary airport shuttle service. Our only complaint was that (at least in the wing we were housed in) the walls must have been very thin. You could not only hear noise, but actually words from the next room.

The villas feature a total of three restaurants and one lounge. Casual poolside dining is available at the Kalapaki Grill, and Kukui's as well as lunches and dinners at Duke's Canoe Club. Aupaka Terrace offers daytime refreshments or evening specialty cocktails, featuring an espresso and ice cream bar. The resort amenities include Hawaii's largest swimming pool and a 20,400 square foot retail shopping center.

The resort offers the Kalapaki Kids Club which focuses on the uniqueness of the Hawaiian Islands and Kaua'i in particular. For example, during the hula classes, the songs that are taught are all from Kaua'i, such as "Aloha Kaua'i." Kids are exposed to the ukulele and various Hawaiian crafts like lei making and lauhala weaving. Reservations need to be made one day in advance. The full day program is available Tuesday through Saturday from 9 am until 3 pm for youthages 5 to 12 years. The program costs $45 and includes lunch, a snack, and a Kalapaki Kids T-shirt.

As for adult activities, there are plenty of those! Special activities and Hawaiian exhibits are scheduled daily including sunrise walk, introduction to snorkeling or windsurfing, or you can even have your portrait done! Exhibits include Hawaiian Woodworking, Ni'ihau shell lei display, Hawaiian quilting, or featherwork. There are eight tennis courts and nearby are two outstanding golf courses designed by Jack Nicklaus. Adjoining the resort, the Kaua'i Lagoons has miles of lagoons. The mahogany launches which used to carry passengers around six islands with exotic wildlife are gone and the animals have been removed as well.
Ask about current package options. *Garden $270; ocean/pool view $325; ocean view $370; ocean view deluxe King suite $599.*

**LANIKAI**
390 Papaloa Rd., Kapa'a, HI 96746. RENTAL AGENTS: Castle Resorts 1-800-367-5004. Maui & All Islands 1-800-663-6962. Kaua'i Vacation Rentals 1-800-367-5025. Two, three story buildings offer eighteen units, half of these are in the rental program. These ocean-front condominiums provide large lanais as well as full kitchens. Property amenities include pool, BBQ area. Located near Wailua State Park Beach and Kapa'a.
*Castle: 1 BR suites w/ kitchen $227-253/207-226; 2 BR suites with kitchenette $183-303/256-276.*

# SOUTH SHORE TO WEST SHORE

## INTRODUCTION

### Koloa-Po'ipu-Lawa'i-Port Allen-
### Hanapepe-Waimea-Kekaha-Koke'e

## WHAT TO SEE/WHERE TO SHOP

This portion of accommodations and sights to see will begin as we head down Hwy. 50 from Lihu'e through Puhi then Hwy. 520 (the tree tunnel) to Koloa, continuing down to Po'ipu and Lawa'i, then following back up to Hwy. 50 (via 530, Lawa'i) eastward to Port Allen, Hanapepe, Waimea, Kekaha, and finally offering a course to the Waimea Canyon State Park and Koke'e State Park. As you follow Hwy. 50 toward Koloa, you will turn left onto Hwy. 520. You will not be able to miss the stunning stand of trees which line the road on either side. Walter Duncan McBryde was landscaping his homestead at the turn of the century when he discovered he had an excess of eucalyptus trees. He donated five hundred eucalyptus (also known as swamp mahogany) to the county and they were planted along Hwy. 520. This famed Eucalyptus Grove, known as the ***Tunnel of Trees,*** has recovered substantially since the hurricane, but a little more time will be required for mother nature to rebuild the canopy effect. In the days before the construction of the Kaumualii Hwy., the tree tunnel was three times longer than its current size. Construction of the highway resulted in the removal of some of the trees, but others remain on their original site along the dirt road through the canefields on the left side as you head to Lihu'e.

A recent addition to transportation alternatives on Kaua'i is the ***Coconut Coast Trolley*** operated by Trans Hawaiian Kaua'i from 10am to 10pm daily. Their most recent (1999) posted fare structure is $2 for a one way ticket or $5 for an all-day pass. Phone 245-5108. Northbound stops include Maui Marriott, Hilo Hattie, Outrigger, Holiday Inn Sunspree, and the Coconut MarketPlace. Southbound stops include Kapa'a Town--ABC Store, Kaua'i Village, and Smith's/Waialealae Boats. A feeder shuttle provides transfer from Po'ipu, Lihu'e and Nawiliwili Harbor. This is a demand type of service and they reserve the right to not stop or pick up at locations based upon lack of demand. They suggest you call and make reservations 245-5108 to insure stops at Hyatt Regency, Embassy Vacation Resort, Kiahuna Plantation, or Sheraton Kaua'i.

If you are staying at the Hyatt end of Po'ipu (Pe'e Road or beyond), the Koloa By-pass at Weli Weli Road now allows you to bypass Po'ipu and go straight into Koloa (and points East or North from there.) Phase II of the By-pass project is underway with a new, express version of this same route expected to completed by November 2000.

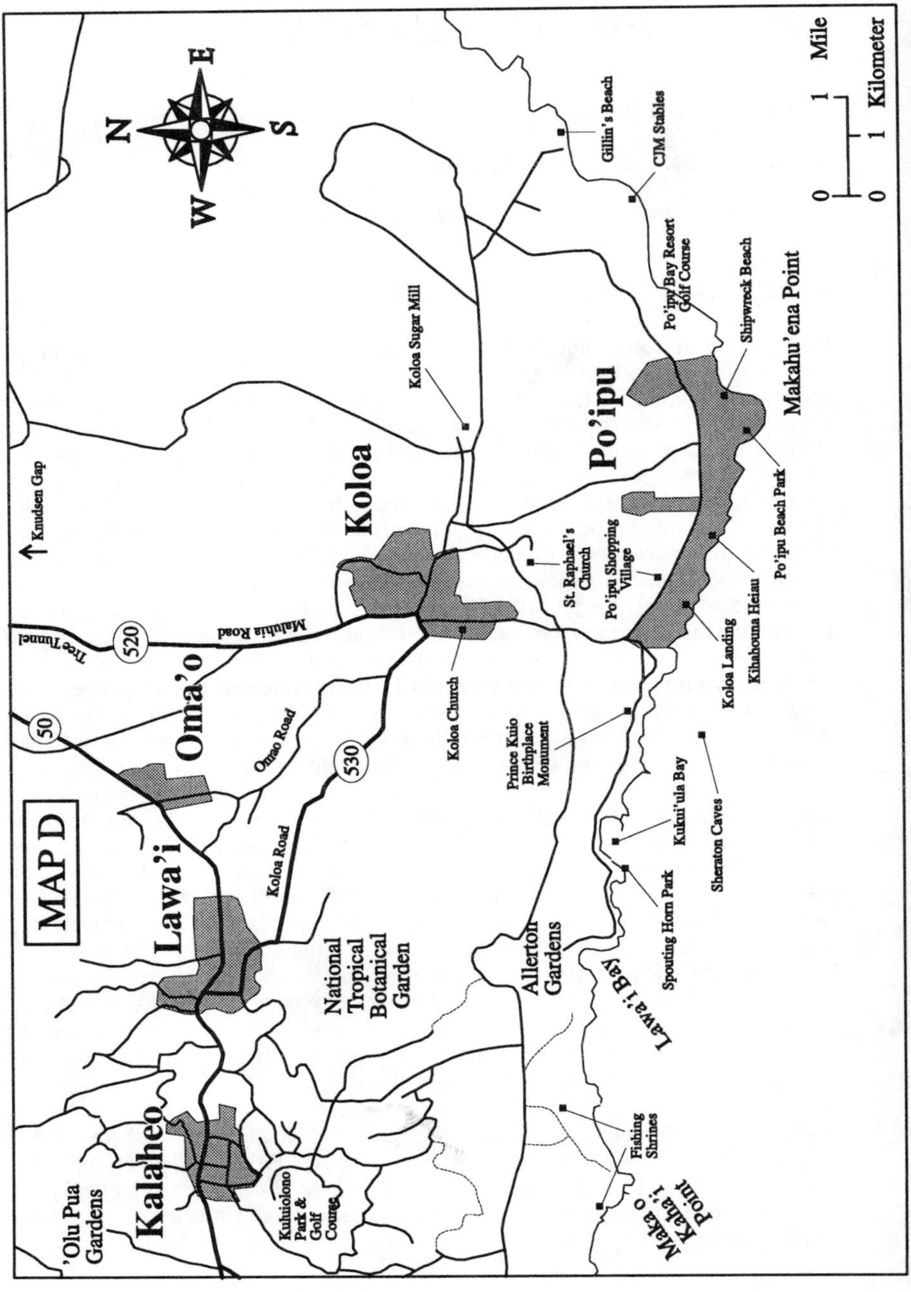
MAP D
N
E
S
W
Kalaheo
'Olu Pua Gardens
Kukuiolono Park & Golf Course
Lawa'i
Oma'o
Koloa
Po'ipu
Knudsen Gap
Tree Tunnel
520
Maluhia Road
50
Omao Road
530
Koloa Road
National Tropical Botanical Garden
Allerton Gardens
Lawa'i Bay
Maka'o Kaha'i Point
Fishing Shrines
Spouting Horn Park
Kukui'ula Bay
Sheraton Caves
Prince Kuio Birthplace Monument
Koloa Church
St. Raphael's Church
Po'ipu Shopping Village
Koloa Landing
Kihahouna Heiau
Po'ipu Beach Park
Makahu'ena Point
Shipwreck Beach
Po'ipu Bay Resort Golf Course
Koloa Sugar Mill
CJM Stables
Gillin's Beach
0 1 Mile
0 1 Kilometer

## *KOLOA*

The last volcanic eruptions occurred on Kaua'i in the Koloa area some one million years ago. Traveling around the area you will see cinder cones still dotting the landscape.

The word Koloa has several meanings, but the most common translation is "place of long cane." The town of ***Koloa*** developed along the Waikomo Stream which provided not only fresh water, but power for the first sugar mills. In 1835, Ladd and Company established the first successful sugar plantation in Hawai'i here. King Kamehameha III leased 980 acres to a Bostonian, William Hooper, for $300 a year. The first mill was built in 1836 in an area known as Green Pond. The mill used large koa logs to grind the cane juice. The second mill was built in 1838 in the same location, but used much-improved iron rollers. Ladd and Company built the third mill in 1841 near the confluence of the Omao and Waikomo Streams. The mill was powered by water and firewood fueled the boilers. The chimney stack at the park across the street from the monkey pod tree in Koloa is all that remains of this third mill which was used until 1913. The monument represents the many varied ethnic groups which contributed their labors to the sugar cane industry. The "new" mill was built in 1913 and continued in production for the Koloa Sugar Company until it ceased operations in 1996. McBryde - Koloa's last incarnation once owned by Alexander & Baldwin - has shifted to coffee production as Island Coffee Company.

From its inception in 1835 and then for 21 years, this was the only sugar cane plantation in the Hawaiian islands. The quaint plantation feel of this town continues to this day. A small strip of shops line the town of Koloa. Tomkats restaurant and Pizzetta are adjacent to several art galleries. One has some interesting old Hawaiiana prints and reprints. Island Soap and Candle Works has opened a second location in Old Koloa Town. Visit them on the web, too, at: <www.handmade-soap.com>

KOLOA

The large monkey pod tree was planted in 1925 and lends its shade to the Crazy Shirts store. This building was originally built by Mr. Yamaka who ran a hotel in the back until the mid 1920's when the Yamamoto family began their store at this sight. Behind this is a small mall area with the Koloa Museum. This small, free, museum depicts the development of the sugar industry in this area. The hours it is open seem to be sporadic.

The best deal in town is behind Sueoka's grocery. The small "snack shop" is reminiscent of the old Azeka's snack shop on Maui. Walk up to the window and order your grinds. Open just for lunch, it is worth the drive back from Po'ipu Beach to pick up a meal!

The Waita Reservoir on the east side of Koloa is the largest reservoir in Hawaii. This man-made body of water was built on marshlands between 1903 and 1906 and covers 370 acres.

The ***Koloa Church***, located on Po'ipu Road, was established in 1835. However, this pristine white church was not built until 1859. The design reflects a traditional New England style, typical of the missionary influence in early Hawai'i.

In Koloa you will find one of Kaua'i's notable historic religious landmarks. More than 150 years ago, in 1841, ***St. Raphael Catholic Church*** opened its doors on Kaua'i. The island's first Catholic church was damaged by Hurricane Iniki, but fortunately was repairable. Other buildings on the property had to be torn down. The original church had walls that were thickly built. A mortar was made by burning sand into lime and it was then mixed with pounded coral. This was used to hold together the rocks that constituted the walls. A reporting of the church's construction was published in a centennial celebration held in 1941: "The gathering of coral was a saga itself. The men and women swam out to the reef from Koloa beach and there they dived under water to break off huge slabs of coral. They would then swim with the slab back to the beach, tie it onto their shoulders and trudge the three miles across the plain to the church." Changes to the original church over the years included the addition of more arched windows and a steeple was added in 1933. St. Raphael was originally a parish school and offered instruction for many years. While the main church seats only 150 persons, you may find three times that many in attendance on Sundays. So, in addition to the rebuilding efforts, the church also has plans for expansion. You might also visit the Lady of Lourdes shrine, built of lava rocks in a secluded spot at the back of the property.

***Koloa Landing***, on the edge of town, was the state's third largest whaling port in the 1800's and was also used for the exporting of raw sugar and sweet potatoes. An inter-island ferry would traverse between the islands, bringing passengers to this port on Kaua'i. The landing as a port sight was abandoned in 1928. Today you can still see the remains of the old mill, and nearby is a sculpture that depicts the history of the area and the various ethnic groups that made their mark on Kaua'i's sugar industry.

## *PO'IPU*

While Po'ipu has no definitive town center, it is none-the-less a wonderful Kaua'i vacation destination. Located on the south shore, there are several excellent accommodations. Po'ipu Beach is located in front of the Kiahuna Plantation. This is one of the island's best all-around beaches for family activities, except during high seas. The Hyatt Regency is located on Keoneloa Beach, fondly referred to as Shipwreck Beach for a long-since-gone wreck that once was beached on this stretch of coastline.

The ***Po'ipu Shopping Village*** is the largest and only real shopping center in this area. You will find eateries ranging from fine dining to very casual including *Roy's Po'ipu Bar & Grill, Keoki's Paradise, Pattaya Asian Cafe, Shipwreck Subs, Plantation House,* and *Amigo's Mexican Restaurant*. There is also a *Crazy Shirts* and some other fashion shops, jewelry stores, and touristy shops with fine arts and gifts. They have free Hawaiian entertainment and Tahitian Dancers Monday and Thursday at 5 pm.

***Prince Kuhio Park*** is located on Lawa'i Beach Road. Prince Kuhio was the youngest son of Kaua'i's Chief David Kahalepouli Piikoli and the grandson of Kaumuali'i, the last King of Kaua'i. His aunt was Queen Kapiolani and Prince Kuhio was adopted by her and grew up in the royal household in Honolulu. The monument at this park marks the birth site of Prince Jonah Kuhio Kalanianaole. Prince Jonah was known as the "People's Prince" because of his achievements for his Hawaiian people. You can see the foundation of Kuhio's parents' home, royal fishpond, shrine, *Hoai Heiau* where the *kahuna* (priests) meditated and lived, and a sitting bench that faced the grounds. He was born in 1871, and elected in 1902 as a delegate to Congress, where he served until his death on January 7, 1922.

Located just to the east of Po'ipu Beach there is a lava rock outcropping known as ***Spouting Horn***. It is named for the shooting geyser of sea water that appears during high tide. The spouting results from the surf washing into the lava tube and being sucked up through a hole in the coastal rock. The geyser reaches heights of as much as 60 feet. This popular tourist attraction is open to the public at no charge. It is easy to find, follow Hwy. 520 to Lawa'i Rd. (also known as Spouting Horn Rd.). Heed the posted signs which caution about the dangerous rocks. Continuing on along Lawa'i Road will lead you to the mouth of the Lawa'i Stream.

If you haven't already, take time to backtrack along Lawa'i Road to Po'ipu Road and head north to the charming town of Koloa. Old ***Koloa Town*** offers lots of interesting historic sights, restaurants, and quaint shopping opportunities.

If you'd like to experience a little of the pleasures of Robinson Crusoe or Swiss Family Robinson, plan an excursion to ***Maha'ulepu Beach***. It was here that King Kamehameha I made his attempt to conquer the island of Kaua'i in 1796. Unfortunately, a storm forced a retreat, but the advance forces of Kamehameha's troops arrived on the island unaware of the order to retreat and were quickly killed.

This is also the beach site where George C. Scott portrayed Ernest Hemingway in the movie *Islands in the Stream.* Maha'ulepu Beach is actually a collection of smaller beaches. Bones of ancient and now extinct flightless birds have been found in caves in this area. The beaches offer a diverse assortment of aquatic activities including fishing, surfing, bodyboarding, body surfing, kayaking, windsurfing, snorkeling, and swimming. The three areas along this beachfront are Gillin's Beach, Kawailoa Bay, and Ha'ula Beach.

Gillin's was named for the supervisor of Grove Farm Company, Elbert Gillin, who arrived in the islands in 1912 and relocated to Kaua'i in 1925 where he built his home. He was the supervisor of the Ha'upu Range Tunnel. Following two hurricanes, all that remained was Gillin's chimney, but the home has now been rebuilt. Several feet below this beach are the Rainbow Petroglyphs. Discovered in January of 1980 when a severe storm took out as much as six feet of beachfront, the petrogylphs were suddenly exposed. Working in reverse, the sea soon chose to cover them up once again. Currents at Kawailoa Bay make it unsafe for swimming or snorkeling. To reach Ha'ula Beach you may park on the east side of Pa'o'o Point and travel to the shore by trail. This area is the south shore's most dangerous beach.

The first beach, Gillin's, on occasion may be good for the experienced snorkeler during calm surf. Ha'ula Beach is often less crowded. Access to these beaches is over private land which is open during daylight hours only, 7 am to 6 pm. The gate is locked at night and no overnight camping is permitted. This private property is owned by the Grove Farm Company. Since access could be denied at any time, please be respectful and take your litter out with you so everyone can enjoy these gorgeous Kaua'i beaches.

Public access is found at the end of Po'ipu Road. Take the dirt road and then turn right onto the cane road. There are no facilities here, so remember to bring your own water. Parking is along side the road.

This area of ***Maha'ulepu*** is important geologically as well as archaeologically. Many of the early Hawaiian archeological sites were destroyed when the land was cleared for sugar cane. However, scientists have enough information to speculate that this area was heavily populated in pre-contact times. (Referring to the period prior to the arrival of Captain Cook.) The area offered the early Hawaiians excellent fishing grounds and a fertile valley making it a very suitable living environment. It was noted by Captain George Vancouver that from this area the glow of numerous campfires could be seen as he sailed past. Further confirmation was found by the many burial sites located in the sand dunes here. Geologically the area lies below Mt. Ha'upu, which is now only an eroded caldera. The sand dunes have born other rich geological treasures including the fossils of extinct birds. They have identified a flightless bird called a rail, several species of geese, and a long-legged owl. John Clark's *Beaches of Kaua'i* notes that, "Several caves in the vicinity contain two extremely rare insects, one a blind wolf spider and the other a blind terrestrial amphipod."

The ***Po'ipu Beach Resort Association*** provides up to date information on accommodations, activities, dining, shopping, transportation, and service in the Po'ipu, Koloa, and Kalaheo areas of Kaua'i. To request a free 36 page brochure. Contact: Po'ipu Beach Resort Association, PO Box 730, Koloa, HI 96756. (808) 742-7444. FAX (808) 742-7887. Toll free 1-888-744-0888. E-mail: info@poipubeach.org or look up their electronic brochure at <www://poipu-beach.org>

## *LAWA'I*

Leaving Koloa and heading eastward on Hwy. 530, you'll travel to Lawa'i. Little is known of early Lawa'i. According to an account by David Forbes in his book, *Queen Emma and Lawa'i*, the early maps and photographs show that the valley was cultivated in taro and later in rice. Queen Emma, the wife of Kamehameha IV, probably first saw Lawa'i during her visit in 1856, but returned for a more lengthy stay during the winter and spring in 1871. On arrival she found the area rather desolate, and compared with the busy life in Honolulu, it must have seemed so. In her correspondence with her family on O'ahu she requested many items to be sent, including plant slips. With these plant starts she began to develop one of the finest gardens in the islands.

Queen Emma leased the Lawa'i land to Duncan McBryde for a span of fifteen years in 1876, however, she reserved her house lot and several acres of taro patch land. According to Forbes, "In 1886, after the Queen's death, Mrs. Elizabeth McBryde bought the entire Ahupuaa for $50,000. The upper lands were planted to sugar cane, and the valley was apparently leased to Chinese rice growers and taro planters."

In 1899, Alexander McBryde obtained the land and with a love of plants, he continued to enlarge and cultivate the gardens which were begun by the queen. Alexander McBryde died in 1935 and the land was sold to Robert Allerton and his son John in 1938. They continued to enlarge the gardens, searching out plants from around South East Asia. Today Lawa'i is a horticulturist's dream, with an outstanding collection of tropical plants. The ***National Tropical Botanical Garden*** is a nationally-chartered non-profit organization that is actually made up of five separate gardens. Three are on Kaua'i, one is on Maui, and another is located in Florida. Each of the gardens has an individual name, but they are sometimes incorrectly referred to individually as the "National Tropical Botanical Garden."

The Lawa'i Garden (National Tropical Botanical Garden Headquarters) is located on Kaua'i's southern shore in the lush Lawa'i Valley, and was the first garden site to be acquired by the National Tropical Botanical Garden. The NTBG headquarter facilities are located adjacent to the Lawa'i Garden. The headquarters complex includes a scientific laboratory, an herbarium housing nearly 30,000 specimens of tropical plants, an 8,000 volume research library, a computer records center, an educational center, and offices for staff and visiting scientists. ***Lawa'i Garden*** is a research and educational garden comprising 186 acres. The garden's extensive collections include tropical plants of the world that are of particular significance for research, conservation, or cultural purposes. Special emphasis is given to rare and endangered Hawaiian species and to economic plants of the tropical world.

Of particular interest is the endangered *kanaloa kahoolawensis* (one of only four in the world). This small, woody plant is known only to exist on Kahoolawe. In 1992 two specimens of this plant were discovered on Kahoolawe. This is the first new genus discovered in Hawai'i since 1913 and two have since been grown from seeds at the NTBG. There is also a collection of familiar household products - sugar, vanilla, cinnamon - all seen here in their natural plant state. Palm oil, sandalwood (for scent), koa (for wood items including canoes and furniture), and cuari (used to make sodium pentathol) can also be seen in their original form. ***Three Springs*** is at the interior of the Lawa'i Garden (toward the mountains). This 120-acre area was acquired as a bequest to the Garden. As yet undeveloped, it will eventually be designed as an additional garden section, emphasizing the beautiful natural land and water features.

The nearby ***Allerton Garden*** is located oceanfront at Lawa'i-Kai, adjacent to the Lawa'i Garden. The entrance, located across from Spouting Horn, is a 14,000 square foot renovated plantation home that was transplanted from West Kaua'i to become the visitor center for the Garden. This was formerly a private 100-acre estate. The beautifully designed garden is managed by the National Tropical Botanical Garden pursuant to an agreement with the Allerton Estate Trust. The gardens, started by Queen Emma, were lovingly developed and expanded over a period of 30 years by Robert Allerton and his son John. The sculpted gardens contain numerous plants of interest, outstanding examples of garden design and water features, as well as Queen Emma's original summer cottage. The cottage was severely damaged by Hurricane Iniki and plans for restoration are underway. The Moreton Bay fig trees here have giant buttress roots and helped create a prehistoric scene for the filming of *Jurassic Park*. While these trees appear ancient, they were actually planted in 1940. Reservations are required for tours of the Lawa'i and Allerton Gardens. Tour fee for the Allerton Garden or Lawa'i Garden is $25 adults, $15 teens (13-18), $10 children (6-12) for each tour. For information on scheduled tours and reservations for either call (808) 742-2623. PO Box 340 Lawa'i, HI 96765.

## *KALAHEO*

The town of Kalaheo was home to many immigrants at the turn of the century. There was homestead land auctioned by the government beginning in about 1910 and was originally used for growing pineapple with Walter McBryde spearheading the pineapple industry. The population was predominantly Portuguese, Hawaiian and Japanese. The name translates to "the proud day." As you enter into the town of Kalaheo you will pass Brick Oven Pizza, thought by many to serve the best pizzas on the island, so stop if you're in the mood for a pizza pie!

To take a short and worthwhile detour you need to turn left onto Papalina Road and head for Kukuiolono Park. Many of the street names are Hawaiian words for parts of the body. For example, *Papalina* means cheek, *Lae* means forehead, *Maka* is eye, and *Opu* is stomach. Glimpse off to your left as you climb the winding road and, if you are fortunate, you'll see a rainbow hanging over Po'ipu. The three huge satellite dishes on the right will warn you that your turn is just ahead. A small white sign on the right is too small and too near the turn off to prepare you for the U turn onto Puu Rd. Enter Kukuiolono Park through the huge rock archway with iron gates. ***Kukuiolono Park*** is a series of gardens with sweeping Pacific and Lawa'i Valley views. This park was built by Walter McBryde, a founding father of the island's pineapple industry. This beautiful, scenic public park is a popular location for wedding ceremonies. There is also a Hawaiian garden which displays some interesting ancient stone artifacts. There are huge rock bowls and a stone with a shape resembling the island called "Kaua'i iki" or Little Kaua'i. It is said by some that if you haven't seen Little Kaua'i, then you haven't seen Kaua'i. The public golf course located here is open 6:30 am-6:30 pm. No tee-offs allowed after 4:30. This is the best golf value on the island with nine picturesque holes costing only $7! Because of the value it may be crowded, but if you tee-off late in the day and don't have time to finish, it may be well worth the green fees. You might like to stop at the Kalaheo Coffee Co. and Cafe, just past the Papalina Rd. intersection and pick up some of their huge sandwiches to enjoy as a picnic up at the park.

***Olu Pua Gardens***, a 12-acre botanic garden estate, is no longer open to the public tours. However, it is available for vacation rental through Kaua'i Vacation Rentals.

## *ELE'ELE and PORT ALLEN*

Just beyond mile marker 14 on the right is a scenic overlook of the Hanapepe Valley. It is a strikingly beautiful vista with the sheer canyon walls in hues of amber, ocher, and red. You will first travel through Ele'ele and Port Allen before reaching the town of Hanapepe, so we'll describe it later.

As you continue toward Waimea, you will note a series of substantial looking electrical poles bordering the road on both sides. These were put in following the devastation caused by Hurricane Iniki and we were told they could withstand wind forces up to 120 miles per hour. As the road curves downhill you will reach the area of Ele'ele. The most notable landmark is the Ele'ele Shopping Center.

A *Big Save* and *Toi's Thai Kitchen* are here. Turn down toward Port Allen to see one of Kaua'i's two seaports. The Coast Guard has boats here and some are "drones" or target ships. They warn "Target Drone, Stay Clear" in large bold letters. Obviously these in the harbor have either not had a turn at being bombed, or they just got lucky with some misses! You can purchase bags of Kaua'i grown coffee and other coffee-related items at the *Kauai Coffee Company and Visitor Center* located between Kalaheo and Ele'ele on a turn off just past the old McBryde Mill. Enjoy free samples of java while you browse their store. Call (808) 335-5497 or 1-800-545-8605.

You may have noticed that the dirt has become redder as you proceed around the southern coastline. The soil contains a good deal of iron. A very clever entrepreneur has taken advantage of this red clay which has a natural property for staining anything that it comes in contact with. You are sure to have seen the "Red Dirt Shirts" at various shops around the island. If you can't wait to visit, you can order by mail. Paradise Sportswear, PO Box 1027, Kalaheo, HI 96741. Send for a copy of their catalog which depicts their many varied styles.

Port Allen has reemerged as a focal harbor for tourists. With the closure of useage from Hanalei Bay, many of the boating excursions to The Napali now depart from this location.

## *HANAPEPE*

Hanapepe, which means "crushed bay," was Kaua'i's largest town back in the 1920's and remained so until about 1947 when it experienced a post-war decline. Two decades later, however, the population had dwindled significantly. The area was rediscovered by the Chinese immigrants who began to grow rice here. Hanapepe was once again one of Kaua'i's busiest towns from World War I through the early 1950's.

KONA COFFEE

During the second World War, this coastal village was alive with thousands of GIs and sailors who were sent from the mainland and the rest of Hawai'i to train for Pacific Theater duty and to shore up Kaua'i's defenses. At this time Hanapepe reached its largest population and boasted restaurants, two theaters, two roller rinks, a dance hall -- and a brothel!

Hanapepe boasts that it is the biggest little town on Kaua'i. Fortunately, Hanapepe feels like a step back in time with its plantation era buildings and slow pace. When the highway was widened it was decided to by-pass the town of Hanapepe and it was probably at that time that Hanapepe began to fade into disrepair. The opening of the Kukui Grove Shopping Center in Lihu'e was another blow to shopkeepers who just could not compete. It is a quaint town that has potential for being a wonderful locale for artisans galleries or such. You may recognize this town for scenes from the made-for-television mini-series *Thornbirds*. Many of the buildings damaged by Hurricane Iniki have not, and may not ever, be repaired. The *Taro Ko Chips* factory is on the edge of town, and you might catch them when they are open. Mr. and Mrs. Nagamine started this business following their retirement and they cook up chips made from taro grown in fields nearby.

*The Green Garden Restaurant* has been hopping since the 1940's when the GI's would stop by for a meal and a piece of their wonderful pie. *Yoshiura's General Store* operated as Mikado until World War II and is a classic. The *Hanapepe Cafe & Espresso* and adjacent *Aloha Angels Gallery* are worth a visit. By 4 pm the town is pretty well closed up. Except for Friday night! A number of new art galleries have been springing up in recent months, optimistic that perhaps this artisan community will soon be discovered by more and more visitors exploring Kaua'i's western shore. And now these local galleries host "Art Night" every Friday (6-9pm) with at least one of them providing refreshments and an art demonstration. Decorative lighting adds to the mood for visitors to enjoy a festive stroll, watch artists doing portraits, and enjoy the hula show and Hawaiian local music.

One of the most fascinating natural sites in Hanapepe is the salt ponds at Salt Pond Beach. The natural flats along this beach have been used by Hawaiians for generations. Today, this site continues to be used for traditional salt making. The resulting product is used for medicinal and cultural purposes. In late spring the wells, or *puna*, are cleaned and the salt making process runs through the summer months. Mother nature has been kind enough to create a ridge of rock between the two rocky points at Salt Pond Beach, resulting in a large lagoon. The area is fairly well protected, allowing for swimming and snorkeling (except during times of high surf) and is popular for surfing and windsurfing as well. This park is well used, because of its protected swimming area, for families and children. This part of the island is often sunny and warmer, even when there is rain on the south and east shore, Salt Pond Beach can be a great day-long excursion. There are picnic areas, restrooms, a rinse off shower, and generally a lifeguard on duty. Camping is permitted with a county permit. To reach the park, turn *mauka* off Kaumualii Hwy. on Lele Rd. then go past the Veterans Cemetery on Lokokai to parking area.

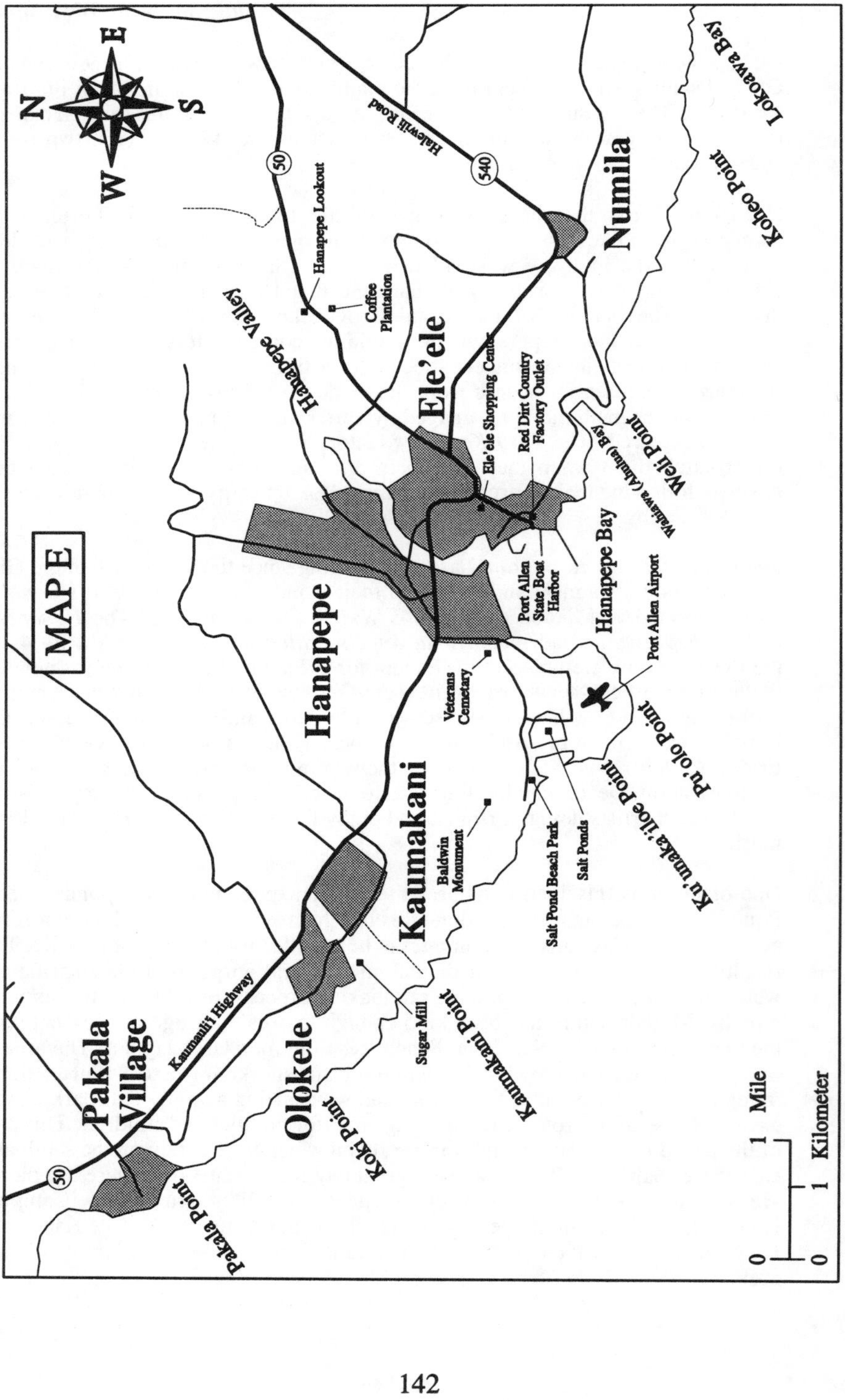
MAP E
N
E
S
W
Pakala Village
Olokele
Kaumakani
Hanapepe
Ele'ele
Numila
Kaumuali'i Highway
Halewili Road
50
540
Hanapepe Lookout
Coffee Plantation
Hanapepe Valley
Ele'ele Shopping Center
Red Dirt Country Factory Outlet
Port Allen State Boat Harbor
Hanapepe Bay
Port Allen Airport
Veterans Cemetery
Baldwin Monument
Salt Pond Beach Park
Salt Ponds
Sugar Mill
Pakala Point
Koki Point
Kaumakani Point
Pu'olo Point
Weli Point
Koheo Point
Lokoawa Bay
0
1
Mile
Kilometer

## *WAIMEA - KAUMAKANI - MAKAWELI*

West Kaua'i is being developed into a valuable tourist destination. Exploring the area (dubbed the West Kaua'i Sugar Heritage Corridor), begins just outside of Hanapepe. Here sugar was king and the story can be viewed along the highway and from connecting roads ... passing through Kaumakani Village, Waimea and Kekaha Town.

Waimea is perhaps the best known, and that is a direct result of the one early adventurer. Captain James Cook first landed in the Hawaiian islands in January 1778 at this site. A monument stands in his honor. In later times, rice was grown in the valleys and swamp, and sugar in the dryer areas that required irrigation. The region also grew taro and raised cattle. As we enter a new millennium, Waimea and the West Kaua'i Sugar Corridor are experiencing an incredible rebirth! Tourists and locals alike are discovering what opportunities can be afforded here!

It is a wonderfully quaint town and with its location on the western coastline, often provides better weather conditions than in other areas of the island. You can pick up a very helpful self-guided map of the Waimea area. It is available at the West Kaua'i Techonology and Visitor Center. It highlights all the places to eat, picnic spots, and beaches, as well as historic sites in or near Waimea including the Russian Fort, Menehune Ditch, and Gulick-Rowell House. We've given descriptions of some of the most notable. Activities in the area include plantation tours at Gay & Robinson and soon to begin are the Koula Valley Tours. Annual events include Christmas in Waimea with its Annual Lighted Christmas Parade, the annual Falsetto Competition and Concert, and the Waimea Town Celebration.

Plantation Lifestyles Walking Tour provides insight into plantation life in 1900. In the future, a museum may be built near the ruins of the old Waimea Sugar Mill. The tour, led by volunteers, includes a visit to the Waimea Plantation Cottages with a collection of relocated camphouses that now serve as visitor accommodations. Reservations are required for the ***Waimea Sugar Mill Camp Museum and Plantation Lifestyles Walking Tour***, a 1 1/2 hour cultural tour in an original sugar plantation village. Limited to 12 people, the tour is currently offered Tuesdays, Thursdays, and Saturdays at 9 am. Cost is $6 adults, $5 seniors 65 and older, and children 12 and under are $3. Waimea Plantation Cottages, PO Box 1178, Waimea, HI 96796. (808) 335-2824

Hawaii's cultural history can be intimately explored through the heart of the sugar plantation. Hawaii's multi-cultural history is due to the need for laborers in the labor-intensive sugar fields of yesterday year. Now you have the opportunity to view field to factory operations at Gay & Robinson. The two-hour bus tour, conducted by Gay & Robinson Tours LLC, is available weekdays and includes the history of the plantation, its operation, processing, the plantation's miles of irrigation systems and views of the private plantation lands. Harvesting operations are seasonal with the months of April through October the best times to visit Gay

& Robinson. Tour routes depend on the day-to-day operations. If you don't have time for the full tour, stop by their office on Kaumakani Avenue and view the historic displays. The office is located in the historic Field Office (circa 1900) on Kaumakani Avenue. From Lihu'e, travel Hwy. 50. Just past mile marker 19, turn left on Kaumakani Avenue with its monkeypod trees and old-fashioned streetlights. It is open 8am-4pm Monday through Friday, with the exception of plantation holidays. Tours are at 9am and 1 pm. All visitors on the tour are required to wear safety equipment to enter the factory. They must also wear pants (shorts are okay), low-heeled, closed shoes and they will be provided with safety glasses and hard hats. Cost of the tour is $30. In the not-to-distant future they will be adding other tours of their ditch systems. For tour information call (808) 335-2824. If you want more information on Waimea, pick up a copy of *Touring Waimea* by Christine Fayé. Available at local bookstores.

Just before you reach Waimea, before crossing the river, is ***Fort Elizabeth*** (also known as the Russian Fort). Built on the mouth of the Waimea River in 1817 by a German doctor, Georg (that's right, no "e") Anton Scheffer, who was employed by the Russian/American Fur Company of Alaska. When he began to fortify his fort the native chiefs grew concerned and notified the king who in turn ordered the Russians out of Kaua'i. There are restroom facilities located here.

Across the river on the other side of the mouth is the ***Lucy Wright State Park***. This beach sight was named for a school teacher who taught in Waimea for more than thirty-five years, Lucy Kapahu Aukai Wright. She was born August 20, 1873 in Anahola. Just past the Waimea River turn right onto Menehune Road.

BREADFRUIT

Follow the road up 1.3 miles to the cliff on the left. You will note the cactus which drapes down over the cliff face. Caverns in the cliff are said to be sacred burial sites of the early Hawaiians. The ***Menehune Ditches*** extend 25 miles up the Waimea River. The construction of it is of unknown origin, and there is some question that the early Hawaiians had the talents to build in this "dressed lava" stone fashion. A much simpler explanation is the legend that it was built in one night by the menehune to irrigate taro patches for the people in Waimea. Today, you can still see a two-foot-high portion of one of the walls that is marked by a plaque. Frankly, the ditches are not as interesting as one might expect. A picturesque sight formed by the lovely stream and the swinging foot bridge is more pleasant. If you are in luck you will see the local people fording the stream to the other side, or perhaps meet the enormous long-haired boar that goes for a walk and a bath in the stream with her owner.

The historic, newly restored ***Waimea Theatre*** building reopened at the end of 1999 as Kaua'i's newest venue for movies, live performances, and conferences. This old-fashioned movie theatre (it seats 250!) is located in the heart of town in a 1938 art deco building -- complete with a glass ticket booth in front -- and is worth a visit just to enjoy the architecture and history.

A good place to begin your Waimea exploration would be at the new ***West Kaua'i Visitor & Technology Center***, 9565 Kaumualii Hwy., Waimea (808) 338-1332. HOURS: Open daily 9am-5pm. Pictorials, graphics, and displays with touch-sensitive screens provide information on all of Kauai's activities, not just Waimea. This high-tech, state-of-the-art 7500 square foot center facility opened in April 1999 with land leased from the Kikia'ola Land Co. for $1 a year for 30 years. They anticipate more than 500,000 visitors to cross through the doors each year. Utilizing the theme, "Enduring Engineering," visitors follow cultural and historic photographs showing the development of engineering on Kaua'i from ancient days to modern times. From the Polynesian voyagers to NASA's most sophisticated techology. Enjoy old photographs of Waimea, back to the days of grass shacks! There is even a photo of the first movie filmed on Kaua'i, *White Heat* by director Louis Weber. (The film has long since been lost or destroyed.) One unusual model is the Pathfinder which is a pilotless aircraft that was flown at an altitude of 80,000 feet over Barking Sands beach. The museum blends the history of the area with information on the nearby Pacific Missile Range Facility. Not an easy task to undertake, but one that seems to work here. They are looking forward to Phase II! In addition to the displays there are several tenants in the facility. Currently they include Oceanit Laboratories, Inc., Solipsys Corpration, Textron Systems and Trex Enterprises.

The monument to ***Captain Cook*** is found in the center of town. It was placed there in 1928 in celebration of the 150th anniversary of Captain Cook's discovery of the islands and his first landing in the islands at Waimea. The statue was placed in Waimea by the state in 1978 commemorating the 200th anniversary of Cook's discovery at Hofgaard Park and in 1987 was moved to its present location.

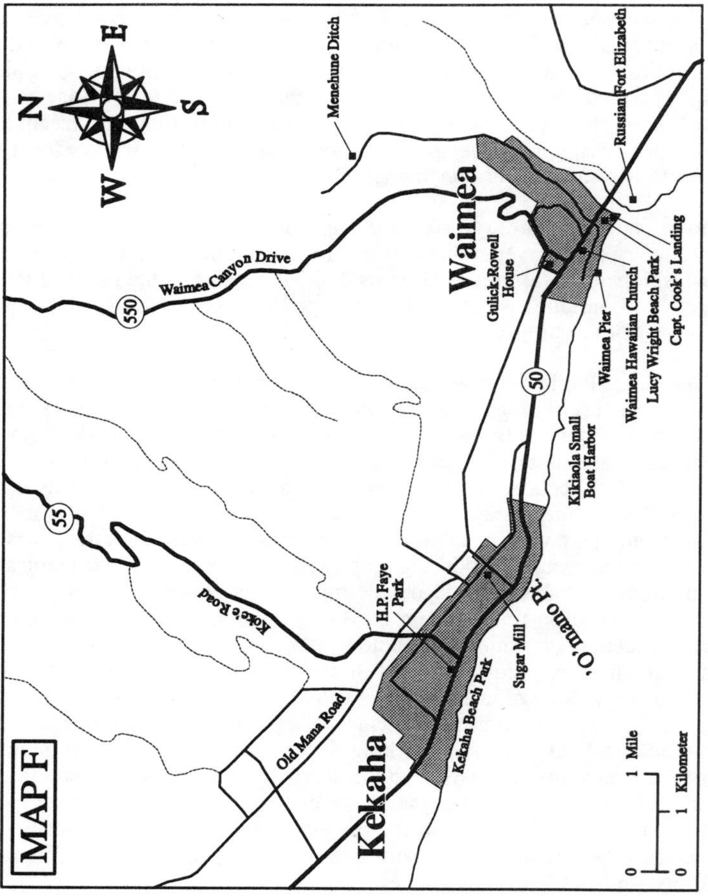
MAP F
N
E
S
W
Kekaha
Waimea
Old Mana Road
Kekaha Beach Park
Sugar Mill
H.P. Faye Park
Koke'e Road
55
550
Waimea Canyon Drive
Menehune Ditch
50
Gulick-Rowell House
Kikiaola Small Boat Harbor
Waimea Pier
Waimea Hawaiian Church
Lucy Wright Beach Park
Capt. Cook's Landing
Russian Fort Elizabeth
'O'mano Pt.
0 1 Mile
0 1 Kilometer

The ***Waimea Hawaiian Church*** was built around 1865 by Reverend Rowell when he had a falling out with the Waimea Foreign Church. It was seriously damaged by Hurricane Iniki and was totally rebuilt. You might wish to visit a Sunday morning church service which is conducted in Hawaiian.

The ***Waimea Foreign Church*** was built about 1859 by Reverend George Rowell. According to John Lydgate in a speech given in the early 1900s, the church was built of sandstone blocks cut from a mile or so away near the beach. They were soft when cut, but hardened when exposed to the air. They were transported by bullock-carts and secured with lime mortar. Pieces of the reef were broken off by divers and a 20-foot lime kiln pit was dug. Workers dragged lehua wood down from the mountains with teams of oxen for the woodwork used in the structure. (By the way, "foreign" in this case means English speaking!)

The ***Gulick Rowell House*** was begun in 1829 by the Reverend Peter Gulick, but was not finished until 17 years later by missionary George Rowell. This is one of the oldest surviving examples of early missionary structures in Hawaii. The 24-inch thick walls provided natural cooling. (Private residence, no public access.)

At Waimea, Highway 550 turns north and heads up to Koke'e and the Waimea Canyon. A description of this area follows. For now, we will proceed northwest along the Kaumualii Hwy, Highway 50, to Kekaha and you can travel up to Waimea Canyon by that route and then return down via Hwy. 550.

## *KEKAHA AND POLIHALE*

On a clear day from the coast near Kekaha, you can enjoy a clear view of Ni'ihau. There is another small island farther to the north called Lehua which is uninhabited. There appears to be a lower island just beyond Ni'ihau. This, however, is part of the island of Ni'ihau. Kekaha Town was built by sugar and was a typical and thriving company town for more than 100 years. Many of the plantation era buildings still remain in and around the mill. Kekaha Sugar celebrated its 100th anniversary in 1998. The Kekaha Sugar Mill is set to close in 2000, with production moving to Lihu'e.

***Kekaha Beach Park*** is a 30-acre stretch of beach with plenty of parking along the highway and restroom facilities. The weather on this part of the island is generally drier, so if you are looking for some sun, visit the western coast. Refer to the beaches chapter for more information on safety conditions for shorelines in this area.

The nearby ***Kikia'ola Harbor*** has become increasingly popular with the new regulations which have eliminated Hanalei Bay as a boat tour departure spot. The Corp of Engineers has $4.6 million set aside for renovations over the next few years.

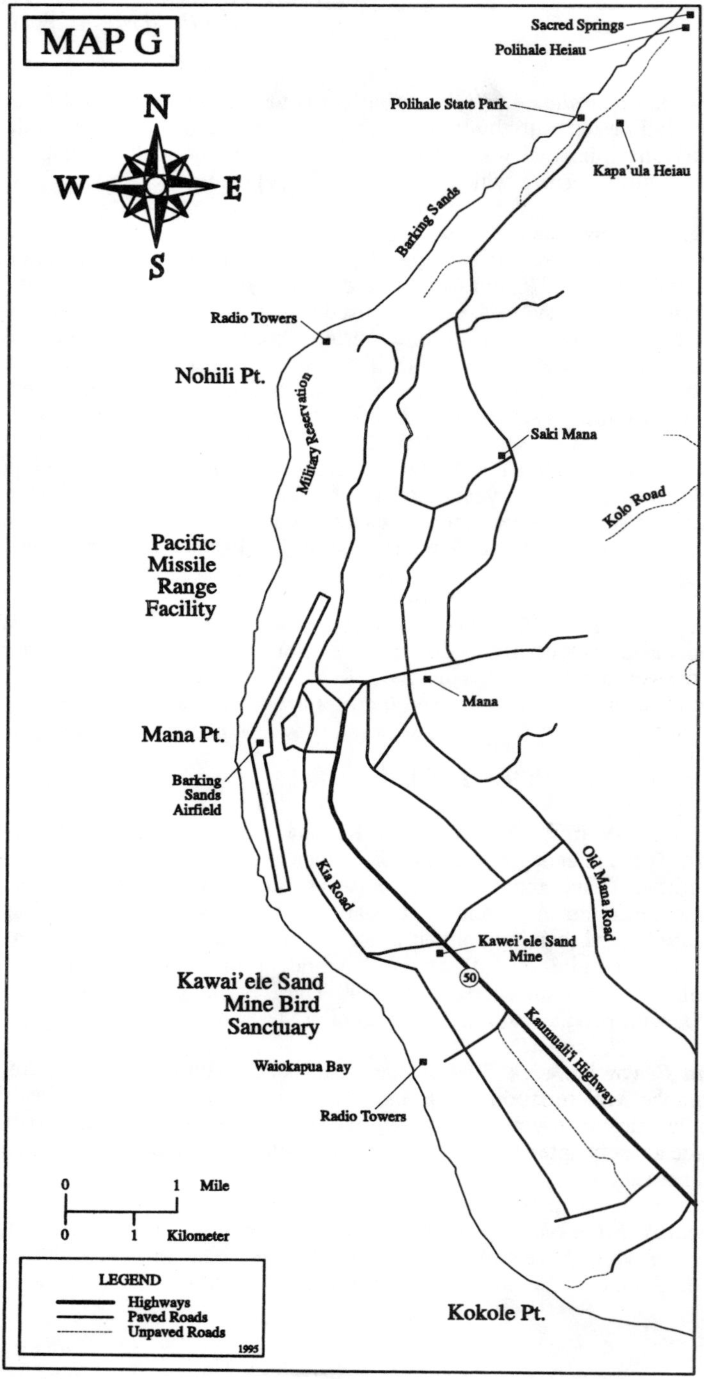
MAP G
N
S
E
W
Sacred Springs
Polihale Heiau
Polihale State Park
Kapa'ula Heiau
Barking Sands
Radio Towers
Nohili Pt.
Military Reservation
Saki Mana
Kolo Road
Pacific
Missile
Range
Facility
Mana
Mana Pt.
Barking
Sands
Airfield
Old Mana Road
Kia Road
Kawei'ele Sand
Mine
50
Kawai'ele Sand
Mine Bird
Sanctuary
Kaumuali'i Highway
Waiokapua Bay
Radio Towers
0
1
Mile
0
1
Kilometer
LEGEND
Highways
Paved Roads
Unpaved Roads
1995
Kokole Pt.

If you continue northward you will reach the area of the Barking Sands Airfield and the ***Pacific Missile Range***. This is a naval base with testing facilities which runs along the Mana shore.

A huge monkeypod tree in the road with a very unofficial sign will advise you that you are almost to Polihale. You may see some cars parked here. If you choose to stop, be careful your wheels don't become mired in the sand! Then proceed by foot over the dunes to a unique natural formation. Known as ***Queen's Pond,*** this is a lagoon protected within the reef. It can be safe for a cool dip, but only when the surf is calm. It is said in ancient times a king of Kaua'i was killed at Barking Sands, and that today the sand still groans when you rub the pieces between your hands. We tried it, maybe you will have better luck! Some say that merely walking on the dry sand will cause the same effect.

It is another few bumpy and dusty miles along the dirt road before it ends at ***Polihale State Park***. (See the beaches chapter for recreational opportunities afforded along the Mana coastline of West Kaua'i.) This beach is unsafe for any water activity, but strolling along the shoreline you should look closely to be fortunate enough to find some of the tiny shells like those that scatter the coastline of Ni'ihau.

If you plan on a visit to Koke'e, it might be a good idea to bring along that sweater, sweatshirt, or lightweight jacket you packed in your bag. The slightly higher elevation can drop the temperature down a few pleasantly cool degrees. While the weather topside may appear overcast from below the mountain, it can also blow through quickly.

Choosing either Hwy. 550 from Waimea or Hwy. 55 from Kekaha you can follow the road as it slowly winds up to ***Waimea Canyon***. We would recommend you go to Kekaha and follow Hwy. 55 from Kekaha up to Waimea Canyon and take the other, Hwy. 550, down from the canyon. This offers an opportunity to enjoy some dramatically different scenery. You might want to take this opportunity to check your gas gauge.

The Koke'e Road from Kekaha, Hwy. 55, was built in 1911, but is in fact a better road than the newer road from Waimea. It is the one used by the tour bus drivers. The Waimea Canyon Road, while newer, is much steeper. After about seven miles you will reach the sign for Waimea Canyon State Park. Another 1/2 mile and the Koke'e Rd intersects with the Waimea Canyon Rd. Just before the road mile marker 9 is the Kukui Trailhead. This is one of many trails which riddle the area and offer outstanding day hiking opportunities. Many are reached by main roads, some are accessible by smaller dirt roads. Another 2 1/2 miles and the road fork will advise you of the turn-off to either Koke'e Park or Waimea Canyon.

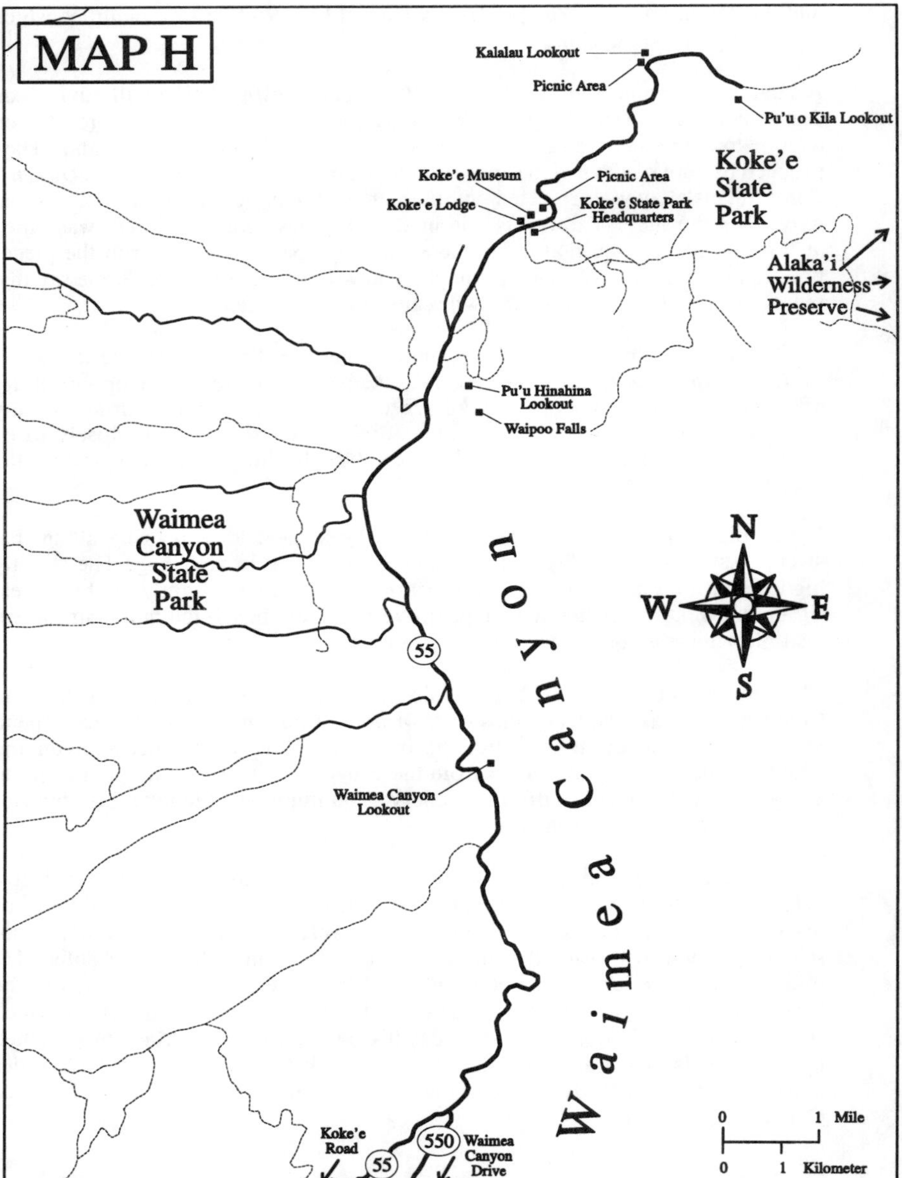
MAP H
Kalalau Lookout
Picnic Area
Pu'u o Kila Lookout
Koke'e State Park
Koke'e Museum
Picnic Area
Koke'e Lodge
Koke'e State Park Headquarters
Alaka'i Wilderness Preserve
Pu'u Hinahina Lookout
Waipoo Falls
Waimea Canyon State Park
Waimea Canyon
N
W
E
S
55
Waimea Canyon Lookout
0
1 Mile
0
1 Kilometer
Koke'e Road
55
550
Waimea Canyon Drive

***Waimea Canyon State Park*** provides unsurpassed opportunities for exploration. Follow Waimea Canyon Drive as it winds its way up 12 miles into the interior of the island, hugging the rim of the canyon for a dramatic panorama. The view of the 3,000-foot deep canyon is staggering. Hues of orange and red are splashed against the tropical green of 1,866 acres of parkland. Mark Twain aptly described this as the *"Grand Canyon of the Pacific."* Contiguous with Waimea Canyon is the Koke'e State Park.

***Waimea Canyon Lookout*** is the first of several lookouts. At an elevation of 3,120 feet, this is a stunning canyon vista. ***Puu Ka Pele Lookout*** is the next stop as you continue to climb. It offers picnic tables and another, slightly different, view of the canyon. *Puu Hinahina* is another vista, viewing out toward Ni'ihau. Near the entrance to Waimea Canyon Park is the trailhead to the ***Iliau Nature Log Trail*** at the Kukui Trail head. This is a good family hike which follows a short .3 mile trail with an overview of the canyon and the waterfall on the far side of the crater. A relative of the silversword plants found on Maui at Haleakala National Park and the Big Island of Hawai'i grows only here on Kaua'i. The *iliau* is an unusual plant which, like the silversword, blooms with a profusion of blossoms which marks the end of its life.

## *KOKE'E*

The ***Koke'e Museum*** is nestled amid one of Kaua'i's most scenic wonders. This museum, the oldest on the island, creates more than 100,000 visitors each year and is the only museum in Hawai'i open every day of the year at no charge. The Museum sponsors two annual festivals. In May, they celebrate "The Banana Poka Festival" and the "*Eo E Emalani I Alaka'i Festival*" attracts hundreds of visitors each October. The museum sponsors the Audubon Christmas Bird Count as well as an assortment of workshops and year-round interpretive programs and exhibits. You might be interested in becoming a *Hui O Laka* member. Contact the Koke'e Museum at PO Box 100, Kekaha, HI 96752. Phone (808) 335-9975, fax (808) 335-6131. And check out the Koke'e Museum's Internet homepage with hiking maps, weather report links, and more to assist in your travel planning. <www.aloha.net/~kokee/>

Adjacent to the museum is a gift store which provides a chance to purchase your own selection of books about Hawai'i's wildlife. ***Koke'e State Park*** offers 45 miles of named hiking trails. The Canyon Trail leads to the east rim of Waimea Canyon and offers a breathtaking view into its depth. The main canyon stretches for 12 miles and drops 3,000 feet. This is an easy trail for even the novice hiker, traversing 1.4 miles. Poomau Canyon Lookout Trail heads through a native rainforest and a series of Japanese plum trees. Awaawapuhi Trail leads through a forest to a 2,500-foot high vista which overlooks cliffs and the ocean. Halemanu-Koke'e Trail offers stunning views of the Napali Coast including Honopu Valley and the Valley of the Lost Tribe.

A short Nature Trail begins at Koke'e Museum and passes through a koa forest. The Alakai Wilderness Preserve encompasses the Alakai Swamp and is adjacent to Koke'e State Park. The swamp is 10 miles long and two miles wide and spans the basin of the caldera. There are pristine nature trails and a boardwalk over the boggy terrain for viewing some of Hawai'i's rarest flora and fauna. The Alakai Swamp Trail passes through bogs and rain forests to the Kilohana Lookout above Hanalei Bay. Koke'e Museum phone is (808) 335-9975.

Continue up Koke'e Road another couple of miles and you will reach the Kalalau and Pu'u o' Kila lookouts. Kalalau Beach, which lies below along the coast, is that part of the Napali which requires an eleven mile hike to reach. On a clear day, this is perhaps the most picturesque location on Kaua'i.

The valley falls below for 4,000 feet and is splashed by waterfalls. *Kaua'i, A Separate Kingdom,* as well as a tale by Jack London, portrays the saga of Ko'olau, his wife, and young son. During the days when leprosy was scourged by forcing the infected victims to be confined to Moloka'i without their family, Ko'olau fled to this valley area. Several others fled as well, but they were eventually tracked down. Ko'olau's son, Kalei, succumbed first to the disease, and later Ko'olau also died from the affliction. His wife, Piilani, buried him in the wilderness. Never infected with this tragic disease, Piilani, returned to Waimea after the death of her husband and son and remarried.

## *BEST BETS*

***Po'ipu Kai*** - several buildings on a large property with nice condo accommodations that are value priced. ***Hyatt Regency Kauai*** - a lovely, tropical resort. ***Whalers Cove*** - a more expensive condominium, but an ideal location. ***Embassy Vacation Resort at Po'ipu Point*** - spacious and elegant with all the amenities of a resort and a condominium combined. ***Kiahuna Plantation*** - Well located, this is a beautiful upscale property with plenty of amenities. ***Waimea Cottages*** - Just what you'd imagine a Hawaiian home to be. For B&B's we would recommend ***Gloria's Spouting Horn*** and ***Po'ipu Inn B&B*** - lovely, but pricey! Also ***Marjorie's Kaua'i Inn*** - a great value.

## *PRIVATE VACATION HOMES*

**HONU KAI VACATION VILLAS**
1871 Pe'e Rd., Koloa, HI 96756. (808) 742-9155. FAX (808) 742-7940. 1-800-854-8363. Email: RJR@Houkai.com Hosts Robert and Patty Rolland offer private oceanfront villas. The property includes a swimming pool and jacuzzi surrounded by a lava rock wall. Brennecke's Beach is 100 yards away. They accept Visa and Master card with a 4% processing fee. All units are non-smoking. A great south shore location! Rates are $175-500.

**MAUKALANI AT LAWA'I**
Write to: 2381 Kipuka Street, Koloa, HI 96756. 1-800-745-7414 (808) 742-1700, FAX (808) 742-7392. Email: catawalt@aloha.net

Po'ipu Beach is a 10 minute drive from this rental home. Rates are $65 per night with a 3 night minimum double occupancy. $10 per night, maximum 4 people. $35 cleaning fee. This one bedroom home is on the second floor of a two story building. A kitchen, laundry facilities and a queen sized bed in the bedroom and queen size sofa bed in the living room. Carol Ann can also assist you with a rental car or wedding photography services.

**PUA HALE AT PO'IPU BEACH**
Write to: 2381 Kipuka Street, Koloa, HI 96756. 1-800-745-7414 (808) 742-1700, FAX (808) 742-7392. Email: catawalt@aloha.net A convenient South Shore location, Po'ipu and Shipwreck beach are less than a 5 minute walk away. "Flower House" features a Japanese waterfall in a tropical garden. Eastern influence is again found in the bathroom where you can enjoy a furo (Japanese style soaking tub). The home features a queen size bed which can be isolated by sliding shoji doors. Four night minimum. Visa or Mastercard accepted for deposit only. No smoking. No children under 8 years. Your hosts are Carol Ann Davis and Walter Briant. *$120 per night. Weekly rate $735 with additional nights $105. Price is for double occupancy, additional persons $10 per day, maximum 4 persons. $40 cleaning fee.*

## *BED & BREAKFAST*

**BAMBOO JUNGLE HOUSE B & B**
PO Box 1301, Koloa, HI 96756. Toll-free 1-888-332-5115, (808) 332-5515. E-mail: serene2@aloha.net or Web: <www.aloha.net/~serene2/> Two to four night minimum. Cleaning fee of $10 for shorter stays. Your hosts are Doug and Judy Beane. The Jungle Room and Safari Suite have full bath with tub or shower and private entrances. *Jungle Room $75; Safari Master Suite $95. The Grass Shack studio features a mini kitchen, full bath and living room at $110.*

**CORAL BY THE SEA B & B**
PO Box 820, Waimea, HI 96796. Mainland or inter-island: 1-800-337-1084, (808) 337-1084. E-mail: Coralsea@Hawaiian.net <WWW> Hosts Fred and Sharon offer guests a fully equipped non-smoking studio in a residential area within one block of sandy beaches and a short drive to Waimea Canyon. Queen-sized bed, sitting room, private bath with shower. A comfy couch is also a sleeper sofa. B&B, in this case, goes back to the original British meaning of "Bed & Bath" (in fact a number of B&B are discontinuing breakfast, or adding it as an option for an extra fee). Bright coral on the outside, a bit dark on the inside (but it keeps it cool) *Three night minimum runs $71.50 includes tax.* (Higher rates for one or two nights.)

**GLORIA'S SPOUTING HORN B & B**
4464 Lawa'i Rd., Koloa, HI 96756 (808) 742-6995. Gloria's B&B opened their doors in June 1986. Completely renovated following Hurricane Iniki, this custom-designed beachhouse features spacious oceanfront guest rooms and Hawaiian rock baths. Each of the five units includes a telephone, TV/VCR, wet bar with sink, refrigerator and microwave, along with a coffee and popcorn maker.

One room offers a unique twig canopy bed. There are complimentary snacks and beverages,beach towels, and mats. The buffet breakfast offers fresh fruits, breads and cereal. Bob Merkle (Mr. Gloria) is a retired minister and can officiate at your wedding on the beach!

The rooms are beautifully appointed, but this lovely property is on the high end of the price spectrum for B&B accommodations. Since children are allowed only ages 14 and above, it is restrictive for families with young children. While it rates quality, we can't give it a star for value. But if you can splurge, look into this one! No charge cards. They also offer condos and apartments at other locations. Three night minimum.
*Rates are based on single or double occupancy $225 ($250 during Christmas) plus tax. Weekly discount of $150 except over Christmas.*

**HALE IKENA NUI**
Mailing address: PO Box 171, Kalaheo, HI 96741. Located at 3957 Ulualii Street in Kalaheo. (808) 332-9005. FAX (808) 332-0911. 1-800-550-0778. Email: pantone@hawaiian.net. <WWW> Hosts Dan and Patti Pantone offer a private suite featuring a full kitchen, queen bed, full size sleeper couch, private phone, washer/dryer. No charge for children 3 and under. Three day minimum.
*Rate is $80 per day for two guests $15 per additional guests. Slightly higher rates for shorter stays.*

**HALE KUA**
4896-E Kua Rd., PO Box 649, Lawa'i, HI 96765. (808) 332-8570. 1-800-440-4353. E-mail: <halekua@aloha.net> <WWW> Two units available, one located above the garage and the other is in a guest house behind the main house. Each features a queen-size bed, full bath, kitchen, queen sleeper sofa in living room. Television, telephone, and washer/dryer. Views of the ocean, Lawa'i Valley, and the mountains, including Mount Kahili. Recently opened three new units, one has 3 BR and a loft, the other is 2 BR.
*Rates $80-95*

**HAWAIIAN HILLSIDE HIDEAWAY**
5086A Puuwai Rd., Kalaheo, HI 96741. (808) 332-9721. Graceleanor Baird offers a ground floor, one bedroom, one bath unit with large living area and private entrance. Two twin beds and queen size sofa bed, mini-kitchen with microwave, compact refrigerator, toaster; TV & VCR. Continental breakfast provided at an extra charge. Non-smokers preferred. Weekly rates available.
*Double occupancy $60 per night ($15 extra person for 3 or more).*

**ISLAND HOME B&B**
1707 Kekaukia St., Koloa, HI 96756. (808) 742-2839. Two units, both with private entrances, microwaves, and compact refrigerators. No children. Swimming privileges at nearby resort pool. Your hosts are Debra van de Taeye and Larry Widhelm. *Single or double occupancy, $90 with breakfast; $75 without.*

**KALAHEO INN ★**
444 Papalina Road, Kalaheo HI 96741. Toll free 1-888-332-6023. FAX (808) 332-5242. Email: chet@aloha.net or website <www.kalaheoinn.com> Units are very clean and in a good location. Each has a kitchenette or full kitchen, TV, VCR, twin or queen beds. There is an on site laundromat. Located in downtown Kalaheo between Po'ipu and the Waimea Canyon. Four or five restaurants are within a few blocks walk. "A rare find for the budget minded vacationer." Hosts are Chet & Tish Hunt.

*Large studios $49 (2), One bedrooms $55 (2), Large 1BR $65 (4), 2 BR $75 (6).*

**KAUA'I COVE COTTAGES**
Reservations: 1-800-624-9945. (808) 742-2562. Email: info@kauaicove.com or website: <www.kauaicove.com> Located a short walk from Po'ipu beaches (or snorkel at Koloa Cove in front). The cottages each feature vaulted ceilings, complete kitchen, private patio. Rates $85 for 2 people.

**MARJORIE'S KAUA'I INN ★**
PO Box 866, Lawa'i, HI 96765. 1-800-717-8838. Call during business hours Hawai'i time 8 am-6 pm. In Hawai'i (808) 332-8838. Email: ketcher@aloha.net and check out their home page at: <http://www.planet-hawaii.com/marjorie> This classifies as an "inn" or "Bed & Bath" rather than a Bed & Breakfast since it does not include daily breakfast. The units have a mini-kitchen and on the first night you'll receive a basket with fruits, homemade banana bread, and juice in the refrigerator and coffee with coffeemakers. Each room is a mini studio apartment with a private entrance. There have been some pleasant changes. The "Sunset View" (formerly the Puka Room) has been expanded which allows for additional length plus a new lanai. The interior space allows for a queen bed plus the existing double size futon sofa bed, microwave, coffee pot, toaster, mini-refrigerator, bar sink, kitchen cabinets, cable TV, telephone, dining tables and chairs, private entrance, private bath. The new area has an open beam ceiling providing an even larger and more spacious feel. A sliding glass door and four more windows offer a fabulous view of Lawa'i Valley and the mountains. The unbelievable breathtaking panoramic view of the Lawa'i Valley is truly spectacular. There is a hot tub in a gazebo at the end of the property and that, too, overlooks the valley. Marjorie Ketcher has travel agency experience and is very knowledgeable about activities. She can assist in choosing and booking the activity that best suits the interests of her guests. Her in-room guide lists markets, area hiking opportunities, eateries and beaches. A good value with a superb view. The view along with Marjorie's personal service makes guests return year after year. *Marjorie's Valley View $88; Tradewind $78; Sunset View Room $88 (2).*

**OLD KOLOA HOUSE**
3327 Waikomo Road, Koloa, HI 96756. (808) 742-2099. Email: keanel@webtv.net or website: www.aloha.net/~keane Your hosts Bob & Linda Keane welcome you to their 100-year-old plantation bungalow, once owned by McBryde Sugar Plantation. The one unit B&B is located two miles from Po'ipu Beach and a short walk to old Koloa town. It features a queen bed, microwave, compact refrigerator, private entrance, and bath. Continental breakfast the first morning in your room. *Two night minimum, $78 per day.*

**PO'IPU BED & BREAKFAST INN**
2720 Hoonani Rd., Koloa, HI 96756. (808) 742-1146 or FAX (808) 742-6843, 1-800-22-POIPU. This B&B includes four bed and breakfast units located in this 1933 plantation inn. All units have private baths, most with whirlpool tub and separate shower, king bed, cable TV and VCR, wicker and pine antiques. Some units have a kitchenette or the option of twin beds. A honeymoon suite features an ocean view, private lanai and whirlpool tub for two plus air conditioning. Handicapped accessible room available. Unfortunately, it appears to have encountered some disrepair over the last months. We understand it is being sold, and hope the new owners will restore it to its former self. We will have to see if the collection of carousel horses will stay! *Prices run $120-$195.*

**SOUTH SHORE VISTA**
4400 Kai Ikena Drive, Kalaheo, HI 96741 (808) 332-9339 or (808) 332-9201, FAX (808) 332-7771 or E-mail: <vista@aloha.net> Located on the hillside of Kalaheo, this one-bedroom apartment has an ocean view and is located only two blocks from a public golf course and park. The unit features a queen-size bed, living area with full-size fold out couch, kitchenette with microwave, oven and utensils, a private deck, and separate entrance. Coffee, tea, and oatmeal provided in the unit. Breakfast provisions stocked in the kitchen for an extra fee. Minimum stay 3 nights. *Room rates run: $59-69*

**(THE) SUGAR MILL COTTAGES**
Located in the Po'ipu Kai Resort on the greenbelt. (808) 742-9369, fax (808) 742-6432 or toll free reservations through the Kalaheo Inn 1-888-332-6023. Website is <www.sugarmillaccomodationspoipu.com> Easy walk to Po'ipu Beach or Shipwreck Beach. On site amenities include a pool, hot tub, and tennis courts. Brand new building (opened end of 1999) in a very good location (the Koloa bypass goes straight through to their street) which adds up to a very good value. Studios $75 (2), One bedroom $90 (4)

**VICTORIA PLACE**
3459 Lawailoa Lane, PO Box 930, Lawa'i, HI 96765. (808) 332-9300. FAX (808) 332-9465. Website: <hshawaii.com/kvp/victoria> Three guest rooms and a studio apartment offer a choice of B & B options. The three main rooms are all charming and look out onto the pool deck. The single room is a little smaller. The sitting area is pleasant with plenty of books and lots of helpful information on touring and dining on Kaua'i. Hostess Edee Seymour is very knowledgeable and eager to share information about the island. No children under age 15.

*Raindrop Room, double bed, single occupancy only $60; Calla Lily Room with queen bed $80; Shell Room with twin beds or king-size is handicapped accessible $80. "Victoria's Other Secret" is a studio apartment with private entrance, king bed and day bed, kitchen $100. Add $10 per room during holiday season (mid-December to mid-January. Additional $15 for one night only.*

## *INEXPENSIVE*

**KOKE'E LODGE CABINS**
PO Box 819, Waimea, HI 96796 (808) 335-6061. Located at an elevation of 3,600 feet the lodge is located in Hawai'i's 4,345 acre Koke'e State Park. A dozen housekeeping cabins furnished with refrigerators, stoves, hot showers, cooking and eating utensils, linens, towels, blankets, and pillows. Size of units vary from one large room which sleeps three, to two-bedroom cabins that sleep seven. Maximum stay is five days and pets are not permitted. Full payment is required for confirmation. *$35-$45 per cabin.*

**KOLOA LANDING COTTAGES**
2704-B Hoonani Rd., Koloa, HI 96756. 1-800-779-8773, (808) 742-1470 or (808) 332-6326. FAX (808) 332-9584. <WWW> Email: dolfin@aloha.net The cottages are set in a tropical garden across the street from the beach. All cottages and studios include microwave, telephone, color cable TV, and full kitchens. Coin operated laundry facilities are on premises. Studios have queen bed. Cottages include one queen bed and one set of twins. The studios can accommodate 2 persons, the cottages sleep four people, with room for 2 extra persons at $10 each sleeping on futons.
*Large cottage $110; Cottages 1-2 persons $95; 3-4 persons $95; studio 1-2 persons $60. Add one time cleaning fee $20-60.*

**PO'IPU PLANTATION**
1792 Pe'e Rd., Koloa, HI 96756. (808) 742-6757, 1-800-634-0263. FAX (808) 742-8681. Visit their website at <www.poipubeach.com> or Email them at: plantation@poipubeach.com

They offer Bed & Breakfast rooms with private bath, lanai and ocean view plus one and two bedroom units. Air conditioned. Laundry room. Outdoor BBQ area and hot tub. Prices are for single or double occupancy. Minimum 2 day stay in condo units, no minimum in B&B. Maximum 3 persons in B&B or 1 BR units, and maximum five persons in 2 BR units.
*B&B Units: $85. 1 BR g.v. from $90; 1 BR lower o.v. from $100; 1 BR upper o.v. from $105 2 BR lower o.v. from $120; 2 BR upper o.v. from $130*

**PRINCE KUHIO**
Mailing address: PO Box 3284, Lihu'e, HI 96766. Property located at: 5061 Lawa'i Rd. RENTAL AGENTS: Po'ipu Connection Realty 1-800-742-2260. R&R 1-800-367-8022. Prosser Realty 1-800-767-4707. Kaua'i Vacation Rentals 1-800-367-5025, Maui & All Islands 1-800-663-6962. Studio, one and two bedroom units. All have microwave ovens, full-size refrigerators, cable TV, and telephones. Guest laundry facility on the ground floor. BBQ, pool. Located next to Prince Kuhio Park in Lawa'i area of Po'ipu. *Studio $70-90; 1 BR $80-110; Two BR penthouse $135/115.*

## *MODERATE*

**ALIHI LANI** ★
2564 Hoonani Rd., Po'ipu, HI 96756. Located at Po'ipu Beach. RENTAL AGENT: Po'ipu Connection 1-800-742-2260, (808) 742-2233. This property has a total of six units. These condos are spacious with full kitchen plus full-size washers and dryers. Outside is a private swimming pool and sunning deck. This attractive property is located on a rocky oceanfront, but it is a short and pleasant walk down to Po'ipu Beach. With only six units in this property, you won't find crowds at the pool!
*Po'ipu Connection Realty has units which require 5 night minimum, plus $75 outcleaning, rate $185-250.*

**GARDEN ISLAND SUNSET VACATION RENTALS**
RENTAL AGENT: Kaua'i Vacation Rentals, 1-800-367-5025. Oceanfront, this 4-plex offers wonderful sunsets and views of Ni'ihau. A short walk to Waimea Town. All units are 2 BR, 1 BTH, and sleep 4.
*Kaua'i Vacation Rental Rates: $650 weekly*

**GARDEN ISLE COTTAGES-OCEANFRONT**
2666 Puuholo Rd., Koloa, HI 96756. 1-800-742-6711. (808) 332-9201. <WWW> These sea cliff cottages are located on a small ocean inlet where the Waikomo Stream meets the ocean overlooking historic Koloa Landing. These are ocean view units. The Hale Waipahu cottages feature open beamed ceilings. A queen bed on the upper main floor and twins on the lower. Four nights deposit required. Also Bed & Breakfast units are available. Extra persons $10.
*Sea Cliff Cottages: studio, one and two bedroom $95-199.*
*Hale Waipahu: Large studio $87-92; Suites $148-197.*

**HALE HOKU**
4534 Lawa'i Rd., Koloa, HI 96756. Phone or FAX (808) 742-1509. This two bedroom, two bathroom unit provides a full kitchen, washer/dryer, cable TV. Outdoor pool, outdoor shower, and BBQ. Minimum 10 day stay during high season. Four person occupancy; additional $15 for fifth guest.
*2 BR 2 BTH $225/200.*

**KUHIO SHORES**
5050 Lawa'i Beach Rd., Koloa, HI 96756. Located near Prince Kuhio Park. RENTAL AGENTS: R&R (800) 367-8022. Prosser Realty 1-800-767-4707 rents a 1 BR oceanfront condominium. Garden Island Rentals 1-800-247-5599.
*Garden Island rents a 1 BR and 2 BR oceanfronts $100-115 plus cleaning fee.*

**LAWA'I BEACH RESORT**
5017 Lawa'i Rd., Koloa, HI 96756. (808) 742-9581. FAX (808) 742-7981. RENTAL AGENTS: Grantham 1-800-325-5701. Maui & All Islands 1-800-663-6962. Suite Paradise 1-800-367-8020. This property has turned into timeshare, but a few units are still in the vacation rental program. Cable TV with HBO, private phone, washer/dryer. Pool, jacuzzi, BBQ grill, limited maid service. Coin-op laundry. Telephones.
*Grantham rates: 1 BR o.f. $249/224*

**MAKAHUENA**

Located in Po'ipu. Mailing address: 1661 Pe'e Rd., Koloa, HI 96756. (808) 742-2482. RENTAL AGENTS: Castle Resorts 1-800-367-5004. Grantham Resorts 1-800-325-5701. R&R 1-800-367-8022. Maui & All Islands 1-800-663-6962. Po'ipu Connection Realty 1-800-742-2260. Seventy-nine condominiums. Resort includes pool, tennis court, jacuzzi, and BBQ area. We stayed in a deluxe 2 BR 2 BTH operated by Po'ipu Connection. It was really oceanfront, with a blowhole right outside our lanai! It was a pleasure to open the double doors into the entranceway and be greeted by such a spacious, luxurious unit. The size was enhanced by wall mirrors and high cathedral ceilings and it seemed "huge" but once we settled in, found it to be comfortable and intimate. The furniture was attractive with warm shades made tropical with lots of cane and bamboo. The bedrooms had shoji (Japanese screen) doors, there were ceiling fans throughout, programmed lighting and A/C controls, wet bar, dishwasher, washer/dryer, microwave, and plenty of dishes and utensils. The unit was clean and fresh with new furniture and nice soft carpet. All units have ceiling fans, full kitchens, and washer/dryer.

*Po'ipu Connection Rates: 2 BR 2BTH deluxe oceanfront $210*
*Grantham Rates: 1 BR distant $169/139; 2 BR distant $87/161;*
*3 BR distant $194/164; 2 BR oceanfront $225/194; 2 BR superior $288/238;*
*Castle Resorts: 1 BR $173-221/146-194; 2 BR $183-243/156-216;*
*3 BR $264-297/286-324*

**NIHI KAI VILLAS**

Located up the hill from Brennecke's Beach. 1-800-325-5701. (808) 642-1412. RENTAL AGENTS: Prosser 1-800-767-4707. Grantham Resorts 1-800-325-5701 (they currently manage front office.) Maui & All Islands 1-800-663-6962. R&R 1-800-367-8022. Suite Paradise 1-800-367-8020. Po'ipu Connection Realty 1-800-742-2260. Garden Island Rentals 1-800-247-5599. Seventy units with one, two and three bedroom. Phones, TV, microwave, kitchens, washer/dryer. Many oceanview. Ocean front swimming pool and tennis courts. Nearby beach is popular for body surfing.

*Garden Island Rates: 1 BR $125 / 2 BR 2 BTH $135 plus cleaning fees*
*Suite Paradise Rates: For minimum 7 day stay, 2BR 2 BTH unit $122-150*
*Rates quoted are from Grantham:*
*1 BR g.v. $161-186/129-149; 1 BR o.v. $186-211/$149-169*
*2 BR g.v. $174-199/139-159; 2 BR o.v. $199-224/159-179;*
*2 BR ocean superior $211-244/169-195*
*3 BR Oceanfront $313-344/250-275*

**PO'IPU CRATER**

2330 Ho'ohu Rd., (808) 742-7260. RENTAL AGENTS: R&R 1-800-367-8022. Po'ipu Connection Realty 1-800-742-2260. Maui & All Islands 1-800-663-6962. Suite Paradise 1-800-367-8020. Grantham Resorts 1-800-325-5701. Thirty condominiums in a garden setting. Each two bedroom, two bath bungalow is furnished with telephone, cable TV, VCR, microwave, washer and dryer, plus full kitchen. Located near Brennecke's Beach. Resort features tennis, swimming pool, sauna, BBQ.

*Grantham: 2 BR 2 BTH garden $136/124*
*Suite Paradise: 2 BR 2 BTH garden $97-118 with minimum of 7 day stay (higher rates for shorter stays) R&R Realty: 2 BR 2 BTH $75-90*

**(ASTON AT) PO'IPU KAI**
1941 Po'ipu Rd., Koloa, HI 96756 (808) 742-6464. RENTAL AGENTS: Managed by Aston Resorts 1-800-922-7866. Suite Paradise 1-800-367-8020. Maui & All Islands 1-800-663-6962. R&R 1-800-367-8022. Prosser 1-800-767-4707. Garden Island Rentals 1-80-247-5599. Suite Paradise 1-800-367-8020. Po'ipu Connection Realty 1-800-742-2260. Grantham Resorts 1-800-325-5701. Maui & All 1-800-663-6962. Pleasant Hawaiian Holidays 1-800-242-9244. Three hundred and fifty condominium units. Seven resorts within a master resort, like a sprawling apartment complex made up of individual buildings -- each with its own Hawaiian name. The privately owned condominiums include Po'ipu Sands, Manualoha, Makanui, Kahala, and The Regency. Lanai Villas and Bayview offer private homes. The buildings and units are all different, but equal in stature and category of accommodations. Two-story townhouses are stylish and modern with a two bedrooms and two bathrooms on the lower (entry level) floor. Roomy bathrooms with luxury shower and tub. Living room, full kitchen and 1/2 bath upstairs. High ceilings, ceiling fans, wet bar, good assortment of small appliances and kitchen utensils. W/D with handy starter supply of detergent, complimentary HBO, private phone. Interior decoration varies with each owner, but island-style furniture is generally very attractive and comfortable. Po'ipu Kai shares Shipwreck Beach with the Hyatt and fronts Po'ipu Beach Park at the other end of the property. A great location for beach aficionados! Shop around, prices vary greatly depending on rental agent (as can quality of the unit.) Prices may reflect location in resort or amenities such as maid service.
*Suite Paradise manages twice as many units as the management agency, Aston, so for best selection check with them first, then compare with Aston rates!*

*Inquire with Aston about special packages, promotionals or Island Hopper Discounts. Aston Rates:*
*1 BR 1 BTH $190-260/235-305;*
*2 BR 2 BTH $260-320/300-375, 2 BR 2 BTH o.f. $350-400/320-370.*

**PO'IPU KAPILI** ★
2221 Kapili Rd., Koloa, HI 96756. ON SITE RENTAL AGENT: Po'ipu Ocean View Resorts (same address) (808) 742-6449, 1-800-443-7714, FAX (808) 742-9162, Email: aloha@poipukapili.com and Website is found at <www.poipukapili.com>

Sixty 1 and 2 bedroom condominiums in seven low-rise oceanfront buildings. The property features a traditional Hawaiian plantation architecture located in the Po'ipu Beach resort community. Kitchens fully equipped including microwave ovens. One bedroom units are 1,200 sq. ft., two bedroom units are 1,800 sq. ft. Laundry facilities are available on the property, but two bedroom units have their own washer and dryer. Oceanview pool, and complimentary tennis courts lighted for night play. The property is very private and the attractive and well cared for grounds add to the appeal. As nice as some other units costing much more. Room and car packages are available. (Christmas holiday rates are higher than the high season rates which follow.)

*1 BR o.v. $195/180; 1 BR o.v. dlx $210/195; 2 BR o.v. $260/245;*
*2 BR o.v. dlx $285/270; 2 BR superior $305/290; Penthouse $400/375.*

**PO'IPU MAKAI**
1677 Pe'e, Po'ipu, HI 96756. Small swimming pool. Located overlooking ocean. RENTAL AGENTS: Prosser 1-800-767-4707. Grantham Resorts 1-800-325-5701. Maui & All 1-800-663-6962. Kaua'i Vacation Rentals 1-800-367-5025. Po'ipu Connection Realty 1-800-742-2260. 15 units. Each unit fronts the ocean. *Depending on the rental agent and unit prices vary greatly! Po'ipu Connection Rates: 2 BR 2 BTH $110-155, 3 BR 2 BTH $140-170.*

**PO'IPU PALMS**
1697 Pe'e Rd., at Po'ipu Beach. (808) 245-4711. RENTAL AGENTS: R&R 1-800-367-8022. Prosser Realty 1-800-767-4707. Po'ipu Connection 1-800-742-2260. Maui & All 1-800-663-6962. There are 12 units in this complex which are located oceanfront. Attractive, homey apartments with two small bedrooms and two baths. The pool and pool deck have been refurbished and the exterior has been freshly painted.
*2 BR 2 BTH $110-$155*

**SUNSET KAHILI**
1763 Pe'e Road, Koloa, HI 96756. 1-800-82-POIPU, (808) 742-7434. RENTAL AGENT: Maui & All 1-800-663-6962. There are 36 condominiums in a five story building. Pool. Full kitchens, television, telephones, ceiling fans, washer/dryer, lanais, and swimming pool. One block to Brennecke's Beach.
*1 BR $110-115/100-120; 2 BR $145-155/140-150*

**WAIKOMO STREAM VILLAS**
Located in Po'ipu. RENTAL AGENTS: Grantham Resorts 1-800-325-5701. Maui & All Islands 1-800-663-6962. Prosser 1-800-767-4707. Sixty 1 and 2 bedroom units in tropical setting. Units have private lanais and are equipped with kitchen telephone, cable TV, VCR, microwave, washer and dryer. Free tennis, BBQ area and an adult and children's swimming pool are amenities.
*1 BR 1 BTH g.v. $124/11 (1-4); 2 BR 2 BTH g.v. $149/136 (1-6)*

**WAIMEA PLANTATION COTTAGES**
PO Box 367, Waimea, HI 96796. (808) 338-1625. 1-800-9-WAIMEA.
RENTAL AGENTS: Managed by Aston Properties 1-800-922-7866. Maui & All Islands 1-800-663-69692. Visa and Mastercard accepted. Each of their cottages, originally built between 1880 and 1950 to house plantation employees, has been fully restored and updated. Located in a lovely grove of palms, these individual houses are just what you'd expect a Hawaiian home to be. There are forty-seven cottages spread among 27 acres.

Their property information sheet includes the following history: "In 1884, Hans Peter Fayé, a Norwegian engineer and farmer, secured a lease from Kalakaua, King of Hawai'i, for about 200 acres of Mana swamp land, where he successfully grew sugar cane. He and nearby planters combined their lands to form the Kekaha Sugar Company in 1898, one of Hawai'i's most profitable cane producers. By 1910, W.P. Fayé, Limited had privately purchased the neighboring Waimea Sugar Mill Company. Today, Fayé's descendants manage Waimea Sugar Mill lands as Kiki'aola Land Company, Ltd."

The Alan E. Fayé Manager's Estate is a two story house circa 1900. This five bedroom home is 4,000 sq. ft. H.P. Fayé's first home, originally in Mana, 20 miles away, was relocated to the entryway where it now serves as the front desk. The property is divided into several areas: Seaside, Historic Mill Camp, Hanawai Courtyard, and Coconut Grove. They also have a 1916 two story beach house and cottage located on the shore of Hanalei Bay available for rent. They now have a Waimea Sugar Mill Camp Museum and Plantation Lifestyles Walking Tour. Reservations are required for this tour which is limited to 12 people. Offered Tuesdays and Saturdays at 9 am. Cost is $6 adults, $5 seniors 65 and older, and children 12 and under are $3. Weekly maid service, color cable TV, telephones, laundry facilities, complimentary tennis, swimming pool. New amenities include a recreation room featuring a large screen television, lounge area, video games, and a gift shop which includes a small museum with Hawaiian arts and crafts and Kaua'i made items.

These units are full of history -- looking at the tiny doors, old fashioned dressers and end tables, and rattan furniture, you can actually imagine what it would have been like to be a plantation worker coming in the back door and putting your "lunch tin" on the oil cloth on top of the tiny table in the quaint kitchen. But the plumbing has been modernized and though the bathrooms are a bit small, they have a great walk-in tiled shower with plenty of room. The lighting fixtures are new, but have an old look. A/C, ceiling fans. tv, stereo, coffee maker and starter packet of coffee. Pool area is spacious and completely open and overlooks the ocean. (It can be noisy what with the gravel driveways, crowing roosters, and squeaky floor boards, but you expect that in an older building and it just adds to the ambiance!)

*1 Bedroom/1 bath cottage with kitchen (2): Grove view $180/160; Superior grove view $190/170; Superior oceanfront $210/190 -- 2 BR/1 bath cottage with kitchen (4): Grove view $235/210; superior oceanfront $270/250 -- 2 bedroom/2 bath cottage with kitchen (4): Superior grove view $245/220 -- 3 bedroom/2 bath cottage with kitchen (5): Superior grove view $270/245; Superior oceanfront $300/270 -- 4 bedroom/3 bath cottage with kitchen (8): Partial ocean view $315/290 -- 5 bedroom/4 bath cottage with kitchen (9): Oceanfront $465/430*

## *EXPENSIVE*

**EMBASSY VACATION RESORT - PO'IPU POINT ★**
1613 Pe'e Rd., Koloa, HI 96756. (808) 742-1888. Managed by Marc Resorts. Reservations: Marc Resorts Hawai'i 1-800-535-0085, toll free FAX 1-800-633-5085, local (808) 922-9700. OTHER AGENTS: Maui & All Islands 1-800-663-6962. Pleasant Hawaiian Holidays 1-800-242-9244. They have 218 units. Some units are timeshare. This is another very pleasant luxury property with architectural style like that of the Moana Hotel on O'ahu. The decor is reminiscent of an English country estate with dark greens accented by antique floral patterns. The bathrooms are spacious with big showers and deep tubs. The units have a full kitchen with washer/dryer, microwave and dishwasher. Rooms have stereos, TVs, VCRs and there is enough game software to keep the kids happy!

Nightly two-hour manager's cocktail party includes beverages and pupus. Coffee in rooms with complimentary breakfast in the Club Room by the pool. Breakfast includes assorted juices, fresh fruit, and breads, but be prepared for the activity talk!! The landscaped pool area and whirlpool are surrounded by sand (that is similar to aquarium gravel) with lawn chairs around the border. One bedroom suites have a king bed and sleeper sofa. The two-bedroom suites have a king bed and two twin beds plus a sleeper sofa in the living room. Health Club features workout equipment, steam and sauna baths. Toddler pool and a nice touch are the many sand toys available for the use of those little guests. Check out the volcanic lava flow out on the beachfront and see the family of green turtles that frolic in the surf. Great amenities that are sure to enhance your vacation! Also Pleasant Holidays and Maui & All Islands all offer some special package rates and free night discounts.
*Marc Resort Year Round Rates: 1 BR g.v. (max 4) $299; 1 BR partial o.v. $340; 1 BR o.v. $385; 1 BR o.f. $450. 2 BR g.v. (max.6) $350; 2 BR partial o.v. $425; 2 BR o.v. $490; 2 BR o.f. $565. Presidential 3 BR 3 1/2 BTH w/ kitchen $1,000.*

**HYATT REGENCY KAUA'I RESORT & SPA ★ (HOTEL)**
1571 Po'ipu Rd., Koloa, HI 96756. (808) 742-1234, FAX (808) 742-1557. Reservations 1-800-233-1234. OTHER RENTAL AGENTS: Pleasant Hawaiian Holidays 1-800-242-9244. Visit the Hyatt Regency website at: <www.kauai-hyatt.com> This Hyatt, while not on as grand a scale as some other Hawai'i Hyatt properties, still has a grand feeling. This property is located on fifty oceanfront acres in the Po'ipu Beach District. The property opened in November 1990. The classic traditional Hawaiian architecture is reminiscent of the 1920s and 1930s. It is very open and elegant, with a regal, Hawaiiana look. Even during high occupancy, this resort doesn't feel crowded. A pleasant surprise are the pools, which are heated. With two swimming pools, three jacuzzis, and another "action" pool with waterfalls, slides, water volleyball, a children's area, and five acres of meandering saltwater swimming lagoons featuring islands, each with its own landscaping -- well, you may decide to never leave the property while visiting Kaua'i. Four tennis courts with pro shop and tennis professional are on the property as well. The Dock offers poolside coffee, beverages, snacks, and light meals. The Seaview Terrace has a comfortable, living room feel, very open and airy with a beautiful view.

The Stevenson's Library is a cruise ship-type bar area, a combination gaming room (complete with pool, backgammon, chess, and more), library, and bar, although very un bar-like. The Ilima Terrace embraces the true Hawaiiana feeling, serving breakfast, lunch, Sunday brunch, and dinner in an open-air arrangement with plenty of foliage and koi filled lagoons. Tidepools restaurant is housed under a thatched roof surrounded by a lagoon island. Dondero's is the fine dining Italian restaurant. The Po'ipu Bay Bar & Grill (in the golf course clubhouse) is now part of the Hyatt.

While the beachfront is pleasant, the winds and surf can come up and make it unsafe for swimming. The Hyatt does post flags advising people of the ocean safety. The guest rooms are light and bright with plantation-style furnishings. As with many Hyatt properties, they offer the Regency Club which are special floors offering special guest amenities such as complimentary breakfast, beverage service, and late afternoon hors d'oeuvres. While damaged from Hurricane Iniki, their restoration was completed and the resort reopened in seven months. The resort offers the ANARA Spa to hotel and non-hotel guests. Salon facilities, exercise room, aerobic and yoga classes, as well as an array of wonderful facial and body treatments can certainly be a memorable part of your Kaua'i vacation holiday! Highly recommended by these authors! See Spas/Fitness Centers in the recreation chapter for more information.

The Hyatt's Wedding department offers extensive wedding services. The wedding coordinator can provide you with an informative list of "10 Helpful Tips for Getting Married on Kaua'i" to help you plan your wedding before you leave home. Unusual and romantic, the resort will even arrange to order a replica of an award-winning Hawaiian bridal gown (*holoku*) for the bride-to-be. The Victorian-styled Hawaiian holoku wedding dress was designed by Maile Jean Amorin, a replica of her grandmother's wedding gown. Wedding packages range from $980 - $1,750. Vow renewal packages start at $730.

The Hyatt Regency Kaua'i has developed an innovative Hawaiian program that is free to the general public. Activities conducted by the Kaua'i Historical Society include the Archaeology and Dune Walk along the 500 yard white sand beach fronting the resort and "Talk Story" sessions which focus on the lore and legends of Kaua'i. Leilani Bond, the Hyatt's *kumu* (respected teacher) oversees the Hawaiiana program. She and the 250 students of her hula halau share their knowledge of Hawaiian culture. Traditional arts and crafts are offered Monday through Friday and include poi pounding demonstrations, modern hula instruction, quilting demonstrations, flower lei-making, and even ukulele lessons. Traditional Hawaiian music is featured each evening in the Seaview Terrace from 6-8 pm. A torch lighting ceremony (accompanied by chanting and traditional hula) is a part of the evening guest entertainment four nights each week. A weekly schedule of the resort's Hawaiian program activities is available at the concierge desk.

Room rates are single/double occupancy. No charge for children 18 and under when sharing their parents room using existing bed space. For additional persons 19 and older, $30 charge per night; $50 per night for the Regency Club. Maximum four adults or two adults and two children per room.

*Hyatt Guest Accommodations: Garden $310; Mountain $340; Lagoon $375; Partial Ocean $415; Deluxe Ocean $455; Regency Club $520*

*Hyatt Suites: Ocean $785; Regency Club Ocean $885; Deluxe $1,250; Regency Club Deluxe $1,350; Presidential $2950.*

**KIAHUNA PLANTATION ★**
Located in Po'ipu. Mailing address: 2253 Po'ipu Rd., Koloa, HI 96756. 1-800-367-7052 from the U.S. and Canada, (808) 742-6411, FAX (808) 742-1698. RENTAL AGENT: Outrigger Hotels & Resorts manages part of the property and Castle the other part ... confusing! The reservation number for Outrigger is 1-800-OUTRIGGER. Castle Resorts 1-800-367-5004. OTHER RENTAL AGENTS: Maui & All 1-800-663-6962. Suite Paradise 1-800-367-8020. Pleasant Hawaiian Holidays 1-800-242-9244. Kiahuna is the largest resort condominium on Kaua'i with 333 units in two and three story buildings and situated on 35-acres of lush gardens and expansive lawns which were once part of Hawai'is first sugar cane plantation. The historic manor house was originally the home of the plantation manager and now is home to Piatti's restaurant.

This is what might be called "Classy Hawaiian." The rooms are very attractively decorated and have the feel of a comfortable beach home. They have high ceilings and are nicely furnished with wicker and wood with the bedroom set off in a cozy nook of its own. The kitchens have coffee makings and a microwave with complimentary microwave popcorn. The property has plenty of amenities as well, the Kiahuna Keiki Club, crafts and Hawaiian activities, and free tours of the grounds. The comforts of a condo and the amenities and convenience of a hotel earn this property a star. One and two bedroom units have various garden view, ocean view, and oceanfront categories. All units include living room and dining room, private lanai, fully equipped kitchen, color TV, video tape player, and ceiling fans. Daily maid service, laundry facilities, complimentary beach chairs and towels, gas BBQs. Pool and ten tennis courts. Free tours available of the incredible cactus in their Moir Gardens and the newer Hawaiian Gardens that are located on this resort property. Excellent location on Po'ipu Beach and even more family-friendly with their Keiki Klub Summer Program! Offered seasonally during busier travel periods at Christmas, Easter, and all summer long, the program is open to children ages 5-12 years. Kids are kept busy learning about Hawaiian culture through lei-making, 'ukulele lessons, hula dancing, and story telling. Other activities include arts & crafts, beach walks, and lagoon fishing. The program is $30 per child for a full day session and $15 for a half-day session. Lunch and afternoon snack are included in the full-day session charge.
*Castle Resorts:*
*1 BR g.v. $175-190; o.v. $310; o.f. $420*
*2 BR g.v. $330-400; o.v. $470; o.f. $635*

*Outrigger:*
*1 BR g.v. $175; royal g.v. $190; partial o.v. $225; o.v. $295; o.f. $400*
*2 BR g.v. $315; royal g.v. $345; partial o.v. $375; o.v. $450*

*Suite Paradise: 1BR 1 BTH garden view minimum stay 7 days $130-158. Shorter stays are more expensive.*

**PO'IPU SHORES**

1775 Pe'e Road, Koloa, HI 96756. 1-800-869-7959, (808) 742-7700. Managed by Castle Resorts. RENTAL AGENT: Castle Resorts (808) 591-2235, FAX 1-800-477-2329, 1-800-367-5004. Maui & All Islands 1-800-663-6962. Thirty-three oceanfront condominiums one, two, and three bedrooms. All suites feature fully-equipped kitchens, color TV, washer/dryer and private lanai. Both the living room and bedroom have oceanviews. The units are more appealing inside than out, with light furniture and walls and attractive lighting. Wood and marble kitchens are fully equipped with microwaves and plenty of counter space. Many of the privately owned units are equipped with VCR's, paperbacks, and even CDs. There is a raised deck area surrounding the pool and a club room complete with kitchen plus magazines and games. The older elevators tended to make a bit of noise, but happily, it was drowned out by the crashing of the waves. While most of the accessible parking area fills up quickly, it is a nice enough property, centrally located and a good value in this price range.
*Castle Resorts rates:*
*1 BR o.f. $2358/207; 2 BR o.f. or dlx o.f. $280-297/257-291;*
*3 BR o.f. $323/287; Penthouse 2 BR 2 BTH oceanfront Suite $383/355*

**SHERATON KAUA'I RESORT**

2440 Ho'onani Road, Koloa, HI 96756. (808) 742-1661. FAX (808) 742-9777. SheratonReservations: 1-800-782-9488. Website: <www.sheraton-hawaii.com>

The Sheraton Kaua'i Resort began welcoming back guests to Po'ipu in early 1998. The resort is situated on 20 acres of oceanfront gardens adjacent to Kaua'i's popular Po'ipu Beach. The resort comprises 413 air-conditioned rooms (including 14 suites) and required five years and $40 million to complete. Three wings, each no higher than four stories, provide guests with ocean vistas and tropical gardens with koi-filled ponds. The Garden Wing is located across the street. The resort's artwork and interiors showcase the traditions of Hawaiian culture and diversity of the island. Guest rooms are decorated in natural earth tones and the rooms' furnishings and fabrics use Hawaiian kapa (bark cloth), lei and floral motifs. The property features guest services and facilities including two swimming pools, massage and fitness center, tennis courts, beach activities booth with rental equipment and instruction, and the Keiki Aloha Club children's center. Two swimming pools are available for guest use, one oceanside with pool slide and two children's pools and a whirlpool. The oceanfront pool and surrounding area feature tropical landscaping and they have done a particularly nice job restoring the surroundings to their natural, simple state of ocean and sand rather than trying to improve on nature and add a lot of complicated, man-made landscaping. The koi ponds, tropical gardens, and waterfalls enhance, rather than detract from the natural landscape. In-room amenities include coffee and coffee maker, mini-refrigerator, complimentary safe, hair dryer, color TV with cable, in-room movies, Sony Play Station and video checkout. They have a daily selection of activities including a massage & skincare center plus full service salon at "Stylists," fitness center and beach activities center at the beachfront pool. Tryout scuba with a free lesson offered twice daily. Hawaiian Arts Classes can be attended in the Garden Lobby (reservations required) and include lei making or hula dancing lessons. Their Hawaiian Cultural Court features displays and demonstrations daily in the Garden Lobby.

The Sheraton Kaua'i Resort entertains young guests with their Keiki Aloha Children's Program. Activities range from lei making and other Hawaiian arts & crafts to kite flying and ukulele lessons. The program is available year round. Price is $45 for a full day of play, $25 for half day. (808) 742-4016.

Guests can enjoy Shells, the resort's signature dining room which hugs Po'ipu Beach and serves breakfast,lunch and dinner. Lighter fare and a panoramic ocean vista (with live local entertainment evenings) are offered at The Point, which has both indoor and outdoor seating. A dramatic tile mural of a canoe paddler carving a path across a cresting wave welcomes guests to this casual dining spot. (Great for sunsets and one of the "happening" nightlife locations) Overlooking tropical gardens and carp-filled pools is Naniwa, a Japanese dinner restaurant which is designed to resemble a traditional Japanese Inn. They serve dinner daily. The Oasis Bar & Grill and The Garden Terrace (the resort's poolside restaurants) serve sandwiches and salads. You'll often find live Hawaiian music as a backdrop here!

Sheraton has followed the lead of other resorts and adding a hotel fee. While this one includes some nice amenities ... it is unclear to these authors why the go about with these charges. Since everyone is required to pay them, why don't they just raise the rates $10? The $10 automatic hotel charge includes free phone calls, continental breakfast, tennis, fitness center, internet, and more.

Check with Pleasant Hawaiian and other "package" retailers regarding air/room packages that include a stay at this lovely resort property.

*Garden $285; Lagoon $365; Deluxe Ocean Front $410; Ocean Luxury $450; Garden Suite $480; Ocean Front Suite $750*

HELICONIA, BIRD OF PARADISE

### (MARRIOTT'S) WAI'OHAI BEACH CLUB AT PO'IPU

2249 Po'ipu Road, Koloa, HI 96756. Prior to Hurricane Iniki, one of the island's loveliest resorts was the Stouffer Wai'ohai Beach Resort. It was hard hit by the hurricane and has remained as a decaying remnant of its former grandeur for seven years.

Following Iniki, the Renaissance took over this piece of real estate and the adjoining Po'ipu Beach Hotel. Plans have finally been announced that call for redevelopment. The old structure will be demolished and a new $50 million resort will be constructed. The property will become a time-share resort, with seven rooms set aside for hotel accommodations. (The hotel rooms are needed to allow the company to make use of resort zoning.)

Construction is planned to begin in the fall of 2000 and will be handled in six phases. The first phase will include 77 units in the central building. The new resort will include several four-story buildings and underground parking. The construction which follows Phase I is termed as being "sales driven." The completely rebuilt resort will be set on almost twelve landscaped acres and include 227 two-bedroom villas, each with more than 1,100 square feet including full kitchens. Plans also call for a restaurant and retail shops.

A *heiau* on the property was destroyed by both Iwa and Iniki and is now partially submerged, so it will not be restored. Some of the plants will be put into storage and others will be given to the community. One of the inside mural walls will be donated to Koloa School. The future of the adjoining Po'ipu Beach hotel property is still in question and as we go to press, it appears that it will remain a skeletal remanant of Iniki. While Marriott owns the land and existing property of the Wai'ohai, the Po'ipu Beach parcel is owned by the Knudsen family and the land was leased by the former owners of the hotel. The property owners and Marriott have thus far been unable to reach any agreements.

### WHALERS COVE ★

Located in Po'ipu. Mailing address Koloa Landing at Po'ipu, 2640 Puuholo Rd., Koloa, HI 96756. (808) 742-7571. Premier Resorts 1-800-367-7052. RENTAL AGENTS: Suite Paradise 1-800-367-8020. Garden Island Rentals 1-800-247-5599. Maui & All Islands 1-800-663-6962. Pleasant Hawaiian Holidays 1-800-242-9244. Thirty-eight units. Oceanside pool. Full kitchen including microwave and dishwasher. Located on a promontory overlooking the ocean. Years ago whaling ships anchored at this cove to unload passengers and cargo. Swimming beach one mile away. The cove fronting the property offers very good snorkeling. Rooms have spacious patio/lanais, are private and beautifully furnished. Third floor units have jacuzzi tubs overlooking the ocean. Discounts for longer stays. *Garden Island Rates: 1 BR $195; 2 BR $225 plus cleaning fees*
*Premier Resort Rates: 1 BR $310-445; 2 BR $375-545*

# *NORTH SHORE*

### *Anahola/Kilauea/Princeville/Hanalei/Ha'ena*

# *INTRODUCTION*

The picturesque beauty of the North Shore is unsurpassed in the Hawaiian Islands. Most of the attractions on this side of Kaua'i revolve around the sights provided by Mother Nature. From botanical gardens to postcard perfect sunsets on the beach, here you can ignore the hustle and bustle and simply relax!

## *KEALIA*

At mile marker 10 you'll see a long stretch of beach that looks pleasant enough, but the water conditions are not safe. The rip currents along this beachfront are very strong. Kealia was another old plantation town and you may still see some of the old plantation buildings that remain. The word Kealia means "salt encrusted" and it was to this beach that the early Hawaiians gathered salt that had evaporated along the beachfront. From Kealia, the road moves inland slightly as you continue around toward Kaua'i's North Shore.

## *ANAHOLA*

Five miles from Kapa'a and just prior to mile marker 14 is what most visitors see of Anahola: ***Duane's Ono Burgers!*** (The best place to get a burger on Kaua'i -- in our opinion.) Duane's Ono Burgers are REALLY onolicious! Across the street is the expanded ***Polynesian Hide-a-way & Haw'n Bar-B-Q Chicken***, a roadside stand that now offers plate lunches and sandwiches along with fresh roasted macadamia nuts. A few steps away is ***Kamaka's*** for shave ice and smoothies. Shave ice starts at $1.50, but splurge and get the big one for $2: it's great - soft as cotton candy with no crunchy ice pieces!

Historically, the hole in the mountain (now partially collapsed) above Anahola on the seaward side carries a legend. It tells that the hole was made by the spear of an early Hawaiian giant. The giant threw it at the King of Kaua'i and missed him, piercing the mountain and leaving the hole. And, of course, another version says it was another chieftain who opposed the king and that Kamehameha threw the spear, which went entirely through the rock behind him.

In more recent history, Anahola suffered the effects of a severe flood in late 1991. The heavy rainfall during the night caused the stream to swell and the subsequent flooding came as a surprise to the residents. Not only property, but lives were lost as well.

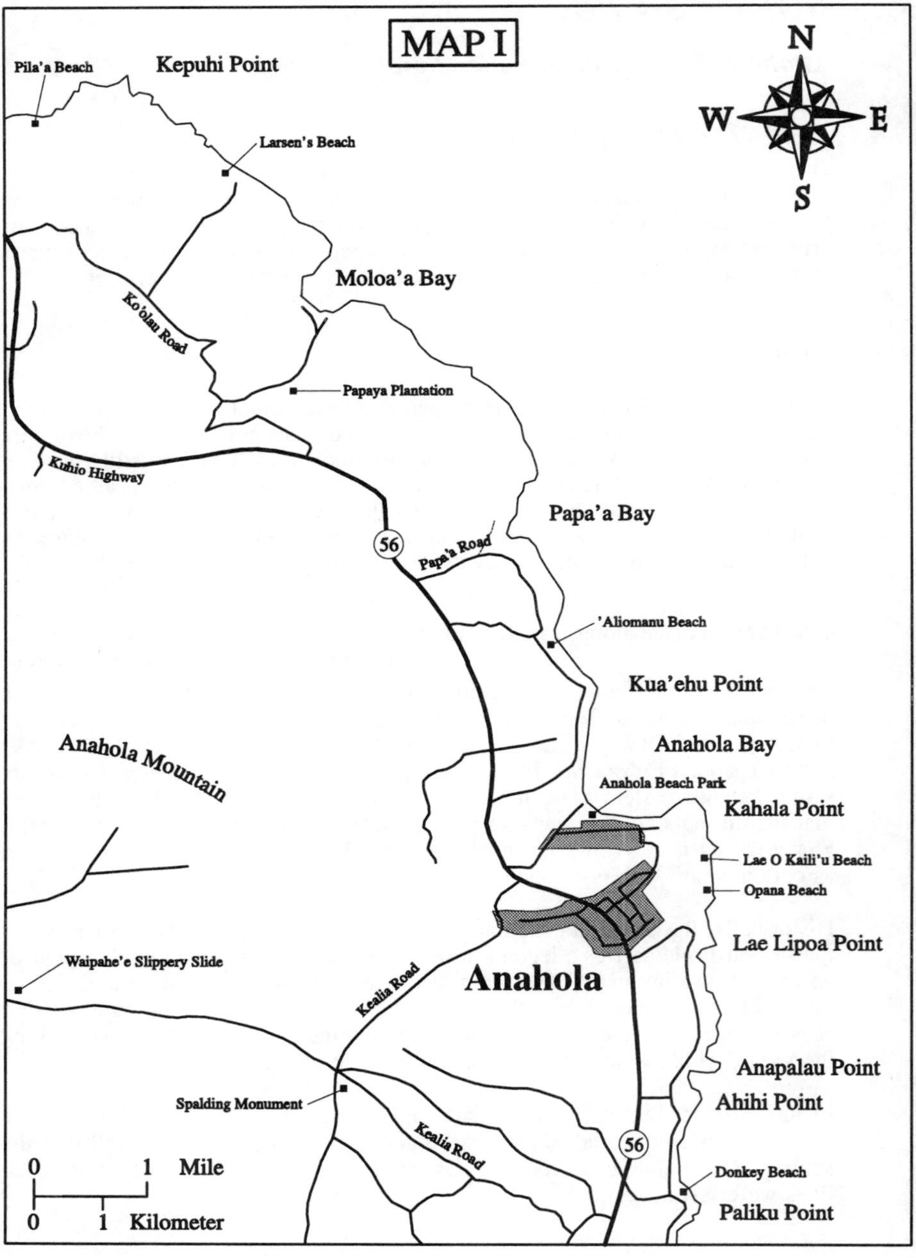
MAP I
N
W
E
S
Pila'a Beach
Kepuhi Point
Larsen's Beach
Moloa'a Bay
Ko'olau Road
Papaya Plantation
Kuhio Highway
Papa'a Bay
56
Papa'a Road
'Aliomanu Beach
Kua'ehu Point
Anahola Bay
Anahola Mountain
Anahola Beach Park
Kahala Point
Lae O Kaili'u Beach
Opana Beach
Lae Lipoa Point
Waipahe'e Slippery Slide
Anahola
Kealia Road
Anapalau Point
Ahihi Point
Spalding Monument
Kealia Road
56
0 1 Mile
0 1 Kilometer
Donkey Beach
Paliku Point

## *MOLOA'A*

This now sleepy community was once thriving. Prior to the turn of the 20th century, sugar cane and pineapple were booming in this region and so was the population. Just past mile marker 16 on Kuhio Highway you'll want to turn right. Turn right onto Ko'olau Road. Then right again onto Moloa'a Road and at the fork in the road keep to the left and continue on past private homes. There is public access to the trail, but parking is limited in front of these homes, so please respect their privacy and "no trespassing."

This is as pristine a bay as you may find on Kaua'i. If you happened to catch the lone airing of the pilot episode of Gilligan's Island a few years back on Fox television, you might recognize this bay. While this bay can be especially dangerous during winter and spring surf, anytime there is high surf, dangerous ocean conditions and powerful rip currents can occur. During periods of calm, you can enjoy swimming, snorkeling, and diving here.

To reach the beaches enroute to Kilauea, Ka'aka'aniu Beach (Larsen's), and Wa'iakalua, will require parking and a short walk to reach. Neither is safe for water activities.

The road moves past dairy farms nestled along the foothills. Signs warn that the roads may flood if there are heavy rains. Following heavy rains, the cattle mire in deep mud, coating their bodies with the rich, red-brown soil. Judging by the sienna hue, it is our impression that these must be the cows that make chocolate milk! As you drive along, can you find profile of King Kong's face or, for those desiring to advance to the expert level of sleuthing, can you spot the transmitting pole disguised as a tree?

## *KILAUEA*

The next stop on the map is Kilauea. You can turn right onto Kolo into town or go a little farther and turn right on Kilauea Road at the Shell Gas Station. A short distance past Kolo Road on your left you will find the ***Guava Kai Plantation and Visitors Center***.

But we are getting ahead of ourselves. If you take this first turn to Kilauea onto Ho'okui, you'll find the *Little Grass Hut* gift shop and *Mango Mama's Cafe*, a former juice and smoothie stand that has expanded to also offer sandwiches, salads, and bagels. Take another left onto Kolo Road and you will pass the ***Christ Memorial Episcopal Church***. This small church has beautiful stained glass windows which were sent from England and a hand-carved altar designed by Mrs. William Hyde Rice. While the church had its origins many years ago, the current structure only dates to 1941. The next major street is Kilauea Road. Turn right here.

Turn to your left onto Oka Street, at the former location of Jacques' Bakery is now the *Roadrunner Cafe & Bakery*. Open for breakfast, lunch, and dinner the interior is designed to resemble a Mexican courtyard. You can also visit their bakery and purchase some taro bread! (808) 828-8226.

A bit further you will pass by ***St. Sylvester's Church*** with its unusual octagonal architecture. Either way you'll reach Kilauea Road and continue down to the lighthouse.

The ***Historic Kilauea Theater*** is expected to open soon (if not already) after years of financial woes which closed their doors. Located in the Kong Lung Center, the historic theater will serve as a community events center. Owners hope to acquire a large screen projector system which can show art house and classic films as well as local theatrical productions. The original theater was built in 1930 and was located across the street from the current theater which was built in 1967.

But first you may wish a brief respite at the ***Kong Lung Center*** in Kilauea. They offer a limited, but distinctive, variety of shopping opportunities. The *Kong Lung Company* is an emporium housed in a restored historic building. Products include a selection of unique, "essential luxury" items. They opened in 1978 and were closed for a year following Hurricane Iniki. They offer Kong Lung's own T-shirts and backpack-style tote bags, swimwear, tableware, and lamps. The Kong Lung Co.'s structure dates back to 1860 when it was a two-story wooden building housing the Kilauea Plantation General store. In about 1918, the Kilauea Sugar Company's plantation manager tore down the old wooden structure. In the early 1940's the plantation rebuilt the structure using a fieldstone construction method which is unique to Hawai'i and the Chew "Chow" Lung store reopened as the new Kong Lung Store. In the early 1970's, the Kilauea Sugar Company closed and the Kong Lung Center was purchased by local businessmen. Following the damage caused by Hurricane Iniki, the decision was made to restore the Kong Lung Co. to the authentic, plantation-style architecture and design that makes the building historically significant. In August 1993, it was placed on the National Register of Historic Places. During the year-long remodel, an old floor-safe was discovered in what is now used as a dressing room. The original butcher's freezer, dating to 1943, is now a large private dressing room. Open 10 am-10 pm daily. Phone (808) 828-1822, FAX (808) 828-1227. *Reinventions*, located up the spiral staircase, is an assortment of new and gently used clothing with a good selection of inexpensive ($12-14) Aloha shirts. (808) 828-1125.

*The Lighthouse Bistro* recently opened at the Kong Lung Center. The adjacent *Kilauea Bakery* and *Pau Hana Pizza* are popular with visitors and local residents alike. Their signature bakery items include Napali brown bread, guava fermented Hawaiian sourdough bread, and tropical fruit layer cakes with whipped cream icing. Tom Pickett (formerly a pastry chef with the Sheraton Princeville) and his wife Katie, opened their business as a bakery only. Adding the pizza business was a natural progression as their popularity increased. They recently expanded and now offer cafe seating inside and a courtyard with a few tables outdoors. Open 6:30 am-9 pm, Monday-Saturday (808) 828-2020.

At the back of the center is the *Island Soap & Candle Works*, a factory and gift shop that makes and sells tropical scented lotions, soaps, and candles. (They also just opened one in Koloa.) Scented with island fragrances like plumeria, torch ginger, or pikake, they are all hand-made using natural ingredients. The "factory" looks like an old-fashioned alchemist or apothecary shop where you can watch their soap and candle products being made on the premises. 1-888-528-SOAP <www.handmade-soap.com> Email: soap@aloha.net

On Saturdays, local farmers gather at the nearby ***Kilauea Plantation Center*** to sell their fresh produce. Fresh vegetables, herbs, flowers, and fruits are available, and most are organically grown. Look for the red flags! Look for expansions of the ***Kilauea Fruit Stand*** which will be increasing in size and offering more varied locally grown produce along with longer hours.

Continuing onto the lighthouse, we will begin with a bit of history concerning the area geographically, the lighthouse, and the wildlife refuge. ***Kilauea Point*** is a remnant of the former Kilauea volcanic vent that last erupted 15,000 years ago. Today, there is only a small "U" shaped portion of the vent that remains, which allows for a spectacular view from the 570 foot ocean bluff. The history of the ***lighthouse*** began in 1909 when the property was purchased for a one dollar token fee from the Kilauea Sugar Plantation Company. The location for the lighthouse was perfectly suited as this grass-covered bluff was surrounded by pounding surf on three sides. Winter swells of twenty feet or more were not uncommon. (We hope you have packed that pair of binoculars!) Work began on the lighthouse in 1912 and was completed in May, 1913, with a light shining to ships 21 nautical miles away. The lighthouse is today on the National Register of Historic Places. The visitor center adjacent to the lighthouse has displays explaining the seabirds and their sanctuaries.

The ***Kilauea Point National Wildlife Refuge*** was established in 1974 and is recognized as Hawai'i's largest seabird sanctuary, a place that is home to more than 5,000 seabirds. This refuge is a nesting site for the red-footed booby, wedge-tailed shearwater, Laysan albatross, and many other species of Hawaiian seabirds. The acquisition of land has continued ever since with this sanctuary now encompassing 203 acres. The refuge was struck hard by Hurricane Iniki. Not only was there much damage to the birdlife and vegetation, but the famous lighthouse was also seriously affected. At Kilauea Point, they reported that about 80% of the native plants suffered damage. On Crater Hill, at least 25% were lost and an additional 50% damaged. Mokolea Point vegetation suffered little damage. Kilauea Point lost the most birds and suffered the worst damage to the habitat. The Kaua'i Natural Wildlife Refuge complex lost 12 of their 20 buildings. There was also damage to the lighthouse visitor center and bookstore, storage buildings, fences, and the water delivery system.

KILAUEA LIGHTHOUSE

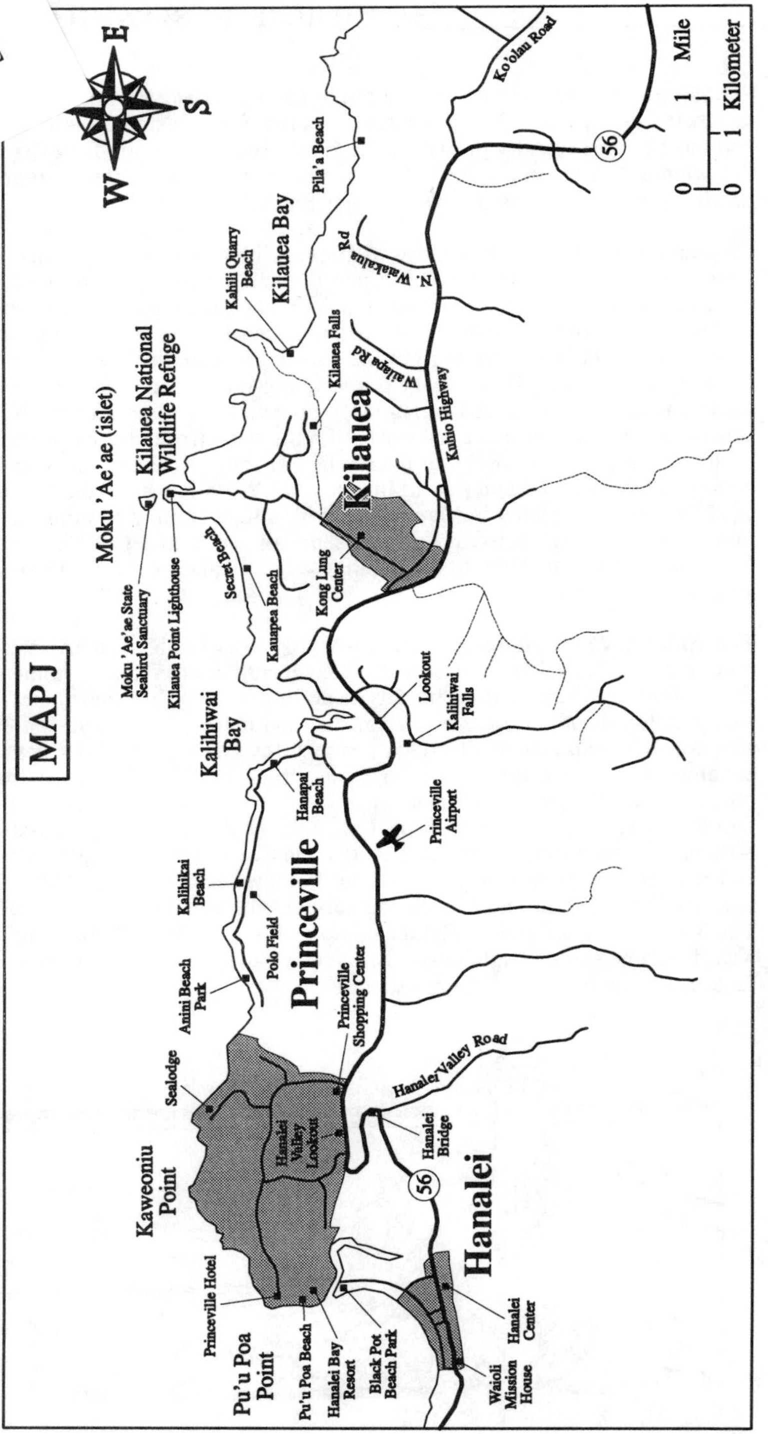
MAP J
W
E
S
Moku 'Ae'ae (islet)
Kilauea National Wildlife Refuge
Moku 'Ae'ae State Seabird Sanctuary
Kilauea Point Lighthouse
Secret Beach
Kauapea Beach
Kahili Quarry Beach
Kilauea Bay
Pila'a Beach
Ko'olau Road
56
Mile
Kilometer
0
1
N. Waiakalua Rd
Wailapa Rd
Kilauea Falls
Kilauea
Kuhio Highway
Kong Lung Center
Kalihiwai Bay
Lookout
Kalihiwai Falls
Hanapai Beach
Princeville Airport
Princeville
Kalihikai Beach
Polo Field
Anini Beach Park
Princeville Shopping Center
Hanalei Valley Road
Sealodge
Kaweonui Point
Hanalei Valley Lookout
Hanalei Bridge
Hanalei
Princeville Hotel
Pu'u Poa Point
Pu'u Poa Beach
Hanalei Bay Resort
Black Pot Beach Park
Waioli Mission House
Hanalei Center

When the lighthouse and support facilities were transferred from the U.S. Coast Guard on February 15, 1985, Kilauea Point became the 425th National Wildlife Refuge. The adjacent Kilauea Point Humpback Whale National Marine Sanctuary was established in 1994. Over 250,000 visitors enjoy the Kilauea Point National Wildlife Refuge visitor center and wildlife viewing areas each year. As many as 1,000 visitors per day may tour the facility over the Christmas holiday. A two-hour guided Crater Hill hike is offered daily, free with the cost of admission to the Refuge. Early reservations are recommended. (Call 828-0168, or sign up at the visitor center.) There is an on-going habitat management program that includes water development, native plant propagation, volunteer conservation group and service club, and nursery activities. Over 200 volunteers donate hours to varied refuge projects. Of the 203 acres, 183 acres are owned, and another 20 acres are conservation easement. ***Kilauea Point***, PO Box 87, Kilauea, Kaua'i, HI 96754, is open to the public daily from 10 am-4 pm, closed some federal holidays. (808) 828-1413. Admission is $2.

Drive back to the highway and head toward Princeville. On the left, just past mile marker 23, turn onto Kuawa Road on the *mauka* side of the Highway, and you can follow it up to a guava plantation.

There are 480 acres of guava orchards under commercial cultivation at the ***Guava Kai Plantation*** in Kilauea, which is considered the "Guava Capitol" of the world. Visit the plantation's visitor center and discover how guava is grown and processed into a variety of treats. Guava has fewer calories and more vitamin C than oranges, and it is also a good source of vitamin A, potassium, and phosphorus. Guava is actually not a citrus, but a berry with a fleshy seed cavity and a thick skin.

The guava can survive in dry or very tropical conditions. The Kilauea orchards receive 100 inches of rainfall each year with temperate 65-80 degree weather that is very agreeable to this crop. During dry months each tree receives up to 75 gallons of water per day. The seedlings were planted in this orchard in 1977 and began producing fruit in 1979. The first commercial yield was in January of 1980 with 2,000 pounds per acre harvested. Today the yield is 5,000 pounds per acre or about 400 pounds of fruit per tree per harvest cycle. The fruit at this plantation is hand-picked and harvested year round on a full-scale crop cycling system.

The fruit meat can vary from white or yellow to orange or pink. The variety grown at the Guava Kai Plantation is a hybrid developed by the University of Hawai'i's College of Tropical Agriculture and has a bright pink flesh and an edible rind. The color in your glass of juice is all natural.

The guava was a native of South America and introduced to the islands in 1791 by the Spaniard Don Francisco de Paula Marin, who was an advisor to Kamehameha I. The guava flourished and many now grow wild in Hawaii.

There is a self-guided tour that includes a view of the orchard and of the processing plants as well as an informative eight minute video. There is a man-made fish pond and an assortment of native Hawaiian plants. The snack bar, only open in the summer months, sells ice cream, juice, breads, and other bakery items that are made with guava.

There are free samples of guava juice, jams, jellies, and coffee. Since they are owned by Mauna Loa, they also sell their products at slightly lower rates than retail outlets. Guava Kai Plantation is open daily 9 am-5 pm. (808) 828-6121.

Back on the Highway and continuing toward Princeville, you'll pass *Banana Joe's*. A landmark you will definitely want to visit if you have a thirst for a fruit smoothie! Better yet, try a "frostie" - a tropical blend of fresh fruit and nothing but fruit, pureed to the consistency of soft serve ice cream. Or try your papaya, banana, pineapple, or mango yet another way - dried in a dehydrator by Joe's father, "Banana" Tom!

At mile marker 25 is a scenic lookout for ***Kalihiwai Falls***. The valley is visible on the makai side of the road and it is a cautious vacationer who must venture down the bridge and over to the other side to view the falls. During the 1957 tsunami, the original bridge was literally lifted up off the foundation and moved 50 - 100 feet up stream. The Kalihiwai Falls is actually two falls, accessible by hike, kayak, or horseback.

You'll want to skip the first sign that says Kalihiwai Road; it no longer goes through. Two miles past the Kilauea Shell Station and between mile markers 25 and 26, take the second turn off to Kalihiwai Road down to ***'Anini Beach***.

'Anini Beach is a popular windsurfing location and can be good for snorkeling during calm surf. This is one of the best beachcombing locations you'll find on the island. The kids will love sifting through the amber sand to find shell treasures! This quiet beachfront community might be an ideal location for a vacation home rental. While the real estate values in this area are sky high, there are some good vacation values available. Sylvester Stallone recently sold his beachfront home here and the oceanfront property that was used in the filming of *Honeymoon in Las Vegas* was also quickly snapped up when it was placed on the real estate market. Both reportedly sold for $1-2 million. The beach park here is nicely maintained, with covered pavilions, ideal for a picnic lunch. Across the road from the beach they have polo matches each Sunday beginning in late April and running through the early fall. There is another birthstone located here.

Back to Kuhio Highway and just before mile marker 26 you will pass the airport on your left (*mauka*) and the Princeville Golf Club will be on your right (*makai*). The breathtaking golf course vistas offered by the Princeville course may tempt even the non-golfer. Even if you aren't a golfer, you might be interested in their health club or restaurant. Suddenly the entrance to Princeville appears on your right and access to all the hotels and condominiums is off of this road. The Princeville Center is located at this intersection as well.

The Princeville Library opened their beautiful new facility in 1999 to become the 50th library in the state system. This attractive new building blends with the Princeville architecture, but has a sleek, modern interior with state-of-the-art computer services and technology systems. Hours: Tues, Thurs, Fri & Sat 9-5, Wed 12-8, closed Sun-Mon. (808) 826-1545.

Continuation along the highway will lead to the Hanalei area and that will be discussed following the Princeville portion.

## *PRINCEVILLE*

Hanalei, ringed with gorgeous bays and beaches, has long been a place of beauty and power. In times past, the surrounding area were *kula* lands - land available to the *maka'ainana* or common person for cultivation and fishing. History provided by the Princeville resort tells us that, "overlooking Hanalei Bay was the plateau which is now known as Princeville - a place of spiritual power or mana. From the hotel's present site to Po'oku, just beyond the highway, there is said to have been one of the largest *hala* (pandanus) groves in all of Hawai'i. The grove was celebrated in many chants and stories, as the *hala* was very important to the Hawaiians. The presence of the tree indicated that there were abundant water sources, and the long leaves provided weaving materials for mats and other household items. Further up O'oku was one of Kaua'i's largest *heiau* or temples of worship.

"The site of the hotel was known as *'pu'upoa'* or *'pu'u pa'oa'* -- *pu'u* meaning mountain and *pa'oa* meaning the staff of the fire goddess, Pele who, when searching for a new home would strike her staff in the earth to create a new crater. Directly below the hotel is a marshy area known as *kamo'omaika'i*, the site of a large fishpond. The Hawaiians were quite adept at raising fish in ponds next to the ocean. There they also built fishing shrines and altars to pay homage to the gods of the reef and the sea. This area, where ancient rockwalls are still visible, is being restored and preserved."

It was in late January of 1815 that the *Behring* went aground at Waimea Bay. The *Behring*, owned by the Russian-American Company, was headed toward Sitka with a load of seal skins when Kaua'i's king, Kaumuali'i, confiscated the cargo. In 1816 a German named Georg (that's right, no "e") Anton Scheffer was selected by the manager of the Russian-American Company, Alexander Andreievich Baranov, to head to Kaua'i to claim their load of pelts. He arrived in Hawai'i in November of 1815 and arrived on Kaua'i in May of 1816. While Georg and his forces were prepared to take back their cargo by force, the king returned the cargo as a show of good faith. The King had hopes of an alliance with the Russian Empire. Schaffer had ideas that were slightly different, his plans were to take over the entire island chain for the Russian Empire. He constructed a fort at Waimea Bay in September of that year and named it after the Russian Empress Elizabeth and ordered two additional forts to be built, one at Hanalei and another in Princeville. His fort on top of Pu'u Poa in Princeville was named Fort Alexander for Tsar Alexander I. After King Kamehameha learned of his plans to overthrow the government, Georg was ordered to depart from the islands. Georg made his stand at Pu'u Poa, but failed in his attempt and shortly thereafter he sailed to Honolulu and then fled the islands. The grassy area just outside of the porte cochere for the Princeville Hotel has only a few rocky outcroppings, for little remained of a fort made of dirt and clay. A kiosk with an interpretative center sits beyond the plateau and also offers a panoramic view of the Pacific Ocean.

A Scottish physician, Robert Crichton Wyllie, came to Kaua'i in 1844 after making a fortune as a merchant in South America. He had not planned on staying in the islands but was persuaded to accept an appointment by King Kamehameha III as minister of foreign affairs, a post he held for 20 years. He desired a manor with the opulence and elegance as those found in his homeland in Scotland and selected Hanalei as the site. In early days, taro was raised here. When Wyllie purchased the property it was a coffee plantation which he converted to a cattle ranch. Later, rice was grown in the area and now it has returned to taro cultivation. In fact, fifty percent of all of Hawai'i's poi comes from the taro root grown here.

The name ***Princeville*** was given in the 1860's when Kamehameha IV and his wife, Queen Emma, visited Wyllie's home and plantation along with their young son, Prince Ka Haku o Hawai'i. Upon his death in 1865, Wyllie bequeathed the estate to a nephew. However the estate was deeply in debt and the young fellow was so overwhelmed that he committed suicide. In 1867 the lands were auctioned off. The area later became a cattle ranch and was then sold in 1968 for resort development. Today the Princeville Resort Community occupies 9,000 acres and is a mix of private homes, condominiums, golf courses, and several hotels.

In 1969, the first major development of the Princeville Resort area began with the State of Hawai'i reclassifying 995 acres from agricultural to urban. There were 532 acres zoned for single and multi-family housing and hotel development, and the remaining 463 acres would become the Makai Golf Club. The 27 hole golf course opened in July 1971 and by 1973, Golf Digest had already selected this course as one of "America's greatest 100 courses." In 1976 the Princeville Airstrip was completed and provided service until 1997. Princeville Air, an affiliate of Hawaiian Helicopters recently (1999) resumed interisland service to O'ahu. By 1983 the Princeville Shopping Center had expanded to 66,000 square feet and construction began that same year on the ***Princeville Resort Hotel***.

The resort opened in September 1985. In 1987 the first nine holes of the ***Prince Golf Course*** officially opened and by July 1990, the full 18-holes of the course were complete. Between 1989 and 1991 renovations and improvements were made to the Princeville Resort Hotel. Following Hurricane Iniki in September, 1992, the hotel was closed for restoration and resumed operation in October, 1993.

The Princeville Resort Hotel is worth stopping by to view. With a European flare, this outstanding resort is located on a picture perfect location in Princeville. Enjoy afternoon tea in their lobby lounge or plan on splurging for Sunday brunch or the Friday evening seafood buffet at their Cafe Hanalei restaurant. See the review of this property under the accommodations section which follows.

In 1865, a small volume was published in Boston. Author Mary E. Anderson had visited the Hawaiian Islands with her grandmother and shared her experiences in print. Stepping back into time, it is a glimpse of the North Shore of Kaua'i, over 130 years ago.

*"We arrived at Hanalei, Kaua'i, about twelve on Tuesday, and were met on the beach by the missionaries, Messrs. Johnson and Wilcox, who escorted us on horseback to the house of the former gentleman. The next morning we breakfasted at Mr. Wilcox's, then at twelve had a meeting in the church, where a goodly number of natives were assembled; among them Kanoa, the governor of Kaua'i, who afterwards dined with us.*

*At three o'clock Mr. Wyllie sent down a boat for a party to take us to his estate called Princeville. It was a delightful row up the river, the foliage on either bank was the richest and most luxuriant we had seen. There was hardly a ripple on the water and no sound was to be heard but the gentle dip of the oars.*

*First, we visited the sugar-mill, which is the finest and most expensive in the islands. There we witnessed the whole process, from the grinding of the cane to the grained sugar. After that we went up to the agent's house, and were cordially welcomed by his family, and shown over the beautiful garden surrounding the house. There was a hedge of lovely roses, with a profusion of fragrant blossoms....The view from the piazza is exquisite. Mountains rise peak above peak in the distance, while a beautiful valley, with its meandering stream, lies at your feet. Tropical trees and lovely flowers are all around you. I do not wonder that Mr. Wyllie is proud of Kikiula Valley, with its waving fields of sugar-cane. He called his estate Princeville after the young Prince of Hawaii, who is now dead. On Thursday morning, bright and early, we started on our travels again. The roads of Kaua'i are better than on any of the other islands. Several members of the party started a little before the others, and rode up Kikiula Valley through Princeville. After a ride of about two and a half miles, we dismounted and ascended a little eminence. What a scene was before us! Far below was the river with its rapids, the course of which we could trace down the valley for some distance. Around us were mountains, on the left a bluff, and before us the Twin Peaks, with cascades in the distance. We galloped back, and soon overtook our cavalcade...We lunched at the house of a German, who kept a small store, and then rode on several miles to Kealia Park, the residence of Mr. Krull, a kind*

*German gentleman, who hospitably entertained us overnight. Mr. Krull has a large dairy which in part supplies the Honolulu market with butter....The grounds about the house are prettily laid out, with two walks leading to a picturesque summerhouse called "Bellevue" from which one looks over an extensive plain to the sea. We slept in a nice grass house, with matting on the side instead of paper. Familiar engravings adorned the walls, and the beds, with their pretty muslin mosquito-curtains, looking inviting enough to the weary traveler."*

Just past the entrance to Princeville Resort area is the ***Princeville Center***. *Chuck's Steak House*, *Foodland* grocery, a medical center, and assorted shops make for interesting strolling. Foodland has a very good deli with hearty sandwiches to take along on your picnic lunch. *Hale O'Java* serves up a great espresso along with pizza, pasta and sandwiches in their outdoor dining area. The owner has *Paradise Grill & Bar* here as well. As you pass the shopping center you are at mile marker 28 on Hwy. 56, which now switches to mile marker 0 as you suddenly change to highway 560. Just past this on the left is the scenic lookout for the Hanalei Wildlife Refuge.

## *HANALEI*

The ***Hanalei Wildlife Refuge*** was established on 917 acres in 1972 and is located in the Hanalei Valley. Unique to many refuges, taro is allowed to be commercially farmed on a portion of the property and one permit is granted for cattle grazing. Administered by the U.S. Fish and Wildlife Service as a unit of the National Wildlife Refuge System, they actively manage the habitat to provide wetlands for endangered Hawaiian waterbirds. There are 49 species of birds, including the endangered Hawaiian black-necked stilt, gallinule, coot, and duck that make their home here. Of the 49 species, 18 are introduced. There are no native mammals, reptiles, or amphibians, except possibly the Hawaiian bat. Historic farming (taro) and grazing practices are compatible with the refuge's objectives and thus are permitted to a limited degree.The refuge is not open to the public, but this interpretive overlook on the state highway allows an excellent photo opportunity. (Hurricane Iniki caused major damage to the facilities and habitat of this refuge and recovery continues.)

About one-half mile past the Wildlife Refuge lookout is another unmarked pull-off area along side the road. It's worth a stop to get a glimpse of this beautiful valley with buffalo grazing in the meadows below. At the base of the hill you'll cross the rustic, circa 1912, one-lane bridge into the Hanalei Valley. (The bridge is periodically closed for hours or even days when heavy rains cause the river to rise and partially submerge the bridge.) You can imagine why Peter, Paul, and Mary chose this magical place for their enchanted dragon, Puff, although they distorted the name slightly -- no doubt for better lyrical flow. Look off to the mountains for the many small waterfalls which glisten down the cliffs. The Hanalei River is a popular location for kayaking.

Many notable personalities have homes in quiet Hanalei. Sylvester Stallone, Michael Crichton, and Graham Nash (of Crosby, Stills, Nash & Young) who has, apparently, an affinity for large plastic cows.

At the first stop in Hanalei town are a couple of shops which merge with the *Hanalei Dolphin*, one of the area's more popular restaurants. *Kai Kane* offers some interesting selections of aloha wear for gentlemen and ladies. Upstairs you'll find surf equipment for sale. The adjoining *Ola's* has glassware and other unusual gift items (and where Christie usually finds something irrestible). *Postcards Cafe* is located in what was once a small museum. This is a small, very attractive restaurant with dining on the veranda or indoors. *Hanalei Town Farmers Market* is a mobile farmers market located on the lot across the street from Postcards and in front of *Kayak Kaua'i*. Michael O'Reilly Rowan offers an array of locally grown, organic fruits and vegetables and is open Tuesday-Sunday from 7 am to 7 pm. His mobile *Hanalei Juice Co.* is "parked" next door. A short hop down the road and you'll find the hub of activity in Hanalei. *Tahiti Nui* is a restaurant that also presents a weekly luau. The *Hanalei Wake Up Cafe* is a little hole-in-the-wall eatery, but offers what may be the best French toast in Hawai'i. The Wake Up is currently open only for breakfast and lunch. *Zelo's* is on this corner of Hanalei and this intersection is now a happening spot. (Zelos is open for lunch and dinner). Their sister restaurant, *Sushi Blues & Grill* (just steps away at the Ching Young Center) now competes with Zelo's with their own live entertainment as does the *Hanalei Gourmet Cafe* across the street

Hanalei means "lei shaped." ***The Hanalei Pier*** is a scenic location, and one you'll no doubt remember if you saw the movie *South Pacific*. The wooden pier was constructed in 1892 and then 30 years later was reinforced with concrete. It was used by the local farmers for shipping their rice until it was closed in 1933. In 1979, the pier joined other landmarks in the National Register of Historic Places. As a result of age, the pier was condemned prior to Hurricane Iniki and was rebuilt afterward. To actually reach the Hanalei Pier and the parking areas along Hanalei Bay turn right on Aku Road or on Malalo Road. Both take you down to Weke Road which runs parallel to the bay.

In 1996, Smithsonian archaeologists began surveying and excavating a wreck in Hanalei Bay at the mouth of the Wai'oli Stream. ***Cleopatra's Barge***, a ship which sank April 5, 1824, was once a royal vessel as well as the first ocean-going passenger ship constructed in the U.S. The Crowinshiled family had the 100 foot ship built in New England in 1816 at a cost of $50,000. In 1820 the ship was sold to Liholiho (King Kamehameha II) in trade for $80,000 worth of sandalwood and was renamed *Ha'aheo o Hawai'i*, or the Pride of Hawai'i. Four years after the purchase, the royal yacht ran aground on a reef and sank (reportedly the captain and crew were drunk when the ship broke free from its moorings). The team was ready to terminate the search when a massive hull timber was located. Further excavation will continue. The current research is supported by the Kaua'i Historical Society and the Princeville Resort Hotel.

Continuing through the town of Hanalei is an assortment of restaurants and shops to meet most of the visitors needs. One shop, *on the road to Hanalei* offers browseable gifts and other items and *Evolve Love Artists Gallery* next door continues where the former Hawaiian Artists Guild left off. A few shops still offer sea excursions along the Napali coast.

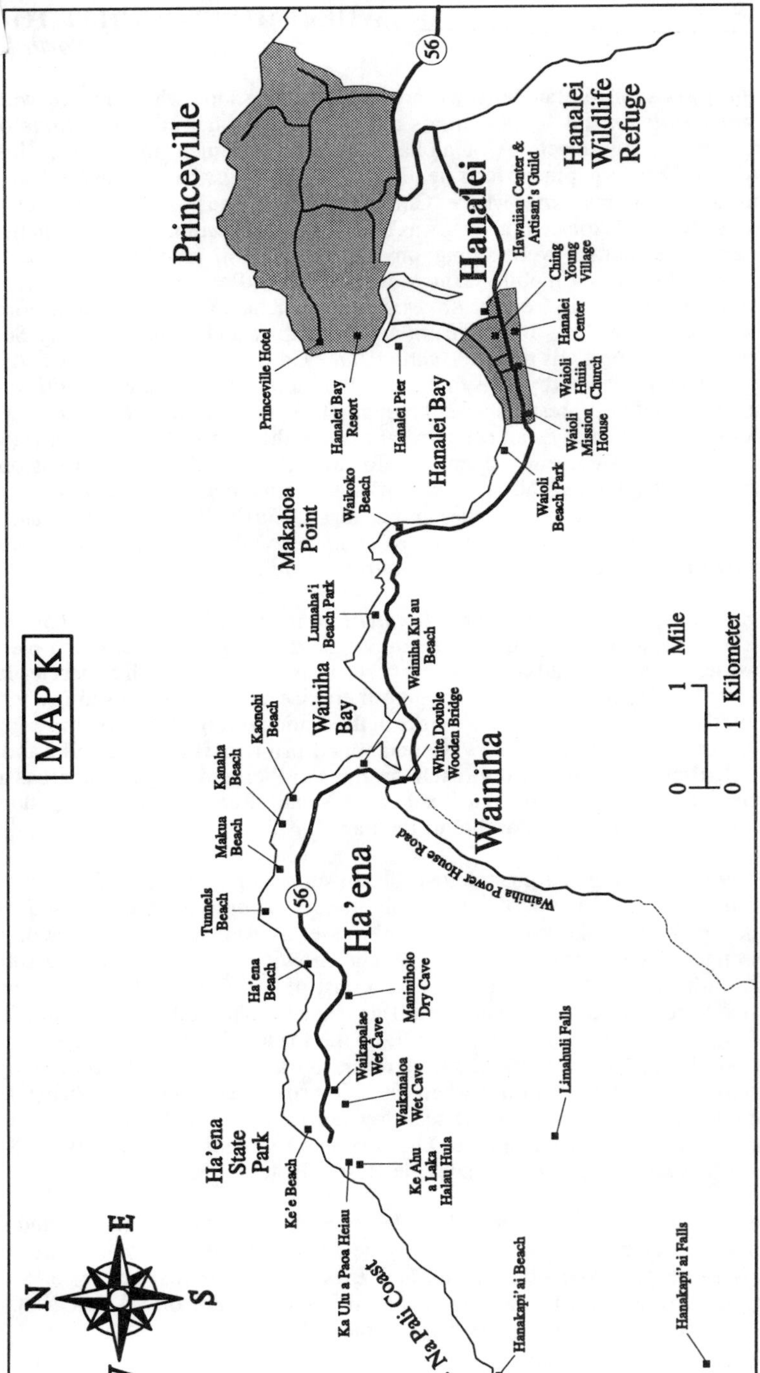
MAP K
Princeville
Princeville Hotel
Hanalei Bay Resort
Hanalei Pier
Hanalei Bay
Hanalei
Hawaiian Center & Artisan's Guild
Ching Young Village
Hanalei Center
Waioli Huiia Church
Waioli Mission House
Waioli Beach Park
Hanalei Wildlife Refuge
56
Makahoa Point
Waikoko Beach
Lumaha'i Beach Park
Wainiha Ku'au Beach
Wainiha Bay
White Double Wooden Bridge
Wainiha
Wainiha Power House Road
Kaonohi Beach
Kanaha Beach
Makua Beach
Tunnels Beach
Ha'ena Beach
Ha'ena
Maniniholo Dry Cave
Waikapalae Wet Cave
Waikanaloa Wet Cave
Limahuli Falls
Ha'ena State Park
Ke'e Beach
Ke Ahu a Laka Halau Hula
Ka Ulu a Paoa Heiau
Na Pali Coast
Hanakapi'ai Beach
Hanakapi'ai Falls
N
E
S
W
0 1 Mile
0 1 Kilometer

| | |
|---|---|
| Islas Vírgenes Británicas ⁜ | 1-800-888-8000 |
| Islas Vírgenes de los EE.UU. (CC) | 1-800-888-8000 |
| Irlanda (CC) | 1-800-55-1001 |
| Italia (CC) ◆ | 172-1022 |
| Japón (CC) ◆ | |
| Para llamar usando KDD | 00539-121◗ |
| Para llamar usando IDC | 0066-55-121 |
| Para llamar usando JT | 0044-11-121 |
| Para llamar usando NTT | 0034-811-811 |
| Jordania | 18-800-001 |
| México (CC) | |
| Para llamar usando Avantel | 01-800-021-8000 |
| Acceso para llamadas por cobrar en español | 01-800-021-1000 |
| Mónaco (CC) ◆ | 800-90-019 |
| Nicaragua (CC) | 166 |
| Nueva Zelandia (CC) | |
| Para llamar usando Telecom NZ | 000-912 |
| Panamá | 00800-001-0108 |
| Paraguay ⁜ | 00-812-800 |
| Perú (CC) | 0-800-50010 |
| Portugal (CC) ⁜ | 800-800-123 |
| Reino Unido (CC) | |
| Para llamar usando BT | 0800-89-0222 |
| Para llamar usando C&W | 0500-89-0222 |
| Rusia (CC) ◆ ⁜ | |
| Para hablar con un operador en ruso | 747-3320 |
| Para llamar usando Rostelcom | 747-3322 |
| Para llamar usando Sovintel | 960-2222 |
| Singapur (CC) | |
| Para llamar usando SingTel | 8000-112-112 |
| Para llamar usando StarHub | 8000-010-002 |
| Sudáfrica (CC) | 0800-99-0011 |
| Suiza (CC) ◆ | 0800-89-0222 |
| Tailandia (CC) ★ | 001-999-1-2001 |
| Taiwan (CC) ◆ | 0080-13-4567 |
| Trinidad y Tobago ⁜ | 1-800-888-8000 |
| Venezuela (CC) ⁜ ◆ | 800-1114-0 |

Si desea obtener una guía completa de WorldPhone, marque el número de acceso de WorldPhone del país donde se encuentra y pídale al operador que le comunique con el Servicio al Cliente. En los EE.UU., llame al 1-800-674-0881.

Servicio automatizado disponible desde la mayoría de los lugares.

(CC) Se pueden hacer llamadas de un país a otro desde la mayoría de los lugares internacionales.
◆ Los teléfonos públicos pueden requerir el uso de monedas o de una tarjeta de llamadas para obtener el tono de marcar.
⁜ Disponibilidad limitada.
▼ Espere al segundo tono de marcar.
◗ Debido a las reglamentaciones vigentes no se permiten llamadas dentro de Japón.
★ No está disponible desde teléfonos públicos.

MCI®

Para más información visítenos en: http://www.mci.com/worldphone

MCI®

**Desprenda** una de estas tarjetas de acceso y guárdela en su billetera.



## LA TARJETA MCI

### Cómo llamar a los Estados Unidos o a otros países

1. Marque el número de acceso gratis de WorldPhone® del país desde donde está llamando.
2. Marque o dele al operador el número de su Tarjeta MCI℠.
3. Marque o dele al operador el número al que desea llamar.

El servicio WorldPhone está a su disposición en más de 125 países, la mayoría de los cuales se enumeran a continuación:

| | |
|---|---|
| Alemania (CC) | 0800-888-8000 |
| Antillas Francesas (CC) | 0-800-99-0019 |
| Argentina (CC) | |
| Para llamar usando Telefónica | 0800-222-6249 |
| Para llamar usando Telecom | 0800-555-1002 |
| Aruba ✣ | 800-888-8 |
| Australia (CC) ◆ | |
| Para llamar usando AAPT | 1-800-730-014 |
| Para llamar usando OPTUS | 1-800-551-111 |
| Para llamar usando TELSTRA | 1-800-881-100 |
| Austria (CC) ◆ | 0800-200-235 |
| Barbados ✣ | 1-800-888-8000 |
| Bélgica (CC) ◆ | 0800-10012 |
| Belice | |
| Desde teléfonos públicos | 815 |
| Bolivia (CC) ◆ | 0-800-2222 |
| Brasil (CC) | 000-8012 |
| Canadá (CC) | 1-800-888-8000 |
| Chile (CC) | |
| Para llamar usando CTC | 800-207-300 |
| Para llamar usando ENTEL | 800-360-180 |
| China ◆ | 108-12 |
| Para hablar con un operador en mandarín | 108-17 |
| Colombia (CC) ◆ | 980-9-16-0001 |
| Acceso para llamadas por cobrar en español | 980-9-16-1111 |
| Costa Rica ◆ | 0800-012-2222 |
| Ecuador (CC) ✣ | |
| Para llamar usando Andinatel | 999-170 |
| España (CC) | 900-99-0014 |
| Estados Unidos (CC) | 1-800-888-8000 |
| Francia (CC) ◆ | 0-800-99-0019 |
| Grecia (CC) ◆ | 00-800-1211 |
| Guatemala (CC) ◆ | 99-99-189 |
| Holanda (CC) ◆ | 0800-022-91-22 |
| Hong Kong (CC) | 800-96-1121 |
| Islas Bahamas ✣ | 1-800-888-8000 |
| Islas Caimanes ✣ | 1-800-888-8000 |
| Islas Filipinas (CC) ◆ | |
| Para llamar usando PLDT | 105-14 |
| Para llamar usando Globe Telecom | 105-14 |
| Para llamar usando Smart | 105-14 |
| Para llamar usando Digitel | 105-14 |
| Para hablar con un operador en filipino para todas las compañías mencionadas anteriormente | 105-15 |


## LA TARJETA MCI

### Cómo llamar a los Estados Unidos o a otros países

1. Marque el número de acceso gratis de WorldPhone® del país desde donde está llamando.
2. Marque o dele al operador el número de su Tarjeta MCI℠.
3. Marque o dele al operador el número al que desea llamar.

El servicio WorldPhone está a su disposición en más de 125 países, la mayoría de los cuales se enumeran a continuación:

| | |
|---|---|
| Alemania (CC) | 0800-888-8000 |
| Antillas Francesas (CC) | 0-800-99-0019 |
| Argentina (CC) | |
| Para llamar usando Telefónica | 0800-222-6249 |
| Para llamar usando Telecom | 0800-555-1002 |
| Aruba ✣ | 800-888-8 |
| Australia (CC) ◆ | |
| Para llamar usando AAPT | 1-800-730-014 |
| Para llamar usando OPTUS | 1-800-551-111 |
| Para llamar usando TELSTRA | 1-800-881-100 |
| Austria (CC) ◆ | 0800-200-235 |
| Barbados ✣ | 1-800-888-8000 |
| Bélgica (CC) ◆ | 0800-10012 |
| Belice | |
| Desde teléfonos públicos | 815 |
| Bolivia (CC) ◆ | 0-800-2222 |
| Brasil (CC) | 000-8012 |
| Canadá (CC) | 1-800-888-8000 |
| Chile (CC) | |
| Para llamar usando CTC | 800-207-300 |
| Para llamar usando ENTEL | 800-360-180 |
| China ◆ | 108-12 |
| Para hablar con un operador en mandarín | 108-17 |
| Colombia (CC) ◆ | 980-9-16-0001 |
| Acceso para llamadas por cobrar en español | 980-9-16-1111 |
| Costa Rica ◆ | 0800-012-2222 |
| Ecuador (CC) ✣ | |
| Para llamar usando Andinatel | 999-170 |
| España (CC) | 900-99-0014 |
| Estados Unidos (CC) | 1-800-888-8000 |
| Francia (CC) ◆ | 0-800-99-0019 |
| Grecia (CC) ◆ | 00-800-1211 |
| Guatemala (CC) ◆ | 99-99-189 |
| Holanda (CC) ◆ | 0800-022-91-22 |
| Hong Kong (CC) | 800-96-1121 |
| Islas Bahamas ✣ | 1-800-888-8000 |
| Islas Caimanes ✣ | 1-800-888-8000 |
| Islas Filipinas (CC) ◆ | |
| Para llamar usando PLDT | 105-14 |
| Para llamar usando Globe Telecom | 105-14 |
| Para llamar usando Smart | 105-14 |
| Para llamar usando Digitel | 105-14 |
| Para hablar con un operador en filipino para todas las compañías mencionadas anteriormente | 105-15 |

At the ***Ching Young Center*** you'll find a variety store, natural foods store, pizza restaurant, and a Big Save Market which has a Subway inside. *Hanalei Mixed Plate* has become a mainstay in downtown Hanalei offering hearty portions of local style plate lunches affordably priced. *Sushi Blues & Grill* is located upstairs. Check out *Paradise Adventures*, operated by Byron and Dot Fears. They are former activity operators and now operate a gift shop and book island activities as well as B&Bs and vacation rentals (over 75 guest lodgings). They specialize in Napali Coast boating and dolphin/whale watching due to their many years in the business. (808) 826-9999 or toll free 1-888-886-4969, fax (808) 826-9998, Email: whales@aloha.net or website <www.paradise-adventures.com>

Across the street, the old Hanalei school has been converted to art and clothing shops and the *Hanalei Gourmet Cafe & Deli*. The school, built in 1926, is listed in the National Register of Historic Places. Adjoining is the Hanalei Center where you'll find *Cafe Luna* and a small Mexican restaurant. Fronting the complex is the old *Hanalei Coffee Company*, *Shave Ice Paradise*, and *Bubba's* burgers. Perhaps the most interesting shop is *Yellowfin Trading*. It is tucked in the back, a little harder to find, but worth the hunt. They have Hawaiiana collectibles and antiques along with some unusual gift items.

Following the road through town, you will pass the green Wai'oli Church and the Wai'oli Mission House. ***Wai'oli Mission House*** is open to the public Tuesdays, Thursdays and Saturdays. Listed in the National Register of Historic Places, the home is open between 9 am and 2:45 pm. The original coral church was built in 1837 with Reverend William Alexander the first clergyman on the North Shore. In 1846, Abner and Lucy Wilcox arrived here as missionaries and while the church was founded in 1834, the present green and white ***Wai'oli Church*** was not built until 1921. The Wilcox family established themselves on the North Shore and it was Abner and Lucy's three granddaughters that initiated the restoration of the church in 1921. The one-hour guided tour is taken on a walk-in basis with donations welcomed at the end of the visit. Sunday services performed in English and Hawaiian are fascinating. To tour the property for groups of twelve or more, please write or call in advance. Call Grove Farm at (808) 245-3202 for more information.

A new landmark in Hanalei is poised along the side of the Kuhio Highway, at the former Hawaiian Tel switching station. An enormous poi pounder, which began as a 1,500 pound boulder, now graces the front yard of the new ***Hanalei Poi Company***. Partners Beno Fitzgerald and Hobey Beck plan to produce enough poi to saturate the Kaua'i market. They will begin by processing 2,000-4,000 pounds of taro each week and increase as demand improves! (Not open to the public.)

The next few miles are dotted with one lane bridges, but just before mile marker 5 is the lookout to *Lumaha'i Beach*. The east end of Lumaha'i Beach, Kahalahala (which means pandanus trees), is where Mitzi Gaynor filmed her famous "wash that man right out of my hair" scene. At mile marker 5 there is a very small pullout along the road that offers an unbeatable photo opportunity.

The ***Lumaha'i Valley*** was once populated with Hawaiians. But it was the Japanese who farmed the first taro. Later immigrants cultivated rice. The 23 square mile area is now used for cattle grazing.

***Wainiha Beach*** is a known shark breeding ground and not recommended for swimming or water activities. Pass the Wainiha "Last Chance" store and pick up a cold drink or sandwich. It was in this valley in the 19th century that 65 persons reported their ethnicity as "menehune." A few miles beyond Wainiha Beach is Powerhouse Road: just before mile marker 7, you'll see the road (and road sign) turn off to climb inland through the valley. The road travels through some beautiful, not-to-be-missed scenery and ends at the Powerhouse. Built in 1906, it served to provide irrigation for the McBryde Sugar Company.

## *HA'ENA*

Here is the last vestige of civilization. The ***Hanalei Colony Resort*** is a quiet get-away and it adjoins *Surt's on the Beach and The Steam Vent Cafe,* the last stop for dining!

Now you are entering the Ha'ena area of Kaua'i. ***Camp Naue***, a four-acre camp operated by the YMCA, is located between the 7 and 8 mile markers. More information on accommodations will follow under rental information.

Mile marker 8 indicates you have reached ***Makua Beach***. You will probably see cars parked alongside the main road and on a short sandy side road. Makua is one of the most popular beaches on the North Shore and is commonly referred to as Tunnels Beach. You can also park down at Ha'ena Beach Park and walk down to Tunnels. While this is among the safest beaches on the North Shore and offers fair snorkeling, there can be strong rip currents even during small surf.

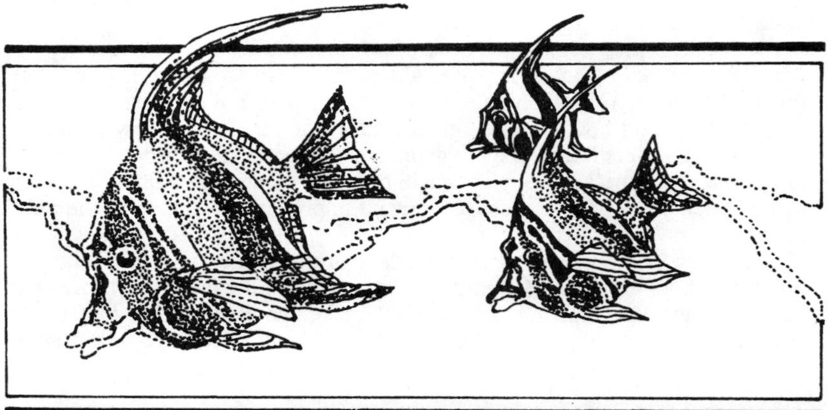


KIHIKIHI

To cite an example: some years ago, we took a boat trip on a day when the surf was fairly calm. One young, muscular male member from our boat tour was caught up in the rip current and while struggling with a face mask which had a broken strap, had to be pulled into shore by one of the crew. Always use caution on Kaua'i's many beautiful beaches. Beauty can be deceptive and we don't want any of our readers to become a statistic! In the past many tour boats and zodiacs that departed from Hanalei would travel up here for a snorkeling trip. (Now new regulations prohibit the departures from Hanalei Bay, so boats coming out of Port Allen don't venture up this far.)

You will notice many of the houses are up on concrete stilts. This area has been struck hard by the tsunamis of 1946 and 1957. The stilts makes it a long walk up to deliver the groceries, but gives the homeowners the added benefits of obtaining limited home owners insurance. Whether this precaution will serve its purpose should another tsunami strike the area, will hopefully never be tested. ***Ha'ena Beach Park*** is a five-acre park maintained by the County of Kaua'i. The foreshore here is steep and therefore the dangerous shorebreak makes it inadvisable for swimming or bodysurfing. Although you may see some bodysurfing done here, it is not for the novice.

Across the road from Ha'ena Beach Park is ***Maninolo Dry Cave***. This lava tube was a sea cave in earlier centuries when the sea was higher. You can travel several hundred yards and emerge at the other end. We were told that the cave was larger before it was filled in with sand by the tsunami that hit the island in 1957. Maninolo Dry Cave, according to one legend, was created by the menehune who had caught a great quantity of fish. There were too many fish to take them all home in one trip, so they carried as much as they could to their home in the mountain planning to return later for the rest of their catch. When they returned they discovered the remaining fish had been stolen. The menehune noticed a small hole in the mountain which was a clue to the path that the fish thieves had taken. The menehune proceeded to dig out the thieves and the result was this dry cave. Another legend credits the goddess Pele who traveled along the Napali coast searching for fire in the earth. She fell in love with Lohiau, the high chief of Kaua'i, but the couple could not be together until Pele found fire beneath Kaua'i, so she began to dig in search of it. She was unsuccessful and left Lohiau to go to the island of Hawai'i. The "caves" were the result of her efforts. The inner room was used as a meeting chamber by chieftains.

***Limahuli Gardens*** is one of three gardens on Kaua'i which are a part of the National Tropical Botanical Garden and is open to the public. It is located 7/10 of a mile from Ha'ena Park and is well marked with a sign and a HVB marker. This magnificent site, surrounded by towering mountains and breathtaking natural beauty, receives an annual rainfall of 80 to more than 200 inches. Within Limahuli Valley are two important ecosystems -- the lowland rain forest and the mixed mesophytic forest. Together these two ecosystems are the natural habitat of over 70% of Kaua'i's (59% of Hawai'i's) endangered plant species. Thus, Limahuli Garden is vitally important as a botanical and horticultural resource. The Garden emphasizes rare and endangered plants of Hawai'i, as well as plants of ethno-botanical value. Limahuli Gardens is also a part of an archaeologically significant site known as the Limahuli complex.

The entire area has a rich history, and a series of ancient stone terraces, believed to be well over 700 years old, are visible at the garden. The oldest taro patches in Hawai'i are also located here.

Limahuli Gardens encompass 17 acres, and was gifted to the NTBG by Juliet Rice Wichman in the mid 1970's. An additional 990 acres behind the garden are set aside as a natural preserve. In 1994 the gardens were opened up to tours on a limited basis. In the future there is the possibility that they may open up a trail to the 800-foot Limahuli Falls. Guided tours are currently available only by reservation for $15. Self-guided tours include a descriptive booklet and the cost is $10 per person. Currently open Tuesday-Friday and Sundays from 9:30 am-4 pm. They have recently added a gift shop which features books, posters, and shirts. Parking area and restroom facilities are available. Picnic lunches are prohibited. (808) 826-1053.

Just beyond Limahuli Steam are the ***Waikapala'e Wet Caves,*** accessible by a short hike up and behind the gravel parking area. One of the caves has a fresh water pool and is a unique phenomenon. The Waikapala'e (the name is commonly thought to mean water of the lace fern) Wet Cave has a cool shady cave known as the blue room. It requires a venture into the chilly waters and, depending on the water height, possibly an underwater swim through a submerged tunnel. This is one adventure we have yet to try, but we are told it is an inspiring experience. (Be cautious, however, many drownings or near-drownings have occurred here.) Apparently the reflection of the light through the tunnel causes the incredible blue effect on the cavern walls. The second wet cave, the ***Waikanaloa Cave***, is located roadside. This cave is salt water and not suitable for swimming. Slightly east of Ke'e, and not far beyond the "Blue Cave" is the area that in the 1960's became the ***Taylor Camp***, owned by the brother of Elizabeth Taylor. The beach chapter, under Ha'ena State Park & Ke'e Beach has this tale of the island's first flower children.

***Ke'e Beach*** is the end of your scenic drive (mile marker 10) and beyond is the Napali Coast, 11 miles of which are accessible by foot along the ***Kalalau Trail***. (Note: Correct spelling is Napali, not Na Pali, as verified by Hawaiian linguist and historian Mary Kawena Pukui.) See the recreation chapter for a brief description of this scenic trail. New rates became effective in 1999. Charges of $10 per person per day for use of campgrounds along the Kalalau Trail.

While some have remarked that this is the most beautiful trail in the world, be forewarned that the Sierra Club rates the 11 mile hike to the Kalalau Valley as a "ten" on their scale of difficulty. The shorter hike to Hanakapi'ai is a partial day hike and more suited to the recreational hiker.

Ke'e Beach currently has a lifeguard (but talk is that the service will be discontinued) and dangerous water conditions. Swimming and snorkeling are only recommended during very calm conditions and then using common sense.

Above the beach, a walk of about 5 or 10 minutes will take you to remnants of ancient Hawaiian villages and the *Kaulu o Laka Heiau*. This sacred altar is set among the cliffs of Napali and was built for Laka, the goddess of hula. It is one of the dramatic sites on the island with views of the cliffs and ocean.

The people of Nu'alolo Kai also left remnants of their shelters. The sandstone slabs were probably used as foundations for a pole and thatch house. The people that lived in this area were agricultural. There is a low boggy area that may have grown taro. The reef fringing the area provide plenty of fish and shellfish for the inhabitants. The Bishop Museum conducted excavations in the area for five years beginning in 1959. They determined that this area had been continuously inhabited from 1380 until 1919. The *heiau* is still used today by hula halaus. Ke'e Beach is the end of your road, but a great place to begin an evening sunset!

## *BEST BETS*

***Princeville Resort*** - elegantly wonderful, what an ideal way to enjoy Paradise! ***Sealodge*** - affordable with an incredible view of the Kilauea lighthouse. ***Hanalei Bay Resort*** - Multiple amenities with views of Bali Hai and a lagoon swimming pool.

## *PRIVATE VACATION HOMES*

The North Shore has a plethora of homes to meet most any need or group size and there are almost as many rental agents to assist you. Following are a few homes that we have toured and found of special interest.

**ANCHORAGE POINT**
Located in Ha'ena. RENTAL AGENT: Na Pali Properties 1-800-715-7273. This 2 BR 2 BTH home is elevated with a spacious living/kitchen/dining room offering a panoramic ocean view. It resembles a large cabin with simple furnishings. One of the bedrooms has an adjoining shower large enough to hold a small party. The location of this is a plus and the ocean view couldn't get much better. There is some need for a bit of updating, but the price is a plus. We enjoyed reading the guest's comments on whale and bird sightings and although they noted "no Charo sightings" (alas!) one did record a "Charo's sister sighting!"
*$1,050-1,250 per week for two, $300 deposit, $85 cleaning fee.*

**HALE KIPA**
1-800-866-2539 or (808) 262-2539. Hosts are Henry and Gloria Drayton. This rental is located on the golf course at Princeville. This two story, three bedroom and 3 1/2 bath home has over 3,000 square feet of living area. Each of the bedrooms have a private entrance. Four televisions will ensure that each guest has their own choice of programming! Pool use at nearby Sunset Drive clubhouse with discount rates to Princville Golf Club. Call for current rates or visit their website: <www.vrsource.com/kipa1.htm>

**JUNGLE CABANA & JUNGLE BUNGALOW**
The Jungle Bungalow & Jungle Cabana are privately situated on 2.25 acres of lushly landscaped jungle alongside a rushing mountain stream with Wainiha Valley as a backdrop. Located a few minutes drive to beaches, 10 minutes to Hanalei or the Napali Coast.

The Jungle Bungalow is a secluded modern structure with charm of a different style. If you seek the "tropical style" and like to kick back in a hammock,listen to birds sing and the sound of the rushing river and think that relaxing in a claw foot tub located outside in a beautiful garden is bliss, then this is the place for you. This two story accommodation sleeps up to five guests. There is a complete kitchen with quality cookware. It provides total privacy for those seeming a bit of quiet romance. Mountain view s and private gardens compliment the tropical atmosphere: 1-2 guests $11; $690 weekly. $10 for each additional guest ($50 per week). <www.paradise-adventures.com/bungalow>

Jungle Cabana is a cozy first class studio-style lodging with about 350 square feet of interior space which is paneled primarily in woven bamboo, trimmed with bamboo accents. It opens up to soothing views of the rushing mountain stream and spectacular Wainiha Pali (cliffs). The tropical Zen-type decor is enhanced with bamboo sofa and furniture. There is a complete kitchen that also offers that rushing jungle stream as a view! The main living space is the "nature that surrounds." Bathing is in a private riverside garden setting with claw foot tub and shower. Here you can surely transcend reality and enjoy a private and romantic setting! 1-2 guests $95; $570 per week.
<www.paradise-adventures.com/cabana>

Byron & Dot Fears. Paradise Adventures, the Kaua'i Adventure Company. PO Box 1379, Hanalei, HI 96714. FAX (808) 826-9998. Toll free 1-888-886-4969. (808) 826-9999. Email: whales@aloha.net

**KALIHIWAI JUNGLE HOME**
Contact: Your Kaua'i Vacation Home, PO Box 717, Kilauea, HI 96754. (808) 828-1626. This 1 BR luxury unit is decorated in Hawaiian art from the 1930s and 40s and offers plush carpeting, a marble fireplace, and marble bathroom with jacuzzi bathtub. The large deck features a double hammock and multiple views that look into the jungle, a waterfall, and the mountains. Situated on one-half acre along the rim of the Kalihiwai Valley jungle, it is located 2 minutes away from 'Anini Beach. Additional discounts on longer stays. *$135 per day, $845 per week plus $45 cleaning fee.*

**KILAUEA LAKESIDE ESTATE ★**
Contact Steve Hunt, 910 The Strand, Hermosa Beach, CA 90254. (310) 379-7842. This estate is situated on a 3-acre peninsula surrounded by a 20-acre fresh water lake with 1,000 feet of lake frontage and a white sand beach. You couldn't get much more private than this! The lake offers boating as well as catfish and bass fishing. The home features 3 large bedrooms and 3 baths, a 2 person spa tub, washer/dryer, DMX stereos, big screen TV, a one-hole golf course, and private botanical garden. Coming soon: two Polynesian-style vacation cottages situated on the adjoining property available for individual rental or along with the estate. High Season rates apply December 15-April 15 and June 15-September 15. Email: shunt@aol.com or website <www.mmv.com/lakeside>
*Rates: $450 per night low season; $550 per night high season.* Rates are for up to six guests. (Discounted rates depending on availability.)

**LANI AINA BEACH HALE** ★
Located beachfront at Ha'ena. RENTAL AGENT: Na Pali Properties 1-800-715-7273. Unlike several other homes we toured, this 2 BR 2 BTH beach cottage was very welcoming. The bathrooms are contemporary and the new bed covers have brightened up the place making the bedrooms more cheery. A large yard offers plenty of room for active youths and roomy front porch and spacious glass doors provide an opportunity to sit and simply enjoy the oceanfront location. *$1,200-1,500 per week. $500 deposit, $100 outclean, sleeps 6.*

**PLANTATION MANAGERS HOME (formerly BONAGUIDI)** ★
Located on Hanalei Bay. RENTAL AGENT: Na Pali Properties 1-800-715-7273. We love it, we love it, we love it. This magical home was built at the turn of the century. Back then it was a ranch house with cattle roaming along the sweeping beachfront on Hanalei Bay. This elegant historic plantation home is furnished with koa wood pieces that are museum quality. With a huge front lawn stretching out to beautiful Hanalei you couldn't ask for more. The living area is roomy with a huge big screen television. The kitchen has been updated with new appliances, yet not so renovated as to destroy the classic style of this old plantation home. A bedroom and bathroom are located off the downstairs foyer and upstairs are a small bedroom and bathroom along with a master suite. The master bedroom offers large patio doors which open onto a small deck with a panoramic Pacific vistas. The master bath is spacious with a huge contemporary footed tub.

We were told that a tsunami that struck some fifty years ago pushed the home several hundred yards farther from the beach. Apparently blessed a second time, Hurricane Iniki caused serious damage to surrounding homes, but amazingly this lovely home was spared all but slight water damage through the oceanfront doors. This sprawling plantation home, located on an oceanfront acre, may not be in your budget, but if it is, the $3,500 per week with $200 cleaning fee is worth it!

## *BED & BREAKFAST*

The following are just a few of the Bed & Breakfast options offered on the North Shore. See the end of this chapter under Rental Agents for companies that offer a wide range of properties around the island.

**HALE 'AHA** ★
3875 Kamehameha, PO Box 3370, Princeville, HI 96722 Phone (808) 826-6733, FAX (808) 826-9052. Toll free 1-800-826-6733. E-mail: <kauai@pixi.com> This is the only B & B overlooking the Prince Golf Course. The upstairs house is reserved for guests; the living room is pretty and pastel with a cozy fireplace and dining area set up for breakfast. Rooms are cushy and comfy, everything is very homey, especially the hospitality of your hostess, Ruth Bockelman. Breakfast is at 8:00, but she puts the coffee on at 7 for early risers who might want it with a muffin or cereal, on the run. But if you wait, you'll be treated to a full spread that includes hot homemade bread (with guava butter), muffins, fresh fruit, granola or cereal; a tropical smoothie, fresh fruit, steamed brown rice with brown sugar, crushed almonds, raisins, and fruit plus a baked apple with whipped cream! Rooms have TV's, mini refrigerators, bathroom amenities and extra towels, and pillow.

Guests are entitled to substantial golf discounts at the course. They take Visa and MC, but sorry, they don't take children. They provide a brochure that is very detailed and informative. The penthouse suite is the top floor of the property with 1,000 square feet of room, separate living area, large whirlpool tub and washer and dryer. Three night minimum stay.
*On the golf course $95; Bali Hai Mountain $88; Honeymoon suite $150; Penthouse $220.*

**HALE HO'O MAHA**
PO Box 422, Kilauea, HI 96754. (808) 828-1341, 1-800-851-0291. E-mail: hoomaha@aloha.net and their website is at: <www.pixi.com/~kauai>

Located in a country farm-like setting (in fact a bull lives just down the road), surrounded by ponds and streams with the ocean and bay just a bit further. The decor is whimsical and eclectic with lots of wood and wood artifacts and an aquarium in the living room. Each room has a personality of its own: the Pineapple Room has a round bed with pineapple bedspread, rugs and knick-knacks, and the romantic guava room has a canopy bed with sheer, wispy draping. Breakfast includes Anahola Granola (made just a few miles away), muffins, and a plate of fresh fruit that not only offers papaya, pineapple, bananas and grapes, but rambutans, too! (They are like lichees with spikes!) Located on 5 acres, this home is within walking distance of two beaches. $20 per night charged for additional person. A 50% deposit is required to confirm your reservation for each room. Visa or Mastercard accepted. Your hosts are Toby & Kirby. *They offer four varied accommodations from $55-$80 per night, double or single occupancy.*

**HALELUIA BY THE RIVER**
PO Box 302, Kilauea, HI 96754. (808) 828-6813. Email: river@aloha.net

Owner Joy Finch provides three studios for vacation rentals. Her focus is Healing Hawaiian Vacations for couples or singles. Here you can stay in one of the river edge rentals, receive massages and go on hikes and island tours.
*Rates are $50 for minimal view, $70 with private lana'i overlooking the river. $90 for a 1 BR with view and full amenities.*

**THE HISTORIC B&B**
PO Box 1662, Hanalei, HI 96714. (808) 826-4622. Email: jbshepd@alolha.ne>

Built in 1901, this home is included in the National and State Historic Registry as the oldest Buddhist mission on Kaua'i. Following years of neglect, the building was scheduled for demolition. In 1985, a few local businessmen banded together and the building was moved across the island and converted into a residence. Over 95% of the original building was able to be saved. Rooms are furnished with antique bedding and *shoji* Japanese screen sliding doors that open onto the long hallway of polished wood. Located next to Postcards Cafe. Walking distance to the beach. Island style breakfasts. Your hosts are Jeff and Belle Shepherd. <WWW> *Room rates $59-68, 2 night minimum.*

**MAHINA KAI BED & BREAKFAST**
Box 699, Anahola, HI 96703. (808) 822-9451, 1-800-337-1134, FAX (808) 822-9451. Email: trudy@aloha.net

Trudy Comba is your host at this Asian-Pacific style home located on a terraced hillside overlooking Anahola Bay. Also on property is a tea house. With a capacity for 12-14 persons, this property could be geared for a small retreat. It can accommodate about 35 people for workshops and meetings. (Note: Additional overnight space at another house across the street could also be arranged.) Breakfast would be included, other meals by arrangement. Three night minimum stay is requested.
*The bed and breakfast rooms rent for $100 single; $125 (2) with breakfast included. Also available is a 2 bedroom apartment that can sleep up to six persons. Rates are $150 for two, $175 (3), and $200 (4-6). Cost to rent the entire Mahina Kai home, which sleeps 14, is $600 per night.*

**MAKAI FARMS**
PO Box 93, Kilauea, HI 96754 (808) 828-1874, FAX (808) 828-0148. Email: makai@aloha.net. <WWW>

Located just outside the town of Kilauea, this small family farm specializes in the growing of orchids. This Bed & Breakfast is located in a building separate from the main house, with ocean and mountain views from the upper level. There is a king-size bed and a sleeper sofa. Downstairs is a kitchen and bathroom. Breakfast fixings are provided and include fruits grown on the farm and freshly laid eggs. Two night minimum. Your hosts are Robert and Michelle.
*$80 per night single or double occupancy.*
*(Deduction of $5 if you choose no breakfast)*

**NORTH COUNTRY FARMS**
PO Box 723, Kilauea, HI 96754, (808) 828-1513. FAX (808) 828-0805. E-mail: ncfarms@aloha.net

North Country Farms is an organic vegetable, fruit, and flower farm surrounded by horse farms. Their redwood guest cottage includes a kitchen for snacks and meals. Your host, Lee Roversi, adds that they are a family of five and love to open their farm to other families. The cottage and farm are completely child-friendly. As the guest house is a separate accommodation, it lends itself very well to a traveling family. *$90 per night.*

**PAVILIONS AT SEACLIFF**
Contact: Estate Manager, PO Box 3500-302, Princeville, HI 96722. (808) 828-1185, FAX (808) 828-1208. RENTAL AGENTS: 'Anini Beach Vacation Rentals 1-800-448-6333 or (808) 826-4000. Homes & Villas in Paradise 1-800-282-2736, (808) 262-4663. Prosser Realty 1-800-767-4707. The property is bordered by the Kilauea Point Wildlife Bird Refuge and Kilauea Lighthouse. The house offers 3 ocean view master suites and 3 1/2 baths. A lap pool with jacuzzi. Washer/dryer, fax machine, plus a complete workout room. (Christie wouldn't mind roughing it for a week or so here, although her co-author is frightened by the phrase "Workout Room!") Minimum 3 night stay. Rates are for up to 6 guests. 10% monthly discount. $1,000 deposit required. *$700/600/day.*

## *INEXPENSIVE*

**(THE) FISH SHACK**
Anahola. RENTAL AGENT: Prosser Realty 1-800-767-4707. In an ever continuing effort to give our readers the most options available, we felt it necessary to include this property. Located on the edge of Anahola Bay. Their flyer notes: a studio "for one or two who like each other." A "vacation" kitchen and full-size bed along with outdoor bamboo shower. *Rental rate: $65*

**HALE MOI COTTAGES**
5300 Ka Haku Rd., PO Box 899, Princeville, HI 96714. (808) 826-9602. RENTAL AGENTS: Marc Resorts 1-800-535-0085. Na Pali Properties 1-800-715-7273. Forty units in two story buildings. Hotel rooms, studio suites with kitchens, 1 1/2 bedroom suites with kitchens. Mountain and garden views. Full kitchens and washer/dryer, except in hotel units.

All have remodeled kitchens and bathrooms. The studios are spacious -- one very large room with a nice, full kitchen. The hotel units are actually mini suites with a small bedroom and living area. A tiny alcove provides some basic kitchen-type amenities: mini-fridge, coffee maker, microwave, eating utensils, glasses, cups, and dishes. The units are an interesting cross between a hotel room, condo unit, private cottage, and small apt.! They are just big "enough" with a charming cottage look, both inside and out. *(Check in at Pali Ke Kua office across the street) Marc Resort Year Round Rates: Hotel Room Mt.V. $119 (2); Studio Suite Mt.V. w/ kitchen $159; One 1/2 Bedroom, 2 BTH Suite Mt.V. $179*

**HANALEI INN**
5468 Kuhio Hwy., PO Box 1373, Hanalei, HI 96714. (808) 826-1506. Owners are Michelle & Parnell Kaiser. Full kitchen, queen beds (3rd person or child okay on futon). Small, cute apartments, clean and well-kept. Outdoor phone for free local calls. Popular with kayakers, hikers, surfers - no couch potatoes here! *$65 per night. (Unit without full kitchen runs $55.)*

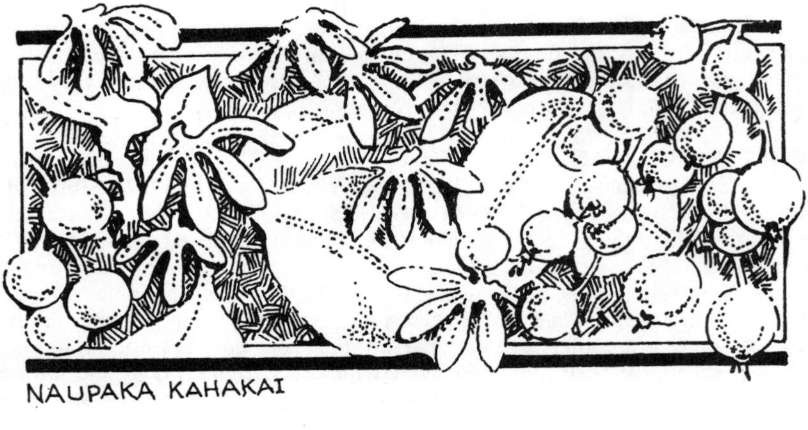

NAUPAKA KAHAKAI

**PANIOLO**
Located in Princeville. RENTAL AGENT: Hanalei Vacations 1-800-487-9833. Studio and 1 BR 2 BTH units. Swimming pool. Short walk to shopping and beach. *Studio and 1 BR units $105-125/$65-95.*

**SANDPIPER VILLAGE**
Located in Princeville. RENTAL AGENTS: Oceanfront Realty 1-800-222-5541. This property offers hotel rooms, 1, 2, or 3 bedroom units. Pool and hot tub. Some 2 bedrooms have loft, and some units have washer/dryer. Not all rooms have phones. *Oceanfront Realty Rates: Garden views as low as $45/night for a studio up to $140 night for 2BR plus loft. Outclean fee charged.*

**SEALODGE ★**
Located in Princeville. RENTAL AGENTS: Carol Goodwin rents her J-7 unit with a fabulous view of the Kilauea Lighthouse (plus other units at Sealodge) Write: 3615 Kingridge Drive, San Mateo, CA 94403 or call (650) 573-0636. Oceanfront Realty 1-800-222-5541. Maui & All Island 1-800-663-6962. Hanalei Vacations 1-800-487-9833. Prosser 1-800-767-4707. Ocean view units located along the bluff at Princeville. The exterior is cedar shake which is reminiscent of accommodations on the Oregon beachfront. While each unit has a different view, those on the farther eastern end have a spectacular view of the Kilauea lighthouse and Pacific coastline. Watch the waves come in over the extensive reef, enjoy the seabirds frolicking in the air currents, or during the winter, enjoy this outstanding viewpoint from which to watch whales. Just make sure you pack your binoculars! The trail down to the beach is marked by a "use at your own risk" sign and is steep and very slippery when muddy and recommended only for the hale and hearty. The trail ends on a rocky shore and you will need to clamor over the rocks to your left to reach the crescent shaped stretch of white sand beach that is the length of a football field. Because of the enormous ‘Anini reef, this piece of coastline is fairly well protected all year from high ocean swell and surf. With all the comforts of home, an outstanding vista, and value priced, you could hardly do better on the North Shore. Carol Goodwin offers great rates: *1BR 1BTH $95; 2BR 2BTH $125 (Cleaning fee charged for stays of less than five nights).*

## *MODERATE*

**ALII KAI I**
Located in Princeville. RENTAL AGENTS: Kaua‘i Paradise Vacations 1-800-826-7782. Hanalei Vacations 1-800-487-9833. Two bedroom, two bath units, some ocean front. Depending on the owners, units furnished with two double beds, one queen, or one king. Most units have sleeper sofas. Some units have full-size washer/dryer. Pool. *2 BR 2 BTH $140-150/120-130.*

**ALII KAI II**
Located in Princeville. On property management 1-800-648-9988. RENTAL AGENT: Kaua‘i Paradise Vacations 1-800-826-7782. Hanalei Vacations 1-800-487-9833. Some units with view of the ocean, others offer mountain vistas. Activity desk. Most units 1100 sq. ft. and have been recently redecorated. Most include microwave, TV, many with VCR and washer/dryer. Pool and hot tub. *2 BR 2 BTH $125/$110.*

**BALI HAI VILLAS**
RENTAL AGENT: Pahio VIP Services (808) 826-8270. This is a vacation ownership property, also known as Timeshare. Bali Hai Villas are one- and two-bedroom condominiums and one of the newest properties in Princeville. Each unit has an entertainment center and whirlpool bath. (Authors note: It would be our guess that Pahio VIP Services would be happy to introduce you to timeshare opportunities at this property during your stay.)
*1BR $145, 2BR $190, 2 night minimum.*

**(THE) CLIFFS AT PRINCEVILLE**
Located at 3811 Edward Rd., Princeville. Managed by Premier Resorts. RENTAL AGENTS: Premier Resorts 1-800-367-7052. Kaua'i Paradise Vacations 1-800-826-7782. Maui & All 1-800-663-6962. Hanalei Vacations 1-800-487-9833. Kaua'i Vacation Rentals 1-800-367-5025. Prosser Realty 1-800-767-4707. There are two hundred and two vacation studios, 1 BR 2 BTH, 2 BR 2 BTH, and even 4 BR 4 BTH units available through some rental agents. There is an onsite activity director with a variety of classes, hula-aerobics, and even a weekly local farmers market. Attend a free movie night or try out your talents at karaoke! Amenities include pool, 4 tennis courts, two jacuzzis, sauna, BBQ area, and a recreation pavilion. Units have ceiling fans, lanais, full kitchens. Daily maid service. Beach nearby. They underwent major renovations in late 1999.
*Prosser: Oceanfront 4 BR/4 BTH $175*
*Premier Resorts: Rates start at $155 for a one-bedroom g.v. with two night minimum required.*

**EMMALANI COURT**
Located in Princeville. RENTAL AGENT: Pacific Paradise Properties 1-800-800-3637, Kaua'i Vacation Rentals 1-800-367-5025. Two bedroom, two bath unit with ocean and golf course views.
*Nightly $175, weekly rate $1050/1200, cleaning fee $75 per stay.*

**HANALEI BAY VILLAS**
Located near the Princeville Hotel. RENTAL AGENTS: Marc Resorts 1-800-535-0085. Na Pali Properties 1-800-715-7273. These condominium units are actually single structures, with views of the golf course, mountains, and Hanalei Bay in the distance. The condos are 2 BR 2 BTH with the upper level providing living area kitchen, dining room and half bath. On the downstairs level are two bedrooms and two bathrooms. Beautifully furnished in pastel hues, lots of extras including lanais off both the top and lower levels.
*Marc Resort Rates:*
*2 BR Dlx 2 1/2 BTH suite w/kitchen mountain view or bay view $249-289, maximum 6.*

**HANALEI COLONY RESORT**
Rental Agent: Hanalei Colony Resort, PO Box 206, Hanalei, HI 96714. (808) 826-6235, FAX (808) 826-9893, 1-800-628-3004 U.S. & Canada. Email: hcr@aloha.net or visit their website: <www.hcr.com> RENTAL AGENT: Prosser 1-800-767-4707.

Hanalei Colony Resort is located on 4.5 acres of beach front, this village of condominiums (13 two-story buildings, each with four condominiums) offers accommodations with 2 bedrooms. Situated just prior to the end of the road at Napali, here is the last vestige of civilization. The rooms are decorated island-style and they are open and airy with fabulous views and the beach in your backyard. This is truly a place to get away from it all because they don't have TV's, stereos, or phones (although there is a telephone by the pool where guests can make complimentary local phone calls). They do offer a weekly complimentary poolside breakfast with tea, coffee, and juice and a selection of fresh fruits and freshly baked pastries. Hotel amenities also include pool and jacuzzi. Twice weekly maid service. Car and condo packages available. Weekly discounts. They also offer wedding coordination service. The Hanalei Colony Resort adjoins Surt's on the Beach and the Steam Vent Cafe, a popular Big Island restaurant "team" which opened here in late 1999. Surt's is open for dinner, Steam Vent for light meals and coffee drinks.

*2 BR g.v. $170/145; o.v. $195/175; o.f. $230/205, premium ocean $265/240. Prosser rents a corner 1BR 1BTH $145*

**HANALEI PLANTATION COTTAGES**
**(AND KAUIKELONI ESTATE)**

Mailing address: PO Box 81, Hanalei, HI 96714. (808) 826-1454, FAX (808) 826-6363. Kauikeloni, the historic plantation home of Albert Spencer Wilcox, has stood for over one hundred years. Wilcox was a successful turn-of-the-century sugar planter and the fourth son of missionaries Abner and Lucy Wilcox. The estate is bounded by the Hanalei River and guests can look out upon an expansive lawn to the waters of Hanalei Bay. Following Hurricane Iniki, the estate was restored with great detail to the historic era of the 1890's. The name Kauikeolani means "vision that come in the early morning mist" and the home was named after Albert's wife, Emma Kauikeloni Napoleon Mahelona. The estate can be booked at $1,000 per day (3 day minimum) or $5,000 per week, 12 person maximum occupancy, and a $350 cleaning fee. Day rates are available for banquets, incentive groups, and weddings. Rates begin at $1,500 for 1-50 people. All day use requires a $200 outclean fee and a certificate of liability insurance. Available for rent are three cottages adjacent to the main home. Historically these small houses served as guest and worker's quarters. Each is set apart from the others: *Umetsu Cottage (beachfront) 1BR, 1BTH (4), $225 night/$1,500 week. Palaka Cottage 2 BR, 1 BTH+day bed (4-6), $200 night/$1,200 week. Plumeria Cottage 3 BR, 1 BTH (6) $350 night/$2,400 week.*

*Two new beachfront cottages have been built to blend with the historic style. Nalu and Paniolo: 3BR, 2BTH (6), $350 night/$2,400 week.*

*3 night minimum on all cottages. Plus $100 cleaning charge on 1-2BDR; $150 cleaning charge on 3 BDR.*

**KAMAHANA**

Located in Princeville. RENTAL AGENTS: Oceanfront Realty 1-800-222-5541. Prosser Realty 1-800-767-4707. Pacific Paradise Properties 1-800-800-3637. Blue Water Vacation Rentals 1-800-628-5533. One and two story condominiums overlooking the golf course. Rooms have high slanted ceilings with ceiling fans which offer lots of sun during the day, though stay cooler at night.

Spacious, airy, modern kitchens are well equipped with all the necessities. The picture windows and sliding glass doors are all around and offer plenty of vistas. Our room had lots of extras, such as a closet full with goodies like books and cards, beach chairs, golf balls and even a boogie board. Since each is privately owned this will vary between units. Small, uncrowded pool area with "rec room" for gatherings. Located next to Sealodge.
*Prosser rents 2 BR 2BTH o.v. or golf/mt. view $85-120 for 2*

**MAKAI CLUB AND MAKAI CLUB COTTAGES**
Located on the first fairway of Princeville's golf course. The Makai Club features one bedroom condo suites with full kitchens, washer/dryers, lanai, TV, and VCR. The Makai Club Cottages are two bedroom cottages with full kitchens, lanais with ocean, golf, or mountain views. *Timeshare property only.*

**PALI KE KUA**
5300 Ka Haku Rd., PO Box 899, Princeville, HI 96714. (808) 826-9066. RENTAL AGENTS: Marc Resorts Hawai'i 1-800-535-0085, toll free FAX 1-800-633-5085, local (808) 922-9700. Hanalei Vacations 1-800-487-9833. Kaua'i Paradise Vacations 1-800-826-7782. Kaua'i Vacation Rentals 1-800-367-5025. Pacific Paradise Properties 1-800-800-3637. Oceanfront Realty 1-800-222-5541. Maui & All 1-800-663-663-6962. Hanalei North Shore Properties 1-800-488-3336. Located on the cliffs at Princeville, adjacent to the Princeville Golf Courses. Ninety eight units in two story wooden buildings with Hawaiian-style roofing. 1 BR units are 763 sq. ft., 2 BR are 1,135 sq. ft. Each unit is like a small, private apartment with a well-equipped kitchen and washer/dryer (with a starter box of detergent). The furniture is light bamboo with fabrics in rich colors and patterns. The units are fresh and particularly clean and well maintained. There are a number of nice appointments such as eyelet edge lace on the sheets and large counter space in both the kitchen and bathroom. Outdoor amenities include pool and jacuzzi. A short walk to a small beach. Winds of Beamreach Restaurant located on property.

*Marc Resorts Year Round Rates:*
*1 BR dlx mt.v. or g.v. $179; o.v. $199; o.f. $229;*
*2 BR dlx mt.v. or g.v. $229; o.v. $249; o.f. $299;*

**PUAMANA**
Located on golf course in Princeville. (808) 826-9768. RENTAL AGENTS: Oceanfront Realty 1-800-222-5541. Prosser Realty 1-800-767-4707. Two bedroom, two bath units, many with ocean views. Swimming pool.
*Prosser Realty offers a 1BR 2 BTH $95*

**THE SHEARWATER**
RENTAL AGENT: Pahio VIP Services (808) 826-8270. This is a vacation ownership property, also known as Timeshare. The Shearwater offers two bedroom condominiums with full kitchen, washer/dryer, entertainment center, and outstanding Pacific Ocean views. Bathrooms have a large tub with spa. (Authors' note: It would be our guess that Pahio VIP Services would be happy to introduce you to timeshare opportunities at this property during your stay.)
*2BR $210, 3 night minimum.*

**WAIOLI VACATION RENTAL**
PO Box 1261, 5539 Weke Rd., Hanalei, HI 96714. (808) 826-6405. E-mail: amadeus@aloha.net <WWW> Claudia Herfurt offers an 800 square foot apartment which is on the lower level of her home. It has a living room, separate bedroom, and outside patio, and BBQ. The bedroom view encompasses Kaua'i's magnificent mountains and waterfalls of Hanalei. A 50% deposit is required to hold reservations, refundable with cancellation 30 days prior to arrival. Located across the road from the beach. *Rates: $750 per week with a $65 cleaning fee.*

## *EXPENSIVE*

**HANALEI BAY RESORT ★**
Located in Princeville. RENTAL AGENTS: Quintus Resorts 1-800-827-4427. Maui & All 1-800-663-6962. Pleasant Hawaiian Holidays 1-800-242-9244. Hanalei Vacations 1-800-487-9833. Oceanfront Realty 1-800-222-5541. Kaua'i Paradise Vacations 1-800-826-7782. The property is now owned and operated by Quintus Resorts with sales and marketing handled by Aston Hotels & Resorts 1-800-922-7866. Built in 1979, it was completely renovated in 1994. The former Hanalei Bay Resort offers three floors with a total of 153 rooms. The former Embassy Suites portion added another 75 one, two, and three bedroom suites on three floors. No elevators. Suites are equipped with a complete kitchen offering a full-size refrigerator, stove/oven, microwave, dishwasher, and coffee maker. Units are spacious and nicely furnished, the suites have both a homey and a luxuriant feel. The high-beamed ceilings have tropical fans. Telephones in both living room and bedroom. The upholstered chaise lounge is romantic, elegant, and comfortable. One bedroom suites are 1,091 square feet with two televisions. Two bedroom suites are 1,622 square feet with two bathrooms and three televisions. Three bedroom suites are 2,085 sq. ft with three bathrooms, four televisions, and service for eight guests. Pay per view television on command is available for all!

There are a lot of free activities for guests: slide presentations, scuba lessons, and a tennis clinic. The on-site Bali Hai restaurant has a spectacular view. Sunday afternoon there is Jazz in the Happy Talk Lounge. The pool and jacuzzi are built in a natural lagoon setting surrounded by waterfalls with an island in the middle. It almost looks like it was there before and the hotel was built around it. The bathrooms are unusually decorated with a Victorian look: green tile and floral decor make it more homey and a lot less sterile than most hotel bathrooms. Resort amenities include the over-sized lagoon swimming pool and eight complimentary tennis courts (some lighted for night play) on the property. Rooms feature balcony, air-conditioning, telephones, and daily maid service. Non-smoking rooms available on request. Hotel rooms are 521 sq. ft. and studios are 570 sq. ft. The Princeville Makai and Prince Golf Courses are adjacent to the property (a total of 45 holes) with golf shuttle service. Conference facilities available. *Quintus Rates: Hotel rooms (1-2) $150-$230; Studio with kitchenette (1-2) $165-240. 1 BR with kitchen mt.v. & o.v. (1-4) $275-300, 2 BR 2 BTH mtv. & o.v. (1-6) $380-500, 3 BR 3 BTH o.v. (1-8) $690; 1 BR Prestige Suite o.v. (1-4) $500; 2 BR Prestige Suite o.v. (1-6) $750, 3 BR Prestige Suite o.v. (1-8) $1,000. 1 BR Suite mt.v. $250, o.v. $270 (1-4); 2 BR Suite mt.v. $350, o.v. $460 (1-6); 3 BR Suite o.v. $650 (1-8). Additional person $20. Room & car packages are also available.*

*Hanalei Bay Resort rates from Kauai Paradise Vacations: Hotel Room or studio $100-190; 1 BR $150-180; 2 BR $210-260; 3 BR $280-350. Rates do not including "outcleaning fee."*

**PRINCEVILLE RESORT ★ (HOTEL)**
PO Box 3069, Princeville, HI 96722. 1-800-826-4400 from the US & Canada, locally (808) 826-9644, FAX (808) 826-1166. For reservations call their toll-free number 1-800-325-3535. Visit their website: <http://www.princeville.com> E-mail: <info@princeville.com> Overnight accommodations can also be booked through Pleasant Hawaiian Holidays 1-800-242-9244

The Princeville Resort opened their 252-room resort in September 1985. The hotel was closed following Hurricane Iniki in September 1992 and reopened in October 1993. Readers of the Conde Nast Traveler have regularly voted the Princeville Resort in the top 50 resorts of the world. In 1996 the hotel was ranked No. 15 in a Conde Nast Traveler's Readers poll with more than 34,000 readers responding. In 1996, Golf Magazine named Princeville as a 1996 Gold Medal Resort.

The Princeville Resort is a stunning property set gracefully on 23 acres on Pu'u Poa Ridge above Hanalei Bay, with Bali Hai mountain forming a majestic backdrop. From the moment you enter the spacious lobby you will feel worlds away. While not traditionally Hawaiian, this hotel is classic elegance with a European flare. The use of water throughout the lobby, above the restaurant, and in the foyer creates reflecting pools that glimmer and glisten. With a lobby so enormous and opulent, it is surprisingly simple to find a quiet corner. Off to one side is the library lounge, a popular spot for taking afternoon tea, reading a good book, or watching the sun slowly sink from either the veranda or a cozy sofa indoors.

The resort comprises three separate buildings that terrace down Pu'u Poa Ridge, reaching from the top plateau of Princeville to the Beach of Hanalei Bay. The lobby and entrance are located on the 9th floor, the pool and beach are on the first floor. A total of six rooms are available for the physically impaired. There is a freshwater swimming pool and three whirlpool spas plus an exercise room and an in-house cinema showing movies daily. A thoughtful addition in the guest rooms is a Do Not Disturb light that you can switch on from next to the bed that glows out in the hallway. The bathrooms are divine, filled with oversize bathtubs, marble double vanities, telephones, and music speakers. In each bathroom there is a "magic" window which electronically changes to allow for view or opaqueness. It is right up there with the Halekulani on O'ahu, a shower with a view! Tasteful additions, such as the fresh orchids in the vase in the bathroom, add that pampered feeling. The view is one of the primary amenities here and from every possible angle of the hotel, they've incorporated that picture perfect setting. The resort is beautiful during the day, but perhaps even more spectacular at night. The Living Room Lounge has a very comfortable and homey feel and you can enjoy afternoon tea while you again get an opportunity to appreciate the view. Inquire about the Princeville Golf Club passes which offer multiple rounds for multiple days at discounts. Resort packages are also available including the Prince Package (which offers golf discounts and Breakfast), Luxury Romance Package, Luxury Taste Package, Luxury Holiday Package.

Cafe Hanalei is much more spectacular than its name seems to indicate. In fact, it doesn't have much at all in common with a "cafe." The bay of Hanalei below and the cliffs best known as Bali Hai create a lovely and romantic dining environment for breakfast, lunch, dinner, or Sunday brunch. Don't miss splurging on dinner here, or better yet, the Friday seafood buffet. The menu is a blend of American, Oriental, Hawaiian and a touch of Italian for good measure. La Cascata offers Mediterranean cuisine seven nights each week. The Beach Restaurant and Bar serves lunch and snacks daily. The resort also has available a very nice selection of meeting and banquet facilities.

Activities include their Hawaiian Cultural program of Hula and Hawaiian implement demonstrations, Hawaiian story telling, and lau hala weaving. Should you feel the need for extra pampering, the Prince Health Club and Spa is located at the Prince Golf and Country Club. Short term membership rates are $12 per person per day, weekly fee $45, two week fee $65, monthly fee $95. All users must be at least 16 years of age. See Spas section in the Recreation chapter for more information.

The Princeville Hotel's Keiki Aloha program is available for children 5-12 years of age and designed with play in mind. Qualified youth counselors plan a full schedule of activities including Hawaiian crafts, sand castle building, beach and pool games, evening movies. There is a charge of $50 per day for the first child and $40 additional child per family. Keiki meals are available and the lunch is charged to the parent's room based on consumption. Daytime program runs 9 am - 3 pm and evening programs run 3pm - 9 pm. Summer program runs June 1 - August 31. For children under age 5, babysitting is available. Current rate is $10 per hour per child plus tax. For children in the same family, an additional cost of $1 per child, maximum 3 children per sitter.

Even if you are not fortunate enough to have the opportunity to stay at this resort, be sure to stop and visit and you are sure to make plans for a stay during another vacation to Kaua'i.

*Mountain/Garden $380; partial o.v. $430; o.v. $535; Prince Junior Suites $625, Executive Suites $1100; Presidential Suites $2,800; and Royal Suite $3,600. Third adult person additional $60 per night.*

**PU'U PO'A**
5300 Ka Haku Rd., PO Box 899, Princeville, HI 96714. (808) 826-9602. RENTAL AGENTS: Marc Resorts Hawai'i 1-800-535-0085, toll free FAX 1-800-633-5085, local (808) 922-9700. Hanalei Vacations 1-800-487-9833. Kaua'i Vacation Rentals 1-800-367-5025. Kaua'i Paradise Vacations 1-800-826-7782. Oceanfront Realty 1-800-222-5541. Maui & All 1-800-663-6962. Hanalei North Shore Properties 1-800-488-3336. Pacific Paradise Properties 1-800-800-3637.

Fifty-six units in four-story buildings with ultra-modern exterior. Pool and tennis court. Units have washer/dryer, ceiling fans, full kitchens, and daily maid service. Renovated in 1999. *2 BR dlx o.v. $249; 2 BR luxury o.v. $299; (max 6)*

# *PRIVATE VACATION HOME RENTAL AGENTS*

**'ANINI BEACH VACATION RENTALS**
PO Box 1220, Hanalei Bay, HI 96714. 1-800-448-6333, (808) 826-4000, FAX (808) 826-9636. E-mail: anini@aloha.net <WWW>

They offer a variety of two, three, and four bedroom rental homes on the North Shore. Prices start at $1,200 per week and go upwards to more than $1000 per day. Give De'an, Phyllis or Jim a call!

**GRANTHAM RESORTS**
3176 Po'ipu Road, Suite 1, Koloa, HI 96756. 1-800-325-5701 (808) 742-7200. Email: info@grantham-resorts.com or website: <www.grantham-resorts.com>

Grantham Resorts offers 100 Po'ipu Beach rental properties ranging from bungalows to oceanfront condominiums.

**HANALEI NORTH SHORE PROPERTIES**
PO Box 607, Hanalei, HI 96714. (808) 826-9622, 1-800-488-3336. E-mail: hnsp@aloha.net <WWW>

Condominium rentals, plus many outstanding cottages and homes. Charo's own beachfront villa is available for vacation rental. It is situated on three oceanfront acres, complete with 4 master suites and 6 baths. Located on Tunnels Beach. Or how about "Club Nash" the premier beachfront estate of Graham and Susan Nash. 4 bedrooms, 3 1/2 baths on Hanalei Bay. This "old Hawaiian" style home was completed in 1992 and runs $4,200-5,000 per week. Other homes from $750-$5,600 per week. Condos from $500 per week.

**HARRINGTON'S PARADISE PROPERTIES**
PO Box 1345, Hanalei, HI 96714. (808) 826-9655, FAX (808) 826-7330. Toll free 1-800-720-9655.

A varied selection of homes and cottages, primarily on the North Shore. Five night minimum stay most of the year, with the exception of summer (one week minimum) and Christmas (two week minimum).

**HOMES AND VILLAS IN PARADISE**
1-800-282-2736, (808) 262-4663, FAX (808) 262-4817. Email: hvhi@aloha.net or website <planet-hawaii.com/homes-villas>

Cottages and a variety of three, four, and five bedroom homes.

**MAUI & ALL ISLANDS CONDOMINIUMS & CARS ★**
PO Box 947, Lynden, Washington 98264. Phone 1-800-663-6962. TOLL FREE FAX 1-888-654-MAUI. Website: <www.mauiallislands.com>

Rental homes on the North Shore and around Kaua'i as well as a large selection of condominiums.

**NA PALI PROPERTIES ★**
PO Box 475, Hanalei, HI 96714. 1-800-715-7273, (808) 826-7272, FAX (808) 826-7665. Email: kauai-1@aloha.net or website: <napaliprop.com>

Specializes in rental homes on the North Shore. They earn a star for having a wide range of selection and prices. They offer quaint cottages, five bedroom homes or even an outstanding historic 3 bedroom home on Hanalei Bay, built in 1904. Prices begin at $450 per week and go up to $2,000.

**PACIFIC PARADISE PROPERTIES**
PO Box 3195, Princeville, HI 96722. (808) 826-7211, 1-800-800-3637.

Rental homes and condominiums in the Princeville area.

**PROSSER REALTY ★**
4379 Rice St., PO Box 367, Lihu'e HI 96766. (808) 245-4711. 1-800-767-4707. FAX (808) 245-8115. E-mail: holiday@aloha.net <WWW>

Prosser Realty gets special mention for having a very interesting selection of rental homes, they also rent condominiums! They promise to find you the best possible vacation accommodations for the lowest possible price.

## *RETREATS/LARGE GROUPS/REUNIONS*

**ISLAND ENCHANTMENT**
PO Box 821, Anahola, HI 96703 (808) 823-0705, toll free 1-888-281-8292. <www.aloha.net/~enchant/Kauai.html> Humberto Blanco runs this accommodation in addition to offering Adventure Tours $75 per person per day. Accommodations are combined with a 6-8 day tour. Their outdoor adventures offer an opportunity to learn and practice the elements of yoga, body/mind techniques, meditation and massage plus swim beneath secluded waterfalls. You can also arrange for a one day custom tour $75. Call for prices on 6-8 day tours.
*$55-65, weekly rates available.*

**KAHILI MOUNTAIN PARK**
PO Box 298, Koloa, HI 96756. (808) 742-9921.
Website: <www.aloha.net/~kas/kmp.htm>

Owned and operated by the Seventh Day Adventist Church. The camp is 20 minutes from Lihu'e airport and 7 miles from Po'ipu Beach. Located on 197 acres. Cabins and cabinettes are available and accommodate up to 6 persons each. The cabinette offers 5 twin beds, 2 that can be made into kings, a kitchenette with a two burner stove and shared bathrooms and showers. $40 double occupancy. The cabin has two twin beds and one double and sleeps up to 4 people. (Two cabins sleep up to 6 persons). Each has 1/2 bath inside and an outdoor private shower. The kitchen includes a two burner stove and small refrigerator. $50 double occupancy. The new cabins have two twin beds and one queen bed, a kitchen with two burner stove. Full indoor bath and shower and screened porch. $60 double occupancy. Each additional person is $6. Laundry on premises. They provide linens (including bedding and towels) dishes, dish soap, cookware.

**KAI MANA**
Contact Sara Cash at (808) 828-1280. Kai Mana is no longer a B&B operation, but the cottage is available as a vacation rental with a 5 night minimum. TV, VCR. Hammock on the lanai and a tennis court out in front. Located in Kilauea overlooking a secluded beach. Rate is $150 nightly, $900 weekly plus tax and a $100 cleaning fee and $250 security deposit (refunded if no damages). Very private with tasteful Hawaiian decor.

**KAUIKEOLANI ESTATE**
PO Box 81, Hanalei, HI 96714. (808) 826-1454. FAX (808) 826-6363. Email: halelea@aloha.net or visit their website at: <www.hanaleiland.com>

The historic plantation home of Albert Spencer Wilcox, successful turn-of-the-century sugar planter and fourth son of missionaries Abner and Lucy Wilcox, has stood for over one hundred years. The estate is bounded by the Hanalei River and guests can look out upon an expansive lawn to the waters of Hanalei Bay. Following Hurricane Iniki, the estate was restored with great detail to the historic era of the 1890's.

The name means "vision that comes in the early morning mist" for this home named after Albert's wife, Emma Kauikeloni Napolean Mahelona. The estate can be booked at the rate of $1,100 per night (3 night minimum) or $6,500 per week, maximum 12 persons, and a $400 cleaning fee. Day rates are available for banquets, incentive groups, weddings. Rates begin for 1-50 people $1,500. All day use requires a $200 outclean fee and a certificate of liability insurance. Also available for rent are their Hanalei Plantation Cottages. (See listings under Accommodations--North Shore/Moderate)

**KEAPANA CENTER**
5620 Keapana Rd., Kapa'a, HI 96746. (808) 822-7968, 1-800-822-7968. Located on six acres. Room with shared bath $55 double, $40 single; room with private bath $70 double, $65 single. Rates include continental breakfast, use of jacuzzis. They also offer space for small group retreats. The yurt is a 24' round structure that can accommodate 3 persons. There is a limit of 12 persons in the house. Exclusive use of the house accommodations, 5 BR without breakfast is $300 per night, an extra $60 per night for the yurt.

**MAHINA KAI BED & BREAKFAST**
Box 699, Anahola, HI 96703. (808) 822-9451. An Asian-Pacific style home located on a terraced hillside overlooking Anahola Bay. The bed and breakfast rooms rent for $100 single, $125 double with breakfast included. Also available is a 2 bedroom apartment that can sleep up to six persons. Rates are $150 for two, $175 for three, and $200 for four to six. Also on property is a tea house and two large meeting areas. With a capacity for 12-14 persons, this property could be geared for a small retreat. Cost to rent the entire facility is $600 per night. Breakfast would be included and other meals could be served by arrangement. Three night minimum stay is requested.

**YMCA**
The YMCA operates ***Camp Naue***. It is located on four beachfront acres between the 7 and 8 mile markers on the State Hwy. past Ha'ena on Kaua'i's North Shore. Office: (808) 246-9090; Camp: (808) 826-6419. They offer two co-ed bunk houses that will sleep up to 50 people and a bath house with hot/cold showers and restroom facilities. The kitchen seats 60 people. They also have a 2 bedroom/1 bath beach cabin which sleeps up to 6 people. The beach cabin may be rented as part of a group reservation or for individual use. The beach cabin must be rented in order to receive exclusive use of Camp Naue. Because of the capacity of the camp, they only accept reservations for groups of 15 or more except for the cabin which requires no minimum but a maximum of 6 people. ***Camp Naue:*** *Bunk Houses -- Kaua'i resident $11 per person/non-resident $12 per person. Tent use -- one person with tent $10. Each additional person in the same tent $7 per person. Cabin (renter furnishes bedding) with group $40 per day, individual rental $50 per day. Kitchen use: $25 per day and is non-refundable.*

**YWCA**
The YWCA operates ***Camp Sloggett***. YWCA of Kaua'i, 3094 Elua Street, Lihu'e, HI 96766. (808) 245-5959, FAX (808) 245-5961, camp phone (808) 335-6060.

The YWCA hostel and campground is located in the heart of Koke'e State Park. The grounds offer 2 acres of open field space, covered fire pit for camp fires, barbecue area, volleyball and badminton nets. Sports and recreation equipment are available.

Henry and Etta Sloggett built the lodge in 1925 as a mountain retreat for their friends and family. Following Henry's death, the Sloggett children generously donated the house and grounds to the Kaua'i YWCA and in 1938 YWCA Camp Sloggett was established.

They offer accommodations in Sloggett Lodge which sleeps 10 in 2 bedrooms (3 people in each) and 4 in the main room. The kitchen facilities offer commercial double ovens and 6 burner stove, 2 refrigerators, cookware, and table settings for 58 people. A covered lanai space of 800 sq. ft. is suitable for dining, meetings, or recreational use. The Weinberg Bunkhouse sleeps 48 people with mixed single and bunk style beds. Two staff rooms sleep 4 each and two common rooms offer space for 16 each. The bathroom has 4 toilets and showers. In April 1995 they opened additional bathrooms and kitchenettes. Camp rates are $15 per person per night for Kaua'i residents. $18 per person per night for Hawai'i residents. Non-residents are charged $20 per person per night. Children age 5 and under are free. A minimum of 5 people weekdays and 8 people weekends. They require 10 people minimum on weekends during peak season May through September. Tent camping is available to Kaua'i residents for $5 per person per night. Hawai'i Residents $7 per person per night. Non-residents $10 per person per night. A 2 night minimum on weekends and 3 night minimum over holidays is required. Kitchenette facilities available. Hostel accommodations are in the Weinberg Bunkhouse and tent sites only and include use of bath and recreational facilities. Barbecue, microwave, and refrigerator are available on the lanai. No reservations. Individuals accommodated on a space available basis.

# *CRUISE LINES*

***CRUISING THE ISLANDS:*** One pleasant way to see the Hawaiian islands is aboard the ***American Hawai'i Cruises*** ship, the *S.S. Independence*. This 1,021 passenger, 682-foot ship provides comfortable accommodations and friendly service during its seven-day sail around the islands. In 1993, American Hawai'i Cruises was acquired by The Delta Queen Steamboat Co. public company, now American Classic Voyages, Co. In late 1999, American Hawai'i Cruises acquired the *Nieuw Amsterdam* from Holland America Line. This new U.S. flag ship will be renamed *ms Patriot* and join the *Independence* in service in December, 2000. The 704-foot *ms Patriot* will offer nine passenger decks, five lounges, two restaurants, a fully equipped spa and fitness center, two outdoor pools and a 230-seat theater. (Note: Two new U.S. flag 1,900 passenger, state-of-the-art cruise ships will enter service in Hawaiian waters in early 2003 and 2004.)

On board either the *Independence* or the *ms Patriot* you'll enjoy some outstanding Hawaiiana programs. Hawaiian costumes, hands-on Hawaiian museum exhibits, cabins with Hawaiian names, traditional Hawaiian church services, menus filled with Hawaiian specialties, and tropical flowers in every room are among the changes which bring the essence of Hawai'i on board. American Hawai'i Cruises has *kumu* (Hawaiian teachers) on board to instruct passengers about the culture and history of Hawaii. Both ships offer fully handicap-accessible suites. Currently the ***S.S. Independence*** departs Honolulu on Saturdays. It travels a seven day route from Honolulu to Nawiliwili, Kaua'i; Kahului, Maui; Hilo, Hawai'i and Kona, Hawai'i. Also available are a number of "Theme Cruises" which range from Big Band cruises to one which combines with Hawai'i's Aloha Festivals. The ship comes into port at each of the major islands for a day (or in some cases two) for touring.

"Beautiful Seas" wedding packages are available for couples who choose marriage aboard ship in Hawaii. It includes the services of an official to perform the ceremony, a small wedding cake, live Hawaiian music, a flower lei and floral headpiece for the bride and a lei or boutonniere for the groom, champagne and keepsake flutes, photography service and a 24 5X7 photos in a souvenir album. The wedding package price is $695 plus cruise fares. See Weddings & Honeymoons in this chapter for information on tests and licenses. For honeymooners that marry on the Mainland on a Saturday, they don't have to "miss the boat" to enjoy a Hawaiian Islands honeymoon cruise. While the normal departures are on Saturday from Honolulu, the "Sea and Shore" honeymoon enables couples to board the ship in Nawiliwili, Kaua'i. After six days on board ship, the honeymooners will enjoy a seventh night at a Waikiki Hotel. American Hawai'i Cruises offers shore excursions which include opportunities for passengers to discover the "hidden" Hawai'i. Trips include the opportunity to hike through a rain forest to discover a hidden waterfall. The idea of a cruise is to give you a taste of each of the islands without the time and inconvenience of traveling by plane in-between islands. In fact, it would be impossible to see all the islands in a week in any other fashion. For additional information contact American Hawai'i Cruises 1-800-765-7000 or FAX (504) 585-0630.

*There are other cruise lines that visit the Hawaiian islands on a less frequent basis. Check with your travel agent.*

# RENTAL AGENTS:

## *BED & BREAKFAST*

**Affordable Paradise**
**Bed & Breakfast, Hawaii**
332 Kuukama Street
Kailua, HI 96734
(808) 261-1693
Fax (808) 261-7315
Email: afford@aloha.net
<WWW>

**All Island Bed & Breakfast**
463 Iliwahi Loop
Kailua, HI 96734
(808) 542-0344
1-800-542-0344
Email: cac@hawaii.rr.com

**Bed & Breakfast Kaua'i**
105 Melia St.
Kapa'a, HI 96746
Liz Hey
(808) 822-1177
1-800-822-1176
Email:heyliz@hawaiian.net
<WWW>

**Bed & Breakfast Hawai'i**
PO Box 449
Kapa'a, HI 96746
(808) 822-7771
1-800-733-1632
FAX (808) 822-2723
Email:
reservations@bandb-hawaii.com
<WWW>
Al Davis & Evie Warner started B&B Hawai'i in 1979!

**GO NATIVE**
On-line guide to B&B Inns of Hawaii with listings by city.
Website:
go-native.com/Hawaii/HI.html

## *CONDOMINIUM AND HOME RENTALS*

**ASTON HOTELS & RESORTS**
2155 Kalakaua #500
Honolulu, 96815
1-800-922-7866
From Hawai'i 1-800-321-2558
FAX (808) 922-8785
<www.aston-hotels.com>

Aston Kaua'i Beach Villas
Aston Kaua'i Coast (Beachboy)
Aston at Po'ipu Kai
Hanalei Bay Resort
Islander on the Beach
Kaha Lani
Waimea Plantation Cottages

**CASTLE RESORTS & HOTELS**
1150 South King Street
Honolulu, HI 96814
(808) 591-2235
1-800-367-5004 US & Canada
FAX toll free 1-800-477-2329
<www.castle-group.com>
Kiahuna Plantation & Beach
Bungalows at Kiahuna
Lanikai Resort
Makahuena
Po'ipu Shores Condominiums

**GARDEN ISLAND RENTALS**
PO Box 57
Koloa, HI 96756
(808) 742-9537
1-800-247-5599
FAX (808) 742-9540
Email: gir@kauai rentals.com
www.KauaiRentals.com

Kuhio Shores
Manualoha
Nihi Kai
Po'ipu Sands at Po'ipu Kai
Whalers Cove
Also many rental homes including Stone House

**GRANTHAM RESORTS**
3176 Po'ipu Rd., Suite 1
Koloa, HI 96756.
1-800-325-5701 (808) 742-7200
www.grantham-resorts.com
Email:info@grantham-resorts.com

Kiahuna
Lawa'i Beach Resort
Makahuena
Nihi Kai Villas
Po'ipu Crater Resort
Po'ipu Kai
Po'ipu Makai
Waikomo Stream Villas
Also rental homes and cottages

**HANALEI VACATIONS**
PO Box 1109, Hanalei, HI 96714
(808) 826-7288
1-800-487-9833
Email: rentals@aloha.net
www.800Hawaii.com

Alii Kai
(The) Cliffs
Hanalei Bay Resort
Kamahana
Pali Ke Kua
Paliwili Cottages
Paniolo
Puamana
Pu'u Po'a
Sealodge
Plus oceanfront cottages

**HARRINGTON'S PARADISE**
PO Box 1345
Hanalei, HI 96714
(808) 826-9655
FAX (808) 826-7330

Rental homes and cottages
Specializes in 2-3 bedroom condos at Po'ipu Kai resort.

**KAUAI PARADISE VACATIONS**
PO Box 1708
Hanalei, HI 96714
1-800-826-7782
Email: kpv1@aloha.net
FAX (808) 826-7673

Alii Kai I & II
(The) Cliffs
Hanalei Bay Resort
Pali Ke Kua
Pu'u Poa

**KAUAI VACATION RENTALS**
3-3311 Kuhio Highway
Lihu'e, HI 96746
1-800-367-5025
(808) 245-8841
Email: aloha@kvrre.
www.kauaivacationrentals.com

(The) Cliffs
Emmalani Court
Garden Island Sunset
Hale Awapuhi
Kapa'a Shore
Lae Nani
Lanikai
Pali Kai
Pali Ke Kua
Po'ipu Makai
Pono Kai
Prince Kuhio
Wailua Bay View

**MARC RESORTS HAWAI'I**
2155 Kalakaua Ave., 7th floor
Honolulu, HI 96815
Hawai'i (808) 922-9700
1-800-535-0085 US/Canada
Toll free FAX 1-800-663-5085
<www.marcresorts.com>
E-mail: marc@aloha.net
Embassy Vacation Resort
Hale Moi
Hanalei Bay Villas
Pali Ke Kua
Pu'u Po'a
Pono Kai Resort

**MAUI & ALL ISLANDS CONDOMINIUMS & CARS**
*US Mail only*
PO Box 947, Lynden, WA 98264
*Canadian Mail only*
PO Box 1089, Aldergrove, BC V4W 2V1
Toll free FAX 1-888-654-MAUI
Local FAX (604) 856-4187
1-800-663-6962 US & Canada
www.mauiallislands.com
Email: paul@mauiallislands.com

Banyan Harbor
(The) Cliffs
Embassy Vacation Resort
Hale Awapuhi
Hanalei Bay Resort
Kaha Lani
(Aston) Kaua'i Beach Villas
(Aston) Kaua'i
Coast Resort (Beachboy)
Kiahuna Plantation
Lae nani
Lanikai
Lawa'i Beach Resort
Makahuena
Nihi Kai Villas
Outrigger Kaua'i Beach
Pali Ke Kua
Plantation Hale
Po'ipu Crater
(Aston) Po'ipu Kai
Po'ipu Makai
Po'ipu Palms
Po'ipu Shores
Pono Kai
Prince Kuhio
Pu'u Po'a
Sunset Kahili
Waikomo Stream Villas
Wailua Bay View
Waimea Plantation Cottages
Whalers Cove
Also private home rentals

**NA PALI PROPERTIES ★**
PO Box 475
Hanalei, HI 96714
Email: kauai-1@aloha.net
website <napaliprop.com>

1-800-715-7273
(808) 826-7272
FAX (808) 826-7665

Specializes in North Shore home rentals $500-$2000 weekly
Ask for Nancy or Jane!

**NORTH SHORE PROPERTIES & VACATION RENTALS**
PO Box 607
Hanalei, HI 96714
(808) 826-9622
1-800-488-3336
FAX (808) 826-1188

Hanalei Bay Villas
Pali Ke Kua
Pu'u Poa
Sealodge
Rental Cottages and homes from beachfront cottages to estates

**OCEANFRONT REALTY**
PO Box 3570
Princeville, HI 96722
1-800-222-5541
Princeville office (808) 826-6585
FAX (808) 826-6478

Alii Kai
(The) Cliffs
Hanalei Bay Resort
Hanalei Bay Villas
Kamahana
Pali Ke Kua
Paliuli Cottages
Puamana
Pu'u Po'a
Sandpiper
Sealodge

**OUTRIGGER HAWAI'I**
1-800-733-7777 US & Canada
0014-800-125-642 Australia
FAX 1-800-456-4329
<www.outrigger.com>
Outrigger Direct (808) 926-0679

Lae nani
Outrigger Kaua'i Beach

**PAHIO VIP SERVICES**
PO Box 3099
Princeville, HI 96722
(808) 826-8270
FAX (808) 826-6715

(Aston) Kaua'i Beach Villas
Bali Hai Villas
Ka'eo Kai
The Shearwater

**PLEASANT HAWAIIAN HOLIDAYS**
1-800-242-9244
6am-7pm Mon-Fri
7am-3:30pm Sat
<http://www.2hawaii.com>

(Aston) Kaua'i Beach Villas
Po'ipu Kai
Embassy Vacation Resort
Hanalei Bay Resort
Hyatt Regency Kaua'i
Islander on the Beach
Kaua'i Coconut Beach Resort
Kaua'i Marriott Resort
Kiahuna Plantation
Outrigger Kaua'i Beach
Plantation Hale
Princeville Resort
Whalers Cove

**PO'IPU CONNECTION**
PO Box 1022
Koloa, HI 96756
(808) 742-2233
FAX (808) 742-7382
Reservations 1-800-742-2260
E-mail: poipu@hawaiian.net
<www.poipuconnection.com>

Alihi Lani
Kuhio Shores
Makahuena
Po'ipu Crater
Po'ipu Makai
Po'ipu Palms
Prince Kuhio

**PREMIER RESORTS**
PO Box 4800
Park City, UT 84060
1-800-367-7052

(The) Cliffs at Princeville
Whalers Cove

**PROSSER REALTY** ★
4379 Rice St. or PO Box 367
Lihu'e, HI 96766
(808) 245-4711
1-800-767-4707
FAX (808) 245-8115
<www.prosser-realty.com>
Email: holiday@aloha.net

Banyan Harbor
(The) Cliffs
Hanalei Colony Resort
Kaha Lani
Kamahana
Kuhio Shores
Nihi Kai Villas
Po'ipu Kai
Po'ipu Makai
Prince Kuhio
Puamana
Sea Lodge
Waikomo Stream Villas
Wailua Bay View
Also homes and cottages

**R&R**
Realty & Rentals
1661 Pe'e Road
Po'ipu, HI 96756
(808) 742-7555
1-800-367-8022
FAX (808) 742-1559
Website:
<rnr-realty-rental.com>
E-mail: <randr@aloha.net>

Kuhio Shores
Makahuena
Nihi Kai Villas
Po'ipu Crater
Po'ipu Kai Resort
Po'ipu Palms
Prince Kuhio
Also rental homes

**SEASIDE KAUA'I**
2337 Nalo Road, Koloa, HI 96756
(808) 742-1165
Toll free 1-800-468-3992
E-mail: <rfarkas@aloha.net>
Po'ipu rental homes/condos

**SUITE PARADISE** ★
1941 Po'ipu Rd.
Po'ipu, HI 96756
1-800-367-8020;
(808) 742-7400
(808) 742-9121
FAX (808) 742-9121
E-mail:
<mail@suite-paradise.com>
www: <suite-paradise.com>

Specializes in "The Best of Po'ipu" Excellent service! Check their weekly condo rates and interisland as well as mainland to Hawai'i airfares and car packages.

Kiahuna Plantation
Lawa'i Beach Resort
Nihi Kai Villas
Po'ipu Crater
Po'ipu Kai
Po'ipu Shores
Whalers Cove

GINGER & ANTHURIUMS

# RESTAURANTS

The cultural diversity of the Hawaiian islands brings many benefits to visitors and residents alike. As immigrants arrived, they brought with them many varied foods from their native lands. Some may be familiar while others will offer an opportunity to sample something new and interesting. The restaurants are divided into the same three sections of the island as the accommodations. This should simplify looking for that perfect place for breakfast, lunch, or dinner based on the location where you find yourself. A little background on some ethnic foods may tempt you to try a few new foods as a part of your dining adventure on Kaua'i.

## *ETHNIC FOODS*

### CHINESE FOODS

*Char Siu:* roasted pork with spices
*Crack Seed:* preserved fruits and seeds - some are sweet, others are sour
*Egg Roll:* a rolled fried pastry with various vegetables, meat or shrimp inside
*Okazuya:* this is a style of serving where you select dishes from a buffet line
*Won Ton:* crispy fried dumpling

### FILIPINO FOODS

*Adobo:* chicken or pork cooked with vinegar and spices
*Cascaron:* a donut made with rice flour and rolled in sugar
*Halo Halo:* a tropical fruit sundae that is a blend of milk, sugar, fruits and ice
*Lumpia:* fried pastry filled with vegetables and meats
*Pancit:* noodles with vegetables or meat

### JAPANESE FOODS

*Fish Cake:* white fish and starch steamed together
*Miso Soup:* soup of fermented soy beans
*Sushi:* white rice with various seafood and seaweed
*Sashimi:* raw fish
*Wasabi:* very spicy green horseradish root used to dip sushi into

### LOCAL FAVORITES

*Plate lunches:* These combinations might include teriyaki chicken, hamburger with gravy or fish, but are always served with rice and a scoop or two of macaroni salad
*Loco Moco:* a combination of hamburger, rice, fried egg and gravy
*Bento:* a box lunch
*Saimin:* Top Ramen -- only better!
*Shave Ice:* flaked ice that can be topped with a variety of flavored syrups, sometimes available with ice cream

### PUERTO RICAN

*Pasteles:* an exterior of grated green banana that is filled with pork and vegetables

### KOREAN FOODS

*Kim Chee:* spicy pickled cabbage flavored with ginger and garlic
*Kal Bi Ribs:* flavored similarly to teriyaki, but with chile pepper, sesame oil and green onions
*Mandoo:* fried dumplings with meat and vegetable fillings

## HAWAIIAN FOODS

*Haupia:* a sweet custard made of coconut milk
*Kalua Pig:* roast pig cooked in an underground imu oven, very flavorful
*Kulolo:* a steamed pudding using coconut milk and grated taro root
*Lau Lau:* pieces of kalua pig, chicken or fish flavored with coconut milk and mixed with taro leaves, then steamed inside of ti leaves
*Lomi Lomi Salmon:* diced and salted salmon with tomatoes and green onions
*Long Rice:* clear noodles cooked with squid or chicken broth.
*Opihi:* these salt water limpets are eaten raw and considered a delicacy
*Poke:* raw fish that has been spiced. A variety of types of fish are used and are often mixed with seaweed; for example, tako poke is raw octopus

# *A FEW WORDS ABOUT ISLAND FISH*

Whether cooking fish at your condominium or eating out, the names of the island fish can be confusing. While local shore fishermen catch shallow water fish such as goatfish or papio for their dinner table, commercial fishermen angle for two types. The steakfish are caught by trolling in deep waters and include Ahi, Ono, and Mahi. The more delicate bottom fish include Opakapaka and Onaga which are caught with lines dropped as deep as 1,500 feet to shelves off the island coast lines. Here is some background on what you might find on your dinner plate.

***A'U*** - The broadbill swordfish averages 250 lbs. in Hawaiian waters is a "steak-fish." Hard to locate, difficult to hook, and a challenge to land.

***AHI*** - The yellow fin (Allison tuna) is caught in deep waters off Kaua'i and weighs 60-280 lbs. Pinkish red meat is firm yet flaky and popular for sashimi.

***ALBACORE*** - This smaller version of the Ahi averages 40 - 50 pounds and is lighter in both texture and color.

***AKU*** - This is the blue fin tuna.

***EHU*** - Orange snapper

***HAPU*** - Hawaiian sea bass

***KAMAKAMAKA*** - Island catfish, very tasty, but a little difficult to find.

***LEHI*** - The silver mouth is a member of the snapper family with a stronger flavor than Onaga or Opakapaka and a texture resembling Mahi.

***MAHI*** - Although called the dolphin fish, this is no relation to Flipper or his friends. Caught while trolling and weighing 10-65 lbs., this is a seasonal fish which causes it to command a high price when fresh. *Beware*, while excellent fresh, it is often served in restaurants having arrived from the Philippines frozen and is far less pleasing. A clue as to whether fresh or frozen may be the price tag. If it runs less than $10-15 it is probably the frozen variety. Fresh Mahi will run more! This fish has excellent white meat that is moist and light. It is very good sauteed.

***MU'U*** - We tried this mild white fish on Maui years ago and were told there is no common name for this fish. We've never seen it served elsewhere.

***ONAGA (ULA)*** - Caught in holes that are 1,000 feet or deeper, this red snapper has an attractive hot pink exterior with tender, juicy, white meat inside.

***ONO*** - Also known as Wahoo. ONO means "very good" in Hawaiian. A member of the Barracuda family, its white meat is firm and more steaklike. It is caught at depths of 25-100 fathoms while trolling and weighs 15 to 65 pounds.

***'OPAE*** - Shrimp

***OPAKAPAKA*** - Otherwise known as pink snapper and one of our favorites. The meat is very light and flaky with a delicate flavor.

***PAPIO*** - A baby Ulua caught in shallow waters -- weighs 5-25 lbs.

***UKU*** - The meat of this grey snapper is light, firm and white with a texture that varies with size. It is very popular with local residents. This fish is caught off Kaua'i, usually in the deep Paka Holes.

***ULUA*** - Also known as Pompano, this fish is firm and flaky with steaklike, textured white meat. It is caught by trolling, bottom fishing, or speared by divers and weighs between 15 and 110 pounds.

## *DINING BEST BETS*

While it is difficult to pick out dining "best bets," we have done our utmost to eat as much as we possibly could to provide you with what we feel is a pretty fair highlight of the most terrific dining options on Kaua'i. If you have some additions to our list, please do write us with your suggestions! After all, each person has their own distinctive tastes, likes, and dislikes. We would love to hear yours!

**BEST SMOOTHIES:** Fruit smoothies at Banana Joe's Fruit Stand or Mango Mamas in Kilauea, and the People's Market in Puhi, near Lihu'e. (Or try the "fruit, the whole fruit, and nothing but the fruit" frosties at Banana Joe's or Hanalei Juice Co.)

**BEST BREAKFAST:** Kountry Kitchen, Kalaheo Coffee Co. & Cafe, Eggbert's, and the Po'ipu Bay Resort Grill and Bar.

**BEST FRENCH TOAST:** Hanalei Wake Up Cafe.

**BEST BREAKFAST VALUE:** Ma's in Lihu'e.

**BEST FINE DINING IN A CASUAL ATMOSPHERE:** Roy's, Gaylord's, and A Pacific Cafe. Beach House

**BEST DINING VALUE:** Eat at one of the local style restaurants!

**BEST VIEW:** Al & Don's has a wonderful view, try it for breakfast. Other views can be enjoyed at the Beach House Restaurant (right on the beach!), Bali Hai with a view of Hamolokama Mountain and Waterfall, and JJ's Broiler overlooking Kalapaki Bay. If you can afford it, Cafe Hanalei at the Princeville Resort wins hands down!

**BEST SEAFOOD:** Generally, fresh fish and seafood are expertly prepared at our three favorite Kaua'i restaurants, Gaylord's, Roy's, and A Pacific Cafe. We also like Keoki's Paradise.

**BEST SUSHI**: We like the variety at Tokyo Lobby and the new creative choices at Sushi Blues. Our readers also recommend Steve's Mini Mart in Kalaheo and Pono Market in Kapa'a.

**BEST APPETIZER/PUPU**: Keoki's or Duke's (especially the calamari!), "The Kiss" at Casa di Amici Po'ipu, Postcards (in Hanalei)) for their innovative vegetarian selections, and Waimea Brewing Co. for their creative sauces and condiments.

**BEST DINNER BUFFET:** Hanalei Cafe at the Princeville Resort and the Ilima Terrace at the Hyatt.

FRI pm's seafood buffet

**BEST ORIENTAL:** Hanama'ulu Restaurant has good food and great ambience as does Restaurant Kintaro. We like Mema Thai Cuisine for Thai and Hong Kong Cafe for Chinese. Also try Tokyo Lobby or for more local-style, Kun Ja's.

**BEST BREAKFAST BUFFET:** The Hyatt Regency Kaua'i Best SPA

**BEST SALAD BAR:** There are very few, but Duke's could hold its own - even with a lot of competition!

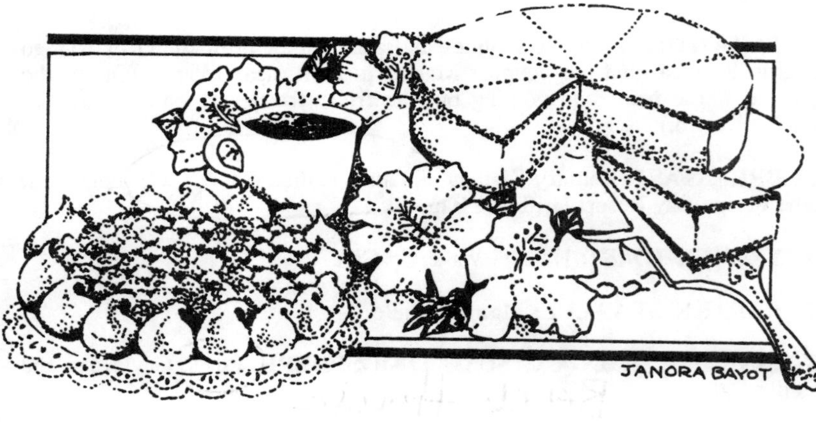

**BEST SALADS:** Warm ahi salad at A Pacific Cafe, the Oriental chicken salad at Princeville Restaurant, or a fresh green salad at Kalaheo Coffee Co. & Cafe. Sushi Blues' garlic sauteed mushrooms are served on a bed of lettuce that absorbs the great garlic-butter-sake sauce and makes it like a hot spinach salad!

**BEST SANDWICH:** The lean turkey Reuben at Joe's (either one), the chicken salad sandwich at Lizard Lounge & Deli, and the healthy, fresh, and colorful veggie sandwich at Mango Mamas.

**BEST PIZZA:** Brick Oven pizza, a long time favorite. Pau Hana Pizza gets points for its variety of unusual toppings!

**BEST MEXICAN:** Tropical Taco or tiny Taqueria Nortenos (called "The Crack") -- we also hear good things about the authentic Mexican fare at Maria's.

**GOOD AND CHEAP:** Hamura Saimin, Sueoka's, Barbecue Inn, and Waipouli Restaurant.

**BEST HAWAIIAN/"LOCAL STYLE":** K.C.L. Barbecue Drive Inn, Lawai Restaurant

**BEST BAKERY:** Kilauea Bakery, Roadrunner in Kilauea or the Bread Box in Kalaheo.

**MOST OUTRAGEOUS DESSERTS:** Roy's Chocolate Souffle, Keoki's Hula Pie, and the pies at Green Garden. We loved the spumoni ice cream cake at Pomodoro and the Toasted Hawaiian "sculpture" at A Pacific Cafe. Camp House Grill has a chewy chocolate chip macadamia nut pie or pineapple cream cheese pie that are both worthy of the calories!

**BEST HAMBURGERS:** Duane's Ono Burgers.

**BEST HAMBURGER EXPERIENCE:** The Whale of a Burger at Whalers Brewpub -- a feast on a bun!

**BEST SHAVE ICE:** Halo Halo Shave Ice in Lihu'e or Kamaka's small roadside stand in Anahola.

**BEST VEGETARIAN:** Papaya's has good casual fare, but Hanapepe Cafe & Espresso and Postcards in Hanalei both offer wonderful gourmet vegetarian dinners. We also hear good things about Caffe Coco.

**BEST MEALS ON WHEELS:** Tropical Taco serves up some great inexpensive Mexican food from their green van in Hanalei. Also Hanalei Town Farmers Market (in their blue truck) is parked in front of Kayak Kaua'i. Owner Michael O'Reilly Rowan offers quality local produce with everything from jabong (Japanese grapefruit) to Kaua'i honey. Their Kaua'i Natural salad dressings and meat marinades are wonderful. Open Tues-Sun 7 am-7 pm (summer), from 9 am in the winter. Michael's Hanalei Juice Company (next door) serves smoothies and juices year round plus sandwiches and salads in the summer.

## *RESTAURANT INDEX*

## *FOOD TYPE INDEX*

**AMERICAN**



**BAKERIES**



**BREAKFAST**



**BUFFETS/BRUNCH**

**BURGERS / SANDWICHES**



**CHINESE-VIETNAMESE-THAI-KOREAN-FILIPINO**

**FAMILY DINING**



**HAWAIIAN/LOCAL STYLE**



**HAWAIIAN REGIONAL/
PACIFIC RIM CUISINE**



**HEALTH FOOD**



**ITALIAN/PIZZA**

KILOHANA

# *RESTAURANT INTRODUCTION*

What do a green van in Hanalei and a restaurant owned by one of the top twelve Hawaiian Regional Cuisine chefs have in common? They both have earned stars! Tropical Taco has been operating for years out of this landmark vehicle on the North Shore and A Pacific Cafe is one of Hawai'i's most highly acclaimed restaurants.

The story begins long ago, in a land far, far, (well not really that far) away. When the first paradise guide was released, we rated the restaurants by one, two, three or four stars. It was quickly apparent that comparing restaurants as different as Tropical Taco and A Pacific Cafe was a problem. Each was wonderful for what it was, but did Tropical Taco deserve only one or two stars because it has no indoor seating, (no outdoor seating for that matter) and only serves lemonade? Thus evolved the solution of recommending a restaurant on a one-star basis. These are our "favored" restaurants or eateries based on their individuality. In their own way, Tropical Taco and A Pacific Cafe meet particular needs. They both provide very good food for the vacation dollar. So as you read through the restaurant chapter, we've highlighted these special restaurants with our mark of excellence -- a ★!

As with our Accommodations section, we've also added additional codes for those who prefer to surf for their Surf & Turf: <WWW> for restaurants with a website; <E> for those with E-mail.

The restaurants have been divided into Central/Eastside which will offer dining options for Lihu'e, Kapa'a, Nawiliwili, and Wailua. The Southern and Western portion of the island includes Po'ipu-Koloa-Lawa'i-Port Allen-Hanapepe-Waimea-Kekaha-Koke'e. Lastly the section on dining on the North Shore features restaurants (and vans) in the towns of Anahola, Princeville, and Hanalei.

We haven't listed the fast food restaurants, McDonald's, Burger King and the like. You'll have no trouble finding them speckled around the island. Just take a breath before you check out the prices.

Heavenly Creations in Anahola (828-1700) seems to be one of the few privately-owned catering companies on Kaua'i offering custom catering and a personal chef for all occasions. However, if you have guests to feed or are planning a party, you'll find that most restaurants -- from KFC to Keoki's, Green Garden to Gaylord's -- offer full catering.

## *CENTRAL/EASTSIDE*

**A PACIFIC CAFE** ★ *Pacific Rim/Hawaiian Regional Cuisine*
Kaua'i Village Shopping Center, Kuhio Hwy. in Kapa'a (822-0013) HOURS: 5:30-9:30 pm. SAMPLING: Menu changes daily, but your "First Taste" might begin with an appetizer like poached scallop ravioli with tobiko pearls (scallop flavor, but with a different texture) and lime ginger sauce, deep fried curried oysters with scallion sauce, firecracker salmon with sweet Thai chile sauce, or their signature tiger eye ahi suhi tempura ($7.75-10.25). Soup might be Thai coconut curry with island fish & shrimp ($6.25) or you might opt for a salad of spicy ahi, grilled Indonesian shrimp with mango vinaigrette, or Japanese eggplant with goat cheese fritter ($8.50-8.95). Entrees from the wood-burning grill might include fire roasted ono with shrimp risotto and Thai coconut green curry sauce (smokey, but lively and flavored with flare!), Moroccan marinated veal chop with cous cous, NY steak with gorgonzola cabernet sauce, grilled swordfish with Thai peanut sauce, or lacquered ahi with mushroom compote & orange soy caramel sauce. Specialties might feature their signature wok-charred mahi mahi in garlic sesame crust with lime ginger sauce, blackened opah with papaya basil sauce & kiwi ginger salsa, mushroom spinach stuffed chicken breast on garlic mashed potato, Chinese roast duck with braised baby bok choy, scallion flat bread & carmelized pineapple glaze, or local style steamed ono with green onion, ginger, cilantro, soy and sizzling sesame oil ($22.50-26.95). For $39, they offer a prix-fixe "tasting menu" where you can select a combination of one of the evening's appetizer, entree, and dessert selections with suggested wines for an additional $16. (A three-course vegetarian menu is available for $29.) If you can't decide on a dessert, a sampling is available ($11 for two people). This is a great way to indulge in the hot macadamia nut tart AND the banana lumpia, AND the chocolate bombe (with macadamia mouse filling), AND (our favorite) the delectable Toasted Hawaiian: white chocolate cake layered with haupia, white chocolate mousse, macadamia nuts, and caramel sauce that looks as distinctively Hawaiian as it tastes! COMMENTS: This is the one you've heard about. (And so has everyone else, so reservations are a must.) Owner Chef Jean-Marie Josselin is one of the twelve acknowledged Hawaiian Regional Cuisine chefs in Hawai'i and has garnered more than his share of accolades and awards since opening in 1990. They grow their own salad greens, vegetables and fresh herbs on their own organic farm often dedicating a night to a special ingredient (fresh mushrooms, for example) throughout a prix fixe menu. Chef Josselin has not only branched out with other award-winning restaurants in Hawaii, but has also written several cookbooks, has a weekly local television show, and a website at <www.pacific-cafe.com>

**AL & DON'S** *American*
Kaua'i Sands Hotel, Kapa'a (822-4221) HOURS: Breakfast 7-9:15 am, Dinner 6-8 pm. No lunch. SAMPLING: Large selection of hot cakes (with a variety of tropical fruit toppings and special coconut syrup), waffles or waffle sandwich, French toast, omelettes, and egg dishes ($3.95-5.75). Senior breakfast specials from $2.95. Dinners include French bread, choice of pasta or whipped potatoes and vegetable ($6.95-9.50). There is spaghetti, roast turkey (or hot turkey sandwich), leg of lamb, chicken stir-fry, mahi mahi, lasagna, pineapple baked ham, or ham & turkey combination dinner. Senior specials nightly from $5.95.

Chocolate dream cake, strawberry shortcake, cream pies, cheesecake, hula pie, or sundaes ($2.25-2.75) COMMENTS: They serve old-fashioned food at old-fashioned prices. Children's menu at half price. Breakfasts are the best bet, but any time before sunset buys you a great beachfront view. Karaoke on weekends.

**ALOHA DINER** *Local*
971-F Kuhio Hwy, Kapa'a, in the Waipouli Complex (822-3851) HOURS: Lunch Mon-Sat 10:30 am-2:30 pm; Dinner Tues-Sat 5:30-9 pm. Closed Sunday; lunch only on Monday SAMPLING: Local plates for lunch and a few more expensive ones for dinner: Kalua pig or lau lau with lomi salmon and rice or poi ($5.75); with chicken luau, haupia or kulolo and tea or coffee for dinner ($8.75). Other lunches include tripe or beef stew and various combinations ($6-7.25). Dinner with additional items as above and in combination ($8.75-10.75). All specials items available a la carte along with won ton and saimin. COMMENTS: You can try luau food without the show - or the expense!

**ARA'S SAKANA-YA FISH HOUSE** *Seafood deli/plate lunches*
4301 Kuhio Hwy., Hanama'ulu (245-1707) HOURS: 8 am-7 pm; Sundays till 5. SAMPLING: Sushi, poke, boiled peanuts or soy beans, kim chee, shrimp, and scallop salad. Plate lunches include rice, potato salad, and kim chee ($4.50-6.50) COMMENTS: Eat in or Take out.

**AUNTIE ONO'S KITCHEN** ★ *Breakfast & Lunch/Homecooking*
1292 Kuhio Hwy., Kapa'a (822-1710) HOURS: Breakfast 7am to noon. Lunch 11 am-2 pm SAMPLING: Two full pages of egg dishes and omelettes offer an unusual variety of meat, cheese, and vegetable combinations (like tomatillo & avocado, fried rice with kim chee, and homemade chorizo) as well as pancakes (including banana or tropical) and French toast ($4.25-7.95). Sandwiches like cod, veggie, tuna, turkey, and egg salad plus burger varieties that include teri, mushroom, bacon, BBQ, chili, patty melt, and pineapple ($3.95-7.95). Fresh fish, chicken or beef stir-fry, meatloaf, saimin, or fried noodles plus chicken or mahi burgers, hot & cold chicken stir-fry salad, and plate lunches run $5.25-7.95. Old-fashioned homemade pies have real flavor; there's nothing plastic or artificial tasting in the coconut or macadamia nut custard or the coconut vanilla or macadamia nut vanilla cream ($3.25). Keiki menu $1.75-3.25.

COMMENTS: The former Ono's Family Restaurant no longer serves dinners or their famous buffalo burgers, but hopes to resume both in the near future. Their service has always been outstanding: friendly, attentive, and enthusiastic. It's as if they are actually glad to see you and enjoy serving you! This is definitely family style with cute, homey decor: knotty-pine with lots of curtains, knick-knacks, and plates on the walls. Dress casual and be comfortable, the workers do. There are no uniforms and sometimes you can't tell the help from the patrons. It's as if you were in someone's home and the guests just get up to help - and the regulars here probably do! To be fair, we have heard disappointed patrons reviewing the restaurant as "oooohnooo" but we found it an "ono" (delicious) and very enjoyable experience.

**AUPAKA TERRACE AND SUSHI BAR** *Breakfast/evening pupus & sushi bar*
Kaua'i Marriott, poolside (245-5050) HOURS: Continental breakfast 6-10:30 am; Appetizers & sushi bar 5-10 pm. SAMPLING: Pastries, bagels, fruit, yogurt, Anahola granola ($1-3.25). In the evening, try the Hawaiian nachos, cheese quesadilla, fish fingers, Volcano wings, shrimp cocktail, jalapeno poppers, burger, teri chicken sandwich, or Caesar salad ($5.95-9.50). The sushi bar offers a variety of sushi & sashimi ($4.50-16) and maki sushi rolls ($5.50-9.50) COMMENTS: An attractive restaurant resembling a large gazebo in a park. Choose from a dozen liqueur coffee drinks and specialty martinis ($6.50-6.75). Cigars and board games available upon request.

**BARBECUE INN** ★ *American/Japanese*
2982 Kress Street, Lihu'e (245-2921) HOURS: Breakfast 7:30-10:30 am; Lunch 10:30-1:30 pm, Monday-Friday; Dinner 5-8:30 Monday-Thursday, 4:30-8:45 Friday & Saturday. Closed Sunday. SAMPLING: Breakfast meats and eggs dishes, pancakes ($2.25-7.50), and Oriental breakfast of miso soup, teriyaki fish, scrambled egg with green onion, rice, and hot tea ($6.95). Burgers, sandwiches, local plates, and Japanese dishes ($3.75-10.95) plus lunch specials: chicken strudel, roast duck or pork, beef cutlet, breaded shrimp platter, and pan-fried tuna steak ($7.25-11.95). Specialty salads include peppered or seared ahi, and Oriental chicken ($10.95-12.95). Dinners offer teri steak or chicken, spaghetti, lobster, garlic shrimp, pork chops and specials like Cajun prime rib, deep-fried coconut shrimp, macadamia nut chicken, seared scallops, cornmeal crusted calamari and their popular baby back ribs. Also Japanese dinners like teriyaki, tempura, yakitori ($7.95-22.95). COMMENTS: Lunch specials include soup or fruit, drink & dessert; dinner also comes with salad. All sandwiches come on their freshly baked bread; you can buy a loaf to take home! The same family has owned the restaurant in he same location since 1940 -- that's 60 years this millennium! It was named by the grandfather and although there are now a few token BBQ items on the menu, the BBQ in the name referred to a hibachi or small grill which was just the regular way of cooking. They have added a few more gourmet-style entrees and now serve champagne or wine, but basically, this is still a nice family-style restaurant (Keiki menu for both lunch and dinner) with booths and curtains and a plantation-style look. Recent renovations have given it a more open spacious look with lighter colors. Generous portions, good value, and friendly, attentive, efficient service. As one of our readers summed it up (in probably our favorite review comment of all time): "If you don't eat here at least once during your stay, you're an idiot!"

**BEEZERS** *Old-fashioned diner/ice cream parlor*
1380 Kuhio Hwy., Kapa'a (822-4411) HOURS: 8 am-9 pm (dinner entrees from 4 pm to 9 pm), sandwiches and desserts till 11. SAMPLING: Breakfast served all day: scrambled eggs, omelettes, Scramble (eggs, mushrooms, onions, peppers, potato with cheese and Picante Sauce), and loco moco ($3.95-7.95) or order from a "serious" selection of burgers ("Cheezer," Boca veggie, chili, egg, char-grilled chicken breast or fresh fish, patty melt) plus turkey club, BLT, cold pastrami, grilled veggie, "Stacker" (ham, roast beef, or fresh-roasted turkey breast), tuna melt, fried egg, grilled ham & cheese, hot dog, peanut butter with jelly, banana, or bacon, and homemade Sloppy Joe or meatloaf sandwiches ($4.95-$7.95). Homemade soup and chili; salads like the Beezers' Ceezer (with grilled chicken

or fish), chef's, turkey, or tuna with homemade dressings ($3.95-$8.95). Dinner entrees and Blue Plate Specials ($10.95-$18) feature chicken-fried steak, fried chicken, fish & chips, fresh fish, meatloaf, open-faced turkey sandwich, fresh fish, and grilled veggie platter. They're served with sides of mashed potatoes, country gravy, and vegetables and if you clean your (real) blue plate, you can have dessert! Quench your thirst with a flavored coke, ice cream soda, egg cream, or black cow then get into the thick of it with a malt (made with old-fashioned malt powder), shake or smoothie ($1.50-4.95). You scream, I scream, the homemade apple, blueberry, or pineapple-pecan crunch pie screams for a scoop of vanilla bean ($4.25) or spend some time on a sundae, on a banana in a split, on a brownie with fudge or with peppermint for a twist ($3.95-7.95). You can make a point of a cone ($2.25-3.95) wedge in a brownie, belly up to the cookie bar, square-off with fudge, or have your cake (carrot, chocolate) and eat it, too ($1.25-3.25). COMMENTS: A Beezer is somebody who loves ice cream and this old-fashioned ice cream parlor is the kind of the place that only a Beezer can love. The decor is "malt shop chic," from the booths in the back to the soda fountain in front. It's one small step up to the shiny counter to order or just to enjoy the photos from the 50's and the collection of labels and logos - and linoleum! - from long ago. Then, after you drink it all in, you know what you can do? Make like a banana - and split!

**BORDERS CAFE ESPRESSO** *Coffee/light meals*
Inside Borders Books at 4303 Nawiliwili Road, Lihu'e (246-0862) HOURS: Monday-Thursday 7:30 am-9:30 pm; Friday-Saturday till 10:30; Sunday 8 am-7:30 pm. SAMPLING: Sandwiches, soups, salads (and combinations), vegetarian chili, eggrolls ($3.25-4.95) Flavored slushies and smoothies ($3.50-3.75). Italian sodas, coffee and tea drinks. Chocolate crumb cake, baklava, brownies, cookies, $.85-3.50. COMMENTS: Small cafe with separate entrance or through Borders. Coffee bar or tables and chairs. Light meals and/or beverages served with plenty of reading material including out-of-town newspapers.

**BUBBA'S** *Burgers*
1421 Kuhio Hwy., Kapa'a (823-0069) HOURS: 10:30 am-6 pm. SAMPLING: Bubbas, double bubbas, hubba bubbas plus hot dogs, corn dogs, and Budweiser beer chili. "Alternative" burgers include fish, chicken, tempeh, and Italian sausage or fresh fish sandwich with pineapple lemongrass salsa ($1.50-5.75). Side orders of Caesar salad, french fries, onion rings, frings (fries and rings), or chili fries ($1.75-3.75). COMMENTS: With a name like Bubba's, you were expecting maybe escargot? They're fun and funny and serve good, old-fashioned burgers to anyone named Bubba. (That means you!) They used to "cheat tourists and drunks", but had to "cease and desist" after receiving a letter from a San Francisco attorney. So now they also cheat attorneys! Not quite as funky as their original location across the street, but still fun at twice the size with an old-fashioned counter and stools, murals and memorabilia on the walls and ocean-view seating on the veranda. They've got another hamburger joint in Hanalei; both locations have take-out and T-Shirts. Buy a hat or shirt and if you wear it when you order your burger, you'll get a free drink! Email: obubba@aloha.net Web: <www.bubbaburger.com>

**BULL SHED** ★ *Steak and Seafood*
796 Kuhio Hwy., Waipouli (822-3791) HOURS: Cocktails from 4:30, Dinner 5:30-10 pm. SAMPLING: Their trademark prime rib is $19.95. Other meaty offerings include garlic tenderloin, beef kabob, teri chicken or top sirloin, Australian lamb rack, garlic chicken, and pork baby back rib ($12.95-20.95). Shrimp, scallops, or crab ($15.95-21.95); in combination with steak or chicken ($14.95-26.95). Catch of the day is always under $20, usually $17-18, lobster at market price. Salad bar (included) offers basic ingredients, but a few unusual items like peas, fresh pineapple and garlic bread. Mud pie for dessert; kids menu of teriyaki chicken ($6.95) or fresh fish ($7.95). COMMENTS: We expected a dark and dingy steakhouse, but this was light and bright; very open with picture windows and a great ocean view. Arrive early for a view table! The food is consistently good and with rice, bread and salad bar, you get a lot for your money.

**BUZZ'S STEAK & LOBSTER** *Steak & Seafood*
Coconut MarketPlace, Kapa'a (822-0041) HOURS: Lunch 11 am-2:30 pm, Dinner 4:30-10:30 pm. SAMPLING: Lunch offerings include soup or salad ($2.95), and mahi mahi, grilled cheese, teri chicken, burgers, and French dip sandwiches ($4.95-6.50). Dinners start with mozzarella sticks, sauteed mushrooms, or teriyaki beef sticks ($4.95-5.95). Dinner, naturally, has steak and lobster, alone or in combinations plus shrimp, seafood plate, fresh fish, baby back ribs, and pastas: Alfredo, primavera, chicken, or shrimp ($9.95-17.95). Prime rib on Fri-Sat only ($18.95). Cheesecake or homemade ice cream pie for dessert ($3.95). COMMENTS: Dinner is served with fresh bread and choice of fries, rice, or baked potato. (For the hearty eater, most dinner entrees can be ordered at lunch.) Buzz's salad bar is also included with your entree ($7.95 a la carte). Early Bird specials from 4:30-6:30 pm are just $8.95 and include the salad bar!

**CAFE ESPRESSO** *"A Micro Bakery"*
1384 Kuhio Hwy., Kapa'a (822-9421) HOURS: Mon-Fri 8 am-2 pm; Saturday till noon; closed Sunday. Light breakfasts: Banana Belgian waffle, quiche, pancakes, breakfast burrito, cinnamon roll, bagels ($2.75-5.75); Hawaiian French toast on fresh-baked sweet bread with coffee or tea, $5. Turkey, tofu, or chicken salad; tuna or PB&J sandwiches on freshly baked honey-molasses wheat bread ($4.85) plus cakes, pies, pastries, juices, smoothies, and coffee drinks ($1.25-3.85). Almond poppyseed or strawberry almond bread, $1.35-1.50 a loaf.

**CAFE PORTOFINO** ★ *Italian*
3501 Rice St., Pacific Ocean Plaza, Nawiliwili (245-2121) HOURS: Dinner nightly 5-10 pm. SAMPLING: Roasted bell peppers, steamed clams, calamari, mozzarella (fried or with tomato), ahi carpaccio, and escargot are offered as antipasti ($8-13.50). Gaspacio, minestrone, or garlic soup ($4). Featured pastas are penne with broccoli & spinach, fettucine with shrimp & mushroom or Alfredo, linguine carbonara, pesto, or with clams, ravioli, canneloni, and lasagna ($13.50-17). Choose veal or chicken parmigiana, marsala, or Portofino style (with shrimp & scallops in lemon sage sauce), or veal piccata, ($18-20) or chicken in wild mushroom sauce, sauteed with artichoke hearts, or a la caccitora ($14.50-15). Specialties include osso buco, Provencale or lemon wine scampi,

and eggplant parmigiana ($15-25). Profiteroles, caramel custard, and tiramisu are some of the homemade desserts ($3.50-5.50). COMMENTS: It looks like an elegant stucco house with paned windows, beamed ceilings and a patio (a lanai where you can dine al fresco overlooking Kalapaki Beach). Nice bar and lounge areas with live music (usually jazz) on weekends. They recently won the prestigious DRONA (Distinguised Restaurant of North America) award for 1999-2000. Food is authentic Italian (and so is owner Giuseppe Avocadi!) with ingredients imported from Italy, then made fresh here. Breads, ice creams, and desserts made on the premises. Everything made to order; cream sauces are fresh, not from premade bases. We love their upholstered swivel dining room chairs. Why hasn't anyone thought of these before?

**CAFFE COCO** ★ *Bistro-style*
369 Kuhio Hwy., Wailua Village (822-7990) HOURS: Breakfast 9 am-noon (Sun till 2); continuous menu till 9 pm. Closed Monday. SAMPLING: Fruit bowl, homemade granola, scrambled egg croissant or egg or tofu burrito, roast veggie omelette for breakfast ($2.50-7.50). Light meals include potstickers, Greek or tofu salad, sandwiches on focaccia bread (BBQ or roast turkey, seared ahi, roast eggplant & cheese) and wraps: tofu & roast veggie, Greek salad or fish ($5.50-8.50). Platters with rice & salad offer spiced tofu, seared fresh fish, macadamia sesame encrusted ahi, pasta del giorno ($10.50-14.50). Morrocan spiced seared fish or tofu, fish burrito, ahi nori wrap, gumbo & rice, homestyle pot pie, sweet potato cakes, spanikopita, pizza, and Thai pumpkin coconut might be some of the blackboard specials. Pumpkin spice cake, haupia pudding with tropical fruit sauce, banana fruit tart, Mexican chocolate tofu pie (vegan), or black mocha ice cream roll are some of the homemade desserts ($3.95). Cool drinks (iced green tea & hibiscus, chai, fruit fizz, or ginger-lemon) are $2. Coffee drinks and espresso. COMMENTS: Caffe and art gallery surrounded by cane fields in a restored plantation home. Eclectic collection of tables and chairs in various corners and cozy nooks inside; garden seating amidst hanging foliage, orchid ferns, and lilikoi shade trees outside. The display case offers savory items like curried vegetable samosa plus homemade pastries and desserts. Not inexpensive, but we've heard nothing but good reviews all around and Christie raved about the Ahi Nori Wrap with warm flour tortilla & wasabi sauce. They feature fresh fish and locally grown-produce -- whatever they have in their garden that day! The browsable Bambulei furniture and gift shop is next door.

**CAMP HOUSE GRILL & BAR** ★ *American/Home Cooking*
Kaua'i Village, Kapa'a (822-2442) HOURS: Breakfast 6:30-11 am, lunch 11 am-9 pm, dinner 5-9 pm. SAMPLING: Breakfast quesadilla, pancakes, omelettes, French toast, biscuits and gravy, eggs benedict, omelettes and a variety of breakfast sandwiches - Monte Cristo with hash browns, or BLT (& egg), pancake or French toast with bacon & eggs ($3.95-8.95). They have early bird specials ($1.99-2.99) before 8 am, but as they say on the menu: After 8:01, No Way! Grilled fish, veggie, BLT, or turkey BLT sandwiches; chili ($3.95-7.95). Lunch and dinner offerings include a variety of burgers, salads, several grilled chicken entrees, BBQ pork ribs, sirloin steak Polynesian, and fresh catch served with soup or salad and choice of side ($7.95-14.95). Dinners of pork chops, prime rib, steak, scampi, or crab leg ($11.95-18.95). They're known for their homemade pies, so if you don't save room for dessert, you'll just have to buy a whole one from the glass case on your way out. Pineapple cream cheese macadamia pie or

chewy chocolate chip macadamia nut sound good enough to eat (and they are!) and so do the cream pies of coconut, banana, and chocolate or the Paradise Pie made with macadamia nut, pineapple and coconut. COMMENTS: It's home cooking all the way and home baking as far as the pies are concerned. Menehune (children's) menu available for lunch and dinner. This new, 3,000 square foot restaurant is owned by Nick Morrison and features the same family-style atmosphere and home-style cooking that have been traditions at the original Camp House Grill for more than a decade. The first Camp House Grill opened in Kalaheo in 1987; the second (Camp House Grill & Cantina) opened in the old Sinaloa location in Hanapepe at the end of 1998.

**CASCADES** *Sandwiches/salads*
Outrigger Kaua'i Beach (245-1955) HOURS: Food service 12-4 pm; bar open till 6. SAMPLING: Bacon cheese, teriyaki or chili burgers ($6.75-7.50), hot dogs ($4.95-6.25), mahi burger, chili burrito, nachos, chili & rice ($3.50-7), fresh fruit or garden salad ($8.75-9.50), fruit stix, Haagen Daz ice cream bar, coffee sodas, shave ice, popcorn, pizza ($1.75-3.25) COMMENTS: Poolside snack bar by the hotel's cascading waterfall. Exotic tropical drinks.

**COCONUT MARKETPLACE:**
(484 Kuhio Highway, Kapa'a) Lappert's ice cream, Tradewinds Bar, and several small restaurants (indicated here) make this shopping center into a kind of extended food court. Some of the larger restaurants and/or those having something particular to recommend them are also listed individually and alphabetically.

**ALOHA KAUA'I PIZZA** (822-4511) Calzone, lasagna, salads, and Italian sandwiches $5.50-7.95 (pizzas to $22.95). Fresh ingredients, turkey meatballs, sausage and sauces from a 120-year-old family recipe have made this an *Entertainment Book* winner several years running.

**BUZZ'S STEAK & LOBSTER** (822-0041) See individual listing.

**EGGBERT'S** (822-3787) See individual listing.

**(THE) FISH HUT** (822-2505) Fish-n-chips plus charbroiled fish, fried seafood (shrimp, scallops, oysters) in combinations with french fries & homemade cole slaw. ($6.95-9.95).

**HARLEY'S RIBS-N-CHICKEN** (822-2505) No surprise, they serve ribs and BBQ chicken!

**KRAZY COCONUT CAFE** (822-9227) Breakfast sandwiches & wraps, French toast, omelettes. Sub sandwiches (turkey, tuna, pastrami, BLT, ham & cheese), and wraps: Greek, Veggie, and Chicken Caesar, Cajun or Cordon Bleu wrapped in flavored tortillas ($4.95-7.95). Espresso, coffee drinks, and smoothies.

**PALM TREE TERRACE** (823-9181) Sandwiches (garlic chicken, pastrami, crab), appetizers (calamari rings, mozzarella sticks, jalapeno poppers) and beef or chicken kabobs, pork chops, steak, shrimp or chicken Alfredo pasta with salad bar. ($4.95-14.95)

**TACO DUDE** (822-1919) Good Mexican food at this wrap around counter. White meat chicken, special seasonings, and healthy preparations make this a cut above. Huge portions moderately priced from $1.75-8 including tax.

**TC'S ISLAND GRILL** (823-9181) Local-style breakfasts plus hot dogs, hamburgers, salads, sandwiches, chili, and teriyaki beef or fried chicken platters $4.95-7.95.

**ZACK'S FAMOUS FROZEN YOGURT AND CAFE** (246-2415) See individual listing.

**DAIRY QUEEN** *Local*
4302 Rice St., Lihu'e (245-2141) HOURS: Mon-Thurs 7 am-9:30 pm, Fri-Sat till 10, Sun 7:30 am-3:30 pm. (Breakfast till 11 am, Dinner after 5 pm.) SAMPLING: Hot cakes, omelettes, waffles, French toast, and egg breakfasts ($3.95-5.25). Sandwiches include hot turkey, BLT, pastrami, club, tuna, and hot dogs ($2.95-5.75); burgers with cheese, bacon, mushrooms, teriyaki, and BBQ or you can get your "burger" made with fish, chicken, or as a tuna or patty melt on rye ($1.20-5.95). Saimin, soup, salads, loco moco ($1.95-5.50) and entrees of pork chops, liver and onions, sweet & sour spare ribs, breaded fish, beef stew, chicken and veal cutlets ($5.45-8.50). Dinners offer rib steak, mahi mahi, breaded shrimp, steak and scampi ($9.50-16.95). For dessert, there are all the familiar Dairy Queen treats like cones, shakes, floats, freezes, and a variety of sundaes ($1.65-4.50). COMMENTS: A lot of food for an ice cream shop; the whole menu is available for take out and they have catering, too. With the closing of the Waimea and Ele'ele DQ's, this is the now the only Dairy Queen left on Kaua'i.

**DANI'S** *Local*
4201 Rice St., Lihu'e (245-4991) HOURS: Breakfast 5-11 am; Lunch 11:30 am-1 pm. Closed Sundays. SAMPLING: Breakfast meats, eggs, and omelettes including kalua pig and Dani's special with fish cake, green onion, and tomato ($4.70-6). Pineapple, banana, papaya hot cakes and sweet bread French toast ($3.60-5.70). Breakfast and lunch specials include combinations of lau lau, kalua pig, beef or tripe stew ($5.20-8.40) and lunch entrees offer hamburger steak, pork chops, roast pork, veal, beef or chicken cutlet, fried shrimp, oysters or scallops, plus burgers and sandwiches ($1.80-6.20). COMMENTS: Popular local coffee shop. Kind of looks like an Elks Lodge Hall without the elk. While Dani's might be a bit brighter (and even cleaner) we recommend driving around the corner to Ma's!

**DELI & BREAD CONNECTION** *Deli/Sandwiches*
Kukui Grove Shopping Center, 3171 Kuhio Highway, Lihu'e (245-7115) HOURS: 9:30 am (from 10 on Sundays) to 7 pm (till 9 on Fridays, 6 Saturdays, 5 Sundays). SAMPLING: Sandwiches on freshly-baked bread or rolls include roast beef, pastrami, corned beef, smoked ham, liverwurst, chicken salad, and crab meat. ($3.98-4.65). French Dip, tuna or chicken with avocado, Reuben, BLT, meatloaf, or club ($4.75-5.85), sub or poor boy with choice of ingredients ($5.70-7.50). Vegetarian sandwiches and daily homemade soups ($2.50-5.50).

COMMENTS: We've heard good things about their fresh (and freshly-made) ingredients and generous portions. They also sell gourmet books, kitchen gadgets, and cookware in an old-fashioned general store setting. Bakery breads include rye, wheat, sour dough, French and their signature Oriental sweet bread plus giant muffins and cookies, cinnamon rolls, manju, brownies, and pies. Indoor and outdoor seating.

**DORI'S GARDEN CAFE** *Sandwiches & sandwiches*
Roxy Square (part of Sunnyside Market) 1345 Kuhio Hwy., Kapa'a (822-0494) HOURS: 8 am-7 pm SAMPLING: Hot or cold corned beef, pastrami, or salami sandwiches on rye ($5.59); gourmet sandwiches include sauteed eggplant, smoked turkey, hummus, and sugar cured ham ($4.79). Homemade soups like vegetable chili, beef stew, chicken noodle, and clam chowder ($2.59-3.79); garden, tuna, or cobb salad ($5.49-5.99). Fruit smoothies in assorted combinations of papaya, strawberry, pineapple, banana, and mango ($2.79) COMMENTS: Small, casual cafe that's a kind of "patio" to the Sunnyside Market next door. The market offers take-home pineapples, mac nuts, and papayas boxed for shipping and also carries snacks, beverages, coffees, candy, and food products along with crafts, gifts, T-shirts, clothes -- even shrunken heads!

**DUKE'S CANOE CLUB** ★ *Steak & Seafood*
Located in front of the Kaua'i Marriott at Kalapaki Beach. (246-9599) HOURS: Lunch and Barefoot Bar menu 11:30 am-11:30 pm. Dinner 5-10 pm. SAMPLING: Pizza, burgers & sandwiches, salads, pupus, and Hawaiian local plates for lunch ($3.95-9.95). Stir fry chicken cashew, pork ribs, fish tacos, roast beef & cheddar sandwich, and grilled mahi Caesar are just a few of the options. Fresh fish, seafood, steaks, and prime rib are still the most popular dinner offerings with almost all entrees priced under $20. All include a very serious salad bar that has a fresh Caesar salad station, fresh greens, and variety of veggies, prepared salads like macaroni, cole slaw, pasta and potato plus warm breads, macadamia lemon muffins, and carrot muffins. A fantastic value with dinner or a meal in itself for $9.95.

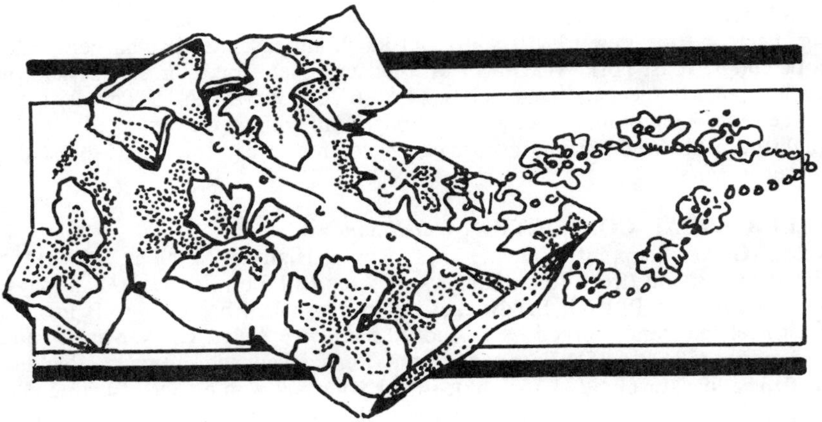

Duke's has been "modernizing" its menu of late with innovative new dishes like Thai seafood coconut curry ($17.95); Linguine with basil and sun-dried tomatoes ($14.95), Thai chicken pizza (with a delicious sweet chile sauce and light, homemade pizza crust) at $8.95; and appetizers of mac nut & crab wonton, poke rolls (with Maui onion), and great, thick sticks of perfectly prepared calamari ($6.95-9.95). Their (Kimo's) hula pie is the best, but the Kona coffee cheesecake can hold its own. Complete keiki dinners under $6. COMMENTS: Named in honor of Duke Kahanamoku (probably the greatest surfer of all time), the restaurant features an extensive collection of Duke memorabilia including photos, an impressive 40-foot outrigger canoe, and three of his surfboards. The lava rock waterfall in the center is a focal point, with stairs alongside and a spacious and attractive area upstairs. There is a separate area with a salad bar and wide plantation-like verandas which overlook the ocean. (Part of the beachfront lanai is portioned off for private parties, a great place to celebrate a special-occasion anniversary or birthday in your own little corner of the world!) Duke's required extensive renovation after Iniki, but the 30-foot waterfall is as spectacular as ever, creating a unique centerpiece as it splashes into a koi pond. Duke's Canoe Club is owned and managed by TS Restaurants which also operates Keoki's Paradise at Po'ipu and several other restaurants in Hawai'i and Southern California including the popular Kimo's and Hula Grill on Maui. Strolling musicians in the dining room; live music and entertainment in the Barefoot Bar on weekends.

**EGGBERT'S FAMILY SPECIALTY RESTAURANT** *Breakfast/lunch*
Coconut MarketPlace, by the water wheel (822-3787) HOURS: Breakfast 7 am-3 pm; Lunch 11 am-3 pm; Dinner 5-9 pm SAMPLING: Eggs Benedict in five styles (combos of veggie, ham, or turkey) and two sizes ($7.45-10.25) or create your own with additional ingredients ($.85-1.50) - all with Eggbert's own Hollandaise made fresh with tangy lemon. Omelette varieties include ham, Portuguese sausage, mushrooms, sour cream & chives, tomato & cheese, and Denver ($4.25-9.95) or you can choose your fillings for $1.85-2.95. Egg plates, pigs-in-a-blanket, French toast (with cinnamon and vanilla), and banana hotcakes round out the breakfast menu ($4.25-6.95). Lunch specialties offer turkey or ham club sandwiches, fried rice "crowned" with a crepe-thin omelette, pork & cabbage, and the definitive brunch dish: Eggbert's Big "O" omelette sandwich with choice of ingredients ($4.75-7.95) Dinner entrees include NY steak, fresh catch, stir frys (fish, chicken, beef, or pork) meat loaf, roast pork, and BBQ chicken ($8.95-14.50). Senior and children's portions available from $5.95. COMMENTS: Eggs Benedict, along with keiki favorites like banana pancakes and pigs-in-a-blanket, are the specialties carried over from their pre-hurricane location in Lihu'e. Their "water-wheel" corner of the Coconut MarketPlace is open and airy with comfortable space between the tables and a veranda that's perfect for people watching.

**ENDLESS SUMMER** *Snacks/farmers market*
3366 Wa'apa Road, (adjacent to Anchor Cove) Lihu'e (246-8854) HOURS: 9 am-9 pm (Monday 9 am-5 pm) SAMPLING: Hot dogs, chili & rice, smoothies, shakes, Lappert's ice cream ($3-5). COMMENTS: Fresh fruit stand and mini-farmers market in front. Try an Endless Summer smoothie with papaya, banana, pineapple, lilikoi, and coconut juice.

**(THE) FISH EXPRESS** *Seafood/fish*
3343 Kuhio Hwy., Lihu'e by Wal-Mart (245-9918) HOURS: 10 am-7 pm Mon-Sat., till 5 pm Sun. SAMPLING: Plate lunches ($5.95), Kalua or lau lau plate ($6.95), seafood lunch ($7.95). Prepared fish with a variety of sauces: Provencal, passion-orange & tarragon, ginger-curry, blackened with guava-basil ($6.95). COMMENTS: Seafood deli with limited seating.

**FLYING LOBSTER** *Seafood*
Kaua'i Coconut Beach Resort, Kapa'a (822-3455) HOURS: 5:30-9:30 pm. SAMPLING: Signature lobster dinners from $21 plus steak, scampi, herb roasted or honey-macadamia chicken, BBQ ribs, and fresh catch, ($13-17); crab legs ($24). All-you-can-eat pasta (with mix and match pastas & sauces) includes a small salad ($8.95). Combination dinners from chicken & ribs to steak & lobster ($14-26). Limited menu of burgers and sandwiches plus Caesar salad with shrimp and appetizers of calamari rings, crab legs, shrimp, hot crab dip with garlic toast or Clams Casino ($4-7.50). Dinners include soup or salad bar, starch and vegetable. Desserts include cakes, pies, ice cream and Kaua'i Coconut Beach Sand Pie ($2.75-4). COMMENTS: Early Bird specials ($12.95) nightly, 5:30-6:30 pm. Friday-Saturday prime rib & seafood buffet ($23.95Adult/$14.50Teen/$12Child). This is called The Voyage Room at breakfast and lunch; see separate listing.

**GARDEN ISLAND BBQ AND CHINESE RESTAURANT** *Chinese/local*
4252 Rice St. in Lihu'e (245-8868) HOURS: Monday-Saturday 10:30 am-9 pm, Closed Sunday. SAMPLING: Chicken, beef, pork & shrimp dishes plus chow mein, BBQ, soups, and combination plates ($3.75-6.95) like lemon chicken, beef curry, pork with bitter melon, shrimp with eggplant, loco moco, BBQ short ribs, sweet & sour spare pork, scallop soup, rainbow tofu soup, and House "Chop Suey Chow Mein!" Burgers and sandwiches ($1.25-2.80). COMMENTS: Good selection of inexpensive local and now Chinese food located next to the thrift store bakery on Rice Street. (This tiny little restaurant recently expanded to about three times its original size so now it is next to the thrift store and next to that and next to that!)

**GAYLORD'S RESTAURANT** ★ *American*
At Kilohana Plantation just outside of Lihu'e (245-9503) HOURS: Lunch Monday-Saturday 11 am-3 pm, Sunday brunch 9:30 am-3 pm, Dinner nightly from 5 pm. SAMPLING: Menus change daily. Innovative lunch salads might include papaya stuffed with shrimp, Oriental chicken, Greek-style roasted vegetable, Caesar with red peppers and mild goat cheese coated with macadamias, or Salpicon: local greens with bell pepper, onion, tomato, ahi, cactus(!), avocado, and feta cheese ($8.95-9.95). Sandwiches come with soup or salad and fries or rice: San Francisco Reuben (on sourdough), turkey and avocado, a variety of burgers, Monte Cristo, and a tasty ground ahi burger with pickled ginger and a special sauce ($7.95-9.95). Signature lunch dishes range from baby back ribs to sweet & sour chicken or try the Farmer's Pie (vegetables under a crust of whipped potatoes), grilled Alaskan salmon, honey-dipped chicken, or capellini pomodoro ($8.95-11.95). Dinners might feature appetizers of coconut shrimp, spicy crab cakes, pan-seared sashimi, hot crab & artichoke heart dip, and honey-baked or garlic brie ($8.95-9.95) and entrees of steak, fresh fish, baby back ribs, rack of lamb, seafood rhapsody, prime rib (regular or blackened), and chicken served Florentine, Greek, or Kaua'i style with papaya,

pineapple, and macadamia nut wine sauce ($17.95-28.95). Sauteed venison is a specialty at $29.95 and the prime rib & lobster duet remains one the most popular double entrees at $36.95. The dessert list is extensive starting with linzertorte, Kilohana mud pie, passion fruit parfait, and double chocolate mousse. Their chocolate truffles are deep fried in coconut on the outside with melting chocolate inside and the homemade banana cream pie tastes of real banana with no synthetic taste or gooey texture ($4.95-7.95). A good selection of premium wines are offered by the glass. For Sunday brunch, entrees are accompanied by a plate of fresh fruit and home-baked cinnamon roll and feature eggs Benedict, spinach quiche, strawberry French toast, tropical Belgian waffle, crepes, banana macadamia pancakes, a variety of pastas, and their signature sweet potato hash with chunks of purple sweet potatoes & chicken breast topped with two poached eggs and Maltaise sauce ($9.95-14.95) COMMENTS: The atmosphere and re-creation of the old plantation living and dining rooms makes this a special place to dine. Unfortunately, the dining area is along the courtyard and on a cool or rainy afternoon or evening they drop the canvas walls with plastic windows. While this helps keep the elements out, it does detract a bit from the ambiance. (Sort of gourmet dining in a tent!) The food is excellent, however, and dining here is certainly worthy of a recommendation, but preferably on a warm and sunny afternoon or early evening to enjoy the full experience of its unique ambiance. (Recently enhanced by the addition of new coconut shell table tops with pedestals, wicker plantation chairs and a second private dining area and roof deck.) Gaylord's has been voted "Most Romantic" restaurant on several of the Travel Channels and is a consistent winner in awards for excellence. Their entrees and salads are highly creative, offering unusual ingredients in wonderful taste combinations. The fresh fish is generally recommended, but could be sold out if you are a late diner. Except for the fresh fish, most dinner entrees are relatively moderate in price and good portions. Desserts are to die-for; the banana cream pie was a special delight, nothing fancy or exotic, just one of those wonderful comfort foods! Added plusses are that they use no frozen or prepared foods on any menu items and the coffee is excellent. We've also heard diners comment that they appreciate having a choice of meat entrees along with the usual island fare of fish and seafood. And praise for the professional and attentive service of the wine steward, Henri Francois Cinq-Mars, has been unanimous! Although we have had readers report inconsistency in food and service in the past, we can now recommend it without reservation! (Well, actually reservations are still a pretty good idea.) They now offer a twice-weekly luau; see LUAU section for more information. <www.gaylordskauai.com>

**HALE KIPA TERRACE** *Buffets/Island style*
Outrigger Kaua'i Beach (245-1955) HOURS: Breakfast 6:30-11 am, buffet to 10:30; lunch 11 am-2 pm, dinner 6-10 pm, buffet to 9:30. SAMPLING: Omelettes, eggs Benedict, guava crepes, papaya strudel, pancakes, sweet bread French toast, Belgian waffle ($4.25-11.75). Fitness offerings of fresh fruit frappe, three-grain pancake, or frittata ($4.75-9.75). Also continental breakfast ($7.25) and buffet ($11.50). Lunch: French dip, ham & turkey club, burger, bay shrimp & crab salad, mahi mahi, club, and lean turkey on grain bread sandwiches ($8.50-10). Caesar, pineapple boat with fruit, or green salad, ($3.25-10.95). Soup ($3.25). Dinners feature steak, prime rib, hibachi chicken, honey glazed stuffed pork chops, prawn tempura, lobster curry, kiawe smoked rack of lamb, fried scallops, ribs, and fresh fish ($13.95-21.95); combos ($19.95-26.95) and

...ter fare (pasta, burger, chicken salad, or vegetable platter) for $8-11.95. Entrees served with baked potato or herbal rice and homebaked papaya bread. Add $3.50 for salad bar. Cakes, pies, mousse, and cheesecake ($3.95-4.95). COMMENTS: Several private alcoves with tables and "bamboo booths" that provide a bit of a plantation look accented by coral, blue, and lavender colors. Buffets change nightly, but always feature prime rib & crab legs along with soup, salad bar, a variety of regional entrees, saute station, and selection of desserts ($24.95A, $12.50C). A la carte, the food is hotel fare and the prices have always been inflated accordingly. Their latest menus, however, have been far more reasonable with plenty to choose from under $15. Wine and beer. Special prices for seniors and keikis.

**HAMURA SAIMIN** ★ *Local* good

2956 Kress, Lihu'e, just off Rice Street (245-3271) HOURS: Mon-Thurs 10 am-11 pm; Fri & Sat till 1 am; Sundays till 9:30 pm. SAMPLING: No surprise, they serve saimin - in small ($3.25), medium ($3.50), large ($3.75), and extra large ($4). Also BBQ, udon, fried noodles ($3.50), and won ton soup ($4.75). Wonton are 2 for $1. Most expensive item on the menu is the shrimp or special (with lots of meat, veggies, and hard boiled egg) saimin at $5. Fresh lilikoi pie, $1.50 a slice. COMMENTS: A tacky shack that looks like a run-down school room inside. There are several U-shaped formica covered counters surrounded by a variety of unmatched stools. The menu is on the wall and is limited, so ordering and receiving your food is quite speedy. A good thing as during peak meal hours you may have to wait for a vacant stool. You'll find friendly local folks explaining directions to Wailua Falls to a youthful European backpacker and next to them a group with mega numbers of kids sitting with chopsticks in hand eagerly awaiting their steaming bowls of saimin. But don't overlook the chicken and beef sticks. At $1 per they are a deal. The meat is a good size portion, moist and very flavorful. Order at least one to accompany your noodles! Hamura Saimin is not only popular during regular meals, but since so many of the clubs have closed down, it's actually become a late-night hang out. Oh yes, and heed the warning posted, no sticking gum under the counter! They serve shave ice (as Halo Halo Shave Ice) Monday-Friday from 10 am-4 pm.

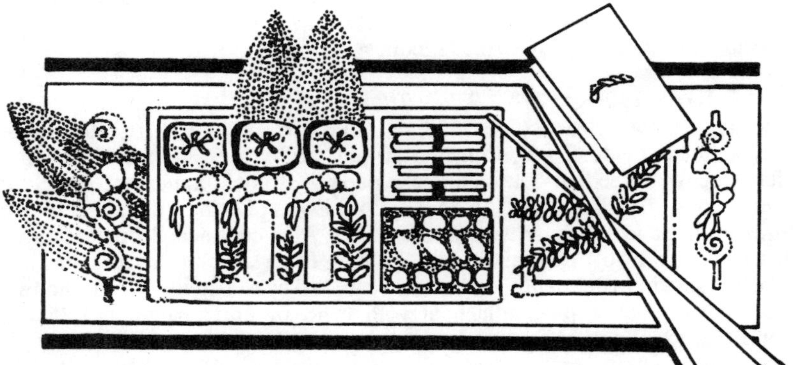

**HANAMA'ULU RESTAURANT, TEA HOUSE, SUSHI BAR & ROBATAYAKI** ★ *Chinese/Japanese*
Hwy. 56 in Hanama'ulu (245-2511) HOURS: Lunch Tuesday-Friday 10 am-1 pm, Dinner Tuesday-Sunday 4:30-9 pm. Closed Monday. SAMPLING: Chinese dishes with noodles, pork, beef, chicken, and seafood plus baked mussels and lobster ($4.50-9.50). Japanese salads, soups, beef, chicken, pork, seafood, and vegetarian specials. ($7-10.25). Also soups and appetizers from pot stickers to robatayaki. Complete dinners (also available for lunch): 9-course Chinese or Japanese for 2 or more $15.75 per person. Special tempura or seafood platters ($13.75-14.75). Chinese, Japanese, or teriyaki plate lunches ($5.75-8); available at dinner for an additional $1.50. Sunday night Oriental buffet from 5:30-8:30 pm features sushi, sashimi, salads, fish, chicken, crab, teri beef, and dessert for $20.95. COMMENTS: The front room is used for lunch and is decorated in a pleasant Oriental style, but the Japanese Dining Room (where you sit on the "floor") towards the back is a fantasy setting that overlooks a beautiful garden with Koi ponds. Restaurant offers robatayaki cooking grilled in front of you as well as a full sushi bar. The food is reliably good and has been for over 75 years! While Hanama'ulu seems to be a spot on the road that people drive thru to get somewhere else, consider making it your dining destination. This is one of the best Oriental restaurants on Kaua'i. And if it were located at a "resort" destination, prices would be a lot more!

**HAWAIIAN CLASSIC DESSERTS** *Bakery/Cafe*
4479 Rice Street, Lihu'e (245-6967) HOURS: Open 6 am-9 pm daily. Breakfast 6-11 am; Lunch 11 am-3 pm; Dinner 5-9 pm. SAMPLING: French toast or pancakes (with apple smoked chicken sausage), omelettes, loco moco, eggs with lup cheong & green onion fried rice, and homemade corned beef hash ($4.50-5.95). Plate lunches ($5.50); ham hoagie, turkey, Hawaiian-style Philly steak sandwiches (with teri beef), and burgers ($5.95-6.95); salads with seared poke, broiled lemon pepper salmon, grilled eggplant, or somen noodles ($5.95-7.75). Dinners start with Buffalo wings, pork ribs, summer rolls, or pot stickers ($5.95-8.50); salads include grilled seafood, Caesar with grilled shrimp, calamari with mango dressing, pulehu beef with tomato lomi lomi, and roasted chicken Oriental ($9.50-10.50). Nightly specials might offer shrimp tempura, miso salmon, ono on somen noodles with sweet chile sauce, or kau gee min over crispy noodles ($12.95 to $16.95). The "plated desserts" are always different and the plates are used as a canvas to feature strawberry decadence, bread pudding with guava butter sauce, chocolate creme brulee, or double chocolate mousse cake (from $5.50). Bakery items range from Danish, muffins, and donuts pastries to cream puffs, eclairs, and fruit tarts ($.85-1.75) as well whole pies and coconut, lemon, chocolate Dobosh (and wedding) cakes. COMMENTS: Upstairs in the pre-hurricane Eggbert's location, the restaurant and bakery retains the "signature" red dirt walls, Indonesian accents, and black & beige geometric designed furniture from its most recent incarnation as a Jean-Marie Josselin cafe. Alcohol- and smoke-free environment. Open kitchens in both the restaurant and behind the dessert bar where you can watch owner and pastry chef Fenton Lee create your "just desserts!" As you'd expect, the sandwiches are all on freshly baked bread and buns, but it seems odd that they charge extra for toast with your breakfast. Early reports from readers give the desserts high marks!

**HIGASHI** *Local*
1415 Kuhio Hwy., Kapa'a (822-5982) HOURS: Mon-Fri 6 am-2 pm, Sat 6 am-1 pm. Closed Sunday. SAMPLING: Two eggs, breakfast meat, rice & toast or omelettes ($3.70). Sandwiches: hamburger (teri or BBQ), egg, tuna, ham, bacon & egg ($2.25-3.10) Saimin, oxtail soup, loco moco, chicken moco $2-3.50. Beef or curry stew, shoyu chicken, roast pork, mahi, beef or pork cutlet ($6-7).

**HIROKO'S OKAZUYA** *Local*
3630 Lalo Road across from the school; turn up the hill just past Nawiliwili Harbor. (245-3450) HOURS: Breakfast and lunch 7 am-2 pm. SAMPLING: Breakfast ($4.50-5); daily plate lunch specials: chicken hekka, pork peas & pimento, fried rice & hot dog, mayo baked chicken, roast beef or pork, sweet & sour meatballs, or mixed plate with two pieces of chicken, two pieces of cooked meat, noodles, luncheon meat, corned beef hash, two scoops rice and one scoop macaroni salad ($5-6). COMMENTS: Sodas and juices. Nothing over $6. Benches outside with soda machine for after hours.

**HONG KONG CAFE** ★ *Chinese* OK
Wailua Shopping Center at 361 Kuhio Hwy. (822-3288) HOURS: Mon-Fri 10:30 am-2:30 pm, 4:30-9:30 pm. Sat-Sun 2:30-9:30 pm. SAMPLING: Lunch and dinner plates and combos include rice, macaroni salad and sweet & sour cabbage: chicken katsu, roast duck, fried shrimp, lemon chicken, BBQ beef stick, fish cutlet, char siu, sweet & sour chicken, and fried stuffed eggplant ($5.25-6.95). Sizzling platters offer seafood, fish, or pepper steak (7.9508.95). Ala carte dishes range from the traditional to the unusual. You can order your mu shu pork ($7.50) with beef, chicken, or vegetables instead -- either way, the portions are generous with plenty of tasty filling and just enough "crepes" and hoison sauce to make everything come out even! Deep fried crab & cream cheese won tons ($4.50) are just one of the ways to start, but the Chinese chicken salad ($6.95) with shredded walnut and crispy noodle is not to be missed. Roast duck is a specialty ($5.45-17.95) as is their spicy eggplant with chicken, minced pork, beef, or shrimp ($6.50-7.50) -- both are excellent choices and worthy signature dishes. Chow mein, lo mein, saimin, and several vegetarian dishes round out the menu ($2.95-7.50). COMMENTS: The color scheme of aqua & black with green & black marble accents give this inviting Chinese restaurant a sleek art deco look. The ambiance is clean and smoke-free, the attractive chairs have comfortable, cushy seats, and there's a colorful aquarium as a focal point. They use fresh Kaua'i products -- fresh fish and vegetables -- and serve purified, filtered water. Everything we tried was excellent (with friendly, efficient service to match) which makes this a surprising and welcome find!

**JJ'S BROILER** *Steak & Seafood*
4416 Rice Street in Anchor Cove Shopping Center (246-4422) HOURS: Lunch 11 am-5 pm, Dinner 5-10 pm, Cocktails 5-11 pm. SAMPLING: Cheeseburgers come with avocado, bacon, mushrooms, pineapple, or chili ($6.95-7.95). Salads include Asian grilled chicken, cobb, Caesar, seafood and spinach, and there's ocean chowder, French onion, or beef & vegetable soup ($4.75-9.95). Sandwiches of pastrami & swiss, turkey club, mahi mahi, fried egg & avocado, teri chicken or beef, steak, French dip, Monte Cristo, and Reuben are available ($7.95-12.95) as are a surprising number of vegetarian offerings: Kaua'i garden or marinated tofu sandwich and vegetable pizza on a flour tortilla.

Before dinner, there are oysters, mussels, escargot, scampi, crab cakes, or Peking chicken tacos ($7.25-9.95). Seafood entrees offer sauteed scallops, baked lobster tail, coconut shrimp, tempura platter, and fresh island fish; char-broiled meats include NY steak, filet mignon, roasted macadamia lamb rack, prime rib, barbeque pork ribs, Cornish hen, and JJ's signature Slavonic steak ($16.95-23.95). Other specialties include black bean shrimp with Asian polenta, spicy wasabi ribeye steak, ahi & crab Napoleon, beef medallions with lobster saute, sugar cane shrimp, chicken fettucine, seafood linguini, tortellini primavera, and baby lamb chops with penne pasta ($15.95-26.95). Entrees include table salad bar and choice of rice. Key lime pie, JJ's sea of chocolate, and double decker ice cream pie are some of the after dinner treats. COMMENTS: Nice outdoor patio and deck for lunch; light cafe menu in the evening. Dinner is served upstairs with a big picture window overlooking the beach. They offer quite a few innovative appetizers and entrees, but their Slavonic steak (filets cooked in wine, butter and garlic) is still the most popular.

**JR'S PLANTATION RESTAURANT** *Steak and seafood*
On Hwy. 56 in Hanama'ulu (245-1606) HOURS: Dinner 5-9:30 pm. SAMPLING: Appetizers include Asian ginger shrimp, escargot, and Cajun stuffed mushrooms ($5.95-6.95); ala carte items (add $4 for salad bar) offer seafood pasta, jumbo burger, roast beef, Hawaiian luau platter, or salad bar ($7.95-10.95). Entrees include salad bar, rice or potato, and homemade garlic bread: NY steak, prime rib, scampi, lamb chops, fresh catch, garlic, Cajun or teri chicken, fried shrimp or their signature Cajun fish & shrimp with ginger scallion sauce ($12.95-18.95). "Little Cowboy" dinners include a trip to the salad bar ($5.95-7.95). Homemade desserts are hula pie; strawberry or blueberry cream cheese pie ($3.50) or try JR's strawberry haupia! COMMENTS: Tropical drinks served with or without alcohol.

**JOLLY ROGER** *American*
Just behind Coconut Plantation MarketPlace next to The Islander (822-3451) HOURS: Breakfast and Sunday breakfast buffet 6:30 am-noon, Lunch 11-4:30 pm, Dinner 3-10 pm. SAMPLING: Omelettes, eggs Benedict, French toast, steak & eggs plus apple pancakes or waffle with cinnamon apples and macadamia nuts ($3.95-7.25). Sunday breakfast buffet has eggs, bacon, sausage, corned beef hash, French toast pancakes, waffles, and fresh fruits ($6.95A, $4.95C). Burgers, salads, and sandwiches including a chicken or tuna avocado melt, French dip, turkey, and mahi mahi ($4.25-7.25). Specialties include teri steak or chicken, fettucini Alfredo with mushrooms or chicken, spaghetti, and stir-fry for lunch ($7.95-9.25), for dinner ($9.75-13.95). Other dinners offer fresh or fried fish, seafood platters, chicken Polynesian, fried calamari, scallops, smothered chicken, and create-your-own combinations ($12.25-14.95). Then there are sundaes, hot fudge cake, or Mauna Kea crunch -- a chocolate chip cookie with sundae toppings ($2.45-3.45). COMMENTS: Familiar chain with a traditional menu, though there are a few creative surprises. Specials like steak & all-you-can-eat shrimp ($10.95) and a senior menu with a choice of teriyaki steak or chicken, ground beef, mahi mahi, ono, sirloin steak, spaghetti, or hibachi chicken for $7.95 including vegetable, potato or rice, soup or salad, and coffee or tea. Food is nothing exotic, but affordably priced with a broad menu offering something for every family member. The breakfast specials are a good value. Karaoke on weekends.

**K.C.L. BARBECUE & CHINESE RESTAURANT** *Local*
3100 Kuhio Hwy., Suite C1; Lihu'e (246-3829) and 971 Kuhio Hwy. in the Waipouli Complex; Kapa'a (823-8168) HOURS: Lunch & Dinner 10:30 am-9 pm. Breakfast (Kapa'a only) 8-11 am; SAMPLING: Eggs, omelettes, loco moco, French toast, or pancakes for breakfast ($3.50-5.95). Burgers, BBQ chicken, shrimp, mahi, or teri beef sandwiches, and hot dogs ($1.25-2.95). Combos ($4.75). Regular and mini portions ($3.95-6.50) of chicken (lemon, katsu, cutlet, BBQ, ginger), roast duck, char siu, mahi mahi, pork chop, loco moco, teriyaki steak, sweet & sour spare ribs, shrimp curry, and combinations (mixed or BBQ mixed plate, bento box, NY steak & garlic shrimp, seafood or chicken combo, and fried chicken) with macaroni salad and rice ($5.95-8.95). Chinese dishes include chop suey, pot roast, chicken with cashew nuts & vegetables, shrimp with straw mushrooms, beef broccoli, pork with bitter melon, chicken with eggplant, shrimp with black bean sauce and squid with ginger & onion ($6.25-6.50). COMMENTS: 'Hard to find a hamburger for $1.35 - or for that matter, mahi mahi, fried shrimp, and scallops for $6.50 - but you can here! It is a kind of funky place, mostly local clientele (who recommend the BBQ mixed plate and the "great Chinese food"). An ideal way to stretch your food budget! Slightly lower prices (amazingly!) at the new Lihu'e location (Opened June, 1999).

**KAHANU SNACK BAR** *Snacks/Sandwiches*
Holiday Inn Sun Spree Resort, Wailua (823-6000) HOURS: 11 am-6 pm. SAMPLING: Mahi mahi or chicken sandwich, cheeseburger, hot dog on Hawaiian sweet bread bun, garden or fruit salad ($4-6.95) plus fries, onion rings, corn dog, ice cream and shakes ($2.50-3.75). Traditional tropical drinks like Blue Hawaii, Tropical Itch, Pina Colada or Chi Chi, and Holiday "Punch" ($6-7.25) COMMENTS: This poolside restaurant also offers an ocean view.

**KALAPAKI BEACH HUT** *Breakfast & burgers*
Overlooking Kalapaki Bay, next to Anchor Cove Shopping Center. (246-6330) HOURS: 7 am-7 pm, breakfast till 10:30. SAMPLING: Breakfast egg or pancake sandwich, loco moco, omelettes, mahi & eggs, buffalo & eggs (really!), Branola French Toast ($3.25-5.95). Lunches feature their flame-broiled burgers with a variety of toppings. They not only come in "basic beef," but they also offer buffalo and ostrich burgers! ($3.95-5.95). Caesar salad; fish & chips; mahi, chicken, tuna, or vegetarian sandwiches ($3.95-$5.75). Try their fresh fruit smoothie with papaya, banana, pineapple, strawberry, and guava - made milkshake-thick for $2.95. Keiki menu ($3.65-4.25). COMMENTS: From Ono Char-Burgers to The Ono Family Restaurant, Steve and Sharon Gerald went on to open Kalapaki Beach Burgers at this location in 1990. Since then, the name has changed to reflect their expanded menu. Casual outdoor setting or buy your burger to go. (And needless to say: very few places offer buffalo burgers - even fewer offer ostrich!)

**KALAPAKI GRILL** *Snacks/light meals*
Located poolside at the Kaua'i Marriott. (245-5050) HOURS: 11 am-4:30 pm. SAMPLING: Grilled burgers, jumbo hot dog, sandwiches (turkey, tuna, grilled chicken), garden, chicken Caesar, or rotelle pasta salad, shrimp cocktail, jalapeno poppers ($4.95-9.95). COMMENTS: Appetizers served in dim sum baskets. Shave ice in 8 flavors, from coconut to lemon-lime ($3.75). Keiki menu ($3.95) Beer, wine & tropical drinks.

**KALENA FISH MARKET** *Local/Korean*
2985A Kalena St. (next to Lihu'e Fishing Supply), Lihu'e (246-6629) HOURS: Monday-Friday 10 am-7 pm, Saturday till 5, closed Sunday. SAMPLING: Kalua, lau lau, or special Hawaiian plate ($5.95); Korean plates (BBQ beef, chicken, or short ribs; meat jun, bi bim bap, fried man doo, kim chee soup) with 2 scoops rice & choice of vegetable ($5.50-6.95). COMMENTS: Fish or tako poke, opihi, lomi salmon, scallop salad, smoked or dried fish, and other pupus from the deli.

**KAPA'A FISH & CHOWDER HOUSE** *Seafood*
1639 Kuhio Hwy. (822-7488) HOURS: Bar open from 4 pm (Early Bird 4-5:30 pm), Dinner 5:30-9:30 pm. SAMPLING: Naturally, they offer chowder (with or without sherry) for $3.50-5.50 or you can also start with escargot, sauteed mushrooms, clams, calamari, shrimp, or Caesar salad ($5.95-14.95). Seafood entrees of cioppino, scampi, sauteed scallops, seafood linguine, calamari "almondine," crab legs, lobster tails, stuffed tiger prawns, coconut shrimp, or seafood platter ($17.95-24.95) and there are also baby back ribs, pork medallions, stuffed breast of chicken, pasta primavera, and several steaks for the landlubber ($14.95-22.95). Combinations ($23.95-28.95). Dinners include salad, starch, and fresh baked bread. Cheesecake (passion fruit or mocha) and mud pie (mint or coffee) for dessert ($4). Tropical and ice cream drinks are a specialty. COMMENTS: A steak and seafood restaurant - hold the steak - that's been around since 1986. The screened Garden Room at the back of the restaurant is airy and full of hanging plants. Children's menu is interesting and more "adult" than most. Early bird specials are a good value: Hawaiian chicken, pork tenderloin, grilled mahi, shrimp Louie, or fish & chips for $11.95. The chowder is good, but it does seem a little chintzy to charge for seconds on bread.

**KAUA'I BREW AND BURRITO** *Mexican*
919 Kuhio Hwy., Kapa'a (823-0330) HOURS: Lunch 11 am-4 pm; dinner 4-9 pm. Closed Sun. SAMPLING: Appetizers include nachos, quesadillas, popcorn shrimp or chicken, cheesy potato, hot dog bites with dipping sauce, ahi poke or sashimi, and spicy chicken wings ($4.95-8.95). Plate lunches with kalua pork, chicken, steak, veggies, fish, or shrimp with beans & rice, and salad ($6.95-7.95). Burritos, tostados, taquitos, chili & rice, or cheese quesdilla ($3.95-7.95). Giant burrito on a 12" tortilla ($9.95). Dinner specials offer fresh catch, grilled shrimp, teri chicken or beef, grilled veggie plate, fajitas, enchiladas, burritos, tacos, tostado, beef or chicken kabobs, and kalua pork plate ($8.95-14.95). COMMENTS: Non-smoking restaurant with good prices and hearty portions. Traditional Mexican favorites and several dishes with a Mexican flair. Their "best" burrito is made with black beans and can be ordered gourmet-style with kalua pork & a ginger cabernet sauce, or try the ocean style ahi or shrimp with white wine & lemon pepper. Beer and wine bar with a good selection of draft beer. Free tokens are given out to children of diners for the video games and on Tuesday nights, kids eat free! (5-9 pm, up to age 12).

**KAUA'I CHOP SUEY** *Chinese*
In Pacific Ocean Plaza at 3501 Rice Street, Nawiliwili (245-8790) HOURS: Lunch Tuesday-Saturday 11 am-2 pm, Dinner Tuesday-Sunday 4:30-9 pm. Closed Monday. SAMPLING: House specials include Kaua'i chop suey with mushrooms ($7.25) or hon too mein for 4-6 persons - a lot of food for the price of $27.25! Also chicken, duck, shrimp, scallop, beef, pork, vegetarian, sweet &

sour, egg, and noodle dishes ($5.45-9.95). Chow mein and noodle soups ($4.05-8.55) as well as rice dishes including special fried rice with chicken, pork, mushrooms, beans, shrimp, and more ($6.55-7.95). Their sizzling rice platters like beef, chicken, scallop or shrimp with lobster sauce (with 10 pieces of jumbo shrimp) are a specialty ($6.95-8.55). COMMENTS: Big Chinese banquet room divided into three areas with round archways and red & gold decor. Service is unhurried - well, slow. They don't have a liquor license, so bring your own if you so choose. The food is nicely seasoned and the sizzling platters (which arrive crackling and steaming) are always fun!

**KAUA'I COMMUNITY COLLEGE/QUEEN VICTORIA ROOM** *lunch*
Kaua'i Community College, inside the Campus Center. (245-8243) HOURS: Wed & Fri at 11:30, 11:45, and 12 noon during Spring and Fall semesters. (The Fall semester also offers tableside cooking on Tues & Thurs.) SAMPLING: Three-course continental and Pacific Rim lunches ($8.50-12.50) are the fine dining options for Spring; Fall is more like a "coffee shop" with diner/truck stop style cooking and casual atmosphere. Salads, sandwiches, and homecooked entrees ($2.95-7) with paper plates, paper napkins, etc. For the fine dining and tableside-cooked lunches, they bring out the "good" china, silver and linen napkins. COMMENTS: Separate dining room offers lunch while school is in session as part of the Culinary Arts program. Students learn all aspects of the restaurant business, they shop, serve, clean, and wait on the tables. The program is only offered during the school year, so be sure and call to check on availability and schedule a reservation.

**KAUA'I KITCHENS** *Local*
Rice Shopping Center, 4303 Rice Street, Lihu'e (245-4513) HOURS: 7 am-2:30 pm, Saturdays 7:30 am-1:30 pm. Closed Sundays. SAMPLING: Sandwiches, plate lunches, bentos, sushi (maki cone) from $1.20 and daily specials: chicken cutlet, fresh corned beef, breaded crab croquette, baked pork chops, roast turkey with stuffing, lemon chicken, seafood curry, fish filet, pork adobo plus Hawaiian, Filipino, and Oriental plates ($4.95-5.95). They also sell Kaua'i Kookies, baked foods and T-shirts retail from the Kaua'i Kookie Kompany. COMMENTS: "Quick Tasty Island Style" that you can eat in or take out. Other locations in Koloa and Waimea.

**KAWAYAN** *Local/Filipino*
1543 Haleukana St., Puhi Industrial Park (245-8823) HOURS: Monday-Saturday 9-9:30 am to 6 pm or later. Closed Sundays. SAMPLING: Pork adobo, pancit guisado, pinkabet, and Thai chicken served daily ($5.75-6.75) along with lumpia and spring rolls (40-65¢). Plate lunches with 1, 2, or 3 choices run $5.75/6.50/6.75 and are featured as daily specials like curry chicken, pork & peas, chicken papaya (Monday), beef senigang, fish or vegetable curry (Tuesday), chow fun, chicken adobo, Thai fried rice with shrimp & pork (Wednesday), pork tocino, Thai curry (Thursday), mongo beans, beef tocino, fried rice (Friday). COMMENTS: They also have halo-halo, shave ice, and frozen appetizers (lumpia, spring rolls) by the dozen.

**(RESTAURANT) KIIBO** *Japanese*
Just off Rice Street at 2991 Umi St. in Lihu'e (245-2650) HOURS: Lunch Monday-Friday 11 am-1:30 pm, Dinner Monday-Saturday 5:30-9 pm. Closed Sunday. SAMPLING: Lunch special with entree, rice, miso soup and salad ($5.25-6.95). Teriyaki chicken, beef or pork plus tempura, sushi, sukiyaki, sashimi, nabe, butterfish nitsuke, saba shioyaki, fried salmon or chicken, ramen, chicken or pork tofu, noodles, fresh fish, and special house bentos ($6-17). COMMENTS: The decor and food are authentic and very traditional, however, better Japanese fare can be found a little farther down the road at Hanamaulu Cafe Tea House & Sushi Bar.

**KING & I THAI CUISINE** *Thai*
Located in the Waipouli Plaza, 901 Kuhio Hwy. (822-1642) HOURS: Mon-Fri lunch 11 am-2 pm; dinner nightly 4:30-9:30 pm, till 10 Fri-Sat. SAMPLING: Start with the spring rolls with fresh mint and cucumber, ready to wrap in lettuce and dip, then try the lemon grass or coconut soup, green papaya salad, or King & I Noodles with shrimp, pork, or chicken ($5.95-8.50). You can choose from red, green, or yellow curry ($6.95-9.25), smell the aroma of jasmine rice, and enjoy the Siam fresh basil, spicy eggplant, ginger fish, garlic shrimp, and other Siam dishes with choice of beef, pork, chicken, shrimp, calamari, tofu, or fish ($6.50-9.25). Thai iced tea or coffee are a must and be sure to try the coconut milk and black rice, the natural color of the herbal rice from Thailand ($2.25). If you don't want to make a decision, they also offer set menus for 2, 3, or 4 ($27.95, $38.95, $49.95) which include five items with rice, tea, and dessert. COMMENTS: As owners (and sisters) Stephanie and Cindy take turns out front and in the kitchen. (Their brother, Mee, owns Mema Thai Chinese Cuisine, and Lemongrass Bar & Grill -- both down the road a few miles -- plus Pattaya in Po'ipu.) The sisters grow their own herbs so when the dish says fresh basil or fresh mint, it really is. Some of the entrees are excellent, a few are mediocre. The green curry is wonderful, perfectly seasoned and an ideal accompaniment with fresh fish. The fried shrimp, however, proved to be too greasy and were all batter and no shrimp. The portions are a little on the small side, but the prices are affordable. Ask your waiter to offer recommendations on entrees!

**(RESTAURANT) KINTARO** ★ *Japanese*
370 Kuhio Hwy., Wailua (822-3341) HOURS: 5:30-9:30 pm Monday-Saturday. Closed Sunday. SAMPLING: Tempura, sukiyaki, and yakitori dinners, one-pot nabemono, broiled steaks, shrimp, mussels, and fish combinations plus complete teppanyaki dinners with appetizer: oysters, chicken or NY steak teriyaki, filet mignon, hibachi shrimp, fish with scallops or lobster tail, and tenderloin steak ($10.95-28.95). COMMENTS: Good mussels and steaks; also hand-rolled sushi and soft-shell crab. Stylized, attractive Japanese ambiance with a sushi bar and aquarium. There are two serving sections: the general (moderately priced) seating area and second, moderately expensive area with teppanyaki tables where you can enjoy your meal cooked before your eyes. While it is a bit more expensive, it is worth it for the show! The service is excellent on both sides.

**KOREAN BBQ** *Korean*
356 Kuhio Hwy. in the Kinipopo Shopping Center, Wailua (823-6744) HOURS: 10 am-9 pm, Wed-Mon. Open Thurs for dinner only 4:30-9 pm. SAMPLING: Combination plates served with four vegetables, macaroni-potato salad, and two

scoops of rice. Kalbi ribs, teri beef, BBQ chicken, fried or rolled mandoo (dumpling), fish jun ($5.25-7.50). Single plates: Stir fry squid or long rice (tofu, chicken, or beef), chicken cutlet or katsu, hamburger steak ($4.35-7.25); also kim chee, miso, and kooksoo soup ($6.35-6.75). COMMENTS: They sell vegetables and kimchee. Also catering.

**KOUNTRY KITCHEN** *American*
1485 Kuhio Hwy., Kapa'a (822-3511) HOURS: Breakfast 6 am-2 pm, Lunch 11 am-2 pm SAMPLING: Pancakes and waffles (plain, strawberry, or banana), French toast, pork chop and eggs, corned beef hash, loco moco, omelettes with cornbread (Polynesian, Denver, ham & cheese, fresh mushroom, hamburger, tuna, chili, or build-your-own), and vegetable, turkey, or traditional eggs Benedict ($3.95-9.50). Lunch fare includes patty melt, BLT, grilled ham & cheese, and tuna sandwiches or create your own burger with your choice of a variety of toppings ($5.25-6.85). Lunch plates of hamburger steak, grilled pork chop, mahi mahi, sirloin steak, or fried chicken served with vegetable, rice or fries and cornbread ($6.85-8.75). Ice cream, and blueberry or apple crisp ($1.75-3.50). COMMENTS: Looks like an old-fashioned coffee shop of the 50's, but with wood, brick, and copper accents. Family-style restaurant, but they do have beer and wine. (Keiki menu $3-3.25) Good breakfasts!

**KUHIO DINING COURT** *American*
Holiday Inn Sun Spree Resort, Wailua (823-6000) HOURS: Breakfast buffet 6:30-10:30 am; Dinner Sun-Thurs 5:30-9 pm, Fri & Sat buffet only 6-9:30 pm, (Not open for lunch). SAMPLING: Breakfast buffet offers fresh fruits, breads & pastries, cereals plus hot selections of eggs, potatoes, pancakes, and breakfast meats ($9.95A, $5C). Dinners begin with shrimp cocktail, sashimi, calamari rings, steamer clams, seafood salad, or chicken Caesar ($7.95-11.50); seafood chowder ($2.25-3.50). Clams linguini, shells & seafood, or vegetarian combo with two sauces & two pastas ($12.50-14.25) plus prime rib, top sirloin, broiled chicken, fresh catch, scampi, mahi mahi, BBQ ribs, or seafood & beef stir fry ($12.75-21.50). Burger, garden burger, fish & chips ($5.95-8.50); pizzas (12.40-15.50). Assorted cakes & pies ($4.25). The Fri & Sat prime rib & seafood buffet has live Hawaiian entertainment ($19.95A, $14.50 ages 13-17, $1 per year ages 6-12) COMMENTS: This former warehouse of a restaurant has become more intimate with the addition of tall wood columns and smaller table groupings. The wood and green accent colors now give it a richer, cozier look and feel., but they still offer affordable family dining: kids under 12 eat free per each adult that orders off the main menu. The adjacent Marketessen offers light meals and snacks -- Danish, fruit, sandwiches, and salads plus ice cream, yogurt, or cake ($1.25-3.75). Box lunches ($4.50).

**KUKUI GROVE SHOPPING CENTER**
(3171 Kuhio Highway, Lihu'e) As the draw of most of these small restaurants is their location in the Kukui Grove Shopping Center, we've listed them here with just a capsule review. A McDonald's Express is also located here and some of the larger restaurants and/or those having something particular to recommend them are also listed individually.

**DELI & BREAD CONNECTION** (245-7115) - See individual listing.

**HO'S CHINESE KITCHEN** (245-5255) Chinese dishes featuring chicken, duck, beef, pork, seafood, soup, chop suey, noodles, and egg specialties $4.75-6.50; combination plates $6.50-39.50 (for 4).

**JONI HANA** (245-5213) Chicken broccoli, pepper steak, pork eggplant, fish, shrimp. Plate lunches, bentos, "local grinds" $4-7.

**KAUA'I BAKERY** (246-4765) Donuts, turnovers, cinnamon buns & local pastries: manju, malasadas plus haupia, lilikoi, and guava cakes.

**MYRON'S** (245-5178 ) Filipino and local food: pork or chicken adobo, tripe stew, chicken papaya, pork & peas, BBQ spare ribs, chicken long rice, lumpia (Plate lunches $5-5.50-6).

**RAMPY'S** (246-2729) - See individual listing.

**YAKINIKU PALACE** (246-0106) - See individual listing.

**ZACK'S FAMOUS FROZEN YOGURT & CAFE** (246-2415) - See individual listing.

**KUKUI'S RESTAURANT & BAR** ★ *Pacific Rim/Buffets*
Kaua'i Marriott Resort, Lihu'e (245-5050). HOURS: Breakfast 6:30-11 am, Lunch 11 am-2 pm, Dinner 5:30-10 pm, Pizza Cafe 12-8:30 pm. Sunday brunch 8 am-2 pm. SAMPLING: Unusual breakfast offerings should wake up your taste buds: shrimp & crab Benedict, vegetable frittata, breakfast burrito (with scrambled eggs, Portuguese sausage & island salsa), macadamia nut pancakes, and Hawaiian sweetbread French toast with sun-dried fruits ($5.25-12.95). Cold buffet ($13.50); full breakfast buffet ($16.50). Lunch begins with sausage nachos, crab & shrimp quesadilla, vegetable rice paper roll, Maui onion soup plus a variety of salads including ceviche, Oriental chicken soba, or seafood Caesar ($5.25-9.25). Entree selections feature Jawaiian chicken, eggplant, or swordfish sandwich, fish tacos, shrimp & crab cakes, mushroom ravioli, burgers, seafood melt, and tempura batter fish & chips ($6.95-15.25). Roasted garlic chicken, brie & asparagus, smoked salmon, and eggplant, artichoke & goat cheese are some of the pizzas ($7.95-15.95). Dinners include seafood crusted mahi mahi, roasted char siu pork, paniolo steak, lemon rosemary chicken, and pasta with seared tiger prawns or garlicky scallops ($15.75-27.95). Chocolate mousse, passion fruit cream tart, chocolate mac nut pie, coconut rice pudding, and Kahlua cheesecake are the desserts ($4.25-5.95). Weekly prix fixe specials with soup or salad, bread with seafood mousse, cheesecake, and coffee ($31.95-32.25). Specialty dinner buffets are featured on the weekend from 5:30-9:30 pm: Friday is prime rib & King crab with Hawaiian music ($28.95), Saturday, Pacific Rim with a keiki hula show ($28.95). Their excellent Sunday brunch with ($26.95) or without champagne ($21.95) offers salads, fresh fruit, cheese, fish and sushi platters, breakfast dishes, hot entrees, an omelette station, Anahola granola and other cereals with a selection of nuts and sweet toppings including an unusual treat of dried tropical fruits. Choose pancakes, French toast or potato pancakes at the griddle station, rotisserie spiced mahi at the Southwest wrap & roll station, prime rib at the carving station or try some of the innovative creations at the sushi bar-like tempura

sushi with lightly fried edges and soft sushi middles! COMMENTS:This open-air pavilion-style restaurant is located at the edge of the resort's 26,000 square-foot pool, the largest in the Hawaiian islands.

**KUN JA'S II** *Korean BBQ*
939A Kuhio Hwy., Kapa'a (821-2088) HOURS: Monday-Saturday 10 am-9 pm. Closed Sunday. SAMPLING: Soup and noodles (with beef, vegetables, squid, dumplings, or tofu); Kalbi ribs, BBQ chicken or beef, egg-battered mahi, sauteed squid, kim chee fried rice with beef ($5.25-6.75). Popular combination plates with BBQ chicken and beef, mundoo (dumplings), or Kalbi ribs ($6.50-7.25). COMMENTS: Entrees served with kim chee, Korean style vegetables, rice, and bowl of soup. They moved from their tiny spot on Rice Street to this expanded, attractive location next to Taco Bell.

**LA BAMBA MEXICAN RESTAURANT** *Mexican*
4261 Rice St., Lihu'e (245-5972) HOURS: 11 am-10 pm; Sunday 4-9 pm. SAMPLING: Seafood salad on a tortilla or taco salad in a shell ($7.95-8.95) plus the usual selection of tacos, burritos, enchiladas and quesadilla (from $1.95 ala carte). The carnitas or carne asada burritos are the house specialties ($6.95) or you can try them as an entree ($11.95). Chile verde, tamales, or chile relleno ($10.95-11.95); fajitas with chicken, steak, or seafood for one ($12.95/16.95) or two people ($19.95/22.95). Homemade flan ($3). COMMENTS: Entradas (entrees) and tortas (sandwiches) come with rice and beans (or steak fries with your sandwich if you prefer.) Take out available, but no liquor license so you are welcome to BYOB. The same owners now have Mi Casita in Old Koloa Town.

**LEMONGRASS BAR & GRILL** *Pacific Rim/Asian*
4-871 Kuhio Hwy., Kapa'a (822-1221 for restaurant & gallery) HOURS: 5-10 pm. Initially open for dinner only, but may eventually offer lunch. SAMPLING: Pacific Rim and Asian cuisine; sushi bar. Appetizers ($5.95-9.95). Dinners from $14.95. COMMENTS Small "house" that faces the highway offers inside and outside dining. The newest venture from the owners of Mema Thai Cuisine and Pattaya is complemented by the Lemongrass Gallery which features "Pacific Fine Collectibles" in a separate building located behind the restaurant. Browse through the unique selection of antiques, sculptures, gifts, art, and accessories before or after your dinner! Gallery opened July, 1999. RESTAURANT SCHEDULED TO OPEN BY SPRING 2000. (NOT OPEN AS WE GO TO PRESS.)

**LIHU'E BAKERY & COFFEE SHOP** *Filipino*
Rice Shopping Center, 4303 Rice St., Lihu'e (245-7520) HOURS: Monday-Friday 5 am-6 pm, Saturday 5 am-4 pm, Sunday 5-10 am. SAMPLING: Unusual Filipino baked goods, also donuts and muffins. Hot Filipino entrees served cafeteria-style from 5 am through lunch ($4-5). COMMENTS: Macaroons, turnovers, and lots of baked goods for under $1.

**LIHU'E CAFE** *Local*
2978 Umi St., Lihu'e (245-6471) HOURS: Lunch only: Tuesday-Friday, 10:30 am-1:30 pm. SAMPLING: Weekly menu specials are chicken hekka, chili dog (Tuesday); roast pork, nishime (Wednesday); pork tofu, chicken curry (Thursday); beef stew, roast turkey, surprise special (Friday). Daily specials vary, but

might include chow fun, sweet & sour spare ribs, or fried chicken ($5/5.50/6 for 1, 2 or 3 choices with rice, kim chee, salad - and tax - included in the price). Teriyaki or chop steak plate ($5.75); Saimin, won ton mein, bento ($2.75-5). COMMENTS: Mostly open at night as a bar & lounge, but they serve lunch from a small buffet table for you to pick up and bring to your booth or table.

**LIZARD LOUNGE & DELI ★** *Sandwiches/Pizza*
Waipouli Town Center, 771 Kuhio Hwy. (821-2205) HOURS: 10 am-2 am. SAMPLING: Pizza by the slice ($2.50-2.75) and a selection of ham, salami, turkey, veggie, tuna, chicken salad, or roast beef sandwiches named after the seven major Hawaiian islands ($4.50). They're served on a large French roll (fresh and soft) with dill pickles on the side. (If you can't decide, Dona recommends asking for a Maui County: 1/2 a Maui - ham, turkey breast, and Swiss cheese - and 1/2 a Lanai with chicken salad and pineapple . . . try to guess the secret ingredient!) Chef salad, buffalo wings, or chicken breast sandwich ($6.50). Smoothies, coffee drinks, and good homemade cole slaw and potato salad. Imported beers and microbrews, modern martinis and tropical drinks like the Po'ipu Passion, Kapa'a Cooler, and a pina colada that they'll put up against any on the island! COMMENTS: No lounge lizards here, despite the cute name! This gathering place is bright and inviting with hanging plants and plenty of seating at tables & chairs or the bar/counter. Live entertainment, electric and steel tip dart boards - even playing cards - make this a popular hang-out for workers, singles, families - just about anyone. The shopping center is safe and well-lit so you can take advantage of the 2 am closing. Personable owner John Butz has done well - even with Dave ("Handsome" Dave as he likes to be called) as a sidekick! In fact, they were planning on expanding and offering a bigger menu with more entertainment, but nothing had been formalized at press time. We'll keep you posted in a future Update.

**L&L DRIVE INN / CHOPSTICKS EXPRESS** *Local*
733 Kuhio Hwy., Kapa'a (821-8880) HOURS: 10 am-10 pm. SAMPLING: At L&L you can get plate lunches (seafood, chicken, pork, and beef) plus burgers, hot dogs, saimin, chili, curry, and stew ($3.50-5.95); combinations plates or prime rib ($5.95-7.15). The incorporated Chopsticks Express "side" offers beef, pork, seafood, chicken, and vegetarian Oriental dishes. Combination plates run $3.95-6.35 for one to three items. Entrees of beef with broccoli, orange chicken, vegetable chop suey, black pepper chicken strips, or sweet & sour pork ($4.95-6.75). COMMENTS: This dual restaurant is (are?) owned by L&L, an O'ahu chain which recently branched to Maui, and now this Kaua'i location which opened in July, 1999. With almost everything under $7, the prices are affordable, but they do seem a little heavy with the rice.

**LOCAL BOY'S DRIVE INN** *Local*
3160 Kuhio Hwy., Lihu'e (246-8898) HOURS: 9:30 am-10 pm. SAMPLING: Sandwiches & burgers ($1.25-2.95); beef, pork, chicken, and seafood plate lunches ($5.35-7.95) and mini-plates ($3.95-4.50); Stir fry & noodles ($6.25-6.75); Snacks like chili, saimin, and beef stew or curry ($2.50-3.95) They also offer "beach paks" with BBQ chicken, teriyaki beef, or BBQ short ribs available raw or cooked ($24.50-28.50) COMMENTS: We didn't drive "in" or sleep over "inn," but still liked the big portions and small prices at the Lahaina (Maui) location of this small local outlet. The Teriyaki Saimin was a surprise: the BIG

chunk 'o meat was a little difficult to negotiate so we tried the Teriyaki Beef sandwich. Yummy! The plate lunch with fried scallops was on the spendy end of the menu ($7.25!), but the scallops were good - not huge, but very tender.

**MA'S** *Local/Homestyle*
4277 Halenani Street, Lihu'e (245-3142) HOURS: Monday-Friday 5 am-1:30 pm, Saturday & Sunday to 11:30 am. SAMPLING: Eggs, omelettes, meats, and waffles or pancakes come plain or with pineapple, papaya, or banana ($5). Lunch entrees include meat loaf, cutlets, fish, fried noodles, tripe stew, curry beef, and Hawaiian specials ($3-6). Sandwiches are around $2 with hamburgers at $1.75, roast beef or pork at $2.50. COMMENTS: Ma's opened in the mid 1960's and you can still see Ma cooking on the griddle in back - sort of a forerunner of Roy's open kitchen concept! The breakfasts are still a bargain - the prices have stayed the same for our last two editions! Try a local variety of spam and eggs for $2. Other breakfasts including omelettes, pancakes, or French toast made with Portuguese sweet bread run less than $5. This is definitely a hole-in-the-wall, greasy spoon restaurant, but that's what makes it so much fun! The service is friendly with the waitress greeting you with a smile and plunking down a big thermos of coffee so you can serve yourself. (The coffee is free with meals!) Big portions and great prices make it popular with locals and returning visitors. Turn off Rice Street onto Kress Street and another left onto Halenani.

**MARGARITAS, A MEXICAN RESTAURANT AND WATERING HOLE** *Mexican*
733 Kuhio Hwy., Kapa'a (822-1808) HOURS: 4-9:30 pm, Happy Hour 4-6. SAMPLING: Nachos el deluxo, Mexican pizzas, quesadillas, flautas, jalapeno poppers, quesadilla, caliente wings ($5.95-7.95); fish tacos, chicken quesadilla (with chipotle & mango salsa), and hickory smoked ribs from the grill; ($9.95-16.95) and salads: taco, chicken taco, or chicken fajita ($11.95-12.95). Entrees include shredded beef, chicken, sirloin, vegetarian, or ahi burritos; chimichanga; beef, chicken, or vegetarian quesadilla; beef & chicken enchiladas or Enchilada Ranchera; and fajitas with beef and/or chicken ($9.95-16.95). COMMENTS: Food is made fresh daily; specials change every few weeks. Live music on Friday and Saturday nights. Good place to watch the sunset during the winter when it goes down between Sleeping Giant Mountain and the coconut grove next door. Good margaritas. There is better Mexican food elsewhere on the island, but this is passable middle-of-the-road cuisine. The menu is large and varied and if you choose to eat on the back porch, the donkey and horse in the adjoining coconut grove might stroll over and say "howdy."

**MARIA'S** *Mexican*
3142 Kuhio Hwy., Lihu'e (246-9122) HOURS: Mon-Fri 11 am-8 pm, Sat 5-8 pm, closed Sun. SAMPLING: A la carte nachos, quesadilla, burritos, tostadas, enchiladas, and tacos ($1.99-4.99). Combination plates with tacos, enchiladas, chile rellenos, taquitos, and veggie or pork sopes ($5.99-7.99). Beer, wine or homemade Sangria ($3-4). Dinners to go serve 2 to 6 people ($15.99-39.99). COMMENTS: Yes, there really is a Maria and she learned to cook traditional family recipes from her grandmother in Jalisco, Mexico. Located next to Seven-Eleven and across from the Lihu'e McDonald's, this small Mexican restaurant doesn't take credit cards, but not to worry: they're also located next to an ATM!

**MARK'S PLACE** *Local*
1610 Haleukana Street in the Puhi Industrial Park (245-2722) HOURS: 10 am-7 pm. SAMPLING: Plate lunches with hamburger steak, beef curry or stew, teri or Korean chicken, loco moco, chicken cutlet or katsu in regular ($5-5.50) or mini ($4-4.50) sizes. Mixed plate with chicken katsu, teri beef, and beef stew ($6). Burgers, and hot teri chicken or beef sandwiches ($2.25-3.50). Daily specials might include garlic & herb ahi, 1/2 roasted chicken with mashed potatoes and corn on the cob, or miso pork with eggplant ($5.50-6.25). Fresh salads change daily; mini or large bento ($4-5.50). Homemade desserts like strawberry Bavarian parfait ($2) or blueberry streusel, haupia bread pudding, and banana nut bread. COMMENTS: We hear good things about this grind "find" off Puhi Road and Hanalima Street. They also offer take-out and catering as "Contemporary Flavors, Inc."

**MELE LOUNGE** *Sandwiches/pupus*
Outrigger Kaua'i Beach lobby (245-1955) HOURS: Sandwiches 12-8 pm; pupus served until 10. SAMPLING: Cheeseburger; hot dog; turkey, ham & bacon club; smoked ham & swiss sandwiches ($6.95-8.50). Crab or pork won tons; spicy chicken wings; potato skins; jumbo onion rings; nachos; and grilled Portuguese sausage on sauteed Kaua'i onions ($4.95-8.75). Tea, espressos, and coffee drinks ($1.75-2.50). Smoothies with rum ($5.25), without ($4). COMMENTS: Cocktail lounge with nightly Hawaiian entertainment.

**MEMA THAI CUISINE** ★ *Thai/Chinese*
361 Kuhio Hwy., at the Wailua Shopping Plaza, Kapa'a (823-0899) HOURS: Lunch 11 am-2 pm Monday-Friday, Dinner 5-9:30 pm nightly. SAMPLING: Appetizers include shrimp rolls, sa-teh, fish cakes, and fried calamari ($6.95-10.95). Salads with beef, calamari, or green papaya (eat it with a mint leaf!) run $6.95-10.95 and soups (Thai ginger coconut, long rice, and spicy lemongrass) are offered at $7.95-14.95. Noodles and rice come in a variety of flavors for $7.95-10.95; with seafood $16.95. Red, yellow, and green curry are offered along with house (panans) curry and Mema's curry ($7.95-16.95) depending on whether you order them with chicken, beef, pork, fish, shrimp, tofu, or seafood. Choose from the same for your entree of Evil Jungle Prince, garlic with coconut, cashew nut or blackbean sauce stir fry (also with calamari), fresh basil eggplant, or ginger oyster sauce, or try pineapple shrimp, lemon chicken, or garlic pork ($7.95-16.95). There are three pages of vegetarian offerings starting with spring rolls, crispy noodles, sa-teh, and laab tofu ($5.95-7.95) and entrees like broccoli tofu, garlic coconut mixed vegetables, pad Thai tofu, and vegetable curry ($6.95-9.95). Dinners for 2, 3, 4, or 6 offer a wide selection and good variety from appetizer to dessert and start at $35.95 for two. COMMENTS: Owner Mei is the brother of Cindy and Stephanie who own King & I. Some folks think Mema is better than King & I, while others think the reverse is true. Mema's is almost twice the size with a more upscale ambiance; the decor is just a bit more creative and festive with plenty of plants interspersed with Thai art and artifacts to create a garden-like setting. Mema's also serves some Chinese dishes as well as Thai. Mee continues to expand with Pattaya in Po'ipu and Lemongrass Bar & Grill (also in Kapa'a).

**(THE) NAWILIWILI TAVERN** *Italian*
At Kalapaki Bay near Anchor Cove Shopping Center. (245-7079) HOURS: Dinner 4-8 pm, bar open till 2 am. SAMPLING: Spaghetti with marinara, meat, spinach & mushroom, white clam, meatballs, and combination sauces, or chicken parmesean ($5-6.75) served with green salad and fresh baked sour dough bread. Daily specials offer spicy sausage & roasted peppers, $6.75 (Mon); baked lasagna; $7.50 (Tues), braised pork chop pizziola; $8 (Wed), eggplant parmesean; $7.50 (Thurs), seafood pasta, $8.50 (Fri); Kalapaki chili, $6 (Sat); scampi chicken, $7.50 (Sun). COMMENTS: Pool tables, darts, and video games. Located in the historic Hotel Koleyama.

**NOE'S GRILLE** *American*
Kaua'i Village, Kapa'a (821-0110) HOURS: 11 am-11:30 pm, Dinner 5-10 pm. SAMPLING: Caesar, cobb, chicken, or seafood salads plus burgers, smoked turkey, club, BLT, pastrami, steak, chicken, and fish sandwiches; shrimp, tuna, or crab melt ($6.50-11.50). Mozzarella sticks, quesadilla rolls, breaded dill pickles, calamari or onion rings, wing dings, and jalapeno poppers for appetizers ($3.95-8.95) and for dinner, NY steak, scampi, mahi mahi, and local style stir-fry with beef, chicken, or shrimp ($13.95-18.95). COMMENTS: Attractive and clean. Friendly bar atmosphere, more like a pub. They offer fresh fish in the evenings: $9.95 in a sandwich or Caesar salad, $15.95 for dinner. Dinners include soup or salad, vegetables, and french fries or rice. Good value and it comes recommended. Great lunch place, too. Nightly karaoke.

**NORBERTO'S EL CAFE** ★ *Mexican*
1375 Kuhio Hwy., Kapa'a (822-3362) HOURS: 5:30-9 pm, closed Sun. SAMPLING: Taquitos, tacos, burritos, quesadillas, nachos, and chimichangas are just some of the items offered ala carte ($2.75-7.45). Dinner specialties include rellenos tampico, burrito rancheros, fajitas made with Kaua'i steak or chicken, and the enchiladas grande with beef, chicken, eggplant - or homegrown Hawaiian taro leaf! ($13-15.45). All entrees come with soup, vegetables, rice and beans, corn chips and salsa. Their homemade desserts have won awards: chocolate cream pie, hula pie, and rum cake ($3-3.50).

COMMENTS: Family operated restaurant since 1977 and one of the oldest on the Kapa'a "strip." People still drive from Kekaha for the bean soup so with such a loyal following, they should be around for another 20 plus years! They serve Mexican beer and a variety of margarita flavors (Midori, passion fruit, and raspberry) available by the glass or by the pitcher. We tried their unique taro enchilada and it was delicious - the taro was cooked just right with a smooth texture and taste that was not too stringy or bitter. The eggplant enchilada was equally tasty getting its flavor (like all their dishes) from the food, not the seasonings. (If you like a bit more "kick" just spoon on the fresh salsa till it's just right!) The chile relleno came highly recommended and we were pleasantly surprised with both the texture (not greasy or overly-fried) and the perfect proportion of chile to relleno: it didn't taste like a fried jalapeno, but it didn't taste like a chile omelette either. Their beef is all locally grown and the beans are made from scratch - no lard or animal fat is used in any of their preparations. This is probably not the absolute best Mexican food we've ever had, but they get a star for their innovative preparations, friendly service, and kitschy (but not too) cantina atmosphere. (We only saw one velvet painting!) It's a fun place that makes for good family dining and they have a kid's menu to prove it. Here's another little plus: bring this book in with you when you dine, they'll take 10% off your food bill! Tell 'em Patti (Norberto's daughter) said so!

**OKAZU HALE** *Japanese/local*
4100 Rice St., Lihu'e (245-6554) HOURS: Open Monday-Saturday 11 am-2 pm, 5-9 pm. SAMPLING: Spicy chicken & egg plant, shrimp & vegetable tempura, teri beef or chicken, pork chops, and chicken cutlet served with rice and tossed salad ($5.95-8.95), half orders ($3.25-4.75). Donburi (rice bowl) with chicken, beef, stir fry, or tempura ($5.25-6.95). Saimin ($3.95-5.95), ramen ($5.50), and sushi ($4-10). COMMENTS: Daily specials include ahi & stuffed cabbage, oxtail soup, stuffed chicken, pot roast, and meat loaf ($5.95-7.95); Saturday night sushi and tempura dinner ($14.95).

**OKI DINER and BAKERY** *Local/Homecooking*
3125 Kuhio Hwy., Lihu'e (245-5899) HOURS: Open 24 hours! Breakfast from midnight to 11 am, the rest of the menu served anytime. SAMPLING: For breakfast, they have omelettes, egg dishes, pancake sandwich, fried rice with meat, and blueberry or banana hotcakes ($3.95-6.95). The rest of the day (and night), there are burgers, sandwiches, saimin or won ton min, fried noodles, and noodle salad ($3-6.95) and local favorites like lau lau, kalua pig, pork adobo, loco moco, spaghetti, kalbi ribs, pork chops, tempura, ginger chicken, and oxtail soup - all served with rice and salad ($5.95-9.95), mini ($3.99-6.99). Beef stew, and fried chicken are the "Politically Correct" favorites of noted politicians ($5.95-6.95). Create your own stir fry from a selection of meats and vegetables ($5.95-7.95), mini ($4.99-5.99). Hearty eater's loco moco or won ton min ($8.95). Keiki menu ($3.95) and bentos ($3.25). Pies from their own bakery with fresh cream topping: lilikoi chiffon, banana or chocolate cream, custard, or "PC" (see above) lime ($1.95 a slice or take home a whole one for $8.95). COMMENTS: It's like a fast and friendly bus station for food: there's a separate stand for shave ice with over two dozen flavors ($1.50-1.75); and a full bakery with coconut or apple turnovers, large cookies, butter mochi, manju, brownies, huge, oversized cream puffs with custard filling, apple squares, and their yummy

specialty pumpkin crunch. And they're open 24 hours! (At press time they were undergoing a complete cosmetic renovation with a new color scheme, bamboo window shutters, carpeting, plants, lighting fixtures, artwork, and a canopied lana'i and were planning to add a selection of Chinese dim sum appetizers and new pupus to their menu.)

**OLYMPIC CAFE** *American with Mexican & Italian*
1387 Kuhio Hwy., Kapa'a (822-5825) HOURS: Breakfast 6-11 am, Lunch, 11am-5 pm, Dinner 5-9:30 pm. SAMPLING: Breakfast burrito or quesadilla, a variety of omelettes and scrambles, coconut pineapple, or blueberry pancakes, and guava jelly-stuffed toast $3.50-7.50. Several burger options plus sandwiches including BBQ or blackened chicken, mozzarella & pesto, tuna, BLT, and chicken avocado club ($5.95-7.50. Caesar, Greek, cobb, tuna, or grilled chicken salad plus several Mexican entrees ($4.95-7.95). Most lunch items available for dinner or begin with fried calamari, bruschetta, spinach-artichoke dip, or roasted garlic spread ($4.95-6.50) and follow with entrees of coconut curry rice, teri chicken, fresh catch, scampi, and a variety of pastas including Caesar salad-style ($8.50-16.95). COMMENTS: Opened June, 1999 in the old Olympic Cafe location, but with a new owner and new color scheme! The former lavender walls are now bright yellow with colorful tapa print chairs that go very well with the bright and colorful books in the used book library for both "browsers and buyers." (And those go very well with the selection of teas, juices, coffee drinks, fresh muffins, and pastries available from the espresso bar.)

**PANDA GARDEN** *Chinese*
831 Kuhio Hwy., Kaua'i Village, Kapa'a (822-0922) HOURS: Lunch 11 am-2 pm; Dinner 4:30-9:30 pm. SAMPLING: Over 100 offerings of both Cantonese and Szechuan dishes. Appetizers, soups, chicken & duck, beef and pork, seafood, eggs, sizzling platters, vegetarian, chow mein, and rice ($6.25-10.95). Scallop with peppery salt ($12.95), lobster with black bean sauce or ginger & onions ($19.95). Steamed island fish, pot roast chicken, beef with sesame sauce, pork hash, shrimp with chile garlic sauce, and tenderloin steak with black pepper are just a few of the diverse selections. Plate lunch specials offer a choice of eight entrees with soup, won ton, and rice for $5.95 and set dinners for 2 to 10 run $24.95 to $179. COMMENTS: They offer both the unusual and the traditional, but seafood is a particular specialty. Their hot, spicy dishes are marked with a star. Beer & wine; take out available. Food is fair to good, but the portions are a bit small. One of our readers was impressed that when requesting no MSG, the waitress wrote it on the top of the check in both English and Chinese, but agreed that while the service was fast and friendly, the food was not worth the price.

**PAPAYA'S NATURAL FOODS** *Natural/Healthy*
831 Kuhio Hwy. at Kaua'i Village, Kapa'a. (823-0190) HOURS: Open 9 am-7 pm, breakfast until 1 pm. SAMPLING: Rosemary potatoes, steamed eggs & brie, multi-grain pancakes, tofu scramble, granola, tofutos rancheros, or frittata to start you off ($2.99-6.50), then a variety of sandwiches and entrees for lunch or dinner: tempeh or tofu burgers, falafel, hummus or Mediterranean salad plate, Thai vegetable stir-fry, baked tofu, veggie pizza, and spinach & herb lasagna ($4.99-7.50). Good selection of muffins, scones, breads, cookies and brownies, and serious desserts ($1.50-3.95). COMMENTS: Teas, coffee drinks and smoothies plus a variety of fat free, sugar free, wheat free, and vegan items. This

is a health food store, too, one of the few where the patrons actually look fit and healthy! Order at the counter, then bring your selections to the tables outside. Yet another new owner so the menu has been revised, but everything is still all organic and still a good value for your dining dollar.

**PARADISE SEAFOOD & GRILL** *Steak & seafood*
1850 Kaumualii, Puhi (246-4884) HOURS: 11 am-3 pm, dinner 5-9 pm SAMPLING: A variety of burgers including fish and chicken plus smoked turkey, chicken salad, and club sandwiches ($5.95-6.95). Caesar salad, fried chicken, lasagna, fish & chips, and seafood: on a platter, in a salad or linguine ($6.25-7.95). Dinner start with steamed clams, fried mushrooms, crab cakes, oysters, mussels, or calamari ($5.95-8.95). Entrees include fresh fish, scampi, baby back pork ribs, crab legs, steak, prime rib, and mushroom or teri chicken ($14.95-23.95). Combos $18.95-21.95). Chocolate cappuccino brownie, mud pie, or cheesecake for dessert ($3.95-4.95). Wine, beer & espresso. Keiki menu ($4.95). COMMENTS: Opened July 1999. Owned and operated by the Hirano family who had the Pasta Pub in Ele'ele over ten years ago. Take-out or seating outside on the lanai or back patio.

**PONY ISLAND CANTINA** *Mexican*
831 Kuhio Hwy. in Kaua'i Village (823-9000 ) HOURS: Lunch Mon-Sat 11 am-2:30 pm; Dinner 4:30-9 pm, Sun noon-8 pm. (Closed Mon-Sat for *siesta* from 2:30-4:30 pm!) SAMPLING: Seared ahi salad, cheese or roast beef quesadilla, an innovative taco, burrito, enchilada and tostada selection (roast beef, chipotle chicken, or vegan) plus their specialty shrimp taco, chile rellenos, and a bowl of organic rice & beans with fresh salsa & homemade cornbread ($3.95-7.95), combination dinners ($11.95-14.95). Desserts range from spiced carrot or apple cake to coconut or macadamia nut flan. COMMENTS: Violet's has closed at the Kaua'i Shopping Village and in its legendary purple place, Pony Island Cantina offers a unique menu of both traditional and eclectic Mexican food. They use local and/or organic produce whenever available. Their specialty is shrimp scampi tacos (sauteed in garlic cheese sauce). They also have fresh ahi burritos and tacos and their vegan entrees are made with an intriguing mix of tofu, carrots, and Hawaiian sweet potato!

**POOR BOY'S PIZZA** *Pizza & Sandwiches*
1384 Kuhio Hwy., #104, Kapa'a (822-7985) HOURS: Mon-Sat 10 am-10 pm, Sun from noon. SAMPLING: Pizza in 12, 16 and 29 inch sizes range from $11.95 for a small cheese to $28.95 for a large supreme or build your own 7" pizza from $5.95. Calzones, stromboli, and Italian or ham & cheese sandwiches on fresh baked bread ($6.95-8.95) plus breaded zucchini, hot wings, or seasoned fries ($2.75-5.95). Strawberry or tropical fruit smoothies ($1.59-3.50). COMMENTS: Named for the financial status of owner Todd O'Herman (and friends) as opposed to the New Orleans sandwich! Take out or delivery available or just sit in front and people-watch in the heart of Old Kapa'a Town.

**PO'S KITCHEN** *Local*
4100 Rice Street, Lihu'e (246-8617) HOURS: 6 am-2 pm, Mon-Sat. SAMPLING: Bento and box lunches in three sizes: small/regular/deluxe for $4.75/5.75/6.75. Box lunches include fried chicken, teriyaki meat, egg roll, rice ball, potato salad, luncheon meat, hot dog, side dish, and pickled cabbage. Also

teriyaki chicken, meat, or short ribs plate lunch and hot entree that changes daily ($4.75-6.75 with rice and salad). COMMENTS: Compared to their former tiny hole-in-the-wall behind the Lihu'e Shell station, these are relatively "deluxe" digs in the Ace Hardware Annex Building. Simple and very inexpensive menu. The fried chicken was a wingette, the luncheon meat, a piece of spam. All the portions in the small bento were appetizer-sized. A good place to sample some unusual local dishes with a lot of small sides and snacks items from 30¢ to $1.

**PUAKEA BAR & GRILL** *American/local*
Grove Farm Golf Course at Puakea (4315 Kalepa St.) across from Kukui Grove Shopping Center (245-8756) HOURS: Sat-Tues 9 am-6:30 pm, Wed-Fri until 7:30. SAMPLING: Burgers, hot dogs,sandwiches (turkey, egg or white meat chicken salad, grilled ham & cheese, roast beef, BLT, club, albacore tuna), fish & chips, chicken Caesar, and chicken or beef taco salad ($4-5.50). Chile & rice, onion rings, spam & cabbage, chicken wings with fries, diced hot dog & onions ($2-3.50). Beer & wine, sodas, raspberry tea, pink lemonade, and snacks ($1.25-3.50). COMMENTS: Small cafe across from the pro shop with counter & table seating. Ask about their monthly discount specials!

**RAMPY'S** *American/Local*
Kukui Grove Shopping Center, 3171 Kuhio Hwy., Lihu'e (246-2729) HOURS: Breakfast Mon-Fri 8-11 am, Sat from 7:30; Lunch Mon-Sat 11 am-3 pm, Dinner Friday only 5-8:30 pm. SAMPLING: Omelettes, waffles, sweet bread French toast, loco moco, grilled pork chops, rice & eggs, saimin, and macadamia or banana pancakes ($4.50-7.50). Plate lunches include teri steak or chicken, chili & rice, mushroom chicken, calamari katsu, and shrimp tempura ($6.95-8.95). Sandwiches (club, BLT, egg or tuna salad, turkey, ham) and Caesar, chef, fruit, or Oriental chicken salads ($5-8.25). Saimin, clam chowder or miso soup ($3.50-5.50). Friday night dinners offer shrimp (tempura, scampi, or stir fry), steak, or mahi, ($11.95-14.95). Plate lunch entrees (with starch and salad) available for dinner ($8.95-10.95). Chocolate or strawberry sundae, and chocolate mousse cake (2.75). COMMENTS: Friday night karaoke from 8:30 pm. Wine & Beer and Rampy's special "Cat's Meow" cocktail with Midori, vodka, orange juice, blended and topped with whipped cream and Bailey's ($5.50).

**ROB'S GOOD TIMES GRILL (ELMER'S PLACE)** *American*
4303 Rice St., Lihu'e (246-0311) HOURS: 11 am-10 pm. SAMPLING: Lots of appetizers/pupus like sauteed mushrooms, chicken sticks, won ton, egg rolls, fresh veggies, fried chicken or zucchini, kalua pork & cabbage, boiled peanuts, chips & homemade salsa ($3-5.95). Sashimi, grilled steak, seared poke, or mixed pupu basket ($7-8.95). Tuna or Oriental chicken salad ($5.25). Pastrami and swiss, mahi, egg salad, tuna, grilled chicken or turkey, BLT, and turkey club sandwiches ($4.50-6.95). Burgers include mushroom, bacon, or chili ($4.95-6.25). COMMENTS: Pub mirrors and beer signs on the walls with satellite TV and a dart board. Music, entertainment and karaoke. (Call for schedule.) During football season, they open at 7 am for breakfast with loco moco, omelettes, or sweet bread French toast. It is still more bar than grill, but now that "Elmer's Place" is doing the food, there are more sandwiches, salads and grilled pupu items. (But you'll have to ask Norine who Elmer is!)

**ROCCO'S ★** *Italian*
4405 Kukui St. in Pacific House Plaza, Kapa'a (822-4422) HOURS: Dinner 4:30-11 pm. SAMPLING: Sauteed or stuffed mushrooms (firm texture and good mushroom taste with just the right amount of garlicky seasoning), white pizza (topped with mozzarella and a side of red marinara sauce), garlic ricotta cheese bread (with lots of both!), antipasta, scampi, or calamari steak are the starters for $3.50-9.50. Caesar salads are a specialty. Made with an exceptionally light tasting olive oil, they are served hot or cold with fresh fish, jumbo shrimp, chicken parmesan, veggies, or Italian meats ($6-12.50). Rock oven pizzas from $10 plus toppings (additional $2-2.50 each) and pasta offerings of ravioli, manicotti (made with spinach pasta), baked cannelloni or lasagna (with lots of bubbling hot cheese), and linguini marinara or Alfredo run $9.95-13.95. Eggplant, chicken, or pork parmesan ($14.95). Additional entrees include scampi, clams, eggplant marsala, and baked or sauteed fresh fish ($14.95-18.95). The fish comes in large portions and the ahi was excellent and surprisingly moist - not an easy thing to do with its tuna texture. Main courses all come with a hot loaf of fresh baked bread and dinner salad. For dessert there's homemade NY style cheesecake or tiramisu ($4.50) COMMENTS: They now have patio seating and the upper level dining mezzanine has been converted to offer a pool table, video games, and a new bar with (occasional) live entertainment until 2 am. This is an upscale, modern version of the old family style pizza restaurants of the 50's and 60's. It's reflected in the ambiance with hanging plants and vines as well as in the prices (which have stayed the same since our last book), complete dinners, large portions, and homecooking by the owner, Richard Senkus. The bread is homemade as are the meatballs. This is a great find -- both a fun "hang-out" and an excellent value family restaurant with or without a family.

**SAMPAGUITA'S/BIG WHEEL DONUT SHOP** *Local*
Old Hanamaulu Trading Post (245-5322) HOURS: Donuts from 4 am to 11:30 am. Breakfast 5 am to "whenevah." SAMPLING: Plate lunches $3.95-4.95; Breakfast: eggs, bacon, and hot cakes $3.60. COMMENTS: These are two different places, but in such a small building that it's almost impossible not to list them together. Big Wheel also serves coffee, makes their donuts fresh, and frequently has a "Sorry out of Donuts" sign in front. Not surprising, since they start serving them at 4 in the morning!

**SEASHELL** *Italian*
Kuhio Hwy., across from the (still dormant) Coco Palms Resort in Wailua. Pomodoro's Iaskolk family still plan to reopen this landmark restaurant (nearly destroyed by the hurricane) as soon as the dust (and insurance claims) finally settle. They'll be serving Italian cuisine for dinner along with oceanfront cocktails and pupus.

**SRI'S CAFE** *Local*
Rice Shopping Center, 4303 Rice St., Lihu'e (246-3910) HOURS: Breakfast 6-9 am, Lunch 11 am-3 pm. Closed Sunday. SAMPLING: Oxtail soup ($4.50-6.75); pork tofu, chicken or beef stew ($4.25). Weekly specials ($5.50) offer roast beef (Mon), roast chicken (Tues), roast pork (Wed), roast duck (Thurs), and roast turkey (Fri). COMMENTS: This tiny local cafe also has guri guri, a local style creamy sherbet (75¢ or $1.25 with ice cream).

**SUKHOTHAI** *Thai/Chinese*
Kapa'a Shopping Center, 1105 Kuhio Hwy. (821-1224) HOURS: 10:30 am-9 pm daily. SAMPLING: Soups (ocean golden, lemongrass shrimp or chicken, long rice, spicy fish) and laab, seafood, papaya, or calamari salads ($6.95-13.95). Appetizers of spring roll, chicken crepe, sa-tay, and fried tofu ($6.95-10.95). Thai entrees include cashew chicken, pad eggplant, coconut chicken or seafood, garlic mixed vegetable, pad ben-ja-lung (shrimp & vegetables), and fish prig prow ($8.95-13.95) and red, green, yellow, pa nang, pineapple, and matsaman curries ($7.95-15.95. Chinese dishes include chop suey, egg fu-young, lemon chicken, garlic calamari, seafood broccoli, pepper steak, Asian fish, stir-fried long rice, or sweet & sour ($7.95-13.95). House specials offer seafood with chile paste, whole snapper with garlic, crispy duck with vegetables, spicy chicken angel and shrimp stuffed with minced chicken in peanut sauce ($13.95-16.95). For dessert there is fried ice cream, tapioca pudding with coconut sauce, or rambutan stuffed with pineapple ($2.50-3.50). COMMENTS: Also Vietnamese and vegetarian dishes. (Anything on the menu can also be ordered vegetarian.) Same menu served all day.

**SUSHI KATSU** *Sushi/Japanese*
3173 Akahi, Lihu'e (246-0176) HOURS: Lunch (sushi only) Tuesday-Sunday 11 am-2 pm, Dinner 5:30-9:30 pm. Closed Monday. SAMPLING: Lunch: Chirashi sushi ($13.95), maki mono roll ($6.95), tekka ju ($11.95), regular ($4) or BIG California roll ($8), and sushi combinations ($6.95-8.95). Special rolls (soft shell crab, spicy ahi, fresh salmon, or inari sushi) priced $3-6.50. Dinner ($8.95-15.95); sushi combination ($17.50); sushi and sashimi deluxe assortment ($21.50)). Udon and soba noodles ($5.95-7.95). Dinners (including soup and rice) feature shrimp tempura, teriyaki beef or chicken, chicken katsu, tempura & sushi, oyako donburi, or catch of the day ($8.95-12.95). Green tea ice cream ($2.50). COMMENTS: This Japanese restaurant and sushi bar is part of the legendary Tip Top Cafe.

**SUSHI-Q** *Japanese/Sushi Bar*
1394 Kuhio Hwy., Kapa'a (822-3878) HOURS: Lunch 11 am-2:30 pm, Dinner 5-9:30 pm. SAMPLING: For lunch or dinner choose chicken teriyaki, unagi or katsu donburi, chicken katsu, shrimp tempura, tempura soba, salmon steak, seafood or char siu ramen, NY steak, or fried chicken ($8.50-14.90). Nabemono ($8.75-16.95). Nigiri, roll or hand roll sushi a la carte: spicy hamachi, salmon skin, snapper, scallop, sake, tako, eel, tekka, vegetable mix ($3-6); specialties include garlic tuna roll, soft shell crab, manbo, tango, and rock & roll ($4.50-9). Sashimi combo ($16.95), sushi & sashimi ($19.95). COMMENTS: Very small restaurant, the sushi bar has seating for only 10 and there are only a handful of tables. Currently they don't have a liquor license, so you are welcome to pick something up at the store and bring it along.

**TERRACE RESTAURANT AT KAUA'I LAGOONS RESORT**
3351 Ho'olaule'a Way at Kaua'i Lagoons Golf Course, Lihu'e (241-6080) HOURS: Breakfast 8-11 am, Lunch 11 am-1:30 pm. (No dinner). SAMPLING: Fruit, cereal, egg dishes, Spanish or kim chee omelette, Hawaiian sweet bread French toast, banana nut hot cakes, crab cake Benedict, steak & eggs ($2.95-9.95). Burgers, sandwiches (curried tuna croissant, BBQ teriyaki sirloin, fresh fish or turkey, ham & cheese); grilled ahi, shrimp, fruit, or chicken Caesar salad

($6.95-8.95); Oriental stir fry (veggie, chicken or shrimp), donburi teri beef or chicken, and double garlic linguine ($8.50-8.95). Luncheon buffet with soup, salads, hot entrees, sandwich bar, and desserts ($11.50) COMMENTS: Attractive setting overlooking a gazebo garden. Lunch too strenuous? Take a break after to relax and refresh in the European spa next door!

**TIP TOP CAFE** *Local*
3173 Akahi, Lihu'e (245-2333) HOURS: Breakfast daily 6:30-11:30 am, Lunch Tuesday-Sunday 11 am-2 pm. SAMPLING: Macadamia or banana pancakes, sweet bread French toast, loco moco, omelettes, bento ($3-6). Burgers, grilled ham and cheese, BLT, and tuna sandwiches ($3.20-4) plus beef stew, saimin and oxtail soup, a popular specialty. Daily specials: meat loaf, corned beef & cabbage, pork tofu, spaghetti, and chili ($5.50-6). COMMENTS: Move over Hard Rock Cafe, the Tip Top souvenir shop has t-shirts and hats! The bakery continues to make their signature items like macadamia nut cookies, cream puffs, and eclairs. This is an especially popular stop for breakfast and lunch. The macadamia pancakes are light and fluffy ("addictive" according to one of our readers) and the French toast is very good. With no entrees priced more than $6, you can't go wrong! They've been in business since 1916 and moved to their present location in the early 60's. The cafe is part of the Tip Top Motel. Their sushi bar and Japanese restaurant, Sushi Katsu is part of the Cafe. (See individual listing.)

**TOKYO LOBBY** ★ *Japanese/Sushi Bar*
Pacific Ocean Plaza, 3501 Rice Street, Lihu'e (245-8989) HOURS: Dinner 4:30-9:30 pm, Lunch Monday-Friday 11 am-2 pm. SAMPLING: Unusual and creative sushi offerings like shrimp tempura roll, Kohaku roll (cream cheese & salmon), Tokyo lobby (tuna & hamachi), spider (soft shell crab), spicy eel or tuna, and the bright and colorful Amigo (tuna, hamachi, salmon) priced $5.50-7.50. Also available are garlic tuna sashimi and green mussels baked with spicy mayonnaise ($5-8.50). Combinations ($8.95-19.95). Tempura, katsu, teriyaki, and cold soba noodle (with tempura or sushi) lunch entrees ($7.95-9.50); donburi, udon noodles ($5.95-11.95). Japanese dinners include nabemono, teriyaki, tempura, katsu, assorted chicken dishes, and combinations ($9.95-14.95). Shabu-shabu $24.95. The specialty is the "Love Boat," a choice of three combination dinners brought to the table in a head-turning artistic Japanese wooden boat at $21.50 per person for 2. Top off your meal with refreshing ice creams in green tea, coconut pineapple, Kona coffee, or Japanese-made red bean. COMMENTS: The tempura was light, crispy and fresh, not mushy or greasy. The sushi was attractively presented in tasty and unusual combinations prepared by Sushi Chef Keiichi. Closed by the hurricane, they reopened in 1993 and won an award right away. They serve both eat-in and take-out sushi regulars as well as a number of Japanese movie stars and ball players. (Harrison Ford became a frequent diner while filming on Kaua'i.) The restaurant is attractively decorated in bright, fresh hues of pink and green with red & black accents in the Japanese pictures and wall hangings. They have expanded and added on a garden room. It's very bright and open, like a conservatory surrounded by big windows on all sides. Jack Ho is the owner, but his Mom, Lin Ho, is the manager and sweet, friendly, gracious hostess. "Mom" talks and visits with everyone who comes in and even if the sushi weren't so good, she'd be well worth the star.

**TROPIX ISLAND BAR & GRILL** *American*
1330 Kuhio Hwy., Kapa'a (822-7330) HOURS: Lunch 12-5 pm, Dinner 5-9:30 pm. SAMPLING: Hawaiian chicken stir fry, sauteed mahi, hamburgers, kalua pork COMMENTS: Tropical drinks, 40 different beers. Big screen TV, video and dart games. They have a new name and the staff is much nicer, but after several attempts, we still weren't able to get any menu information other than on a generic flyer.

**VOYAGE ROOM** *Breakfast/Lunch/Sunday Brunch*
Kaua'i Coconut Beach Resort, Wailua (822-3455) HOURS: Breakfast 6:30-10 am, to 9 am Sunday (Brunch 10 am-1:30 pm), lunch 11 am-1:30 pm. SAMPLING: Breakfast buffet with fruit, pastries, breads, cereals, eggs, breakfast meats, and potatoes ($10.75 Adult/$8.50 Teen/$5.50 Child). Also a la carte omelettes, pancakes, Belgian waffle, or roast beef hash Benedict ($6.25-9.50). For lunch, there are sandwiches of turkey, ham, tuna or chicken salad, fresh catch, and burgers ($5.50-9.50) plus saimin bowl or ravioli ($6.50-7.50), and fruit, cobb, chef's, Greek, and chicken or shrimp Caesar salads ($5.50-9.25). Island style iced tea is available with cane sugar and pineapple and there are a variety of cakes, pies, and ice creams for dessert ($2.75-3.75). COMMENTS: Some of the hotel packages include the breakfast buffet with your room which is a real bonus. At $16.95, the Sunday brunch is a good value offering a carving station of roast meats plus sushi, salads, Belgian waffles, omelette station, hot entrees, selection of pies and cakes, and an ice cream sundae bar ($12.95 for teens, $1 per year for children 6-11). The restaurant stays the same, but the name changes at dinner when it becomes the Flying Lobster (See separate listing.)

**WAH KUNG CHOP SUEY** *Chinese*
Kinipopo Shopping Village, 356 Kuhio Hwy. (822-0560) HOURS: Daily 4:30-8:30 pm, Lunch Tuesday-Saturday 11 am-2 pm. SAMPLING: Soups, poultry, chop suey, chow mein, gau gee, won ton, seafood, beef and pork, egg, vegetables, and rice. Lunch specials of three items plus rice $5-6, pupu plate with fried chicken & shrimp, won ton, and egg roll $8.50. Roast duck, beef or pork tofu, lup chong (Chinese sausage), shrimp fu young, sweet & sour pork, scallop soup, pot roast chicken ($5.50-6.50). Abalone with black mushrooms, seafood with vegetables ($7.95). COMMENTS: Small take-out place with a few tables and chairs. Combination and dinner plates posted on the wall, so you don't have to read, you can just point. While it looks (and it is) pretty dinky, the food is very good and so are the prices! Food is Cantonese style with a few exotic dishes thrown in and the prices make it a good option for filling up those hungry appetites that always seem to develop after a day at the beach.

**WAILUA FAMILY RESTAURANT** *Local/American*
361 Kuhio Hwy., Wailua Shopping Plaza (822-3325) HOURS: Breakfast 6:30 am-12 noon; lunch 10 am-4 pm, dinner menu from 10 am till 9:30 or 10 pm. SAMPLING: Breakfast: eggs, pancakes, French toast, ham & turkey Benedict, loco moco, omelettes ($2.99-7.99). Burgers and sandwiches (corned beef, fish, club, patty melt, French dip, BLT, and salads ($5.99-6.99); stir fry or combination platters of steak, fish, chicken, or shrimp ($6.99). Dinners offer similar combinations plus dozens more with seafood, ribs, pork, and beef ($8.99-14.99). T-bone or prime rib ($16.99-17.99). All-you-can-eat salad buffet has more than just salads: there's soup, a seafood bar, taco bar plus puddings and cookies.

Offered ala carte for $7.99-8.99 or $3.99 with dinner. COMMENTS: Senior dinners ($9.99 including salad bar) and children's menu ($2.99-3.99) served all day from 10 am. This is Sizzler gone "local." The salad bar is still a good value (which now includes options like pig's feet!) and the Sizzler ambiance has been uh, enhanced both inside and out with a "death by twinklelight" display.

**WAILUA MARINA RESTAURANT** *American*
5971 Kuhio Hwy., Wailua River State Park Building B. Located near to Smith's Tropical Plantation in Kapa'a (822-4311) HOURS: Lunch 10:30 am-2 pm, snacks and sandwiches 2-4 pm (summer only), dinner 5-9 pm. Closed Monday. SAMPLING: Chinese chicken, pineapple boat and chef's salads and BLT, tuna, egg, turkey, French dip, ham, pastrami, mahi mahi, club, burger, steak, BBQ or teri chicken, Reuben and Monte Cristo sandwiches ($6.50-8.95). Many dinner entrees available for lunch ($6.75-9.95). Baked stuffed pork chop (with stuffing) or chicken (with plum sauce), Chinese style steamed mullet, char-broiled calamari, prawns or ahi stuffed with crab meat, prime rib, sauteed seafood, teriyaki steak, scampi, filet mignon, spaghetti, or spare ribs ($10-17.50). Oxtail soup ($9); shrimp, steak & chicken mixed plate ($11.75). Hot lobster salad is a specialty ($20). Desserts ($2.25-2.75) include homestyle cream pie (coconut, macadamia nut, or chocolate), ice cream pies (mud, fudge, brownie, or spumoni) or lilikoi chiffon pie (like key lime, only better!) COMMENTS: Yonezo and Gladys Arashiro's restaurant (the only one overlooking the Wailua River) has been in operation since 1968 - outlasting most other Kaua'i restaurants. Not a typical tropical meal. The stuffed pork chops are big and thick, but you can cut them without a knife! The fish is always fresh and priced at least a couple of dollars less than it would be anywhere else. With more than three dozen entrees on the dinner menu, you are sure to find something for everyone. There are extra long tables for families or groups, with a separate banquet room and cocktail lounge. Seating on the lanai can be more pleasant, however. Wall murals may amuse the younger kids in your family, one across the back wall has 3-D sea turtles, shells, and fish. Don't let the tour buses scare you away!

**WAIPOULI DELI & RESTAURANT** ★ *American/Local/Oriental*
771 Kuhio Hwy., Kapa'a (822-9311) HOURS: Breakfast & lunch 7 am-2 pm, Dinner Mon-Sat 5-9 pm. SAMPLING: Eggs with breakfast meats, pancakes, French toast, and homemade corned beef hash ($2.99-5.89). Lunch entrees of shrimp tempura, roast pork, chop suey, chow mein, pork tofu, beef broccoli, fried chicken, pork or chicken cutlet, liver with bacon and onions, beef or chicken hekka, mixed plate ($5.99-6.99). Homecooked rice bowl $2.99. Burgers and burger platters, sandwiches, and saimin ($1.99-5.99). Dinners include fries or rice, salad, and iced tea or coffee. Beef stew, egg fu yung, BBQ teriyaki steak, beef tomato and most of the lunch entrees at slightly higher prices ($8.69-13.99). COMMENTS: Small local restaurant. Children's half order portions available on lunch and dinner entrees. When a restaurant is always packed, you know they must be doing something right. The service is very friendly, the food is good to great, the prices are reasonable -- an excellent dining value.

**WHALERS BREWPUB** *Pacific Rim Beer Cuisine*
Beyond the Marriott at Fashion Landing Shopping Center at Kaua'i Lagoons, Lihu'e (245-2000) HOURS: Lunch 11:30 am-2:30 pm; Dinner 5-10 pm; Sunday brunch 10 am-3 pm. SAMPLING: For lunch, try the blackened chicken pasta,

Amber ale batter fish & chips, teri chicken, pork ribs, or saimin along with a variety of sandwiches: turkey club, Philly chicken, roast beef, salmon bagel, or specialty spiced mahi ($7.95-10.95). Fresh fish or garlic stir fry with tofu, shrimp or chicken ($12.95-14.95). Dinner entrees also include fiery shrimp harpoons, lamb chops, NY steak, and Hawaiian mixed grill ($15.95-23.50) Their signature "whale of a burger" is a specialty for both lunch and dinner. Also soups, salads, and pupus that include egg rolls, calamari rings, teri chicken skewers, chicken quesadilla, and nachos ($4.95-8.95). COMMENTS: This open air microbrewery is located at the back of Kaua'i Lagoons offering a spectacular view of the ocean with the lighthouse in the background. Casual lana'i seating outside; attractive wood booths inside. There's a pool room upstairs and they have live music on the weekends. Their trademarked Pacific Rim Beer Cuisine incorporates the flavors of nine (brewed-on-the-premises) ales in a lot of their menu items especially pupus like the beer-batter fish, coconut shrimp bites, and flowering onion. Other seasonings range from Asian to Cajun and when they say they have "One Whale of a Burger" they mean it! This isn't a hamburger, it's a buffet on a bun! The 20 ounces of ground beef is served on a huge, homebaked bun and served on a platter filled with a ton of fries, an assortment of onions, tomato, lettuce and other good, fresh toppings for your burger plus a variety of condiments. The platter is so big it almost hangs off the edge! And the best part is that it feeds two (or more) for only $18.95. They also have a Beer and Brunch Buffet every Sunday that includes all nine microbrews plus salads, carved prime rib, omelettes, and a variety of hot entrees and desserts for $19.95.

**WILCOX HOSPITAL CAFETERIA** *American/local*
3420 Kuhio Hwy., Lihu'e (245-1164) HOURS: Breakfast 6:30-9:30 am; Lunch & Dinner 10 am-7 pm. SAMPLING: Eggs, omelettes, cereals, cinnamon roll, coffee cake, muffins ($.80-1.70). Soup $1.65; somen noodle $2; pork lau lau $2.35. Daily entrees - seafood stir fry, grilled cod, turkey with stuffing, beef macaroni casserole, kalua turkey, chicken & mushroom, Swiss mushroom veggie burger - average price $3.10. Healthy dietician's choice $3.80. Pudding, pies, and jello (of course!) for dessert ($1.30-2) COMMENTS: No, we haven't gone off the deep end! We had heard good things so we checked and the hospital said it receives so many calls about their cafeteria that they are planning to install a hotline to call for the day's menu specials. They also have a salad & sandwich bar (mix and match at 29¢ per oz., then bring to the register to weigh for your total) and a cappuccino machine. You don't have to check in to check it out!

**YAKINIKU PALACE** *Japanese/Korean/Chinese*
Kukui Grove Shopping Center, 3171 Kuhio Highway, Lihu'e (246-0106) HOURS: Daily 10:30 am-8 pm. SAMPLING: BBQ beef, pork or chicken, fried shrimp, short ribs, chicken teriyaki, chicken katsu ($8.99); combinations ($10.50). Appetizers, tempura, stir fry, steamed fish, noodle dishes, pot stew, sweet and sour chicken or pork and spicy soups ($5.99-11.95). Korean, Japanese, and Chinese entrees ($9.99-13.99. Marinated yakiniku from $14.50; family dinner for 2, 3 or 4 ($14.99-$16.99 per person). Entrees served with soup, rice & vegetable side dishes. Wine, beer & sake. COMMENTS: We haven't tried this Oriental restaurant, but from the looks of it, we wouldn't hesitate: it is immaculate - possibly the cleanest restaurant we've ever seen! And besides, we like the Japanese doll that sits by the doorway in her display case, greeting customers as

they come in, then thanking them as they leave - in three different languages! (In short: pretty neat and pretty neat!)

**ZACK'S FAMOUS FROZEN YOGURT AND CAFE** *Sandwiches/Salads* Kukui Grove Shopping Center, Lihu'e (246-2415) and Coconut MarketPlace, Kapa'a (822-2112) HOURS: Kukui Grove open Mon-Thurs & Sat 11 am-5:30 pm, Sun till 5, Fri till 9. SAMPLING: The MarketPlace location is a small outlet with ice cream, yogurt, espresso, coffee drinks, and desserts (frosted brownies, mac nut cheesecake bars, apple bits, cookies, and lilikoi pie). Kukui Grove offers those along with a more substantial menu of hot dogs, hamburgers, vegetarian specials, soups, salads (Caesar, chicken sesame, or chicken papaya) plus ham, French dip, roast beef, and chicken sandwiches and beef, ham or veggie wraps ($2.75-4.95). Pizza ($2.69-2.99). A variety of chili ($2.69-3.29) or stuffed baked potatoes including bleu cheese, chili, hot dog, broccoli, cheese, and bacon bits for toppings ($3.49-5.29). Chicken and ham plates come with pineapple-papaya sauce and a fresh papaya slice ($5.25). COMMENTS: Lots of homemade touches like soups (Portuguese bean, green papaya chicken), cole slaw and potato salad, desserts (lilikoi pie is a specialty), and fresh salads with homemade bleu cheese and other dressings -- even homemade croutons!

# *SOUTH SHORE*

**AMIGO'S MEXICAN RESTAURANT** *Mexican*
Po'ipu Shopping Village (742-2449) HOURS: 11 am-9 pm SAMPLING: Nacho quesadilla, or taquito appetizers ($4-6); Mexican black bean chicken salad ($7). Burrito varieties include fresh fish or potato and entrees (with rice and beans) feature carne asada, flautas, chile relleno, chimichanga, chile verde, taquitos, tostada, and fresh fish tacos ($7.50-8.50). Several good vegetarian options ($4-5.50). COMMENTS: Beverages include refills for 50¢. Dine in or take out. Authentic Mexican food in a casual atmosphere. (In their words, "owned and operated by *real Mexicans.*")

**BEACH HOUSE RESTAURANT ★** *Pacific Rim*
Lawa'i Beach Road on the way to Spouting Horn (742-1424) HOURS: Dinner 5:30-10 pm. SAMPLING: While new owners were making changes, Chef Linda Yamada just kept doing what she's always done: creating and preparing innovative dishes for Beach House diners. At press time, she had just begun to put together an all new menu with plans to offer such appetizers as grilled artichoke, shrimp "pulehu," crab cakes, and a "taster" of ahi prepared as sushi, in a taco, and in a hash spring roll. Seafood minestrone plus scallop & green papaya or Kaua'i asparagus salad are also some of the possible starters ($6-12). New entrees might include Asian duck breast, crispy sesame chicken, lemongrass crusted sea scallops, "local" paella with shrimp, scallops, fresh catch & ham, and seared pork chops with lehua honey & whole-grain mustard glaze. From the kiawe grill, you might look for coriander marinated lamb chops, grilled ahi with black bean chili sauce, fire-roasted eggplant cannelloni, NY steak with truffles, grilled ono with caper pesto, or Kaua'i shrimp with spinach & mushrooms ($18-29). Dessert options ($6-7), might be Kahlua poi cheese cake, warm chocolate tart with white chocolate gelato, coconut butter mochi "sundae," fruit quiche, sorbetto martini, or apple banana "Foster." COMMENTS: As we go to press, the new owners are planning a renovation that will include new carpets and furniture, painting, and an overall upgrade of this long-standing restaurant. New visuals will offer Jan Kasprzycki artwork to enhance the "old" visuals of the oceanfront park just steps away from the picture windows. You can't get much closer to the ocean than this, although you might find comparable views at SeaWatch or the Plantation House - which just happen to be the new owners' popular and successful restaurants on Maui! On this reputation alone, the star stays!

**BETTY'S KITCHEN** *Local*
9643 Kaumalii Hwy. Waimea (338-1018) HOURS: Breakfast 6:30-10:30 am (from 7 am on Sunday), Lunch & Dinner 10:30 am-9 pm Sun-Thurs; till 9:30 Fri & Sat.) SAMPLING: Blueberry and banana pancakes plus lots of international omelettes from $4.95. A variety of burgers and hot dogs ($1.40-2.75), 1/4 lb. burgers ($3.20-4.10). Sandwiches include egg, club, ham & turkey, grilled ham & cheese, and tuna ($1.25-3.90). Tuna or chef's salad ($4.50); saimin, chili & rice, loco moco ($2.35-3.40); Plate specials of hamburger steak, BBQ ribs, pork adobo, and kalbi, teriyaki, or honey-dip chicken ($4.25-5.50). For dessert, they offer Napoleon turnover and strawberry shortcake and since this used to be a Dairy Queen, a variety of ice creams: cones, shakes, floats, sundaes, and banana splits ($1.40-4.15) COMMENTS: Former Dairy Queen location.

**BRENNECKE'S** *Steak and Seafood*
Po'ipu Beach Park (742-7588) HOURS: Lunch 10 am to 4 pm, Dinner 4-10 pm, Happy Hour 11 am-5 pm daily. SAMPLING: Burgers, sandwiches, soups, and salad bar served till 10 pm ($4.95-10.50). Pupus all day, too: ceviche, sashimi, nachos, black and blue ahi, teri chicken sticks, Oriental or local style samplers ($6.95-12.95). Dinner choices include scampi, vegetables, or mussels with pasta, prime rib, NY steak, shrimp skewers, Oriental chicken stir-fry, Hawaiian spiny lobster, and fresh fish ($13.95-$22.95). COMMENTS: Excellent children's menu ($3.95-7.95) and early bird specials (4-6 pm) starting at $6.50. Salad bar has some interesting items, like whole red skinned potato salad, baby corn, pasta salad, and a good choice of dressings. Stir-fry was tasty with big pieces of chicken and the kiawe broiled opakapaka was flavorful. In the past we thought the prices seemed a tad high for such a casual atmosphere, but they haven't gone up in four years (in fact, some have gone down) and besides, everything comes with a salad bar and a right-on-the-beach view (at the renovated Po'ipu Beach Park) so it makes it easy to justify. Brennecke's also has T-shirts and a Beach/Activity Center and Beach Deli downstairs.

**BRICK OVEN PIZZA** *Italian*
2555 Kuhio Hwy., Kalaheo (332-8561) HOURS: 11 am-10 pm Tuesday-Saturday, 3-10 pm Sunday, closed Monday. SAMPLING: Whole wheat or white crust with the usual pizza toppings plus homemade Italian sausage, lean beef & green onions, imported anchovies, smoked ham & pineapple, salami, and bay shrimp. from $9.45 (small cheese) to $28.30 (large "super"). Pizza breads and hot sandwiches with sausage, seafood, meats and vegetables, or "pupu" pizza: pizza dough with garlic & cheese and a side of pizza sauce or dressing for dipping ($3.30-6.70), green veggie, or chef's salads ($2.15-6.55). Desserts include aloha pie or ice cream sundae cups ($.80-2.85). Beer & wine. COMMENTS: Hearth baked pizzas at this family owned operation which has been pleasing residents and visitors alike since they opened in 1977. Good homemade sausage and excellent pizza crust, soft and doughy, but beautifully browned - like a soft pretzel. The garlic butter on the crust is an added flavor treat - just don't try to taste it with a cold . . .

**CAMP HOUSE GRILL** ★ *American/Home Cooking*
Kaumualii Hwy., Kalaheo (332-9755) HOURS: Breakfast 6:30-10:30 am (to 11 weekends and holidays), Lunch/Dinner 10:30 am-9 pm. SAMPLING: Breakfast quesadilla, pancakes, omelettes, French toast, biscuits and gravy, eggs Benedict, omelettes and a variety of breakfast sandwiches - Monte Cristo with hash browns, or BLT (& egg), pancake or French toast with bacon & eggs ($3.95-8.95). They have early bird specials ($1.99-2.99) before 8 am, but as they say on the menu: After 8:01, No Way! Grilled fish, veggie, BLT, or turkey BLT sandwiches; chili ($3.95-7.95). Lunch and dinner offerings include a variety of burgers, salads, several grilled chicken entrees, BBQ pork ribs, sirloin steak Polynesian, and fresh catch served with soup or salad and choice of side ($7.95-14.95). COMMENTS: They're known for their homemade pies, so if you don't save room for dessert, you'll just have to buy a whole one from the glass case on your way out. Pineapple cream cheese macadamia or chewy chocolate chip macadamia nut sound good enough to eat (and they are!) and so do the cream pies of coconut, banana, and chocolate or the Paradise Pie made with macadamia nut, coconut,

and pineapple. The burgers are good, but the ribs are outrageously good! This looks like a funky neighborhood diner, but it is bright, spacious and naturally, it's comfortable and casual. It's home cooking all the way and home baking as far as the pies are concerned. The children's menu is available for lunch and dinner and it is no secret this is a family place. (Other locations in Hanapepe and Kapa'a,)

**CAMP HOUSE GRILL & CANTINA** ★ *American/Home Cooking/Mexican*
3959 Kamualii Hwy., Hanapepe (335-5656) HOURS: Breakfast 7:30-11:30 am (till noon Sat & Sun.), lunch 11 am-9 pm, dinner 5-9 pm. SAMPLING: Breakfast quesadilla, pancakes, omelettes, French toast, biscuits and gravy, eggs Benedict, omelettes and a variety of breakfast sandwiches - Monte Cristo with hash browns, or BLT (& egg), pancake or French toast with bacon & eggs ($3.95-8.95). They have early bird specials ($1.99-2.99) before 8 am, but as they say on the menu: After 8:01, No Way! Grilled fish, veggie, BLT, or turkey BLT sandwiches; chili ($3.95-7.95). Lunch and dinner offerings include a variety of burgers, salads, several grilled chicken entrees, BBQ pork ribs, sirloin steak Polynesian, and fresh catch served with soup or salad and choice of side ($7.95-14.95). Mexican specialties come with rice & beans: mahi mahi tacos, chile rellenos, burras, cheese or chicken enchiladas, and "chivichungas" ($10.95-12.95). Chicken or fish soft tacos ($2.50-3.95). Dinners of pork chops, prime rib, steak, scampi, or crab leg ($11.95-18.95). Save room for a piece of their famous homemade pie ($3.50). Pineapple cream cheese macadamia, chewy chocolate chip macadamia nut, coconut, banana, chocolate, and Paradise Pie made with macadamia nut, pineapple and coconut are also available whole to take home. COMMENTS: This, the second in the Camp House Grill "dynasty," opened in the old Sinaloa location at the end of 1998 hence the addition of Mexican food on the menu. They also offer live entertainment on Friday and Saturday nights. (The original Camp House Grill opened in Kalaheo in 1987, and the newest at Kaua'i Village in early 1999.)

**CASA DI AMICI PO'IPU** *Italian cross-cultural*
2301 Nalo Road, Po'ipu (742-1555) HOURS: Dinner only 5:30-930 pm SAMPLING: Start with a Caesar, mista, or Asian salade with fresh fish or an appetizer like gorgonzola polenta or four-cheese risotto ($8-11). Entree specials might include fennel crusted lamb with orange-hoison-ginger sauce, salmon & shrimp in lobster-cognac sauce, porcini-crusted chicken breast in cherry port wine, or mahogany-glazed salmon with jalapeno tequila aioli and black bean chinitos ($22-27). There's also a full page of pastas and sauces to mix and match ($18-22; light portions from $13) plus lasagna, fettucine putanesca, and linguine primavera ($19-24). Chicken or veal (prepared marsala, picatta or gorgonzola) also come in light ($17-18) or regular portions ($21-23). COMMENTS: Yes, you're on an island, but if you can imagine you're taking a long drive in the country, this looks like just the type of place you'd be happy to find at the end of the day. Actually you'll find it if you turn left above the curve just past Po'ipu Beach Park. Approach from the front porch to an old fashioned wood building that looks like it was once someone's home. Walls have been knocked down to give it a more open-air feeling, but the lava rock and wood beam ceilings remain along with the 400 gallon salt water aquarium that divides the dining room from the friendly bar. The "Casa" moved here from its long-time Kilauea location in November 1999, but owner/chef Randall Yates has kept the popular menu and

offers old favorites along with new innovations: Bacio (the Kiss) of boursin cheese in phyllo crust remains a signature appetizer; the spicy Fettucini Nero with Italian sausage ($21) and filet mignon with a light and dark peppercorn sauce from Campania ($23) still reflect the generous use of seasoning in the sauces that have strong flavor, yet never overpower. At press time, they were just settling in, but hope to resume baking and selling the big, round Tuscan loaves of "Rustic Italian" bread as well offering the nightly piano music that have always been two of the restaurants most popular and distinctive "attractions."

**DA IMU HUT CAFE** *American/local*
3771 Hanapepe Rd., (335-0200) HOURS: Breakfast 8-10:30 am, Lunch 10:30 am-2 pm, Dinner 5-8:45 pm (Fri till 9:45) Closed Saturday and Sunday. SAMPLING: French toast, omelettes, meat, egg & rice plates ($4-5.50). Local plates: Hamburger steak, teri beef or chicken, saimin (fried or bowl), kalua or lau lau ($4.95-6.50). "Burgas," egg or tuna sandwich ($1.75-3.50)

**DA'LI DELI & CAFE** *European Deli & Bakery*
Old Koloa Town (742-8824) HOURS: 7am-4 pm Mon-Fri; Sat from 8 am, Sun 8 am-2 pm (breakfast till 10:30, Sat. & Sun. till 11) SAMPLING: German pancakes, French toast, frittata, lox platter, bagelwich, granola, fruit plate, or egg breakfast ($4.95-8.50) Create your own sandwich from a choice of deli meats, cheeses, toppings, and condiments on a variety of freshly baked breads ($3.95-6.95). Specialty sandwiches include marinated eggplant on focaccia, turkey with cranberry relish, Italian sub, or spinach & smoked turkey wrap plus quiche, and Greek, chef's, or curry chicken salad ($3.60-6.95). Breads, flavored bagels, pies, tortes, cookies and other baked goodies from the bakery plus coffee drinks and smoothies. COMMENTS: Everything is baked fresh on the premises. Sandwiches are all served on their home-baked bread using organic vegetables and fresh deli meats. They even roast their own turkey and make their own traditional boiled-in-water bagels!

**(THE) DOCK** *light meals and snacks*
1571 Po'ipu Rd., at the Hyatt Regency (742-1234) HOURS: 10:30 am-5 pm. SAMPLING: Deli sandwiches, burgers, salads (Caesar, grilled or Oriental chicken, pasta, chef's, tuna and a signature Smoked Seafood Salad with Lilikoi Vinaigrette) plus and grilled specialty sandwiches like BBQ chicken, garden burger, fresh fish, spiced beef on focaccia and a Reuben wrapper. $3.50-8.50. Ice cream, frozen yogurt, cookies, fresh fruit $2.50-4. COMMENTS: Located poolside. Keiki meals available.

**DONDERO'S** *Italian*
Hyatt Regency Kaua'i, Po'ipu (742-1234) HOURS: 6-10 pm. SAMPLING: Antipasti consists of porcini mushroom crepes; beef carpaccio; bruschetta; fresh triangle pasta with shrimp, asparagus & mushrooms, speidini of prawns & artichokes; minestrone soup; artichoke with crab fondue, and several salads including portabella mushroom & goat cheese ($5.50-12.50). Pastas include ricotta cannelloni with walnuts; veal rigatoni; seafood spaghettini; fettucine with roasted chicken, porcini mushroom, prosciutto & parmesan cream sauce and risotto with grilled vegetables ($16.50-26.75). Veal scallopini with lobster; osso buco; chicken stuffed with spinach, mushroom & fontina cheese; filet medallions with marsala sauce; risotto-crusted fresh fish with lobster & shrimp cannelloni;

and cioppino ($24-28.25. Desserts ($5.50) include tiramisu, fresh fruit torte, amaretto cheesecake souffle, chocolate-chocolate torte, or Zuppa Inglaise (translation: "English Soup"), the Italian version of English trifle. COMMENTS: Extensive wine list. Decor is an upscale Italian version of a Mexican cantina: tiled floors with "hand-painted" stucco walls and "real" three-dimensional seashells stuck on over painted-on shells. There's a colorful mural at the back and outside dining is on a villa patio. The color scheme is dark green and white and somehow it all worked - it was fun, yet fancy, about the closest thing to fine dining that there is in Kaua'i. Both appetizers and desserts can be ordered in sampler plates, a real plus when there are so many good things to try. The food is Italian with a difference that should appeal to purists as well as the more adventurous Italian food lover. While dining is casual on the Garden Isle, they do request men wear shirts with collars. Reservations suggested.

**ESPRESSO USA** *Coffee drinks & light meals*
The Courtyard, Old Koloa Town (742-7925) Email: <netcafe@aloha.net> HOURS: Mon-Fri 8 am-4 pm; Sat-Sun till noon. SAMPLING: Fresh pastries, salads, sandwiches (tuna, beef, ham, turkey, ham rolls, hot dogs), ice cream, desserts and snacks plus espresso, cappuccino, and latte ($1.25-3.25). COMMENTS: Comfortable "play" room with tables and chairs, chess set, TV, books, local arts & crafts, and a bulletin board. Access to email and internet, $3 per 1/2 hour, $5 per hour.

**GREEN GARDEN** ★ *Local plus*
Hanapepe Town (335-5422) HOURS: Breakfast 8:30-10:30/11 am (from 8 am on Saturday and 7:30 am Sunday), Lunch 11 am-2 pm, Dinner 5-9 pm. Closed all day Tuesday. SAMPLING: Breakfast of eggs, breakfast meats, waffles, hot cakes, and French toast ($3.65-4.95). For $5.20 you can have dessert for breakfast: a waffle with ice cream, whipped cream, coconut, and strawberry topping! Lunch sandwiches include salad, fries, and beverage and offer roast pork, mahi melt, burgers, and a variety of clubs ($5.95-6.95). Entrees also include vegetables and feature chicken chow mein, shrimp tempura, sweet & sour spare ribs, and BBQ chicken ($6.75-7.95) and specials like seafood curry, breaded liver, or chicken tofu. Shrimp Louis, tuna, or chef's salads ($6.75-6.95). Dinners are complete with homemade soup, salad, rice or potatoes, vegetables, rolls, and beverage. Appetizers include a choice of escargot stuffed mushrooms, shrimp cocktail, mussels, sashimi, or pupu platter ($3.95-6.95). They offer some of the same lunch entrees at only slightly higher prices as well as kiawe broiled pork chops, steaks, kabobs, or chicken peppercorn as well as Chinese, Japanese or Hawaiian plates, breaded liver, rack of lamb, and teri chicken. Posted specials, too, like roast turkey or pork, prime rib, steamed crab legs, fresh fish, chicken cutlet, or their "house special" baked seafood salads ($8.95-20.95). Lobster ($26.95). They're known for their "mile-high" pies like coconut or macadamia cream, chocolate, and especially the lilikoi ($2). COMMENTS: This family owned restaurant has been here since 1948 serving an eclectic mix of local, homestyle, and gourmet meals in large portions for small prices. Wine & tropical drinks. Good selection of children's choices. The salad bar, given the inflated prices of fresh produce on Kaua'i, is a real value! ($6.50 for lunch, $7 for dinner, $2.50 with entree.) Very casual with the spacious garden look of a

large greenhouse. The long family-style tables are popular with tour bus groups and perhaps negates an intimate dining experience. But the portions are generous,the menu is broad, the atmosphere pleasant, the prices reasonable and the pies fabulous!

**GRINDS ESPRESSO** *Bakery/Pizza/Espresso*
Ele'ele Shopping Center (the old Dairy Queen building) (335-6027) HOURS: Mon-Sat 5:30 am-9 pm (pizza slices from 10:30 am until closing) SAMPLING: Skillet breakfasts with potatoes, green pepper & potatoes or rice with a choice of meat (sausage, salami, pepperoni) plus omelettes, French toast, and burger, steak, or mahi mahi breakfast ($3.75-6.50). Sandwiches ($4.50-6.75) on homemade bread are served hot (chicken club, bacon & pineapple, mahi mahi, salami & pesto cream cheese, burgers) or cold (Italian, smoked turkey & jack cheese, veggie, ham & cheddar). Salads include an organic Caesar, chicken & walnut, and chef's ($6.75-7.50). "Haole" local plates (that means no spam!) offer mahi, BBQ or Cajun chicken, and shoyu beef or chicken ($6.75-7.25). Pizzas in 15" and 18" sizes from $12-23. Espresso and coffee drinks, smoothies, Italian sofas ($1.50-4.25) COMMENTS: The old Dairy Queen has been spruced up and even has patio seating with lattice work and flowers.

**HANAPEPE CAFE & ESPRESSO** ★ *Gourmet Vegetarian* South.
Located in old Igawa Drugstore at 3830 Hanapepe Road (335-5011/335-8544) HOURS: Breakfast Tuesday-Saturday 8-11 am, Lunch 11 am-2 pm. Dinner served Friday & Saturday 6-9 pm. SAMPLING: Breakfast naturally begins with espresso and other coffee drinks and there are multi-grain waffles and pancakes, homemade oatmeal, home fries, and baked frittatas ($4.25-9). Lunch includes soups and salads, healthnut or grilled vegetable sandwich, pasta, and garden burgers with various combinations of pesto, sundried tomatoes, sauteed mushrooms, and artichoke hearts ($5-8.25). Dinners change monthly and might include an appetizer of stuffed tomatoes, ricotta dumplings, roasted goat cheese cakes,

or seared polenta salad ($7.25-11.75) or entrees like vegetable & potato Charlotte, vegan lasagna with layers of sliced potatoes & pasta with lentils, garbanzo bean flour cakes with eggplant & tomatillo relish, quesadilla with pesto & portobello mushrooms, purple sweet potato quiche with raisins, cheese & sauteed mushrooms, or puree of onion with fresh spinach. ($13.25-18.75). Desserts include macadamia nut creme brulee, passion fruit bread pudding with raspberry sauce & vanilla ice cream, tiramisu, and chocolate cake with lilikoi glaze ($6-6.50). COMMENTS: Owners Larry Reisor and Chris Ayers offer gourmet vegetarian dinners that even meat eaters like. They're made with a French and Italian flair and with such fresh, flavorful vegetables that most don't know anything's "missing." (In fact, 90% of their customers aren't vegetarian!) The dishes are creative and colorful, mixing and matching ingredients for bursts of flavor that are both familiar and exciting. BYOWine. Live music on dinner nights with regular or Hawaiian slack key guitar. Reservations recommended. <www.hanapepe.com>

**HOUSE OF SEAFOOD** *Fish/Seafood*
1941 Po'ipu Road at Po'ipu Kai Resort (742-5255) HOURS: 5:30-9:15 pm. SAMPLING: Steamed clams, shrimp cocktail, Oysters Rockefeller, and crab stuffed potato are a few of the appetizers ($8.50-9) or warm up with French onion soup or Wailua clam chowder ($4.50-6). Entrees feature fresh fish as well as Scallops Po'ipu, lobster & shrimp curry, seafood pasta, crab stuffed prawns, abalone, paella, cioppino, and bouillabaisse ($20.50-43.50). Meat lovers aren't left out, several steaks are offered alone or in seafood combinations ($25-40). Several adult-style steak and seafood offerings are available on the keiki menu ($7-13). COMMENTS: The long-room dining area has beautiful wood floors and large open windows which allow the evening breezes to come in. They do offer quite an extensive seafood menu so chances are they will have something on the menu that you haven't ever tried before. However, given that the meals are a la carte, when you add soup and/or salad to your bill at $3-6 or more each, your meal is going to become pretty expensive.

**ILIMA TERRACE** *Island style*
Hyatt Regency Kaua'i, Po'ipu (742-1234) HOURS: Breakfast 6-11 am (buffet till 10), Sunday Brunch 10:30 am-2 pm, Lunch 11 am-2:30 pm, Dinner 6-9 pm. SAMPLING: Assorted cereals, fruits, pancakes, Belgian waffles, banana French toast, smoked salmon plate, omelettes (4-12.50) and a daily breakfast buffet ($16.75) or Sunday Champagne Brunch ($28.95). Lunch starts with a sashimi sampler, smoked chicken quesadilla with sweet chile cream, buffalo wings, Thai summer rolls, or a variety of salads: cobb, pasta, fruit, Caesar, or sesame shrimp & seafood ($6-15). Burgers, pizza, pasta, or entree specialties like Korean chicken, seared ahi loin steak, prawn noodles, or red hot chicken spaghetti along with healthy offerings such as red lentil chili, grilled salmon salad, or whole wheat tortilla chicken sandwich ($6-16). Limited dinner menu with pizza, sandwiches and salads ($6-11.50) or a nightly buffet ($28.95) that includes salad bar, breads, fruits and cheeses, pastries, and hot food depending on the night: Sunday/Thursday, prime rib; Monday/Friday, Hawaiian seafood; Tuesday, Italian; and Wednesday/Saturday, surf & turf for $28.95. COMMENTS: Dinner buffets are an affordable way to experience the luxury of dining at the Hyatt and their healthy, natural cuisine options are a plus. Recently remodeled with richer, warmer colors that give it a more upscale look. Reservations suggested.

**ISLAND TERIYAKI** *Local style*
Old Koloa Town Center (742-9988) HOURS: Sunday-Wednesday 11 am-12 am; Thursday-Saturday till 1:30 am. SAMPLING: Plate lunches or papaya-teriyaki grilled chicken, beef, or fish are served with rice, macaroni salad, or ginger cole slaw ($5.95-7.95). Their signature dishes are served in a bowl on top of rice or mashed potatoes, or in a "wrap" surrounded by a plain, sun-dried, or spinach tortilla. Try American (chicken salad or steak); Asian (fish, veggie stir-fry, beef with hoison sauce, or chicken with curry, coconut, or peanut sauce); Latin (grilled shrimp, fish with papaya salsa, Mexicana, or quesadilla-style); Mediterranean (steak & peppers, roasted eggplant, or lemon-dill fish); or Local (kalua pig, saimin, or loco moco) $4.95-7.95. Po'ipu kabobs, barbecue sticks, fresh smoothies, and shave ice $1.95-3.95. COMMENTS: When Pizzetta moved from here to bigger digs down the block, owners Cathy Halter and her son, John, retained the location and opened this new day & late night, take-out spot for innovative food items that are local - and beyond!

**JOE'S COURTSIDE CAFE** ★ *Salads/Burgers/Sandwiches*
Located at Kiahuna Tennis Club, Po'ipu (742-6363) HOURS: Breakfast 7-11 am, Lunch 11 am-2 pm. SAMPLING: Pastries, breads, and healthy fruits, along with eggs Benedict, loco moco, Huevos Rancheros, French toast, Anahola granola, banana macadamia pancakes and their popular tofu scramble, are the breakfast options or you can create your own omelette from a list of ingredients. For lunch, choose your ingredients for a personalized salad or opt for a Caesar with grilled chicken breast or Portuguese bean soup ($3.50-7.95). Sandwiches include turkey club, tuna & jalapeno melt, vegetarian, South Shore steak sandwich (like a Philly), and a great, lean, turkey Reuben or try a burger, hot dog (with Cleveland Stadium mustard!) or tasty chicken avocado with jack cheese hot off the grill ($5.25-9). Try the chocolate toffee or lilikoi ice cream pie for dessert ($3.50). COMMENTS: "Eat at Joe's" for some great sandwiches in an open air restaurant and bar. The gazebo-style house has a tented roof and overlooks the tennis courts. Tennis not your game? Read on . . .

**JOE'S ON THE GREEN** ★ *Salads/Burgers/Sandwiches*
Located at the Kiahuna Golf Course in Po'ipu. (742-9696 ) HOURS: Breakfast 7:30-11:30 am, lunch 11:30 am-2:30 pm. Dinner Thursdays only, 5:30-8:30 pm. Cocktails and pupus till 6 on weekends. SAMPLING: Breakfast specials include Joe's special scramble made with ground beef, eggs, and taro leaf; homemade corned beef hash served in a crisp potato skin; and a variety of tropical fruit pancakes. For lunch, try the grilled turkey Reuben or chicken Philly sandwich; Mediterranean grilled eggplant salad; or the fresh, local fish and chips. ($4.75-8.50) Dinner (and great sunsets!) are offered on Thursday nights. The lively and inventive menu features some surprising combinations that really work: prawns wrapped in phyllo with banana curry sauce; kalua pork and lomi salmon ravioli; and fresh mahi mahi in coffee lime beurre blanc sauce are just a few of the Thursday night specials. ($14.95-21.95). COMMENTS: No longer just a snack bar, the wide, open-air bar and pleasant seating area is now enhanced by a "real" restaurant thanks to new owner Joe Batteiger, the personable and gregarious Joe of Joe's Courtside Cafe above. The country club setting overlooks the golf course and offers a great panoramic view. Live Hawaiian music on Thursday nights.

**JOHN'S PLACE** *Sandwiches/burgers/ice cream*
9875 Waimea Road, Waimea (338-0330) HOURS: Breakfast 6-11 am, from 7 Sat-Sun. Lunch daily 11 am-5 pm. Closed for dinner. SAMPLING: Breakfast burrito, croissant sandwich, omelettes, French toast ($3.95-6.95) Bagels, pastries, fruit, and assorted coffee drinks ($1.60-2.50). Sandwiches on their own home-baked bread (turkey & avocado, grilled ham or tuna & cheese, roast beef), chicken, tuna, veggies, or fish "wrapped" in a tomato or spinach tortilla, burgers, hot dogs, fried chicken, burritos, soft tacos, fish & chips, and Caesar salads ($4.25-6.75). Daily soups ($2.50-3). Smoothies, shakes, floats, or Cappuccino Blast ($2.75-3.75) Shave ice ($1-2). COMMENTS: The "in" (and only) place in Waimea for "healthy" foods and more with ice cream parlor seating. Tropical ice cream and smoothie flavors include, guava, mango, and Ling Hing Mui. (Sample a Waimea Sunset smoothie with strawberries, bananas, guava juice and vanilla ice cream.)

**KALAHEO COFFEE CO. & CAFE** ★ *Sandwiches & Salads*
2436 Kaumualii Hwy., Kalaheo (332-5858) HOURS: Monday-Friday 6 am-4 pm (Saturdays from 6:30); Sundays 7 am-2 pm. SAMPLING: Breakfast ($2.95-6.75) is served till 11 offering Anahola granola, scrambled egg sandwich, pastries, pancakes, Belgian waffles, breakfast burrito tortilla wrap, and "Bagel Bennys," but you can build-your-own omelettes till 3:30. Lunch is served from 10:30 with Kaua'i grown salads (with bulgar wheat, herb chicken, or Oriental veggie) homemade soups, and deli or grilled sandwiches like hot pastrami, tuna melt, Cajun tofu & eggplant, chicken & bulgar salsa wrap, grilled Reuben, turkey burger, or fresh vegetable on focaccia ($4.75-7.95). Ice cream shakes and pastries including muffins, scones, cinnamon rolls, cheesecake, apple pie, carrot cake, and chocolate raspberry cake. And of course they have plenty of coffees and teas. COMMENTS: The fresh salads are excellent and the sandwiches are piled high. Owners Kristina and John Ferguson have the perfect place to stop after a visit to the Canyon for a late lunch and/or leisurely cup of coffee or to pick up some lunch to eat up at Kukuiolono Park! Email: <java@kalaheo.com> Website: <www.kalaheo.com>

**KALAHEO STEAK HOUSE** *Steak/Seafood*
4444 Papalina Road (332-9780) HOURS: Dinner 6-10 pm. SAMPLING: Mussels or clams by the pound, artichokes, mushrooms, calamari , or teriyaki steak stix will start you off ($4.50-6.25) and they're followed by dinners of steak, pork, poultry, prime rib, seafood, or combinations you can choose ($14.95-24.95). Cornish game hen, teriyaki pork tenderloin, and Kalaheo shrimp are some of the more unusual offerings and all come with all-you-can-eat of good, hearty salad topped with white beans, homemade Italian dressing & crumbled bleu cheese and fresh, but over-nuked rolls (from The Bread Box bakery across the street) plus baked potato or rice. For dessert, there's rum cake and/or ice cream plus a hot fudge sundae and a daily cheesecake ($3.75-3.95). COMMENTS: Nice wood decor with hanging plants. Located in a quiet, residential neighborhood. The portions are ample and a good value; their Portuguese soup with a house salad makes a satisfying light supper.

**KAUA'I KITCHENS** *Local*
Koloa Road (near Big Save), Koloa (742-1712); 9861 Waimea Road, Waimea (338-1315) HOURS: Koloa 7 am-2:30 pm, Waimea 6 am-2 pm. SAMPLING: Sandwiches, plate lunches, bentos, sushi (maki cone) from $1.20 and daily specials: chicken cutlet, fresh corned beef, breaded crab croquette, baked pork chops, roast turkey with stuffing, lemon chicken, seafood curry, fish filet, pork adobo plus Hawaiian, Filipino, and Oriental plates ($4.95-5.95). They also sell Kaua'i Kookies, baked foods, and T-shirts retail from the Kaua'i Kookie Kompany. COMMENTS: "Quick Tasty Island Style" that you can eat in or take out. Also located at Rice Shopping Center in Lihu'e.

**KEOKI'S PARADISE** *Steak & Seafood*
Po'ipu Shopping Village (742-7534) HOURS: Dinner 5:30-10 pm; Cafe menu for lunch; also seafood and taco bar 11 am-11:30 pm. SAMPLING: Sashimi, fisherman's chowder, and Thai shrimp sticks with guava cocktail sauce to start ($3.95-8.95) and entrees of fresh fish (with several preparations), pesto shrimp macadamia, Pacific Rim rigatoni (with seafood), steaks, Koloa pork ribs, Balinese chicken (in garlic and lemon grass), and vegetarian lasagna ($10.95-19.95). Ice cream, triple chocolate cake, and "The Original Hula Pie" from Kimo's (still the best!) from $2.95-4.95. The Cafe menu has burgers and sandwiches (chicken, steak, roast beef, Reuben); fish tacos, nachos, chicken quesadillas, and a selection of pupus from the dinner menu as well as their superb calamari strips ($3.95-9.95). Hawaiian local plates (pork, fish, and chicken) are $9.95. COMMENTS: This is one of the popular TS restaurant chain that also owns Duke's Canoe Club here on Kaua'i and in Waikiki as well as Kimos's and Hula Grill on Maui. The food is good and a good value, just don't go expecting "A Pacific Cafe" cuisine. All dinners are under $20 (except for a hefty prime rib at $23.95) and all come with Caesar salad, a basket of hot rolls and carrot muffins, and herbed rice. Appetizers are worth the extra few dollars, especially the calamari: the thick strips are about perfect in taste and texture. (Only on their cafe menu, but if you ask, they'll be happy to serve them for your dinner pupu.) The atmosphere at Keoki's is creative with plenty of family appeal. The lagoons with koi, waterfalls, and plenty of lush greenery in this open air, multi-level restaurant create a setting reminiscent of Disney's Jungle Land (albeit without any mechanical elephants or alligators.) The kids will love eating in the tropics! Arrive between 5 and 6 pm for a selection of early bird specials. Reservations are always a good idea even though they may not be quite as busy during low season.

**KOKE'E LODGE** *American*
3600 Koke'e Road, Waimea (335-6061) HOURS: 9 am-3:30 pm. SAMPLING: Continental and light breakfasts, quiche, cornbread, muffins ($2.35-6). Lunch sandwiches on 12-grain bread from $6. Pear, Greek, or Moroccan salads, $7.25. plus Koke'e Lodge specialties like chili, Portuguese bean soup, cornbread; also carrot cake and lilikoi or coconut pie ($3-5). Wine and Kaua'i beer. COMMENTS: Rustic atmosphere and good place to stop on the way to Waimea Canyon. Considering you're in what seems to be in the middle of the Hawaiian wilderness, the food is remarkably good. Nothing like a bowl of bean soup with a side of cornbread to warm you up on a cool afternoon adventure in upcountry Kaua'i!

**KOLOA FISH MARKET** *Fresh fish/plate lunches*
5482 Koloa Road, Koloa (742-6199) HOURS: Monday-Friday 10 am-6 pm, Saturday till 5, closed Sunday. SAMPLING: Smoked fish, seared ahi, poke, lomi lomi salmon, scallop salad, and other deli items. Lunch specials: one choice/$5.25; two choices/$5.75; lau lau & kalua pig/$5.95. Sides of macaroni and rice. Sushi and sashimi trays $3.25-3.99. COMMENTS: Tiny market at the west end of Koloa Town Center; mostly take-out, but a few tables and chairs outside. Owned by the former chef at the Sheraton. A great little find!

**KUPONO CAFE AT THE ANARA SPA** *Health food*
1571 Po'ipu Rd., at the Hyatt Regency (742-1234) HOURS: 6 am-2 pm. SAMPLING: Fresh fruits, cereals, and tropical muffins along with fresh fruit juices and smoothies ($2.75-$7.50). Low-fat lunches include red lentil chili with yogurt & baked corn chips, garden burger, and island-grown salads ($5-8.50). COMMENTS: Located right at the spa so you can enjoy a healthy breakfast or lunch after indulging in a facial or massage, working out in their fitness room, or swimming laps in their 25 yard lap pool. (Although it sounds like an appropriately ethereal and Oriental name, ANARA is actually an acronym for A New Age Restorative Approach.)

**LAWA'I RESTAURANT** *Local/Oriental*
3687 Kaumualii Hwy., Lawa'i (332-9550) HOURS: Mon-Fri 10 am-9 pm, Sat-Sun from 9. SAMPLING: Extensive menu (about 300 items!) of local and Oriental dishes: soup, pork, beef, poultry, seafood, chop suey, eggs, vegetarian, saimin, cake noodles, salad, sushi roll, Filipino dishes, curries, Japanese dishes plus sandwiches, steaks and seafood. Chinese sausage, crispy duck with plum sauce, ham & egg fu yung, seafood spaghetti, duck noodles with vegetables, chicken papaya, sukiyaki don, shrimp tempura, fish teriyaki, BBQ meatballs ($5-10.75). Full seafood, Chinese, or steak combo dinners ($10-15.50). COMMENTS: This small eatery, which opened in 1985, is particularly popular with local residents. There are three pages full of dishes on their printed menu and even more on the blackboard. Try their tasty ginger fried chicken!

**LINDA'S RESTAURANT** *Local*
3840 Hanapepe Road, Hanapepe (335-5152) HOURS: Open Mon-Fri 10:30 am-1:30 pm, Tues-Fri, 5:30-8:30 pm. SAMPLING: Continuous menu features a variety of burgers (mushroom with Swiss, teri beef or chicken) plus tuna, egg, or grilled cheese sandwiches ($1.80-3.40) as well as miso soup, samin, and won ton min ($3-5.50) Plate specials served with rice, macaroni salad, and hot vegetable: teri chicken or beef, loco moco, mahi mahi, pork chop, veal cutlet, beef stew, and honey dip chicken ($4.70-6.85). Fried saimin specials offer many of the same entrees as well as chicken cutlet, wing ding, chicken katsu, and breaded teri beef or chicken ($5.85-6.30). Daily specials might include roast beef, shoyu chicken, meat loaf, chicken hekka, and baked mahi ($6-6.50). COMMENTS: Small coffee shop that celebrated 30 years of business in 1999!

**MI CASITA** *Mexican*
5470 Koloa Road, Old Koloa Town by the post office (742-2323) HOURS: Mon-Sat 11 am-9:30 pm; Sun 4-9 pm SAMPLING: Pork, beef, or chicken burritos, beef or chicken chimichanga ($8.95-9.95). Fajitas for 1 or 2 ($12.95-22.95) with chicken, steak, seafood or a "Fiesta" combination. Specialties include Enchiladas

Rancheras, chile verde, carnitas, chile relleno, enchiladas, tacos, taquitos, and tostadas ($7.50-11.95). Taco salad or seafood salad in a shell plus a variety of nachos, quesadillas, potato skins, and buffalo wings appetizers ($5.95-8.95) COMMENTS: This sister (hermana) restaurant of La Bamba in Lihu'e doesn't have a liquor license, but invites you to BYOB.

**NANIWA** *Japanese*
Sheraton Kaua'i Resort, 2440 Ho'onani Road, Po'ipu (742-1661) HOURS: Dinner 5:30-9:30 pm. Closed Monday & Friday. SAMPLING: Start with ahi carpaccio, sliced beef with citrus ponzu sauce, smoked salmon with fresh fruit/prosciutto ham with asparagus, chilled tofu, tempura, seafood lau lau, and a variety of sushi including Hawaiian roll poke style ($6.95-9.95. Assorted sashimi or sushi ($18.95-22.95). Glass noodle, seafood, or Manoa leaf & papaya salad ($6.50-8.50). Dinner entrees of beef striploin steak, broiled chicken, butter fish, assorted tempura or sushi, buckwheat noodles with tempura plus fresh fish or lobster & crab. Ala carte $16.95-22.95); complete dinners with salad, miso soup, rice and pickled vegetables ($22.95-28.95). East-West desserts range from ujikintoki (ice cream, shaved ice & red azuki beans) to cappuccino grasse (coffee gelatin with ice cream and Kahlua); mitsumame (fruit, gelatin, ice cream & azuki beans) to haupia with fresh fruit ($4.50-5.95). Beer, wine & sake. Saturday night Japanese buffet (5:30-9:30) features sushi, sashimi, salads, entrees, cold seafood, tempura station, and desserts ($31.95). COMMENTS: This is the same name as their pre-Iniki Japanese restaurant. Naniwa blends Hawaiian ambiance into a Japanese inn setting surrounding by koi ponds and lagoon gardens. The food reflects the same blend of Japanese with Hawaiian (and European) touches. Like the other restaurants at the resort, the ambiance is upscale, but not intimidating.

**OASIS BAR & GRILL** *Lunch*
Poolside at Sheraton Kaua'i Resort, 2440 Ho'onani Road, Po'ipu (742-1661) HOURS: 11:30 am-6 pm SAMPLING: Sandwiches, salads, fresh fruit and ice cream ($2.50-6.95). Hot items include fried chicken, jalapeno poppers, nachos, burgers, pizza, hot dog (or turkey dog), fish burger,chicken fingers, buffalo wings, and chicken teriyaki sandwich ($4.95-9.95). COMMENTS: Casual poolside restaurant close to the beach. (The Garden Terrace -- open only during high season -- also offers snacks and light meals.)

**PACIFIC PIZZA & DELI** *Pizza*
9652 Kaumualii Hwy. (part of and adjacent to Wrangler's Steak House across from Big Save), Waimea (338-1020) HOURS: 11 am-9 pm SAMPLING: A variety of "international" pizzas in small, medium, large ($8.95-19.95) sizes and calzone from $4.75-6: Pacific (seafood), Japanese, Portuguese, Mexican, Veggie, Thai, Hapa Haole (pesto with sun-dried tomatoes, mushrooms, zucchini, Canadian bacon -- and Hawaiian pineapple) Lomi Lomi (salmon), and Filipino (with homemade langanizsa sausage). Deli sandwiches (on choice of bread) or cold wraps rolled in a tomato-basil tortilla come in turkey, ham pastrami, roast beef, and tuna ($5.25). Seafood wrap $6.25. House salad ($3.50) plus special deli salads sold by the pound. COMMENTS: Eat in or take out.

**PATTAYA ASIAN CAFE** *Thai & Chinese*
Po'ipu Shopping Village (742-8818) HOURS: Lunch 11:30 am-2:30 pm Monday-Saturday; Dinner nightly 5-9:30 pm. SAMPLING: Spring or summer rolls, fish cakes, sateh, calamari, mee krob appetizers ($6.95-10.95). Lemongrass or Thai ginger coconut soup with chicken or seafood ($7.95-14.95); Fresh papaya, shrimp, or beef salad ($6.25-10.95). Lemon chicken, stir fried eggplant, broccoli with oyster sauce, pad Thai noodles, Evil Jungle Prince, garlic with coconut, pineapple with curry sauce, stir fried bell pepper,and a variety of curries are the entrees ($7.95-16.95). COMMENTS: Mee Choy, owner of Mema Thai Cuisine in Wailua, also owns this casual outdoor cafe in Po'ipu and has recently opened Lemongrass Bar & Grill in Kapa'a. His sisters own King & I in Waipouli -- the family keeps branching out!

**PIATTI** ★ *Pacific Mediterranean*
Kiahuna Plantation in Po'ipu (742-2216) HOURS: Dinner 5:30-10 pm; pupus and drinks from 4 pm. SAMPLING: Menu changes seasonally, but your dinner might start with ceviche tacos, smoked ono or salmon carpaccio, arugula & roast beet salad, wok-seared scallops (with peanuts & bok choy in a delicious lemongrass ginger coconut curry sauce), "porcupine" shrimp with shredded phyllo (served with chile sesame dipping sauce), duck pipikaula salad with poha vinaigrette, or Hawaiian mixed plate ($5.95-13.95). Gourmet pizzas from the wood-burning oven are light with fresh herbs and vegetables or spicy grilled chicken ($10.95-13.95) and the pastas are flavorful with everything from ginger scallion sauce on the smoked duck and chicken ravioli to pesto and pinenuts in the lasagna to spices

and breadfruit, and a hint of green tea in the penne with seafood ($15.95-20.95). Entrees might include rotisserie chicken with tangerine hoison sauce, seafood lau lau, peanut crusted lamb chops, filet wrapped in pancetta, or sugar cane pork tenderloin ($16.95-26.95). For dessert, there's carrot bread pudding, gingersnap streusel cobbler, rocky road sundae, chocolate hazelnut decadence, roasted banana macadamia torte, the "Kauai Slide" ice cream pie, or "Pole Hale Campfire S'mores," a gourmet version of the childhood favorite ($6.25-6.95). COMMENTS: The bounty of fresh vegetables in the lasagna, the moist and flavorful chicken, and the subtle taste sensation of fresh-picked herbs (from Kiahuna Plantation's own garden) were key to our giving Piatti a star after our very first experience. Very impressive, especially for a chain! Although California-based, they have done an excellent job of adapting their original Italian menu to reflect island flavors and now offer even more of an international variety: their panko crusted/pan seared ono was served with dried cherry ginger cider vinaigrette, avocado sauce & toasted pine nuts; the pork tenderloin was served on a stick of sugar cane (like a pork popsicle!) with tamarind plum sauce, candied garlic, and Thai rice musubi. Both dishes had a "sense" of sweetness, but the ultimate taste was savory; the pork even more smokey from its marinade and grilled preparation. The presentations (though still fairly horizontal) offer some creative fun when you find colorful bits of (orange) sweet potato in the mashed; rice & peanuts under the scallops, or roasted sweet potato under your ono. (Like a culinary treasure hunt!) Our only complaint was that the sauces were so good there just wasn't enough to make it to that last bite. The lovely plantation atmosphere of the historic 1930's Moir House adds charm with just a touch of whimsy: if you're trying to find the restroom, a simple "Yes" above the doorway answers your unspoken question.

**PIZZETTA** ★ *Italian*
Old Koloa Town Center (742-8881) HOURS: 11 am-10 pm, bar open till 12:30. SAMPLING: Distinctive salads (blackened chicken celery, chop chop, and Caesar with blackened chicken or bay shrimp); unusual burgers such as Italian sausage, eggplant parmigiana, meatball, and blackened chicken; and Panini (Italian sandwiches): grilled bread is covered with combinations of meat and vegetables like salami, provolone, roasted peppers, eggplant, blackened chicken, artichoke hearts or marinated, grilled sirloin tip. ($6.95-10.95). Pizzas include the usual toppings plus barbecue or blackened chicken, shrimp, pesto, spinach, sun-dried tomato, homemade Italian sausage, artichoke hearts, and pineapple (from $10.95 medium cheese to $23.95 large meat lovers or chicken supreme). Calzones, mozzarella or pepperoni sticks, stuffed mushrooms, spinach & artichoke dip (with focaccia bread) or tapenada ($3.95-5.95); Minestrone soup, Greek Caesar, or chop salad ($2.95-7.95). Entrees include ravioli, lasagna, pasticcio, chicken or eggplant parmesan, baked penne, chicken cacciatore, beef tenderloin steak, and fresh fish. Pasta specials offer lemon chicken sauce, spicy puttanesca (tomato, garlic, capers, olives), fettucini (Alfredo or clam sauce), penne (primavera or with Italian sausage) and a choice of spaghetti ($7.95-14.95). Cheesecake, ice cream, chocolate decadence, and a perfectly textured tiramisu are some of the desserts ($3.95-5.95). COMMENTS: They recently expanded (1999) and moved into the old Koloa Broiler location with renovating and remodeling that included relocating the bar to make room for a pizza take-out counter in front. Pizza by the slice ($2.75-3.25) also available at the window. Full beverage selection with

Italian sodas, tropical iced tea, juices, espressos, and coffee drinks as well as wine and beer. The owner/chef duo of Cathy Halter (La Griglia) and her son, John Halter (both are both!) have joined forces and you'll find the best of both Italian worlds at this new location. We were unable to review this new hybrid by press time, but with a combination of her homemade sauces and pastas from La Griglia and his variety of Pizzetta pizzas, we will just go ahead and presume they are still star-worthy. La Griglia is now closed, but their Island Teriyaki (just down the block) also opened at the end of 1999 and offers a unique menu of international and local-style tortilla wraps and rice bowls.

**(THE) PLANTATION HOUSE** *Pizza/Sandwiches*
Po'ipu Shopping Village (742-7373) HOURS: Breakfast 7-10 am, lunch 11 am-3:30 pm, dinner 5-10 pm SAMPLING: French toast, Belgian waffles, and buttermilk-taro or banana macadamia nut-taro pancakes plus loco moco and omelettes ($4.95-6.95) Starters for lunch (or dinner) include salmon & shiitake mushroom spring rolls, shrimp & mushroom saute, hot wings, crab cakes, or veggie wrap ($5.25-9.25). Shrimp club, mahi tempura, grilled vegetable, or teri chicken sandwich; entrees of Atlantic salmon, shrimp or chicken linguine, or mahi & chips are priced slightly less for lunch ($10.95-13.75); dinner entrees are served with soup or salad and include NY steak, fried chicken, sweet chile shrimp, pork chops, and Hawaiian BBQ chicken ($14.75-18.75). Pizzas offer unusual toppings like rock shrimp & roasted eggplant, spinach & bacon, fresh vegetables, and the popular chicken & shiitake mushroom (medium or large, $12.50-21.75). COMMENTS: Several name changes and renovations later, what originally began as Rusty's now has the look of a family-style plantation house with paniolo ambiance and seating outside on an old-fashioned porch. A display case inside offers bakery goodies -- cookies, brownies, muffins, and bags of local-style (crunchy) cinnamon toast.

**(THE) POINT** *Lounge/Appetizer & Dessert menu*
Sheraton Kaua'i Resort, 2440 Ho'onani Road, Po'ipu (742-1661) HOURS: Open 3 pm-1 am; grill 4-10 pm, late menu 10 pm. SAMPLING: Hot and cold appetizers (suitable for grazing!) include crusted seared ahi, cheese plate, prawns, and sashimi plus nachos, wons tons, chicken wings, burgers, fish or chicken sandwich, and tempura ($4,95-9.50) Their drink menu offers some creative choices in liqueur coffee drinks, alcoholic (and non-) tropical, and martinis plus beer & wine, ports, cognacs, and cigars. Try the Banana Paradise with macadamia nut liqueur, banana cream, vodka & Bailey's or the Menehune Magic with mango cream, cranberry juice & Stoli Razberi. COMMENTS: So what is The Point? It's an airy, poolside lounge that offers appetizers (enough for a light meal) and an extensive drinks menu in an upscale Hawaiian atmosphere with live music - jazz, Hawaiian - and other entertainment. A special cigar room with pool table is located next door. Tall, glass windows surround both The Point lounge and the adjacent Shells restaurant offering the dramatic ocean waves as a panoramic backdrop.

**PO'IPU BAY BAR & GRILL** *Breakfast & Lunch*
Just past the Hyatt on the golf course at Po'ipu Bay Resort (742-1515) HOURS: Breakfast 6:30-10:30 am, Lunch 10:30 am-3 pm. (Sandwiches & pupus Thurs-Fri 3-7 pm, till 11 on Sat.) SAMPLING: Variety of breakfast meats and egg dishes

plus loco moco, eggs Benedict, omelettes, corned beef or crab hash with poached eggs, Belgian waffle, cinnamon rolls, and great selection of tropical & fruit pancakes: banana, macadamia, mango, berry, and raisin! ($6.25-8.75). Japanese breakfasts ($12.95-13.95). Lunch options include salads (Caesar, grilled salmon or eggplant), sandwiches (grilled ahi, Korean BBQ steak, hot dog, club, crab melt), and burgers ($4.75-10). Korean and Hawaiian plate lunches ($9-9.50). Buffalo wings, chili, calamari, nachos (regular or criss-cut potato), ahi sashimi, and spicy onion rings are some of the pupus ($5-8.50). For dessert there's mud pie, apple pie, and ice cream. ($3.50-5) COMMENTS: Windows all around with views of the golf course. Looks like an old fashioned hotel dining room or dining room of a country club. Their breakfast menu seems like a natural for brunch so we're hoping they'll take the hint and serve some of these items later in the day. (Well, Dona does so she won't have to get up so early!) Good reviews on the breakfast for quality and price (especially the eggs Benedict and home fries) and we liked the Asian-style cole slaw and garlicky criss-cut french fries served with their sandwiches. Now part of the Hyatt Regency, they have added pool tables, a dart board, video games and plenty of sports-filled televisions as well as live entertainment from 8-11 pm on Saturdays.

**POMODORO ★** *Italian*
Rainbow Plaza in Kalaheo (332-5945) HOURS: 5:30-10 pm. SAMPLING: Antipasti of calamari fritti, mozzarella marinara, or prosciutto and melon ($6.50-9.50), a variety of pastas - spaghetti, ravioli, cannelloni, manicotti, baked penne, and lasagna, the house special ($10.50-16.95) and Pomodoro specialties like veal parmigiana, pizzaiola, piccata, or scallopini; eggplant or calamari parmigiana, scampi, chicken cacciatore, and chicken saltimbocca, an unusual change from veal ($15.95-19.95). Italian desserts like zabaliogne, tiramisu, and spumoni are featured. COMMENTS: Surprisingly attractive tables and settings for its nondescript shopping plaza location. Separate cocktail lounge. Their food is fresh and flavorful, everything is made to order. This is one of those "finds" we wish we had found sooner! The food was wonderful -- the lasagna deserved its designation as house special; it was made with both beef and sausage and just the right amount (lots!) of cheeses. The calamari was perfect in texture and preparation, and the spumoni ice cream cake easily became one of our Best Bets! The service was excellent (both personable and efficient) and we appreciated the attention to the "little" things -- like napkins under our water glasses! Entrees are served with pasta, vegetable and homemade garlic focaccia bread. Moderate prices (even the veal entrees are under $20) with plenty of items on the menu for the children to enjoy. Owned and operated by the Iaskolk family from Salerno, Italy; they still plan to reopen the old Seashell Restaurant (in Kapa'a) a soon as the Coco Palms settlements will allow. (And we'll be there when they do!)

**POOLSIDE GRILL & BAR** *Snacks/Light meals*
Located at the Embassy Vacation Resort--Po'ipu Point. (742-1888) HOURS: 10:30 am-8 pm SAMPLING: Home-style burgers (including ahi and chicken), sandwiches (turkey, tuna, PB&J), salads (turkey Caesar, penne pasta, fresh fruit), honey-dipped chicken, fish & chips, nachos, saimin ($3.95-8.95). Pizza ($8.95-12.95). Ice cream treats from sundaes to Melona melon bars: a creamy melon popsicle that's become a "serious" local addiction! ($2-5.85). COMMENTS: This is a new (summer '99) addition the Embassy's unique sand beach pool. Wally Wallace of Gaylords' restaurant oversees the daily functions and their Executive

Chef, Andy Althouse, sees that the menu is constantly evolving to appeal to all guests -- not only adults with kids, but kids with taste!

**ROY'S PO'IPU BAR & GRILL ★** *Euro-Asian*
Po'ipu Shopping Village (742-5000) HOURS: 5:30-9:30 pm. SAMPLING: Dim sum and appetizers include potstickers, crispy coconut shrimp sticks, escargot cassoulet, and spring rolls with curry mango sauce ($5.95-8.50). Lemongrass grilled chicken, green apple & bleu cheese,and grilled portabella mushroom & roasted eggplant are a few of the salads ($4.95-6.95). Kiawe wood oven baked pizzas (Mongolian short rib, Cajun shrimp, eggplant & tomato, pesto summer squash) are priced $5.95-7.25. Roy's entrees feature Chinese duck with lilikoi mango sauce, parmesan crusted lamb shank, imu roasted pork pot roast, garlic mustard grilled short ribs, and lemongrass crusted shrimp with Thai peanut curry sauce ($16.95-19.25). There are also nightly specials in every category: wine steamed clams, shrimp & fish cakes with spicy sesame chile butter sauce, or blackened tomato soup with avocado mousse ($4.50-8.95), wood roasted rack of lamb with five spice Kona coffee sauce, sesame crusted ono with wakame miso shrimp sauce & soba noodles, and kiawe-grilled filet mignon with black bean chile sauce ($19.95-24.95) are just a few examples. Their nightly "mixed plates" offer a chance to try two entrees as one ($25.95-29.95). Roy's signature dessert is the dark chocolate souffle, literally swimming in rich chocolate plus there's apple and macadamia nut strudel, blueberry cheesecake, lilikoi custard tart, key lime brulee, or chocolate mousse toffee bars ($5.75-6.25). COMMENTS: Once the newest, this Po'ipu location is now just one of over a dozen restaurants owned by trendsetter and chef Roy Yamaguchi who first gained accolades and the attention of food critics and celebrities at his Hawai'i Kai location. He opened a successful second location in Kahana, Maui, along with a sister restaurant, Nicolina, that he named after his daughter. Apparently they learned something from Kahana and have enclosed the kitchen behind huge glass windows: you can still enjoy watching the chefs as they prepare your meal, without having to be overwhelmed by the noise. (If you are a lip reader, you might enjoy figuring out what those chefs are really saying!) The executive Chef John P. Sikhattana holds the culinary reins here offering one set menu with a second menu of nightly specials. A rust and green theme is carried throughout and when the weather allows, the side panels are opened up to make it a bit more open air. They have also added courtyard seating across the way with seating around the bar that alleviates some of the overcrowding and offers a small bistro feel in an engaging social atmosphere. No view in either section, the food is the main attraction: the "wild mushroom spinach cream cheese raviolis" ($5.95) sound like a mouthful, but they are fresh and light -- satisfying without being too filling. By the time we ordered the lemongrass crusted hamachi with roasted banana curry & mango chutney ($23.95), they had to substitute opah for the hamachi, but we were impressed that they were able to replace one of the more unusual Hawaiian fish with yet another. With the lemongrass and curry to cut the banana and mango, the taste was subtle -- balanced and not too sweet. This was one of the daily specials which are all designed around the best and freshest ingredients each day. The lilikoi tart was tangy and fresh and the toffee bars (with chocolate mousse &, peanut butter toffee layered between a chocolate torte and glazed with ganache) were a delicious mix of flavors and textures While the primary service at Roy's was appropriately friendly and efficient, the support team was not only

too numerous, but just a bit too attentive. It seemed that after each bite there was someone on the wait staff checking in to make sure everything was okay -- and it was a new person each time! We approached the previous management on this one complaint (that we had also gotten from several readers), and although it has been toned down, a further relaxing of the apparent "rules" of hyper-efficiency and obligatory enthusiasm would make for a much more comfortable and enjoyable experience -- for both the diner and the wait staff!

**SHELLS** *International*
Sheraton Kaua'i Resort, 2440 Ho'onani Road, Po'ipu (742-1661) HOURS: Breakfast 6:30-11 am; Sunday Brunch 10 am-2 pm; Dinner 5:30-9:30 pm. SAMPLING: Ala carte breakfast omelettes, egg dishes, corned beef hash, French toast, pancakes, Belgian waffles, fresh fruit, cereals, and "heart healthy" selections ($3.95-13.95); continental breakfast ($10.95); buffet $15.95. Dinners begin with appetizers like crab & prawn cake, ahi carpaccio, oysters Rockefeller, tropical fruit cocktail, shrimp with poha sauce, and gazpacho or Maui onion soup ($3.50-7.50). Salad bar $9.95; $4.95 with ala carte entree. Choice of complete dinners (with salad, dessert, and beverage) or a la carte: prime rib, grilled lamb chops, roasted pork loin (with hoison citrus sauce), filet mignon, macadamia-crusted chicken breast, or fresh fish plus pasta primavera, cannelloni, seafood fettucine, prawn scampi, Oriental pasta with tofu ($14.95-27.95 ala carte/$23.95-32.95 dinners). They also offer a Friday Night Seafood Buffet (5:30-9:30) with sushi, salads, and cold seafood plus hot fish and seafood entrees, a shrimp tempura station, beverages, and desserts including hot chocolate souffle with a variety of sauces and toppings ($34.95). Keiki menu $2.50-7.95. COMMENTS: This is a luxury resort that really is suited for families: the restaurants are attractive, but not upscale and intimidating. The focal point of both Shells and The Point lounge is not the interior decoration, but the tall, glass windows that offer the ocean as a full-wall natural mural. You can dress up, but you can also bring the family!

**SHIPWRECK SUBS & ICE CREAM** *Sandwiches & Ice Cream*
Po'ipu Shopping Village (742-7467) HOURS: 11 am-6 pm. SAMPLING: Create your own 6" or 13" subs on fresh white or wheat bread with turkey, roast beef, ham, pastrami, salami, tuna, or egg plus choice of Swiss, provolone, cheddar, jack or pepper jack cheese and condiments. With 1 meat ($4.75-6.50), 2 meats ($5-6.75), or 3 meats ($5.25-7). Potato and pasta salad $1.30. Ice cream $2.40-3.85. COMMENTS: They have a kid's special for ages 12 and under: $3.25 for peanut butter and jelly with chips and a small soda. We have had good reports from readers who have been particularly pleased with their fresh breads, meats sliced to order, friendly service, and reasonable prices.

**SUEOKA'S** ★ *Local*
Located in Koloa next to Sueoka's Grocery Store (742-1112) HOURS: Monday-Friday 9:30 am-3 pm, Saturday 9:30 am-4 pm, Sunday 10 am-3 pm. SAMPLING: Plate lunches, sandwiches and burgers, local foods. COMMENTS: What a delight to still find a local walk-up restaurant. Much like the old Azeka's Market on Maui, this small, unobtrusive structure on the side of the grocery store not only has REALLY cheap food (prices haven't changed since our last edition and it was cheap then!), but it is REALLY good too. A chance to sample some local dishes, they serve a variety of plate lunches with specials that change daily.

The specials are listed on papers stuck on the window and as they sell out of that item, they pull the paper off. You'll see plenty of local folks picking up their lunch during their break. Hamburgers begin at $1.05 (up just 10¢ and the only price change in four years!), grilled cheese $1.50, fishburger $1.60, or saimin at $1.40. The teriyaki sandwich seemed like a splurge costing a whopping $2.50. It was not a huge sandwich, but very tender and flavorful, and at this price you could order two! Plate lunches like fried chicken, tripe stew, and teriyaki still run $3.25-4.15. No place to sit and eat, so we recommend you take your order over to the beach and enjoy a bargain meal with oceanfront dining.

**TAQUERIA NORTENOS** ★ *Mexican*
Located in Po'ipu Plaza (742-7222) HOURS: 11 am-10 pm Monday- Sunday. Closed Wednesday. SAMPLING: Mexican fare, still nothing much over $6 (with add-ons); most items priced $2-4. COMMENTS: Burritos and the works. The usual enchiladas, tacos, tostadas, et al, plus chalupas (crispy corn cups filled with beans and cheese), and bunuelos - dessert chips sprinkled with cinnamon sugar. This is the epitome of a hole-in-the-wall restaurant. The few tables in a small room behind the walk-up counter are a joke, resembling a large closet that they converted. But don't be misled. This place has really great food! The prices appear average, but wait until you see the portions!! You can fill up and then some for $6 or less. Since the ambiance isn't much, grab some food to go and head to one of Kaua'i's beautiful parks or beaches.

**TIDEPOOLS** ★ *Seafood & Steak*
Hyatt Regency Kaua'i, Po'ipu (742-1234) HOURS: 6-10 pm. SAMPLING: The menu changes frequently, but you might start with almond shrimp cakes, fried oysters, ahi sashimi, grilled sweet chile shrimp & ahi, "Kauaian" ribs, or mussels & clams ($7.50-9.50). Follow up with Kaua'i onion soup or clam chowder and Caesar (with crisp onions and Puna goat cheese); Kaua'i onion and tomato, fresh fruit, or green salad ($5-7.50). Then enjoy a wide selection of entrees: there's pan-fried somen noodles with grilled tofu & vegetables or a "cupboard" of potato, vegetable, and noodle dishes for the vegetarian ($17.50-18.50) and filet mignon, prime rib, pork chops, or roast chicken from the grill ($22-27.50). Specialties of the house include charred ahi sashimi, shrimp & crab strudel, skewered shrimp scampi, seafood mixed grill, Tidepools' signature macadamia nut crusted fish, ($24.50-29), and live Maine lobster ($34). Fresh Hawaiian fish is prepared several ways and a variety of meat & seafood combination plates are offered for $34. Desserts range from warm apple tart to mud pie; ginger creme brulee to white chocolate cheesecake ($5-5.50). COMMENTS: They offer contemporary Hawaiian cuisine featuring Kaua'i grown products like onions and sweet corn plus vegetables and herbs from an Omao farm, Chinese noodles from Kaua'i Noodle Factory, island-grown fruit, and Hawaiian fish. The choice of entree combinations is a great way to taste and sample - a diverse selection of menu items can really make dining an experience! (If they're available, try some of the more unusual fish offerings like hebi, ehu, or monchong.) Selected entrees are available for the kids in your family at half price, making this rather expensive dining choice a more affordable one. While the children in your traveling party will enjoy the Robinson Crusoe atmosphere, the adults will enjoy fine dining in a romantic setting. The restaurant is built like a series of grass-thatched Polynesian huts over a tranquil lagoon - it definitely puts you in the mood for fish! It kind

of looks like Humuhumunukunukua'pua'a Restaurant at the Grand Wailea on Maui, but thank goodness this one is easier to pronounce! Call ahead for reservations.

**TOI'S THAI KITCHEN** *Thai*
Ele'ele Shopping Center, near Hanapepe (335-3111) Hours: Lunch 10:30 am-2:30 pm, Dinner 5:30-9 pm. Closed for lunch on Sunday. SAMPLING: Soups (such as tom yum, long rice, tofu, and saimin) are served with rice, papaya salad, and dessert ($5.95-14.95). Appetizers include spring rolls, mee krob, and deep fried tofu plus salads with beef, pork or chicken; shrimp, mahi mahi or calamari, and beef, chicken or pork laab ($7.95-9.95). Pad Thai, Thai fried rice, lad na, and fried noodle with broccoli are offered with pork, beef, chicken, shrimp, mahi, calamari, tofu, or vegetables ($8.95-11.95). Dinner entrees include green papaya salad and choice of jasmine, brown, or sticky rice: jub chai, buttered garlic nua, satay, ginger sauce nua, nua krob, cashew chicken, or shrimp, panang chicken and red, green, yellow, or Matsaman curry ($10.95-15.95). (These types of dishes simply drive the computer spell checker nuts!) Toi's Temptation (choice of meat simmered in coconut milk and chile paste with lots of lemon grass) is a specialty as is Pinky in the Blanket: deep fried shrimp marinated in white wine and wrapped in rice paper with satay peanut sauce ($10.95-15.95). American plates (chicken, pork, mahi, or shrimp with fries, salad, and dessert) available for the gringo ($8.95-10.95). Lunch menu features the same items as dinner, most at $1-3 less. COMMENTS: Attractive decor. Cute chairs with dark green pillows; bright flower pots on each table and individual lace curtains on the windows. Karaoke at 9:30 with late night pupus till 1 am: $5 for saimin, pork won ton, calamari, or onion rings, wing dings, poppers, fried mushrooms; $8 sashimi Friday & Saturday.

**TOMKATS GRILLE AND BAR** *American*
Old Koloa Town Center (752-8887) HOURS: 11 am-10 pm, Happy Hour 4-6 pm. SAMPLING: Nibblers like fried onion rings, mushrooms, mozzarella sticks, or zucchini plus chicken fingers, calamari rings, jalapeno poppers, and buffalo wings ($4.95-7.50). Caesar, seafood, and "Kobb" salads; good choice of burgers and sandwich traditions like a patty melt, Reuben, French dip, BLT, turkey "Klub" or ham & cheese ($5.50-8.50). Hawaiian, Italian, paniolo, or teri chicken sandwiches ($6.25-6.95). Homemade chili ($2.50-4). Also seafood or steak kabobs and rotisserie chicken plus nightly dinner specials (from 5 pm) like barbecue pork ribs, steak, chicken marinara or seafood linguine, fresh "Katch" or prime rib ($8.50-16.95). Wash it all down with a White Tiger, Banana Cow, or a Mai Tai made with passion fruit and guava juice. COMMENTS: The name of the restaurant was derived from the first names of owners, Tom and Kathy Podlashes, and Katnip is behind the bar. Casual outdoor seating on wood decks in a rustic garden setting. Very good desserts and Tom makes the carrot cake himself! Menu for Kittens 12 and under.

**WAIMEA BREWING CO.** ★ *Cross-cultural Brew Pub*
9400 Kaumalii Hwy. at Waimea Plantation Cottages (338-9733) HOURS: 11 am-9 pm, bar & brewery till 11. SAMPLING: Start with such innovative appetizers as Caribbean jerk seared ahi "sashimi" with fire roasted corn salsa, Kalua duck

lumpia with black bean hoison sauce, taro leaf goat cheese dip, fiery chicken wings with blue cheese papaya dipping sauce, Gado Gado chicken skewers with peanut sauce, or the "twisted" Caesar salad with grilled lettuce (!) and their own non-traditional dressing ($4.75-6.75). Burgers topped with everything from bleu cheese to fried egg plus grilled fish, chicken or portobello mushroom sandwiches ($6.75-8.95). "Big Plates" of mango-stout baby back ribs, fresh catch, kalua pork, or Mediterranean roasted chicken ($12.95-15.95), and keikis can order a PB&J, grilled cheese, hot dog, or popcorn chicken off the Short Pants Club menu ($3.50). Nightly dinner specials might offer appetizers of lemongrass crusted ahi satay or smoked marlin lasagna ($8.95-10.95) with entrees like "quill" pasta with Kekaha shrimp (served with tomato, lime & Hawaiian chile pepper sauce and cilantro mac nut pesto), herbed mahi with spicy passion fruit sauce, or grilled ono with green curry-lime leaf beurre blanc ($15.95-19.95). Roasted banana cheese-cake, lilikoi poundcake, and "Chocolate is my Master" are the desserts ($3.50-4.75). COMMENTS: This restaurant location has finally found its niche with a plantation-style ambiance that is attractive, but not too upscale and food that has just the right balance of familiarity and creative innovation. There are petroglyph designs throughout and the bar is made from red dirt (cemented and polished) with a view of the gleaming brew tanks. The patio deck has old-fashioned "park bench" chairs. The hardwood floors are smooth and polished and so are the gold faucets and fixtures in the bathrooms! Chef Todd Oldham makes his own condiments and spices so you'll find your burger served with guava chile or roasted pepper ketchup, your fresh fish with wasabi aioli sauce or your sandwich with jalapeno & beer mustard or wasabi pickled ginger mayo. And there's also their "Damn Good Fries" with hand-harvested Hawaiian salt, bok choy cabbage or Java slaw, and "beginners" kim chee! You can wash it down with a tart, fresh lilikoi margarita, but you'll probably opt for one of the handcrafted brews like the Pakala Porter, Alalakai Stout, West Side Wheat or Napali Pale Ale ($2.75-3.25 or $5 for a sampler of 4). They and also have brew label t-shirts and some really cool mugs with their petroglyph logo designs.

**WONG'S RESTAURANT OMOIDE DELI & BAKERY** *Chinese*
Hanapepe (335-5066) HOURS: Deli open 8 am-9 pm; Wong's dinner service 5-9 pm. Closed Monday. SAMPLING: In the deli: breakfasts of eggs, pancakes, and omelettes ($3.50-6.75), appetizers of spring roll, won ton, gau chee, loco moco, fried shrimp ($4.50-7.50), sandwiches, burgers, spam ($2.85-3.50), saimin ($6.50), lunch & dinner plates like spare ribs, oyster chicken, or beef broccoli ($5-6.50) and dinner specials like roast pork and NY, chop, or pepper steak ($8-12.85). Char siu pork or roast duck from $7.25 lb. The bakery has pies (lilikoi or chocolate chiffon, mac nut cream custard, pumpkin) cakes (haupia, guava, chantilly, "chocolate dream"), plus cheesecake (raspberry, fudge, "turtle pecan"), and almond float from $1.40 to $8 for whole pies, $10.50-12 for cream cakes. Wong's has an extensive Chinese dinner menu with chicken, duck, beef, pork, egg, seafood, vegetarian, and noodle dishes. Crispy skin chicken, "duck-in-the-nest," Mongolian beef, pork with eggplant, shrimp fu young, steamed sea bass with ginger & onions, Szechwan tofu, and roast pork saimin are just a few examples ($6-9). "Gringo" steak and shrimp entrees ($10-24). COMMENTS: The restaurant is a banquet room that also does a lot of parties and catering. They're famous for their lilikoi chiffon pie and we've heard good things about the sea bass entrees.

**WRANGLER'S STEAKHOUSE** *Steak and seafood*
9652 Kaumualii Hwy. (across from Big Save), Waimea (338-1218) HOURS: Mon-Fri Lunch 11 am-5 pm; Dinner Mon-Sat 5-8:30 pm. Closed Sunday. SAMPLING: Burgers, sandwiches, fresh fish ($6.75-11.25) or the "Kau Kau Tin" lunch: Oriental shrimp tempura, teriyaki chicken and Japanese pickled vegetables served in a plantation workers tin ($8.25). Dinners offer scampi, crab legs, chicken cordon bleu, pork chops, BBQ ribs, and seafood platter ($14.95-19.95). Mexican entrees include enchiladas and burritos ($10.25-11.75) and a variety of steaks are served broiled, pan-fried, sizzling (their house specialty), or in seafood combinations ($16.25-19.95). Keiki menu ($6.5). COMMENTS: This really is a steak "house" serving meals in several distinctive rooms with a gift shop in the den. Their Pacific Pizza & Deli is also in the same building.

## *NORTH SHORE*

**AMELIA'S** *Sandwiches/Snacks*
At Princeville Airport, 3541 Kuhio Hwy. (826-9561) HOURS: 12 noon-8 pm; Music and dancing till 2 am Fri-Sun. SAMPLING: Turkey, ham, tuna, BBQ beef, roast beef, or French dip sandwich $6, hot dogs, chili, nachos ($4.50-5). COMMENTS: Like a neighborhood roadhouse with more character than most bars enhanced by interesting Amelia Earhart decor and great view. TV with satellite sports.

**BALI HAI RESTAURANT** ★ *Traditional with Pacific Rim touches*
Located at the Hanalei Bay Resort, 5380 Honoiki Road (826-6522) HOURS: Breakfast 7-11 am, Lunch 11:30 am-2 pm, Dinner 5:30-10 pm. SAMPLING: Unusual island-style items for breakfast like sliced bananas with coconut cream, macadamia nut waffles, or the Taro Patch Breakfast with two eggs, Portuguese sausage, poi pancakes, and taro hash browns ($3.75-12.50). Lunch offers Kaua'i

onion soup, smoked tofu salad, quiche, island papillotte (fresh fish steamed in a banana leaf), chicken Hanalei (breaded with peanuts and panko), and a good selection of sandwiches: Reuben, seafood salad, turkey club, and burgers ($4-12.75). Save your decision-making energy for later and start your dinner with a pupu platter of pork ribs, chicken skewers & prawns katsu or sashimi, shrimp cocktail & diced ahi "fiesta" ($14.75). Follow with a Caesar or vegetable salad with chicken or shrimp ($6.50-10.95) or go straight to one of the special fresh fish preparations - pan seared over a crispy crab cake with sweet potatoes, sauteed with papaya & pineapple salsa, or broiled with coconut milk, sweet chile & peanut sauce ($25). Steaks, lamb chops, chicken linguini, or shrimp & scallops are some of the other dinner options ($15.95-32). Children-sized portions on selected items. If you want to end with a dessert, banana lumpia, passion fruit mousse cake, coconut macadamia tartlett, fresh berries & Grand Marnier cheesecake, tropical fruits in a pastry shell, or creme brulee are the choices ($6-10). COMMENTS: Whatever you order, it comes with a stunning, panoramic view of the Bay and Hamolokama (Bali Hai) Mountain and Waterfall They now bake all their own breads and in addition to the above, the pastry chef offers a different dessert each night. Their special flambe desserts are still available on special occasions.

**(THE) BEACH** *Sandwiches/Salads*
Princeville Resort (826-2763) HOURS: 11 am-5:30 pm. SAMPLING: Turkey club, NY steak, fresh fish, tuna in pita, wrapped Caesar chicken sandwich, or Black Angus burger ($12.95-14.95). Cobb, Caesar, grilled chicken (with avocado, papaya & fresh berries), or taco salad ($11.95-16.95). Spring rolls, buffalo wings, nachos, crabmeat quesadilla, or ahi trio plate ($9.95-16.95) COMMENTS: Wine & beer and a good selection of tropical drinks. Keiki menu ($3.95-7.95) and desserts ($3.50-5.95).

**BUBBA'S** *Burgers*
Hanalei Center on Kuhio Hwy. (826-7839) HOURS: 10:30 am-6 pm, till 8 pm in the summer. SAMPLING: Bubbas, double bubbas, hubba bubbas plus hot dogs, corn dogs and Budweiser beer chili. "Alternative" burgers include fish, chicken, tempeh, and Italian sausage ($1.50-5.75) or fresh fish sandwich with pineapple lemongrass salsa ($1.50-5.75). Side orders of Caesar salad, french fries, onion rings, frings (fries and rings), or chili fries ($1.75-3.75). COMMENTS: With a name like Bubba's, you were expecting maybe escargot? They're fun and funny and serve good, old-fashioned burgers to anyone named Bubba. (That means you!) They used to "cheat tourists and drunks", but had to "cease and desist" after receiving a letter from a San Francisco attorney. So now they also cheat attorneys! Smaller than their Kapa'a location which expanded and relocated across the street. (It's not as funky, but still fun at twice the size with an old-fashioned counter and stools, murals, and memorabilia on the walls and ocean-view seating on the veranda.) Both locations have take-out and T-Shirts. Buy a hat or shirt and if you wear it when you order your burger, you'll get a free drink! Dona had a good cheeseburger at Kapa'a, but Christie thinks they cheat travel writers! (She checked out the food here at Hanalei and thought her teriyaki burger was pitiful. It was difficult to even find the burger patty in the sauce!) Some really rave about Bubba's, but we think the drive back to Anahola is worth a bettah burger at Duane's. <www.bubbaburger.com> Email: obubba@aloha.net>

**CAFE HANALEI** ★ *Pacific Rim with Japanese specialties*
Princeville Resort (826-2760) HOURS: Breakfast 6:30-11 am, Lunch 11 am-2:30 pm, Dinner 5:30-9:30 pm; Breakfast Buffet to 10:30 am (9:30 Sundays), Sunday Brunch 10 am-2 pm. (Sushi bar menu: Tues-Wed & Sat-Sun, 5-9:30 pm) SAMPLING: Order an a la carte breakfast ($4.50-13) or sample their buffet featuring crepes, pastries, fruits, omelettes, pancakes, and breakfast meats ($20-.95). For lunch there are salads (stir fry chicken, cobb, soba & somen noodle, fresh fruit), burgers and sandwiches (club with avocado, grilled chicken on focaccia, fresh albacore, vegetarian wrap) for $11.50-16.95 and Japanese entrees ($14.95-18.95). Dinner appetizers include Thai curry & coconut soup, crab cakes, spinach salad wrap, salmon tartar, ahi trio plate, coconut prawns, and California rolls ($6-16). Entrees feature seafood curry, steak & prawns, hoison barbecue lamb chops, Hawaiian bouillabaisse, grilled chicken breast, fresh fish or Japanese unaiu: fresh water eel with miso soup, pickled vegetable, and green salad. ($20-34). They also offer a set three-course dinner with your choice of appetizer, entree, dessert, and beverage for $43.95. For dessert try a duo of Kona coffee & ginger creme brulees, chocolate torte, Thai tapioca with jellied berries, or lilikoi cheesecake ($5.50-7.50). Sunday Brunch offers an elegant buffet for $31.95; $38.50 with champagne. There are salads, fresh seafood, sushi, pastas, hot entrees, carved roast beef, an omelette bar, fruit crepe bar, waffle bar, and plenty of desserts. Keiki menu $2.50-6. COMMENTS: Nestled deep down below the opulent lobby at the foot of two elegant staircases, this restaurant has the perfect view of Hanalei Bay with the perfect full-length picture windows to gaze and glory in it unencumbered. The Friday night Seafood Buffet (5:30-9:30 pm) is a pricey $43.95, but worth the splurge. An entire buffet of hot seafood dishes range from shrimp lasagna to crab & lobster sausage, seafood paella to bouillabaisse, salmon en croute to escargot with curry butter. There are at least a dozen choices before moving to the cold seafood display filled with sushi, sashimi, fresh Dungeness crab, shrimp, and mussels and seafood salad selections from spicy calamari to bay shrimp with cilantro and avocado. Save room for the barbecue, where a chef will cook your fresh fish to order. We had a selection of fresh ono or salmon or a skewer of scallops and prawns. Oh, did we mention dessert?

**CAFE LUNA** *Northern Italian*
Hanalei Center (826-1177) HOURS: Lunch 11:30 am-5 pm, Dinner 5-9:30 pm. SAMPLING/COMMENTS: We've always enjoyed the ambiance here: the wood tables and stucco walls give the indoor restaurant an Italian bistro feel, but you can also choose to eat in the courtyard nestled in a "sunken" wood patio. We also enjoyed the Northern Italian cuisine . . . unfortunately, Cafe Luna was recently sold and in speaking to the new owner, it is evident that he knows as little about operating a restaurant as he does about holding a polite conversation. We were hoping to find out the basic menu concept as well as any new ideas or changes that might be forthcoming to help get the information out to our readers. We were rudely informed that they didn't need our "help" which we have to assume means that they don't need or want our recommendation (or your business either) and we are happy to oblige. You're on your own on this one! (Let us know if you receive better treatment.)

**CHUCK'S STEAK HOUSE** *Steak and Seafood*
Princeville Shopping Center (826-6211) HOURS: Lunch 11:30 am-2:30 pm Monday-Friday, Dinner nightly 6-10 pm. SAMPLING: Lunch offers a good selection of burgers and salads (including shrimp and/or crab Louie) plus several hot and cold sandwiches (turkey Swiss, teri beef or chicken, BBQ prime rib, tuna melt, or shrimp, crab & bacon;) plus fries, skins, or rings. ($3.75-12.50). Start your dinner with mushrooms saute, steamed artichoke, or shrimp cocktail ($4.95-8.95). Entrees include salad bar, bread, and rice: fish, shrimp, crab, and Hawaiian spiney lobster plus prime rib, top sirloin, barbequed pork ribs, and several steak and seafood combinations ($16.95-26.95); crab or lobster at market price. There's always mud pie for dessert ($3.95) or a choice of daily specials. COMMENTS: It's called Chuck's Steak House and they have that and seafood, too. They also have a children's & senior menu with slightly smaller portions of teri chicken, BBQ ribs, hamburger, or shrimp Hanalei for $8.95-13.95 including salad bar. A senior couple we spoke to gave it a (clean) "thumbs up" even after their ribs, thanks to the finger bowl that they thought was a nice touch. (And we all agreed that you can't trust anyone who doesn't eat ribs with their fingers!) Casual, rustic look with a lot of wood. Live Hawaiian music on the weekends (Thursday-Saturday). The same owner also operates Amelia's.

**DUANE'S ONO BURGERS** ★ *Burgers*
On the highway in Anahola (822-9181) HOURS: Monday-Saturday 10 am-6 pm, from 11 am on Sunday. SAMPLING: The teriyaki burger is the biggest seller here, but there are lots to choose from: BBQ, blue cheese, avocado, mushroom, and combos like "Duane's Special" (1,000 island, grilled onions, pickles, sprouts, cheddar & Swiss) or the "Local Girl" (teriyaki, Swiss cheese, pineapple). Burgers are priced from $3.90-6.20 and there are sandwiches, too. Fish, chicken, patty melt, tuna, grilled cheese, and a new veggie burger ($2.75-6.75) and side orders of fries, onion rings, or salad are $1.80-3.10. They have keiki burgers and sandwiches as well as some great shakes including marionberry - not the former mayor of DC, but a yummy combination of boysenberry and blackberry ($2.95). COMMENTS: The prices haven't changed since 1993 and the burgers are still piled high with lots of "stuff," like a Dagwood burger. Try the fries with the special seasoning they have on the counter - ono! The outdoor tables also have a great mountain view. These burgers are worth the drive, from whatever side of the island you visit. The teriyaki isn't strong and salty, but...just right! You'll know you are in Anahola when you see the line outside the little red building. (By the way, don't go looking for Duane; the Cords and the Jacobsens own it now and you'll probably see one of them working behind the counter.)

**HALE O'JAVA** *Sandwiches/Salads*
Princeville Center (826-7255) HOURS: Breakfast 6:30-10:30 am, Lunch 10:30 am-2:30 pm. (Pizza 11 am-9 pm.) SAMPLING: Breakfast options include Belgian waffles, French Toast (made from their homemade egg bread), cereals, and omelettes ($3.75-6.95); pastries and muffins from $1.65. Sandwiches (panini) on focaccia bread in combinations of roast beef, turkey, Black Forest ham, meatballs, artichoke hearts, tomatoes, roasted peppers and provolone, fontina or fresh mozzarella cheese ($5.50-6.95); salmon, capers, red onion, and cream cheese on light rye ($7.95). Also enjoy soup and/or salad bar from $3.50; pizzas

($13.50-19.50). Gelato, cakes, pastries, and homemade fruit pies ($2.75-4.50). Smoothies and gelato milk shakes ($3.50-4.95) The usual hot coffee drinks (as well as Italian coffee) plus wine and beer. COMMENTS: Generally good food, but a bit expensive for what you get. Table service or you can order at the counter and serve yourself. The espresso is served in huge Italian style cups and it is perfectly wonderful sitting in the courtyard with a steaming mug and one of their tasty paninis. (Panini is simply the Italian word for sandwich which explains why you'll see so many varieties: regular, fried, on focaccia bread. . . all called "panini" - like in France, croissant just means "toast"!) The menu has been pared down quite a bit and doesn't seem as varied or as interesting as before. Live jazz every Wednesday (6:30-9 pm); flamenco guitar Tues. & Thurs. from 4-6. Owner Dave Davies also operates Paradise Bar & Grill in the same complex.

**HANALEI DOLPHIN** ★ *Steak and Seafood*
Hanalei (826-6113) HOURS: Lunch 11 am-3:30 pm, Dinner 5:30-10 pm. Pupus served all day: 11 am-10 pm. SAMPLING: Lunch sandwiches (teri chicken, chilled fish salad, fresh fish, calamari, or tempeh veggie burger) on Kaiser roll or Dolphin squaw bread ($6-7). Dolphin salads (with lettuce, cabbage, and bean sprouts) are topped with calamari, chicken, fish, or fish salad ($8-9). Appetizers include ceviche, seafood chowder, artichoke, and stuffed mushrooms ($5-7). Seafood entrees of fresh fish, calamari, scallops, shrimp, and crab plus chicken, steak, and "surf and turf" combinations ($16-26). Homemade dessert selections change daily, but they always have Dolphin ice cream pie ($5) with banana, mac nut & coconut ice cream in an Oreo cookie crust. COMMENTS: Quite a few of the entrees are under $20 (fresh fish runs $22-24) and come with salad, fries or rice and bread. They also offer menehune (kid) portions ($11.50-16.50) or light dinners: broccoli casserole, seafood chowder or salad & bread ($9-14). Pretty reliable food, but nothing exotic or Pacific Rim! They don't take reservations and unless you arrive early, you will probably have a wait. Put in your name and spend your time browsing through the adjoining gift and clothing stores. The food is hearty, some of the sauces are a bit on the heavy side, but the salads are a very pleasant surprise. Served family style in a bowl, the mixed greens are accompanied by homemade garlic croutons and an assortment of dressings you can add yourself. They have a fish market, too, open from 11 am-8 pm.

**HANALEI GOURMET** ★ *Sandwiches/Salads*
5161 Kuhio Hwy. Old School Building at Hanalei Center (826-2524) HOURS: Breakfast 8-11 am; Lunch 10:30 am-4:30 pm, pupus & grilled sandwiches until 5:30, dinner 5:30-9:30. SAMPLING: Basic sandwiches like turkey, roast beef, corned beef, chicken salad, and tuna ($4.95-6.50) on fresh baked bread with "the works." More gourmet varieties ($6.95-7.95) include Oregon bay shrimp (open-faced with melted jack cheese and remoulade sauce), ahi with dill mayo, ginger chicken, and roasted eggplant & red pepper with provolone cheese, a sour cream-lime-cilantro sauce and sweet red onions. Gourmet burgers with gorgonzola or avocado with bacon ($5.95-7.95). Salads include chicken in papaya or avocado boat, Hanalei Waldorf with mango vinaigrette, and Oriental ahi pasta ($4.95-8.95). Pupus include Asian crab cakes, ahi nachos, crab-stuffed mushrooms, sauteed mussels, and artichoke toast -- broiled with their unusual and flavorful

artichoke dip and lots of gooey cheese ($3.50-8.95); boiled shrimp from $7.95 (to $18.95 for a full lb.) Pastas include eggplant or seafood marinara, Greek, or gorgonzola chicken. Breakfast offerings include Huevos Santa Cruz, muesli, bacon & egg sandwich ($4.50-7.50) or fruit, bagels, and pastries from $1.50. COMMENTS: The roasted eggplant sandwich was excellent - fresh, innovative, and full of flavor -- and the gorgonzola chicken had a tasty grilled flavor that went well with the cheesy Alfredo sauce. In fact, just about everything we tried was good! The place is generally busy, from first thing in the morning with people at the bar by 9 am with others enjoying piping hot coffee and pastries at the lana'i tables. Specials are written on the blackboard left over from when it was a schoolroom. We didn't sample any of the bakery selections (carrot cake, lilikoi mac nut bundt cake, hot brownie ala mode, toffee crunch ice cream pie) but the lunch fare and dinners were all very good and served in hearty portions. (Which is probably why we haven't been able to sample the desserts!) Thursday night is Fish Taco Night: tempura beer batter fish taco with lots of rice and black beans ($9.50). Early bird specials offer $2 off all major entree selections from 5:30-6:30 pm. "Big Tim" is still the personable and proud owner and they still have live entertainment nightly.

**HANALEI JUICE COMPANY** *Sandwiches & salads*
Next to Hanalei Town Farmers Market in front of Kayak Kaua'i in Hanalei. HOURS: Tues-Sun 7 am-7 pm (summer), from 9 am in the winter. SAMPLING: Fresh "squeezed" juices (carrot, apple, beet, celery, banana, guava, pineapple, lilikoi) and 100% fresh fruit smoothies and "frosties" ($3-3.75) Food offered summer only (June-Sept.). Salads with 7 different combinations of greens and all organic produce plus sandwiches of smoked turkey, provolone, or tuna made fresh to order on homemade bread ($3-5). Muffins, carrot cake, white chocolate macadamia cookies ($.75-1.25). COMMENTS: Owner Michael O'Reilly Rowan has expanded his farmers market to include light meals and juices -- a natural extension since he's got all the fresh ingredients right there! Enjoy the Juice Company *now*, or buy from the Farmers Market for *later* -- you'll find quality local produce with everything from jabong (Japanese grapefruit) to Kaua'i honey and their Kaua'i Natural salad dressings and meat marinades are wonderful.

**HANALEI MIXED PLATE** *Hawaiian/Chinese/Thai*
On Kuhio Hwy. at Ching Young Village, Hanalei (826-5531) HOURS: 10:30 am-8:30 pm. Closed Sunday. SAMPLING: Kalua pork & cabbage, shoyu ginger chicken, and vegetable stir fry or chow mein (all with white or brown rice) are just some of the mixed plates ranging from $4.95 for one choice; $5.95 for two, $7.95 for three. Vegetarian Thai coconut curry, creamy garlic basil mahi mahi, grilled Cajun ahi, or grilled sesame chicken are some of the specials from $6.95. Sauteed mahi mahi, Kalua pork, grilled ahi, and teri or shoyu chicken sandwiches ($6.95-10.95); Chicken or mahi mahi Caesar and garden salads ($6.95-9.95). Corn dog, chili dog, or hot dog; cheeseburger, tempeh, garden, or buffalo burger ($4.95-6.95). Baskets with fish, chicken, shrimp or spring rolls, $6.95-8.95 with chips. (Any two combo for $10.95.) COMMENTS: Mostly take-out with a small patio area for eating in (out?). This is one of a very few places left that has Bison-on-a-bun! (A little coarser and meatier, but not at all tough or chewy.)

Mixed plates are a good value; the vegetables are fresh and colorful - it's hard to decide when they all look so appetizing! Fresh ahi and mahi mahi dishes and sandwiches are served all summer Owners Rudy & Shanda Bosma also operate Two Frogs Hugging, an unusual import gift shop in Kapa'a which is where they got their new teak furniture when they remodeled this small, but pleasant outlet.

√ **HANALEI WAKE UP CAFE** ★ *Hawaiian/Mexican* ok

Aku Road (826-5551) HOURS: Breakfast daily 6-11:30 am, Lunch Mon-Sat 11:30 am-2:30 pm. SAMPLING: For breakfast, there's homemade granola, pancakes, French toast, veggie tofu, a scrambled egg quesadilla, and build-your-own omelettes ($4.25-6.85). Or try Christie's personal favorite: custard French toast made with Portuguese sweet bread and topped with pineapple, coconut, and whipped cream ($5). For lunch, there is veggie, tofu, chicken, or ahi stir fry ($6-7.95), plate lunches with chile pepper ahi or chicken, hamburger steak, teri chicken, chicken cutlets, or charbroiled ahi ($5.50-8). Chinese chicken, Caesar and garden salads, or sandwich choices of BLT, ham & cheese, tuna melt, beef or veggie burgers, and ahi ($5-6.95). Mexican entrees offer taco or enchilada plates with choice of chicken or ahi ($6.75-8.25). COMMENTS: Small coffee shop-type restaurant, family-owned and operated by Brando, Kaula, Keoki and their Mom, Lani. The custard French toast called "Over The Falls" is to die for, and while it appears to be a small portion, it is plenty filling, really more custard than toast. The breakfast quesadillas are good-sized portions that should appease those hearty morning appetites. The Mexican meals are flavorful, not too heavily spiced, and served in ample sized portions. The motif here is "surf" from he photos and trophies to the video playing on the television. The atmosphere is still VERY casual (though meals are no longer served on paper plates) -- most folks look like they just walked in from the beach and left their surfboards on the front stoop.

**KILAUEA BAKERY & PAU HANA PIZZA** ★ *Bakery/Pizzeria*

Kong Lung Center on the road to the Lighthouse (828-2020) HOURS: 6:30 am-9 pm, pizza from 11 am. Closed Sundays. SAMPLING: Croissants, cinnamon buns, scones, and other freshly-baked pastries plus unusual breads like limu sourdough with sea algae, sun-dried tomato and fresh basil, poi bread, feta cheese and sweet red bell pepper, Hawaiian sourdough (fermented from a guava starter), and Na Pali brown bread made with fennel, caraway, orange rind, and cocoa. Pizzas are just as innovative with a lot of unusual toppings and combinations: "Barbequed Chicken" (BBQ chicken, roasted onions and red peppers, mushroom, and mozzarella cheese), "Classic Scampi" (tiger prawns, tomato, roasted garlic, capers, asiago and mozzarella cheeses), and "Billie Holiday" (smoked ono, swiss chard, roasted onions, gorgonzola rosemary, sauce and mozzarella cheese) priced $10.95S/16.95M/23.75L. Regular pizzas are priced by size and toppings and run from $7.25 (small cheese) to $27.85 (large with six toppings) or try their Abrezone, an open-faced vegetable calzone baked in French bread dough! They have a tasty selection of cream cheese spreads with everything from mango-pineapple to red pepper & garlic to tapenade or hummus to put on your bagel. They also have coffee drinks and espressos ($1.50-3.50). Pizza/salad lunch specials run $5.95. COMMENTS: Pastries and breads baked daily. Pizza crust is extra crispy and the staff are extra nice. Owners Tom and Katie Pickett started the bakery in their home, expanded, then added pizza. If you don't have a big appetite or a family, you can order pizza by the slice. Or try their flavored breadsticks in chile pepper, garlic butter, or sesame & alae (red) salt: they make a great made-on Kaua'i gift to take home! Their signature bakery items include the afore-mentioned sourdough and Na Pali brown breads and tropical fruit layer cakes with whipped cream icing. Tom Pickett (formerly a pastry chef with the Sheraton Princeville) and his wife Katie, opened their business as a bakery only. Adding the pizza business was a natural progression as their popularity increased. They recently expanded to twice the size and now offer a full service espresso bar with cafe seating inside and a courtyard with a few tables outdoors.

**KILAUEA FARMERS MARKET** *Sandwiches & salads*
Next to Kong Lung Center in the Kilauea Theatre Building (828-1512) HOURS: Lunch counter 10 am-3 pm; Store & take-out deli hours 8:30 am-8:30 pm SAMPLING: Sandwiches served on freshly-baked Kilauea Bakery bread: turkey, roast beef, ham & cheese, fresh fish, pastrami, PB&J or PB&H (peanut butter, banana & honey), chicken salad, or subs. Hummus, tabouli, pasta, pesto, 3-bean, tofu, and garden salads. Homemade soups with garlic toast (fish, minestrone, chicken noodle, and chowder with corn fresh off the cob). Daily specials might feature quiche, stir fry, chicken fajita, stuffed baked potato, or curry made with authentic Indian spices. Desserts include tofu pie, banana delight, mousse, mango cheesecake, organic fruit crisps (apple, apricot, nectarine peach), and a variety of dessert breads like banana, pumpkin, ginger-carrot, poppyseed, and coffee cake. Prices from $2.75 to $6.50. COMMENTS: This small lunch counter and kitchen is located inside a gourmet grocery store which offers everything from organic coffees, Thai cooking ingredients, microbrew beers & organic wines, and local organic produce. Whatever's fresh, they'll make something out of it -- fresh to order or specials pre-packaged daily for take-out!

**LA CASCATA** *Italian*
Princeville Resort (826-2761) HOURS: 6-10 pm. SAMPLING: Antipasto beginnings include kobocha squash soup with pistachios, beef carpaccio, crispy calamari, seared ahi Nicoise salad, potato-crusted crab cakes, arugula salad with pear, gorgonzola cheese & walnut vinaigrette, espresso-lacquered lamb chop, or tomato & eggplant Napoleon ($6.95-13.50). Seafood linguini, smoked chicken ravioli, rack of lamb, stuffed chicken breast, veal picatta, grilled ahi with mushroom risotto, swordfish with cous cous, and snapper with spinach gnocchi are the entrees prepared with an Italian accent ($22.95-32.50). The desserts are varied: mango cheesecake, cappuccino creme brulee, Tia Maria parfait, tiramisu, chocolate cake with lilikoi puree, or macadamia nut pie ($5.95). COMMENTS: Dinners begin with focaccia bread squares and olive oil or tomato and garlic tochu sauce to dip them in. A complete three course dinner is available with your choice of appetizer, main entree, dessert, and coffee beverage for $43.95 per person. They have an extensive selection of wines, by the glass and by the bottle. Keiki menu $2.50-6. The food is good, but you'll pay the price -- slightly more forgivable with its extraordinary panoramic view of Hanalei Bay.

**LIGHTHOUSE BISTRO** *Pacific Rim with an Italian flair*
Kong Lung Center, Kilauea (828-0480) HOURS: Lunch 11 am-2 pm; Dinner 5:30-9 pm. SAMPLING: Soups, salads, hamburgers, chicken sandwiches, or fish tacos range from $6-10 for lunch. For dinner, start with tossed antipasto (served on wild greens), Jawaiian seared scallops, artichoke picatta, or chicken sateh with peanut sauce ($9.95-11.95). Caesar (with fish or chicken), mescalun, or garden

salad; seafood bisque ($4.95-13.95). Fettucini Alfredo, tri-colored tortellini (with sun-dried tomato pesto), or pasta marinara ($10.95-12.95) Entrees (served with soup or salad) include stuffed shrimp in phyllo, filet au poivre (in peppercorn brandy sauce), mango cherry chicken breast, seafood linguini, rib eye steak, chicken pesto, or Cajun BBQ shrimp ($16.95-24.95). Fresh fish ($22.95) is offered broiled (and served with tropical salsa), blackened, sauteed, or pan-seared with mango sesame sauce. COMMENTS: New owners have added a more plantation-style look and feel to the former Casa de Amici. (Matt Ernsdorf worked at the old Casa for 13 years and Michael Moore was a cook at Zelo's.) They feature premium well drinks and personally choose all their wines, offering a different selection each night. Live entertainment Thursday-Saturday. Opened at the end of 1999. NOT OPEN AS WE GO TO PRESS.

**(THE) LIVING ROOM ★** *Afternoon Tea/Hors d'oeuvres/Desserts*
Princeville Resort (826-2760) HOURS: Afternoon Tea 3-5 pm, Hors d'oeuvres 5-9:30 pm (Sushi bar Tues-Wed & Sat-Sun) Desserts 5-10:30 pm). SAMPLING: An exquisite Afternoon Tea offers tea sandwiches, scones with Devonshire cream and strawberry preserves, English tea bread, miniature pastries, fresh fruit tarts and, of course, a lovely, hot "cuppa" for $18. Prawn cocktail, California rolls, crab cakes, vegetable crudite, ahi trio plate, spring rolls, Caesar salad, cheese plate, or even a cheeseburger or grilled sirloin are offered as hors d'oeuvres or a light supper ($8.95-19.95). Maki and nigiri sushi ($4-9.95), sashimi ($8.50-12.50). Desserts are from the hotel's Hanalei Cafe: a duo of Kona coffee & ginger creme brulees, chocolate torte, Thai tapioca with jellied berries, lilikoi cheesecake ($5.50-7.50). COMMENTS: Wine & beer, tropical cocktails, brandies & cognacs, and a selection of cigars are also available to enjoy with nightly entertainment from 7-11 pm. This is such a charming and elegant room that you really don't have to do anything but delight in the view from the comfortable, intimate groupings of couches and chairs. It does look and feel like a living room, but one belonging to someone a whole lot richer than anyone we know!

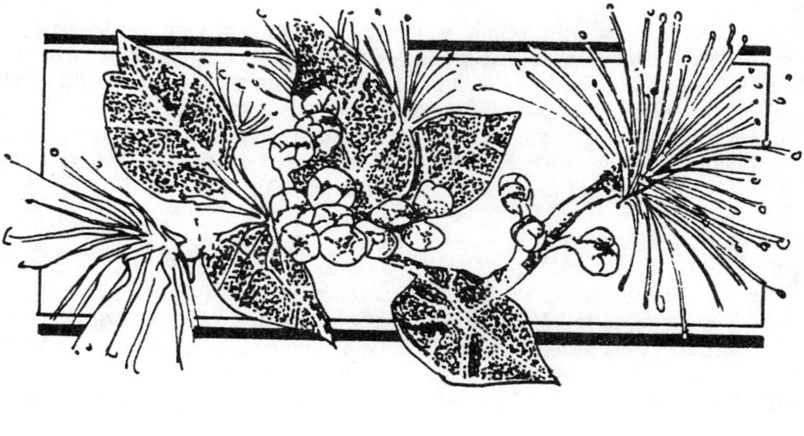

**MANGO MAMAS CAFE** *American*
Kilauea roadside: Kuhio Hwy & Ho'okui Road (828-1020) HOURS: 7:30 am-6 pm. SAMPLING: Fresh fruit and vegetable juices & smoothies (just juice & fruit -- no additives) in tropical combinations of mango, banana, pineapple, coconut, guava, and passion fruit. ($3-5.50) Sandwiches (avocado, hummus, rice or soy cheese, PB&J, ham, turkey, tuna), wraps, vegetarian tamales, veggie or tempeh burgers ($3.50-5) Fresh fruit, salads, and soup. Sprouted wheat and spelt (wheatless) bagels with various toppings, organic granola, Suzi's pastries ($1.25-3.50), flavored coffees, coffee drinks, tea and chai (extra spicy with ginger!) from $1.25-3.75. COMMENTS: This former smoothie and juice stop is now a cafe. The friendly staff is young, and enthusiastic and if we had a category for "prettiest sandwich" this would be it: Light green avocado, with orange carrot shreds, red tomato, and dark green lettuce piled up on "basic beige" bread in a bright yellow wrapper! Fresh, colorful, filling -- and delicious!

**NEIDE'S SALSA & SAMBA** *Mexican/Brazilian*
Hanalei Center (826-1851) HOURS: 11 am-9 pm. SAMPLING: Quesadillas, burritos, enchiladas, tostadas and chimichangas plus Huevos Rancheros, carne asada, steak ranchero, and fish tacos. ($6.95-11.95). Brazilian dishes (6.95-13.95) include vegetarian (pumpkin stuffing) or chicken *panqueca* (crepe), *muqueca* (fresh catch with coconut sauce, shrimp and cilantro), *ensopado* (baked chicken and vegetables, *bife acebolado* (steak and onions) or *bife a cavalo* (steak with an egg on top) COMMENTS: Neide might have salsa and samba -- even an interesting menu with good prices -- but she doesn't seem to have very much aloha. Luckily the staff is nice, but we hope the food is better than the owner's unfriendly attitude.

**OLD HANALEI COFFEE COMPANY** *Coffee/Pastries & Light Lunches*
5183 Kuhio Hwy. in the Hanalei Center (826-6717) HOURS: 7 am-6 pm (summers till 8). SAMPLING: In addition to flavored coffees, they offer espresso, lattes, cappuccinos, frosted or hot mochas, teas ($1.75-3.50 with free refills on most of the "basic" beverages), smoothies ($3.50-3.75) waffles and bagels plus muffins, mac nut brownies, cookies, pies, and cakes, all baked fresh daily. Lemon bars and "aloha bars" (macadamia nut crust with chocolate chips and toasted coconut) are popular, quick snacks. COMMENTS: Waffles served 7:30-11:30 am. Start with a plain waffle ($4.95) and add toppings like papaya, banana, kiwi, mango, raspberries, blueberries, strawberries, coconut, mac nuts, chocolate chips, and whipped cream for 50¢ each or try a Kaua'i waffle "pre-created" for $6.45 with papaya, banana, mac nuts, and whipped cream. The menu offerings are very limited, but what they have is good. Casual and pleasant atmosphere -- homey with curtains and a small selection of gifts. They also offer mail order coffees from their Island Java Roasting Co. (888-4 KAUAI 4).

**PARADISE BAR & GRILL** *American*
Princeville Center (826-1775) HOURS: 11 am-10 pm. SAMPLING: Start with peel & eat shrimp, spring rolls, teri chicken skewers, jalapeno poppers, potato skins, soup, or salad ($3.50-8). Fish or shrimp & chips, chicken strips, or crab cake "nuggets" plus steak, fish, teri chicken sandwiches, and burgers ($5.95-8.95). Dinner entrees (served from 5 pm) include rice and baked potato and two steamed vegetables: Fresh fish, rib-eye steak, teri chicken, garlic shrimp, sauteed

beef tips, crab legs, vegetable platter ($12.95-15.95) or combine any two for $17.95. COMMENTS: Beer & wine, fruit smoothies, and the basic tropicals plus a featured micro brew draft of the month. (There's also a keiki menu, $2.50-3.95). Owner Dave Davies also operates Hale O'Java in the same complex.)

**PIZZA HANALEI** *Pizza*
Ching Young Village (826-9494) HOURS: 11 am-9 pm. SAMPLING: Combinations or choose your toppings from pepperoni, homemade sausage, Canadian bacon, pineapple, bell pepper, meatless sausage, onion, mushroom, jalapeno, fresh garlic, zucchini, pesto, and more. Small, medium, or large from $10.75-34.45. Slices (served all day - only cheese at night) or side of garlic bread ($2.25-2.85). Spinach lasagna, pizzarito (pizza ingredients rolled up in a pizza shell like a burrito), Caesar or garden salad ($3.95-6.95). COMMENTS: Pizza Hanalei has been here for twelve years. Their pizzas are all hand made to order. Sauce is homemade as are the crusts: whole wheat with sesame seeds or white. Well, it sounds good doesn't it? It even looks good. However, we tried the pesto pizza and could have sworn there was fish on it. The sesame coated crust looked wonderful, but it was dry as a board. One bite was enough! Others report they have enjoyed the pizza here, but we'd suggest you hop in the car and head back to Kilauea for Pau Hana pizza.

**POLYNESIAN HIDE-A-WAY & HAW'N BAR-B-Q CHICKEN** *Hawaiian*
4409 Kuhio Hwy., Anahola (821-8033) HOURS: Sun-Mon 11 am-4 pm; Tues-Sat 10 am-5 pm. SAMPLING: Huli-Huli chicken, teri beef, Bar B-Q pork, fish, and grilled cheese sandwiches $3.50-4.50, burgers $4.75-7, and "island favorites" including pork or chicken lau lau, kalua pig, loco moco, smoked meat, and hamburger steak $6-7. COMMENTS: Dine in or take-out at this former roadside stand that now offers plate lunches and sandwiches along with fresh roasted macadamia nuts! They're flown in daily from the Big Island and roasted fresh on the premises. Priced per bag: $3.50 (1/4 lb.), $6 (1/2 lb.), $11 (1 lb.)

**POSTCARDS** ★ *Seafood/Gourmet Vegetarian* OK
5075A Kuhio Hwy., Hanalei (826-1191) HOURS: Breakfast 8-11 am (Sundays till noon or later); Dinner 6-9 pm. No lunch. SAMPLING: Design your own omelette; try the tofu scramble, breakfast burrito, homemade granola, or 7-grain hot cakes; or have a "Bowl of Potatoes" (red roasted with onions, garlic and cheese) or their signature 7-grain English muffin topped with tempeh strips, sauteed greens, and Hollandaise over red roasted potatoes ($5-10). Dinners begin with taro fritters, sesame-crusted prawns with teriyaki plum sauce, seared ahi, Thai summer rolls, or "rocket-shaped" salmon strips ($8-11). Caesar (with eggless dressing) or Kaua'i-grown salads ($5-8) can be ordered with crostinis or prawns for $3.50-9 additional. Entrees feature Thai coconut curry, seafood or primavera pasta, and Taj Triangles -- peas, carrots & potatoes with Indian spices in phyllo pastry ($15-22). Fresh fish ($23-26). Desserts include ginger-spice cheesecake, pineapple upsidedown cake, chocolate raspberry torte, lilikoi mousse, and mac nut pie ($6) as well as some delectable non-dairy offerings. COMMENTS: The taro fritters were delicious! Served with a mound of papaya salsa, they looked a bit like crab cakes, but with a dark brown crust dusted with cornmeal. The "Salmon Rockets" (strips rolled in layers of nori and lumpia) were cut to offer a nice chunk of texture, each a tasty flavor bite inside the crispy crust. The Taj Triangles were a perfect combination of textures and flavors: the flaky pastry with

vegetable filling and exotic curry flavor was light yet satisfying. (Think of a gourmet comfort food with the most basic of vegetables made exoticly Indian inside a trio of mini-Cornish pasties - and you'd still come up short!) The Hawaiian sea bass special ($26) was just that: a special artistic presentation of blackened fish served with papaya cream sauce, colorful tropical salsa (made with big chunks of papaya, tomatoes & pineapple), garlic string beans, and macadamia nut rice. The sea bass had a subtle blackened crust and the flavorful rice had bits of real nuts! Even the mashed potatoes were a cut above flavored with garlic & herbs with chunks of potato and skin left in. The desserts were unbelievable - literally! Who could believe that the macadamia nut pie could be thick with nuts yet taste so light or that the vegan French chocolate silk pie had neither eggs nor milk? The restaurant was charming (it once housed the old Hanalei Museum); the food was innovative and expertly prepared. But what could we do to set it apart? Let's see . . . famed San Francisco Chef Jeremiah Tower (of "Stars" restaurant) noted that there was "a new star in Hanalei" and "star" diners Robert Redford, Terrance Stamp, Meryl Streep, and Dylan McDermott (not to mention "*Star Wars*" director George Lucas) apparently agree. That's it -- a star!

**PRINCEVILLE RESTAURANT & BAR** ★ *American/Oriental*
Just before Princeville at the Princeville Golf Club. (826-5050) HOURS: Breakfast 8-11 am, Lunch 11 am-3 pm. SAMPLING: Breakfast sandwich, loco moco, omelettes, Belgian waffle, French toast, or banana pancakes topped with macadamia nuts or blueberries ($5.25-8.50). For lunch ($4.95-9.50) they have burgers, sandwiches (French dip, Reuben, teri chicken, or grilled ahi), local style plates, and variety of Chef's Specials. Salads are excellent: The Oriental chicken is fresh and crisp, so big it covers the entire plate and the wasabi sesame dressing is fantastic! The seared ahi is served on fresh greens and goes great with their papaya seed dressing. All the portions are really big. They have also added a number of heart-healthy selections for spa-goers (yogurt, granola, veggie burgers) along with mineral & oxygen enhanced water! On Monday nights they offer a special menu of Japanese cuisine and sushi from 5:30-8:30 pm (Dinners $14.95-17.95). On "Pau Hana Fridays" there is a limited pupu and sushi menu with draft beers and karaoke from 6 pm. The Sunday Sports Brunch Buffet (9:30 am-2 pm) has eggs Benedict, breakfast meats, an omelette station, green salad, chicken and beef entrees, sushi, cheese blintzes, potatoes, rice, fruit, cereal, assorted Danish, and desserts with beverage/beer included for $18.95 (Children $8.95). COMMENTS: This is the restaurant formerly known as Prince . . . they've changed the name to avoid any confusion, but it remains confusing in other areas, like in how to describe it! You'll find it downstairs in a cool atrium with palm trees, ceiling fans, and garden furniture in pink and green, yet the elegant building looks like a mini version of the Princeville Resort with a gorgeous view of the golf course. It's like fun food in a fine atmosphere. (So what's a casual restaurant like you doing in a marble and glass place like this?)

**ROADRUNNER BAKERY & CAFE** *Mexican*
2430 Oka Street, Kilauea (828-8226) HOURS: Breakfast 8-11 am, Lunch 11 am-5 pm, Dinner 5-8 pm. SAMPLING: Huevos Rancheros, omelettes, breakfast burra, pancake sandwich, French toast, special cheese hash browns (with onion & tomato or salsa & guacamole), chile relleno & eggs ($4.95-9.95); handmade bagels and breakfast pastries ($1.75-2.50) and espresso bar. Start lunch (or dinner) with taquitos, nachos, chicken flauta, ahi salad, or jicama, almond & chile

salad ($6.95-9.95) followed by chicken, pork, beef, fish, veggie, or tofu tacos and burras; ($6.75-7.75). Black Dog burra with pork & grilled taro ($7.25). Fish, tempeh, or beef burgers are served on freshly-baked taro buns ($6.25-7.95). A variety of sopes, tostadas, fajitas, enchiladas, or combination plates are available for lunch ($6.95-12.95) and/or dinner ($8.95-16.95): Enchiladas Mole Poblano (chicken, cheese, or eggplant made with traditional mole sauce or chile relleno & Hawaiian fish taco with pineapple salsa are among the entrees. Kids' menu priced ($3.50-5.95). COMMENTS: The huge metal mixers (leftover from the former Jacques Bakery) are part of the Mexican courtyard decor along with hand-painted murals on the walls. Step around the corner to their adjoining bakery for taro, rye-molasses, and multi-grain bread as well as Danish, coffee cakes, and a variety of oversized cookies from coconut macaroon to chocolate-chile (spicy like chocolatey gingerbread -- wait for the kick!)

**STEAM VENT CAFE** *Lite meal & coffee drinks*
Kuhio Hwy. next to Hanalei Colony Resort in Ha'ena (826-0055) HOURS: 6:30 am-8:30 pm. SAMPLING: Portuguese bean or chicken dumpling soup ($3.95), sandwiches (health nut with peppers, feta & spinach, roast beef, turkey with cranberry lime sauce, Black Forest ham & cheddar), and Caesar, Greek, "Captain Cook" (with turkey, ham & cheddar), or garden salads ($4.95-7.95). Espresso and coffee drinks ($1.45-3.25). Breads (eight cut), muffins, cookies, mac nut pastry or bar ($.59-1.99). COMMENTS: Freshly-made sandwiches wrapped and ready for take-out plus limited seating. Located inside Surt's on the Beach (see listing that follows) where the old Charo's gift shop was. These "unidentical twin" restaurants started in Volcano on the Big Island and opened here in late 1999.

**SURT'S ON THE BEACH** *French / Thai fusion*
Kuhio Hwy. next to Hanalei Colony Resort in Ha'ena (826-0055) HOURS: Lunch 11 am-4 pm, Dinner 5-9:30 pm. SAMPLING: Asian lunch specialties offer chicken, spring rolls, calamari salad to start ($5.95-6.95) followed by entrees of beef panang, Oriental pasta, and a variety of curries ($7.95-11.95). From Europe, there's stuffed escargot, green salad or Caeser with anchovies or chicken breast ($4.95-12.95) as well as pasta primavera, chicken eggplant, prosciutto fettucine, cheese ravioli with chicken, or Dutch steak with potato ($9.95-14.95). Most of the lunch offerings are available for dinner (at the same prices) along with (Asian) eggplant chicken, or sauteed squid with basil and (European) beef stroganoff, lobster ravioli, NY steak, chicken (carbonara, puttanesca, marsala), scampi, and calamari steak ($11.95-19.95). Chef's specials (fresh fish, steak Diane, leg of lamb, peppered salmon) include a salad ($24.95). "De-surt's" include hot (liquid!) creme brulee, poached pear, chocolate brownie, and original or mango tiramisu ($3.95-4.95). Wine, beer, tea, and coffee drinks. COMMENTS: The restaurant "team" of Surt's and Steam Vent Cafe originated at Volcano on the Big Island and opened here in the old Charo's location in late 1999 (too late for us to review). Chef Surt Thammountha (Oh, that's where they get the name!) began at Michel's in Honolulu before collaborating with owners Brian & Lisha Crawford who also operate several vacation rental properties on the Big Island including Chalet Kilauea and the Lodge at Volcano.

**SUSHI BLUES & GRILL** *Sushi / Pacific Rim*
Ching Young Village, Hanalei (826-9701) HOURS: Dinner 5:30-9:30 pm (Closed Monday) SAMPLING: Naturally, appetizers include sashimi ($11.95-12.95); sushi ($3.75-7.50); and combinations ($14.95-17.95) as well as Thai spring rolls, crab stuffed mussels, shrimp & vegetable tempura, oyster shooters, soft shell crab salad hand roll, and garlic sauteed mushrooms served on a bed of lettuce that absorbs the great garlic-butter-sake sauce and makes it like a hot spinach salad! ($5.95-8.95). Oriental, Caesar, spicy tuna, salmon skin, and tempura shrimp salad ($4.95-11.95). Entrees come with miso soup, julienne vegetable tempura, and 3-piece California roll and feature miso chicken saute, stir fry, scallops in cilantro pesto cream, coconut shrimp with Thai chile plum sauce, kiwi teriyaki chicken, and tenderloin filet with raspberry peppercorn sauce ($13.95-21.95). Fresh fish is served grilled with garlic sake cream, wok-charred with mango BBQ glaze, or sauteed with Chinese black bean. Desserts include green tea or mango ice cream, chocolate mousse cake, or mud pie ($3.50-4.95). COMMENTS: Brought to you by "those wonderful folks" at Zelo's Beach House, this is the latest of the popular sushi "plus" restaurants. (Although possibly the first and only on Kaua'i!) You can have your sushi and eat dinner, too, or mix and match to have just one -- or the other! The sushi is innovative, tasty, and offered in beautifully artistic presentations with swirls of color and design in each sushi piece. Chef Masa's signature Crunchy Roll is made with tempura shrimp, chili sauce & tobiko eggs and rolled in tempura flake roll; the Grasshopper Roll has BBQ eel & mac nuts in a seaweed flake roll; the Sushi Cake is spicy shrimp wrapped in raw ahi, kind of a cross between sushi and sashimi. There's a full page of sakes (or try a sampler of 4 for $12), 15 specialty martinis, international beers plus wines and tropicals. There is live music several nights a week ranging from blues to jazz to Hawaiian swing band dance music. (Call for current days and times.) We liked the food, we liked the cool name, and we were impressed that the couple next to us drove all the way from Po'ipu just for the sushi! In fact, we were almost star-struck, but unfortunately, felt the service could have been more personalized and less by "rote."

**TAHITI NUI** *American/Hawaiian/Thai*
Kuhio Hwy., Hanalei (826-6277) HOURS: Lunch & dinner 11:30 am-9 pm, Luau on Wednesday at 6 pm (separate entrance and admission). SAMPLING: Crispy duck, stuffed shrimp, lobster in black bean sauce, and fresh fish with ginger or coconut garlic sauce are some of Tahiti Nui's special entrees for $16.95-19.95. COMMENTS: Tahiti Nui celebrated 35 years of business in 1999. They still have the old-fashioned (50's style) Polynesian Bar with the South Seas style bamboo walls and ceiling fans and the lana'i out front facing the highway is still a great place to people watch - it seems to be a national pastime with North Shore locals! Unfortunately, their recent experiment of combining with a Thai restaurant came to an end just as we went to press and we were unable to get any information about their subsequent plans for returning to their original menu or for any (re)renovating of the restaurant. (For information on their luau, see section on Luaus at the end of this restaurant chapter.)

**TROPICAL TACO** ★ *Mexican*
What's green and has no address? The Tropical Taco van! This is like the truck and the stop in one. HOURS: Wed-Sat 11 am-4 pm. SAMPLING: Tacos, tostadas, and burritos made fresh daily; prices range from $1 for a bigger-than-bite-size piece of fresh fish to $8 for the fat jack burrito. The tropical taco (fresh fish or beef) is made with a thicker, "plushier" tortilla that you can order deep fried or just warmed up ($6-7). If you're thirsty, it's lemonade or nothing. COMMENTS: Cash or traveler's cheques only! Owner Roger Kennedy has been serving Mexican food from his van since 1978. There is no lard in the beans, no "frozen" in the fish, and the fresh salsa is made with just-picked chiles. It's so popular there's always a line out the "window" and soon there may be one out the door! That's right, a real door! Tropical Taco will be moving into permanent digs in the new Halele'a Building at 5088 Kuhio Hwy.(next to the liquor store) scheduled to open in April, 2000. But don't worry: the van will be parked right in front and continue to open for business -- as unusual! (The "wheel-less" van is not open as we go to press; call 635-TACO for hours and additional information.)

**VILLAGE SNACK & BAKE SHOP** *Deli/Bakery/Coffee Shop*
Ching Young Village, Hanalei (826-6841) HOURS: Breakfast 6-11 am, Lunch 11 am-4 pm (Sundays till 3 pm.) SAMPLING: Breakfast sandwiches, eggs, pancakes, rice, spam. loco moco ($2.75-5.95). Tuna melt, teri beef or chicken, BLT, sandwich; burgers, hot dogs ($2-4.50). Side orders from $1; plate meals (fried or chile pepper chicken, hamburger steak, teri beef) or fish & chips, $5.95. Beach or picnic lunch to go includes sandwich, soda, fruit, or salad ($5.95). COMMENTS: The bakery offers coconut, macadamia or banana cream pies plus their signature lilikoi chiffon pie. Carrot cake, apple cobbler, brownies, and oversized cookies, $1.50.

**WINDS OF BEAMREACH** *American*
Located at Pali Ke Kua, Princeville (826-6143) HOURS: 5:30-9:30 pm. SAMPLING: Appetizers include sashimi, poke, steamed clams, and chicken teriyaki ($7.95-8.95). Entrees are served with soup or salad & fresh baked rolls: medallions of pork tenderloin with peppercorn sauce, macadamia nut or garlic herb chicken, seafood pasta marinara, pineapple shrimp, beef or chicken stir-fry, fresh fish, seafood pot, NY steak, filet mignon ($14.95-23.95). For dessert, there's Tahitian lime pie, macadamia cream pie, chocolate or rum caramel sundae, and hula pie ($4.50). Early bird specials (5:30-6:30) offer fresh fish kabob, chicken teriyaki, beef or chicken stir-fry, hamburger steak, or linguini Alfredo from $10.95. COMMENTS: Fresh fish steamed Hawaiian style with fresh ginger, garlic & green onion is a specialty. The teriyaki steak is also popular. Owner Diane Anakalea makes all the desserts, salad dressings, and a lot of the soups. Her husband tends bar and their three children serve as wait and bus help. A real family establishment! No ocean view here, but they do overlook the pool so at least there's water as well as a nice view of the mountains. Our ultimate test of a meal is the fish and the coffee. Both were average: the fish was fresh, but the seasoning was flat. The poi rolls were yummy and the salad was a pleasant mix of leaf lettuce with homemade dressings. The Tahitian lime pie was a disappointment resembling lime sherbet with walnuts on it.

**ZABABAZ CAFE** *Tropical/Vegetarian/Vegan*
Located in the Ching Young Village, Hanalei (826-1999) HOURS: 9 am-7 pm. SAMPLING: Organic vegetarian dishes like lasagna, enchiladas, quiche, veggie burgers, potato or green salad, hummus wrap, and several Thai items. Fresh bakery goodies include their popular brownies and oatmeal chocolate chip cookies. The cornbread and banana walnut bread are made with maple syrup instead of sugar. They also have Lappert's ice cream as well as smoothies, juices, and espresso drinks. Prices average $3-6. COMMENTS: Small style vegetarian cafe and juice bar located in the old (original) Ching Young Store. Limited seating at picnic tables with benches. (Is Hanalei trying to get a corner on the restaurants with "Z" names? Read on . . .)

**ZELO'S BEACH HOUSE** ★ *International/Mexican*
Ching Young Village, Hanalei (826-9700) HOURS: Lunch 11 am-3:30 pm, Dinner 5:30-10 pm, Happy Hour 3:30-5:30 pm with limited lunch & pupu menu SAMPLING: Stuffed baked potato, lunch omelette, fish & chips, fish tacos, or all-you-can-eat spaghetti ($7.50-11.95); entree-sized chicken or fish Caesar, Mediterranean, or Chinese chicken salad ($8.95-12.95). Philly steak, turkey club, or French dip sandwiches; tuna, hummus, Cajun chicken, or seafood quesadilla wraps ($7.25-9.95) plus an extensive variety of beef, chicken, or fish burgers ($5.95-8.95). Dinner entrees feature crab stuffed fresh fish, Hawaiian chicken, coconut shrimp, rib-eye steak, baby back pork ribs, fresh fish tacos, seafood fajitas, beer battered fish & chips, and mushroom-smothered chicken ($12.95-23.95) plus a variety of pastas: smoked salmon linguini, sun-dried tomato rigatoni, fettucini Alfredo (or with Cajun chicken, fresh fish, or seafood artichoke picatta), cheese raviolis, chicken pesto tortellini, linguini with clams and toasted pine nuts, or all-you-can-eat spaghetti ($9.95-20.95). No room for dessert? Put the rest in a doggie bag and order carrot cake, macadamia nut cream pie, chocolate suicide cake, or grasshopper pie ($3.50-4.95) COMMENTS: Their logo is the Greek symbol for "exuberance" - and it shows! The food was surprisingly good with unexpected touches like warm bread with herb garlic butter, baked potato included with dinner, and more than ample portions. We sampled several of their daily specials, the mixed seafood on pasta was a selection of fresh fish and seafood and none of it was overcooked. The seared salmon was excellent; ditto the lemon picatta seafood preparation. The portions are enormous, and not just judging by our standards. We saw quite a few "doggie bags" going out the door. The same owners now have Sushi Blues and Grill just down the road apiece.

## *LUAUS*

**GAYLORD'S ("REFLECTIONS OF PARADISE")**
Kilohana Plantation, Lihu'e (808) 245-9595
Luau guests gather outside on the Kilohana Estate grounds and pick up their mai tais as they enter the historic Carriage House for the luau dinner and show. After dinner, a cloud of mist draws your attention to the stage as your MC, Mikela, introduces the opening number: a medley of 1940s Hapa Haole songs accompanied by hula dancers in colorful cellophane skirts. A group of talented musicians guides you through a travelogue of Polynesian, Hawaiian, Tahitian, and Maori dances culminating in a Samoan Fire Knife Dance. The best and most unusual numbers in the show also centered around fire -- literally!

In one intriguing bit of choreography, bowls of fire were featured as intimately as dancing partners. Then in the poi ball number (an already mesmerizing display of talent and skill), the excitement was enhanced with twirling poi balls on fire! The costumes were attractive and well-designed especially the skirts made from a provocative collection of leaves and bark with color and texture that certainly made for a unique fashion statement. And by popular demand (well, Dona and Christie's) they have now added more male dancers to the show line-up. The buffet consisted of kalua pig, mahi mahi, teriyaki beef, pineapple chicken, fried rice, imu baked sweet potato, fresh vegetables, poi rolls, sweet bread, and a variety of salads and fresh fruit. We were disappointed in the food in our first review, but found it had improved. (For one thing, they 86'd the green jello and replaced it with a much more interesting and appealing strawberry guava!) The macaroni-potato salad was actually quite good, with chunky bits of potato and a well-textured dressing and the strawberry papaya was particularly sweet and tasty. The fried rice was spicy and tasted like it might have had Portuguese sausage in it. The teri beef was good and tender, but the chicken was big pieces on the bone and was a bit messy to eat. The pig was good with poi in tiny little white cups and the taro rolls were a nice touch. Tropical fruit filled cakes, and a potentially interesting imu-baked rice pudding were the desserts. They have all new tables and chairs that make it easier for getting in and out. After the show, the dancers and Chief Manu, the fire dancer, greet the guests and pose for photos. The luau is offered Mondays and Thursdays at 6:30 pm. At press time, this was the lowest priced luau on the island and we were told they had no immediate plans to raise the prices. Adults $49; senior discount for 55 and over, $45. Children 6-14 are $20; children under 6 are free. They also do group and wedding luaus as well as special luaus with turkey for holidays.

**HYATT REGENCY KAUA'I ("DRUMS OF PARADISE")**
1571 Po'ipu Road, Po'ipu (808) 742-1234
The luau program includes Hawaiian crafts and displays and a cocktail social along with the Hawaiian buffet and Polynesian show of music and dance. The buffet begins with fresh sliced tropical fruits; Garden Isle greens with cucumber, tomatoes and carrots topped with croutons and grated cheese with papaya seed dressing; lomi lomi salmon; spinach, pipikaula and macadamia nut salad; and poi. Entrees of hulu huli chicken; fresh island fish with macadamia nut butter; kalua pig, and teriyaki steaks are offered with stir fry vegetables; Hawaiian sweet potatoes; steamed island rice; rolls and butter. Pineapple cake, bread pudding, and haupia (coconut pudding) are the desserts. The luau is held outside in the Grand Gardens every Sunday and Thursday at 6 pm. Adults $59.95, Juniors (13-20 years) $39.95, Children (6-12 years) $29.95 and children under 5 are free.

**KAUA'I COCONUT BEACH RESORT LUAU ★**
Coconut Plantation, Kapa'a (808) 822-3455 extension 651. <www.kcb.com>
This luau has received the "Kahili" Award from the Hawai'i Visitors Bureau for its "Keep it Hawai'i" program. Featuring only the dances, legends, and lore of Kaua'i, it also provides the visitor with the opportunity to witness *kahiko* hula, one of the most ancient forms of this cultural dance. The show is choreographed by Kumu hula (master) Kawaikapuokalani Hewett. The dancers are beautifully dressed and make some very speedy costume changes. They put the pig in the imu at 10:45 in the morning, so if it works out with your schedule, stop by the

Luau Halau Pavilion and see how it is done. The luau begins at 6 pm with the blowing of the conch shell, torchlighting ceremony, and a shell lei greeting. Seating is family style, however, and a little too crowded to make it comfortable to get in and out of your seat. Haupia and fresh pineapple are on the table when you arrive. The buffet is a pleasant mix with fried rice, mahi, kalua pork, baked taro, teriyaki beef, and tropical chicken combined with fresh fruits and assorted salads. The kalua pork was wonderful and the teriyaki beef was surprisingly moist and flavorful. The chicken was in a sweet and sour sauce that seemed just too sweet. Dessert options were coconut cake, haupia, and a pasty, flavorless rice pudding. Arrive early and wait in line for the better seats. Open bar throughout the evening. They do have smoking and non-smoking sections. At press time, the cost was $52.00 for adults, $30 for teens 12 to 17 and $20 for children 3 to 11, but prices were expected to change. Changes were also planned for their Family Night (currently offered every Monday, Tuesday, Friday, and Saturday) with one child accompanied by an adult paying full price admitted free. (Additional children charged at the regular child rate.) Seniors (55 years) $47.50. Held nightly; advance reservations are needed.

**PRINCEVILLE RESORT BEACHSIDE LUAU ("PA'INA 'O HANALEI")**
5520 Ka Haku Road, Princeville (808) 826-2788.
Held poolside under a pavilion (and partial tent) with Hanalei Bay as the backdrop, this luau begins with the blowing of the conch shell and participation in a traditional luau ceremony. The food is better than most with a buffet of kalua pig, chicken lau lau, grilled marinated chicken with macadamia nut sauce (tender strips of chicken breast in a tasty sauce), mahi mahi with lemon seaweed sauce, soba noodles with vegetables, and ginger & lemongrass marinated beef. There was also rice and Hawaiian (purple) sweet potatoes. Two excellent salads were featured: cold roasted vegetables and a salmon combination that was part grilled and part lomi lomi style - a delicious blend of textures, flavors - and colors! Other Hawaiian-style salads included tako with kim chee, cucumber and seaweed, bean sprout & watercress, as well as "gringo" greens and fruits. The dessert table featured pineapple upside down cake, haupia, imu-baked rice pudding, large cookies, and slices of banana bread attractively dusted with powdered sugar. Beer, wine, and mai tais. The entertainment features *Ho'ike Nani 'O Ke Kai* (A Show of Splendor by the Sea) in a program that offers kahiko hula along with a paniolo number, *The Hawaiian War Chant*, and ultimately, two fire knife dancers, one of whom creates (with slight-of-hand dexterity) a sudden "line of fire" at his feet - very impressive! The luau is priced at $59.50 for adults, $30 for children 6 to 12, and a substantially discounted rate of $47.50 for seniors (65 years). Held Monday, Wednesday, & Thursday at 6 pm.

**SMITH'S TROPICAL PARADISE**
174 Wailua Rd., Kapa'a (808) 822-4654
Smith's luau grounds are located on their 30-acre botanical and cultural garden. The luau begins with a traditional imu ceremony at 6 pm, but the gates open an hour early for touring of the grounds - on your own or on an optional guided tram tour. They have an open bar with live music which opens at 6:15 and closes at 7:30, serving beer, wine, and mai tais. Dinner is served at 6:30; an all-you-can-eat buffet of Garden Isle greens, poi, jello, three-bean, nimasu, and macaroni salads, Oriental fried rice, lomi salmon, fresh fruits, kalua pig, teriyaki beef, adobo chicken, sweet & sour mahi mahi, hot vegetables, snowflake and sweet

potatoes, hot vegetables, and haupia, coconut cake, and rice pudding for dessert. At 8:00, Madame Pele introduces the luau show with a fiery welcome in the garden's covered lagoon amphitheater. The "Golden People of Hawaii" is an International Pageant depicting dances and songs from the South Pacific. Featured are Tahiti, China, Japan, the Philippines, New Zealand, and Samoa, in addition to Hawaii. The luau is held Monday, Wednesday, and Friday at a cost of $52 for adults, $27 for ages 3-12 years, and $18 for children 3-6 years. International Pageant luau show alone $14 Adult/$7 Child. Reservations are required.

**TAHITI NUI LUAU**
Kuhio Hwy., Hanalei (808) 826-6277
This North Shore luau is offered twice a week on Wednesdays and Sundays at 6 pm. Held indoors in the back of the Tahiti Nui restaurant, it is a narrow room with long tables and a stage at the end. This is a family-style luau and there are always lots of kids. The food is authentic - no glitz or glamour - casually displayed in serving trays and Tupperware-like dishes; it's as if you went to someone's home for a luau dinner and the guests took turns getting up to perform. This is a small luau room (as luaus go) with the advantage that you have a good view of the stage from most any table and they are not so packed together that it is difficult to get in and out of your seat. (Important when you want to hit that buffet line!) A more intimate and local luau with a friendly atmosphere. They cook the pig in an imu out in back, not a very attractive pit, but then it *is* authentic imu cooking. The menu is an all-you-can-eat Tahitian and Hawaiian buffet with mai tais. Buffet items feature kalua pig, fresh fish, teriyaki chicken, Poisson Cru, chicken with coconut milk, fish or chicken lau lau, sweet potatoes, poi, lomi salmon, green salad, potato/macaroni salad, fresh fruit slices, garlic bread, haupia, and chocolate cake. Admission prices have jumped quite a lot since our last book, the only difference seems to be that they now include free mai tais instead of just one alcoholic drink: $52 adults; $30 teens (12-17), $20 children (3-11) with one child admitted free when accompanied by full paying adult.

WILIWILI

## *NIGHTLIFE*

Gilligan's at the Outrigger offers diverse evening entertainment ($5 cover); Comedy Club Thursday & Saturday with top headliners ($12 at door, $10 in advance, $5 for buffet patrons). Thursday Beach Party, Friday Retro Night. The Disco also has dancing until 2 am on Friday & Saturday nights.

Hap's Hideaway on Rice Street in Lihu'e is a sports bar.

The bar at Keoki's Paradise seems to be a popular hang out for locals and visitors. Live contemporary Hawaiian music Thursday-Saturday.

Jazz in the Happy Talk Lounge at Hanalei Bay Resort is a Sunday afternoon tradition from 3-7 pm and they hope to establish another tradition with their Aloha Friday "happy hour" from 4-6:30 pm with special pupus and drinks. Also live entertainment Mon-Sat from 6:30-9:30 pm.

Live Hawaiian music on the weekends (Thurs.-Sat.) at Chuck's Steak House.

Hanalei Gourmet has nightly entertainment - recommended by our readers for great musicians and singers.

Karaoke at Rob's Good Times Grill and Rampy's (Kukui Grove Shopping Center) in Lihu'e; JR's in Hanama'ulu; and Noe's Grille and Bar or Jolly Roger in Kapa'a.

Stevenson's Library at Hyatt is a quiet retreat with a large aquarium, chess tables, and bookcases. Read, browse, or just relax and soak up the atmosphere! The library is open from 6 pm to 1 am with jazz nightly from 8 to 11.

Live entertainment, electric and steel tip dart boards and other games at the Lizard Lounge and Deli at Waipouli Town Center.

Enjoy Hawaiian music and other nightly entertainment in the Living Room Lounge of the North Shore's Princeville Hotel.

Sushi Blues in Hanalei has entertainment several evenings a week usually jazz on Wednesday, blues on Friday & Saturday, and Hawaiian swing music on Sunday.

Live Hawaiian music at Joe's on the Green during their Thursday night dinners from 5:30-8:30.

Jazz at Hale O'Java, Wednesday nights 6:30-9 pm. (Flamenco guitar Tuesdays & Thursdays, 4-6 pm.)

Live music (8-11 pm) Friday & Saturday at Margaritas Mexican Restaurant & Watering Hole in Kapa'a.

Po'ipu Bay Bar & Grill is open Thursday-Saturday evenings with live music (and a pupu menu) from 8 pm.

Live entertainment Thursday-Saturday at the Lighthouse Bistro in Kilauea.

Duke's Canoe Club hosts Tropical Friday every week from 4-6 pm with live music and tropical drink & food specials. Live music in the bar Thursday-Sunday night from 9-11:30.

Amelia's at the Princeville Airport has TV with satellite sports plus music and dancing Friday-Sunday till 2 am

JJ's Broiler has live music Thursday-Sunday at their Anchor Cove location.

Lihu'e Cafe Lounge has dancing on Friday & Saturday, Karaoke on Tuesday & Thursday, and free pool on Monday & Wednesday.

Listen to guitar music on the weekends at Hanapepe Cafe & Espresso and the Royal Coconut Grove lounge at Kaua'i Coconut Beach Resort.

Whalers Brewpub offers a variety of live music: reggae, rock and more from both local and mainland bands.

STILSON
JBAYOT

# BEACHES

## *INTRODUCTION*

Kaua'i, being the oldest of the major Hawaiian islands, has beaches that have been worn with time. Because of this, you will not find exotic dark sand beaches, but rather those of golden sand that has been gently polished over millions of years. If you are the active beach-goer who likes to snorkel or swim or the type that prefers to find a quiet shady beachfront spot, Kaua'i offers a diverse selection.

We have not given a full description of every beach on the island but focused on those that were either the most beautiful or offered the best activities. Wherever possible, we have used the true Hawaiian names for the beaches, while including the local names as an aside. For more information on Kaua'i's beaches, the ultimate book is *Beaches of Kaua'i and Ni'ihau* by John R.K. Clark, published by University of Hawai'i Press. This reference will provide you with everything you want to know and perhaps a little bit more!

"It has been calculated that 44% of its coastline is fringed by fine white sand beaches, double the percentage of any other Hawaiian Island." (Excerpt from *Ten Years, 250 Islands* by Ron Hall.) With ratings of average, outstanding, and world class, Ron Hall has rated Kaua'i as world class in sandy beaches, coastal spectacle, and island scenery. Most are accessible by foot, three are accessible by water only, and six are by water or by trail. Fifteen of the beaches have public facilities. Kaua'i has more linear miles of sandy shore line than any of the other major islands, approximately 113 miles.

Following is a two page map of Kaua'i which depicts the location of the most popular beaches around the island. For further directions, refer to the enlarged area maps located in the Where to Stay - What to See section of this guide.

As with all of the Hawaiian islands, the beaches of Kaua'i are publicly owned and most have right-of-way access; however, the access is sometimes tricky to find and parking may be a problem! Please note public access to some Kaua'i beaches is on or through private property and the state of Hawai'i exempts landowners from liability. In other words, you may use their land, but they are NOT responsible - YOU are! Parking areas are provided at most developed beaches, but they are often small. Some have lifeguards on duty.

In any parking lot (but even to a greater degree in the undeveloped areas where you will have to wedge your vehicle along the roadside), it is vital that you leave nothing of importance in your car as the occurrence of theft, especially at some of the more remote locations, is high.

At the larger, developed beaches, a variety of facilities are provided. Many have convenient rinse-off showers, drinking water, restrooms, and picnic areas. A few have children's play or swim areas. The beaches near the major resorts often have rental equipment available for snorkeling, sailing, and boogie boarding, and some even rent underwater cameras. These beaches are generally clean and well maintained. (See CAMPING for information about beach facilities.)

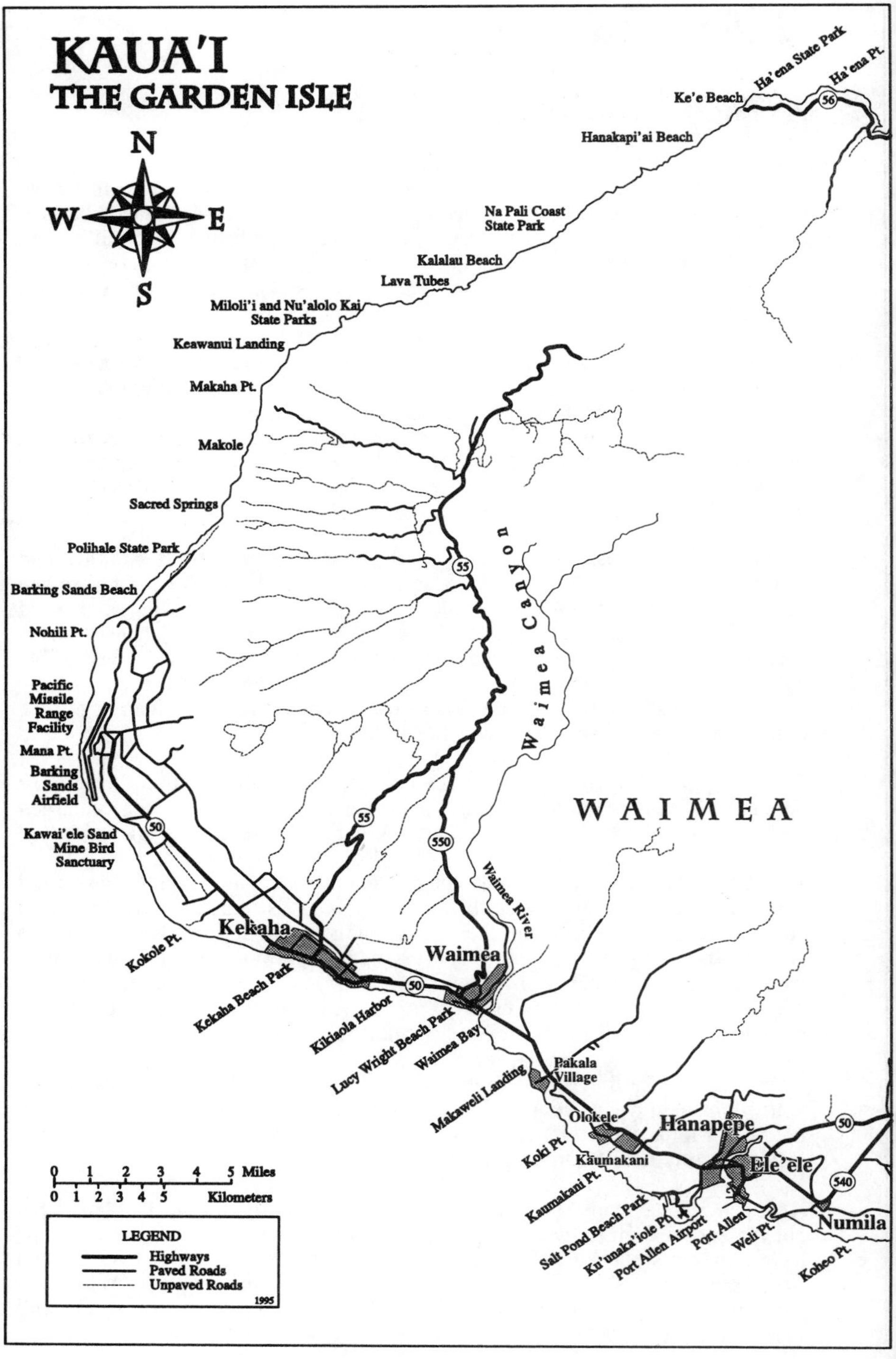

KAUA'I
THE GARDEN ISLE
N
W
E
S
Ha'ena State Park
Ha'ena Pt.
Ke'e Beach
56
Hanakapi'ai Beach
Na Pali Coast
State Park
Kalalau Beach
Lava Tubes
Miloli'i and Nu'alolo Kai
State Parks
Keawanui Landing
Makaha Pt.
Makole
Sacred Springs
Polihale State Park
Barking Sands Beach
Nohili Pt.
Pacific
Missile
Range
Facility
Mana Pt.
Barking
Sands
Airfield
Kawai'ele Sand
Mine Bird
Sanctuary
55
550
50
Waimea Canyon
WAIMEA
Waimea River
Kekaha
Waimea
Kokole Pt.
Kekaha Beach Park
Kikiaola Harbor
Lucy Wright Beach Park
Waimea Bay
Makaweli Landing
Pakala
Village
Olokele
Hanapepe
Ele'ele
540
Numila
Koki Pt.
Kaumakani
Kaumakani Pt.
Salt Pond Beach Park
Ku'unaka'iole Pt.
Port Allen Airport
Port Allen
Weli Pt.
Koheo Pt.
0 1 2 3 4 5 Miles
0 1 2 3 4 5 Kilometers
LEGEND
Highways
Paved Roads
Unpaved Roads
1995

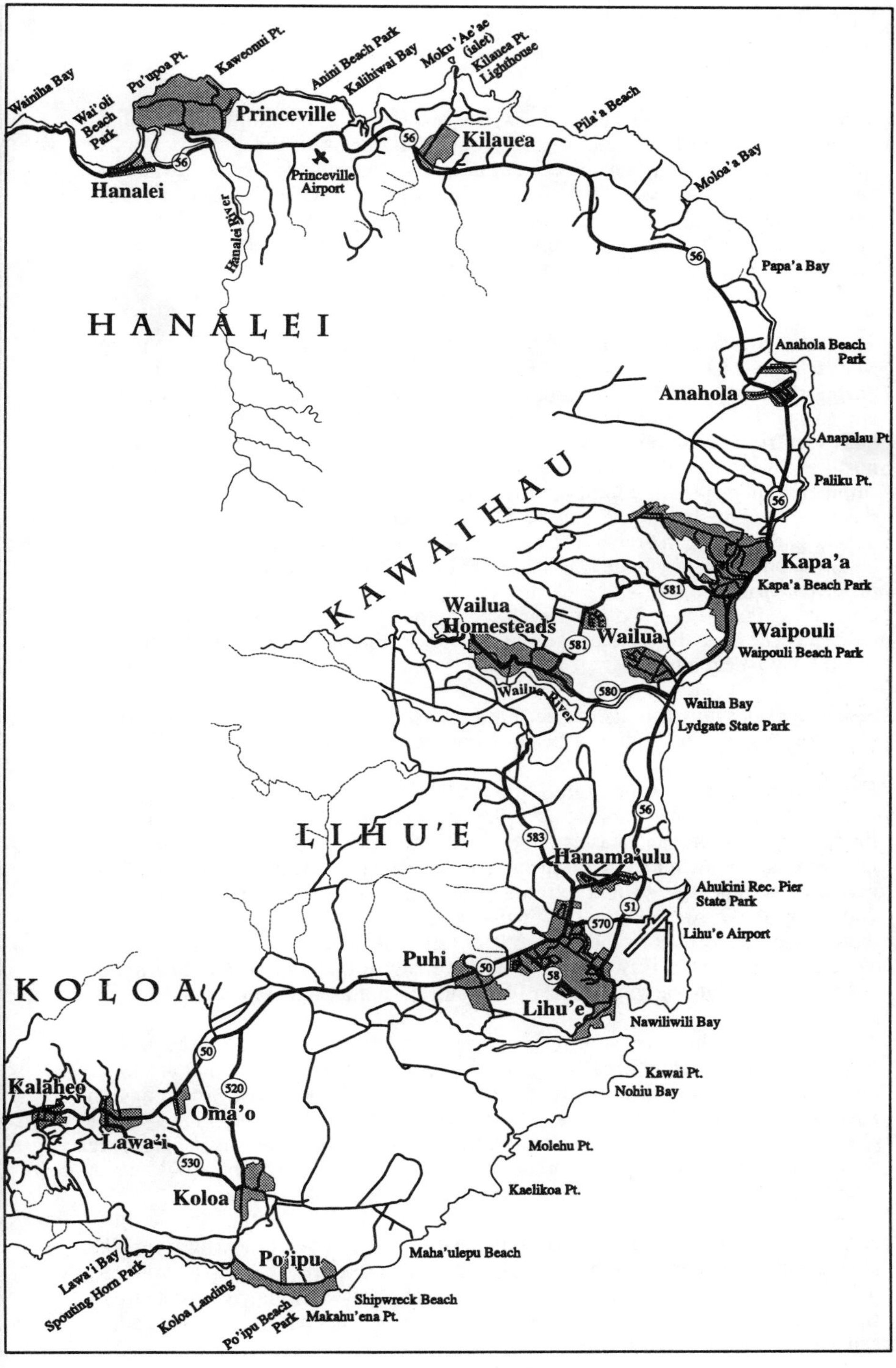
Wainiha Bay
Wai'oli Beach Park
Pu'upoa Pt.
Kaweonui Pt.
Anini Beach Park
Kalihiwai Bay
Moku 'Ae'ae (islet)
Kilauea Pt. Lighthouse
Princeville
Kilauea
Pila'a Beach
Hanalei
Princeville Airport
Hanalei River
Moloa'a Bay
Papa'a Bay
HANALEI
Anahola Beach Park
Anahola
Anapalau Pt.
Paliku Pt.
KAWAIHAU
Kapa'a
Kapa'a Beach Park
Wailua Homesteads
Wailua
Waipouli
Waipouli Beach Park
Wailua River
Wailua Bay
Lydgate State Park
LIHU'E
Hanama'ulu
Ahukini Rec. Pier State Park
Lihu'e Airport
Puhi
Lihu'e
Nawiliwili Bay
KOLOA
Kawai Pt.
Nohiu Bay
Kalaheo
Oma'o
Lawa'i
Molehu Pt.
Koloa
Kaelikoa Pt.
Maha'ulepu Beach
Po'ipu
Lawa'i Bay
Spouting Horn Park
Koloa Landing
Shipwreck Beach
Po'ipu Beach Park
Makahu'ena Pt.
56
581
580
583
51
570
50
58
520
530

Kaua'i's most gentle beaches in the winter are found on the Southern coastline. While the Princeville/Hanalei region receives the brunt of most of the tropical weather, storms can affect the condition of the beaches all around the island. Seasonally, there is also a great change in the island's beaches. While any beach you visit may be calm and idyllic in the summer, there may be high and treacherous surf during the winter months. Unlike Maui, whose southern and western beaches form part of a protected area sheltered by the islands of Kahoolawe and Lana'i, Kaua'i has beaches which are more exposed.

The North Shore of Kaua'i has higher surf during the months of October through May. On the east coast, high surf from the east and north is also more frequent during the same months. The south shore also receives high surf from the west and east and heavier rain during the winter months of October through May, and high surf from the south can occur April through September. High surf from the north and west will affect the west shore beaches October through May and the summer southern swell will affect the west side April through September. Even on a very calm day, there can be an unexpected wave surge. (Many of the beaches have changed dramatically as a result of Hurricane Iniki; some will never be the same again.) Lydgate and Salt Pond Beaches have two sea pools which are protected from the surf and ideal for young children. You'll find lifeguards on duty at Lydgate Park, Po'ipu Beach, Salt Pond, Ke'e, and Hanalei Pavilion. Other beaches may be manned with life guards during the busier summer months or on busy weekends.

Seasonal conditions can also affect the beach itself. Sand is eroded away from some beaches during winter to be re-deposited during the spring and summer.

Here are some basic water safety tips and terms. Most of the north and west shore beaches of Kaua'i do not have the coral reefs or other barriers which are found on the south and eastern shores. These wide expansive beaches pose greater risks for swimmers with strong currents and dangerous shorebreaks. You may see swimmers or surfers at some of the beaches where we recommend that you enjoy the view and stay out of the water. Keep in mind that just because there is someone else in the water, it doesn't mean it is safe. Some of these surfers are experts in Hawaiian surf, and we advise that you do not take undue risks. Others might be visitors just like you, but not as well informed!

A *shorebreak* is the place where the waves break directly on the shore, or very near to it. Smaller shorebreaks may not be a problem, but waves that are more than a foot or two high may create hazardous conditions. Most drownings on Kaua'i happen at the shorebreak. Conditions are generally worse in the winter months. Even venturing too close to a shorebreak could be hazardous, as standing on the beachfront you may encounter a stronger, higher wave that could catch you off guard and sweep you into the water.

A *rip current* can often be seen from the shore. They are fast moving river-like currents that sometimes can be seen carrying sand or sediment. A rip current can pull an unsuspecting swimmer quickly out to sea and swimming against a strong rip current may be impossible. Unfortunately, these currents are another leading cause of drownings in Kaua'i.

*Undertows* happen when a rip current runs into incoming surf. This accounts for the feeling that you are being pulled. They are more common on beaches which have steep slopes.

We don't want to be alarmists, but we'd prefer to report the beaches conservatively. Always, always use good judgment.

*Kona winds* generated by southern hemisphere storms cause southerly swells that affect Po'ipu and the southern coastline. This usually happens in the summer and will last for several days. This condition can cause unusually high summer surf.

*Northerly swells* caused by winter storms northeast of the island are not common, but can cause large surf, particularly on the northern beaches at 'Anini Beach Park, Kauapea Beach, Kaka'anui Beach, and the beaches at Princeville and Hanalei.

Based on drowning records from 1970 through 1988, according to *The Kaua'i Guide* to Beaches by Pat Durkin, the five most dangerous beaches, listed in order of drownings are Hanakapi'ai, Lumaha'i, Wailua, Hanalei, and Waipouli. Other beaches with high incidents of drownings are Polihale, 'Anini, Kalalau, and Kealia. Pat Durkin notes that "drowning statistics are also a reflection of a beach's popularity. For instance, if Wainiha and First Ditch [Kekaha] were as popular as Lumaha'i or Polihale, they would probably have higher drowning rates, as conditions are similar." (*Kaua'i Guide to Beaches* is published by Magic Fishes Press, PO Box 3243, Lihu'e, HI 96766.)

Kaua'i's ocean playgrounds are among the most benign in the world. There are only a few ocean creatures that you should be aware of. We will attempt to include some basic first aid tips should you encounter one of these. Since some people might have a resulting allergic reaction, we suggest you contact a local physician or medical center should you have an unplanned encounter with one of them.

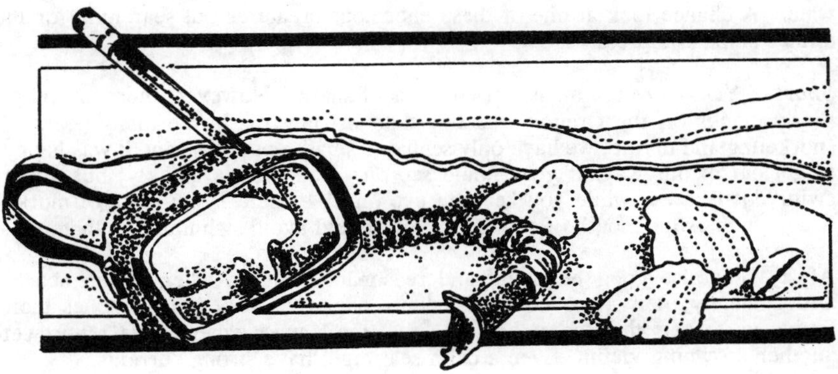

Only once (and that was on Maui) have we seen Portuguese Man-of-War. These very small creatures are related to the jellyfish and are propelled by the wind. The one time we encountered these beautiful sea creatures, they had been blown in by an unusual wind and covered the beach with glistening crystal orbs filled with deep blue filament. If they are on the beach, assume they are also in the water and stay out. On rare occasions they will be seen drifting in the ocean during a sea excursion and the staff will change snorkeling destinations if this is the case. The sting is unpleasant, so don't touch! If you are stung you can use vinegar to help neutralize the venom. Diluted ammonia or baking soda is said to provide a similar effect, or try out the local remedy which is urine.

In the water, avoid touching sea urchins: the pricking of one of the spines can be painful. You will need to check carefully to be sure all of the spine has been removed.

Coral is made up of many tiny living organisms. Coral cuts require thorough disinfecting and can take a long time to heal.

Cone shells look harmless enough, they are conical and in colors of brown or black. The snails which inhabit these shells have a defense which they use to protect themselves and also to kill their prey. Their stinger does have venom and it is suggested that you just enjoy looking at them. Cleaning the wound and soaking it in hot water for 30-90 minutes will provide relief.

Eels live among the coral and are generally not aggressive. You may have heard of divers who have "trained" an eel to come out, greet them and then take some food from their hands. We don't recommend you try to make an eel your pal. While usually non aggressive, their jaws are extremely powerful and their teeth are sharp. And as divers know, sea animals could mistake any approach or movement as an aggressive or provoking act. Just keep a comfortable distance, for you and the eel. Also, should you poke around with your hands in the coral, they might inadvertently think your finger is some food. This is one of the many reasons you should not handle the coral. Eels are generally not out of their home during the day, but a close examination of the coral might reveal a head of one of these fellows sticking out and watching you! At night, during low tide, at beaches with a protective reef, you might try taking a flashlight and scanning the water. A chance look at one of these enormous creatures out searching for its dinner is most impressive.

***Sharks?*** Yes, there are many varied types of sharks. However, there are more shark attacks off the Oregon coastline than in Hawai'i. In the many years of snorkeling and diving, we have only seen one small reef shark, and it was happy to get out of our way. If you should see one, don't move quickly, but rather swim slowly away while you keep an eye on it! If there is any area of murky water, such as the mouth of any river, you should avoid swimming in that area.

Always exercise good judgment and reasonable caution when at the beach. Unfortunately, it is a too common occurrence when a person stretches their limits, or forgets their common sense that the Kaua'i papers must report yet another drowning victim. Even a calm sea might have strong currents.

Here are some additional ***beach safety tips***:

1. "Never turn your back to the sea" is an old Hawaiian saying. Don't be caught off guard, waves come in sets with spells of calm in between.

2. Use the buddy system, never swim or snorkel alone.

3. If you are unsure of your abilities, use floatation devices attached to your body, such as a life vest or inflatable vest. Never rely on an air mattress or similar device from which you may become separated.

4. Study the ocean before you enter; look for rocks, shorebreak, and rip current.

5. Duck or dive beneath breaking waves before they reach you.

6. Never swim against a strong current, swim across it.

7. Know your limits.

8. Small children should be allowed to play near or in the surf ONLY with close supervision and should wear flotation devices. And even then, only under extremely calm conditions. The protected pools at Lydgate and Salt Pond are safer alternatives.

9. When exploring tidal pools or reefs, always wear protective footwear and keep an eye on the ocean. Also, protect your hands.

10. When swimming around coral, be careful where you put your hands and feet. Urchin stings can be painful and coral cuts can be dangerous and you can also damage or injure the coral. Yes! Coral is living!!

11. Respect the yellow and red flag warnings when placed on the developed beaches. They are there to advise you of unsafe conditions.

12. Avoid swimming in the mouth of rivers or streams or in other areas of murky water.

Paradise Publications and the authors of this guide have endeavored to provide current and accurate information on Kaua'i's beautiful beaches. However, remember that nature is unpredictable and weather, beach, and current conditions can change. Enjoy your day at the beach, but utilize good judgment. Paradise Publications and the authors cannot be held responsible for accidents or injuries incurred.

Surface water temperature varies little with a mean temperature of 73.0 degrees Fahrenheit in January and 80.2 degrees in August. Minimum and maximum range from 68 to 84 degrees. This is an almost ideal temperature (refreshing, but not cold) for swimming and you will find most resort pools cooler than the ocean.

# *BEST BETS*

We would really like to be able to give you the definitive list of the best beaches on Kaua'i. Unfortunately, that is not possible. It will depend on seasons and ocean conditions. Remember, generally, that the south shore has better beach conditions in the winter and the North Shore has better conditions in the summer.

**BEST SNORKELING:**
Beginners - SOUTH SHORE: Po'ipu Beach
NORTH SHORE: 'Anini during calm surf
Intermediate - Makua Beach (Tunnels)

**BEST WINDSURFING:**
Beginners - 'Anini
Intermediate - Makua Beach (Tunnels) or Maha'ulepu

**BEST FOR CHILDREN:**
Lydgate Beach Park and Salt Ponds

**BEST FOR SWIMMING:**
Po'ipu and Salt Ponds

**BEST FOR SUNSETS:**
Ke'e Beach, Pakala Beach

**BEST FOR SUNRISES:**
Lydgate or Maha'ulepu

**BEST FOR TIDEPOOLS:**
Kealia Beach

**BEST FOR BEACHCOMBING:**
Wainiha, Nukole, Ka'aka'aniu, Waialkalua Iki, Kauapea, 'Anini, Kealia

The following beach index refers to a variety of beaches and beach parks. Some of them are not true beaches. For example, Spouting Horn is a beautiful beach location, but only for viewing and not for any aquatic activities. Be sure to read all the descriptions of the beaches, even those with which have no recreational activities, yet are accessible and beautiful Kaua'i destinations.

The stars ★ indicate beaches which are recommended for family activities. They are more protected and some have lifeguards on duty.

## *BEACH INDEX*

# *WESTERN SHORE*

## *Waimea, Kekaha, and Polihale*

### POLIHALE BEACH / BARKING SANDS BEACH

The Polihale State Park extends for five miles along the eastern shore and encompasses 140 acres. Large dunes are formed along the back of the beach that can reach up to 100 feet high. You'll know you have arrived at Barking Sands when you see the military installation. The Pacific Missile Range is operated by the Navy, but there are no state signs posted.

The Polihale State Park marks the southern end of the Napali. Dangerous surf conditions preclude swimming, etc. And be sure to bring shade with you, because you won't find much here!

More than 100 years ago, the sand from this area was studied at the California Academy of Sciences and it was discovered that it had small holes or "blind cavities." The resulting vibration of these unusual sand grains causes a sound that is said to be that of barking or singing when rubbed between the hands. Hence the name for this beach area.

We couldn't make it bark! What do you think? A similar anomaly occurs on one beach on O'ahu and another on Ni'ihau. A few other places in the world have sand with this remarkable skill. After you've tried making the sand bark, you might try searching the shoreline for the extremely small shells used in making the necklaces of Ni'ihau. The same currents that bring them ashore on Ni'ihau, also bring some to this stretch of coastline.

In the middle of the beach park, about 3.5 miles along the cane road, is an area cleared of coral. Named the Queen's Pond or the Queen's Bath it is reportedly named for Leilani, the queen of Kaua'i who bathed here. The legend has it that when a chief from O'ahu asked for her hand, a battle ensued between the O'ahu chief and the chief of Kaua'i. After the battle, Leilani was so distraught that she poisoned herself and turned into a seabird. They say you can still hear the groans of pain from this battle in the sand.

While you may see locals driving along the beach, this is not advisable. Not only will the rental car companies not be pleased should you become stuck, but there is also a plant unique to this area that is threatened by beach driving. The Ohai is an endangered beach plant found only in Hawai'i. On Kaua'i, the only place these 30 foot shrubs grow is at Polihale and officials fear that the damage caused by beach traffic is further endangering the survival of this species.

The *Polihale Heiau* is a four terraced temple found on the slopes above the beach, almost indistinguishable after the centuries of erosion. This *heiau* was sacred to Miru, the God of Po. It was said that the oceans below Polihale was the land of the dead. You can see the sculptured cliffs at the end of the beach.

In the early days the grass houses on this side of the island were all small and made of grass. There was one large living room and two doors on opposite sides. Eric Knudsen, an early pioneer on Kaua'i, recalled that his father was curious as to why all the houses were built with their gable-ends east and west and doors facing toward the mountains and towards the sea. The obvious reason might be for tradewinds to create cool breezes through the home, or perhaps for those wonderful ocean and mountain visits. However, when he questioned a fellow he was told, "Why, you know that Po, the abode of the dead, lies under the ocean just outside Polihale, where the cliffs and the ocean meet and the spirits of the dead must go there. As the spirits wander along on their way to Po, they will go around the gable-end of a house but if the house stood facing the other way, the spirits would walk straight through and it would be very disagreeable to have a spirit walk past you as you were eating your meal. In fact we can always tell when a battle has been fought by the number of spirits passing at the same time." And be sure to bring some shade with you, because you won't find much here!

*Recommended for:* An opportunity to experience the vast barking sands, picnics, a glimpse at the south end of the Napali, and a nice long drive!
*Facilities:* Picnic pavilions, showers, restrooms
*Access:* Follow the Kaumuali'i Highway at Mana to the end and then follow signs along the cane roads approximately five miles. There are no state signs posted, but some smaller, difficult to read signs might be noted along the way.
*Camping:* Camping is allowed, but permits from the state are required.

**KEKAHA BEACH**

This is a 15 mile stretch of coastline reaching from Kekaha to Polihale located on the western end of the town of Kekaha and along the Kaumuali'i Highway. Along the roadside the beachpark is attractive and includes facilities nearby. Several decades ago, this shoreline had severe erosion problems. In 1980 a seawall was constructed along the roadway. Strong rip currents are generated here during high surf that is particularly dangerous during winter and spring months. Surfers occasionally enjoy the surf at a couple of locations along this beachfront. If the wind is blowing up at Polihale, chances are you might find you can enjoy your picnic lunch with less sand in your sandwich here at Kekaha. Shorebreak and rip currents all year make this a dangerous beach for water activities. However, it is an excellent beach for sunsets or a picnic lunch.

*Recommended for:* Picnics, beach play, and sunsets
*Facilities:* Picnic pavilions, showers, restrooms
*Access:* Follow the Kaumuali'i Highway past Kekaha
*Camping:* No camping

**LUCY WRIGHT BEACH PARK**

Lucy Kapahu Aukai Wright was born August 20, 1873 in Anahola. She was a well-loved school teacher in Waimea for thirty five years until her death in 1931. This beach is dedicated to her memory. An earlier very notable visitor arrived at this beach site. Captain James Cook landed here on his arrival to the Sandwich Islands in January 1778. Because of the location of this beach on the west side near the mouth of the Waimea River, the beach collects assorted debris and the water is murky. It is not popular for sunbathers or swimmers, but you might see surfers offshore.

*Facilities:* Restrooms, showers, parking area, picnic tables at Waimea Pier
*Access:* On the Waimea side of the bridge over Waimea River, turn mauka on Lawa'i Rd. off Kaumuali'i Hwy. and follow to the park
*Camping:* By county permit on grassy area

**RUSSIAN FORT ELIZABETH HISTORICAL PARK**
On the east bank of the Waimea River is another of the Russian Forts built by Georg Anton Scheffer during the years of Russian trading on Kaua'i. Georg had his sights set on conquering the islands of Hawai'i in the name of Russia, but when the Kamehameha learned of this he was quickly expelled in 1817. This 17 acre site is now the Russian Fort Elizabeth State Historical Park.

*Facilities:* Restrooms and a pavilion with historical information

**PAKALA BEACH**
Great offshore waves make this a popular summer surfing spot. You might enjoy watching the surfers demonstrate their skills. A wonderful location to enjoy a Hawaiian sunset.

**SALT POND BEACH PARK**
The natural flats along this beach have been used by Hawaiians for generations. Today, this site continues to be used for traditional salt making. In late spring the wells or puna are cleaned and the salt making process runs through the summer months. Mother Nature has been kind enough to create a ridge of rock between the two rocky points at Salt Pond Beach, resulting in a large lagoon area that is fairly well protected, except during times of high surf. Popular for surfing and windsurfing as well. And, because of its protected swimming area, this is an ideal spot for families and children. A lifeguard is generally on duty.

*Recommended for:* Swimming and snorkeling most of the year, except during high surf. Popular for surfing and windsurfing as well
*Access:* From the Hwy. turn onto Lele Road, past the cemetery, turn right onto Lokokai St. From the Hwy. Lele Rd is marked Hwy. 543. You can also follow the signs to the animal shelter, which will get you almost to the beach.
*Facilities:* Picnic areas, BBQs, restrooms, rinse off showers, lifeguard
*Parking:* Paved parking area
*Camping:* With county permit

**HANAPEPE BEACH PARK**
The Hanapepe Beach Park has a picnic area, restrooms, showers, and parking, but is not recommended for beach activities.

**PORT ALLEN**
Port Allen has restroom facilities and boat launching. Hanapepe Bay is the second largest port on Kaua'i. Port Allen has little to offer in the way of a beach or beach activities. However you might enjoy stopping in at the Red Dirt Shirt Factory near the harbor. Also in the harbor are Target Drones warning that all stay away. (These are boats used for bombing practice!)

*Access:* In Ele'ele turn mauka off Kaumuali'i Hwy on Waialo Rd., follow it to the parking area at the boat launch

# *SOUTHERN SHORE*

## *Po'ipu, Koloa, Lawa'i and Kalaheo*

**SPOUTING HORN**

There are a number of places around the Hawaiian islands that have the perfect conditions to form a blow hole. The best displays at Spouting Horn are during high surf when the water and air rushing together make a fine display. The geyser can reach heights of 60 feet. As you'll note by the many cars, tour buses, and vendors booths, this is a popular visitor destination. There is no access to the ocean. "Do Not Enter" signs post the danger of being on the rocks should you attempt to descend down. The obvious danger is that you could be hit by a wave and pulled down. There is a legend about a sea monster which once lived in the area. Listening to the groaning sounds made by the water as it courses underneath the rocky ledge, you can imagine that there truly must be a dragon or other mythical creature sighing and moaning. The sound effect happens even without the hole blowing. Many years ago it was noted that the salt spray was damaging to the crops. So during one night, we were told, an unscrupulous fellow was sent to blow up the hole, widening it so that the force of the spray would be lessened.

*Recommended for:* Enjoying one of nature's wonders, a blow hole!
*Facilities:* Restrooms, vendors selling their wares
*Access:* Enter from Hwy 520, the road forks into Po'ipu Road on one side, Lawa'i Road on the other. From Lawa'i Road (also known as Spouting Horn Road) it is two miles and located along the roadside
*Parking:* Large paved parking area

**BEACH HOUSE PARK**

Located along side the road, this narrow beach is primarily usable only during low tide. Swimming and snorkeling can be good during low surf. The reef makes good snorkeling even for the beginner. This is a very, very small beachfront located right off the road, tucked between hotels and the restaurant with plenty of traffic going past. Not a very scenic or picturesque beach location.

*Recommended for:* Swimming and snorkeling during calm surf
*Facilities:* Restrooms, showers, and paved parking area across the road from the beach.
*Access:* Enter from Hwy. 520, the road forks into Po'ipu Road on one side and Lawa'i Road on the other (also known as Spouting Horn Road). It is not as far down as Spouting Horn and is located across from the Lawa'i Beach Resort

**PRINCE KUHIO PARK**
This beach park is dedicated to Prince Jonah Kuhio Kalaniana'ole. He was born in 1871 and in 1902 was elected to be a delegate to Congress, where he served until his death on January 7, 1922. He was known as the "People's Prince" because of his achievements for his Hawaiian people. You can see the foundation of Kuhio's parent's home, the royal fishpond, and *Hoai Heiau*, where the *kahuna* (priests) meditated and lived, and a sitting bench that faced the grounds.

***Prince Kuhio Park*** is located on Lawa'i Beach Road. Prince Kuhio was the youngest son of Kaua'i's chief David Kahalepouli Piikoli and the grandson of Kaumuali'i, the last King of Kaua'i. His aunt was Kapiolani and Prince Kuhio was adopted by Queen Kapiolani and grew up in the royal household in Honolulu. The monument at this park marks his birth site.

*Recommended for:* Swimming, snorkeling and sunning during low tide and calm seas. During high tide, it becomes just a park, with no beach!
*Facilities:* Public restrooms
*Parking:* Paved parking area

**KOLOA LANDING**
In the height of the early plantation days, Koloa Landing was the departure and arriving port for passenger and cargo vessels as well as whaling ships. Today Koloa Landing is a remnant of history, this old boat launch is now used as a departure for beach scuba dives. No facilities.

**PO'IPU BEACH** ★
This is the beach in front of the Kiahuna Plantation. Several nearby hotel resorts are still awaiting their future, three years following Iniki. This beach also suffered heavily from Hurricane Iniki and has not returned to its finest form. Still, it is good snorkeling as a result of the offshore reef. Boogie boarding is popular here and you might see surfers riding the waves farther out. Windsurfers enjoy this site as well. Dangerous water conditions during high surf.

*Recommended for:* Snorkeling and swimming during calm seas, stay inside the reef area
*Access:* The east end of Ho'onani Road
*Facilities:* Only a rinse-off shower, lifeguards sometimes on duty

**WAI'OHAI BEACH**
This beach was the site of the Knudsen home until construction began on the Wai'ohai Resort in 1962. Vlademar Knudsen was the son of the premier of Norway, who first went to California and made a fortune in the gold rush before relocating to Kaua'i and making a second fortune as founder of Kekaha Sugar Company.

Anne Sinclair was the daughter of Elizabeth Sinclair, none other than the same lady who purchased the island of Ni'ihau in 1864. Anne Sinclair and Vlademar Knudsen married in later years. The site on Wai'ohai was selected by Anne Knudsen for her beach house. This is actually a part of Po'ipu Beach.

*Recommended for:* This sandy beach is good for surfing, swimming, and snorkeling during calm seas. High surf generates dangerous conditions
*Access:* No real access until the old Stouffer's (soon-to-be Marriott) reopens. Can be reached from adjoining beach
*Facilities:* Only those found at nearby Po'ipu Beach Park
*Parking:* Dirt parking lot next to Brennecke's

**PO'IPU BEACH PARK ★**

Po'ipu Beach Park is a four acre stretch of land fronting the eastern section of Po'ipu Beach as well as Brennecke's Beach. In the spring of 1997, the popular Po'ipu Beach park was restored. New pavilions, comfort stations, sidewalks and showers were installed. This park has been the center-piece of the Po'ipu Beach resort area for decades, but most of its facilities were wiped out by Hurricane Iniki.

Popular for families with young children and novice swimmers there is one section of the park that is particularly safe. In this area an offshore reef provides substantial protection to the shoreline. Another benefit is that a lifeguard is on duty seven days a week. This site is also popular with surfers, swimmers and snorkelers. Snorkeling around the right side of Nukumoi Point is very good. The beach is protected by Nukumoi Point and a shorebreak on the east. Bodyboarders are attracted to the waves offshore. High surf can occur April through September.

Here you will find another one of Hawai'i's eight tombolos. Without knowing it was something special, you probably wouldn't have noticed it at all. This is a strip of sand which connects two pieces of land. There are only eight tombolos in all of Hawai'i. On the rocky volcanic shore to the east be on the lookout for green sea turtles frolicking in the waves.

*Recommended for:* Swimming and snorkeling during calm seas
*Access:* Turn mauka off Po'ipu Rd. then west onto Ho'owili Rd
*Facilities:* Restrooms, rinse off showers, lifeguard, playground
*Parking:* Paved parking area

**BRENNECKE BEACH**

Hurricane Iwa in 1982 changed the configuration of this beach and Iniki did further damage. The shorebreak onto the rocks with little beachfront remaining can be hazardous to the boogie boarder. At one time this beach was so popular for sunbathing that it was called Bikini Beach and it offered what was considered by many to be the best body surfing on Kaua'i. In an effort to give Mother Nature a little hand in the restoration of this beach, Kaua'i residents have obtained a county permit to dump sand on the beach above the high water mark. It is hoped that this will help the beach to begin the slow restoration process a bit more quickly. Resort and community groups have begun donating funds toward the purchase of sand. Brennecke's Beach Center rents beach equipment.

**KEONELOA BEACH (SHIPWRECK BEACH)**

This sandy shore fronts the Hyatt Regency. Keoneloa and Maha'ulepu are a part of the same beach. It is commonly referred to as Shipwreck Beach for the long-gone ship that ran aground years ago. Hurricane Iwa took away the remains of the wreck, but the motor may still be occasionally visible. A good spot to watch surfers and windsurfers, but swimming, even during calm seas, may not be advised. The Hyatt does erect flags to indicate the condition of the surf, but still use your own good judgment.

*Recommended for:* Sunning, watching the windsurfers and surfers
*Access:* A road runs between the Po'ipu Bay Resort Golf Course and the Hyatt
*Facilities:* Public restrooms, shower facilities for Hyatt guests
*Parking:* Paved parking area at bottom

**MAHA'ULEPU BEACH**

It was here that King Kamehameha I made his attempt to conquer the island of Kaua'i in 1796. Unfortunately, a storm forced a retreat, but the advance forces of Kamehameha's troops arrived on the island unaware of the order to retreat and were quickly killed. This is also the beach site where George C. Scott portrayed Ernest Hemingway in the movie *Islands in the Stream.* Maha'ulepu Beach is actually a collection of smaller beaches. They offer a diverse assortment of aquatic activities including fishing, surfing, bodyboarding, body surfing, kayaking, windsurfing, snorkeling, and swimming. The three areas along this beachfront are Gillin's Beach, Kawailoa Bay, and Ha'ula Beach. Gillin's was named for the supervisor of Grove Farm Company, Elbert Gillin, who arrived in the islands in 1912. He relocated to Kaua'i in 1925 and built his home at this beach. He was the supervisor of the Ha'upu Range Tunnel. Following two hurricanes, all that remained was Gillin's chimney, but the house has since been rebuilt. Several feet below this beach are the Rainbow Petroglyphs. Discovered in January of 1980 when a severe storm took out as much as six feet of beachfront, the petrogylphs were suddenly exposed. Working in reverse, the sea soon chose to cover them up once again. Currents at Kawailoa Bay make it unsafe for swimming or snorkeling. To reach Ha'ula Beach you may park on the east side of Pa'o'o Point and travel to the shore by trail. This area is the south shore's most dangerous beach.

*Recommended for:* The first beach, Gillin's, on occasion may be good for the experienced snorkeler during calm surf. Ha'ula Beach, is on private land and tends to be less crowded. If you would like information getting permission to fish, phone the Grove Farm Office at (808) 245-3678.
*Access:* Daylight hours only, sunrise to sunset. The gate is located at night. No overnight camping is permitted. This is private property owned by the Grove Farm Company which allows public day time use. Since access could be denied at any time, it is requested that you take all your litter with you and be respectful of the right to use these gorgeous beaches of Kaua'i. Take the dirt road at the end of Po'ipu Road and turn right onto the cane road.
*Facilities:* None
*Parking:* On the side of the road

# *EASTERN SHORE*

## *Nawiliwili, Lihu'e, Wailua, Kapa'a*

### KALAPAKI BEACH

This site is of historic significance in surfing history as the location where ancient Hawaiians practiced the skill of bodysurfing. The wave conditions continue to attract surfers and body surfers and the gentle off-shore slope makes it a good option for swimmers during calm seas. During periods of high surf, surfers come out in droves. However, we advise that you leave the high surf to the experienced surfers.

William Harrison Rice and Mary Sophia Rice, arrived on Kaua'i as missionaries in 1841. Their son William Hyde Rice purchased the land around this beach from Princess Ruth Ke'elikolani and here he built his home. Later, the Kaua'i Surf Hotel was built on this wonderful beachfront. In 1987 Amfac sold 175 acres and leased an additional 208 acres to Hemmeter-VMS Kaua'i Company. The result was the Westin Kaua'i Resort with an architectural style that some found outrageous, but most thought was garish. Hurricane Iniki virtually destroyed the resort and while the lagoons opened the next year, the hotel sat empty for more than two years. Marriott picked up the option and in 1994 began renovating the property into a blend of hotel and timeshare condominiums. With the large town of Lihu'e nearby and the close proximity to the Marriott Resort, you are likely to find this beach more populated than most. This beach is better protected than some, except during east swells, but caution is advised at all times.

*Recommended for:* Swimming, windsurfing, and bodyboarding during low surf conditions
*Access:* Beach access is at the left side of the bay or through the Nawiliwili Park public access on the right.
*Parking:* Public parking area at the west end next to the stream which enters this bay
*Facilities:* BBQ grills, restrooms, rinse-off showers.

### NININI BEACH

There are two beaches located here. Both can be affected by high surf and Kona storms. Snorkeling at the larger sandy stretch can be good when the ocean is calm. During high surf enjoy the bodysurfers. Sometimes it is referred to as Running Waters Beach because of the irrigation runoff that once occurred here. Nearby you'll see the Nawiliwili Light Station located at the point. This area is popular with shore fishermen catching reef fish.

*Recommended for:* Snorkeling on calm days (only for the experienced)
*Access:* Turn at Ahukini Rd. follow the dirt road 2.6 miles to Ninini Point
*Parking:* No parking

**HANAMA'ULU BEACH PARK**

A lovely picnic location, however, the bay waters are murky. The *Beaches of Kaua'i* by John Clark notes that, "Hanama'ulu Stream crosses the southern end of the beach, discharging its silt-laden waters into the bay." He also adds that "mullet and sharks, particularly juvenile hammerheads, are also found in the bay." Facilities include tables, toilets, pavilion, barbecue, and showers in this 6.5 acre park. Camping is permitted at this county park under the trees in self-contained mobile campers or tents. A lovely location for a daytime picnic, this isn't a safe park to visit after dark.

*Recommended for:* Picnics
*Access:* Located 1/2 mile from Hanama'ulu Town.
*Parking:* Plenty available

**NUKOLE**

Nukole means "beach of the kole fish," and is the proper Hawaiian name. This beach stretches from Hanama'ulu Bay to Lydgate Park for approximately two miles. It is often referred to as Nukolii, after a dairy that once had cattle grazing in the area. Archeological events suggest that prior to that there was a Hawaiian settlement. The Outrigger Kaua'i Beach, located on this beachfront, maintains the public beach park pavilion and adjoining bathrooms. You may see local residents trying their hand at fishing, surfing and even diving on this beachfront. Swimming and snorkeling are not recommended at any time of the year.

*Recommended for:* Sunbathing, beachcombing, and sunrises
*Access:* Turn mauka on Kaua'i Beach Drive, which leads to the Outrigger Hotel to reach the southern portion of the beach
*Parking:* Parking area for about five cars
*Facilities:* A county park with the pavilion, rinse off showers and restrooms maintained by the Outrigger Hotel

**LYDGATE BEACH ★**

This forty acre "state" park is dedicated to Reverend John Lydgate, who, more than a century ago founded the Lihu'e Union Church and was a force in the establishment of public parks and historic sites on Kaua'i. Wailua was once the home of the island's royalty. The banks of the Wailua River were a sacred area in ancient Hawai'i and a favored dwelling place reserved for the kings and high chiefs of Kaua'i. Near the mouth of the river in Lydgate Park are the remains of a *heiau* that was a place of refuge for those who had broken a taboo. Two large pieces of smooth stone (where women of royal blood or high chiefly rank gave birth) are located on the river's North Shore. Nearby is *Holoholoku Heiau*, believed to be the oldest *heiau* on Kaua'i. About 25 years ago the breakwater was added which created two protected pools, ideal for swimming. The pools have a sandy bottom. Plan on bringing along some bread to feed the fish. Generally there is a lifeguard on duty. You may see windsurfers at this beach during south or Kona winds. While this is called a state park, it is actually maintained by the county.

*Recommended for:* Swimming for adults and children within the protected pools. Not advised beyond the pools. Good location for beginning snorkelers to try out their skills.
*Access:* South of the Wailua River turn mauka on Leho Drive, then continue mauka on Nalu Rd. If you are heading North, the turn off is easy to spot, heading south there is no marked entrance. Heading north it is just past the Wailua Golf Course, heading south, if you get to the golf course, you've missed it!
*Parking:* Large parking area
*Facilities:* Restrooms, rinse off showers, BBQs, picnic pavilions, wonderful playground for kids! Lifeguard may be on duty.
*Camping:* Permits for camping available from the county

**WAILUA BEACH**
A half-mile stretch of beach from the Wailua River north. It is located across the Highway from the Coco Palms Resort (which in 1999 had still not reopened since Iniki) and is the beach which fronts the Lae nani condominiums. *The Beaches of Kaua'i* by John R.K. Clark explains that the surfers shorebreak is called Horners, named after Albert Horner, a pineapple industry pioneer. His mansion was built on this beachfront in 1929 and was later moved by new owners Mel and Pauline Venture to an inland location in Wailua. Dangerous currents much of the year make this beach advisable only for walking and sunning. There are lots of resorts located along here and Al & Don's restaurant has a nice oceanview location. There is one small protected pool at Alakukui Point, which during calm surf is safe for wading. Also at Alakukui Point are some remnants of an old *heiau*.

*Recommended for:* Beachcombing, walking, sunning
*Access:* All along from Lydgate to River to Kapa'a
*Parking:* Parking area near Wailua Bridge and limited parking on Papaloa Rd.
*Facilities:* Phones

**WAIPOULI BEACH**
This narrow strip of beach runs from the Coconut Plantation Resort to the Waika'ea Canal in Kapa'a. The Kaua'i Coconut Beach Resort is located on this beachfront. While the pedestrian trail among the ironwood trees above the shoreline is popular for joggers or walkers, the beachfront is covered by beach-rock and very strong offshore currents make it unsafe for swimming year round. Some marginal swimming might be pursued at the southern end of the beach, but even then, only under very calm surf conditions. A popular fishing location.

*Recommended for:* Swimming is marginal in the summer months
*Facilities:* Only for hotel guests

**KAPA'A BEACH PARK**
With its location nearer to civilization and the adjoining canal used as a boat launch, you are likely to find this beach more populated. Kapa'a Beach has encountered severe shoreline erosion over the last 30 years. You'll note that some human measures have been made to stop the erosion, such as jetties at the mouth of the canal. In the evening you might want to stroll down the beach (on a moonlit night) and perhaps you'll be lucky enough to see fishermen practicing *lamalama* (torch fishing).

*Recommended for:* A few areas of the beach offer adequate swimming when the surf is calm, but not especially recommended. Shore fishing is popular here. Great sunrises!
*Access:* Turn toward the ocean off Kuhio Hwy. at Niu Street, near the Kapa'a ballpark
*Parking:* Parking area
*Facilities:* Restrooms, rinse off showers, public swimming pool

**KEALIA BEACH**
Once the town of Kealia was a thriving plantation town, complete with a train depot, and at the nearby landing an inter-island steamer would stop for passengers. Today it is not much more than a stretch along the highway. The word Kealia means "salt encrusted." (Interesting to note that almost every Hawaiian island has a beach named Kealia!)

*Recommended for:* Tidepools during low tide, strong rip currents make it unsafe for water activities, particularly dangerous during high surf.
*Access:* Hwy. 56 at mile marker 10
*Parking:* Parking along the roadside
*Facilities:* None
*Camping:* No

**DONKEY BEACH**
This is one of the few beaches for which we could find no Hawaiian name. Apparently before the advent of machinery, mules were used to haul cane seed to the fields. Some say that there were only mules and no donkeys at all, but whichever the case, the name Donkey Beach stuck. Located 1 1/2 miles from Kealia Beach, it is a very pastoral setting. Here you will find a popular body and board surfing location, however high surf in winter and spring months can create dangerous rip currents and shorebreaks. There is no public access to this beach, but beachgoers, oblivious to the "No Trespassing" sign continue to find this beach. Its inaccessibility has made this beach the site for nude sunbathing. Nude sunbathing is not legal in Hawai'i and periodic arrests are made. During 1999 local residents hired "security guards" to dissuade nude sunbathing.

*Recommended for:* Fishing
*Access:* There is no public access
*Parking:* Only along the road at mile marker 11
*Facilities:* None

**ANAHOLA BEACH and 'ALIOMANU BEACH**
This is a popular park during the summer for local residents. There is a reef and pockets of sand that create pools that are pleasant for the kids. Anahola Stream is found at the north end of the beach. 'Aliomanu Beach is at the north side of Anahola Beach. Both are located on Anahola Bay. It is widely used by fishermen and *limu kohu*, a popular seaweed is harvested here.

*Recommended for:* Fishing, picnics, swimming (watch for currents)
*Access:* Hwy. 56, look for Anahola Road
*Parking:* parking lot
*Facilities:* Picnic tables, rest rooms, rinse off showers, camping

# *NORTHERN SHORE*

## *Hanalei, Kilauea, and Princeville*

**MOLOA'A**

This is as pristine a bay as you may find on Kaua'i. If you happened to catch the lone airing of the pilot episode of *Gilligan's Island* a few years back on Fox television, you might recognize this bay. (If you want to see this episode, we recommend taking the Hawai'i Movie Tour!) This was also the filming location for *Castaway Cowboys* with James Garner. While this bay can be especially dangerous during winter and spring surf, anytime there is high surf dangerous ocean conditions and powerful rip currents can occur. During periods of calm, you can enjoy swimming, snorkeling, and diving here. We understand there is a hiking trail along the cliff on the left of the bay. We haven't investigated.

*Recommended for:* Snorkeling and swimming only during periods of calm
*Access:* Just past mike marker 16 on Kuhio Highway as you head toward Princeville. Turn right on Ko'olau Road, then turn right again onto Moloa'a Road. At the fork in the road, keep to the left following along the road in front of private residences to the public access trail. Parking is limited in front of these homes, so please respect their privacy and "No Trespassing."

**KA'AKA'ANIU BEACH (LARSEN'S BEACH)**

L. David Larsen, a Swedish born plant pathologist, arrived in Hawai'i in 1908 and later managed the Kilauea Sugar Plantation. This beach was named for the site upon which he built his home. Dangerous rip currents and a shallow rocky shore make this unappealing for swimmers. The offshore reef is a popular location for the harvesting of *limu kohu*, a type of seaweed. During times of low tide you may see the harvesters at work or net throwers catching fish. The county access, purchased in 1979, was sold under the condition that the access not continue all the way to the beach. This was done in hopes of making the beach less attractive and therefore less populated, so it will take a little bit of effort to reach this sandy crescent. Once you reach the head of the path, it will take you less than 10 minutes to walk down to the beachfront.

*Recommended for:* Beachcombing, watching seaweed being harvested, fishing
*Access:* 1.2 miles from the north intersection of Ko'olau Rd and Kuhio Hwy. there is a public access. A 5-10 minute hike to reach the shoreline.

**WAIALKALUA IKI BEACH**

Dangerous rip currents at Waialkalua Iki make it a lovely spot to visit, and a popular fishing location, but inadvisable for water activities. In 1911 on the hill overlooking the ocean, a *heiau* was discovered. There is a trail from the valley up to this archeological site. The twin beach, Waiakalua Nui is just slightly east and is covered with beach rock.

*Recommended for:* Beachcombing
*Access:* Near the end of North Waiakalua Rd. is a public access to the shoreline down a steep trail that requires a 5-10 minute walk
*Facilities:* This is a private beach so there are no facilities and no public parking

## KILAUEA POINT NATIONAL WILDLIFE REFUGE

The Kilauea Point National Wildlife Refuge was established in 1974. The acquisition of land has continued ever since and this sanctuary now encompasses 203 acres. The refuge was struck hard by Hurricane Iniki. Not only was there much damage to the birdlife and vegetation, but the famous lighthouse was also seriously affected. At Kilauea Point, they reported that about 80% of the native plants suffered damage. On Crater Hill, at least 25% were lost and an additional 50% damaged. Mokolea Point vegetation suffered little damage. Kilauea Point lost the most birds and suffered the worst damage to the habitat. The Kaua'i Natural Wildlife Refuge complex lost 12 of their 20 buildings. There was also damage to the lighthouse visitor center and bookstore, storage buildings, fences, and the water delivery system. There are only eight tombolos within the Hawaiian islands and one example may be found here at Kilauea Point. A tombolo is not an unusual musical instrument or an Italian sausage, but rather an unusual beach condition. This is a strip of sand (or sandbar) connects two pieces of land - the shoreline to an island, for example. You can view it at the base of Makapili Rock where it connects the rock to the shoreline. Construction began on the 52 foot lighthouse in 1912 and it was not until 1976 that it was put out of commission. Admission is $2. KPNHA (Kilauea Point Natural History Association) is a non-profit corporation dedicated to environmental interpretation, education, protection, and enhancement. Membership information can be obtained by writing: KPNHA, PO Box 87, Kilauea, HI 96754. (808) 828-1413. Open 10 am-4 pm. closed some Federal Holidays.
*Access:* Turn off Kuhio Hwy. where the large sign indicates Kilauea Lighthouse
*Facilities:* Bookstore, restrooms, visitor center, charge for admission
*Parking:* Large paved parking area

## KAUAPEA BEACH (SECRET BEACH)

This 3,000 foot long beach lies between Kalihiwai Bay and Kilauea Point. It's access is a little tricky given that you cannot see the beach from the highway and the access is not clearly marked. The beautiful people of the 1960's referred to it as Secret Beach, and it is still called this today. Dangerous water conditions due to winter and spring high surf make water activities during these times ill advised. During calmer summer months, you may find a wide variety of beach activities including surfing, bodysurfing, and bodyboarding. There is a fresh water stream and you can see whales in the winter; dolphins in the summer. Again, possibly because of inaccessibility, you should be advised that nude sunbathing does occur at this beach site. Remember that nude sunbathing is not legal in Hawai'i and periodic arrests are made. From this beach you can see Moku'ale'ale Island, a bird sanctuary and part of the Kilauea Refuge.

*Recommended for:* Beachcombing, bodysurfing, or bodyboarding during summer periods of low surf.
*Access:* One-half mile west of Kilaueau, from the Kuhio Hwy., turn onto Kalihiwai Road which dog legs to the left. Off to the right is a dirt road with an embankment on either side. Travel down the road and there is a parking lot. Then take the trail leading to the beach. The trail down to the beach requires a 10 minute hike.
*Facilities:* None
*Parking:* Parking area along the roadside.

**KALIHIWAI BEACH**
This crescent of white sand is fringed with ironwood trees. You'll see board-surfing in the summer. Dangerous during the winter, so stay out of the water and just watch the surfers. Stay away from the mouth of the river, where rip currents may occur. Kayaking up the river can be done except during heavy rains or flooding.

*Recommended for:* Body surfing, swimming, and snorkeling only on calm summer days, fishing
*Access:* Take the Kalihiwai Road (eastern exit)
*Facilities:* Picnic tables
*Parking:* At the beach under the ironwood trees

**'ANINI BEACH PARK**
Apparently this beach was called Wanini, but sometime during the years, it was abbreviated. (One story tells that the "W" just fell off the sign, so they changed the name of the beach rather than repairing the beach sign.) With a two mile offshore reef, this beach is popular for varied types of fishing (pole, spear, throw-net) and also seaweed harvesting. Snorkeling, windsurfing, beachcombing, reef walking, and boating are also to be found here. Water conditions are very dangerous during high surf which causes strong rip currents. Many drownings and near drownings have occurred here over the years. This beachfront was the location for several scenes in *Honeymoon in Vegas.* You can see the top of the blue tile roof from the road near 'Anini Beach Park.

*Recommended for:* Windsurfing, swimming only during very calm summer surf. Stay away from the west end of the beach where there is a channel. Snorkeling can be good here during the summer. Stay inside the reef, same with swimming.
*Access:* Follow Kuhio Highway to Kalihiwai Road and take Anini Road to the beach
*Facilities:* Picnic facilities, showers, restrooms
*Parking:* Long stretch of grass for parking with an open area next to it for boats and trailers
*Camping:* With county permit

**PRINCEVILLE**
Princeville is a 2,000 acre tract of land lying between Hanalei Bay and 'Anini Beach. The resort development began in 1968 and is composed of condominiums, private homes, and several hotels. Most of the development sits along the bluffs with only four small beaches. One is located below the Sealodge condominiums, another below the Pali Ke Kua condominiums, and a third below Pu'u Poa which is sometimes called Hideaways (actually just a separate section of this same beach, but located on the other side of a cliff). The fourth is at the base of the Princeville Resort. There are several accesses to the Princeville shoreline. Seven accesses are available through the Hanalei Bay Resort. None of these beaches are safe for winter time water activities. The Princeville Hotel Resort is located on the hill called Pu'u Poa. Below is the Pu'u Poa Beach which stretches about 1,200 ft. between the resort and the mouth of the Hanalei River. Only during calm summer surf will you find an opportunity to snorkel amid the reef. Pu'u Poa is the best of the three Princeville beaches. Kayaks can be rented at the Beach Activities Center at the Princeville Hotel Resort to explore the river. Public access to some beaches on Kaua'i is via private property. You can use the access, but you are responsible for any liability.

*Access to Pu'u Poa Beach:* Below the Princeville Hotel. Swimming and snorkeling only during calm summer months at Pu'u Poa Beach. Limited swimming and snorkeling at Kenomene and Kaweonui Beaches during calm surf in summer months. Some parking for beach guests at the Princeville Hotel.

*Access to Kaweonui Beach (at Sealodge condominiums):* The trail starts at the west end of the Sealodge parking lot. A hike of 10-15 minutes down a very steep goat-like trail is required to reach the shoreline. Please be aware that this trail is very dangerous and slippery and it remains muddy even when it is not raining. Use it strictly at your own risk. No facilities.

*Access to Kenomene Beach (at Pali Ke Kua condominiums):* Just before the gate at the Princeville Hotel there is a path down to the beach. This beach is also know as Hideaways. It will take a 5-10 minute walk down the stairs and trail to reach this beach. Guests of Pali Ke Kua have a private trail to another (separate) part of Kenomene Beach. No facilities.

**HANALEI BAY**
The Hanalei Bay begins its two mile sandy stretch at Pu'u Poa and ends at the Makahoa Point toward the west. A small number of beaches and beach parks line this area, including Black Pot Beach, Hanalei Beach Park, Waikoko Beach, and Wai'oli Beach Park. There are three parking areas. The Pier located here was actually condemned before Hurricane Iniki and has since been rebuilt.
*Access:* Turn right on Aku road and another right turn on Weke Road

**BLACK POT BEACH**
One of the few Kaua'i beaches with no true Hawaiian name, this site was dubbed "Black Pot" for the huge cooking pot that was shared by fishermen. Black Pot Beach Park is located where the Hanalei River meets the ocean on the eastern end of the bay. A popular site for local residents to gather, their furor was raised when, in late 1967, it was announced by new owners of the property that they planed to build a condominium. In 1973 it was sold to the county.

*Recommended for:* Swimming, bodyboarding, surfing, windsurfing, and kayaking during calm summer surf
*Parking:* Parking only along the bay on Weke Road
*Facilities:* Restrooms, showers, lifeguard on duty seasonally
*Camping:* With county permits

**HANALEI PAVILION BEACH PARK**
Hanalei means "lei shaped." The Hanalei Pier, is a scenic location, and one you'll no doubt remember if you saw the movie *South Pacific*. The wooden pier was constructed in 1892 and then 30 years later was reinforced with concrete. It was used by the local farmers for shipping their rice crops to market until it was closed in 1933. In 1979 the pier joined other landmarks in the National Register of Historic Places. A lifeguard is sometimes on duty at Hanalei Beach Park during busy weekends. The beach can be calm and serene during low summer surf, but extremely treacherous during winter and spring high surf.

*Recommended for:* Picnics anytime, summertime swimming
*Access:* Turn right on Aku Road, and a second right onto Weke Road
*Facilities:* Picnic tables and restrooms. Lifeguard at the Hanalei Bay Beach.
*Parking:* Areas of compacted sand are located for parking at various intervals along the beach

**WAIKOKO**
Waikiko, which means "blood waters," is the last of the beaches along Hanalei Bay. It offers an offshore reef, making this narrow beach a good place for children to swim. The offshore water is very shallow, in fact, too shallow for most adults.

*Recommended for:* Snorkeling during calm seas and good swimming for children in the shallow, reef protected ocean. During times of high surf you can enjoy watching surfers on the outer edge of the Waikoko Reef.
*Access:* Located along Highway 56, a half mile past mile marker 4
*Facilities:* None
*Parking:* Along side the road

**LUMAHA'I BEACH**
This beach is tucked beneath some lush cliffs and became famous for a well known scene in the 1957 film *South Pacific*. Actually, it was the eastern end of this beach, which has a separate name, Kahalahala (which means pandanus trees), where Mitzi Gaynor filmed her famous "wash that man right out of my hair" scene. A more scenic stretch of beach is hard to imagine. Unfortunately, this is one particularly dangerous stretch of coastline. The width of Lumaha'i Beach is said to vary as much as 360 feet with the seasonal movement of the sand from one end to the other. With the steep shore comes the danger of high surf, dangerous shorebreak and strong currents. There is no protective reef, so the ocean drops off very quickly. The nearby Lumaha'i River may rise dramatically as a result of flash floods. This, in combination with the danger of rough waves, makes even wading along the shore not advisable. You may see body or boardsurfers enjoying this beach, but when the surf becomes even slightly rough, you'll see that even the experts stay out of the waters. With the danger of rogue waves, most common during high surf, again, even wading is not recommended.

You may have heard of *o'opu*, a unique freshwater fish which spends its first few months in the sea before returning to the freshwater stream. They have adapted well to their surroundings by using their lower front fins as a suction cup to hold onto rocks, even those extremely steep rock walls which form waterfalls. Using its tail to propel themselves, the *o'opu* travels slowly upstream. The adults come down the Lumaha'i stream (and others on Kaua'i) in late summer and fall, spawn and then the young head for the ocean. The young (larvae) mature into juveniles called *hinana* and return to their freshwater origins and migrate upstream. These interesting marine creatures are found nowhere beyond Hawai'i and are highly valued for their meat.

*Recommended for:* Enjoying the view, and an outstanding photo opportunity at the 5 mile marker post or at several other small pullouts along the road. Swimming is safe at Kahalahala only on the VERY calmest of summer days.
*Access:* Along the Highway at 4 mile marker before the bridge and parking along the 6 mile marker nearer the river
*Facilities:* None
*Parking:* Very limited along the roadside

**WAINIHA BEACH PARK**
The term Wainiha means "unfriendly." This wide beach has no reef, so it is completely unprotected from the open ocean. High surf, therefore, creates very dangerous conditions as a result of rip currents and shorebreaks. Numerous drownings and near-drownings have been reported here. The water is murky as a result of the Wainiha stream and not recommended for any water activities. The stream cuts back into the valley reaching the Wai'ale'ale Crater. Given the heavy rainfall that comes down from the crater, unexpected flash floods can and do occur in the stream. Hence, swimming here is not advisable. Since there is no protecting reef, beachcombing on the dry sandy shore can be good!

A few miles beyond is Powerhouse Road, the turn0off to climb inland through the valley. The road travels through some beautiful, not-to-be missed scenery and ends at the Powerhouse. Built in 1906 it served to provide irrigation for the McBryde Sugar Company. Where the road ends, the trail begins: a hiking trail known as the Powerhouse Trail.

*Recommended for:* Beachcombing
*Facilities:* No facilities
*Parking:* Off road parking only, near mile marker 7

**KEPUHI BEACH**
You may, perhaps, be thinking that you are seeing double. Yes, there is also a Kepuhi Beach on the south shore. This North Shore stretch of beach is actually three beaches: *Wainiha Ku'au Beach*, *Kaonohi Beach*, and *Kanaha Beach*. There is a series of reefs which make this area popular for throw netting. The beach point at Kaonohi is the location of the YMCA Camp Naue. These beaches frequently have strong currents that are especially dangerous during high surf. Not recommended for water activities except on very calm days. Again, the high surf and dangerous currents have caused many drownings and near-drownings over the years.

*Recommended for:* Summertime swimming on days of calm surf
*Access:* Along highway 56 there is access on Alamo'o Road and Alealea Road, just before mile marker 8
*Facilities:* None
*Parking:* Parking off road among the ironwood trees

**MAKUA BEACH (TUNNELS BEACH)**
You are not likely to find most people referring to this stretch of beach by its Hawaiian name. This popular beach is better known as "Tunnels Beach" and named for the underwater caves here. Located on Ha'ena Point, it is one of the more popular beach sites on the northern shore of Kaua'i. While the shoreline has much beachrock (making it less attractive to swimmers) the offshore reef offers good snorkeling during calm surf.

During the spring and winter time high surf, there are very strong rip currents at Makua Beach. Even during low surf, the current offshore can be treacherous. During high surf this beach is a popular surfing spot, but only for the expert. The surf break on the outer reef is often referred to as Tunnels. You may also see fishermen using spears or nets along the reef.

You may recognize this beach as the major location for the television mini-series *The Thorn Birds.*

*Recommended for:* Watching windsurfing and boardsurfing, swimming and snorkeling during periods of low and calm sea, and beachcombing during high seas. Very dangerous during winter months.
*Access:* Two public accesses, one at the east side of Ha'ena Point, the other to the west. You'll find the first at .3 miles past mile marker 8 on Hwy. 560 and the second 1/2 mile past the same marker.
*Facilities:* None
*Parking:* Limited parking off Kuhio Hwy.

**HA'ENA BEACH PARK**
This is a five acre park maintained by the County of Kaua'i. In past times, this beach (then called Maniniolo which means "traveling manini fish") was a *hukilau* site where fishermen would come and throw their nets out into the sea and pull their catch onto shore. This is different from net fishing which you might see done by a single fisherman. (Today the *hukilau* style of fishing is never done - except at local luaus! You are probably familiar with the *Hukilau* song and hula that are often performed.)

The foreshore here is steep. The resulting shorebreak is dangerous and makes it unsafe for swimming or bodysurfing. Although you may see some bodysurfing done here, it is not for the novice.

Across the road from Ha'ena Beach Park is ***Maninolo Dry Cave***. This lava tube was a sea cave in earlier centuries when the sea was higher. You can follow the tube several hundred yards and emerge at the other end. We were told that the cave was larger before it was filled in with sand by the tsunami that hit the island in 1957.

Following another 2/10 of a mile past Ha'ena State Park and just beyond Limahuli Steam are the ***Waikapala'e Wet Caves,*** accessible by a short hike up and behind the gravel parking area. One of the caves has a fresh water pool which is a unique phenomenon. The Waikapala'e (the modern translation means water of the lace fern) Wet Cave has a cool shady cave known as the blue room. In the past it required a venture into the chilly waters and and a swim through a submerged tunnel. This area, however, is posted as no swimming due to the dangers of this. Apparently the reflection of the light through the tunnel causes the incredible blue effect on the cavern walls. Besides being posted as no swimming, it is also posted that the freshwater, as is the case in all freshwater pools, can be contaminated. Leptospirosis is a viral disease spread by the urine of infected wild animals passed through the soil and into the water system. Symptoms can be severe and include fever, headache, chills, body aches and may not reveal themselves for several weeks after being infected with the virus.
*Recommended for:* Swimming and snorkeling in the summer with calm surf, particularly dangerous during winter months.
*Access:* Located on the Wainiha side of Ha'ena
*Facilities:* Restrooms, showers, picnic pavilions
*Camping:* Permits available from the county
*Parking:* Parking along the roadside

**HA'ENA STATE PARK and KE'E BEACH**
Highway 56 goes as far as this beach before it ends. This is the beginning of the Napali Coast and Napali Coast State Park, which is only accessible by boat or by hiking trail. Swimming here is only advisable during very calm conditions. The 230 acres of Ha'ena State Park include a number of ancient archeological sites. Remnants of ancient Hawaiian villages and the *Kaulu o Laka Heiau* can be found here. This sacred altar is set along a series of tiers on the cliffs of Napali and was built for Laka, the goddess of hula. It is one of the dramatic sites on the island with views of the cliffs and ocean. The *heiau* is still used today by hula halaus.

John Clark's guide to the beaches of Kaua'i tells the story of the Taylor Camp, which was populated by over 100 flower children during the 1960's and 1970's. Howard Taylor, who happens to be the brother of Elizabeth Taylor, offered refuge at his seven acre property for their "hippie" community when they were evicted from a public beach park and threatened with jail time. (Apparently the commune members shared a communal shower and one open air toilet.) If you're over 40 years old, you may remember the *puka* shell fad. It began when these hippies gathered shells, made holes in the center (*puka* means hole) and strung them to make necklaces. Elizabeth Taylor, donning one of these necklaces (a gift from her brother), created a craze which virtually wiped out all of the shells on all the beaches in Hawaii. Great story, eh! Comb the beach for your own shells and you'll have a little piece of this legend. Now back to the hippies who continued to run free and naked, pile trash (to the point of seriously polluting the ocean), and then turned to the cultivation of marijuana for their income -- well, it was a happy ending for the beach. Howard Taylor left, turning the land deed over to the state in 1974 and after several years, the hippies were finally evicted and the state took over the park in 1977. At the very end of the beach park is Ke'e Beach and is best visited during the week when the crowds aren't as large. There can be good swimming and snorkeling, but again (are you tired of hearing this?) only if the surf conditions are calm.

Stay inside the lagoon as the area beyond the reef can have strong currents. If the parking lot is full (and it often is on weekends) follow the dirt road that veers to the right. There has been a lifeguard on duty here, but as we go to press there is talk of cuts which would eliminate the lifeguard at this beach. Ke'e may look familiar to you for it is where the final scene of *Body Heat* was filmed starring Kathleen Turner.

*Recommended for:* Good swimming and snorkeling at Ke'e in the summer with very calm surf, great sunsets
*Facilities:* Restrooms, showers
*Access:* Located at the trail head to the Napali Coast
*Parking:* Parking areas near the end of Kuhio Highway. If the lot at Ke'e is full, continue on the dirt road and there is more parking beyond the restrooms.

**NAPALI COAST STATE PARK**
"Napali" means "the cliffs." You will often see it written as "Na Pali" but Hawaiian Place Names, written by authoritative historian Mary Kawena Kukui, spells it as one. And thus we follow her advice. Remember in using this term, don't say The Napali Cliffs, for that would mean, "The cliffs cliffs." This 6,500 acre state park is composed of dramatic cliffs, dense rainforests, and lush coastal valleys. There are 15 miles of shoreline between Ke'e Beach and Polihale Beach on Kaua'i's eastern shore. There are a total of five major beaches within this state park: Hanakapi'ai, Kalalau, Honopu, Nu'alolo Kai and Miloli'i. The Hanakapi'ai Beach can be reached in a day's hike. It is a distance of two miles from Ke'e and may take from 30 minutes to two hours to reach. Remember to pack plenty of drinking water, and include sunscreen lotion and a hat, along with comfortable shoes. It might be recommended to also include a small first aid kit with an ace support bandage. You may find remnants of a fishing village and a farming community which once resided here. Due to the remoteness of this coastline, beach lovers need to use extra caution. Sadly, it is perhaps at the Kalalau Beach that more drownings occur, **per visitor**, than anywhere else on the island of Kaua'i. As mentioned before, this is a remote wilderness area and help would be a long time in reaching you should you become ill or injured.

As with other North Shore beaches, surf and currents are extremely hazardous. A hike to this beach is recommended for summer when the trail has had time to dry out from spring rains and the ocean is calmer. Another trail which travels two miles inland from the beach and will take you to the Hanakapi'ai waterfall. The falls flow down for about 300 feet to the pool below. Avoid swimming beneath the falls, and resist the urge to drink the water (all fresh water in Hawai'i should be purified before drinking). It is also advisable that you bring along some mosquito repellent!

There is an 11-mile trek along the steep cliffs of the Kalalau Trail to Kalalau Beach. Due to the rugged terrain and steep elevations, it may well take an entire day to reach the beach. The Kalalau Valley was called the Valley of Healing Light by the ancient Hawaiians. Remember to treat any *heiaus* with respect.

Again, the summer months are most advisable. The area was inhabited until 1919. In the late 1960's and early 1970's the area was repopulated, this time by hippies. With serious sanitation problems the state implemented a program which limited access to the area by restricting the number of camping permits. Boat and helicopter landings also came under restrictions. Camping is allowed only at the shoreline at Kalalau and water is available for cooking and drinking following purification, i.e. boiling. With no fronting reef and strong currents, it is dangerous to swim here at any time of the year.

The remaining three of Napali's beaches are only accessible by boat. Camping is permitted in areas of the state park. Permits are not required for day hikes.

**HANAKAPI'AI**

We recommend you simply stay out of the ocean here. This North Shore beach is particularly dangerous, and the #1 beach for drownings between 1970 and 1988. This, combined with the remoteness of this shoreline, means that beach lovers need to use extra caution. As mentioned before, this is a remote wilderness area and help would be a long time in reaching you should you become ill or injured.

The Hanakapi'ai Stream flows into the ocean at this sandy beachfront. The rivermouth has dangerous rip currents. Summer trades can cause the current to be especially hazardous. Conditions are even more dangerous during winter months. Even the Department of Land and Natural Resources recommends you avoid the ocean. There are some ponds along the stream for a quick dip, but keep an eye out above the valley as rain in the uplands can result in flash flooding of the streams. A reminder, as with any freshwater on the island, it needs to be boiled or otherwise treated before drinking. Also see the recreation section of this book under camping for more information on this beach area.

*Recommended for:* Scenic beauty only
*Facilities:* Toilets
*Access:* A two mile trek from the trail head at Ke'e Beach, at the NW end of Kuhio Hwy. It is not recommended that you park and leave your car overnight. Several companies can arrange to drop you off and pick you up.
*Camping:* By permit with the state

**KALALAU BEACH**

The trail from the Hanakapi'ai Valley to the Kalalau Valley is a difficult one and should not be attempted as a day trip. An 11 mile hike from the trail head at Ke'e Beach, it traverses along scenic ocean cliffs with significant elevation changes (meaning a lot of ups and downs!). The beach is long and narrow during the summer, but with close shorebreak, it is unsafe at all times of the year. During the winter, the beach disappears. No water activities can be recommended for this location. This is one of Kaua'i's five most dangerous beaches, based on incidents of drowning. As with other valley beaches, the Kalalau Stream mouth area is subject to rip currents. (As we reported in the last edition, the Kaua'i daily newspaper continues to report weekly drowning or near-drownings. Recently, a woman drowned while wading in ankle deep water when she was pulled off balance by a rip current.) Also, be alert to the possibility of flash floods during rainfall in the upper region. This is the last beach accessible by foot along the Napali Coast. The remaining beaches are accessible only by boat. See the Recreation and Tours section of this book under *Camping* for more information on this beach area.

*Recommended for:* Scenic beauty only
*Facilities:* Toilets
*Access:* Eleven strenuous miles on foot along the Napali Coastline from the trail head at Ke'e Beach at the NW end of Kuhio Hwy. It is not recommended that you park and leave your car overnight. Several companies can arrange to drop you off and pick you up.

**HONOPU and NUALOLO KAI BEACHES**

Accessible only by boat, Honopu has no facilities and camping is not allowed. Nualolo is a popular summer destination for the charter boats - even more well used since the charter companies are departing from Port Allen rather than Napali. Several companies have state permission to land at this beach, others must anchor offshore. Snorkelers need to stay clear of the shallow reefs due to the danger of surges.

*Recommended for:* Snorkeling at Nualolo Kai during calm summer months
*Facilities:* Toilets and picnic tables
*Access:* Charter boats during the summer months, especially Nualolo Kai

## *NA NAI'A HULAHULA*

*The Dancing Dolphins*

**Ne'e papa like lākou,**
**me ta maita'i.**
**Nā Nai'a hulahula**
**i lila i Hā'ena**

**Nā pua 'o ta moana tai,**
**'oia nā ānela ki'ai,**
**Nā Nai'a hulahula**
**i lila i Kē'ē**

**Ha'aheo e Nāpali,**
**i ta holo titī,**
**Na Nai'a hulahula,**
**i lila i Hanakāpī'ai**

**He mele teīa nou**
**nā Nai'a hulahula,**
**Ha'aheo e Nāpali,**
**na pua 'o ta moana tai**

*Their graceful moves,*
*all in unison.*
*The dancing Dolphins,*
*there at Ha'ena*

*Flowers of the sea,*
*the guardian angels.*
*The dancing Dolphins,*
*there at Ke'e*

*Pride of Napali,*
*swiftly moving.*
*The dancing Dolphins,*
*there at Hanakapi'ai.*
*Tell the story,*
*the dancing Dolphins.*
*Pride of Napali,*
*flowers of the sea.*

Used with the permission of Chucky boy Chock

# RECREATION AND TOURS

## *INTRODUCTION*

Kaua'i, The Garden Isle, has much to interest the outdoorsman or outdoorswoman. Whether it is the land, the air, or the ocean that beckons, there are a variety of activities to tempt even the die-hard lounge chair athlete. This chapter lists activities in alphabetical order.

There are a number of agencies on Kaua'i that can assist you with booking the recreational activity of your choice. Pick up a free copy of the *Beach & Activity Guide Kaua'i*. They list companies which give 5%, 10% or 15% discounts if you book directly.

(Authors' note: "Napali" means "the cliffs." You will often see it written as "Na Pali" but *Hawaiian Place Names*, written by authoritative historian Mary Kawena Kukui, spells it as one. And thus we follow her advice.)

## *BEST BETS*

For great snorkeling try Lydgate or Po'ipu Beach on the South Shore or Makua Beach (also known as Tunnels) on the North Shore.

Take a helicopter tour and get a spectacular view of Kaua'i.

The golf aficionado will delight in the Prince Course at Princeville. Rated as the Number One course by Golf Digest, it is well deserved. Excellent play and outstanding scenery!

If the whales are in residence, take advantage of a whale watching excursion to view these beautiful mammals a bit more closely.

For an underwater thrill consider an introductory scuba adventure, no experience necessary.

For an eye-popping, spectacular aquatic adventure, take a tour of the Napali coast.

Take a tour up the Wailua River by kayak to the Fern Grotto.

View the Waimea Canyon, one of the most spectacular of Mother Nature's creations.

Hike along the Kalalau Trail, but keep in mind, this 11 mile trek along the rugged Napali coastline is not for the novice hiker.

The Grove Farm tour is, in our opinion, the island's best cultural experience. Reserve your space long before your arrival, they take very small groups.

Enjoy a hiking excursion in the summer months with an interpretative guide from the Koke'e Natural History Museum.

Spend a day, or part of one, at the ANARA Health Spa at the Hyatt Regency Kaua'i.

Take a bottle of something bubbly and watch a romantic sunset at Ke'e Beach or Pakala Beach.

Take advantage of an incredible golfing value on a picturesque course, the 9 hole Kukuilono Golf Course. Start your play about 3pm, miss the crowds, and if you don't finish you won't feel bad: green fees is a bargain at only $7!

The horticulturist or amateur gardener will not want to miss visiting one or all of the island's lovely botanical gardens.

Here is an outline of some of the activities that might be enjoyed on the island of Kaua'i, along with the price you might expect to pay. Remember to always check the local brochures for coupons, and don't be afraid to ask if they are running a special offer!

| | | |
|---|---|---|
| Helicopter tour (55-60 minutes) | from | $150 |
| Napali coast ocean excursion | from | $ 75 |
| Sunset sail along the coastline | from | $ 59 |
| Deep sea fishing (1/2 day trip) | from | $ 95 |
| Fresh water fishing (1/2 day trip) | from | $105 |
| River kayak (1/2 day guided) | from | $ 60 |
| Scuba diving (2-tank w/equipment) | from | $100 |
| Hawaiian luau | from | $ 50 |
| Horseback riding (3 hour) | from | $ 90 |
| Land tours (around the island guided bus tours) | from | $ 65 |
| Golf (nine holes) | from | $ 7 |
| Golf (eighteen holes) | from | $ 18-145 |

***AIRPLANE TOURS*** - Also see Helicopter Tours (Princeville Air operates commuter service to Honolulu ... see Hawai'i Helicopters, their parent company.)

Kumulani Air/Fly Kaua'i - scenic airplane tour in a 5-passenger Cessna 206. They also offer charter tours statewide in their 9 passenger Piper Chieftain. 1 hour $89 adult, $59 child; 45 minute flight $49 all seats. Three-island air tour runs $139/$99. An aerial tour of all islands including a volcano tour $240, or a tour which includes a ground tour on Moloka'i $240. (808) 246-9123.

## *BICYCLING / MOTOR BIKES*

Kaua'i Coasters - Offers 12 miles of scenic downhill biking from Waimea Canyon to the coast. Includes bikes, gear, guides, and breakfast at the crater rim. Their motto: "We've been going downhill since we started!" (808) 639-2412. Email: coast@aloha.net

Hawaiian Riders - Rent mountain bikes, mopeds, Harley Davidsons, or exotic automobiles. Rent a hummer for $499/day! Located in Kapa'a across from McDonald's. (808) 822-5409.

Outfitters Kaua'i - Offers mountain bike rentals for your own exploration along with car racks, kid's seats, helmets, and plenty of directions. They have a number of biking tours and biking combined with other adventures including hiking and kayaking. Their Bicycle Downhill Canyon to Coast is a guided trip available for sunrise or sunset tours Monday through Friday ($70). 2827A Po'ipu Rd., Po'ipu Beach, HI 96756. (808) 742-9667, 1-888-742-9887. FAX (808) 742-9667. Email: info@outfitterskauai.com or website <www.outfitterskauai.com>

## *BILLIARDS*

Garden Island Billiards is an air-conditioned, smoke-free billiard parlor that offers ten full size tables. Open daily 6pm until midnight. Located next to Anchor Cove Shopping Center, 3366 Wa'apa Rd. (808) 245-8900. They now have liquor and offer ice cold beer. A smoking room is available. Another popular place for pool is at the Stevenson Lounge at the Hyatt Regency. Pool also available at the Nawiliwili Tavern and Sheraton Lounge (The Point).

***BOAT TRIPS*** See "Sea Excursions" and "Snorkeling"

## *BOWLING*

Lihu'e Bowling Center - 28 lanes open daily at 4303 Rice St., in the Rice Shopping Center. They are a smoke-free environment!! Regular rates are $2.95, league bowlers (with card) $2.65, Juniors $2.15, shoes $1.50. Ask about specials. Snack bar features kid-friendly foods including burgers, pizza, clam chowder, and cinnamon toast. Open 9am-midnight Mon-Sat, Sundays noon to midnight. (808) 245-5263.

## *BRIDGE*

Everyone has a passion. You know, that hobby or recreational activity which, in your estimation, exceeds all others? Well, if the game of bridge is yours, then you are in luck on Kaua'i! Visitors are invited to stop by any of three bridge clubs around the island. Locations and playing times vary. Contact Mable Haas at (808) 822-5373 or Colleen Lawshe at (808) 332-9738.

## *CAMPING*

When planning your camping vacation on Kaua'i, remember that space is very limited at the most popular campsites, so make arrangements well in advance. See the section on hiking for more information on some of these areas.

***CAMPING EQUIPMENT:*** Pedal and Paddle in Hanalei. Backpacking and Camping Gear as well as kayak rental and beach equipment rental. (808) 826-9069.

### *STATE PARKS*

Camping permits are available from the State of Hawai'i at (808) 274-3444 or by writing 3060 Eiwa Street, Lihu'e, HI. Cost is now $10 per night per person for camping at the beachparks on the Napali coast and $5 for other campgrounds. All campgrounds, except the parks along the Napali Coast, are equipped with restrooms, showers, drinking water, fireplaces, and picnic tables. There are restrictions as to the number of nights you are allowed to camp, and permits for the Kalalau Trail/Napali Coast are in high demand and you should make application months in advance. We understand that permits may be obtained through correspondence, however, you may be required to submit photocopies of your identification (passport, driver's license, etc.) for each adult (age 18 or older) and the names and ages of minors in your group. Permits are issued Monday through Friday (except Holidays), 8am to 4pm only at the Lihu'e office.

Note that it is unwise to leave cars at the trail head when hiking into the Napali coast area.

These uninhabited valleys on the northern coastline were once the home for hundreds, if not thousands, of Hawaiians. Residents inhabited some of these valleys until the early 1900's and several archaeological studies have been conducted in this region.

**Hanakapi'ai**
The road on the Northern Coastline ends at Napali State Park. Here is the launching site for two of Kaua'i's most incredible hikes. Be sure to wear good sturdy hiking boots, or if you wear tennis shoes, bring old ones as the dirt and mud will cause permanent staining to your footwear.

The trip to Hanakapi'ai Beach can be reached in a day. It is a distance of two miles from Ke'e and may take 1 1/2 to 2 hours to get there. You may find remnants of a fishing village and a farming community which once resided here. Due to the remoteness of this coastline, beach lovers need to use extra caution. Sadly, it bears repeating, but Kalalau Beach has more drownings (per visitor) than anywhere else on the island of Kaua'i. As mentioned before, this is a remote wilderness area and help would be a long time in reaching you should you become endangered. As with other North Shore beaches, surf and currents are extremely hazardous. Even the Department of Land and Natural Resources recommends you avoid the ocean. A hike to this beach is better in summer when the ocean is calmer (albeit still very dangerous) and the trail has had time to dry out from spring rains. The trip to the beach will reward the hiker with outstanding coastline vistas. A side trip that you can take is to follow the Hanakoa Valley along an unmaintained trail for another two miles to the Hanakapi'ai waterfall. The falls flow down about 300 feet to the pool below. Avoid swimming beneath the falls, and resist the urge to drink the water (all fresh water in Hawai'i should be purified before drinking). The upper half of this trail is more difficult, with boulders and fallen trees to negotiate and should be hiked only in good weather to avoid the danger of flash floods. It is also advisable that you bring along plenty of mosquito repellent! Contact the State Parks Department for overnight camping permits.

**Kalalau State Park**

It is an 11-mile trek along the steep cliffs of the Kalalau Trail to Kalalau Beach. Due to the rugged terrain and steep elevations, it may well take an entire day to reach the beach. As you leave Hanakapi'ai Valley, the hiking becomes more strenuous, climbing 800 feet in elevation. After passing through the Ho'olulu and Waiahuakua Valleys, you enter the Hanakoa Valley which is home to many native lowland forest plants. Camping is available near the Hanakoa Stream. In the late 1800's there were terraces of coffee plants grown here (and a few stragglers remain). These cleared areas are now campsites. There is an unmarked 1/3 mile trail to Hanakoa Falls, but unmaintained trail has eroded in some places making hiking hazardous. The next five miles of trail travel through a section which offers a little protection from the sun. Crossing the Kalalau Stream near the mouth of the valley will reward the weary hiker with a small waterfall. Camping is allowed only by this sand beach. During the summer, sea caves just beyond the waterfall can be used as shelter, but during winter and high surf, they are filled with water. An easy two-mile trail follows the Kalalau Valley and ends at a pool in the stream. The Kalalau Valley was called the Valley of Healing Light by the ancient Hawaiians. Remember to treat any *heiaus* you find with respect. The area was inhabited until 1919 and taro was grown here. Now the valley is filled with wild Java plum, guava, and a mango tree or two. In the late 1960's and early 1970's the area was again populated, this time by hippies. With serious sanitation problems the state implemented a program which limited access to the area by restricting the number of camping permits. Boat and helicopter landings also came under restrictions. Camping is allowed only at the shoreline at Kalalau and water is available for cooking and drinking following purification, i.e. boiling. With no fronting reef and strong currents, it is dangerous to swim here at any time of the year. Hiking is best during the summer months, but it is also more difficult to obtain a permit.

**Miloli'i State Park**
A part of the Napali Coast State Park. These forty acres are equipped with a restroom and picnic area, and offers camping and small boat access. Located on Kaua'i's eastern shore. Accessible only by boat, weather permitting.

**Nualolo Kai**
No camping until further notice and day use permit is required. It is accessible by small boat only, weather permitting. Many tour boat operators use this oceanfront for snorkeling trips as a part of their Napali boat tours. In the late 1950's, Dr. Kenneth Emory working on behalf of the Bishop Museum, began a project to study the Nualolo Kai area. The valley contained all the materials to sustain a substantial population. The bark of the *hau* tree was used for making twine and this very soft wood was well suited for canoe outriggers and fires. The streams offered fresh water shrimp and along the shore were *opiis* (limpets) and *pipipis* (black shellfish). Salt was gathered from the seas and the *kukui* tree was useful for a variety of needs of the early Hawaiian people. For example, canoe hulls could be made from the wood of the *kukui* and the nuts, high in oil, were strung together made an imperfect, but adequate candle. The bark was also used to dye fishing nets. The leaves of the pandanus trees (*lauhala*) were woven into mats. Another tree, the *noni*, has medicinal properties that were valuable for the early Hawaiians. Robert Krauss, during a trip to visit Dr. Emory in the valley while he was excavating wrote in his book, *Here's Hawai'i,* ...the "gnarled tree with the lumpy fruit is the *noni*. It has medicinal properties. The Hawaiians tied *noni* leaves over boils for drawing out infection. The green juice from the crushed pulp of a young *noni* apple, used as a gargle, is good for sore throat. Taken internally it will cure fish poisoning." It is unknown why the Hawaiians left this valley, but Emory speculated their leaving may have been influenced by the arrival of the early missionaries who preferred to have their congregations more centralized.

**Polihale State Park**
Where the Napali meets the west side of Kaua'i is where you'll find Polihale. It is a desert-like climate and there are pavilions which offer some shade from the hot rays of sun. Showers, restrooms, and barbecues can also be found here.

**Koke'e State Park**
The cooler climate of upcountry Kaua'i will give you a very different camping experience compared to the beachfront facilities. Many nearby trails throughout the park offer varied daytime excursions. Hikes range from a 1/10 mile walk that leads to an overlook of Waimea Canyon to a 3-1/2 mile trail through forested terrain. Trails into the neighboring forest reserves include Nualolo, Awaawapuhi, Honopu, Pihea, and Alakai Swamp Trails. During June and continuing through September, the Koke'e Natural History Museum offers a series of guided hikes in the scenic uplands of West Kaua'i. Hikes (each Sunday and Wednesday), are led by one of the trained volunteers of the Koke'e Natural History Museum. The hikes vary in length and in difficulty and since space is limited, they ask that you call ahead to reserve your spot. A small donation is requested. Tours include a hike along cliff and canyon trails to Waipo'o Falls, hikes along the fairly strenuous Pihea Trail or a family hike along Berry Flats Trail. Along the way your interpretative guide will explain about the flora and fauna you encounter

along your hike. For information on cabin rentals contact Koke'e Lodge, PO Box 819, Waimea, HI 96796. (808) 335-6061. Cabins are $35 and $45 plus tax. Information on the trails in Koke'e Park can be obtained from the Division of Forestry, Department of Land and Natural Resources, 3060 Eiwa Street, Lihu'e, HI 96766.

## *COUNTY PARKS*

Contact Kaua'i County at (808) 241-6660 or write Division of Parks and Recreation, 4444 Rice Street, Suite 150, Lihu'e, HI 96766. Permits purchased at office $3 per night per adult, or permits are available at the campgrounds from park rangers at $5 per night for each adult. Youth under 18 no charge. Permits may be purchased by mail, but require 30 working days advance. Office hours are Monday through Friday 8am-4:15pm.

**Ha'ena Beach Park**
Camping is permitted across Ha'ena dry cave, under the trees. The 4.7 acre park has pavilions, toilets, showers, tables, and barbecue grills. Swimming is unsafe.

**Hanalei Beach Park**
2.47 acres with toilets, tables, barbecue grill, and swimming. Open only on Fridays, Saturdays and holidays.

**'Anini Beach Park**
Easy access to campsites makes this a good choice for families. Facilities include a pavilion, restrooms, showers, barbecues, and picnic tables.

**Hanama'ulu Beach Park**
Located 1/2 mile from Hanama'ulu Town. Facilities include tables, toilets, pavilion, barbecue, and showers in this 6.5 acre park. Camping is permitted under the trees in self-contained mobile campers or tents.

**Niumalu Beach Park**
Located two miles from Lihu'e. No camping allowed, open for day use only.

**Lucy Wright Park**
Campsites can be seen from the main highway on your left; 4.48 acres with toilets and showers.

**Salt Pond Beach Park**
This six-acre park has picnic pavilions, tables, toilets, and showers. This campground was closed for a time. Call to see if they are open and allowing campers.

## *CANOES*

Hawaiian Sailing Canoe trips offered ... see Hanalei Watersports listing in Scuba section.

## *CULTURAL TOURS:* See Museums

## *DANCING*

There are two dance groups that are active on the island. USABDA which is a national organization and the Hawaiian Ballroom Dance Association. For information on events contact Janine at her email address: jb@aloha.net

There are also dance opportunities, in limited degrees, at The Point at the Sheraton in Po'ipu, and Gilligan's at the Outrigger.

## *DINNER AND SUNSET CRUISES*

HoloHolo Charters -- '61 *HoloHolo*, power catamaran custom built on Kaua'i. Large trampolines or huge open air cabin. They offer a Ni'ihau & Napali Super Tour (7 hours, $140 adults; $109 children includes continental breakfast, buffet lunch and snorkeling). Napali Sunset Tour (3 1/2 hours $79/60). Aboard their 48 foot sailing catamaran *Leila* you can enjoy their Napali Sail (6 hours $99/75) or Sunset Champagne Sail (2 hours $59/45). Seasonal whale watching. Only children ages 6 years and older for excursions, 4 years and older on sunset trips, no "expecting" mothers. Office located at the Ele'ele Shopping Center. Departs Anchor Cove, Nawiliwili. (808) 335-0815. Website: <www.holoholo-charters.com>

KILAUEA LIGHTHOUSE

## *ECO TOURS*

Keiki Adventures Kaua'i, Nature/Eco-Tours for kids -- Tours include a hike at a moderate pace and distance for keikis, swimming in hidden waterfall pools, guided snorkeling tour including instruction, healthy lunch and snacks, rain gear, day packs. This company specializes in ECO tours for kids with guides explaining Hawaiian history as well as background on the native Hawaiian rain forest, coral reef life and scenic sights such as Waimea Canyon. Japanese Interpretation available. 1-800-232-6699 (808) 822-7823.

Na Pali (Eco) Adventures - ★ They are dedicated to the understanding and protection of our eco system. (Their boats use 100% recycled fuel made from cooking oil!) Their guided trip along the Napali coast is led by a trained naturalist. They use motor-powered, hard-body catamarans (passenger maximums of 26 and 35) that provide a smoother and drier ride than the inflatables or rafts, but there are still provide plenty of thrills! The morning trip is 5 hours with snorkeling and sightseeing and includes a full lunch $115 adults, $86.25 youth. The afternoon trip is sightseeing only and is $100 adults, youth $75 and includes appetizers. Call direct and receive a $10 discount on adult fares (some restrictions apply). The operators are genuinely concerned with the welfare of whales and other aquatic life and it shows in the way they run their cruise. If the whales are out there, they'll find them. An underwater microphone allows you to hear the whales' musical conversation. In addition to whales (in season), you might also be treated to a pod of dolphins swimming along your boat, green sea turtles floating like huge army helmets upon the water, or if you look quickly, you may spot a flying fish. We were fortunate during our excursion to be greeted by Kaua'i's rarest aquatic animal. On first sighting, the monk seal appeared to be lounging in the water, however, on the return trip he appeared in another bay giving us what appeared to be a smile! Realizing that there are estimated to be only three monk seals living in the waters around Kaua'i, our captain felt that we had seen the same seal twice and that they rarely see them more than a couple times of year. Ours was a lucky trip indeed. Departs from Port Allen Harbor. PO Box 1017, Hanalei, HI 96714. (808) 826-6804. FAX (808) 826-7073. 1-800-659-6804. Website: <www.napali.com> E-mail: <napali@pixi.com>

## *FISHING*

### *FRESH WATER*

Kaua'i offers some diverse fishing options. In addition to ocean excursions, you anglers will delight to learn that Kaua'i offers some outstanding freshwater fishing! Area reservoirs are home to several varieties of bass including the peacock bass (otherwise found only in Columbia and Venezuela). Since there is no restocking program, your outfitter will release all fish that are caught. Several areas are stocked with rainbow trout, although trout season is limited to the first 18 days of August and then only on weekends and holidays through September. And did you know that the largest body of fresh water in Hawai'i is found on Kaua'i? The 422 acre manmade reservoir is Lake Waita. With a potential to cover 841 acres, only Halali'i Lake on Ni'ihau would win out as being larger, however, it is not continually full. Check with the Department of Land and Natural Resources, Division of Aquatic Resources at (808) 274-3344 regarding licensing for freshwater fishing. Ask about seasonal trout fishing at Koke'e!

Cast & Catch - They offer fresh water bass guided trips aboard their 17 1/2' boat to catch large-mouth bass, peacock bass and small-mouth bass. Beverages and tackle supplied. Hotel and airport pick-up available!! A four hour trip is $105 for the first person, $175 for two, $240 for three or more. Eight hour trips also available. (808) 332-9707.

JJ's Big Bass Tour - Sample bass fishing at one of the various reservoirs of Kaua'i. They supply tackle and refreshments along with hotel pick-up. The 17 foot monarch bass boat accommodates up to three people. A half day trip for one person is $100, full day $170, two persons $170 half day, $280 full day. (808) 332-9219, pager (808) 654-4153.

***OCEAN***

On sport fishing charter boats in Hawai'i, the practice is that generally the boat retains the rights to any fish caught. This may come as a surprise to those of you anglers from other parts of the country. (Although they will often cut enough for you and your family to enjoy for dinner.) You might wish to check with your boat captain/crew before the trip to determine their policy. Half day trip runs $75-$90.

'Anini Fishing Charters - They charge $95 per person for shared charter for a 1/2 day, $105 for 3/4 day, and an eight-hour fishing excursion runs $135. They have 7 trolling lines and bottom fishing available aboard their 33 ft. twin diesel boat. Bob Kutkowski is the owner/operator of *Sea Breeze V.* (808) 828-1285.

Hana Pa'a Charters - Captain Tim and Julie Hale invite you aboard their 38' Bertram. Exclusive and shared charters, night fishing, whale watching. Departs Nawiliwili Small Boat Harbor. (808) 823-6031. (808) 635FISH

Hanalei Sport Fishing & Tours - Ralph Young has been in the tour boat business for a good piece of time. The year 1999 was a turbulent one for boat operators with new legislation forbidding departures in motorized vessels from Hanalei Bay and Hanalei River. As the year ends, this company is one of just a few to continue operations with a temporary continuance for their 13 passenger, 28' power catamaran. It is unclear how long the temporary permits will be issued ... but for now, it is business as usual! (808) 826-6114.

Kai Bear Sportfishing Charters - Located at Nawiliwili Harbor, the *Kai Bear* is a 38-foot Bertram Convertible Sportsfisher. It offers two staterooms with a galley at your disposal and adjacent salon with sofas, chairs, dining table, stereo, VCR, and television plus it is air-conditioned. (On their 8-hour charter *only*, fish are guaranteed! You'll receive your choice of a 3-5 lb. portion of the catch, or a $20 gift certificate for a fish dinner at one of Kaua'i's fine restaurants.) This is a professional outfit, with the crew in uniform. While it may be the most expensive on Kaua'i, it certainly sounds civilized enough to make fisherwomen out of these authors! Maximum is six passengers. 4 hours $550, 6 hours $750, 8 hours $950 for private. Ask about their special for $149 each for four passengers for four hours. (They also have a 42' Bertram that departs Port Allen.) (808) 826-4556.

McReynolds Fishing Charters - Shared and exclusive charters on their 30' Napali style Wilson fishing boat named *Ho'omaika'i*, which means to make good or thanksgiving. Half and fully day trips. (808) 828-1379.

Sea Lure Fishing Charters - Charters also available aboard their 28 ft. Radon Sportsfisher. They provide all gear and light refreshments. Departs Nawiliwili Harbor. (808) 822-5963.

Sport Fishing Kaua'i - Operate a 28' *Vida Del Mar II* and 38' *Kaua'i Kai*. Half day trip $95, 3/4 day trip $135. <www.fishing-kauai-hawaii.com> (808) 742-7013.

True Blue Charters - 55' Delta vessel *Konane Star* equipped with microwave, TV, VCR, hydrophone (whale listening device), hot and cold freshwater showers, restrooms. Half-day share trips (4 hr) $95-175, 3/4 day (6 hr) $125-225 (price reflects number of anglers). Exclusive charters $650-800. Spectators on share trips half price. Departs Nawiliwili Small Boat Harbor Slip #112. They also operate Island Adventures, kayak trips and Rainbow Runner Sailing aboard a 42' trimaran. (808) 245-9662. FAX (808) 246-9661. Website: <www.kauaifun.com> Email: funkauai@hawaiian.net

***FISHING SUPPLIES:***

*Lihu'e Fishing Supply*, 2985 Kalena St. If the "big one gets away," you can always go next door to the Kalena Fish Market! (808) 245-4930.

## *GARDEN TOURS* -- See Museums

## *GOLF*

Kaua'i offers seven 18-hole golf courses at five different locations, plus one 9-hole course and one 10-hole course! Each course takes advantage of mountain and oceanviews and utilizes the natural elements of the island to add character to each course.

***Stand-by Golf*** is a great option for you golfers interested in some serious savings. They feature discounted rates at public and private courses. They sell unsold tee times beginning about 6pm until 9pm for the next day of play and after 7 am for the same day. They book your game at a guaranteed price and time. Discounts range from 10% on the lowest priced courses up to 33% and more. Prices always include the cart. Currently they are only offering one course, Kiahuna, but with luck they'll be adding more! Definitely worth a phone call. They don't book municipal courses, however. Bookings are handled by telephone and you pay with a credit card. 1-888-645-BOOK.

**GROVE FARM GOLF COURSE AT PUAKEA**
4315 Kalepa Street, Lihue, HI 96766 This golf course is built on more than 200 acres of historic property which was once a sugar cane field. It is unusual with its massive ravines, lakes, and volcanic cliffs. Definitely more to the course than you might expect for central Kaua'i! Course rating is 76.2 with slope rating of 135. There are four tee boxes. Designed by architect Robin Nelson, the course is adjacent to the lot on which *Jurassic Park: The Lost World* was filmed. Reservations for the 10-hole course (yes that is TEN) can be made 30 days in advance. Lessons available. $60 for 20 holes, $35 for 10 holes, twilight play $40. Website: <www.golfgrovefarm.com> (808) 245-8756

**KAUA'I LAGOONS GOLF CLUB**
Facilities include a driving range, pro shop, putting green, restaurant, and bar. Tee times can be made 29 days in advance by calling toll free 1-800-634-6400 or locally (808) 241-6000. Rental clubs and shoes available. PO Box 3330 Kalapaki Beach, Lihu'e, HI 96766. (808) 241-6000, or 1-800-634-6400.

***Kiele Course***
This 18-hole, par 72 course is 7,070 yards and was designed by Jack Nicklaus. The course features deep ravines, ocean cliffs, and a wedding chapel. Each hole is named for an animal and a white marble statue of the animal adorns each tee. Golf Digest rated this course #3 in Hawai'i and #88 in the United States. With the nearby Kaua'i Lagoons Chapel by the Sea, perhaps this is the perfect course for the groom-to-be to combine a few holes of golf before or after the ceremony! General public $145, Marriott guests $113, Juniors (17 and under $65)

***Mokihana Course (formerly Lagoons Course)***
Designed by Jack Nicklaus, this 18-hole course (par 72) has 6,942 yards of play. This course was renamed in 1999 in honor of the mokihana, the "official flower" of the island of Kaua'i and underwent some soft renovations with enhancements to the landscaping. This course is less demanding than Kiele, but the Scottish

links style course is popular with the recreational golfer. It has a forgiving layout with wide fairways and four tees for all skill levels. Green fees general public $100; Marriott guests $73, Juniors (17 and under) $42.

**KIAHUNA GOLF CLUB**
Located in Po'ipu. Robert Trent Jones, Jr. designed this 18-hole, par 70 course. Kiahuna features ocean and mountain views, as well as some surprises. Lava rock walls, a huge lava tube, a Blind Eye Spider cave, and other Hawaiian archaeological sites add to the personality of this course as it winds around remnants of an ancient Hawaiian Village. Championship 6,353 yards. Facilities include driving range, pro shop, putting green, snack shop, and bar. Green fees, including cart run: $75 morning, $55 after 11am, twilight play $40. 2545 Kiahuna Plantation Drive, Koloa, HI 96756. (808) 742-9595.

**KUKUIOLONO GOLF COURSE ★**
Located in Kalaheo. This public course is situated on top of Kukuiolono Park and the fourth and fifth holes have spectacular views. This course features ample fairways, a Japanese garden, and ancient Hawaiian rock structures. Play is on a first-come basis, no reservations. The 9 holes are a par 36, with 2,981 yards of play. Facilities include a driving range, pro shop, putting green, and snack shop. Golf club rentals available. At $7 for all day play, it is hard to go wrong. This course is usually very crowded. We suggest you tee off about 3pm: you get through a fair part of the course (and see that spectacular view at the 4th and 5th hole) and for the price it doesn't matter if you don't finish. Carts are optional at $6. (808) 332-9151. Open 6:30am-6:30pm. no tee-offs after 4:50pm.

**PRINCEVILLE GOLF CLUB**
Located at the Princeville Resort. PO Box 3040, Princeville, HI 96722. (808) 826-3580. 1-800-826-4400.

***Makai Course***
Designed by Robert Trent Jones, Jr., this is actually three courses rolled into 27 holes: The Lakes, The Ocean, and The Woods are each nine holes, par 36 with the clubhouse at the hub. With waterfalls, beaches, mountains, and the spectacular Mt. Makana (Bali Hai) as backdrops, it's a spectacular setting. Facilities include driving range, pro shop, putting green, and snackbar. The Prince Course has been listed in Golf Digest Top Resort Courses and in America's 100 Greatest Golf Courses for the last 16 years. The Makai Course has hosted the LPGA Women's Kemper Open more than once. $115 regular rate, $97 for Princeville area guests, $87 for Princeville Hotel guests. Twilight rate (after 1:30pm) is $70. Sunset rate (after 4pm) is $39. An additional round is $32. Club rental $32, shoe rental $12, riders fee $25.

***Prince Course* ★**
The Prince Golf Course opened in 1990. The 18-holes are a par 72 with 7,309 yards of play. Scenic vistas include the rugged cliffsides and the famous "Bali Hai" location. The course fits snugly along the cliffsides of Kaua'i's North Shore with hole #13 featuring a waterfall backdrop. With a USGA course rating of 75.3, this course is ranked as the most challenging in the state. However, multiple tees on each hole accommodate the casual golfer as well. Driving range, pro shop, putting greens, restaurant, and bar are available. Golf Digest ranks this

course #1 in the state of Hawai'i and in the top 50 in the United States. It is one of eleven courses in the U.S. to have a 5-Star rating. The Prince Course charges $155 standard, $124 for Princeville area guests, and $105 for Princeville Hotel guests. Matinee Rate begins at noon for $99.

**PO'IPU BAY RESORT GOLF COURSE**
Po'ipu Bay Resort Golf Course is an 18-hole championship course situated on 210 oceanfront acres adjacent to the Hyatt Regency Kaua'i Resort and Spa. This course opened in April 1991 and is a Scottish links style course with a par 72 designed by Robert Trent Jones, Jr. It boasts some outstanding ocean vistas and seven holes with water hazards. Set between lush mountains and rugged ocean bluffs, the course includes over 35 acres of landscaped tropical plants and flowers. An archeological site that has been incorporated into the course. During winter, golfers can even catch glimpses of the whales as they pass off-shore. And don't be surprised if you see some *nene* geese wandering about. Over the years Po'ipu Bay has won numerous awards and has consistently been rated among the top golf courses in the U.S. and Hawai'i. In 1999 they were rated the #1 golf course in Hawai'i on the Gold List as chosen by the readers of Conde Nast Traveler. Since 1994 the course has played host to the annual Grand Slam of Golf. Current golf course special rates and packages include "Round and a Round and a Round Golf" where guests can include three rounds of golf, including cart and driving range practice for $250 (Hyatt guests pay $210) Afternoon Delight is for play starting after 12:00 noon and no later than 3pm for $100. Twilight special is play starting after 3pm for $50 for nine holes or as many holes as daylight will allow. They also feature a Junior Golf Special Rate for $45 for kids between the age of 8 and 17 years when accompanied by a paying adult. Inquire about their daily clinics and lessons. Facilities include a driving range, pro shop, clubhouse (with restaurant, lounge, and snackbar), putting green, and practice sand bunkers. 2250 Ainako St., Koloa, HI 96756. (808) 742-8711. Golfers can also reserve tee-times through the internet! The online book service is operated through EZLinks Golf, Inc. at <www.ezlinksgolf.com> For more information on the Po'ipu Bay course check out the website at <www.kauai-hyatt.com//golf.html>

**WAILUA MUNICIPAL GOLF COURSE**
18-holes, 6981 yards, par 72. Considered by some to be the best municipal course in the state, it is located on the eastern shore in Kapa'a. With shaded ponds, Pacific Ocean views, and a very low green fees, this may be a great option for the budget traveler. Facilities include a driving range, pro shop, putting green, restaurant, and bar. $25 weekday, $35 on weekends and holidays. Ask about their afternoon specials. Club rental $15. Charge is $14 per cart (cart is optional). Write: 3-5351 Kuhio Hwy., Lihu'e, HI 96766. (808) 241-6666.

## *HANG GLIDING*

Birds in Paradise is an opportunity to experience hang glider ultralight flying. Tandem instructional tours are offered in these powered ultralights and a wing mounted video of your flight is available. Mini-Lesson 25-30 minute $95; Cross Country Lesson 50-60 minutes $165. Longer lessons available. (808) 822-5309, FAX (808) 822-5309. <WWW> E-mail: <birdip@aloha.net>

## *HELICOPTERS*

A helicopter tour will set you back some bucks, but it may be an experience that is worth every penny. If you do take a flight, we suggest that you wait until mid-way in your island vacation, even a little longer, before experiencing the island by helicopter. It is much more interesting to see the island's landmarks by air having first had a close hand look at them on land. It is a chance to view some wonderful sights that can be seen only by air. Helicopters fly around Kaua'i in a clockwise direction, so seating on the right side of the craft offers the best viewing. However, the seat assignment is based on weight and yes, they sometimes have you step on a scale to make sure you are honest. Some helicopter companies are owner-operated and brochures often talk about the owner's flying experience. In some cases, this may not be the person piloting your helicopter tour. In other cases, you'll find that it is indeed the owner that operates each and every tour. Flights depart from Lihu'e Airport and Princeville Airport. The State Department of Transportation recently added the Port Allen Airport (also known as Burns Field) near Hanapepe to the list.

Some revisions in regulations regarding kids! Children 1-35 lbs. must have an "infant" life preserver. Children 36-90 lbs. must have a "child" life preserver. Over 90 lbs. are considered an adult and must have an "adult" life preserver. Up to a child's second birthday, they are permitted to sit on the parent's lap. For a single engine flight over water EVERYONE **must** wear a vest. For a twin-engine flight over water, a vest is not required, but must be easily accessible. On Kaua'i, most tours include a scenic pass along the Napali. Due to weather conditions, and just the view vantage point, the flights must be able to fly out over the water. The only company on Kaua'i currently operating a dual rotor helicopter is Hawai'i Helicopters. While most young children don't go on helicopter trips, we were told that there are lots of infants that go as "lap riders." So inquire if you are traveling with a babe in arms, or want to take a youngster up!

Air Kaua'i Helicopter Tours ★ - Chuck DiPiazza and staff fly air conditioned AStars with a two way intercom and custom bubble windows providing exceptional visibility. They are also equipped with a compact disc player and a special noise cancelling system. They offer one concise tour, a 1-hr deluxe air experience that includes Waimea Canyon, Napali, and Wai'ale'ala for $179. (Mention this book and your price will be $159, Sam said so!) The ride is seamless, no jerky stops and starts, with just the right music and narration to accompany a comfortable flight. Our pilot skillfully flew close to the magnificent Napali, flying in and out between layers and ridges, so close you could almost reach out and touch them. These are canyon views you've never seen! Kaua'i has magnificent scenery, and seeing it by helicopter is definitely an option to be considered during your island vacation. (808) 246-4666. 1-800-972-4666. FAX (808) 246-0101. E-mail: <heliop@aloha.net>

Bali Hai Helicopter Tours - Departs from Port Allen Airport. Owner-operated by James Lee and his staff. Family discounts. 4 passenger Bell 206B Jet rangers. helicopters. Cost is $120 for 45-55 minute trip, $159 for 1 hour. Discounts if you book directly. PO Box 1052, Kalaheo, HI 96741. (808) 335-3166, 1-800-325-TOUR. <WWW> E-mail: <blh@aloha.net>

Hawai'i Helicopters ★ - Departs Princeville Resort or Port Allen. These folks fly AStars out of two locations. This dual landing pad affords them an opportunity to do a couple of fun and interesting tours! The Garden Isle Special (Princeville or Port Allen) soars into Wai'ale'ale Crater for a chance to marvel at 2,000 foot waterfalls and then descend into the Waimea Canyon. Round it off with some spectacular Napali coastline ($135; 45 minutes). Garden Isle Deluxe (Princeville or Port Allen) features Wai'ale'ale Crater, Waimea Canyon and a bit more of the secret hidden beauty ($179; 60 minutes). Hanalei Adventure (Port Allen departure) Soar into the famous Waimea Canyon, past the inaccessible Napali Coast and Mt. Namolokama before landing at Princeville for a Garden Stop and a chance to see some of the lush beauty of Hanalei. Reboard the helicopter and continue on to the Hanalei Valley. ($159; 70 minutes). Kaua'i Cross Island (departs Princeville) is a longer adventure. Start in Princeville and enjoy an aerial tour of Hanalei Valley and Wai'ale'ale before a landing in Port Allen. A shuttle driver picks you up and your land excursion begins in Hanapepe town. You're on your own to enjoy the buildings which date back to the 1800s, and visit art galleries and other interesting shops. Then another short jaunt to a restaurant before you are transported to Salt Pond Beach Park. Hawaiians have been manufacturing salt from the sea for 2000 years and they continue today. The waters are calm (lifeguard, too) and are believed, by some, to have therapeutic properties. In any case, it is a good chance for a post-lunch snooze in the sun and then another ride back to the helipad for a second aerial tour, this time along the Napali and Waimea Canyon. ($179; 2-3 hours). This last tour is a real find for those that have settled their roots into the North Shore for their vacation. Not just a ride, but an adventure! We tried it and we recommend it! 1-800-994-9099. Kaua'i (808) 826-6591. <www.hawaii-helicopter.com>

In early 2000, Princeville Air (part of Hawai'i Helicopters) began offering nonstop service between the Princeville Airport and Honolulu International Airport. At press time, we were advised that a nine passenger, twin-engine Navajo Chieftain would be used with service expected to be twice daily. Fares will be similar to those offered by Aloha and Hawaiian Airlines from Lihu'e to Honolulu. Flight time will be less than 60 minutes. Hawai'i Helicopters operates a commuter service between Kapalua and Moloka'i and Lana'i with a 24-passenger Sikorsky S-61. It is the largest passenger helicopter in the state. 1-800-994-9099. On Kaua'i 826-6591. Website: <www.hawaii-helicopter.com> If you arrive at the Princeville Airport from Honolulu, Avis is the only rental car company. Check with your hotel or Princeville Air about shuttle service. 1-800-994-9099. (808) 826-6591. <www.hawaii-helicopter.com>

Inter-Island Helicopters - Operates Hughes 500 with two sit-up-front and two-sit-in-back seats, each have their own window. They like to fly with the doors off so photos will come out clear and their two-way intercom allows communication between pilot and other passengers. They fly from Port Allen Airport in Hanapepe. The one-hour tour covers Olokele Canyon, 3 valleys of the Waimea Canyon, then over Koke'e to Napali Coast. They also have a 1 hour & 45 minute Waterfall Adventure tour that includes a stop at their private landing pad and a short walk on the boardwalk to the Pu'u Ka Ele waterfall with time for a picnic lunch and a quick swim in the pond. Waterfall weddings also available! 1 hour tour $150 per person. Waterfall Tour $225 per person. Wedding Waterfall tour 2 hours $1300. (808) 335-5009.

Island Helicopters - Flies AStar helicopters and also a 6 passenger A-Star. Depart from Lihu'e. They specialize in just one tour, the "Kaua'i Grand" and the cost is $185. PO Box 831, Lihu'e, HI 96766. (808) 245-8588, 1-800-829-5999. <WWW> Email: island@aloha.net

Jack Harter Helicopters - Flies Bell Jet Ranger. Jack originated helicopter tours on Kaua'i. Their 60-65 minute flight runs $165, 90 minutes $235. (808) 245-3774. 1-888-245-2001E-mail: jharter@aloha.net

Ni'ihau Helicopters - Flies an Augusta helicopter which departs from Hanapepe. The flight circles Ni'ihau and lands briefly on one of the beaches. They are a little difficult to reach with short office hours and tour offerings are limited. PO Box 370, Makaweli, HI 96769. (808) 335-3500. FAX (808) 338-1463.

Ohana Helicopter Tours - Flies AStar, departures from Lihu'e. Owner-pilot Bogard Kealoha is Hawaiian-born and was raised on Kaua'i. A 50 minute Mokihana tour is $144, Maile tour runs 65 minutes and is $184. (808) 245-3996. Email: ohana1@aloha.net or website <www.planet-hawaii.com/ohana>

Safari Helicopters - Flies AStar, departs Lihu'e. Their three and four camera video/sound system with two-way intercom captures your trip with pilot's narration. PO Box 1941, Lihu'e, HI 96766. (808) 246-0136, or toll free 1-800-326-3356. <WWW> E-mail: <info@safariair.com>

South Sea Helicopters - Departs Lihu'e Airport, flies Bell Jet Ranger. Choose between a 45-50 minute "Kaua'i Special Flight", a 55-60 minute "Golden Eagle Flight" or a 70-75 minute "Flight of the Canyon." 1-800-367-2914. (808) 245-2222. Email: 2SSH@gte.com

Will Squyres Helicopter Tours - Will Squyres began his company in 1984 with twenty-two years of flying experience. He uses 6 passenger A-Stars. During their 60-65 minute tour you will visit the Waimea Canyon, the Napali Coastline, Wai'ale'ale Crater and, the famous *Jurassic Park* waterfall, as well as settings used in many other films made on Kaua'i. Cost is $149. (808) 245-8881 or (808) 245-7541.

## *HIKING*

Also see section on *CAMPING* in this chapter for detailed information on several hiking trails.

The Hawai'i State Department of Land and Natural Resources, Division of Forestry & Wildlife has Kalalau trail maps. You will need to send a self-addressed stamped envelope with your request and a small fee for handling. Call or write for requirements to the Department of Land and Natural Resources, Division of Forestry and Wildlife, 3060 Eiwa St., #306, Lihu'e, HI 96766. (808) 274-3433.

Humberto Blanco operates Island Enchantment Kaua'i River Side Retreat as well as offering Adventure Tours. Accommodations are combined with a 6-8 day tour. Their outdoor adventures/hikes are combined with an opportunity to learn and practice the elements of yoga, body/mind techniques, meditation, and massage. You can also arrange for a one-day custom tour at $75 per person. 1-888-281-6292. (808) 823-0705. <www.aloha.net/~enchant/Kauai.html>

Kaua'i Mountain Tours - Mike and Terri Hopkins have reached an agreement with Grove Farm lands for a van tour with short walks to lookout points. The half day trips go to Kilohana Crater where a 360 degree island view is afforded. Then it continues toward Koloa and on to Maha'ulepu. PO Box 3069, Lihu'e, HI 96766. (808) 245-7224. <WWW>

Kaua'i Nature Tours offers day trips with short hikes led by experienced scientists. Choose from a number of interpretative tours, including an Island Ecosystem Tour, a Po'ipu/Mahaulepu Coast Hike, an Island Geologic History Excursion, a Napali Coast Hike into Hanakapi'ai Valley and a Kaua'i Beach Tour to a selection of Kaua'i's world famous beaches. "No need to have a background in science, the only requirement is a curiosity about the Earth's natural environment and its interactive human occupants." These unique tours include transportation, a picnic lunch and refreshments. Most of their tours leave from Po'ipu Beach Park at 9am and return by 4pm. Also available are week long adventure vacations. PO Box 549, Po'ipu, HI 96756. 1-808-842-8305. 1-888-233-8365. Email: teok@aloha.net or website: <www.teok.com>

Princeville Ranch Hiking Tours - they are now also offering hiking tours. The hike starts out at an area known as Green Hill and then continues through the ranch to Kalihiwai Falls. The 3 1/2 mile trek takes about 3 1/2 hours. Another tour goes down the ridge toward Hanalei Valley. They provide daypacks, water bottles, tabis (special Japanese shoes for walking through water) and even rain gear (just in case). Private Rides also available. PO Box 888, Hanalei, HI 96714. (808) 826-7669. Email: prha@aloha.net

The Sierra Club publishes a quarterly newsletter, *Malama*, available by subscription for $7 per year. A sample of the newsletter can be received by writing them, including a $1 fee and a self-addressed and stamped envelope. Also available is *Hiking Softly in Hawai'i*, a guide to the enjoyment of the Hawaiian wilderness with useful information on how to obtain hiking and camping permits, etc. Available for $4 from the Sierra Club. Sierra Club, Hawai'i Chapter, PO Box 2577, Honolulu, HI 96803. Visitors can write to the Kaua'i group a couple of months prior to their arrival and request a schedule by sending a self-addressed stamped envelope and a $1 fee. Bob Nishek on Kaua'i (808) 822-9238, has offered to provide our readers with the latest hiking information. Advance registration is necessary for all outings in the event of last minute changes due to inclement weather. They suggest a $3 donation for each person participating in the outings. Several excellent references are available for the interested hiker. See ordering information at the back of this guide. Craig Chisholm is the author of *Kaua'i Hiking Trails*, *Hawaiian Hiking Trails,* and *Hawai'i: The Big Island Hiking Trails*. His guides provide excellent topographical maps, good directions, and detailed information including the number of calories you can expect to burn, time required to travel the trail round trip, and elevation.

During June and continuing through September, the Koke'e Natural History Museum offers a series of guided hikes in the scenic uplands of West Kaua'i. Hikes are twice weekly and are led by one of the trained volunteers of the Koke'e Natural History Museums. The hikes vary in length and in difficulty and since space is limited, call ahead to reserve your spot. A $2 donation is requested. Tours include a hike along cliff and canyon trails to Waipo'o Falls, hikes along the fairly strenuous Pihea trail or a family hike along Berry Flats Trail. Along the way your interpretative guide will explain about the flora and fauna discovered on your hike. For dates and times of hikes call (808) 335-9975.

**Kalalau Trail**

This time-worn trail of eleven miles starts next to Ke'e Beach at the end of Hwy. 56. There you will find parking, bathrooms, and showers. A sign at the beginning of the trail will provide you with all the pertinent information you will need for your hike. (Maps, permits, mileage, restrictions, etc.) The first two miles/one hour to Hanakapi'ai and additional 1.8 miles/45 minutes to Hanakapi'ai Falls is as far as most people go. Though this hike is relatively short, it is strenuous so it is advisable to bring your own drinking water and snacks. The first half of the Kalalau Trail is more lush with many native plants interspersed with wild orchids and ginger along with papaya and mango trees. Ancient terraced rock walls used for taro-growing are visible and in surprisingly good shape. Further along this pristine coast, there are prehistoric valleys of green velvet, cascading waterfalls, ancient Hawaiian *heiaus*, turquoise water, and ominous sea cliffs. During whale season, these magnificent creatures can be spotted from the trail as they breech out of the water. The coastline is beautiful with incredible vistas from many promontories all the way into Kalalau. This final destination has a refreshing waterfall for bathing. Hikers venturing on from Hanakapi'ai will need overnight camping permits which you can get from the State Parks Office.

Following is the Awaawapuhi Trail, one of twenty-nine trails in *Kaua'i Hiking Trails*, reprinted here with permission. Author Craig Chisholm comments that this trail takes a bit more effort than some, but "it is well-marked and the view at its end is, in my opinion, the most impressive in Hawai'i." This trail is located in the Koke'e area. It is 2 1/4 hours up and 1 1/2 hours down. Round trip on this is 6.5 miles. The highest point is 4,100 feet and the lowest point is 2,560 feet. While this trail may be a bit rugged for the family travel with younger children, there are many other trails outlined in Chisholm's that are less strenuous and of shorter duration.

**Awaawaphui**

Awesome views of the Napali Coast and its isolated, hanging valleys make this trail one of the best for photography in Hawai'i. The trail descends 1,500 feet through native dryland forests to twin viewpoints above the sheer cliffs that drop into the remote Awaawapuhi and Nualolo Valleys. The floors of these rarely visited valleys are accessible only by water and then only after difficult climbing from the sea. However, the viewpoints provide good vantage points of the valleys and the great fluted walls enclosing them. The sight is memorable, especially if you sit at the viewpoints and watch the sunlight and shadows play on the cliffs and sea near dawn. Every morning helicopters flutter like dragonflies in and out of the steep-cliffed valleys below.

The Division of Forestry and Wildlife has marked many endemic plants along the route and has published an interpretive guide which is available at the office in Lihu'e or the Koke'e Museum.

**Route:** From Koke'e State Park Headquarters go 1.6 miles up Highway 550 toward the Kalalau Lookout. The trail-head is on the left, in the Napali-Kona Forest Reserve, across from a dirt road and just before the 17-mile mark on the Highway. At first the broad trail leads north and goes up a little. It then descends (with switchbacks), generally in a northwesterly direction. Along the way there are many numbered and labelled endemic bushes and trees. At approximately 3 miles form the start, the Nualolo Cliff Trail, which is a connector from the Nualolo Trail, leads in from the left (south). Soon after this junction, the Awaawapuhi Trail ends at the metal-railed viewpoints overlooking the sea, great cliffs, white-tailed tropic birds, and the inevitable 8am helicopters. Do not go close to the rims of the canyons. The small stones covering the hard surfaces on the eroded areas, like ball bearings on concrete, provide treacherous footing. The drop to the valley floor on either side is between 1,500 and 3,000 feet, depending on the bounce. The plants in the native dryland forest are rare and the danger of fires extreme; thus, neither overnight camping nor fires are permitted. Water is unavailable.

## *HORSEBACK RIDING*

Horseback riders are afforded the opportunity to enjoy some of Kaua'i's most breathtaking scenery. On the North Shore, you can take a four-hour ride to a mountain waterfall. Near Waimea, visitors can enjoy the island's only ocean rides while watching the sun sinking slowly over the island of Ni'ihau. At Po'ipu Beach, a three-hour breakfast trail ride encompasses scenic views of the ocean, beaches, and mountains.

CJM Country Stables - Owner Jimmy Miranda and his crew will take you into hidden valley ranch land, past secluded beaches and bays to discover the picturesque beauty of Kaua'i on horseback. Three times weekly is the Ultimate Breakfast, this three hour ride runs $75. Monday, Wednesday and Friday at noon is the picnic and swim ride, a 3 1/2 hour trip for $90. Daily at 9:30am and 2pm they do a two hour ride for $65. Po'ipu (808) 742-6096, FAX (808) 742-6015.

Espirit De Corps Riding Academy - Three hour ride includes trotting and cantering $99. Longer rides include an all day excursion. Private rides with longer arena lesson are available for the less experienced rider. Private lessons are also available. PO Box 269 Kapa'a, Kaua'i, HI 96746, or (808) 822-4688. Email: riding@kauaihorses.com <www>

Princeville Ranch Stables / Adventures on Horseback - A family owned business since 1978, Donn and Gale Carswell offer trail trips to a maximum of six riders per group. Minimum age is 8 years. All riders must be in good physical condition. Weight limit restrictions, 180 lbs. for women, 220 pounds for men. Long pants recommended, closed shoes are a must. $115 per person for their two hour *paniolo* ride and $160 for their Hapalaka Excursion. The waterfall ride involves riding and a short, steep hike (without the horse) down to the base of the falls (about 10 minutes). Including a picnic lunch and a swim, the trip takes about four hours. Cost is $110. Experience what it takes to be a *paniolo* (cowboy) on their Princeville Ranch Cattle Drive and round up a herd of cattle at sunrise and drive them back across ranchland to their pen. Observe their border collies (Buster, Lani and Jumbo) assist in the moving of the herd. Only once a week. $125 per person. 'Anini Bluff Ride $100 per person. (Hawai'i State Law, by the way, prohibits horseback riding on the beaches.) Panoramic Hanalei Mountains and Valley trip is $55 per person.

Princeville Ranch Stables also has a new tour on a horse-drawn wagon. They take tours out to the bluffs overlooking A'nini Beach for a sunset barbecue. The tour includes Hawaiian entertainment, legends, and a history of the area. Another trip is on horseback to Kalihiwai Falls. (808) 826-6777.

## *HUNTING/SHOOTING RANGES*

For hunting information on Kaua'i contact the Department of Land & Natural Resources, Wildlife Division. They can help you with enforcement and licensing information as well as hunting guidelines. (808) 274-3433.

The Hunting Shop of Kaua'i is a full service fire arms and hunting shop, including archery. Only authorized Matthews dealer. They also do repairs. 3156 Ohana in Lihu'e. (808) 245-3006.

Ni'ihau Helicopter Safari, Ltd. Exclusive full day hunting of wild boar and feral sheep on the privately owned island of Ni'ihau. Owned and operated by the Robinson family, they also operate Ni'ihau Helicopters. Participants must have a Hawai'i State hunting license, which Ni'ihau Safari will assist in acquiring. Office hours are 8am-2pm, Monday through Saturday. PO Box 370, Makaweli, HI 96769. (808) 335-3500, FAX (808) 338-1463.

Shooter's Paradise is a indoor shooting range. Firearm Safety training courses offered. (808) 246-4967.

## *JET SKIING*

This water recreational activity is not permitted on Kaua'i.

## *KAYAKING*

With its many navigable rivers, Kaua'i is a jewel for the kayaker. You can choose an adventure on your own, take a guided tour, or go on a group expedition. There are sea kayaking adventures to be enjoyed, but they are recommended for the experienced kayaker or with a guided excursion group. Since 1999, Kayaking the Wailua River has been under debate. It was felt that there was overuse of the river. Kayak companies who previously rented and delivered kayaks to the river for independent excursions were no longer allowed to deliver. We'll keep you posted in THE KAUA'I UPDATE as the industry and government continue their debate.

## *Kayaking*

In your next game of trivial pursuit, if you should have the question, "How many rivers are there on Kaua'i?" you could answer five, six, seven, or nine and probably be correct. After exhaustive research and pure conjecture, we decided that it depends on the weather and who you ask. The problem seems to be the determination of just what is a stream and what is a river. A river is usually considered larger than a stream, but how much larger? After a heavy rain, a stream may certainly look river-like. The Hawai'i Visitors Bureau, Parks and Recreation Department, and various maps and guidebooks all have their own answer. The Hawai'i Visitors Bureau goes with seven. It seems there are five that can be agreed upon as being "rivers" by most of these sources: Waimea, Hanapepe, Wailua, Hanalei, and Wainiha. The others are more often called streams: Lumaha'i, Huleia, Kalihiwai, and Makaweli. However, the Huleia and Kalihiwai are referred to by some as rivers. In any case, there are several streams/rivers perfect for kayaking: The Waimea, Hanapepe, Huleia, Wailua, Kalihiwai, and Hanalei. Each can be navigated for only about three miles. The Waimea River, Kaua'i's longest, can be accessed in Waimea at the Lucy Wright Park. This is the location where Captain James Cook first set foot in the islands in 1778. Each river has its own personality and differing picturesque scenery. The Huleia River passes the Haupu Ridge with views of the Boar Head mountains, as well as passing by the Menehune Fish Pond and the Huleia National Wildlife Refuge. The Kalihiwai River/Stream, with its mouth at Kalihiwai Bay near Princeville, travels through lowland areas of Kaua'i. The Hanalei River twists through the valley past fields of taro. The Wailua River is accessible from Wailua State Park and you can reach and enjoy Fern Grotto State Park along the banks. Depending on the seasons and surf, sea kayaking locations will vary. In the summer months, the North Shore may often be calm and perfect for various skill levels of kayakers. The Napali coast trip is a 16-mile kayak adventure and can be accomplished in one day or more, depending on weather conditions and camping permit availability. In the winter, the southern shore offers many options. For more information, pick up a copy of *Paddling Hawai'i* by Audrey Sutherland at local bookstores.

## *KAYAK RENTALS AND GUIDED TOURS*

Choose a guided tour, or rent equipment and explore one of Kaua'i's beautiful rivers at your own pace.

Island Adventures - This outfit features a 2 1/2 hour guided kayak excursion on the Hulei'a River, site of the legendary Menehune Fishpond. The Hulei'a River is in the heart of the 241 acre Hulei'a National Wildlife Refuge with four endangered bird species under protection here. The river is famous as a location for scenes from movies including *Raiders of the Lost Ark* and *The Lost World*. Each person is taught kayak control during a safety briefing. Trip includes picnic snack with juice. Departs Nawiliwili Small Boat Harbor for morning or afternoon excursion. $48 adults, children 4-12 half price. This is their 22nd year on Kaua'i. They also operate True Blue Charters (fishing) and Rainbow Running (sailing/snorkeling). (808) 245-9662. FAX (808) 246-9661.
Email: funkauai@hawaiian.net

Kayak Ecotour - "A True Kayak Experience" - They take small groups (no more than 8) to hidden waterfalls, quiet rivers, lonely beaches, and enchanted ponds. "Please bring your boy/girl scout's attitude, bathing suit, sports or beach footwear, hat, suntan oil, camera and an open mind." The price includes a gourmet sandwich and beverages for the family, kayaks, and all the equipment. $75 adults. Half price for children under 10 years. They also do kayak rentals. <www.kauai-kayaking.com> or call them at (808) 639-7718 or 822-9078.

Kayak Kaua'i Outbound - Their one or multiple day guided tours are available year round. They can be geared for the active adventurer or for the whole family. Napali $130, Secret Falls $80, Blue Lagoon $55, Kipu Kai $105. Or rent your own kayak! Also surfboard rentals, hiking and camping equipment rentals, bicycle rentals. Kapa'a (808) 822-9179, Hanalei (808) 826-9844, 1-800-437-3507.

Kaua'i Water Ski & Surf - Kayaks are among the variety of equipment available for rent. Single or two-person kayaks rentals (currently you have to get your rental kayak to the river.) Kinipopo Shopping Village. Monday-Saturday 9am-9pm. (808) 822-3574. 1-800-344-7915. Email: surfski@aloha.net

Outfitters Kaua'i - Owners Rick and Julie Haviland have one and two person kayaks. Information and maps on kayaking locations are provided. Six days a week they offer a Paddle Jungle Stream & Waterfall Hike ($80) During the summer, they offer their Napali Coast Sea Kayak Tour ($135). They also have recently entered into an agreement with Grove Farm and W.H. Rice Ltd. for permission to cross their land for a new tour. The tour begins with a two mile kayak trip up the Huleia River, then a walk along agricultural roads and renovated trails to Hidden Valley. The area is interpreted and its history, folklore and legends are explored before they return on a couple of the old Westin canoes that have been transformed into double hull vehicles with small 4-stroke outboards. (808) 742-7421, 1-888-742-9887. FAX (808) 742-9667. Email: info@outfitterskauai.com or website <www.outfitterskauai.com>

Paradise Outdoor Adventures - Rental bikes and kayaks; also guided kayak trips. Operating since 1989. Located at the north end of Kapa'a. (808) 822-1112.

Paradise River Rentals - They are located at the Kilohana Planation in Lihu'e. They offer self-guided tours of Kaua'i's six top kayaking rivers. Kayak rentals also include safety equipment, maps, a cooler, and a picnic tarp. Also ecotours with kayaking, snorkeling, and hiking. One or two person kayaks available. (808) 822-1112. Email: kayaks@aloha.net or website: <www.kayakers.com>

Pedal and Paddle - They offer summertime guided trips of Napali. River trips are self-guided. Daily rentals of single and two-person kayaks available. Located in Hanalei at the Ching Young Village. (808) 826-9069.

Wailua River Kayak Adventures - Rentals $14.99-39.99 (call and boats are delivered to the river). Fern Grotto Scenic Paddle Trip each morning or afternoon $50 per person for the 3 1/2-4 hour trip. Morning or afternoon tours to Secret Falls Tour $75 per person 4-5 hours. Email: cleaveclan.org.hgea. <www> (808) 822-5795, FAX (808) 822-5795.

## *LAND TOURS*

Kaua'i Backroads - A new tour from Aloha Kaua'i Tours! They depart for a half-day tour twice daily at 8am and 1pm from Kilohana Plantation. Travel former cane roads in the comfort of an air-conditioned 4-wheel drive van to remote areas. Learn about Kaua'i's history as you travel scenic backroads up to Kilohana Crater, past reservoirs and old Koloa Town to the rugged coastline of Maha'ulepu, then take the tunnel through the Mount Haupu Range and back to the plantation home. A photographer's dream. Adults $48, children $42. (808) 245-8890. 1-800-452-1113.

Kaua'i Mountain Tours - These 4X4 mountain van tours last 6-8 hours and include picnic lunch. $86.40 adults, $60 children. Tours go beyond the normal land excursions in their twelve passenger air-conditioned 4X4 vans. They place an emphasis on Hawaiian history and culture as they travel back roads in the Pali-Kona Forest reserve and Koke'e State Park. *Load up a 4X4 air-conditioned mountain tour van with eager visitors and set out with Doug to discover the backroad beauty of "upcountry" Kaua'i. An island native, our guide was well versed in Hawaiian culture, history, as well as the flora of the region. Explore Koke'e State Park and the Pali-Kona Forest. While you can hike in on many of these roads to the lookouts we visited, the four-wheel drive vehicle can get you much closer to the lookouts! This is an excellent option especially for those who might be unable to do some strenuous trekking. Nothing was more than a light walk. The van was cool and comfortable, although there was some expected jostling that occurs over the rough back roads. Doug had said that he could talk for the entire seven hours of the trip, and indeed he kept his promise. Examining different types of flowers, learning about their uses, and viewing the majestic Waimea Canyon from several different vantage points was broken up by a leisurely picnic lunch. A fine spread of lunchmeats, fruits, salads & cookies. Even straw mats were provided for those who wanted to stretch out a bit. While many choose to drive up to Waimea independently, you'll miss out on learning about some of the secret treasures that Kaua'i has to hold!* (808) 245-7224. <www.alohakauaitours.com> 1-800-452-1113.

Kaua'i Paradise Tours - Island sightseeing in six passenger van to Waimea and Kalalau or the North Shore. Combine land tour with helicopter trip for additional $129 or Fern Grotto Boat Cruise for additional $15. Narration available in English or German with owner/tour guide Max Dereyl. Tours $66-88. PO Box 3927, Lihu'e, HI 96766. (808) 246-3999, FAX (808) 245-2499.

Polynesian Adventure Tours - They do Waimea Canyon, Wailua River, and North Shore (Hanalei Bay, Ha'ena Caves, Lumahai Beach, etc.) tours and combinations thereof. $50-60. (808) 246-0122.

Robert's Hawai'i - They offer full and half day tours to scenic parts of the island. (808) 245-9558, 1-800-831-5541.

Trans Hawaiian - Three trips available: 1) Hanalei and Ha'ena Tour visits the Wailua River and its ancient temples, Opaeka'a Falls, Kilauea Lighthouse and Refuge, Lumahai Beach, Hanalei Bay, the wet and dry caves at Ha'ena, and Ke'e Beach 2) Waimea Canyon Tour which tours Nawiliwili Harbor, the Menehune Fishpond, Russian Fort Elizabeth, Waimea Town, Waimea Canyon, Kalalau Valley Lookout, and Spouting Horn. 3) Waimea Canyon/Wailua River Tour is a full day trip that circles the island from the Eastern shore to the Northern. Prices quoted vary depending on pick-up location. Ask about discounts for children. This company also operates the Coconut Coast Trolley. 1-800-251-5692. (808) 245-5108.

## ***LUAUS*** See chapter on Restaurants.

## ***MOVIES/MOVIE RENTALS*** (Also see Theater)

The Coconut MarketPlace has a twin theater with bargain prices for matinees (before 6). (808) 821-2324.

Kukui Grove Cinemas have two screens in their theater adjoining the Kukui Grove Shopping Center. Phone (808) 245-5055 to hear a recording.

The Princeville Hotel has complimentary movies for hotel guests shown four times daily in their small, private cinema. Non-resort guests who come to the hotel to dine can receive complimentary cinema passes for that evening.

Waimea Community Theatre is now fully restored and offers a variety of films and live productions. Phone (808) 885-5815.

If you have a VCR at your accommodation, there are plenty of options for renting movies. If you don't have a machine you can rent one of those as well. Blockbuster videos is the biggest chain on the island. They have their main outlet at 4-771 Kuhio Hwy. at Waipouli Town Center in the mall next to Foodland. They do have drop off boxes at other places around the island. It is about $5 for a three-day rental. (808) 822-7744. Other video stores are scattered around the island. Check the grocery stores, too, Foodland in Princeville has a good selection.

### *HAWAI'I MOVIE TOUR*

If you are a movie buff, or even if you're not, you are sure to enjoy one of Kaua'i's newest island tours. ***Hawai'i Movie Tours*** travels around the north and eastern shores of the island with a guided narrated tour of some of Kaua'i's most famous movie locations. Ground tours combined with air and sea tours are also available. They have arranged special permission to visit private estates and other hidden places not open to the public. As you travel around the island, their on-van video equipment shows clips of just a fraction of the movies filmed on Kaua'i. (And commercials, too!) The film snippet provides an ideal introduction to the scenic location you are about to visit. Trust us, it would be impossible to visit many of the filming scenes on your own.

Their daily trip begins at 8:45am and ends at 2pm and runs $85 plus tax. Pickup available at east and south side resorts. With their Deluxe Tour you enjoy a hearty and healthy picnic lunch at a beach, take a 90 minute river cruise to the Fern Grotto and end your day with a Hawaiian luau. (Deluxe Tour is $295 and available only Wednesday and Friday.) Book early as this is a popular tour and often sells out. Maximum 10 people per tour. Their office is located behind Beezers in Kapa'a. Phone (808) 822-1192 or toll free 1-800-628-8432.
Email: tourguv@hawaiian.net or website at <www.hawaiimovietour.com>

### *MOVIES MADE ON KAUA'I (Courtesy of Hawai'i Movie Tours)*

Some of these will be familiar names and as for others, well, there is good reason they never made it big on the big screen!

1998: Six Days, Seven Nights; Mighty Joe Young
1997: George of the Jungle
1996: The Lost World-Jurassic Park 2
1995: Outbreak
1994: North
1993: Jurassic Park
1992: Honeymoon in Vegas
1991: Hook
1990: Flight of the Intruder, Lord of the Flies
1987: Throw Mama From The Train
1986: Islands of the Alive
1983: The Thorn Birds, Uncommon Valor
1981: Behold Hawaii, Body Heat
1981: Raiders of the Lost Ark
1979: Seven, Last Flight of Noah's Ark
1978: Deathmoon, Acapulco Gold
1977: Fantasy Island, Islands in the Stream, King Kong, Waterworld (television)
1974: Man with the Golden Gun, Castaway Cowboy
1970: The Hawaiians
1969: Lost Flight
1968: Yoake No Futare, Lovers at Dawn
1966: Hawaii
1965: Lt. Robinson Crusoe, U.S.N, Operation Attack, None But The Brave

1963: Gilligan's Island (pilot episode), Donovan's Reef
1962: Girls! Girls! Girls! (original title Paradise Hawaiian Style), Diamond Head

1961: Blue Hawai'i, Seven Women From Hell
1960: Wackiest Ship in the Army
1958: South Pacific
1957: Forbidden Island, Jungle Heat, Voodoo Island
1956: Beach Head, Between Heaven and Hell, She Gods of Shark Reef, Thunder Over Hawaii
1953: Miss Sadie Thompson
1951: Bird of Paradise
1950: Pagan Love Song
1933: White Heat

## *MUSEUMS/GARDEN TOURS/CULTURAL TOURS*

Kaua'i offers some of the finest garden and cultural tours in the Hawaiian chain. Be sure to find time to take in at least one of the following varied options.

The ***National Tropical Botanical Garden*** is a nationally-chartered, privately funded, non-profit organization. It is the nation's only tropical botanical garden chartered by the U.S. Congress. Headquartered on Kaua'i, its principal mission is research, conservation, and education relating to the world's tropical plants. The NTBG consists of five distinct gardens in the Hawaiian Islands and in Florida. The three Kaua'i gardens are: Lawa'i, Allerton and Limahuli, with another on Maui. Each of the gardens has an individual name, but they are sometimes incorrectly referred to individually as the "National Tropical Botanical Garden."

The ***Lawa'i Garden*** (National Tropical Botanical Garden Headquarters) is located on Kaua'i's southern shore in the lush Lawa'i Valley, and was the first garden site to be acquired by the National Tropical Botanical Garden. In discussion of the Lawa'i Garden, we would like to provide a little background on the area. Little is known of early Lawa'i. According to an account by David Forbes in his book, *Queen Emma and Lawa'i*, the early maps and photographs show that the valley was cultivated in taro and later in rice. Queen Emma, the wife of Kamehameha IV, probably first saw Lawa'i during her visit in 1856, but returned for a more lengthy stay during the winter and spring in 1871. On arrival she found the area rather desolate, and compared with the busy life in Honolulu, it must have seemed so. In her correspondence with her family on O'ahu she requested many items to be sent, including plant slips. With these plant starts she began to develop one of the finest gardens in the islands. Queen Emma leased the Lawa'i land to Duncan McBryde for a span of fifteen years in 1876, however, she reserved her house lot and several acres of taro patch land.

According to Forbes, "In 1886, after the Queen's death, Mrs. Elizabeth McBryde bought the entire Ahupuaa for $50,000. The upper lands were planted to sugar cane, and the valley was apparently leased to Chinese rice growers and taro planters." In 1899, Alexander McBryde obtained the land and with a love of plants, he continued to enlarge and cultivate the gardens which had been begun by the queen. Alexander McBryde died in 1935 and the land was sold to Robert Allerton and his son John in 1938. They continued to enlarge the gardens, searching out plants from around South East Asia. Today Lawa'i is a horticulturist's dream, with an outstanding collection of tropical plants.

The NTBG headquarter facilities are located adjacent to the Lawa'i Garden. The headquarters complex includes a scientific laboratory, an herbarium housing nearly 30,000 specimens of tropical plants, an 8,000 volume research library, a computer records center, an educational center, and offices for staff and visiting scientists. ***Lawa'i Garden*** is a research and educational garden comprising 186 acres. The garden's extensive collections include tropical plants of the world that are of particular significance for research, conservation, or cultural purposes. Special emphasis is given to rare and endangered Hawaiian species and to economic plants of the tropical world.

Of particular interest is the endangered *kanaloa kahoolawensis* (one of only four in the world). This small, woody plant is known only to exist on Kahoolawe. In 1992, two specimens of this plant were discovered on Kahoolawe. This was the first new genus discovered in Hawai'i since 1913. Two *kanaloa kahoolawensis* have since been grown from seeds at the NTBG. There is also a collection of familiar household products - sugar, vanilla, cinnamon - all seen here in their natural plant state. Palm oil, sandalwood (for scent), koa (for wood items including canoes and furniture) and cuari (used to make sodium pentathol) can also be seen in their original form. ***Three Springs*** is at the interior of the Lawa'i Garden (makai or toward the mountains). This 120-acre area was acquired as a bequest to the Garden and is yet undeveloped. It will eventually be designed as an additional garden section, emphasizing the beautiful natural land and water features.

The nearby ***Allerton Garden*** is located oceanfront at Lawa'i Kai, adjacent to the Lawa'i Garden. The new visitor entrance is at Spouting Horn. This was formerly a private 100-acre estate. The beautifully designed garden is managed by the National Tropical Botanical Garden pursuant to an agreement with the Allerton Estate Trust. The gardens, started by Queen Emma, were lovingly developed and expanded over a period of 30 years by Robert Allerton and his son John. The sculpted gardens contain numerous plants of interest, outstanding examples of garden design, and water features, as well as Queen Emma's original summer cottage. The cottage was severely damaged by Hurricane Iniki and plans for restoration are underway. The Moreton Bay fig trees here have giant buttress roots and helped create a prehistoric scene for the filming of *Jurassic Park*. While these trees appear ancient, they were actually planted in 1940.

Reservations are required for tours of the Lawa'i and Allerton Gardens. Tour fee is currently $25 for each tour. For information on scheduled tours and reservations, call (808) 332-7324. PO Box 340 Lawa'i, HI 96765.

The ***Limahuli Gardens***, in Ha'ena, on Kaua'i's North Shore is an area of overwhelming natural beauty. Located one-half mile past the nine-mile marker on Kuhio Highway #560, this is another branch of the National Tropical Botanical Garden (NTBG). This lush garden offers a walking tour that leads you uphill through a 15-acre garden and forest to a beautiful viewpoint overlooking the ocean. You will see ancient taro terraces, many of the plants introduced to Hawai'i by the early Polynesians, as well as plantings of native Hawaiian species and the pristine Limahuli Stream. Their guided tours are 1 1/2 - 2 hours long. A self-guided tour is available and you also need to allow a couple of hours. Advanced reservations are required for all tours and they request that visitors meet promptly for their tours. If you must cancel your reservation, they request a phone call at least two hours in advance of your scheduled tour. All visitors are met by the National Tropical Botanical Garden staff at the garden's entrance. Parking area and restroom facilities are available. Picnic lunches are not allowed on the grounds. Guided tours are offered Tuesday at 1pm and Sundays at 10am at a cost of $15. Self-guided tours are available for $10 per person on Tuesdays at 10am, Wednesdays at 10am and 1pm, Thursdays at 10am and 1pm, and Sundays at 1pm. Phone (808) 826-1053 for information.

The ***Children's Discovery Museum*** on Kaua'i has temporary exhibitions and programs at locations all over the island. For information on what and where call them at (808) 823-8222.

***Grove Farm Homestead*** ★ in Lihu'e is an example of the old style of plantation living. This was the plantation home of George N. Wilcox until 1978. A fascinating two and one half hour tour is given. This, in our opinion, is the best cultural tour on the island. Tours by advance reservation only. Admission $5. Currently tours are offered Monday, Wednesday, and Thursday 10am and 1:10pm. Call to verify schedule. PO Box 1631, Lihu'e, HI 96766. (808) 245-3202.) For additional information see WHERE TO STAY/WHAT TO SEE *Central/Eastside*.

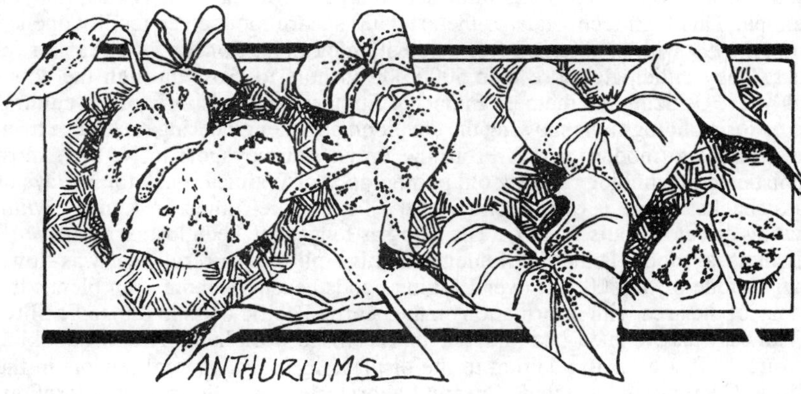

There are 480 acres of guava orchards under commercial cultivation at the ***Guava Kai Plantation*** in Kilauea, which is considered the Guava Capitol of the world. Visit the plantation's visitor center and discover how guava is grown and processed into a variety of treats. Guava has fewer calories and more vitamin C than oranges, and it is also a good source of vitamin A, potassium, and phosphorus. Guava is actually not a citrus, but a berry with a fleshy seed cavity and thick skin. The guava can survive in dry or very tropical conditions. The Kilauea orchards receive 100 inches of rainfall each year with temperate 65-80 degree weather that is very agreeable to this crop. During dry months each tree receives up to 75 gallons of water per day. The seedlings were planted in this orchard in 1977 and began producing fruit in 1979. The first commercial yield was in January of 1980 with a 2,000 pounds per acre harvested. Today the yield is 5,000 pounds per acre or about 400 pounds of fruit per tree per harvest cycle. The fruit at this plantation is hand-picked and harvested year round on a full-scale crop cycling system. The fruit meat can vary from white or yellow to orange or pink. The variety grown at the Guava Kai Plantation is a hybrid developed by the University of Hawai'i's College of Tropical Agriculture and has bright pink flesh and an edible rind. The color in your glass of juice is all natural. The guava was a native of South America and it was introduced islands in 1791 by the Spaniard Don Francisco de Paula Marin, who was an advisor to Kamehameha I. The guava flourished and many now grow wild in Hawaii. There is a self-guided tour that includes a view of the orchard and the processing plants as well as an informative eight minute video.

There is a man-made fish pond and an assortment of native Hawaiian plants to enjoy as your stroll the grounds. The snack bar, open only in the summer months, sells ice cream, juice, breads, and other bakery items made with guava. There are free samples of guava juice, jams, jellies, and coffee. Since they are owned by Maunaloa, they also sell their products at slightly lower rates than retail outlets. Guava Kai Plantation is open 9am-5pm. (808) 828-6121.

A good place to begin your Waimea exploration would be at the new ***West Kaua'i Visitor & Technology Center***, 9565 Kaumualii Hwy., Waimea (808) 338-1332. HOURS: Open daily 9am-5pm. Pictorials, graphics, and displays with touch-sensitive screens provide information on all of Kaua'i's activities, not just Waimea. This high-tech, state-of-the-art 7500 square foot center facility opened in April 1999 with land leased from the Kiki'aloa Land Co. for $1 a year for 30 years. They anticipate more than 5000,000 visitors to cross through the doors each year. Utilizing the theme, "Enduring Engineering," visitors follow cultural and historic photographs showing the development of engineering on Kaua'i from ancient days to modern times. From the Polynesian voyagers to NASA's most sophisticated technology. Enjoy old photographs of Waimea, back to the days of grass shacks! There is even a photo of the first movie filmed on Kaua'i, *White Heat* by director Louis Weber. (The film has long since been lost or destroyed.) One unusual model is the Pathfinder which is a pilotless aircraft that was flown at an altitude of 80,000 feet over Barking Sands beach. The museum blends the history of the area with information on the nearby Pacific Missile Range Facility. Not an easy task to undertake, but one that seems to work here. They are looking forward to Phase II! In addition to the displays there are several tenants in the facility. Currently they include Oceanit Laboratories, Inc., Solipsys Corporation, Textron Systems and Trex Enterprises.

***Kaua'i Sugar Plantation Tours*** - Hawaii's cultural history can be intimately explored through the heart of the sugar planation. Hawaii's multi-cultural history is due to the need for laborers in the labor-intensive sugar fields of yesterdays. Now you have the opportunity to view field to factory operations at Gay & Robinson. The two-hour bus tour, conducted by Gay & Robinson Tours LLC, is available weekdays and includes the history of the plantation, its operation, processing, the plantation's miles of irrigation systems, and views of the private plantation lands. Harvesting operations are seasonal with the months of April through October the best times to visit Gay & Robinson. Tour routes depend on the day-to-day operations. If you don't have time for the full tour, stop by their office on Kaumakari Avenue and view the historic displays. The office is located in the historic Field Office (circa 1900) on Kaumakani Avenue. From Lihu'e, travel Hwy. 50. Just past mile marker 19, turn left on Kaumakani Avenue with its monkeypod tress and old-fashioned streetlights. It is open 8am-4pm Monday through Friday, with the exception of plantation holidays. Tours are at 9am and 1 pm. All visitors on the tour are required to wear safety equipment to enter the factory. They must also wear pants (shorts are okay), low-heeled, closed shoes and they will be provided with safety glasses and hard hats. Cost of the tour is $40. In the not-to-distant future they will be adding tours of the Koula Valley. Phone (808) 335-2824. For more in-depth information on Waimea, pick up a copy of *Touring Waimea* by Christine Fayé. Available at local bookstores.

The family-owned and operated business, ***Kamokila Hawaiian Village*** ★, was open when we were in the area. We were more than pleasantly surprised by the quaintness and authenticity of the village. The admission fee of $5 included a guided tour and we were a bit after the start, but joined up with Lopaka and four other guests. You definitely need a guide to explain the meanings of each of the various thatched structures and their uses. He broke open a coconut for us to sample (the young green spoon ones!), plucked us a flower for our hair, and even a guava off the tree to eat. Dashing between huts to avoid the off and on again rainshowers, Lopaka played the ukulele and sang as we explored the birthing place, the sleeping huts, and other accounts of early Hawaiian life. It is what the Polynesian Cultural Center on O'ahu can never be ... a personalized interpretive center. Nothing commercial here! You can buy a lei for $2 or a freshly made pandanus hat for just a little bit more. (Okay ... so Lopaka DOES have some of his CDs available ... and we even bought one!) Located opposite Opaeka'a Falls, the Kaumo'o Road entrance is just past the Wailua Bridge.

The ***Kaua'i Museum*** is located in downtown Lihu'e. Through murals, artifacts, and artwork, discover how the islands have changed since Captain Cook's arrival at Waimea in 1778. The Museum Shop specializes in Hawaiian Island memorabilia, Hawaiian books, and local crafts. They also have rotating exhibits so there will be something new and different every time you visit. Open weekdays 9am-4:30pm, Saturday 9am-1pm, closed Sunday. The first Saturday of the month is free admission day and it features special family events and activities. Admission $5, senior admission $4, children under 17 are free. (808) 245-6931.

Started in late 1999 (too late to review for this edition) was a ***guided walking tour of Kapa'a***. It is run by volunteers and meets at the Kaua'i Historical Society History Shop (Kamamura Building in Kapa'a). Price is expected to run $15 with a tour that goes through the older part of town, exploring the history of sugar, pineapple, cultural influences, significance of buildings with antidotes, explanations of native plant life, fishing, plantation life and a stop at Pono Kai Resort which used to be a cannery! The History Shop has history related gift items such as books, local art and their own KHS logo shirts (808) 821-1778.

The ***Kaua'i Historical Society Museum***, formerly at the Coco Palms, now at 4396 Rice Street, Suite 101. Admission free by appointment. See page 94 of this guide for additional information. (808) 245-3373.

Kiahuna Plantation offers free self-guided tours of their ***Moir Gardens*** (or *Pa'u a Laka Garden*) or *Hawaiian Gardens*. Guided tours are available as well. Phone (808) 742-6411.

***Kilohana*** is reminiscent of the grandeur and elegance of an earlier age. At the time when sugar was king on the island and prosperity reigned, plantation owners would build luxurious homes. One of the grandest on Kaua'i was the home of Gaylord Parke Wilcox and is known as Kilohana. Built in 1935, it was designed by a British architect named Mark Potter. The grounds were carefully landscaped and inside furniture arrived from the exclusive and expensive Gump's in San Francisco. Today, in addition to the gift shops, galleries, and Gaylord's Courtyard Restaurant, you'll find several tour options for this 35 acre estate. The Canefield Tour is a step back into the history of sugar cane on Kaua'i. A horse-drawn wagon helps return you in time to 1835. The Carriage Ride is a romantic excursion around the grounds, with a short narration. The rides are available daily from 11am-6:30pm, cost is $8 adults and $4 children. Horse drawn Sugar Cane Tours are twice daily by advance reservations, cost is $21 adults and $10 children. For information phone (808) 246-9529. Admission to Kilohana and its beautiful grounds is free. Kilohana and the shops open daily at 9:30am. Gaylord's serves brunch Sunday 9:30am-3pm, lunch Monday-Friday 11am-3pm and dinner from 5pm. Located just outside Lihu'e, travel east along Kaumualii Highway, Route 50. Kilohana is on your left just before the town of Lihu'e. If you are arriving from the north or east, travel Kuhio Hwy., Route 56 south and west through Lihu'e. Bear right at the traffic light at the end of Kuhio Hwy. Kilohana will be 1.4 miles down Kaumualii Highway on your right.

***Koke'e Natural History Museum*** contains geographic maps of Kaua'i along with exhibits of native plant and bird species. Admission is free, but donations are accepted. They regularly offer free or inexpensive guided hikes and other interesting annual activities. (808) 335-9975.

At the Kukui Grove Shopping Center in their ***Exhibition Hall*** you'll discover a cooperative effort between the Garden Islands Arts Council, the Kaua'i Society of Artists and the shopping center. Their Exhibition Hall regularly features the most creative and energetic efforts of the art community. This year (2000), for example, the Exhibition Hall will welcome "Chalk Talks" where artists will be challenged to create temporary works of art on the sidewalk using colored chalk. Other planned activities include a fall "Lights, Lanterns and Luminaries" and an event called "Hello, Mr. Postman" where artists will design unique and innovative mail receptacles. Sounds fun!

***Olu Pua Gardens and Plantation Estate*** is located on the way to Waimea Canyon, one mile past Kalaheo. This plantation estate was once the residence for the Alexander family back in the 1930's. It was designed by Hawai'i's foremost architect, C.W. Dickey. The Alexander family ancestors first arrived in the islands as missionaries, later founding Kaua'i's largest pineapple plantation. The estate is located on twelve acres. The estate is now closed to the public, but available for lease through Kaua'i Vacation Rentals.

***Wai'oli Mission House*** was the home of island missionaries Abner and Lucy Wilcox. This 19th century New England-style home was shipped in pieces from Boston around Cape Horn to Kaua'i. The home features beautiful koa wood furniture and other items from the period. Open to the public Tuesdays, Thursdays, and Saturdays from 9am-2:45pm. Wai'oli Mission House Museum in Hanalei was built of coral limestone blocks in 1837. Guided tours are available at no charge. Donations appreciated. PO Box 1631, Lihu'e, HI 96766. (808) 245-3202.

***Waimea Sugar Mill Camp Museum and Plantation Lifestyles Walking Tour.*** Reservations are required for this historical and informative tour which is limited to 12 people. Volunteers lead a tour which begins at the administration building of the Waimea Plantation Cottages. The tour is currently offered Tuesdays and Saturdays at 9am and lasts about one hour. Cost is $6 adults, $5 seniors 65 and older, and children 12 and under are $3. PO Box 1178, Waimea, HI 96796. (808) 338-0006.

## *POLO*

You might not expect to find this recreational option on an Hawaiian island, but polo season begins in late April and runs through September. Matches are held each Sunday at the 'Anini Polo Field, 3pm. The field is located across the road from 'Anini Beach. Access via Kalihiwai Road.

## *RENTAL EQUIPMENT*

Outfitters Kaua'i - Biking and kayking equipment. (808) 742-7421.

Paradise Outdoor Adventures - Rents bikes and kayaks. (808) 822-1112.

Pedal and Paddle in Hanalei. Backpacking and Camping Gear as well as kayak rental and beach equipment rental. (808) 826-9069.

## *RIVER EXCURSIONS*

Also see section on Kayaking.

Smith's Tropical Paradise cruises up the Wailua River to the famous Fern Grotto. Trips operate daily starting at 9am. The last boat departs at 2:30pm or 3:30pm, depending on the day of the week. Trip duration is 1 hour and 20 minutes. Current scheduled departures are every half hour from 9am-11:30am and 12:30pm until 3pm. Additional 3:30pm departure on Monday, Wednesday and Fridays. No reservations needed, just arrive 15 minutes before departure. They are located at the mouth of the Wailua River. Adults $15, children 2-12 $7.50. Fern Grotto Cruise information phone (808) 821-6892 or 821-6893. For information on Smith's Tropical Paradise phone (808) 821-6895 or 821-6896. For their Wedding Department phone (808) 821-6887 or 821-6888.

Wai'ale'ale Boat Tours Inc. presents Fern Grotto Cruises. A 1 1/2 hour tour up the Wailua River which includes music, hula, historical facts, and legends. Adults $15, children $7.50, senior discounts. Trips start at 9am and there are currently nine trips daily. (808) 822-4908.

## *RUNNING*

Kaua'i has no official running organization. If you'd like to know more about marathons or running events, see the EVENTS section of this guide or try calling the Kaua'i Athletic Club, Foot Locker, or Dan's Sports Shop as they usually have entry forms for any current running events.

## *SCUBA DIVING*

Scuba divers can explore the General Store, a 65-80 foot deep reef with a variety of marine life and a 19th century steamship, or the Sheraton Caves which have interesting lava formations and plenty of green sea turtles. At Koloa Landing, divers might discover bottles or fittings from old whaling ships and parts of the train track that once ran between Koloa and the area's sugar mill. On the North Shore there are underwater lava tubes and archways. While on the eastern shore, divers can explore the wreck of the *Lukenbach*, a German freighter that sank 40 years ago. Off Ni'ihau there are 130 foot deep reef walls with abundant marine life, considered by some to be the best diving in Hawai'i.

Popular shore diving beaches include Makua Beach (Tunnels) on the North Shore and on the southern shore, Koloa Landing and Prince Kuhio Park in Po'ipu. If you'd like to do an introductory scuba dive, a boat dive on Kaua'i will run you $70-90. Shore dives are available from several dive companies. Dive Certification takes several days; some offer PADI while others offer NAUI. The cost of certification on Kaua'i runs $295-$425. A few dive companies offer prescription masks. Most of them offer a three-tank dive to Ni'ihau ($235) a little steep, but quite an adventure to a reef wall. One dive shop suggested that visitors with limited time do "PADI" dive preparation on the mainland and they can then be certified on Kaua'i in just two days. Classes are generally no more than six persons. Private lessons, which run slightly more, are also available. Many of the following dive companies also rent gear.

Bubbles Below - Offers scuba charters that specialize in marine biology. Their 35 ft. vessel, *Kaimanu*, takes out only eight divers at a time. They do a variety of dives including a multi-level drift dive. Also available are night dives. They do Ni'ihau dives, but warn that the rougher channel conditions make this trip only for the hearty and the 20-mile open-ocean crossing usually takes an hour to go across and an hour and a half to come back. Included are three tanks at three different locations. This trip is only available twice weekly. If you are interested in underwater photography, they have a professional camera system and they charge $50 for a roll of 24 photos with negatives included. Night and Twilight dives are two-tank dives for $100. Morning or afternoon dives are four-hour trips and are two-tank dives at two locations. Equipment is available for rent including wetsuits, regulators, and buoyancy compensators. The all day Ni'ihau trip is $200. Owners Linda and Ken Bail have years of experience. Linda began her scuba diving experience at age six and has instructed divers since 1977 as a NAUI course director, and PADI master scuba diver trainer. Ken has been a NAUI instructor and PADI master scuba diver trainer since 1982. They share their love for the marine environment and include the marine ecosystem in their briefing. (808) 822-3483. <www> Email: kaimanu@alolha.net

Dive Kaua'i Scuba Center - Dive tours, boat charters, equipment rentals, introductory dives and PADI certification. Scuba tours $78-98 shore dive, $95-115 boat dive, PADI certification $350-395, introduction to scuba $98. Equipment rental by day or week. 976 Kuhio Hwy., Kapa'a, HI 96746. (808) 822-0452. Email: divekauai.com.

Fathom Five Divers ★ Full service dive store and PADI certification. Introductory dives from one of their two 26' dive boats. They visit more than 20 dive locations ranging from 30 to 90 feet. Some dive sites include Sheraton Caves, General Store, Ice Box, Brennecke's Ledge, Turtle Bluffs, and Zack's Pocket (named after their Hawaiian boat captain who discovered this site). Their dive sites are only 10-15 minutes from the harbor, which makes a two-tank boat dive a half day trip and provides adventures for the experienced and beginning divers. Maximum of six divers. Introductory two-tank boat dive, no experience necessary $135 includes class, dives, and gear. Introductory shore dive with one-tank $95. Their 4 or 5 day course for PADI certification includes lectures, diving each day, and two boat dives on the last day. $369 includes it all. Open water check out dives available $230. (808) 742-6991. <www.fathom-five.com>

Hanalei Water Sports - Offers PADI scuba certification. They have daily guided snorkel and scuba tours as well as rentals. Located on the beach at the Princeville Hotel, they conduct their dives from the shore or offer special dive tours to Tunnels Reef, Koloa Landing, or Ahukini Landing. Guided snorkeling tour (1 hour) includes pool lesson, equipment, and wet suit $35, surf lessons (2 hours) including equipment also available. Outrigger Canoe Tours 1 1/2 hours up the Hanalei Bay and River $55 adults, $45 child or a sunset canoe tour $65. Scuba dives $105-140 for introductory dives, certified divers $75-125. (808) 826-7509 or contact David Takeda at (808) 826-4581 or Paul Frazier at (808) 639-9011.

Mana Divers Scuba - They are a Padi dive center located at the Hyatt Regency Kaua'i and Kaua'i Marriott Resort and Beach Club. They choose from several dive sites depending on conditions. They offer introductory dives, Eco-informed guided dives, PADI instruction and specialty dives, private tours and differently abled dives, and night dives for certified divers. Their Discover scuba diving experience is for mature guests 8 years and older, cost is $35 for 1 1/2 to 2 hours. It is a chance to get a little hands-on dive at a minimal cost.

The experience can include a lagoon (resort pool) dive and the fee can later be applied to an ocean dive if desired. Refresher dives ($85). Introductory dives $110/75 based on weather permitting. Offered to mature guests 12 and older. Guests who do not require the lagoon lesson are charged the lesser fee. Maximum depth 40 feet, average depth 20 feet. (808) 742-9849. 1-800-DIVENOW. FAX (808) 742-2458. Email: manadivers@hawaiian.net

Ocean Quest Watersports - This is a shore diving operation which means your entry is off the beach as opposed to off a boat. Owners Jeannette and George Thompson specialize in small groups, no more than 4 persons, and offer excursions for beginners or advanced divers. North shore eco tours are their summer specialty; south shore tours in the winter. Diving tours are also available for the "Differently Abled." They include dives at Tunnels, Ahukini, and Koloa landing and other advanced sites can be arranged. Certified guided tours are $70-85, introductory lessons are $85. Certification runs $350-395 per person. One tank night divers are available for certified divers $50-60.
(808) 822-3589. 1-888-401-3483. FAX (808) 822-3616.
Visit their website at: <www.hawaiian.net/~ocnqst>

Seasport Divers - Excursions depart aboard their 32 ft., 12-passenger boat from the Kukui'ula Boat Harbor. With 26 different dive sites to choose from, they can address all levels of diving enthusiasts. They offer a morning (8am-noon) or afternoon (1pm-5pm) two-location dive or an evening (6pm-9pm) one-tank dive. Underwater videos will be filmed by the divemaster and are available for $39.95. They also offer 35 mm camera rentals. Two-tank dives including equipment run $110, two-tank dives without equipment $90, One-tank night dive with equipment $75. Introductory boat dive with previous pool lesson $130. Snorkeler or rider $49.95. Shore dives for non-certified divers run $110 for a two-tank resort dive. Open water certification takes 3-4 days and runs $350. They also offer Referral dives and Advanced certification. They offer complimentary pool lessons daily. Call for the scheduled lesson nearest to your location. Reservations are suggested. They can also offer Ni'ihau Island dives. Also available are watersport equipment rentals including snorkel gear, boogie boards, beach chairs, and scuba gear. (808) 742-9303, (808) 742-7288, 1-800-685-5889 or FAX (808) 742-6636. <www.kauaiscubadiving.com> E-mail: <seasport@pixi.com>

Nitrox Tropical Divers and Sunrise Scuba Adventures - No swimming skills are required for this diving experience. They do shore dives and outfit you in shallow water where the scuba gear becomes weightless. They conduct all dives from a calm beach and keep the group size down to six divers. The minimum age for all scuba activities is 12 years, with parental consent. All beginners are required to participate in a FREE scuba orientation in calm shallow water prior to the ocean dive. Prices are $98 for intro dive tour for uncertified divers. $98 for shore or boat dive for certified divers. PADI certification available. They are a PADI 5-STAR enriched air facility. Email: doctrox@aloha.net or <www.sunrisescuba.com> (808) 822-7333.

Wet 'n Wonderful - Free introductory scuba lesson, refresher courses, PADI certification, wetsuits (It might be Hawaii, but it gets cold down under!) Shore dives and night dives. Owner operator Chris E. Norman. We tried to make inquiries on prices and schedules, but never received a reply. (808) 822-0211.

## *SEA EXCURSIONS* -- Also see Snorkeling

Sea excursion options on Kaua'i are more limited than on some of the other islands, but what makes it special on the Garden Island are the intimacies of the trips. Most use small boats, with as few as 6 people with maximums of 25, so that the experience is much more personal.

Depending on the time of year, the roughness of the water can vary greatly. If you are concerned about motion sickness, there are several over-the-counter medications that you could discuss with your doctor. Dramamine has been used by millions of people for years, however those folks we have met that have used this for motion difficulties have been so significantly affected by the sleepiness (which is a side effect for some individuals) that they can virtually sleep away the entire trip. While this might be an option for avoiding discomfort, they can't be having nearly as much fun as those of us who are alert! Bonine is another motion medication that can be purchased over-the-counter that, for some people, has less of a drowsiness effect. Ginger, which can be purchased in capsules at health food stores is recommended as a preventative for motion sickness as well. Check with your physician as to what options might work for you (and with your health conditions and with other medications you may already be taking). Using simple techniques such as keeping your eye on the land and avoiding a heavy, greasy meal before a boat trip are the only precautions most people need to use! A final note which bears mentioning! Most of these small craft DO NOT have bathroom facilities on-board. In some cases, there might be a "lua" (Hawaiian word for toilet) but it may not be available for public use. The larger boats will have facilities. We recommend you ask when booking!

The end of the century saw some dramatic changes in boating on Kaua'i. State regulations have permanently changed commercial boating on the North Shore. As of September 1999, motorized commercial boats are no longer permitted to depart from Hanalei, by the Governor's mandate. One sail boat remained in operation, but with a permit due to expire and not renewed (according to Mayor Kusaka and the County of Kaua'i Planning Department). As it stands now, Hanalei commercial tour boating is just a wonderful memory of days gone by -- a dream that was reality, and now a definite disadvantage for those staying on the North Shore! Those boating companies who have managed to stay in business have had to relocate their operations to the west coast of the island. Departures are now primarily from Port Allen, with a few departing other small west side harbors. This means that the boating trips are a bit longer, with more time required to reach the Napali from that side of the island ... and a VERY long trip from those staying on the North Shore to drive over to the west side. (Note: There is no road that travels around the island. On the North Shore the road ends at Ke'e Beach and on the west it goes out to Barking Sands Beach. In between are the Napalis!)

And, by the way, "Napali" means "the cliffs." You will often see it written as "Na Pali" but *Hawaiian Place Names*, written by authoritative historian Mary Kawena Kukui, spells it as one. And thus we follow her advice. Remember in using this term, don't say The Napali Cliffs, for that would mean, "The cliffs cliffs."

Blue Dolphin Charters, Ltd. - Snorkel, sun, fish, eat, try out their water slide, and scuba aboard their 56' sailing trimaran *Tropic Bird*. Winter four-hour excursion includes a continental breakfast and sandwiches for lunch and runs $85 snorkeling, $110 scuba. Summer 6 hour Napali tours $105 snorkeling, $130 scuba. Seasonal two-hour sunset cruises. They'll be adding a new boat soon! (808) 742-6731. (808) 742-6029. Departs from Port Allen. E-mail: <donnely@aloha.net>

Bluewater Sailing - Recently they have added a new Napali experience. Aboard their new 42 ft. all aluminum, Navy reconnaissance hull power boat, the *Northwind* is certified for 32 passengers, but 20 are "invited." Cushioned shaded seating in the open-air cabin or outside deck seating. A swim step and fresh water showers are added conveniences for snorkelers and all gear is provided along with a deli box lunch and soft drinks. Five hour Napali Coast Experience $110 adult, $85 children 5-12 years. Two hour sightseeing/whale watching (seasonal) adult $60, child 5-12 years $55. Or choose their snorkeling trips aboard their 42' Pearsen ketch, *Lady Leanne II*. Half day snorkeling/sailing with light meal, $105 adults/$85 children (5-12 years). Evening 2 hour sunset sail with snacks and sodas, $60. The "Express" departs from Port Allen. The sailing excursions depart from Hanalei in the summer, Port Allen in the winter. Exclusive charters available for either vessel. PO Box 1318, Hanalei, HI 96714. (808) 828-1142. FAX (808) 828-0508. Email: bluwat@aloha.net or visit their website at <www.sail-kauai.com>

Captain Andy's Sailing Adventures - Sail aboard the 55' catamaran *Spirit of Kaua'i*. Seasonal whale watching. This vessel was designed and built for Capt. Andy in the Virgin Islands, then tested out on the 12,000 mile trek to Kaua'i. Two tours daily to the Napali, 5 1/2 hours, $109 per person, 5-12 year olds $79. Friday sunset cruises include appetizers, cocktails and live music. $40 for adults, youth 5-12 $34, children under 5 are free. Departs Port Allen. PO Box 876, Ele'ele, Kaua'i, HI (808) 335-6833. FAX (808) 335-6838.

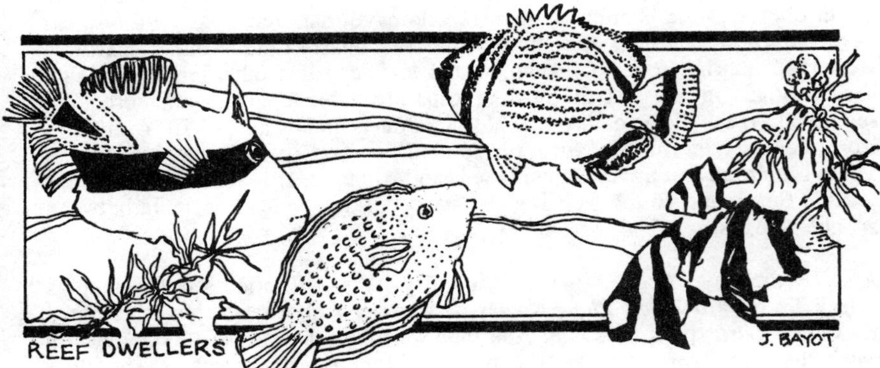

Catamaran Kahanu - Tours the Napali coastline in their power 36 ft. catamaran. Maximum 18 passengers. Covered area and private restroom. There are power engines on this catamaran so you can cruise near the coastline. Whale tours offered seasonally. Four and one half hour trip $95 adults, $75 children 5-11 years. Departs Port Allen. 420 Papaloa Road, Kapa'a, HI 96746. 1-800-422-7824, (808) 335-3577. Email: kahanu@hawaiian.net <www>

Kaua'i Sea Tours - Due to new regulations, Hanalei Sea Tours has been renamed Kaua'i Sea Tours and relocated to West Kaua'i. They sail out of Port Allen Harbor. The ride to the Napalis from this direction is 1 1/2 hours. The morning excursion is 5 1/12 hours and includes a beach landing at Nualolo Kai with a narrated hike of the area and time to snorkel. Cost is $115 and a $10 discount if you call and book direct. Their afternoon trip is 4 1/2 hours with no beach landing and is $95 with the same $10 discount for direct booking. Discounts for children. PO Box 51004, Ele'ele, HI. 1-800-733-7997, (808) 826-PALI. Email: seatours@aloha.net <WWW>

HoloHolo Charters -- '61 *HoloHolo*, power catamaran custom built on Kaua'i. Large trampolines or huge open air cabin. They offer a Ni'ihau & Napali Super Tour (7 hours, $140 adults; $109 children includes continental breakfast, buffet lunch and snorkeling). Napali Sunset Tour (3 1/2 hours $79/60). Aboard their 48 foot sailing catamaran *Leila* you can enjoy their Napali Sail (6 hours $99/75) or Sunset Champagne Sail (2 hours $59/45). Seasonal whale watching. Only children ages 6 years and older for excursions, 4 years and older on sunset trips, no "expecting" mothers. Office located at the Ele'ele Shopping Center. Departs Anchor Cove, Nawiliwili. (808) 335-0815 Website: <www.holoholo-charters.com>

Kaua'i Z-Tour - The 10-passenger *Ho'o Kahi* and 16-passenger *Makaio* are custom built zodiac boats with cushioned seating. Snorkeling, dolphins, sea turtles, seasonal whalewatching, sea caves and arches with waterfalls. They pride themselves on being Kaua'i's smallest company which affords them the opportunity to customize their trip for your needs. Lunch and snorkel gear included. Five-hour whalewatch (seasonal) Kipu Kai snorkel/lunch $90 adults, children 5-12 years $70. Five-hour Napali snorkel/lunch $120 adults, $90 children. Two trips daily. Chris Turner, owner. PO Box 1082, Kalaheo, HI 96741. (808) 742-6331. FAX (808) 332-9177. Email: ztourz@hawaiian.net. Website: <www.ztour@ztouz.com>

Kaulana Pali Kai Tours -- Group or private charters. Sunset cruises, snorkeling, whale watching aboard this 25' Bayliner Trophy. Freshwater shower and enclosed toilet. Departs Kiki'aola Harbor in Kekaha. Their Napali run costs $96 per person for the 4 1/2 - 5 hour cruise including lunch and refreshments. PO Box 1230 phone (808) 639-2780 or (808) 337-9309.

Liko Kaua'i Cruises - Departing from Kiki'aola Harbor, but check-in at their office in Waimea. Board their 49' power catamaran with bathroom, fresh water shower, and shaded area for a 4 hour snorkel excursion. Cost is $95 for adults, $65 for youth ages 4-14 years. Sunset sightseeing cruise three times each week with appetizers and soft drinks $75 adults, $45 children. Seasonal whale watching. PO Box 18, Waimea, HI 96796. 1-888-SEA-LIKO, (808) 338-0333. Email: liko@aloha.net

Na Pali (Eco) Adventures - ★ They are dedicated to the understanding and protection of our eco system. (Their boats use 100% recycled fuel made from cooking oil!) Their guided trip along the Napali coast is led by a trained naturalist. They use motor-powered, hard-body catamarans (passenger maximums of 26 and 35) that provide a smoother and drier ride than the inflatables or rafts, but there are still provide plenty of thrills! The morning trip is 5 hours with snorkeling and sightseeing and includes a full lunch $115 adults, $86.25 youth. The afternoon trip is sightseeing only and is $100 adults, youth $75 and includes appetizers. Call direct and receive a $10 discount on adult fares (some restrictions apply). The operators are genuinely concerned with the welfare of whales and other aquatic life and it shows in the way they run their cruise. If the whales are out there, they'll find them. An underwater microphone allows you to hear the whales' musical conversation. In addition to whales (in season), you might also be treated to a pod of dolphins swimming along your boat, green sea turtles floating like huge army helmets upon the water, or if you look quickly, you may spot a flying fish. We were fortunate during our excursion to be greeted by Kaua'i's rarest aquatic animal. On first sighting, the monk seal appeared to be lounging in the water, however, on the return trip he appeared in another bay giving us what appeared to be a smile! Realizing that there are estimated to be only three monk seals living in the waters around Kaua'i, our captain felt that we had seen the same seal twice and that they rarely see them more than a couple times of year. Ours was a lucky trip indeed. Departs from Port Allen Harbor. PO Box 1017, Hanalei, HI 96714. (808) 826-6804. FAX (808) 826-7073. 1-800-659-6804. Website: <www.napali.com> E-mail: <napali@pixi.com>

Na Pali Catamarans - 32' power catamaran *Kamahele Kai*, 16 passengers. Four-hour sightseeing tour of the Napali Coast $125. Still departing out of Hanalei Bay on a temporary permit. (808) 826-6853.

Na Pali Explorer - Enjoy a Napali excursion on the comfortable adventure raft *Na Pali Explorer*. This 48' rigid hull inflatable is mounted on Scarab ocean racing hulls and is powered by twin Volvo turbo supercharged diesels which each generate 230 horsepower. Needless to say, the *Na Pali Explorer* gets to where it is going pretty quickly, cruising at 25 knots and the potential to reach 33 knots. This vessel offers a smoother, more comfortable ride than the zodiac-type raft experience. Capacity is 49 passengers, but we're advised they take only 35. The five and a half hour tour includes deli sandwiches and beverages. There is also a chance to swim and snorkeling (gear provided) on a protected reef with a beach landing at Nualolo Kai, an ancient Hawaiian fishing village (weather permitting). Comfort features include a canopy for shade, and padded seating. Their expert naturalists share little-known facts about marine life and Hawaiian places along the way. Cost is $118 for adults, $70 for children 5-11 years. Seasonal whale watching. 1-800-335-9909, (808) 335-9909, FAX (808) 335-0188.

Rainbow Runner Sailing - 42' Kantola design Trimaran, maximum of 18 passengers. Departs Nawiliwili Small Boat Harbor or Kalapaki Beach, weather permitting. A one-hour Kalapaki Fun Sail $35 adult/$25 children. High performance speed sailing. Includes soft drinks/juices. Their Nawiliwili Sunset is $45 adults, $30 children and includes champagne, Kilauea Bakery bread sticks and fruit. Whale watching seasonally. Lighthouse Sail n' Snorkel is $59 adults, $30 children and is two hours including continental breakfast. Kipu Kai Sail Snorkel n' Picnic is $85 adults, $59 children. Duration is 4 hours and includes gourmet picnic lunch, soft drinks and juices, snorkel equipment. All trips include performance sailing and seasonal whale watching. They also operate True Blue Charters for those avid fisherfolks and Island Adventures for kayaking fans. PO Box 1722, Lihu'e, HI 96766. (808) 245-9662. FAX (808) 246-9661.
Email: funkauai@hawaiian.net

Captain Sundown - Six hour Napali Adventure Sail every morning (showing you the whole Napali Coast, dolphins, flying fish, with snorkeling and lunch). Three hour Bali Hai Sunset sail every evening. Sailing from Hanalei since 1971 taking only 15 passengers per trip on sailing catamaran Ku'uipo. Winter whales guaranteed. PO Box 697, Hanalei, HI 96714. (808) 826-5585. E-mail: sundown@aloha.net Website: <www.captainsundown.com>

***SNORKELING*** -- Also refer to Sea Excursions which precedes this section

Since weather conditions and ocean conditions cause very dramatic differences in the snorkeling conditions from day to day, a dive shop is a great place to find the tip for the best spot of the day. The staff is friendly and they are eager to ensure you have a great snorkeling experience. If weather conditions are just right, Tunnels on the North Shore is a wonderful snorkel spot. Po'ipu Beach on the South shore will be of interest to the novice and intermediate snorkeler.

You can purchase a disposable underwater camera. You'll get some interesting souvenir photos, but the quality isn't nearly as good as the real thing. One snorkeling trick we learned about was to use vaseline on the mustache to help seal the mask. Several areas around the island have fish that are accustomed to being fed. In fact, they almost expect it! They enjoy bread or try the dried packages of noodles. One source (in days gone by) recommended that we try peas. Thinking it would be healthier for the fish than white bread, we gave them a try. The fish were not too interested and then we learned that the uneaten peas would wash up on the shore making a squishy, smelly mess. We were also told that the fish have trouble digesting the outer coating of the pea. A number of dive shops (and Safeway) carry a little package of smelly fish food pellets. The price tag is a couple of dollars for two tubes of food. You can cut off one end of the plastic tube-bag and slowly shake out the pellets. However, many folks are discouraging feeding the fish at all. It can make them more aggressive and it provides a false habitat.

Kids will take to snorkeling with little effort. The only difficulty might be in their excitement when they spot the fish for the first time. They may forget they have a snorkel in their mouth when they try and shout out their glee. Christie's son became very adept at talking with his snorkel in his mouth, and hearing his words come out the top of his snorkel was a constant source of amusement. For the child who lacks confidence, use water wings for extra buoyancy. A life jacket, of course, is even more security. An adult may find taking a paddle board out and positioning themselves over the top of it (face in the water on one side and feet in the water on the other) a way to get over their initial jitters. Rest assured that snorkeling is much, much easier than swimming. Even easier than walking! All you have to do is float and breathe! Lydgate is a fine beach for the novice child snorkeler. It has a very sheltered area which will inspire confidence. Perhaps the most difficulty for a beginning (child or adult) snorkeler is just getting into the water. Waves make this a more difficult task. Once in the water and enjoying the sights, they'll wonder why they never tried it before.

Po'ipu Beach is generally good for beginning snorkelers as well. For intermediate snorkelers Ke'e, Hideaways, or Tunnels can be good during calm summer surf. The dive shops can advise you which locations are best at the time of your visit. Rental equipment is available at a number of locations around the island. With snorkel gear you will get what you pay for. Prices range from $4-5 a day and up. Silicon gear is preferred, but you generally won't find that at the economy prices. If you plan on adding snorkeling to your list of regular recreational activities, you may find it worthwhile to bite the bullet and invest in your own set of gear. You can pick-up an inexpensive set of fins, mask, and snorkel for a child at Longs drug store, Costco, Big Kmart, or Walmart.

Also refer to the Sea Excursions section for snorkeling trips which are available from various departures around the island. Also see SCUBA.

Fathom Five - Half day boat trips are available to secluded snorkeling sites off the south side. Also scuba available. (808) 742-691.

Hanalei Sport Fishing & Tours - 28' Power Catamaran offers sport fishing as well as snorkeling, and sunset sails. As we go to press, still departing from Hanalei Bay! (808) 826-6114

Hanalei Surf Company - Offers a range of rental equipment: mask, fins, and snorkel, $20 per week; boogie board, $30 per week; wet suits, $4 per day. Optical masks available. Located at 5161 Kuhio Hwy. (808) 826-9000.

Makana's Charters & Tours - A 4 1/2-5 hour tour of Kaua'i's Napali coastline aboard their 32-foot power catamaran. Snorkeling equipment included. Current special $99. Deli lunch provided. Departs Port Allen Boat Harbor. They go to a protected snorkeling location restricted to the smaller boats. Reservations (808) 822-9187.

Mana Divers Scuba - These folks work out of the Hyatt Regency in their 5 acre salt water lagoon and at the Kaua'i Marriott which boasts the largest freshwater pool in Hawaii. Their "Discover Scuba" beginning diver program is offered at both these locations as well as pool lessons for kids 8-11 in their "Bubblemaker" program. They also offer shore and boat dives. Their boat features a large swim platform for easy water access and their hot water shower is a real treat! (808) 742-9849. Website: <manadivers.com> or write them at Email: manadivers@hawaiian.net

Pedal and Paddle Hanalei - Basic rentals for regular or optic mask and snorkel set is $5 day/$20 a week (but the good news is their rental week is eight days long!) (808) 826-9069.

SeaFun Kaua'i - SeaFun is a shore based, half-day, guided snorkeling tour. Some of the islands best snorkeling is inside protective reefs where boats cannot go. Transportation (from most hotels), including wet suit, instruction from the auctions, snacks and drinks are included. An underwater video of your tour is available for an additional $32.50. Experienced snorkelers will appreciate learning more about the environment from Marine Biologist Tara Leota. They snorkel off Lawa'i Beach and Prince Kuhio Park. $66 adults (age 13 and up), $50.40 children (5-12 years). (They also operate Kaua'i Mountain Tours, guided four-wheel drive adventures.) PO Box 3069, Lihu'e, HI 96766. 1-800-452-1113, (808) 245-6400, FAX (808) 245-4888. <www.alohakauaitours.com> E-mail: <tours@GTE.net>

Snorkel Bob's has shops at 4-734 Kuhio Hwy. (808) 823-9433 and Koloa at 3236 Po'ipu (808) 742-2206.

True Blue Charters & Ocean Sports - Join them aboard their 55' Delta vessel, *Konane Star* and 42' Kantola design Trimaran. Maximum of 18 passengers. Departs Nawiliwili Small Boat Harbor or Kalapaki Beach, weather permitting. One-hour Kalapaki Fun Sail $35 adult/$25 children. High performance speed sailing. Includes soft drinks/juices. A good way to see if you like boating! Their Nawiliwili Sunset is $45 adults, $30 children and includes champagne, Kilauea Bakery bread sticks and fruit. Whale watching seasonally. Lighthouse Sail n' Snorkel is $59 adults, $30 children and is two hours including continental breakfast. Kipu Kai Sail Snorkel n' Picnic is $85 adults, $59 children. Duration is 4 hours and includes gourmet picnic lunch, soft drinks and juices, snorkel equipment. All trips include performance sailing and seasonal whale watching. They also operate True Blue Charters for those avid fisherfolks and Island Adventures for kayaking fans. PO Box 1722, Lihu'e, HI 96766. (808) 245-9662. FAX (808) 246-9661. Email: funkauai@hawaiian.net

## *SNUBA*

Snuba Tours of Kaua'i - Snuba, as it sounds, is a blend of snorkeling and scuba. The air source is contained within a floatation raft that follows you as you move beneath the ocean. The guided underwater tour includes personalized instruction, fish food, and equipment, $55 per person. They dive from Lawa'i Beach. (808) 823-8912. Email: snuba@aloha.net <www.hshawaii.com/kvb/snuba>

## *SPAS & FITNESS CENTERS*

Also see "Retreats" in Accommodations section.

Ever considered taking a vacation from your vacation? Well, have we got a tip for you! Let's face it, shopping, beaches, terrific dinners, more shopping, fabulous lunches, more shopping...well, you know, can get pretty tiring! Indulge yourself in a day at the ***ANARA Spa*** at the Hyatt Regency. (ANARA is an acronym for "A New Age Restorative Approach"). When you consider the amenities, it is one great value and you deserve it! Select a facial, half-hour or 50-minute massage, or perhaps an herbal wrap. With any of their pampered treatments you'll get a full-day pass to enjoy their spa facilities.

We'd recommend getting there in advance of your appointment. There are ladies' and mens' facilities which are private, as well as some co-ed facilities. The co-ed area offers a complete exercise room and a lap pool, or for the less aerobically inclined, enjoy some sun or shade on lounge chairs around the pool, have a light lunch, or relax in a jacuzzi. In both the womens' and mens' facilities you'll find a private jacuzzi tub, 12-jet jacuzzi shower, eucalyptus steam room, sauna, multi-person jacuzzi, lava rock shower garden, and more lounge chairs. Get in that relaxation mode and then enjoy your therapy treatment. When you are finished, there is more time to choose from the aforementioned facilities before freshening up with their specially formulated mango scented shampoos, conditioners, and body soaps. Make it a whole day event!

Prices for daily spa membership inclusive with any spa/salon treatment: hotel guests $15/non-guests $20. Massage therapy or skin care treatments runs $55-130. Loofah scrubs, personal training sessions, herbal wraps and other services $35-90. Can't decide? Try a mini-day at ANARA for $215, or the ANARA Sampler for $115 or discover the new you with the 6 hour "Day at ANARA" for $325. Open daily from 6am-8pm.

Salon services are also available. Any salon services over $40 includes a complementary ANARA spa membership for that day. Advance (808) 742-1234 for reservations.

Kai Mana - Shakti Gawain, author of books including *Creative Visualization*, and *Living in the Light* offers week-long "intensives" in Kilauea at her Kai Mana estate. The week long programs are $2,000 plus tax per person or $3,500 per couple plus tax per person. Included are group sessions, classes and two massages by a licensed practitioner. (415) 388-7140. (Kai Mana no longer operates a B&B, but the cottage is available for rental. See North Shore accommodations.)

Kaua'i Athletic Club - They offer aerobics, racquetball, handball, freeweights, and have now added Cybex equipment. Other facilities include a swimming pool, jacuzzi, pro shop, child care, and deli that features low-cal and low-fat options. Hours Monday thru Friday 6am-9pm, Saturday and Sunday 8am-5pm. Single day visit $12. Weekly and monthly unlimited passes also available. (808) 245-5381.

Princeville Health Club and Spa - Located at the Prince Golf and Country Club on the Northern Shore in Princeville. Available amenities are massages, facials, seaweed wrap, and aromatherapy treatments along with their complete health and fitness facility. Passes start at $15 per day (for hotel guests only), weekly rates run $45, and monthly passes are $95. The "Spa Experience" includes: use of whirlpool sauna, steam room, 25 meter lap pool, personal locker, robe, unlimited classes, one hour lomi lomi massage for $130 Princeville Hotel Guest, Spa Guest $140. Spa admission is included in regular Prince and Makai Golf Course green fees. Unlimited daily exercise classes including body conditioning, step aerobics, aquacize and yoga are offered. Spa hours are Monday-Saturday from 9am-6:30pm. Sunday 9am-4:30pm. (808) 826-5030.

## *SURFING*

Hanalei Surf Company rents fiberglass surfboards for $15 per day, $65 per week. Soft surfboards $12 per day, $50 per week. Boogie boards rent for $5 per day, $20 per week. They are located at 5161 Kuhio Hwy. (808) 826-9000.

Margo Oberg's Surfing School. Located between the Kiahuna Plantation and the Sheraton in Po'ipu. Margo won world titles seven times between 1968 and 1981. Her school has been operating now for well over 25 years. (808) 742-8019. Three times daily lessons are offered at $45 per person with 6-7 in a class. Private lessons $75.

Kayak Kaua'i Outbound offers Hawaiian surf boarding lessons, $35 per hour lesson. Kapa'a (808) 822-9179; Hanalei (808) 826-9844, 1-800-437-3507. Email: <outbound@aloha.net>

Progressive Expressions, Inc. in Koloa since 1974. They manufacture and sell surfboards, bodyboards, and surfing accessories for all ages. 5420 Koloa Road. (808) 742-6041.

Windsurf Kaua'i also offers surfing instruction and rental equipment. (808) 828-6838. (See Windsurfing for more information)

## *TENNIS*

Kaua'i County has eight municipal public tennis courts. Available courts are in Waimea, Kekaha, Koloa, Kalaheo, Lihu'e, Wailua Homesteads, Wailua Houselots, and Kapa'a New Park. Many hotels have courts available for public and guest use.

The Tennis Garden at the Hyatt Regency Kaua'i Resort and Spa has 4 plexipave courts and a pro shop. Open 7am-6pm, court fees are $20 per hour. Daily instructional clinics (9:30-10:30am) run $20 per person for an hour and a half (3 person minimum), $25 per hour (two person minimum) or private at $30 per half hour or $50 per hour. Club memberships are available. The Tennis Garden also offers bicycle, beach chair, and cooler rentals. Phone (808) 742-1234 ext. 4990. The tennis facilities are available for non-hotel guests, too!

Other tennis facilities on Kaua'i:

Hanalei Bay Resort (808) 826-6522
Kaua'i Lagoons Racquet Club (808) 241-6000
Kiahuna Tennis Resort (808) 742-9533
Po'ipu Kai Tennis Complex (808) 742-1144
Princeville Resort Tennis Complex (808) 826-3620

## *THEATER*

The Kaua'i Community Players does several productions annually for children and adults. If you're on the island in December, check out their breakfast with Santa! Call (808) 245-7700 for more information on plays and dinner theater productions.

Kaua'i Community College of Performing Arts opened their $12 million theater in the fall of 1995. The theater complex was almost complete when Hurricane Iniki destroyed it. The hall seats 550 persons and adds an exciting dimension to theater possibilities on Kaua'i. Currently they offer approximately six concerts throughout the year.

The Kaua'i International Theater opened in the fall of 1999. The theater features air conditioning and a 62 seat capacity. Artwork of local artists is on display as well. They plan on six shows per season with each show running about 4 weeks. They anticipate guest performers and other entertainment in-between productions so there will be lots happening here. The new theater is located in Kapa'a in the Kaua'i Village. (808) 821-1588.

Check with the Kaua'i Marriott Resort about their Dinner Theater. Held several times each month, it begins with a no-host cocktail party at 6pm, and a dinner buffet of 6:30 with assorted salads. One past musical program opened with selections from Les Miserables which was followed by the main entree buffet and songs from Guys and Dolls. It ended with a dessert buffet and Phantom of the Opera. The production ended shortly after 10pm. The show changes so audiences can come back and enjoy new songs for continuing family entertainment. Call the Marriott (808) 245-50505 or musical director Jona Clark (808) 7842-6511. Cost is $65 inclusive of tax and tip.

Waimea Theatre reopened in 1999. It's history began on September 2, 1938 when it opened for the first time featuring the 20th Century Fox production, "Josette," a romantic film with Robert Young and Simone Simon. At the height of the art deco period, the 500 seat theater was a frame structure with a concrete front. It appeared that its fate was sealed in 1972 when the rural movie house closed and was converted into warehouse and retail space. Nature struck with force when Hurricane Iniki destroyed the decorative marquee in 1992. Over the course of six years, preservation and patience have saved the landmark structure. The fully restored theatre offers a variety of films and live productions. Phone (808) 885-5815.

## *WATERSKIING*

Kaua'i Water Ski & Surf Co. - Rates run $100 per hour, $55 per 1/2 hour. They travel up the Wailua River. Mondays through Fridays 9am-5pm. Surf shop at Kinipopo Shopping Village. (808) 822-3574.

## *WHALE WATCHING*

Whale watching is seasonal, officially December 15 through May 15, although a few stragglers may linger into May and some anxious for those warm waters of the Hawaiian islands may arrive a bit ahead of schedule. The best vantage points for whale watching are from one of the boats that make excursions out in search of these magnificent mammals. You can also view them from above during a helicopter tour. As for a best bet, we would recommend one of the condos above the bluff at Princeville or the Northern most point of the island at the Kilauea lighthouse.

## *WILDLIFE REFUGES*

As you pass the Princeville Center you are at mile marker 28 on Hwy. 56, which now switches to mile marker 0 as you suddenly change to highway 560. Just past this on the left is the scenic lookout for the ***Hanalei Wildlife Refuge***. The Hanalei Wildlife Refuge was established on 917 acres in 1972 and is located in the Hanalei Valley. Unique to many refuges, taro is allowed to be commercially farmed on a portion of the property and one permit is granted for cattle grazing. Administered by the U.S. Fish and Wildlife Service as a unit of the National Wildlife Refuge System, they actively manage the habitat to provide wetlands for endangered Hawaiian waterbirds. Historic farming (taro) and grazing practices are compatible with the refuges' objectives and thus permitted to a limited degree. There are 49 species of birds, including the endangered Hawaiian black-necked stilt, gallinule, coot, and duck that make their home here. Of the 49 species, 18 are introduced. There are no native mammals, reptiles, or amphibians, except possibly the Hawaiian bat. The refuge is not open to the public, but an interpretive overlook on the state highway just north of the refuge allows an excellent photo opportunity. Hurricane Iniki caused major damage to the habitat of this refuge and recovery continues.

Located along the Huleia River is the ***Huleia National Wildlife Refuge***, which is home to the endangered koloa duck. In 1973, 241 acres were purchased to provide a water bird habitat. The lands, once taro and rice fields, are now breeding and feeding grounds for a variety of waterfowl. The refuge is located in a relatively flat valley along the Huleia River which is bordered by a steep wooded hillside. There are 31 species of migratory birds which inhabit the area and 18 of these species were introduced.

A special permit is issued annually to a commercial kayaking business for access through an upland portion of the refuge. The refuge, adjacent to the Menehune Fish Pond, is not open to the public, however, a view of it from the overlook along the road is possible.

*Wildlife Refuge*

The ***Kilauea Point National Wildlife Refuge*** was established in 1974 and is recognized as Hawai'i's largest seabird sanctuary, a place that is home to more than 5,000 seabirds. This refuge is a nesting site for the red-footed booby, wedge-tailed shearwater, Laysan albatross, and many other species of Hawaiian seabirds. The acquisition of land has continued with this sanctuary now encompassing 203 acres.

The refuge was struck hard by Hurricane Iniki. Not only was there much damage to the birdlife and vegetation, but the famous lighthouse was also seriously affected. At Kilauea Point, they reported that about 80% of the native plants suffered damage. On Crater Hill, at least 25% were lost and an additional 50% damaged. Mokolea Point vegetation suffered little damage. Kilauea Point lost the most birds and suffered the worst damage to the habitat. The Kaua'i Natural Wildlife Refuge complex lost 12 of their 20 buildings. There was also damage to the lighthouse visitor center and bookstore, storage buildings, fences, and the water delivery system. Today, the center is fully restored.

When the lighthouse and support facilities were transferred from the U.S. Coast Guard on February 15, 1985, Kilauea Point became the 425th National Wildlife Refuge. The adjacent Kilauea Point Humpback Whale National Marine Sanctuary was established in 1994. Over 250,000 visitors enjoy the Kilauea Point National Wildlife Refuge visitor center and wildlife viewing areas each year. As many as 1,000 visitors per day may tour the facility during the peak of the holiday seasons. There is an on-going habitat management program that includes water development, native plant propagation, service club, and nursery activities. Over 200 volunteers donate hours to varied refuge projects. Of the 203 acres, 183 acres are owned, and another 20 acres are conservation easement.

The refuge is open to the public daily from 10am-4pm, closed some federal holidays. ***Kilauea Point***, PO Box 87, Kilauea, Kaua'i, HI 96754. (808) 828-1413. Admission is $2.

LAYSAN ALBATROSS

## *WINDSURFING*

Once again, weather conditions will determine where this activity is best suited. 'Anini is the best for beginners. Located near Princeville, it offers a lagoon with protected waters and steadily blowing winds that make it ideal for the beginning or intermediate windsurfer. Advanced windsurfers enjoy Tunnels on the North Shore or what they refer to as the YMCA Beach located 1/4 mile past The North Shore Grille and Mahaulepu on the South Shore.

'Anini Beach Windsurfing - Windsurfing rentals $50 for day. Three hour lessons $65. (808) 826-9463.

Windsurf Kaua'i - Located on the North Shore with instruction at the 'Anini lagoon. Celeste Harvel is a master instructor who offers state-of-the-art beginning windsurf boards. These boards are a foot shorter, 11' as opposed to the conventional 12' board, which allows for easier maneuvering. The boards are also just slightly wider. The 'Anini lagoon has a maximum depth of seven feet and 10-20 knot winds year round. Half of the lagoon is designated for windsurfers, the other half for swimming and snorkeling. Lessons for first timers run $75 for a three-hour class with a maximum of 6 people in the class. This phase of instruction includes learning how to steer, sail, and come back to shore. The second level class is the same price and length, but completes certification. This three-hour instruction includes learning how to jibe, beach start, and rig. The equipment makes windsurfing easy for everyone. For the less athletic individual, Celeste utilizes a 15 square foot sail with a 4 1/2 foot boom which is very manageable. She has custom equipment for children and can teach anyone five years and up. She also offers extensive windsurf equipment rental. Rental equipment is $75 all day, $50 half day or $25 per hour. In the winter, spring, and fall Celeste also offers surfing lessons at Hanalei Bay. Windsurfing lessons offered weekdays at 'Anini Beach. She also teaches physically handicapped folks! PO Box 323 Hanalei, HI 96714. (808) 828-6838.

# RECOMMENDED READING

Aikin, Ross R. Kilauea Point Lighthouse: The Landfall Beacon on the Orient Run. Kilauea Point Natural History Association. 1988.

Alexander, Arthur C. Koloa Plantation, 1835-1935, a history of the oldest Hawaiian sugar plantation. Honolulu: Honolulu Star Bulletin. 1937.

Anderson, Isabel Weld Perkins. The Spell of the Hawaiian Islands and the Philippines. Boston: The Colonial Press. 1916.

Anderson, Mary E. Scenes in the Hawaiian Islands. Boston: Cornill Press. 1865.

Barrhre, Dorothy. Hula, Historical Perspectives. Honolulu: Bishop Museum. 1980.

Beekman, Allan. The Ni'ihau incident: the true story of the Japanese fighter pilot. Honolulu: Heritage Press of Pacific. 1982.

Begley, Bryan. Taro in Hawai'i. Honolulu: The Oriental Publishing Co. 1979.

Bennett, Wendall Clark. Archaeology of Kaua'i. Honolulu: Bernice P. Bishop Museum Bulletin. Kraus Reprint Co. 1971.

Bird, Isabella. Six Months in the Sandwich Islands. Tokyo: Tuttle. 1988.

Boom, Bob & Christensen, Chris. Important Hawaiian Place Names. Hawai'i: Bob Boom. 1978.

Borg, Jim. Hurricane Iniki. Honolulu: Mutual Publishing. 1992.

Chisholm, Craig. Hawaiian Hiking Trails. Lake Oswego: Fernglen Press. 1994.

Chisholm, Craig. Kaua'i Hiking Trails. Lake Oswego: Fernglen Press. 1991.

Clark, John R. K. Beaches of Kaua'i and Ni'ihau. Honolulu: University of Hawai'i Press, 1990.

Day, A. Grove. Hawai'i and its People. New York: Duall, Sloan, Pearce. 1955

Ellis, William. Journal of William Ellis (1794-1872). Honolulu: Advertiser Publishing Co. Originally published in 1917. Reprinted in 1963.

Fayé, Christine. Touring Waimea. Kaua'i Historical Society. 1997.

Fielding, Ann. Hawaiian Reefs and Tidepools. Hawai'i: Oriental Pub. Co.

Forander, Abraham. Hawaiian Antiquities and Folk-Lore. Honolulu: Bishop Museum Press. 1919.

Forbes, David. Queen Emma and Lawa'i. Kaua'i Historical Society. 1970.

Franck, Harry A. Roaming in Hawai'i: A Narrative of Months of Wandering Among the Glamourous Islands That May Become our 49th State. New York: Grosset & Dunlap. 1937.

Gay, Lawrence Kainoahou. Tales of the Forbidden Island of Ni'ihau. Topgallant Publishing Co. 1981.

Gay, Roland Lalana Kapahukaniolono. Hawai'i, Tales of Yesteryear, a collection of Legends and Stories. R. Gay Co. 1977.

Golf Hawai'i: the complete guide. Windward Promotions. 1991.

Haldey, Thelma Road guide to Koke'e and Waimea Canyon State Parks. Honolulu: Bess Press. 1993.

Haraguchi, Paul. Weather in Hawaiian Waters. 1983.

Harrison, Craig Seabirds of Hawai'i: Natural History & Conservation. NY: Comstock Pub. 1990.

Hawai'i Audubon Society. Hawai'i's birds. Honolulu: The Society. 1993.

Hazama, Dorothy. The Ancient Hawaiians. Honolulu: Hogarth Press.

Hoverson, Martha ed. Historic Koloa: A guide. Koloa: Friends of Koloa. 1988.

Hume, Kathryn Cavarly. Robert Allerton Story, 1873-1964. John Gregg Allerton. 1979.

Hurricane Iwa Hits Hawai'i. Lubbock, TX: C.F. Boone. 1982.

Joesting, Edward. Kaua'i: The Separate Kingdom. Honolulu: University of Hawai'i Press. 1984.

Judd, Gerrit. Hawai'i, an Informal History. New York: Collier Books. 1961.

Kaua'i Bicentennial Committee. Waimea, Island of Kaua'i 1778-1978. 1977.

Kaua'i Historical Society. The Kaua'i Papers. Kaua'i. 1991.

Kelly, Marion. Pele and Hi'iaka visit the sites at Ke'e, Ha'ena, Island of Kaua'i. Honolulu: Bernice P. Bishop Museum Press, 1984.

Klass, Tim. World War II on Kaua'i Historical Research by Tim Klass. Kaua'i Historical Soc. 1970.

Knudsen, Eric Alfred. Kanuka of Kaua'i. Tongg. 1944.

Kndusen, Eric. Teller of Tales. Honolulu: Mutual Publishing. 1946.

Knudsen, Valdemar. Koolau, Outlaw: a story about the Na Pali Coast. Koloa: V. Knudsen. 1976.

Kramer, Raymond J. Hawaiian Land Mammals. VT: C.E. Tuttle Co. 1971.

Krauss, Bob. Grove Farm Plantation: the biography of a Hawaiian sugar plantation. Palo Alto, CA: Pacific Books. 1984.

Krauss, Robert. Here's Hawai'i. New York: Coward-McAnn, Inc. 1960.

London, Jack. Stories of Hawai'i. Honolulu: Mutual Publishing. 1965.

Ludwig, Myles. Kaua'i in the Eye of Iniki. Hanalei Bay, Kaua'i: Inter-Pacific Media. 1992.

McSpadden, J. Walker. Beautiful Hawai'i. New York: Thomas Y. Crowell, 1939.

Morey, Kathy. Kaua'i Trails: Walks, Strolls, and Treks on the Garden Island. Berkely, CA: Wilderness Press, 1991.

Moriarty, Linda. Ni'ihau Shell Leis. Honolulu: University of Hawai'i Press. 1986.

O'Malley, Anne E. Miracle of Iniki: Stories of aloha from the heart of Kaua'i. Honolulu: Bess Press. 1993.

Pratt, Douglas. Enjoying Birds in Hawai'i. Honolulu: Mutual Publishing. 1993.

Pukui, Mary and Korn, Alfons. Echos of Our Song. Honolulu: University of Hawai'i Press. 1973

Pukui, Mary Kawena et al. The Pocket Hawaiian Dictionary. Honolulu: The University of Hawai'i Press. 1975.

Pukui, Mary Kawena. Tales of the Menehune. Honolulu: Kamehameha Schools Press. 1985.

Rice, William Hyde. Hawaiian Legends. Honolulu: Bishop Museum Press. 1977.

Smith, Robert. Hawai'i's Best Hiking Trails. CA: Hawaiian Outdoor Adventures. 1991.

Smith, Robert. Hiking Kaua'i. Long Beach, CA: Hawaiian Outdoor Adventures. 1989.

Smith, Walter James. Legends of Wailua. Kaua'i Printers. 1955.

Stepien, Edward R. Ni'ihau, A Brief History. Published by the Center for Pacific Island tudies, 1988.

Stevenson, Robert Louis. Travels in Hawai'i. Honolulu: University of Hawai'i Press. 1973.

Tabrah, Ruth. Kaua'i, The Unconquerable Island. Las Vegas. K.C. Publications. 1988.

Tabrah, Ruth. Ni'ihau, the last Hawaiian Island. Kailua, HI: Press Pacific. 1987.

Tanimoto, Charles Katsumu. Return to Mahaulepu Personal Sketches. C.K. Tanimoto. 1982.

Tava, Rerioterai. Ni'ihau: the traditions of a Hawaiian island. Honolulu: Mutual Publishing. 1989.

Titcomb, M. Native Use of Fish in Hawai'i. Honolulu: University of Hawai'i Press. 1952.

Valier, Kathy. On the Na Pali Coast. Honolulu: University of Hawai'i Press. 1988.

VanHolt, Ida Elizabeth Knudsen. Stories of Long Ago: Ni'ihau, Kaua'i, O'ahu. Daughters of Hawai'i. 1985.

Westervelt, W.D. Myths and Legends of Hawai'i. Honolulu: Mutual Publishing Co. 1987.

Wichman, Juliet Rice. A Chronicle and Flora of Ni'ihau. Nat. Tropical Botanical Garden. 1990.

Wichman, Frederick. Kaua'i Tales. Honolulu: Bamboo Ridge Press. 1985.

Wichman, Frederick. Polihale and other Kaua'i legends. Honolulu: Bamboo Ridge Press. 1991.

Wisniewski, Richard A. The Rise and Fall of the Hawaiian Kingdom. Honolulu: Pacific Basin Enterprises. 1979.

# ORDERING INFORMATION

**Available from Paradise Publications are books and videos to enhance your travel library and assist with your travel plans, or provide a special gift for someone who is planning a trip! Prices are subject to change without notice.**

***MAUI AND LANA'I: Making the Most of Your Family Vacation*** by Dona Early & Christie Stilson. This guide is packed with information on over 200 condos & hotels, 350 restaurants, 50 great beaches, sights to see and travel tips for the valley island. The island of Lana'i is included. Here the visitor will enjoy fine dining, local eateries, remote beaches, wonderful hikes and peaceful enchantment. *"A down-to-earth, nuts-and-bolts companion with answers to most any question."* L.A.Times. Almost 500pgs, maps, $15.00, Eighth edition. Copyright 1998.

***KAUA'I, A PARADISE FAMILY GUIDE: Making the Most of Your Family Vacation*** by Dona Early & Christie Stilson. You're holding it in your hand, but if you need another copy of this information packed guide which describes almost 200 island accommodations, 150 restaurants, plenty of secluded beaches, plus recreation and tour options ... we'd be happy to supply one! Maps, illustrations, $16.95. Sixth edition. Copyright 2000.

***HAWAI'I: THE BIG ISLAND, A PARADISE FAMILY GUIDE*** by John Penisten. Outstanding for its completeness, this well-organized guide provides useful information for people of every budget and lifestyle. Each chapter features the author's personal recommendations and "best bets." In addition to comprehensive information about island accommodations, you will find a full range of water, land and activities and tours from which to choose. Then enjoy dining at one of the more than 250 restaurants which range from local style drive-ins to fine dining establishments. Sights to see, beaches, and helpful travel tips. 300 pages. $15.00 5th ed. Copyright 1999.

**UPDATE NEWSLETTERS!** *THE MAUI UPDATE* and *THE KAUA'I UPDATE* are quarterly newsletters published by Paradise Publications that highlight the most current island events. Each features late breaking tips on the newest restaurants, island activities or special, not-to-be missed events. Each newsletter available at the single issue price of $2.50 or a yearly subscription (four issues) rate of $10. Canada $12 per year.

***FREE!*** A free copy of Paradise Publication's quarterly newsletter, ***THE MAUI UPDATE***, is available by writing Paradise Publications (Attention: Newsletter Dept.) 8110 S.W. Wareham, Suite 306, Portland, OR 97223, and enclosing a self-addressed, stamped, #10 envelope.

***MAPS!*** A great addition to your travels is a full-color topographical map by cartographer James A. Bier. Maps are available for $3.95 each for the islands of O'ahu, Maui, Kaua'i, Lana'i & Moloka'i and the Big Island of Hawai'i.

***MORE MAPS!*** *Haleakala,* Earth Press Topographical Map is a must-purchase if you are planning to enjoy this park in-depth. Water resistant, too! $3.95

***VIEWBOOKS*** Doug Peebles is quite possibly Hawai'i's best photographer, and his finest photography has been showcased in these full-color paperback books. Ideal for the armchair traveler or trip planner, these affordable pictorial guides are wonderful souvenirs and great gifts. Choose from these five: HAWAI'I (Big Island), MAUI, KAUA'I, O'AHU, VOLCANOES. Each is 10 x 13. 32 pages, $7.95.

***THE NEW CUISINE OF HAWAI'I.*** This 150 page hardcover cookbook is subtitled "Recipes from the Twelve Celebrated Chefs of Hawai'i Regional Cuisine" and that about sums it up. The culinary wizardry of Roy Yamaguchi, Jena-Marie Josselin and others are shared in this fascinating cookbook. Color photographs highlight each chef's magic touch. 1994. $30.

***COOKING WITH ALOHA.*** Discover the flavors and smells of the Hawaiian islands in your own kitchen with this easy-to-follow cookbook. Appetizers to desserts are covered. An inexpensive guide to cooking your favorite Hawaiian foods. 9 x 12, paperback, 184 pages, $9.95.

***HAWAIIAN HIKING TRAILS*** by Craig Chisholm. This very attractive and accurate guide details 49 of Hawai'i's best hiking trails. Hikes for every level of ability. Includes photography, topographical maps, and detailed directions. An excellent book for discovering Hawai'i's great outdoors! 152 pgs., $15.95. 1994. ***KAUA'I HIKING TRAILS*** by Craig Chisholm. Fernglen Press produces this quality 160 page book features color photographs, topographical maps and detailed directions to Kaua'i's best hiking trails. $14.95.

***HIKING MAUI*** by Robert Smith. Discover 27 hiking areas all around Maui. 5 x 8 paperback, 160 pages. $10.95. Also by Robert Smith. ***HIKING KAUA'I,*** over 40 hiking trails throughout Kaua'i. 116 pages, $10.95. ***HIKING HAWAI'I (The Big Island),*** 157 pages, $10.95. Black & white photographs and maps. Compact and easy-to-use.

***DIVING AND SNORKELING GUIDE TO THE HAWAIIAN ISLANDS.*** 6 x 9. 108 pages. 24 maps. 1991. $11.95.

***DIVERS GUIDE TO MAUI*** A popular guide for many years, written by local resident Chuck Thorne. A comprehensive guide to over 50 locations for snorkeling and diving on Maui. $9.95.

***NEW POCKET HAWAIIAN DICTIONARY.*** Resolve just what those Hawaiian words mean and how to pronounce them! $4.95.

***MARK TWAIN IN HAWAI'I: Roughing It In the Sandwich Islands.*** Samuel Langhorne Clemens visited the Hawaiian Island for four months in 1866 as a correspondent for the newspaper the *Pacific Coast*. He later used excerpts for his personal narrative *Roughing It*. A fascinating account of old Hawai'i. 106 pages. $4.95.

## COMPUTER/VIDEO *(All Videos are VHS format)*

**HAWAIIAN PARADISE** -- by International Video Network. More than a travel log, this is one of the best of many, many videos we have reviewed. The journey covers all six of the major Hawaiian islands, Kaua'i, Hawai'i, Lana'i, Moloka'i, Maui and O'ahu. The narrative begins with the formation of the Hawaiian islands and deviates from the average video by exploring the culture, legend, lore and history of the island. The lover of Hawai'i will learn new and interesting island facts and points of history and the new comer to Hawai'i will be thrilled with this visual taste of the islands. The next best thing to being there. $29.95. 90 minutes.

**FOREVER HAWAI'I** -- This 60 minute, video portrait features all six major Hawaiian islands. It includes breathtaking views from the snowcapped peaks of Mauna Kea to the bustling city of Waikiki, from the magnificent Waimea Canyon to the spectacular Halakeala Crater. A lasting memento. 1992. $24.95. **FOREVER MAUI** -- An in-depth visit to Maui with scenic shots and interesting stories about the Valley Isle. An excellent video for the first time, or even the returning Maui visitor. $19.95. **FLIGHT OF THE CANYON BIRD** -- An inspired view of the Garden Island of Kaua'i from a bird's eye perspective; an outstanding 30 minute piece of cinematography. This short feature presentation explores the lush tropical rainforests surrounding Wai'ale'ale (the wettest spot on earth), the awesome Waimea Canyon and the Napili Coastline. The narration explores the geologic and historic beginnings of the island. A lasting memento or gift! Each tape is 30 minutes. Cost $19.95 per tape.

**KUMU HULA: KEEPERS OF A CULTURE** -- This 85-minute tape was funded by the Hawai'i State Foundation on Culture and Arts. This beautifully filmed work includes hulas from various troupes on various islands, attired in their brilliantly colored costumes and explores the unique qualities of hula as well as explaining the history. $29.95.

**HULA - LESSONS ONE AND TWO** -- "Lovely Hula Hands" and "Little Brown Gal" are the two featured hulas taught by Carol "Kalola" Lorenzo who explains the basic steps of the hula. A fun and interesting video for the whole family. 30 minutes. $29.95.

**SHIPPING**: In the Continental U.S.-- Please add $4 for 1 to 2 items (books or videos). Each additional item over 2, please add $.50. Orders shipped promptly by US first class mail. If you'd prefer items shipped bookrate mail, we'll be happy to quote you shipping costs. Canadian Orders -- Please add $4 for the first book and $1 each additional book/tape. Orders shipped U.S. airmail. Federal Express or overnight mail services are available.

Include your check or money order/Visa or Mastercard information and send to:
**PARADISE PUBLICATIONS, 8110 S.W. Wareham, Portland, OR 97223 -- PHONE (503) 246-1555 or FAX (503) 977-3391**

*EMAIL: Paradyse@worldnet.att.net*

## PARADISE PUBLICATIONS ORDERING INFORMATION.............

***SHIPPING:** In the Continental U.S. Please add $4 for the first item, $1 for each additional item, maximum of $6. Orders shipped promptly U.S. Mail first class priority mail. Bookrate mail is $2 for up to three items. Overnight airmail service available. Call for quotes. Orders to Canada, Alaska or Hawai'i $4 for the first item, $1 for each additional, $6 maximum. Orders shipped small parcel U.S. airmail. Outside U.S., call or write for quote. A GIFT? We can ship items directly and include a personal gift card.*

| TITLE | QUANTITY | PRICE |
|---|---|---|
| | | |
| | | |
| | | |
| | | |
| | | |
| | | |
| | | |

SHIP TO: SHIPPING: ____________________

________________________________

________________________________ TOTAL: _________

________________________________

We accept Visa or Mastercard. For payment by checks, please be sure it is in U.S. Funds.

Visa/Mastercard #________________________________ Expiration ________

Name as shown on card

________________________________________________

Signature________________________________________

Begin MAUI / KAUA'I newsletter subscription with:
(Spring/Summer/Fall/Winter) 200__ issue.

***Paradise Publications, 8110 SW Wareham, Portland, OR 97223***

***(503) 246-1555** EMAIL: Paradyse@worldnet.att.net*

## *INDEX*

## *READER COMMENTS!!*

*If you have comments, corrections or opinions about the information included in this publication, we would love to hear from you!*

*Write to Dona Early and Christie Stilson*

*Paradise Publications*

*8110 S.W. Wareham Circle, Portland, OR 97223.*

*Or send e-mail to: Paradyse@worldnet.att.net*

*MAHALO!*